A History of the Mishnaic Law
of Agriculture: Kilayim

BROWN UNIVERSITY
BROWN JUDAIC STUDIES

Edited by

Jacob Neusner
Wendell S. Dietrich, Ernest S. Frerichs,
Sumner B. Twiss, Alan Zuckerman

Number 26

A History of the Mishnaic Law
of Agriculture: Kilayim
Translation and Exegesis

by Irving Mandelbaum

A HISTORY OF THE MISHNAIC LAW OF AGRICULTURE: KILAYIM

Translation and Exegesis

by

IRVING MANDELBAUM

Scholars Press

Published by
Scholars Press
101 Salem Street
Chico, California 95926

A History of the Mishnaic Law
of Agriculture: Kilayim

Translation and Exegesis

by
Irving Mandelbaum

Figures 4 and 5 taken from J. Feliks, *Mixed Sowing,*
Breeding and Grafting, © 1967 by Dvir Publishing
Company. Used by permission of publisher.

Library of Congress Cataloging in Publication Data

Mandelbaum, Irving.
    A history of the Mishnaic law of agriculture.

    (Brown Judaic studies ; no. 26)
    Includes also translation and exegesis of
Tosefta Kilayim.
    Bibliography: p.
1. Mishnah. Kilayim–Commentaries. 2. Tosefta.
Kilayim–Commentaries. 3. Agricultural laws and
legislation (Jewish law) I. Mishnah. Kilayim.
English. 1981. II. Tosefta. Kilayim. English. 1981.
III. Title. IV. Series.
BM506.K63M36   296.1'23   81-1462
ISBN 0-89130-465-7 (pbk.) AACR 2

Printed in the United States of America

For My Parents

Publication of this book is made possible with the support of The Max Richter Foundation, in honor of Professor David R. Blumenthal.

TABLE OF CONTENTS

Page

PREFACE

This study examines Mishnah-Tractate Kilayim (Diverse-Kinds),
the fourth treatise in Mishnah's Division of Agriculture (*Seder
Zera^{c}im*). The tractate presents an extended essay concerning
the scriptural prohibitions against commingling different categories of plants, animals, or fibers (Lv. 19:19, Dt. 22:9-11).
For each of these types of agricultural items Mishnah supplements
Scripture's rulings in three ways: 1) by establishing criteria
for distinguishing among different classes, 2) by defining what
constitutes the commingling of such classes, and 3) by determining
how to keep these categories separate and distinct from one
another. Although Mishnah's regulations clearly depend upon their
scriptural antecedents, the conception of the law which they express is distinctive to Mishnah. In the tractate's view it is
man, using his powers of observation, who determines what is
orderly and what lies in confusion. Unlike Scripture, which takes
for granted the existence of an established and immutable order,
Mishnah calls upon man to create order based upon his own perception of the world around him.

My purpose in presenting a translation and exegesis of
Mishnah-Tractate Kilayim is to discover the original meaning of
the tractate. What I want to know is the sense which the formulators of the tractate's laws wished their rules to convey. I
make no attempt to establish what laws pertaining to diverse-kinds
meant either prior to their formulation in Mishnah or afterwards,
in the course of the long history of Mishnah-exegesis. Since my
work does not take into account these possible earlier or later
layers of meaning, I am able to focus upon those issues which
are of greatest concern to the actual framers of the tractate, the
rabbis of the second century, A.D. My search for the original
meaning of Mishnah Kilayim thus contributes towards the larger
task of describing and interpreting early rabbinic Judaism.

Both the translation and exegesis of Mishnah Kilayim are di-
rected towards this goal of discovering the original meaning of
the tractate's laws. The translation closely renders into English
the formulaic language and syntactic patterns of the Hebrew text.
My exegesis then opens with a careful analysis of these formal
and literary traits which are underlined by the translation. Here
I show how the formulation of the tractate's rules draws our
attention to those issues which the authorities behind the rules
deem to be of central importance. At this stage it becomes

ix

possible to explain the substance of the laws in terms of these larger issues. This I maintain brings me to those points which Mishnah's framers intended to make through their rulings. Once I have made clear these larger concerns, moreover, I am able to identify the one central issue, or problematic, which has generated them, and so stands behind the tractate as a whole.

Although my study is primarily concerned with Mishnah's Tractate Kilayim, I also present a translation and exegesis of Tosefta Kilayim, an early commentary to our treatise. I include Tosefta in this study because among rabbinic documents it bears a unique relationship to Mishnah. Although it is separate from Mishnah, it totally depends upon the latter for its redactional order, and often employs Mishnah's own formal traits and legal principles in formulating its rulings. Tosefta therefore deserves to be treated in accord with its implicit claim to be a companion-document to Mishnah. For this reason I insert a translation and discussion of Tosefta's pericopae after the mishnaic pericope to which they refer. The purpose of this treatment of Tosefta is simply to explain the latter's exegesis of Mishnah.

It is with deep and heartfelt gratitude that I express my appreciation to those people who helped make this work possible. Foremost among these stands Professor Jacob Neusner, who has patiently guided this study from its inception to its present form. His searching questions, incisive criticism, and insightful suggestions have stimulated me to produce a work far more thorough and lucid than would otherwise have been the case. Dr. David Goodblatt (Haifa University) and Dr. Geza Vermes (University of Oxford) served as readers for the dissertation, and I greatly value their comments and suggestions. My teachers in the Department of Religious Studies at Brown University have contributed immeasurably to my personal and intellectual growth, and so merit thanks for their substantial (if often intangible) influence upon the present work. For their continuing interest in me I would like to thank Professors Wendell S. Dietrich, Ernest S. Frerichs (Dean of the Graduate School), Horst R. Moehring, John P. Reeder, Jr., Sumner B. Twiss, Jr., J. Giles Milhaven, and B. Barry Levy (now of McGill University). Mrs. Lois Atwood, Administrative Assistant, has also helped in many ways towards making my graduate career a pleasant one.

I have also benefitted from the comments, criticism and collegiality of fellow students in the Brown University graduate seminar in Judaic Studies, in which the present work was originally read (1974-77, 79-80). These include: Professors Charles Primus, University of Notre Dame; Tzvee Zahavy, University of Minnesota; Jack N. Lightstone, Concordia University; Richard S. Sarason, Hebrew Union College-Jewish Institute of Religion; Joel Gereboff, Arizona State University; Martin Jaffe, University of Virginia; Peter Haas, Vanderbilt University; Rabbi David Eisenman, Mr. Leonard Gordon, Mr. Avi Habibi, Mr. Alan Peck, Mr. Michael Rosen, and Mr. Howard Essner.

In the course of writing the present work I have been fortunate to have had the opportunity to spend several years at the University of Oxford. My teachers there introduced me to new areas of study and in many ways enriched my academic and personal life. I am grateful to Dr. Geza Vermes, Dr. Sebastian Brock, Rev. Symeon Lash (now of the University of Newcastle), and Professor Mary Boyce (University of London) for all that they have taught me.

I am grateful as well to the various institutions which helped support me during my career as a graduate student. Brown University offered me tuition scholarships in 1974-76, and a teaching assistantship in 1976-77. The Memorial Foundation of Jewish Culture awarded me a Doctoral Dissertation Grant in 1976-77, and the National Foundation for Jewish Culture provided a Comprehensive Examination Grant for the summer of 1977. In addition, the Oxford Centre for Postgraduate Hebrew Studies awarded me Junior Fellowships for the years 1978-80. I greatly appreciate the generosity of the Centre and its principal, Dr. David Patterson, in this regard.

Mrs. Elaine Haste and Mrs. Dody Giletti carefully typed a difficult manuscript, and are to be commended for their efforts. Mr. Douglas Rose skillfully drew the illustrations which appear in the work. My thanks also go to Jenny Godfrey, now my wife, who provided assistance and personal support during the closing stages of the preparation of this study. I am further grateful to the Max Richter Foundation and its president, Dr. Jacob Neusner, for a grant making possible the publication of this work.

Finally, I cannot adequately express the thanks which I owe to my parents, Alice and Myer Mandelbaum. Through their continuous support and encouragement they have taught me much concerning the value of learning and scholarship. This work stands as a tribute to their patience and understanding.

October 14, 1980   Irving Mandelbaum
4 Hešvan, 5741

TRANSLITERATIONS

א	=	'	מ,ם	=	m
ב	=	b	נ,ן	=	n
ג	=	g	ס	=	s
ד	=	d	ע	=	c
ה	=	h	פ,ף	=	p
ו	=	w	צ,ץ	=	ṣ
ז	=	z	ק	=	q
ח	=	ḥ	ר	=	r
ט	=	ṭ	שׁ	=	š
י	=	y	שׂ	=	ś
כ,ך	=	k	ת	=	t
ל	=	l			

Ah. = 'Ahilot

Albeck = H. Albeck, *The Six Orders of Mishnah. I. The Order of Seeds* [Heb.] (Jerusalem and Tel Aviv: Bialik Institute and D^{e}vir, 1957).

Albrecht = see Beer-Holtzmann

Alcalay = R. Alcalay, *The Complete Hebrew-English Dictionary* (Tel Aviv: Massadah, 1965).

Arak. = ^{C}Arakin

Avi-Yonah, *Carta's Atlas* = M. Avi-Yonah, *Carta's Atlas of the Period of the Second Temple, the Mishnah, and the Talmud* [Heb.] (Jerusalem: Carta, 1966).

Avi-Yonah, *Historical Geography* = *Historical Geography of Palestine from the End of the Babylonian Exile up to the Arab Conquest* [Heb.] (2nd ed; Jerusalem: Bialik Institute, 1951).

A.Z. = ^{C}Abodah Zarah

B = Mishnah *Zera^{c}im*, Ms. Berlin 93; see Zachs, I, pp. 77-78.

B. = Babylonian Talmud

B.B. = Baba' Batra'

BDB = F. Brown, S.R. Driver, and C.A. Briggs, eds., *A Hebrew and English Lexicon of the Old Testament* (1907; rpt. Oxford: Clarendon Press, 1952).

Beer-Holtzmann	=	G. Beer and O. Holtzmann, eds., *Die Mischna: Text, Übersetzung und ausführliche Erklärung* (Giessen: A. Töpelmann, 1912-). *I. 4. Seder Zeraim: Kil'ayim: Text, Übersetzung und Erklärung*, by K. Albrecht (1914).
Bek.	=	Bekorot
Ber.	=	Berakot
Bert.	=	Obadiah of Bertinoro, Mishnah commentary; in the Romm ed. of Mishnah.
Bes.	=	Beṣah
Bik.	=	Bikkurim
Blackman	=	P. Blackman, trans., *Mishnayot. I. Order Zeraim* (2nd. ed; New York: Judaica Press, 1964).
B.M.	=	Baba' Meṣi^{c}a'
Bokser	=	B.M. Bokser, *Samuel's Commentary on the Mishnah: Its Nature, Forms and Content. I. Mishnayot in the Order of Zera^{c}im* (Leiden: E.J. Brill, 1975).
B.Q.	=	Baba' Qamma'
C	=	Mishnah, MS. Cambridge 470.1, printed in W.H. Lowe, *The Mishnah on which the Palestinian Talmud Rests* (1883; rpt. Jerusalem: 1967); see Zachs, I, p. 67.
Cant.	=	Canticles
Cn	=	Mishnah, early printed edition of unknown origin, probably Constantinople or Pisaro, c. 1516 (photocopy: Jerusalem: Makor, 1970). See Zachs, I, pp. 82-83.

Columella	=	Columella, *De Re Rustica*, trans. H.B. Ash, E.S. Forster, and E. Heffner. The Loeb Classical Library (London and Cambridge, Mass.: W. Heinemann Ltd., Harvard University Press, 1941-55). Three volumes.
Dalman	=	G. Dalman, *Arbeit und Sitte in Palästina* (1928-42; rpt. Hildesheim: Georg Olms, 1964). Eight volumes; Seven parts.
Danby	=	H. Danby, trans., *The Mishnah* (London: Oxford University Press, 1933).
Dem.	=	Dema'i
Douglas	=	M. Douglas, *Purity and Danger: An Analysis of the Concepts of Pollution and Taboo* (London: Routledge and Kegan Paul, 1966)
Dt.	=	Deuteronomy
Eben-Shoshan	=	A. Eben-Shoshan, *HaMilon HaHadash* (Jerusalem: Kiryat-Sefer, 1969). Seven volumes.
Ed.	=	CEduyyot
Epstein, *IAL*	=	Y.N. Epstein, *Introduction to Amoraitic Literature* [Heb.] (Jerusalem: Magnes Press, 1962).
Epstein, *ITM*	=	Y.N. Epstein, *Introduction to the Text of Mishnah* [Heb.] (2nd ed.; Jerusalem: Magnes Press, 1964). Two volumes.
Erfurt	=	Tosefta, Ms. Erfurt; cf. Lieberman, *TZ*, pp. 8-11.
Erub.	=	CErubin
Ex.	=	Exodus

Feldman	=	Feldman, *Şimḥé HaMishnah* (Tel Aviv: 1962).
Feliks, *Agriculture*	=	J. Feliks, *Agriculture in Palestine in the Period of the Mishna and the Talmud*. [Heb.] (Jerusalem: Magnes Press, 1963).
Feliks, *The Animal World of the Bible*	=	J. Feliks, *The Animal World of the Bible*, trans. Pinḥas Irsai (Tel Aviv: Sinai, 1962).
Feliks, *HaḤai BaMishnah*	=	J. Feliks, *HaḤai BaMishnah* (Jerusalem: Institute for Mishnah Research, 1972).
Feliks, *Mar'ot HaMishnah*	=	J. Feliks, *Mar'ot HaMishnah* (Jerusalem: Midrash Bnei Siyon, 1967).
Feliks, *Mixed Sowing*	=	J. Feliks, *Mixed Sowing, Breeding and Grafting* [Heb.] (Tel Aviv: D^{e}vir, 1967).
Feliks, *Plant World of the Bible*	=	J. Feliks, *Plant World of the Bible* [Heb.] (Tel Aviv: Massadah, 1957).
Finkelstein, Sifré Dt.	=	L. Finkelstein, ed., *Sifre on Deuteronomy* (Berlin, 1939; rpt. New York: Jewish Theological Seminary, 1969).
First printed ed.	=	Tosefta, *editio princeps*. Venice, 1521.
Forbes	=	R.J. Forbes, *Studies in Ancient Technology*, IV (2nd ed.; Leiden, E.J. Brill, 1964).
Geniza fragments	=	Mishnah Mss. fragments from the Cairo Genizah; listed by Zachs, I, pp. 87-112.

Gereboff	=	J. Gereboff, *Rabbi Tarfon* (Missoula: Scholars Press, 1979) (page numbers refer to Brown University Ph.D. dissertation, 1977).
Ginzberg	=	L. Ginzberg, "Beiträge zur Lexikographie des Aramaischen," in Samuel Krauss, ed. *Festschrift Adolf Schwartz* (Berlin: R. Löwit, 1917).
Git.	=	Giṭṭin
Gn.	=	Genesis
GRA	=	Elijah b. Solomon Zalman ("Hagaon Rabbi Eliyahu" or "Vilna Gaon"; Lithuania 1720-1797), Mishnah commentary in Romm edition of Mishnah (Vilna, 1908, and numerous reprints); Tosefta emendations, in Romm ed. of Babylonian Talmud (Vilna, 1886, and numerous reprints)
Graser	=	S.R. Graser, trans., *The Edict of Diocletian*, in Tenney Frank, ed., *An Economic Survey of Ancient Rome* (Baltimore: Johns Hopkins Press, 1940), volume 5, pp. 305-421.
Green	=	W.S. Green, *The Traditions of Joshua b. Hananiah*. Unpublished Brown University Ph.D. dissertation, 1974.
Hag.	=	Ḥagigah
Hal.	=	Ḥallah
Harrison, Masefield, and Wallis	=	S.G. Harrison, G.B. Masefield, and Michael Wallis, *The Oxford Book of Food Plants* (London: Oxford University Press, 1969).

Hartmann and Kester	=	Hudson T. Hartmann and Dale E. Kester, *Plant Propagation: Principles and Practices* (2nd ed.; Englewood Cliffs: Prentice-Hall, 1968).
Hazon Yehezquel	=	Yehezquel Abramsky (1886-1976), *Tosefta Hazon Yehezquel I. Zera^cim* (1925; rpt. Jerusalem, 1971).
HD	=	Hasdé David. David Samuel b. Jacob Pardo (1718-1790), *Sefer Hasdé David* [Tosefta Commentary]. *I. Seder Zera^cim* (Livorno, 1776; rpt. Jerusalem, 1971).
Hill	=	Albert F. Hill, *Economic Botany: A Text-Book of Useful Plants and Plant Products* (2nd ed.; New York: McGraw-Hill, 1952).
Hillel	=	Hillel b. Eliaqim, Commentary to Sifré, in *Sifré. . .with the Commentary. . .of Rabbenu Hillel b. Eliaqim*, ed. S. Koleditsky (Jerusalem, 1958).
Hor.	=	Horayyot
Hul.	=	Hullin
Ish-Shalom	=	M. Ish-Shalom (Friedman), ed., *Sifré debe Rab* (Vienna, 1864; rpt. Jerusalem, 1967).
Israelstam	=	*The Babylonian Talmud: Seder Zera^cim II*, translated into English with notes, glossary, and indices under the editorship of Rabbi Dr. I. Epstein (London: Soncino Press, 1948). Kilayim is the work of J. Israelstam.

Jastrow	=	M. Jastrow, *A Dictionary of the Targumim, the Talmud Babli and Yerushalmi and the Midrashic Literature* (1904; rpt. New York: Pardes Press, 1950).
Jones	=	A.H.M. Jones, "The Cloth Industry in the Roman Empire," in P.A. Brunt, ed., *The Roman Economy* (Oxford: Basil Blackwell, 1974), pp. 350-364.
Josephus	=	Flavius Josephus, *The Jewish War*, trans. H. St. J. Thackeray, in *Josephus*, Loeb Classical Library (London and New York: W. Heinemann and G.P. Putnam's Sons, 1927), volumes 2 and 3.
K	=	Mishnah, Ms. Kaufmann A50; photocopy: G. Beer, *Faksimile-Ausgabe des Mischnacodex Kaufmann A50* (The Hague, 1929; rpt. Jerusalem: Makor, 1969); cf. Zachs, I, pp. 65-66.
Kel.	=	Kelim
Ker.	=	Keritot
Ket.	=	Ketubot
Kil.	=	Kilayim
KM	=	Joseph b. Ephraim Karo (1488-1575), *Keseph Mishnah*. Commentary to Maimonides, *Mishnah Torah*; in standard editions of latter.
Knowles	=	P.F. Knowles, "Safflower-- Production, Processing and Utilization," in *Economic Botany* 9 (1955), pp. 273-299.

Kosowsky	= C.Y. Kosowsky, *Thesaurus Mishnae* [Heb.] (Jerusalem: Massadah, 1956). Four volumes.
Kosowsky, *Tosefta*	= C.Y. Kosowsky, *Thesaurus Tosephtae* [Heb.] (Jerusalem, 1932–61). Six volumes.
KP	= Estori Parḥi (ca. 14th century), *Kaftor VaPeraḥ*, work on medieval Palestine and its agriculture. Cited by Lieberman, *TK*.
Krauss	= S. Krauss, *Talmudische Archäologie* (Leipzig: G. Fock, 1910). Two volumes.
L	= Palestinian Talmud, Ms. Leiden (Codex Scali 3); photocopy: Jerusalem: Makor, 1976; see Zachs, I, p. 72.
Lv.	= Leviticus
Lewin	= B.M. Lewin, ed., *Otzar HaGeonim* (Haifa: 1930).
Lieberman, *Greek*	= S. Lieberman, *Greek in Jewish Palestine* (New York: Jewish Theological Seminary, 1942).
Lieberman, *Hellenism*	= S. Lieberman, *Hellenism in Jewish Palestine* (New York: Jewish Theological Seminary, 1950).
Lieberman, *TK*	= S. Lieberman, *Tosefta Kifshuṭah: A Comprehensive Commentary on the Tosefta. I. Order Zera^c im* (New York: Jewish Theological Seminary, 1955). Two volumes.

Lieberman, *TM*	=	S. Lieberman, ed., *The Tosefta According to Codex Vienna, with Variants from Codices Erfurt, London, Genizah Mss. and Editio Princeps (Venice 1521). II. The Order of Mo^ced* (New York: Jewish Theological Seminary, 1962).
Lieberman, *TZ*	=	S. Lieberman, ed. *The Tosefta According to Codex Vienna, with Variants from Codex Erfurt, Genizah Mss. and Editio Princeps Venice 1521. I. The Order of Zera^cim* (New York: Jewish Theological Seminary, 1955).
Löw	=	I. Löw, *Die Flora der Juden* (Vienna: R. Löwit, 1926). Four volumes.
Lv.	=	Leviticus
M.	=	Mishnah
Ma^cas.	=	Ma^caśerot
Maim., *Code*	=	Maimonides (Moses b. Maimon, 1135-1204), *Mishnah Torah*. Standard edition, six volumes; particularly *Laws of Diverse-Kinds*, in *The Book of Agriculture*.
Maim., *Comm.*	=	Maimonides, Mishnah Commentary, in J. Qappaḥ, trans. and ed., *Mishnah with the Commentary of R. Moses b. Maimon. I. Zera^cim-Mo^ced* (Jerusalem: Mossad HaRav Kook, 1963).
Mak.	=	Makkot
Makh.	=	Makhshirin
MB	=	Samuel Avigdor b. Abraham Karlin, *Minḥat Bikkurim*. Tosefta commentary (1842); in Romm ed. of Babylonian Talmud.

Me.	=	Me^cilah
Meg.	=	Megillah
Me'iri	=	Menaḥem b. Solomon Meiri (1249-1306), *Beth HaBeḥirah on the Talmudical Tractate Shabbat*, ed. Isaak S. Lange (1965; rpt. Jerusalem, 1971).
Mekilta de Rabbi Ishmael	=	J.Z. Lauterbach, ed., *Mekilta de-Rabbi Ishmael* (Philadelphia: Jewish Publication Society, 1935-49). Three volumes.
Men.	=	Menahot
Mid.	=	Middot
Miq.	=	Miqva'ot
Mn	=	Babylonian Talmud, Codex Munich 95; photocopy: Hermann L. Strack, *Talmud Babylonium Codicis Hebraica Monatensis* (Leiden, 1912; rpt. Jerusalem: Makor, 1971). See Zachs, I, pp. 69-70.
Morinaga	=	Toshitaro Morinaga, "Germination of Seeds under Water," *American Journal of Botany* 13 (1926), pp. 126-140.
M.Q.	=	Mo^ced Qaṭan
MR	=	Ephraim Isaac of Premsyla, *Mishnah Rishonah*. Mishnah commentary (1882) in Romm edition of Mishnah.
Ms.	=	Manuscript (plural: Mss.).
M.S.	=	Ma^caśer Sheni
MS	=	Solomon b. Joshua Adeni (1567-1625), *Melekhet Shelomoh*. Mishnah Commentary in Romm edition of Mishnah.

Mt.	=	Matthew
N.	=	Mishnah, *editio princeps* (Naples, 1492; photocopy: Jerusalem: Makor, 1970). See Zachs, I, pp. 81-82.
Naz.	=	Nazir
Ned.	=	Nedarim
Neg.	=	Nega^{c}im
Nesiv	=	Naftali Ṣevi Yehudah Berlin (1817-1893), commentary to Sifré, in *Sifré...^{c}Emeq HaNeṣiv* (Jerusalem, 1959-61). Three volumes.
Neusner, *Eliezer*	=	J. Neusner, *Eliezer b. Hyrcanus: The Man and the Tradition* (Leiden: E.J. Brill, 1973). Two volumes.
Neusner, *HMLHT*	=	J. Neusner, *A History of the Mishnaic Law of Holy Things* (Leiden: E.J. Brill, 1978-). Four volumes thus far.
Neusner, *HMLP*	=	J. Neusner, *A History of the Mishnaic Law of Purities* (Leiden: E.J. Brill, 1974-77), 22 volumes.
Neusner, *Pharisees*	=	J. Neusner, *Rabbinic Traditions about the Pharisees before 70* (Leiden: E.J. Brill, 1971). Three volumes.
Nid.	=	Niddah
Noth	=	M. Noth, *Leviticus*, trans. J.S. Anderson. The Old Testament Library (Philadelphia: Westminster Press, 1965).
Nu.	=	Numbers.
O	=	Mishnah, Ms. Oxford 393, Order *Zera^{c}im*; with Maimonides' commentary, autograph. See Zachs, I, pp. 76-77.

Oh.	=	'Ohalot
Or.	=	^{C}Orlah
Ox.	=	Babylonian Talmud, Ms. Oxford 366, Orders *Zera^{C}im* and *Mo^{C}ed*. See Zachs, I, pp. 68-69.
OZ	=	Isaac b. Moses of Vienna (ca. 1180-1250), *Or Zaru^{C}a*. Cited by Lieberman, *TK*.
P	=	Mishnah, Ms. Parma De Rossi 138 (photocopy: Jerusalem: Makor, 1970). See Zachs, I, pp. 66-67.
Par.	=	Parah
Pe.	=	Pe'ah
Percival	=	J. Percival, *The Wheat Plant: A Monograph* (London: Duckworth and Co., 1921).
Pes.	=	Pesaḥim
Philo	=	Philo Judaeus, *Works*, trans. F.H. Colson, G.H. Whitaker and R. Marcus. Loeb Classical Library (London and Cambridge, Mass.: William Heinemann Ltd. and Harvard University Press, 1929-53). Eleven volumes.
Pliny, *Historia Naturalis*	=	Pliny, *Natural History*, trans. G.H. Rackman *et al*. Loeb Classical Library (London and Cambridge, Mass.: W. Heinemann and Harvard University Press, 1938-49). Ten volumes.
PM	=	Moses b. Simeon Margoliot (d. 1781), *P^{e}nei Moshe*, commentary to Palestinian Talmud; in Zhitomir ed. of latter.

Porton	=	G. Porton, *The Traditions of Rabbi Ishmael* (Leiden: E.J. Brill, 1976-). Three volumes thus far.
Post	=	George E. Post, *Flora of Syria, Palestine and Sinai*, ed. J.E. Dinsmore (2nd ed.; Beirut: Armenian Press, 1932). Two volumes.
Pr	=	Mishnah, Ms. Paris 328-329 (photocopy: Jerusalem: Makor, 1970). See Zachs, I, p. 79.
Primus	=	C. Primus, $^{c}Aqiva's$ Contribution to the Law. I. $Zera^{c}im$ (Leiden: E.J. Brill, 1977).
QA	=	Aaron Ibu Ḥayyim (d. 1632), *Qorban Aharon, Perush LaSefer Sifra* (Dessau, 1749; rpt. Jerusalem, 1970).
Qappaḥ	=	See Maim., *Comm.*
Qid.	=	Qiddushin
Qin.	=	Qinnim
R	=	Palestinian Talmud, Ms. Rome 133, Order $Zera^{c}im$ and tractate *Soṭah*. See Zachs, I, p. 73.
Rabad	=	Abraham b. David of Posquières (twelfth century) glosses to Maimonides, *Mishneh Torah*; in standard edition of latter.
R.H.	=	Rosh Hashanah
Ribmas	=	Isaac b. Melchizedek of Siponto (c. 1090-1160), Mishnah commentary; in Romm edition of Babylonian Talmud.

Ridbaz	=	David b. Solomon ibn Abi Zimra (1479-1573) *Ridbaz* (more commonly known as *Radbaz*), commentary to the books of *Asservations, Seeds, Holiness and Judges* in Maimonides, *Mishneh Torah*; in standard editions of latter.
Rosh	=	Asher b. Yeḥiel (ca. 1250-1327), Mishnah commentary; in Romm ed. of Babylonian Talmud.
RSV	=	Revised Standard Version of the Old Testament.
S	=	Palestinian Talmud, according to R. Solomon Sirillo, Ms. British Museum 403. See Zachs, I, pp. 73-75.
Sanh.	=	Sanhedrin
Sarason, *Demai*	=	R.S. Sarason, *A History of the Mishnaic Law of Agriculture. III. A Study of the Tractate Demai. Part I: Commentary* (Leiden: E.J. Brill, 1979).
Sarason, "Mishnah and Scripture"	=	R.S. Sarason, "Mishnah and Scripture: Preliminary Observations on the Law of Tithes," published in W.S. Green, ed., *Approaches to the Study of Ancient Judaism, II* (Missoula: Scholars Press, 1980).
Sefer Ha'Eshkol	=	Abraham b. Isaac of Narbonne (ca. 1110-1179), *Sefer Ha'Eshkol*, work of halakic codification. Cited by Lieberman, *TK*.

Sens	=	Samson b. Abraham of Sens (twelfth-thirteenth centuries), Mishnah commentary; in Romm ed. of Babylonian Talmud.
Shab.	=	Shabbat
Shav.	=	Shavuot
Sheq.	=	Sheqalim
Shev.	=	Shevi^{c}it
Sifra	=	cf. Weiss, *Sifra*.
Sifré Dt.	=	cf. Finklestein, Sifré Dt.
Sirillo	=	Solomon b. Joseph Sirillo (died ca. 1558), commentator on Palestinian Talmud; cited by Lieberman, *TK*.
Sn	=	*Mishnah Zera^{c}im*, Ms. Sassoon 531. See Zachs, I, p. 68.
Soler	=	J. Soler, "The Dietary Prohibitions of the Hebrews," *New York Review of Books*, June 14, 1979 (26:10), pp. 24-30.
Sot.	=	Soṭah
Suk.	=	Sukkah
T	=	Mishnah *Zera^{c}im*, Yemenite ms. of J. Qappaḥ. See Zachs, I, pp. 80-81.
T.	=	Tosefta
Ta.	=	Ta^{c}anit
Tam.	=	Tamid
TAS	=	*Tosafot Anshé Shem*, anonymous nineteenth century Mishnah commentary; in Romm edition of Mishnah.
Tem.	=	Temurah
Ter.	=	Terumot

Theophrastus, *Historia Plantarum*	=	Theophrastus, *Enquiry into Plants*, trans. A. Hort (London and New York: W. Heinemann and G.P. Putnam's Sons, 1916). Two volumes.
TK	=	See Liebermann, *TK*.
Tm	=	Mishnah *Zera^{c}im*, Yemenite ms. of R. Maimon. See Zachs, I, pp. 80-81.
Toh.	=	Ṭohorot
Tos.	=	Tosafot
T.Y.	=	Ṭebul Yom
TYB	=	Baruch Isaac b. Israel Lipschütz (1812-1877), *Tif'eret Yisra'el Bo^{c}az*, supercommentary to TYY; in Romm edition of Mishnah.
TYT	=	Yom Tov Lipman Heller, (1579-1694), *Tosafot Yom Tov*, Mishnah commentary; in Romm ed. of Mishnah.
TYY	=	Israel b. Gedaliah Lipschütz (1782-1860), *Tif'eret Yisra'el Yakhin*, Mishnah commentary; in Romm edition of Mishnah.
Uqs.	=	^{c}Uqṣin
V	=	Babylonian Talmud, *editio princeps*, Venice 1520-23 (photocopy: Jerusalem: Makor, 1967-72). See Zachs, I, pp. 83-84.
Varro	=	Varro, *On Agriculture*, trans. W.D. Hooper, rev. H.B. Ash. Loeb Classical Library (1934; revised and reprinted, London and Cambridge, Mass.: W. Heinemann and Harvard University Press, 1967).

Vienna	=	Tosefta, Ms. Vienna Heb. 20. See Lieberman, *TZ*, pp. 11-12.
Weiss, Sifra	=	I.H. Weiss, ed., *Sifra debe Rab* (1862; rpt. New York: Om, 1846).
White	=	White, E.B., *Roman Farming* (Ithaca: Cornell University Press, 1970).
Wilson, *Clothing*	=	L.M. Wilson, *The Clothing of the Ancient Romans* (Baltimore: Johns Hopkins Press, 1938).
Wild, "Flax-hackle"	=	J.P. Wild, "The Roman Flax-hackle (AENA)", in *Museum Helveticum* 25 (1968), pp. 139-142.
Wild, *Textile Manufacture*	=	J.P. Wild, *Textile Manufacture in the Northern Provinces* (Cambridge: Cambridge University Press, 1970).
Windfuhr	=	G. Kittel and K.H. Rengstorf, eds., *Die Tosefta: Text, Übersetzung und Erklärung Vi.1. Kelim-Ahilot-Negaim*, by W. Windfuhr (Stuttgart: Kohlhammer, 1960).
Y.	=	Yerushalmi, Palestinian Talmud
Yad.	=	Yadayim
Yev.	=	Yevamot
Y.T.	=	Yom Ṭob
Zab.	=	Zabbim
Zachs	=	N. Zachs, ed., *M. Zera^{c}im* (Jerusalem: Makhon HaTalmud HaYisraeli HaShalem 1972-75). Two volumes.

Zeb.	=	Zebaḥim
Zohary	=	M. Zohary, *A New Analytical Flora of Israel* [Heb.] (Tel Aviv: Am Oved, 1976).
Zuckermandel	=	M.S. Zuckermandel, ed., *Tosephta, based on the Erfurt and Vienna Codices* (Trier, 1881-82; revised edition with Supplement by Saul Lieberman, Jerusalem, 1936-39; rpt. Jerusalem: Wahrmann, 1970).

i. The central thesis of the tractate

Mishnah Kilayim examines the scriptural prohibitions against commingling different classes of plants, animals, or fibers. While agreeing with Scripture's basic premise that different classes must be kept separate from one another, the tractate brings to its subject a conception of the law which is unknown to Scripture but distinctive to Mishnah as a whole. Specifically, Mishnah Kilayim maintains that it is man who both defines what constitutes a class and determines how to keep the different classes distinct from one another. Man thus imposes upon an otherwise disorderly world limits and boundaries which accord with human perception of order and regularity. In the tractate's view, then, what appears to man as orderly becomes identified with the objective order of the world. In presenting this conception of the law of diverse-kinds, the tractate Kilayim expresses views which are paralleled elsewhere in Mishnah. The tractate's interest in the human role in the ordering of mundane and ordinary things mirrors the emphasis placed by other mishnaic treatises[1] upon the part played by man in defining the boundaries of the sacred. These other tractates claim that human thought and action affect the susceptibility of objects to either holiness or its opposite, uncleanness. As I shall explain below, Mishnah Kilayim applies the same principles to the ordering of the mundane realm that other mishnaic tractates apply to demarcating the bounds of the sacred.

Mishnah's divergence from Scripture becomes striking when we turn to the actual texts of the biblical rules. These laws are found in two sources:

Lv. 19:19

"You shall keep my statutes. You shall not let your cattle breed with a different kind (*kl'ym*[2]); you shall not sow your field with two kinds of seed; nor shall there come upon you a garment of cloth made of two kinds of stuff (*kl'ym š^cṭnz*[3])."

Dt. 22:9-11

"You shall not sow your vineyard with two kinds of seed, lest the whole yield be sanctified (*tqdš*), the crop which you have sown and the yield of the vineyard. You shall not plow with an ox and an ass

1

together. You shall not wear a mingled stuff
($š^c\!\!tnz$), wool and linen together."

Although there are differences between the two sources, both
versions of the rules agree that it is prohibited to commingle
plants, animals, or fibers of different kinds. First, both
Leviticus and Deuteronomy prohibit the sowing of different classes
of seeds among one another (the topic of Chapters One through
Three of Mishnah), although Deuteronomy prohibits only the sowing
of seeds in a vineyard (the topic of Chapters Four through Seven
of Mishnah). Second, both sources prohibit the joining together
of animals of different kinds (the topic of Chapter Eight of
Mishnah). Leviticus, however, refers specifically to the mating
of such animals, while Deuteronomy speaks of yoking them together
to pull a plow. Finally, the wearing of a garment composed of
commingled kinds of fibers is also prohibited by both sources,
although Deuteronomy takes "mingled stuff" to refer to a mixture
of wool (an animal product) and linen (a plant product) alone (as
discussed in Chapter Nine of Mishnah). In each case, then, the
two sources agree in prohibiting the commingling of different
classes, while differing as to the specific act of commingling
which is forbidden.

A comparison of the different formulations of the law, in
any event, adds little to our investigation of the larger meaning
of the scriptural laws of diverse-kinds. What we do want to know,
on the other hand, is how each of the pentateuchal sources interprets the significance and purpose of these laws. It is difficult
to learn anything about the views of D, for the context of its
laws, a catalogue of rules dealing with unrelated topics, offers
no insight into D's understanding of these laws. By contrast,
a study of the context of the rules in the Holiness Code of
Leviticus yields important knowledge of P's views of the laws of
diverse-kinds. Leviticus 19 consists of a list of rules headed
by the command *You shall be holy; for I the Lord your God am holy*
(Lv. 19:2). According to the catalogue's redactor, then,
observance of the laws of diverse-kinds, like observance of the
other rules of the catalogue, makes Israel holy. The laws are
therefore to be interpreted in the context of the priestly understanding of the relationship between order and holiness. By
examining this relationship we shall be able to put into perspec-
tive Mishnah's divergence from the views of Scripture.

In the view of the priestly circles which stand behind P,
order is a precondition of holiness. This notion is clearly
reflected in P's account of the creation (Gn. 1:1-2:4a). P
describes the making of a well-ordered, hierarchical world. Each

type of creation is brought forth in order of ascending importance,
with (among living things) plant life appearing first (Gn. 1:11-12),
then animal life (Gn. 1:20-25), and finally man (Gn. 1:26-27).
All living things, furthermore, were created *each according to
its kind* (Gn. 1:11-12, 21, 24-25).[4] Creation is thus an act
of ordering, the purpose of which is to make the world perfect
and thus prepare it to be made holy. The actual act of the
sanctification of the world then takes place on the Sabbath
(Gn. 2:1-3). The point of P's laws in Leviticus, then is to
prevent the confusion of those classes and categories which were
established at the creation. P thus commands man to restore the
world from its present condition of chaos to its original orderly
state, and so to make the world ready once again for sanctification.

Although Mishnah takes up P's general interest in order,
it clearly diverges from P's view that the task of man is to
restore the original order of creation. For, as we have already
stated, Mishnah claims that it is man, and not a set of already
established rules, who decides what is orderly and what is confused. This claim leads the tractate to examine issues which
are wholly unknown to P. For example, Scripture would maintain
that wheat and barley may not be grown together in the same
field, for the growth of two kinds in a single field would con-
fuse the distinctions between these two kinds. By contrast,
according to Mishnah the commingling of different classes is prohibited only if the resultant mixture appears to man to contain
a confusion of kinds, but not if the different kinds are arranged
in an orderly manner. Mishnah thus permits one to grow wheat
and barley in the same field, provided that each kind is allowed
a substantial amount of area, and so appears to be sown in a
separate area unto itself (cf. especially M. 2:6 and 2:9).
Unlike Scripture, then, which is concerned with the absolute
separation of different classes, Mishnah attempts to determine
how different kinds may be kept distinct from one another as
they grow together. Mishnah's views concerning the role of man
in establishing order thus raise new and interesting issues in
the law of diverse-kinds.

Mishnah's divergence from P becomes even more interesting
when one takes into account the historical context of the two
documents. Both P and Mishnah take shape in the aftermath of
historical catastrophes. P was compiled during and after the
exile which followed the destruction of the First Temple, while
Mishnah was redacted primarily after the failure of the Bar
Kokhba rebellion (132-135 A.D.), a disaster which erased

the Jews' last hope of regaining and rebuilding the Temple. It
is thus noteworthy that both P and Mishnah respond to these
similar historical circumstances with an interest in restoring
order to a world which to them appears to lie in utter confusion.
It is striking, therefore, that these two documents should disagree concerning the nature of the order which they intend to
restore. What is important to P is that the world should be returned from its present condition of confusion to its original,
ordered state, as God had created it. P thus responds to the
crisis it perceives by calling for a return to an unchanging,
perfect world. By contrast, Mishnah underlines man's power to
impose order upon the world, a capacity which is unaffected by
historical events. In spite of the occurrence of catastrophes
and disasters, man retains the ability to affect the world around
him through such ordinary activities as sowing a field. While
P thus has man confront confusion by reconstructing the ideal
order of creation, Mishnah regards man as imposing his own order
upon a world in a state of chaos, and so, in effect, as participating in the process of creation.

ii. The structure and contents of the tractate

The first stage in the analysis of Mishnah Kilayim is a
consideration of the tractate as a whole. By examining the logic
which governs the organization of the tractate's materials, we
may understand how the redactors of the tractate viewed the rela-
tionships among the themes and topics which they present, and so
identify the central propositions which they develop. Having
determined first how the tractate's redactors related one idea to
the other, we may begin the exegesis of the text with the same
understanding of the tractate as a whole which is held by the
redactors themselves.

Mishnah Kilayim is organized topically, considering in turn
plants (Unit I), animals (Unit II), and fibers (Unit III). In
each case Mishnah discusses permitted and prohibited ways of
commingling different classes. The most important unit is
the first, which develops the tractate's thesis that a mixture
is prohibited only if it produces the appearance of a confusion
of diverse-kinds. The tractate's redactors, in fact, could have
completed their treatise at the conclusion of this unit, for, as
we shall see, Units II and III do not introduce into the
tractate any major principles dealing with the laws of diverse-
inds. These two units serve only to include in the tractate
Scripture's remaining two topics, the commingling of animals or

fibers of different kinds. It appears, then, that the primary
interest of the tractate's redactors concerns issues relating
to the commingling of different classes of plants alone.

I. *Plants: Growing together different kinds of plants.*
    1:1-7:8
    A. *Plants which are or are not considered diverse-kinds with
        one another.* 1:1-6
    1:1 Wheat and tares, etc., are not considered diverse-kinds
        with one another (six pairs in all).
    1:2 A chate melon and a musk melon, etc., are not considered
        diverse-kinds with one another (eight pairs in all).
  1:4A-C Fruits of the tree: Pears and crustaminum pears, etc.,
        are not considered diverse-kinds with one another (two
        pairs in all).
  1:4D-F Apples and Syrian pears, etc., even though they resemble
        each other, are considered diverse-kinds with one
        another (three pairs in all).
    1:5 A radish and a rape etc., even though they resemble
        each other, are considered diverse-kinds with one
        another (three pairs in all).
    1:6 A wolf and a dog, etc., even though they resemble each
        other, are considered diverse-kinds with one another
        (seven pairs in all).

        Unit I opens at A with a catalogue listing different kinds
of plants which may or may not be commingled. This catalogue
sets the stage for the remainder of the unit, which discusses
various types of commingling. B discusses grafting, an act which
Scripture neglects to prohibit. C and D, respectively, discuss
sowing together different classes of plants in a field (Lv. 19:19),
or growing such plants together in a vineyard (Dt. 22:9). The
unit as a whole, therefore, consists of a proem (A), a non-
scriptural prohibition against commingling different kinds of
plants (B), and discussions of two scriptural prohibitions (C-D).
As we shall see below, Units II and III continue C-D's treatment
of the scriptural prohibitions of diverse-kinds.
        A's catalogue lists pairs containing items which resemble
one another. At issue in A, therefore, is whether one may
commingle items, which, when mingled together, do not produce
the appearance of confusion. A presents two opposing views of
this question, with M. 1:1-4C maintaining that such plants
may be commingled, while M. 1:4D-6 disagrees. We shall take up

in our commentary the problems relating to the interpretation of
these sublists. Both M. 1:1-4C and M. 1:4D-6 are organized
topically, as the former treats, grain, vegetables, and fruits,
while the latter deals with fruits, vegetables, and animals.
This last, anomalous category is surprising, for we would have
expected grain to follow vegetables and so form the pattern
a-b-c-c-b-a. I cannot explain why the catalogue of animals is
included in A's list. It may serve simply to signify the
completion of the list as a whole.

B. *Grafting one kind of plant onto another.* 1:7-9D

1:7   Prohibition of grafting a tree or vegetable of
       one kind onto a tree or vegetable of another
       kind, *vs.* Judah: They do graft a vegetable
       onto a tree.

1:8   Illustrations of the above prohibition.

1:9A-D He who buries turnips or radishes under a vine
       does not scruple lest he has transgressed the
       laws of diverse-kinds, etc.

As pointed out above, B's discussion of the prohibition of
grafting is not mentioned by Scripture. The unit is placed here
so as not to interrupt Mishnah's discussion of the four scriptural
prohibitions of diverse-kinds: 1) sowing different kinds of
plants in a field (C), 2) sowing grain or vegetables in a vineyard (D), 3) mating or yoking together animals of different
kinds (Unit II), 4) commingling wool and flax (Unit III). M. 1:7
opens B with a general prohibition against grafting trees or
vegetables onto one another, which M. 1:8 then illustrates.
M. 1:9A-D appropriately closes the section with a discussion
of an ambiguous case, a graft which appears to take place but
does not actually occur.

C. *Sowing together different kinds of crops.* 1:9E-3:7

   1. *Sowing together different kinds of crops in the
      same space.* 1:9E-2:5

1:9E-H Sowing two kinds of seed simultaneously: He who
        sows a grain of barley together with a grain of
        wheat, this is considered diverse-kinds, *vs.* Judah.

2:1-2   A *se'ah* consisting of seeds of one kind and con-
        taining a quarter-*qab* of seeds of another kind--

he shall lessen the quantity of the latter
kind, *vs*. Yosé: He shall sift them out completely.

2:3-5 Sowing two kinds of seed sequentially: If his
field was sown with wheat, and he decided to sow
it with barley, he waits for the wheat to take
root, overturns it, and sows the barley + two
further cases.

2. *Sowing together different kinds of crops in adjacent
spaces.* 2:6-3:3

2:6 He who wishes to lay out his field in narrow beds
of every kind + Houses-dispute: How large must
the beds be?

2:7 If a row of wheat enters an adjacent field of barley,
it is permitted, since the row looks like the end
of the field of wheat + two further cases concerning
the borders of fields.

2:8 They do not flank a field of grain with mustard or
safflower, but only a field of vegetables.

2:9 He who wishes to lay out his field in patches of
every kind--he lays out twenty-four patches *per
bet se'ah*, one to a *bet rova*^{c}, and sows a different
kind in each. Dispute between Meir, sages, and
Eliezer b. Jacob: How many patches may be sown
with mustard?

2:10 Everything contained in a *bet rova*^{c} is reckoned as
part of it: the ground required for a vine, etc.
Grain of one kind sown in a field of grain of another
kind requires a *bet rova*^{c} of area, etc.

2:11 Grain which leans over grain of another kind, etc.,
is permitted, except for the Greek gourd (which
becomes tangled up with the other kind) + Meir.

3:1 A garden-bed measuring six handbreadths square--
they sow five kinds in it, four along the sides and
three in the middle, *vs*. Judah.

3:2 They do not sow seeds of grain, but only those of
vegetables in a garden-bed.
A border which became diminished in height is fit,
since it was fit from its inception.

3:3 If a row of vegetables enters an adjacent field
of vegetables of another kind, etc.
If his field was sown with one kind of vegetable,
and he wished to plant in it a row of vegetables
of another kind + dispute between Ishmael and

[C]Aqiva: How large must the row be? + Judah.

3. *Sowing together different kinds of crops in*
adjacent spaces. Special case: Trailing plants.
3:4-7

3:4   He who plants two rows each of chate melons,
        gourds, etc.,--it is permitted. One row each--it
        is prohibited, since they do not appear to be
        planted in autonomous fields.

3:5   A man plants a chate melon and a gourd in the same
        hollow provided that each leans to a different side.

3:6   If his field was sown with onions and he wishes
        to plant in it rows of gourds + dispute between
        Ishmael and [C]Aqiva: How much space must be left
        between the two kinds? + sages.

3:7   Gourds planted in a field of vegetables require
        the same area as vegetables planted in a vegetable-
        field of another kind. A row of gourds planted in
        a field of grain requires an area of tillage of six
        handbreadths *vs.* Yosé: Four *amot* + debate: Do
        gourds require more area of tillage than does a vine?

C's treatment of the sowing of different kinds of crops in
a field (Lv. 19:19) begins the tractate's discussion of the
scriptural prohibitions of diverse-kinds. At issue in C is the
manner in which crops belonging to different kinds may be commingled without violating the laws of diverse-kinds. This problem
is treated in two parts, with C1 considering the sowing together
of different kinds of crops in the same space, and C2 considering
the sowing together of such crops in adjacent spaces. C3 then
goes over the ground of C2, this time with regard to the special
case of trailing plants. These plants differ from other crops
in that they tend to spread out over adjacent plants, and so must
be separated from the latter by a fixed distance. C3 thus serves
to introduce D's discussion of sowing crops among vines, which
similarly must be distanced from adjacent plants.

Let us now examine each of C's subunits in detail. C1's
discussion of sowing seeds of different kinds in the same area
opens at M. 1:9E-H, with a general rule concerning the number
of such seeds which, if sown together, render the sower liable
under the laws of diverse-kinds. M. 2:1-2 then proceeds to the
more complex case of sowing a mixed assortment of seeds at the
same time. Mishnah now asks an entirely separate question, *viz.*,
whether one may sow different kinds of seeds together if one does

not thereby produce the appearance of confusion. Once we have
considered the sowing of different kinds of seeds at the same
time, M. 2:3-5 turns to discuss the question of sowing different
classes of seeds in sequence.

From C1's treatment of sowing different classes of plants in
the same space C2 turns to a discussion of sowing such plants in
adjacent spaces. This section is constructed from two formal
subunits, M. 2:6+2:9, concerning various ways of arranging many
different kinds of plants in a field, and M. 2:7+3:3, dealing
with the case of a row of one kind of plants which extends into
a field containing another kind. M. 2:7 has been separated from
M. 3:3 and inserted between M. 2:6 and M. 2:9 because of M. 2:8.
The latter glosses both M. 2:7's discussion of the borders of a
field and M. 2:9's treatment of the mustard plant, and so had to
be placed in close proximity to both pericopae. M. 2:7-8 could
not, however, have been placed after M. 2:9, for the latter is
closely followed by M. 2:10-11. M. 2:10 glosses M. 2:9's discussion of a *bet rova*[c], while M. 2:11 supplements M. 2:10's own
treatment of different kinds growing in adjacent spaces. M. 2:7-8
therefore could only have been placed immediately before M. 2:9.
M. 3:1-2 turns from M. 2:6-11's discussion of sowing different
kinds of plants in a field to consider sowing such plants, vegetables in particular (M. 3:2), in a garden-bed, a miniature
version of a field. Reverting to the issues of the opening of
the section, M. 3:3 supplements M. 3:1-2's discussion of vegetables
with a reprise of M. 2:7, dealing this time with vegetables
instead of grain. M. 3:3 thus serves to tie together the entire
section.

As we have already mentioned, C3 offers a reprise of C2,
dealing this time with trailing plants. C3 consists of two
parts, M. 3:4-5, considering the planting of different kinds of
trailing plants with one another, and M. 3:6-7, discussing the
planting of a single kind of trailing plants among grain or
vegetables. The debate at M. 3:7, comparing the distance which
must separate a gourd from adjacent plants to that which must
set off a vine from nearby plants of other kinds, provides a smooth
transition to D's discussion of sowing crops among vines.

    D. *Sowing crops among vines.* 4:1-7:8
        1. *Permitted sowing of crops in a vineyard.* 4:1-5:4
    4:1-4   Sowing within or around a vineyard: Houses-disputes:
           How large must bald spot, outer space be in order
           to be sown with grain or vegetables. Definition of
           various areas and structures in a vineyard.

4:5   Definition of a vineyard: Houses-disputes:
       He who plants a row of five vines--House of
       Shammai: It is considered a vineyard. House of
       Hillel: It is not a vineyard unless it contains
       two rows + further Houses-dispute making same
       point.

4:6-7 Rulings concerning particular arrangements of
       vines, all presupposing the view of the House of
       Hillel.

4:8-9 He who plants two rows of vines--How much space
       must separate the rows if one wishes to sow between
       them? + further cases dealing with three rows,
       vineyard.

5:1   Special cases of vineyards: A vineyard laid
       waste, or irregularly planted: Under what circum-
       stances are they considered vineyards?

5:2   A vineyard which is planted with less than four *amot*
       separating the rows + dispute between Simeon and
       sages: Is it considered a vineyard?

5:3-4 Autonomous areas within a vineyard: A ditch, wine-
       press, etc.: Is one permitted to sow grain or
       vegetables in them?

    2. *Prohibited sowing of crops in a vineyard.* 5:5-5:8

5:5   He who plants vegetables in a vineyard or allows
       them to grow renders liable to destruction forty-
       five vines. Under what circumstances? Etc.

5:6   He who sees vegetables in the vineyard--he need
       not pluck them until he reaches them; but he may
       not leave them and return, since he would thereby
       indicate his approval of their growth.

5:7   If seeds accidentally enter a vineyard, the vines are
       not liable to destruction as long as the owner does
       not actually see the seeds go into the vineyard.

5:8   He who allows thorns to grow in a vineyard + dispute
       between Eliezer and sages: Does he render the vines
       liable to destruction? Discussion concerning the
       status in a vineyard of other plants not usually
       grown for food.

    3. *Permitted sowing of crops near vines: Special cases.*
       6:1-7:2

6:1   Definition of an espalier and determination of its
       area of tillage + Houses-disputes: From what part of
       the espalier is the area of tillage measured? +
       Yohanan b. Nuri.

6:2   An espalier which projects from a terrace--how much
       of the ground below may not be sown? Eliezer b.
       Jacob: If he can harvest it from the ground, it is
       regarded as if it were on the ground, etc. +
       Eliezer.

6:3-5 He who trains a vine over some laths of latticework,
       he shall not put seed under the remainder of the
       laths. Further cases of barren and fruit trees
       serving to support the vine. Definition of a
       barren tree.

6:6   Gaps of an espalier--they must measure eight *amot*
       and a little more in order to be sown. Definition
       of a gap of an espalier.

6:7   An espalier which projects along a wall from a
       corner and stops--they allow its area of tillage
       and sow the rest, *vs.* Yosé.

6:8-9 Reeds, blossoms, etc., which project from an
       espalier: Is it permitted to sow opposite them?

7:1   He who sinks a vine-shoot into the ground--if there
       are not three handbreadths of soil on top of it,
       he may not put seed upon it.

7:2A-C He who sinks three vine-shoots, and their roots are
       visible--Eleazar b. Sadoq: If there are from four
       to eight *amot* between them, they combine to form a
       vineyard, etc.

7:2D-F Discussion of items near which it is prohibited
       to sow but which do not render liable to destruction
       the grain or vegetables sown near them.

    4. *Prohibited sowing of crops near vines: Special cases.*
       7:3-8

7:3   These prohibit but do not render liable to destruc-
       tion: The remainder of the waste-state of the
       vineyard, etc. (four items in all). But the area
       under the vine, etc. do render liable to destruction
       (three items in all).

7:4-5 He who trellises his vine over his neighbor's grain,
       he has rendered it liable to destruction, etc., *vs.*
       Yosé and Simeon: A man does not render liable to
       destruction that which is not his own + Yosé:
       ma^ca&eh attributing rule to ^cAqiva.

7:6   The usurper who sowed a vineyard, and it left his
       possession--the rightful owner must cut down the
       sown crop immediately, etc.

7:7   A wind which hurled vines on top of grain--he
       shall cut down the vines at once, + further cases.
       At what point in their growth do grain, grapes
       become liable for destruction?

7:8   A perforated pot containing seeds of vegetables or
       grain, but not an unperforated pot, *vs.* Simeon:
       Both unperforated and perforated pots are prohibited
       from being placed in a vineyard, but they do not
       render the vines liable for destruction.

D discusses a second scriptural prohibition, the rule against
sowing grain or vegetables in a vineyard (Dt. 22:9). D presents
a balanced treatment of this rule, dealing first with the permitted ways of sowing crops in a vineyard (D1), and then with the
consequences of sowing crops in a vineyard in a prohibited
manner (D2). D3 and D4 then respectively supplement D1 and D2
with a discussion of special cases, and so form an appropriate
conclusion to the section.

Let us now consider each part of D in detail. At the center
of D1 stand two sets of Houses-disputes. M. 4:1 (heavily
glossed at M. 4:1-4) deals with the minimum size required of areas
in or around a vineyard in order to be sown with grain or
vegetables without creating the appearance of confusion. M. 4:5
then discusses the number of rows, and the number of vines within
these rows, that are required to form a vineyard. Although this
definition of a vineyard is logically prior to M. 4:1's discussion
of areas in or around a vineyard, D1's redactors chose to place
M. 4:1 first because M. 4:5 introduces a new subunit concerning the
rows of a vineyard. M. 4:6-7 supplements M. 4:5 with a discussion
of secondary questions relating to the number of rows and vines
required to form a vineyard, while M. 4:8-9 turns to the question
of sowing between the rows of a vineyard. D1 thus first discusses the question of sowing grain or vegetables in areas in or
near the vineyard (M. 4:1-4), and then considers the problem of
sowing such plants among the actual rows of the vineyard (M. 4:5-9).
M. 5:1-2 further supplements M. 4:5-9's treatment of the rows of
a vineyard with a discussion of irregular arrangements of vineyards. Finally, M. 5:3-4 returns to the concerns of the opening
of the section, asking again whether certain areas within a vineyard may be sown with grain or vegetables. In this instance,
however, the spaces are set apart from the vineyard not by their
size, as in M. 4:1-4, but by their height or depth.

From D1's treatment of permitted ways of sowing crops in a
vineyard, D2 turns to discuss the consequences of sowing crops

in a vineyard in a prohibited manner. D2 opens at M. 5:5 with a
rule concerning the number of vines which must be destroyed when
grain or vegetables (which must also be destroyed [Dt. 22:9]) have
been sown nearby in a prohibited manner. M. 5:6-8 then qualifies
this rule, asking whether one must take into account the intentions of the owner (M. 5:6-7) or the presumed purpose for which
the crops have been grown (M. 5:8).

D3 returns to the concerns of D1, considering again the
sowing of crops near vines in a permitted manner. In this case,
however, the vines do not grow in a vineyard, but are arranged
in other patterns. D3 discusses two such arrangements of vines,
with M. 6:1-9 dealing with vines trained upon a supporting
structure, while M. 7:1-2 treats vines which have been sunk into
the ground to create new plants. M. 6:1-9 asks whether crops may
be sown in the vicinity of vines which are trained upon a supporting structure. Dealing with both an espalier (a row of
trained vines; M. 6:1-2+6-9) and an individual trained vine
(M. 6:3-5), this subunit systematically considers the possibility
of sowing crops in various areas around the vine. M. 6:1-2 opens
the subunit with a discussion of the areas directly opposite
(M. 6:1) and under (M. 6:2) the supporting structure of an
espalier. Interpolated into this discussion of a row of trained
vines, M. 6:3-5 supplements M. 6:2 with a discussion of sowing
under a structure which supports a single vine. At issue in
M. 6:3-5 is whether the vine takes over the aspect of the entire
supporting structure, so that one cannot sow crops even under that
part of the structure which does not support the vine. Having
thus treated the areas surrounding the vines and their supporting
structure, we then proceed at M. 6:6-7 to discuss those areas
which are actually aligned with the vines, whether in the middle
(M. 6:6) or at the end (M. 6:7) of a row. M. 6:8-9 concludes
the subunit with an ambiguous case, asking whether reeds or
blossoms which project outward from an espalier are regarded as
integral to the latter, so that it is prohibited to sow under
them.

D3's second subunit, M. 7:1-2, discusses a pattern of vines
which is created by sinking vine-shoots into the ground to
grow new roots. Like M. 6:1-9, this subunit deals with both a
single vine (M. 7:1) and a row of vines (M. 7:2A-C). At issue
in M. 7:1 is whether one may sow crops above a sunken shoot
without allowing the roots of the crops to become attached to
the sunken vine and so create a prohibited graft. M. 7:2A-C then
turns to a separate question, asking whether a row of new vines
may combine with their parent vines to form a vineyard. M. 7:2D-F

closes the subunit by introducing the concern of D4, *viz.*, prohibited means of sowing crops near vines which do not render the
latter liable to destruction. Although M. 7:2D-F thus turns to an
entirely new problem, the pericope is linked to M. 7:1-2C in
two ways. First, both M. 7:2D-F and M. 7:1-2C contain sayings
attributed to Eleazar b. Ṣadoq (M. 7:2F, M. 7:2A-C). More
importantly, however, Eleazar b. Ṣadoq's saying at M. 7:2D-F
supplements M. 7:1's discussion of the sunken vine-shoot, and so
provides an even stronger link to the rest of the subunit.

Reverting to the concerns of D2, D4 presents a series of
exceptions to the latter's general rule that one must destroy
crops and vines which grow together in a prohibited manner.
In D4's cases, by contrast, one need not destroy such crops and
vines, even though it is prohibited to grow them together in the
first place. D4 presents three different types of cases where
this rule holds. First, M. 7:3 lists specific areas in the
vicinity of vines which may not be sown with crops but which do
not render these crops liable to destruction. M. 7:4-7 then discusses cases in which either human (M. 7:4-6) or non-human
(M. 7:7) agents cause diverse-kinds to grow without the owner's
knowledge or permission. In these instances the crops do not
render the vines liable to destruction, but the owner may not
maintain the growth of diverse-kinds once he discovers them.
Finally, having considered at M. 7:1-7 cases in which the crops
actually grow together with the vines, we turn at M. 7:8 to a
case in which this point is ambiguous. Now the crops grow in a
perforated pot which is placed in a vineyard. At issue, therefore,
is whether the crops are regarded as growing in the vineyard,
so that the vines are liable to destruction, or whether it is
prohibited to place the pot in the vineyard, but the vines need
not be destroyed. With this case of doubt, M. 7:8 concludes both
D4 and D as a whole.

To summarize, Unit I is laid out in a highly logical manner.
A presents a catalogue of plants which may or may not be
commingled, and so serves to introduce B-D's discussion of the
various ways of commingling plants which clearly belong to two
different classes. This latter subunit first considers a method
of commingling which is not mentioned in Scripture (B), and then
turns to its primary concern, the scriptural prohibitions against
commingling different kinds of plants in a field (C) or in a
vineyard (D). C and D are themselves well-structured. C asks
how different classes of plants may be sown together in a field,
whether in the same space (C1) or in adjacent spaces (C2). C3
then goes over the ground of C2, but this time dealing with the

special case of trailing plants, and so serving to introduce D's
discussion of a similar plant, the grapevine. D presents both
sides of the question of sowing crops in a vineyard, considering
first the permitted ways of sowing crops and vines together (D1),
and then the consequences of commingling such plants in a
prohibited manner (D2). D3 and D4 then repeat the same sequence.
Unit I is thus arranged in a thoroughly rational way, with both
the unit as a whole and each of its primary subunits structured
according to their own respective principles of organization.

II. *Animals: Mating or yoking together animals of different kinds.*
   8:1-6
   8:1   General rules concerning the different types of
            diverse-kinds: Diverse-kinds of the vineyard
            differ from diverse-kinds of seeds in that one may
            not derive benefit from them. Diverse-kinds of
            garments are prohibited only from being worn.
            Diverse-kinds of animals are permitted to be reared
            and maintained, and are prohibited only from being
            bred.
   8:2   Prohibition against joining together domesticated
            and wild, clean and unclean animals with one another
            to plow, draw a vehicle, or be led.
   8:3   Both he who leads a wagon drawn by animals of
            different kinds, and he who sits in it incur forty
            lashes, *vs.* Meir, who exempts the one who sits.
            A third animal may not be tied to the harness of a
            wagon drawn by a different kind of animal, even
            if the third animal does not actually draw the wagon.
   8:4A-B   Further discussion of this last principle.
   8:4C-E   Judah: All offpsring of a female horse, and a male
            ass are permitted with one another, and *vice-versa*.
            But the offspring of a female horse are not permitted
            to be mated with the offspring of a female ass.
   8:5A-B   Special types of mules: The mule of unknown parentage,
            etc.
   8:5C-6   Classification of special cases of animals: Are
            they considered man or animal, wild or domesticated?

Unit II's discussion of commingling different kinds of
animals opens the tractate's brief treatment of the two remaining
scriptural prohibitions of diverse-kinds. As we shall shortly
see, Unit III takes up the last such prohibition, the rule
against commingling different classes of fibers. At the head of

Unit II stands a list of rules relating to each of the four
scriptural prohibitions of diverse-kinds   (M. 8:1). This catalogue
serves to link Unit II to Unit I, for the first of its rules
deals with diverse-kinds of the vineyard, the subject of ID, while
the last concerns the topic of Unit II, diverse-kinds of animals.
The remainder of Unit II is organized according to the two
scriptural rules against commingling different kinds of animals.
M. 8:2-4B discusses the yoking together of different classes of
animals to do work (Dt. 22:10), while M. 8:4C-G deals with the
mating of animals of different kinds (Lv. 19:19).

III. *Fibers: Mingling wool and linen.*   9:1-10

   9:1A-C   Three rules concerning wool and linen: The laws of
            diverse-kinds prohibit only a garment composed of
            wool and linen; only garments composed of wool or
            linen are susceptible to uncleanness through
            plagues; priests wear only garments composed of
            either wool or linen to serve in the Temple.

   9:1D-H   Camel's hair and sheep's wood which were hackled
            together--if the majority is camel's wool, they may
            be mixed with flax, etc.

   9:2   Items which are not subject to the laws of diverse-
            kinds, because they only resemble wool and linen,
            or because they are not designed to serve as garments.
            Prohibition against wearing garments of diverse-
            kinds either temporarily or without intending them
            to serve as garments.

   9:3   Hand-towels, etc. (three items in all) are not subject
            to the laws of diverse-kinds, since they are not
            made to serve as garments, *vs*. Eliezer. But barber's
            towels are prohibited.

   9:4   Shrouds and a pack-saddle of an ass, items not usually
            worn by man, are not subject to the laws of diverse-
            kinds. One may not, however, place a pack-saddle on
            his shoulder and use it for carrying items, as it
            then functions like a garment.

   9:5-6   Clothes-dealers and tailors may bear garments of
            diverse-kinds in the course of their work, provided
            that they do not intend to use them as garments.

   9:7   Garments (presumably of foreign provenance) which must
            be examined for diverse-kinds before being worn: A
            birrus, *bardaicus*, etc., (four items in all) + Yosé.

9:8   A further general rule: Nothing is prohibited on
       account of the laws of diverse-kinds except wool
       and flax which have been spun or woven together +
       exegesis of "$sha^c atnez$" in Dt. 22:11 + homiletical
       exegesis by Simeon b. Eleazar.

9:9   Felted stuffs composed of wool and linen are prohi-
       bited, because they are hackled together. A fringe
       of wool fastened onto a garment of flax is prohi-
       bited, because the wool interlaces the web of the
       garment, + Yosé, and further discussion of different
       types of fastening (three cases in all).

9:10   Further discussion of fastening--three cases.

Unit III takes up the remaining scriptural prohibition of
diverse-kinds, the law against commingling different classes of
fibers (Lv. 19:19, Dt. 22:11). M. 9:1A-C introduces the unit
with three rules concerning wool and flax, the only two fibers
which may not be commingled (Dt. 22:11). The unit then considers,
in logical sequence, commingling fibers of different kinds (M.
9:1D-H) and wearing garments of diverse-kind (M. 9:2-7). M. 9:8-
10 concludes the unit with a discussion of the secondary issue,
asking whether items of wool and linen which are connected to
one another in various ways combine to form a mixture of diverse-
kinds.

In summary, we have seen that while Mishnah Kilayim follows
a topical agendum established by Scripture, it treats these
topics in accord with its own approach to the laws of diverse-
kinds. Although the tractate discusses all of the scriptural
prohibitions against commingling different kinds, it chooses
fully to examine only those laws which are of interest to it, *viz.*,
rules concerning the commingling of different kinds of plants (I).
By contrast, the units concerned with animals (II) and garments
(III) are brief, and appear in the tractate only because they
are found in Scripture. We have earlier seen that the tractate's
discussion of the law begins from a distinctively mishnaic conception of order, and so raises issues which are entirely unknown
to Scripture. Within its scriptural framework, therefore, Mishnah
Kilayim presents its own treatment of the law of diverse-kinds.

iii. Goals and Methods of Exegesis
    A. *Commentary to Mishnah*

In my commentary to Mishnah Kilayim I present both a new
translation of the tractate and a fresh exegesis of its rulings.

To consider the former first, the translation attempts to render each pericope of the tractate into intelligible English, while at the same time replicating its literary and formal traits. With this translation, then, the reader is able to follow my analysis of the literary and formal traits of each pericope, from which, as we shall shortly see, the exegesis of the law directly follows.

To translate a pericope I first divide the Hebrew text into its smallest intelligible units of thought. These units I label with the letters of the alphabet (A,B,C,...), thus enabling the reader both to see the component parts in which the pericope expresses its thoughts, and to follow my analysis of these parts in the exegesis. In translating each unit of the pericope I also attempt to find terms in English which correspond to the text's formulaic language, and to maintain as well the syntax of the pericope's rulings, thus rendering in English the pericope's formal traits. Finally, to ensure that my rendering is readable as well as accurate, I frequently insert explanatory language into my translation, placing such interpolations into square brackets. Through these methods I arrive at a translation which reproduces in a lucid manner the style and substance of the Hebrew text. I thus enable the reader immediately to see the layout of each pericope and to determine what exegetical difficulties are posed by the pericope's formal and literary traits. These difficulties I discuss in the exegesis which follows the translation of each pericope.

In my exegesis I aim to discover what the rules of each pericope of the tractate meant to the authorities who formulated them. What I want to know is simply the basic point which the framers of these rules intended their words to express. To gain such an understanding of these rules I first observe the pericope's formal traits, for it is through these traits that the authorities behind the unit attempt to draw our attention to those issues which are of primary concern to them. These larger issues generally are not stated in the pericope itself, but rather implicitly inform the unit's rules. It is thus only by noting the use of formal characteristics by the framers that I am able to draw out the unit's central issue and so gain a point of entry into the exegesis of the pericope as a whole.

The formulators of a pericope use several techniques to highlight those issues which are important to them. For one thing, they may present two balanced rules containing matching but opposing apodoses. In this manner these authorities draw our attention to the contrast between the two apodoses and hence to

the issue which produces that contrast. In my exegesis I explain
the position taken by these two rules with regard to this issue.
Alternatively, the main issue of a pericope may become clear
through the repetition or variation of syntactic patterns on the
part of the formulators of the small units. By repeating a distinctive syntactic pattern, the creators of a pericope implicitly
indicate that a single principle applies to all of the diverse
cases exhibiting that arrangement. These authorities thus lead
us to ask what the different cases all have in common. Having
determined this common factor, I then explain in my exegesis the
meaning of each rule cast in this single pattern. Finally, by
repeating a syntactic pattern and then varying it, a pericope's
framers point out an exception to the previously-stated principle.
In so doing they indicate to us that their interest centers
about this exceptional case and the issue which it raises. With
the identification of this issue I am able in my exegesis to
explain each rule of the pericope in terms of its relationship
to this central concern. It is through the use of repetition
and contrast that the pericope's formulators underline the key
issues of their construction.[5]

In addition to using balanced formulations and recurrent
syntactic patterns, as we have just seen, a pericope's formulators underline their main point by presenting their materials
in certain standard forms. Of particular importance to our
tractate, with its frequent discussion of plants or animals
belonging to different species of the same genus, is the list, a
catalogue of different items sharing a certain trait or common
status. By enumerating these items in a list, the tractate's
formulators effectively draw our attention to that unstated
feature which these items have in common, namely, their genus.
It is through reference to this common characteristic that my
exegesis explains the presence on the list of its diverse members.

Another form which frequently appears in our tractate is
the dispute. In its primary formulation the dispute consists
of a superscription followed by two opposing opinions, although
it may also be produced by a rule followed by an opposing gloss.
In either case the point of the dispute emerges through the
contrast of its two opinions, both of which relate to some larger,
unstated issue. This issue reveals not only what stands at the
center of the dispute but also what is not contested by the two
sides, that is, the premises which the two parties to the dispute
hold in common. It is this common ground which makes possible
the dispute, a discussion of a gray area of law. In my exegesis

I explain both the issue under dispute and what the two sides take for granted.

Finally, we note that in a few instances the disputes of our tractate are followed by debates. These debates serve to raise questions concerning the logical consistency within Mishnah's law as a whole of the positions of the antecedent dispute. As in the case of the dispute, the issue of the debate emerges through the contrast of the opposing opinions. In my exegesis I interpret the positions of both sides with reference to this central issue.

Having followed the formulation of a pericope to its main issue, I turn my attention to those rules which stand outside of the small unit's primary formal construction. What I want to know is whether these rules serve the pericope's main point, e.g., by introducing or illustrating it, or whether they are related only tangentially to the pericope's central concern. By first identifying this important issue, I am able to explain each of the pericope's rules in terms of its relationship to this issue and its function within the small unit.

To summarize, what I present in my commentary is the original meaning of each pericope of the tractate, the sense which the small unit held for the authorities who created it. By paying close attention to the pericope's formulation, I am able to discover the issue which stands at the center of the small unit, and which thus informs each of this unit's rules. With the identification of this issue I am able to explain each pericope solely in its own terms, within the limits of its own language and syntax. Drawing the meaning of a rule from the latter's own formulation alone, my exegesis offers the sense which the rule's formulators intended their words to convey.

In addition to explaining the meaning of the tractate's individual pericopae, I analyze how these small units have been redacted together to form larger thematic units and, ultimately, the tractate as a whole. I want to discover the principle by which the redactors of the tractate shaped their materials into well-ordered structures of ideas. To understand the organization of these constructions I first determine how discrete pericopae are arranged to constitute formally coherent units dealing with a single theme. Discussing this one theme, such units are marked by the distinctive syntactic pattern which recurs throughout it. I then attempt to discover the logic by which the redactors of the tractate have linked these thematic units together in order to develop a single principle or topic. I present this analysis of thematic units at the beginning of my commentary to each chapter of the tractate. Although these

chapters of the printed editions of the tractate frequently do
not correspond to the thematic units constructed by the tractate's
redactors, for the reader's convenience my commentary here
follows the traditional divisions of the standard Hebrew text.
In introducing each chapter I simply indicate how its materials
are divided into the redactors' thematic units.

To analyze the tractate as a whole, I stand back from its
discussions of larger principles and topics and consider its
overall structure. My goal here is twofold. First, I want to
know whether a single, generative issue, or problematic, stands
behind the rulings of the tractate. Second, I attempt to discover whether the tractate's discussion of this problematic, as
well as its treatment of secondary issues, unfolds in a logical
and orderly way. In raising these questions my aim is to determine
whether the tractate has a single, major point which it wishes to
express in a cogent and articulate manner. This analysis of the
tractate, which I have already presented earlier in the Introduction, shows that our tractate does present a disciplined treatment
of a single problematic. Like its thematic units, the tractate
constitutes a well-ordered and coherent treatment of its subject.

It remains for me to discuss the importance of earlier
commentaries to the tractate for my study. I frequently make use
of these earlier works, which both explain difficult passages in
the text and render explicit the larger principles which stand
behind Mishnah's rulings. I am able to draw upon these commentaries
even though I differ with classical exegetes in my understanding
of how Mishnah was composed. We must now determine what this
difference is, and why it does not prevent me from using these
commentaries. Classical exegetes regard Mishnah as a seamless,
unitary document, and so pay little attention to the manner in
which its rules have been formulated and then redacted together.
By contrast, I do not assume that Mishnah is the product of a
single hand. For this reason I carefully observe the text's forms
and formulary paterns, which indicate to us how the tractate's
different pericopae were composed and so enable us to interpret
each of these small units in its own terms. In spite of taking
this approach to Mishnah I am able to engage in discourse with
the classical exegetes. What makes this dialogue possible is the
nature of Mishnah's own composition. Each pericope of the document has its own logic, and so can be explained without reference
to any other small units. Because these pericopae are autonomous
of one another, I am able to agree with classical exegetes
concerning the interpretation of a pericope even though I disagree
concerning its relationship to the rest of the tractate. For

this reason I am able to incorporate into my own work the results
of their efforts.

What enables me to make use of classical exegesis, however,
also determines the limits of such use. Although each of the
tractate's pericopae may be explained in its own terms, classical
exegetes frequently fail to confine their explanations to the
issues raised by these small units themselves. Rather, these
commentators seek to understand what a rule means in relation to
laws found in other rabbinic documents, such as Tosefta, the
legal *midrashim*, and the Babylonian and Palestinian Talmuds.
Since they consider all rabbinic rulings to belong to a single,
wholly-consistent body of law, these exegetes attempt to harmonize
each of the tractate's rulings with laws found in these other
sources. What they want to know is how a rule informs the meaning
of laws belonging to these other compilations, and how these
latter rules in turn affect our understanding of the tractate's
rulings. Because of this goal, classical commentators often
introduce into their explanation of a rule issues drawn from
other sources, and so frequently do not explain a rule in terms
of its own formulation. For this reason classical exegesis does
not always offer me what I want to know, namely, the meaning which
a rule held for its creators. What earlier commentaries do provide, however, is a range of possible meanings of a law. From
among these possibilities I may select that meaning which,
following my own exegetical methods, I consider to be the sense
which the rule's formulators intended it to convey. It is in this
manner that classical exegesis offers valuable assistance to
my work of exegesis.

B. *Commentaries to Tosefta, Sifra and Sifré Dt.*

Together with my commentary to Mishnah Kilayim I present a
translation and exegesis of the corresponding tractate of Tosefta,
with each pericope of Tosefta following the pericope in Mishnah
to which it relates. A commentary to Mishnah, Tosefta relies
upon that document for its redactional order, agendum of issues,
and many of its legal principles as well. Tosefta may therefore
be understood only when read together with Mishnah. Since my commentary to Mishnah provides the most appropriate context for an
investigation of Tosefta, I have taken it upon myself to treat
the latter document as well.

My commentary to Tosefta differs from my discussion of
Mishnah principally in that its primary aim is to make clear the
relationship between these two documents. To this end, in

translating Tosefta's pericopae I italicize those passages
which cite Mishnah, placing in square brackets the references
to the original source. My exegesis then aims to interpret
each rule of Tosefta as it relates to Mishnah's laws. For the
most part Tosefta's rules either cite and gloss Mishnah's laws
or complement these rulings with related materials which carry
them forward in a new way. In only a few cases does Tosefta
present pericopae which are autonomous of Mishnah, and these I
interpret in their own terms. In all of these cases my interpretation of Tosefta applies to the document the same methods that
I employ in explaining Mishnah, and makes use of the classical
commentaries to Tosefta in the same way that my study of Mishnah
uses earlier exegesis. Among the classical exegetes of Tosefta
I make extensive use of the work of S. Lieberman.[6] Like the
classical exegetes to Mishnah, Lieberman serves the purpose of
my commentary by presenting a broad range of possibilities for
the meaning of Tosefta's rules.

In addition to the commentary to Tosefta I include a
translation and exegesis of those pericopae from Sifra (to
Leviticus) and Sifré to Deuteronomy (Sifré Dt.) which are relevant
to certain pericopae of Mishnah Kilayim. These documents aim
to demonstrate that even if a Mishnaic rule does not appear to
be based upon Scripture, it may be deduced only through a highly
formalized exegesis of the biblical text. In line with this goal
Sifra and Sifré Dt. often cite Mishnah's rulings, which rarely
appear with scriptural support, and attempt to link these to
scriptural proof-texts. Because the point of these pericopae
cannot be understood without a knowledge of Mishnah's rulings,
I treat them along with my commentary to Mishnah. As in the
case of Tosefta, my commentary to Sifra and Sifré Dt. attempts
simply to explain the point which these documents make with regard
to Mishnah. In my translation I underline the citations of Mishnah
with a dotted line, while my exegesis explains the principles of
scriptural exegesis by which Mishnah is linked to Scripture.

C. *Texts and Editions*

My translations of Mishnah and Tosefta Kilayim depend
primarily upon the texts and translations of modern scholars. My
rendering of Mishnah follows the text edited by H. Albeck.[7] I
insert into this translation (in parentheses) variant readings
from manuscripts and early printed editions as recorded by N. Zachs
in his critical edition of *Zera^c im*.[8] Foremost among the English
translations which I regularly consult, and often cite (in

brackets), is that of H. Danby.[9] I also make occasional use
of the renderings of P. Blackman[10] and J. Israelstam.[11]

In translating Tosefta I follow Ms. Vienna, which has
been published by S. Lieberman.[12] Lieberman's critical apparatus
provides variant readings from Ms. Erfurt and the first printed
edition, while in his commentary he frequently cites alternate
readings found in other rabbinic documents and in the classical
commentaries. I cite other important readings from the commentaries of Samson of Sens and GRA (found in the Romm edition of
the Babylonian Talmud).

For my translation of Sifra pericopae I use the text of
I.H. Weiss;[13] while for Sifré Dt. I rely on the edition of L.
Finkelstein.[14] I cite the biblical verses which occur in these
two documents in the translation of the Revised Standard Version
(RSV), modifying this rendering only when it is necessary to
clarify a particular point of scriptural exegesis. All scriptural
citations are consistently italicized.

KILAYIM CHAPTER ONE

Chapter One of M. Kilayim opens with lists (M. 1:1-6) which state whether or not certain plants or animals are considered diverse-kinds with one another. The redactor presents these lists as an introduction to chapters 1-7 of the tractate, which concern the prohibition of sowing diverse-kinds. The outline of the lists is as follows. M. 1:1-3 presents a list of twenty pairs of plants which are not considered diverse-kinds with each other, and thus may not be planted or cross-bred with one another. M. 1:1 concerns grains and legumes, while M. 1:2 and M. 1:3 deal with a variety of vegetables. It is clear that this list is a composite, for M. 1:3 contains a short sublist attributed to ^cAqiva, while the rest of M. 1:1-3 is given anonymously. It is possible that this anonymous part of the list is a composite as well. M. 1:4 is then set apart from the foregoing catalogue by its superscription, which reads, "And [in regard to the fruit of] the trees." M. 1:4 contains two sublists, with the first describing fruits which are not considered diverse-kinds with one another, and the second discussing fruits which are so considered. By placing M. 1:4 between M. 1:1-3 and M. 1:5-6, the redactor thus links the former's list of items which are not considered diverse kinds with the latter's catalogue of items which are regarded as diverse-kinds. M. 1:5 proceeds to list vegetables which are considered diverse-kinds, and M. 1:6 describes animals which may not be cross-bred with one another. Although the subject matter of M. 1:6 (animals) differs from that of M. 1:1-5 (plants), M. 1:6 is similar to the other lists in respect to both form and substance.

M. 1:7-8 is a brief, autonomous unit concerning prohibited grafts. The redactor has placed this unit as an appendix to M. 1:1-6, apparently because he wanted to present his briefer material before the more lengthy section on sowing diverse-kinds (Chapters Two and Three). M. 1:7 describes four general categories of prohibited grafts, three of which M. 1:8 then illustrates with specific examples. M. 1:9A-D, although apparently autonomous of M. 1:7-8, actually supplements the unit with an additional example of a graft. However, the case involves only an apparent graft rather than a real one, so that the actions described in

M. 1:9A-D are actually permitted. The redactor has then ended
the discussion of grafts by presenting an exception to the
general law.

The chapter ends with M. 1:9E-G, which is autonomous of
M. 1:9A-D. M. 1:9E-G presents a fundamental law (glossed and
opposed by Judah) defining the minimum act for which one is
liable for sowing diverse-kinds of seeds, and so introduces
Chapter Two, which opens with a discussion of sowing mixed seeds.

1:1

A. (1) Wheat[1] and tares[2]
B. are not [considered] diverse-kinds with one another.
C. (2) Barley[3] and two-rowed barley,[4]
    (3) rice-wheat[5] and spelt,[6]
    (4) the broad bean[7] and the French vetch,[8]
    (5) the red grasspea[9] and the grasspea,[10]
    (6) and the hyacinth bean ($pwl\ hlbn$)[11] and the Nile cowpea[12]
         ($\check{s}^c w^c yt$; R: $\check{s}^c w^c ym$, O: $\check{s}^c w^c yn$),
D. are not [considered] diverse-kinds with one another.

                                        M. Kil. 1:1

Chapter One presupposes the prohibition of Lv. 19:19, which
states that one may not sow different kinds of seeds in the same
field. M. 1:1-3 lists pairs of plants which are exempt from
this prohibition. Each pericope deals with a different group
(or groups) of plants and may be considered independently.

M. 1:1 consists of two lists (A and C), each followed by
the same subscription. A-B contains a single pair, while C-D
includes five pairs, five being a good mnemonic number. As we
shall see, however, it is more likely that we have a single list
composed of two groups of three, for the plants may be divided
in this way according to botanical families. The subscription
then belongs only at D, and B is unnecessary. It is possible
that the subscription was placed after the first two plants
named in M. in order to inform us that the law applies to pairs
of plants (TYT, GRA). Without B we might have thought that all
of the plants of M. are not considered diverse-kinds with one
another. The subscription is repeated at B in order to tell us
that only the members of one pair may be planted together.

We turn now to the law of M. Before we may consider the
significance of the particular plants listed in M., we must first
discuss the underlying conception of the pericope as a whole.
Why are the members of each pair of plants not considered to be

diverse-kinds with one another? This question may be answered
in one of two ways. According to one explanation (following
Maim., *Comm.*[13]) the point of M. is that, although the members
of each pair belong to two different kinds, they are similar
in appearance and thus are not considered to be diverse-kinds with
one another. This interpretation maintains, then, that it is
necessary only that a field not appear to be sown with diverse-
kinds, whether or not it is actually sown with seeds of different
kinds. Alternatively, Maimonides presents the opposite view in
his *Code* (*Diverse-Kinds* 3:1-2) as follows:

> There are kinds (*mynyn*) among seeds where
> one kind will become separated into many forms
> (*ṣwrwt*) because of a difference in locations and
> [in] the type of work [i.e. cultivation] which
> they do [in] the land; until it [i.e. the single
> kind] appears as two kinds. And although [the
> two forms] are not similar to one another, because
> they [belong] to one kind they are not [considered]
> diverse-kinds with one another.
> And there are among seeds two kinds which are
> similar to one another, and the forms of both of
> them are almost a single form; and even so, because
> they [constitute] two kinds, lo, these are pro-
> hibited [to be sown] with one another.

Maimonides then proceeds to illustrate the first rule with the
lists of M. 1:1-3, and the second with the catalogue of M. 1:5.
Maimonides here apparently interprets M. 1:1-3, which gives no
reason for its ruling, together with M. 1:5, which explicitly
states that, although the members of each of its pairs resemble
one another, they are considered to be diverse-kinds with each
other. M. 1:1-3 is thus understood as presenting a contrasting
list of plants which are not considered to be diverse-kinds with
one another even though they do not resemble one another.
According to this interpretation, then, it is important that a
field not actually be sown with diverse-kinds, regardless of its
appearance. It is not necessary, however, to read M. 1:1-3
together with M. 1:5. In addition, we shall immediately see
that the members of each pair actually do resemble one another.[14]
We therefore prefer the first interpretation given above.

The plants of pairs (1)-(3) all belong to Graminae, or the
grass family. Wheat and tares (1) belong to different genera
(*Triticum* and *Lolium*, respectively), but they resemble each other
in both their seeds and their leaves.[15] Tares are often found
growing in wheat fields.[16] Its seeds may germinate even several
years after having been planted, so that its growth could not
always be prevented. This may help explain why it was not prohibited to have wheat and tares growing in the same field.[17]

The members of the pair (2) are types of barley (genus *Hordeum*). Ordinary barley has four or six rows, as opposed to the two rows of two-rowed barley. The difference between them lies in the fertility of the spikelets (the small ears of grain). Each node on a barley stalk has three spikelets, each of which produces two seeds. In two-rowed barley, only the middle spikelet is fertile, while in ordinary barley, either two or all three of the spikelets produce seeds.[18] The plants are similar in all other respects.

Rice-wheat and spelt (3) are both types of wheat (genus *Triticum*), though they are presumably both considered diverse-kinds with the wheat of pair (1). The stalks and pales (the leaves covering the seeds) of rice-wheat and spelt are similar.[19]

The plants of pairs (4)-(6) belong to Papilionaceae, or the pea family. All of the plants of these pairs have their seeds in pods. The broad bean and the French vetch belong to the same genus (*Vicia*) and, according to Feliks, are "systematically and morphologically close."[20] The red grasspea and the grasspea (5) belong to the same genus (*Lathyrus*) and therefore presumably resemble each other. The hyacinth bean (or variety thereof) and the Nile cowpea (6) belong to different genera, and Feliks does not explain how they resemble each other. In Y. 1:1 (27a) they are both considered type of beans (*pwl*) (cf. GRA, long commentary).

1:2

A. (7) A chate melon[21] and a musk melon[22]

B. are not [considered] diverse-kinds with one another.

C. R. Judah says "[They are considered] diverse-kinds."

D. (8) Lettuce[23] and hill-lettuce[24] (*ḥzrt glym*; alternatively: *ḥzrt gnym* [garden-lettuce[25]]),

(9) chicories[26] and wild chicories,[27]

(10) leeks[28] and wild leeks,[29]

(11) coriander[30] and wild coriander,[31]

(12) mustard[32] and Egyptian mustard,[33]

(13) and an Egyptian gourd[34] and a *remuṣah*,[35]

(14) and a cowpea[36] (lit.: Egyptian bean) and an asparagus bean[37] [omitted by B. Pes. 39a[38]],

E. are not [considered] diverse-kinds with one another.

M. Kil. 1:2 (A-C: Y. Kil 1:2 (27a);[39]

D (8)-(13) + E: B. Pes. 39a)

M. 1:2 continues the list of plants which may grow
together. A presents a single pair, followed by the subscription
at B. C glosses A-B and creates a dispute. D presents seven
pairs of plants, which may be divided into groups of one (8),[40]
three ((9)-(11): cultivated v. wild species), and three ((12)-
(14): one plant in each pair is known as an Egyptian variety).
If wild mustard is read for Egyptian mustard in (12), then we
have a list of five (8)-(12) and two (13)-(14). If (14) is
dropped, as it is in B. Pes. 39a, then we have a list of five and
one.

The chate melon and the musk melon (7) belong to the same
genus and species (*Cucumis melo*) of Cucurbitaceae, or the gourd
family. Feliks argues that they produce good hybrids and therefore are not considered diverse-kinds.[41] Judah in C considers
the chate melon and the musk melon to be diverse-kinds with one
another (cf. M. Ter. 2:6, where he expresses the same opinion).

The plants of pairs (8)-(11) belong to various different
families of plants. As we have noted, though, each pair is made
up of a cultivated and wild species ((8) may or may not stand
alone). The plants of pairs (8)-(9) belong to Compositae, or
the composite family. Lettuce and hill-lettuce belong to a
single genus (*Lactuca*), as do chicory and wild chicory (*Cicorium*),
so that there is presumably a resemblance between the members
of each pair. The leek and the wild leek (10) belong to the
genus *Allium* of Liliaceae, or the lily family. Coriander and wild
coriander (11) belong to different genera (*Coriandrum* and *Bifora*,
respectively) of Umbrellifrae, or the parsley family. They resemble
each other in several respects, however, including height (½ m.),
the shape of their leaves, their white flowers, smell, and taste.
They differ only in the shape of their seeds.[42]

Each of the pairs (12)-(14), as we mentioned, contains an
Egyptian plant. Mustard and Egyptian mustard (12) belong to
different genera (*Brassica* and *Sinapsis*, respectively), of
Cruciferae, or the mustard family. The plants are similar in
appearance,[43] with the major differences being that the Egyptian
mustard plant is shorter than the mustard plant and has larger
white seeds, while the seeds of the latter plant are smaller
and are black.[44] Both the Egyptian gourd and the *remusah* (13)
are identified as varieties of the calabash gourd (*Lageneria
vulgaris*, of Cucurbitaceae, or the gourd family).[45] The cowpea
and the asparagus bean (14) both belong to the same genus (*Vigna*)
of the Papilionaceae, or the pea family, and therefore presumably
resemble each other.

A. All of the pairs which the sages enumerated--
B. one kind with its own kind (*myn bmynw*) are not [considered] diverse-kinds with one another.
C. And the rest of the wild vegetables (*yrqwt śdh*; Erfurt: *yrqwt* ["vegetables"]) and garden vegetables--
D. one kind with its own kind (*myn bmynw*) are not [considered] diverse-kinds with one another.

> T. Kil. 1:1a (p. 203, ll. 1-2)
> (Remainder of T. 1:1 cited below
> and at p. 39)

T. consists of two apocopated sentences, A-B and C-D, which have identical apodoses and thus form a unitary composition. A-B comments on the list begun in M. 1:1, and it tells us to read that list by pairs. The phrase *myn bmynw* (B) apparently means that both members of a single pair are considered to be of the same *myn*, or kind, and therefore are not considered diverse-kinds with one another. This implies that two plants which belong to different pairs are not of the same kind and are considered diverse-kinds. It should be noted that the concept of *myn* is introduced by T., for this term does not appear in the list of M. 1:1-3.

C-D offers a generalized law based on M. 1:2D, pairs (9)-(11). Each of these pairs contains one cultivated and one wild species of the same plant. C generalizes and adds all similar pairs to the list of specific pairs of M.

H. "(1) Chate melons and gourds,[46]
   "(2) and watermelons[47] and musk melons,
I. "are not [considered] diverse-kinds with one another;
J. "and they give heave-offerings and tithes from one for the other,"
K. the words of R. Meir [Erfurt: R. Meir and R. Judah].
L. R. Judah and R. Simeon [Erfurt: R. Yosé and R. Simeon] say,
M. "They are [considered] diverse-kinds with one another,
N. "and they do not give heave-offerings and tithes from one to the other."

> T. Kil. 1:1c (p. 203, ll. 3-6)

T. 1:1c is related to M. 1:2 and we shall compare the two pericopae below. T. presents an Ushan dispute about a doublet consisting of two pairs of gourds. H presents the plants at issue. I contains the same subscription as those of the list

begun in M. 1:1. J introduces a new legal consideration (cf.
M. Ter. 2:6). M-N opposes and balances I-J.

H lists four plants which belong to different genera of the
gourd family (Cucurbitaceae). The members of each pair are
somewhat similar to each other, although it is not clear to me
to what extent this is the case. There is certainly no close
resemblance, and this may be the reason for the dispute as to
whether or not the members of each pair are considered diverse-
kinds with one another.

Let us now compare T. to M. 1:2A-C, using the following
chart:

M. 1:2A-C	*T. 1:1c*
1. The chate melon and the musk melon	1. "The chate melons and the gourds and the water-melons and the musk melons
2. are not [considered] diverse-kinds with one another.	2. "are not [considered] diverse-kinds with one another;
3. ---	3. "and they give heave-offerings and tithes from one for the other,"
4. ---	4. the words of R. Meir.
5. R. Judah says,	5. R. Judah and R. Simeon say,
6. "They are [considered] diverse-kinds."	6. "They are [considered] diverse-kinds with one another,
7. ---	7. "and they do not give heave-offerings and tithes from one for the other."

T. differs from M. in three ways. First, the list of T.
at (1) includes the gourds and the watermelons, which are not
found in M. Second, T. mentions the law concerning heave-offerings
and tithes, which M. lacks, at (3) and (7). Finally, T. has
attributions to Meir, Simeon and Judah at (4) and (5), while M.
has only the attribution to Judah.[48] We see, then, that T.
presents an alternate version of M., including additional plants,
a secondary legal consideration, and additional attributions.

We now turn to the law of T. Meir's opinion in T. H-K
conflicts with the law of M. Kil. on two separate points. First,
Meir states that the chate melons and the gourds are not

considered diverse-kinds. M. Kil. 3:4-5, however, implies
that they are so considered.[49] This conflict may be explained
in one of two ways. It is probably that M. Kil. 3:4-5 simply
agrees with the view of Judah (T. L-N) rather than that of Meir.
Alternatively, the gourds do not belong at all on the list of
T.[50] The gourds may have been mistakenly included in the list
of the three melons only because the same four plants are grouped
together elsewhere in M.-T.[51] According to this explanation Meir
does not oppose the law of M. Kil. 3:4-5, for he does not discuss
the gourds at all.

The second legal problem concerns the status of the musk
melon and the chate melon. T. H places the chate melon and the
musk melon in different pairs, so that Meir's ruling implies that
they are considered diverse-kinds with one another. For it is
only if two plants belong to the same pair that they are not
considered diverse-kinds. If, however, they belong to different
pairs, the implication is that they are so considered.[52] Meir
then opposes the law of M. 1:2A-B, which states that the chate
melon and the musk melon are not considered diverse-kinds. Again
this conflict may be explained in one of two ways. It is probable
that Meir simply opposes the law of M. Alternatively, Lieberman[53]
suggests that H be read not as a list of two pairs but as adding
gourds and watermelons to the list of M. 1:2A-C. In effect,
therefore, Lieberman maintains that each of the first three items
is paired with the fourth. In other words, Meir says that
neither chate melons nor gourds nor watermelons are considered
diverse-kinds with musk-melons. According to this explanation,
then, Meir agrees with the law of M. 1:2A-B.[54] This reading
is difficult, however, for it assumes that T. is read differently
than M. (i.e. so as not to concern pairs). We therefore prefer
the first interpretation presented above.

1:3

A. (15) A turnip[55] and a rape (*npwš*; many mss.: *npwš*),[56]
    (16) and a kale[57] and a garden cabbage[58] (*trwbtwr*; Danby,
        Israelstam, Albeck: cauliflower),
    (17) the spinach beets[59] and garden sorrels,[60]
B. are not [considered] diverse-kinds with one another   [Missing
    in many mss.[61]].
C. Added (*hwsyp*) R. Aqiva, "(18) A garlic[62] and a chive,[63]
                        (19) an onion,[64] and a shallot,[65]
                        (20) and a lupine[66] and a yellow
                            lupine,[67]

D. "are not [considered] diverse-kinds with one another."

M. Kil. 1:3

M. 1:3 concludes the list begun in M. 1:1.[68] It adds two
groups of three to this list, making the sum total twenty pairs
of grains and vegetables. M. 1:3 consists of two sublists, A
and C, each followed by the same subscription. B is missing in
many mss. Epstein[69] also deletes B, maintaining that C was
inserted parenthetically into the list consisting of A + a subscription, so that only one subscription is necessary.

A is actually composed of a pair ((15)-(16)) and a single
item (17), for the former is given in the plural, while the
latter appears in the singular. The plants of pairs (15)-(16) all
belong to the genus *Brassica* of Cruciferae, or the mustard family.
The turnip and the rape (15) are similar in respect to their
leaves, bulbs, and taste.[70] The kale and the garden cabbage (16),
both leafy cabbages, are varieties of the same species (*Brassica
oleracea*) and resemble each other. Feliks is not certain of the
identification of *trwbtwr* as the garden cabbage, and others identify
it as the cauliflower, another variety of the same species.

Each of the two plants of pair (17) belongs to a different
family. The spinach beet belongs to Chenopodiaceae (the goosefoot family) while garden sorrel belongs to Polygonaceae (the
buckwheat family). The two plants, however, are similar in
appearance.[71] I can see no botanical relationship between this
pair and the other two pairs of A.

[C]Aqiva adds another triplet in C. The plants of pairs (18)-
(19) all belong to the genus *Allium* of Liliaceae, or the lily
family, and therefore resemble each other. The plants of pair
(20) both belong to the genus *Lupinus* of Papilionaceae, or the
pea family, and are similar in appearance. The main difference
between them is that the lupine has white flowers, in contrast
to the yellow flowers of its counterpart.[72] Again, I can see no
botanical connection between the third pair of the list and the
other two pairs. Perhaps both pairs (17) and (20) are single
items which are attached to the end of their respective lists.

MR suggests that [C]Aqiva's list in C differs from the list
which ends at M. 1:3A. C actually lists plants which do not
resemble each other but are still not considered diverse-kinds.
In this way MR attempts to explain why [C]Aqiva would add to an
existing list (as *hwsyp* implies). It is more likely, however,
that [C]Aqiva had an independent list, which the redactor joined
to M. with *hwsyp*. The redactor apparently understood the list

to contain plants with the same characteristics (i.e. that they are not diverse-kinds) as the plants listed in M. 1:1-3A.

A. *Added (hwsyp) R. ^CAqiva,*
   "(1) *The garlic and the chive,*
   (2) *and the onion and the shallot,*
   (3) *and the lupine and the yellow lupine*
   [yellow lupine omitted in Erfurt] [= M. 1:3C]."
B. Said R. Simeon, "R. ^CAqiva repeated the tradition only
   (*l' hyh r[by] ^cqyb' šwnh 'l')* [GRA omits 'l' and reads:
   R. ^CAqiva did not repeat the tradition] in regard to these
   [first] two pairs,
C. "But ('l') the lupine and the yellow lupine are not
   [considered] diverse-kinds with one another."

                              T. Kil. 1:2 (p. 203, ll. 6-8)

A cites ^CAqiva's list of M. 1:3C, but without a subscription. Simeon then glosses A in B-C, thus attesting it to Usha. Simeon's comment is somewhat difficult. He maintains that ^CAqiva repeated the tradition only with respect to the first two pairs (B), but that, by contrast, the plants of the third pair are not considered to be diverse-kinds with one another (C). Simeon thus implies in C that ^CAqiva regards the members of each of the first two pairs to be diverse-kinds with each other. M. 1:3C-D, however, states that ^CAqiva did not consider any member of the three pairs to be diverse-kinds with its counterpart. Simeon therefore appears to assign to ^CAqiva a position which is contrary to the one attributed to him in M. 1:3C-D.

This difficulty may be resolved in one of two ways. It is possible that Simeon had before him a different version of the subscription, one which read "are [considered] diverse-kinds with one another."[73] Simeon then states in T. that this ruling applies only to the first two pairs on the list, while the contrary ruling (.e., that they are not considered diverse-kinds with one another) holds for the last one. Alternatively, GRA[74] omits 'l' from B, and so reads the latter as: "R. ^CAqiva did not repeat the tradition in regard to these first two pairs." According to this interpretation Simeon maintains that ^CAqiva did not rule at all concerning the first two pairs on the list, so that M.'s subscription (M. 1:3D) applies to the third pair alone. Now although both of these explanations are possible, we prefer the first one, for it allows us to interpret the pericope as it stands, and, unlike the second, does not require us to emend the text of T.

The only other possibility of explaining T. involves reading
B and C as independent of each other. Simeon only says B, and
argues that only the first two pairs belong on ^{C}Aqiva's list, but
not the third. C then contradicts Simeon, for it says that the
third pair is also not considered diverse-kinds, and also belongs
on ^{C}Aqiva's list. According to this interpretation, we have a
saying (B) which is immediately glossed by a contradicting statement (C). This would be an unusual way of transmitting a tradition, and it is therefore unlikely that this interpretation is
correct.

1:4

A. And in [regard to] the tree:
B. (1) Pears[75] and crustaminum pears,[76]
    (2) and quinces[77] (*pryšym*) and hawthorns[78] (^{c}*wzrrym*),
C. are not [considered] diverse-kinds with one another.
D. (1) An apple[79] and a Syrian pear[80] (*ḥzrd*: B, C, L, K
    are corrected to read *ḥzrr*; V, Cn, N, S read *ḥzrt*; O, P
    read ^{c}*wzrd*; Geniza fragments[81] read ^{c}*zrr* or ^{c}*wzrr*),
    (2) peaches[82] and almonds,[83]
    (3) jujubes[84] and wild jujubes,[85]
E. even though they are similar to one another,
F. they are [considered] diverse-kinds with one another.

M. Kil. 1:4

As the superscription (A) shows, our chapter now proceeds
to a new issue, the grafting of diverse-kinds of fruit-trees.
M. 1:4 presupposes the prohibition of grafting a bud from one
fruit-tree onto a fruit-tree of another kind (cf. T. 1:34, M. 1:7,
and Maimonides, *Code, Diverse-Kinds* 1:5). M. consists of a
statement of its theme (A) and two lists of fruit (B-C and D-F).
B-C contains two pairs which are not considered diverse-kinds,
and D-F lists three pairs which are so considered, making a total
of five pairs of fruits. B-C has the same literary structure
as the list of M. 1:1-3, with a list followed by a subscription.
The structure of D-F is similar to that of the list of M. 1:1-3
except for E, which glosses D+F. The two opposing subscriptions,
C and F, balance each other.

The trees represented by the fruits of pairs[86] B(1)-(2) all
belong to the rose family (Rosaceae). The two members of B(1)
belong to the same genus (*Pirus*) and resemble each other. The
quince and the hawthorn (B(2)) belong to different genera (*Cydonia*
and *Crataegus* respectively). There is some question as to the

identification of the *pryš* as the quince, since the latter is
larger than the hawthorn, and the two do not closely resemble
each other.[87] Löw[88] maintains that the *pryš* is a medlar, which is
similar to the hawthorn. Feliks,[89] however, rejects this identification because of descriptions of the fruit in various sources
(cf. B. Ber. 43b, T. Suk. 2:9, and B. Suk. 31a-b). Following
R. Jonah's identification of the *pryš* as *'sprglyn* (= Arabic *'sprgl*)
(Y. Kil. 1:4), Feliks suggests that the hawthorn may have been
considered an inferior variety of the quince.[90]

Although we have assumed that B lists two pairs, this is not
necessarily the case. Y. 1:4 (27a) presents a dispute between
Rav and Joshua b. Levi as to whether B contains two pairs or a
single group of four. Y. apparently concludes that B speaks of
two pairs. However, the four fruits are grouped together in other
contexts in M.-T. Zera^Cim (M. Ma^Cas. 1:3, T. Shev. 7:16), and it
is possible that B should be read as a list of four.

D+F presents three pairs of fruit-trees which are considered
diverse-kinds, even though, as E notes, the members of each pair
resemble each other. The fruit-trees of pairs D (1)-(2) belong
to the rose family (Rosaceae; cf. B (1)-(2)). Feliks identifies
the *ḥzrd* of D (1) as the Syrian pear, although he admits that
he is uncertain about this identification.[91] Both the Syrian
pear and the apple belong to the genus *Pirus*, and therefore
resemble each other. According to Feliks the Syrian pear is
not edible, and it would make sense to graft an apple bud onto its
tree.[92] Peaches and almonds (D (2)) belong to the same genus
(*Prunus*) and are similar in appearance (e.g., certain varieties of
peaches have a smooth peel like the shell of an almond). The
jujube and the wild jujube (D (3)) belong to the genus *Zizyphus*
of the buckthorn family (Rhamnaceae), and resemble each other.
I do not see any botanical relationship between this pair and
the first two pairs of this list.

Following E, Maimonides (*Code, Diverse-Kinds* 3:4) explains
the law of M. 1:4D-F as follows:

> And thus [i.e., it is the same as we saw above in the
> case of seeds] in [regard to] the tree, where there
> are two kinds which are similar to one another in
> [their] leaves or fruits, [but] since they are two
> kinds, lo, they are [considered] diverse-kinds.

Maimonides then lists the fruits of M. 1:4 as examples.[93]

A. In the district (*tḥwm*) of Ariah[94] they used to graft apple

    [buds] onto Syrian pear (*'zrd*; Lieberman corrects to *'zrr* =

    Y.'s *ḥzrr*) [trees].

B. A certain student [once] found them [performing this grafting].

C. He said to them, "You are forbidden [to do this]."

D. They went and cut them [i.e., the buds] off.

E. And they came and asked at Yavneh.

F. They [i.e., the sages] said, "Correctly (*yph*) did that student say."

> T. Kil. 1:3 (p.203, ll. 8-10)
> (Y. 1:4 (27a))

G. In the irrigated fields (*šwqy*) of Sepphoris they used to graft crustaminum pear [buds] onto pear [trees].

H. A certain student [once] found them [performing this grafting].

I. He said to them, "You are forbidden [to do this]."

J. They went and cut them [i.e., the buds] off.

K. [Erfurt, first printed ed.: And] they came and asked at Yavneh.

L. They [i.e., the sages] said, "Whoever met you was none other than [one] of the students of the house of study (*by rb*) of Shammai."

> T. Kil. 1:4 (pp. 203-204,
> ll. 11-13) (Y. 1:4 (27a))

T. 1:3-4 presents two stories which give precedents for the law of M. 1:4. T. 1:3 concerns the law of M. 1:4 D(1), while T. 1:4 deals with M. 1:4 B(1). The two stories clearly were formulated together, for they have the same literary structure, and the language of B-E is identical to that of H-K. The two stories differ mainly in F and L, for in the former the student's words are praised, while in the latter the student is called a Shammaite. The student's ruling in F follows M. 1:4 D-F, while that of L opposes that of M. 1:4 B-C. T. thus supports the view of M. 1:4 by praising one who agrees with it and calling a Shammaite one who opposes the rule.

1:5

A. (1) A radish[95] and a rape[96] (*npwṣ*; many mss.[97] *npwš*),

    (2) mustard[98] and wild mustard,[99]

    (3) a Greek gourd[100] with an Egyptian [gourd][101] and [Geniza fragments[102] add: with] the *remuṣah*,[103]

B. even though they are similar to one another,

C. they are [considered] diverse-kinds with one another.

> M. Kil. 1:5

M. Kil. 1:5 offers the same type of list as that found in
M. 1:4D-F, for it lists plants which are diverse-kinds with each
other in spite of a similarity in appearance. M. presents two
pairs and a group of three (= two pairs), making the total number
of plants seven. We note that one plant of each pair also
appears on the list of M. 1:1-3. We shall first discuss the
characteristics of the plants of M. 1:5 and then determine the
relationship between M. 1:5 and M. 1:1-3.

All of the plants of pairs (1)-(2) belong to the mustard
family (Cruciferae). The radish and the rape belong to different
genera (*Raphanus* and *Brassica*, respectively). In Y. 1:5 (27a)
Jonah maintains that while the two vegetables are similar in
respect to both their leaves and their fruits, they are considered
diverse-kinds because of a difference in taste. Accordingly,
taste becomes the ultimate criterion for determination of diverse-
kinds (cf. MR to M. 1:1[104]).

Mustard and wild mustard (pair (2)) also belong to different
genera (*Brassica* and *Sinapsis*, respectively). The latter is
similar to the former (and, incidentally, to Egyptian [or white]
mustard as well) in its yellow flowers, leaves and taste.[105]
Feliks says that the wild mustard differs from white mustard in
the shape of its root,[106] although he does not say whether it
differs in this respect from ordinary (= black) mustard as well.

All plants of group (3) are varieties of the calabash gourd
(*Lageneria vulgaris*, of the gourd family [Cucurbitaceae]).[107]
The Greek gourd is an African variety while the Egyptian gourd
and presumably the *remuṣah* are Asian. Although the two varieties
are presumably similar to each other,[108] there are important differences between them. The stalks of the African variety spread
out 10-15 m., while those of the Asian variety extend only 3-10 m.
In addition, the leaves of the latter are split into lobes, while
the leaves of the former are not.[109] These differences probably
account for M.'s ruling that the two varieties are considered
diverse-kinds. We may note that, according to M., the Egyptian
gourd and the *remuṣah* are not considered diverse-kinds (following
GRA; cf. M. 1:2D). Nehemiah opposes this ruling in T. 1:5, as
we shall shortly see.

Let us now compare the plants listed in M. 1:5 to those of
M. 1:1-3, using the following chart:

M. 1:1-3 (= are not diverse-kinds)			*M. 1:5 (= are diverse-kinds)*	
M. 1:1	(1)-(6)		---	
M. 1:2	(7)-(11)		---	
	(12)	mustard	(2)	mustard
		Egyptian mustard		wild mustard
	(13)	Egyptian gourd	(3)	Greek gourd
		remuṣah		Egyptian gourd and
				remuṣah
	(14)	cowpea		---
		asparagus bean		---
M. 1:3	(15)	turnip	(1)	radish
		rape		rape
	(16)-(20)		---	

The list of M. 1:5 corresponds to pairs (12), (13), and (15) of M. 1:1-3. One plant from each of these pairs (or in the case of (13), both plants) is combined with another plant to form a pairing of diverse-kinds. In effect, M. 1:5 supplements M. 1:1-3, for it states that while plant A of M. 1:1-3 is not considered diverse-kinds with plant B, it is considered diverse-kinds with plant C. If we are correct in supposing the underlying rule of M. 1:1-3 to be that plants which resemble each other are not considered diverse-kinds, then M. 1:5 provides a list of exceptions to that rule. That is, M. 1:5 lists those plants which do resemble each other but are nevertheless considered diverse-kinds.[110]

E. (1) Dill[111] and fennel,[112]
    (2) coriander and celery,[113]
F. even though they are similar to one another,
G. they are [considered] diverse-kinds [when they grow] with one another.

T. Kil. 1:1b (p. 203, ll. 2-3)

T. 1:1b adds two pairs to M. 1:5's list of plants which resemble each other but are still considered diverse-kinds. The plants of these pairs were all used as spices, and thus are similar to (and, in the case of coriander, identical with) some of the plants listed in M. 1:2. T. thus links M. 1:5 to M. 1:2. All four plants belong to different genera of Umbellifrae,[114] or the parsley family. Dill and fennel resemble each other, although the latter is taller and has larger leaves.[115] Celery appears somewhat similar to coriander, but according to Feliks[116] there

are important differences between them (e.g., smell). The law
of E-F states that these plants, in spite of their similarities,
are considered diverse-kinds. We note that, although this list
is presumably also to be read in pairs, as we have done, it is
also possible that we have a list of four separate items, which
may be read differently (cf. T. 1:1c).

A. R. Nehemiah says, "Aramean and (w) Egyptian gourd[s]
    are [considered] diverse-kinds with the remuṣah."
    [first printed ed.: "Aramean and Egyptian gourd[s] and a
    Greek gourd are [considered] diverse-kinds with the remuṣah."
    Erfurt and GRA: "Aramean and Egyptian gourd[s] are [con-
    sidered] diverse-kinds [Lieberman adds: with] the Greek
    gourd, and are [considered] diverse-kinds with the remuṣah."
    B. and Y.: "[The] Aramean gourd [L: The desert gourd],
    which is the Egyptian gourd, is [considered] diverse-kinds
    [with] the Greek gourd, and is [considered] diverse-kinds
    with the remuṣah."]

                          T. Kil. 1:5 (p. 204, 13-14)
                          (B. Ned. 51a, Y. Kil. 1:2 (27a))

     T. 1:5 presents a saying of Nehemiah which opposes the law
of M. 1:5 in regards to at least one pair of gourds. We shall
follow Lieberman and take Erfurt's reading as the best one.[117]
The saying then reads that both the Aramean and the Egyptian
gourds are considered diverse-kinds with both the Greek gourd
and the remuṣah. As for the gourds themselves, we have already
identified all but the Aramean gourd, which does not appear in
M. 1:5. The only identification of it which we could find
appears in the versions of B. and Y., where it is said to be
identified with the Egyptian gourd. It is also possible, however,
that the Aramean gourd is another Asian variety of the calabash
gourd. If this is so, then Nehemiah says that the Asian varieties
(Aramean and Egyptian) of the calabash gourd are diverse-kinds
with the African variety (Greek) and the remuṣah.
     We shall now compare Nehemiah's opinion in M. 1:2 and
M. 1:5. The following chart shows how the law differs in respect
to each pairing of the Egyptian gourd, the Greek gourd and the
remuṣah.

Pairs of Gourds	*M. 1:2*	*M. 1:5*	*T. 1:5 (Neḥemiah)*
(1) Egyptian remuṣah	not diverse- kinds	---	diverse-kinds
(2) Greek Egyptian	---	diverse-kinds	diverse-kinds
(3) Greek remuṣah	---	diverse-kinds	not diverse-kinds

We first note that the rule of M. 1:2 and M. 1:5 are consistent
with one another. The Greek and Egyptian gourds are considered
to be diverse-kinds with each other (M. 1:5), and so the *remuṣah*,
which is not considered to be diverse-kinds with the Egyptian
gourd (M. 1:2), is regarded as being diverse-kinds with the Greek
gourd (M. 1:5). Now Neḥemiah agrees that Greek and Egyptian gourds
are considered diverse-kinds with one another. He disagrees,
however, concerning the status of the *remuṣah*, maintaining that
the latter is regarded as diverse-kinds with the Egyptian gourd,
rather than with the Greek variety. Neḥemiah perhaps reasons
that both the *remuṣah* and the Greek gourd have a bitter taste,[118]
and that it is this characteristic, rather than any traits shared
by the *remuṣah* and the Egyptian gourd, which determines the
status of the *remuṣah*. If this interpretation is correct, then
Neḥemiah apparently follows the principle that taste is a criterion for determining diverse-kinds (cf. our discussion of the
radish and the rape of M. 1:5).

A. Five things were said concerning the Greek gourd:
   (1) It is prohibited to train it (*'swrh bsykwk*; Y.:
        'yn mskkyn 'wth) over plants (*zr^{c}ym*),
   (2) its stalk [is considered its handle up to a] handbreadth,
   (3) it prohibits in any amount,
   (4) and it conveys uncleanness and interposes before
        uncleanness,
   (5) and [= omitted by Erfurt and Sens] he who prohibits
        [himself] by a vow [lit.: he who vows] from [eating]
        the gourds, is only prohibited from [eating] the Greek
        gourd alone.
                    T. Kil. 1:6 (p. 204, ll. 14-17)
                    (Y. Kil. 2:11 (28b)[119])

     T. supplements M. 1:5 with a list of five different rules
which pertain to the Greek gourd. (1) states that one may not
train (i.e., guide the growth of) the plant of the Greek gourd
over other plants. This ruling refers to M. 2:11, which states

that the only plant which must not be allowed to hang over or lean
on other plants is the Greek gourd. The Greek gourd is a climbing
plant which may spread out 10-15 m. (see above, p. 38), and, if
it is trained over other plants, it may easily become entangled
with them. One would then not be able to tell how close to the
other plants the Greek gourd is actually planted,[120] and the field
would appear to be planted with diverse-kinds.[121]

(2) refers to the statement in M. Uqs. 1:6 that "the stalk
of a gourd [is considered its handle up to a] handbreadth."
Following T. Ned. 3:6 (see item (5) below), Lieberman[122] maintains
that this law applies specifically to Greek gourds. The law
concerns the stalk of an unclean gourd. The part of the stalk
which is within a handbreadth of the gourd is considered its
handle (yd), as it is reasoned that one must grasp a handbreadth-
length of the stalk in order to take hold of the gourd. As the
handle of the gourd, this part of the stalk may convey uncleanness
to the gourd or receive uncleanness from it, although it is not
considered part of the actual gourd.[123] The part of the stalk
which is more than a handbreadth away from the gourd is not considered its handle and is not affected by its uncleanness.

(3) refers to M. Orl. 3:7. The sages there list the Greek
gourd as one of six items, which, if they are prohibited and
become mixed up in a larger group of permitted items, cause the
entire group to be burnt. These prohibited items are not neutralized
in the larger group because such items are usually sold individually and not in large quantities (Maimonides, *Comm.*, *ad. loc.*).
According to M. the Greek gourd becomes prohibited if it is
grown in a vineyard.[124] The gourd must then be burnt, because
according to the laws of diverse-kinds of the vineyard one must
burn both that which is planted in the vineyard as well as the
surrounding vines.[125]

M. Oh. 8:1 lists the Greek gourd among those things which
convey uncleanness and interpose before it (4). Neusner[126]
explains that the plants listed in M. are inedible, are attached
to the ground (and so insusceptible [TYT]), and have large leaves
which may form tents. We shall see that Bar Qappara, in another
list of rulings cited in Y. (see below), regards conveying
uncleanness and interposing before it as two separate properties.[127]

(5) cites T. Ned. 3:6. The law concerns to which gourds
one refers when he vows not to eat "gourds." T. says that
"gourds" refer only to Greek gourds and that the vow does not
prohibit other types of gourds. In ordinary usage, then, "gourd"
means the Greek gourd.[128]

Bar Qappara, cited in Y. 2:11 (28b), presents a different
version of a list of rulings concerning the Greek gourds. His
list contains seven items:

A. Bar Qappara teaches (*tny*) [lit. repeats] seven
    [rulings concerning the Greek gourd]:
    (1) They do not train it over plants,
    (2) and it conveys uncleanness,
    (3) and interposes before uncleanness,
    (4) and [the length of] its handle is a handbreadth,
    (5) and they give it [the full area required for]
         its tillage,
    (6) and it is [considered] diverse-kinds with the
         Aramean gourd,
    (7) and it is [considered] diverse-kinds with the
         remuṣah.
B. And he does not teach [that the Greek gourd] prohibits
    [in any amount];
C. and he does not teach [concerning] vows.

Bar Qappara thus includes T.'s (1), (4) (counted as two rulings),
and (2), in the same order that Y. cites T. He omits (3) and
(5) (cf. Y. B-C) and includes three other laws. The first
is at Y. (5), which says that one allows the Greek gourd the full
area required for its tillage. This ruling refers to M. Kil. 3:7 (PM),
which states that a single gourd must be given an area the size
of fourth of a *qb* (so that it should not spread over other
plants; cf. M. Kil. 2:11).[129] Bar Qappara also adds (Y. (6)-(7))
that the Greek gourd is considered diverse-kinds with both the
Aramean [= Egyptian (?)] gourd and the *remuṣah* (= M. 1:5). This
ruling is counted as two laws, so that the list totals seven.
We may note, however, that since the two laws concerning diverse-
kinds (Y. (6)-(7)) and the two which concern uncleanness (Y. (2)-
(3)) may each also be considered as one law, Bar Qappara's list
may be reduced to five items.

1:6

A. (1) A wolf[130] and a dog,[131]
    (2) a wild dog[132] (*hklb hkpry*) [Geniza fragments,[133] O:
         hkwpry; S, K: *kwpry*] [alt. translation (Blackman):
         village dog] and the jackal,[134]
    (3) goats[135] and gazelles,[136]
    (4) Nubian ibexes[137] and fat-tailed sheep,[138]

(5)   a horse[139] and a mule,[140]

(6)   a mule and an ass,[141]

(7)   an ass and an Arabian onager,[142]

B.   even though they are similar to one another,

C.   they are [considered] diverse-kinds with one another.

M. Kil. 1:6

M. Kil. 1:6 presents seven pairs of animals which are considered diverse-kinds in spite of a similarity in appearance.   This
list of animals augments M. 1:4D-5's discussion of fruits and
vegetables to which the same rule applies.   M. apparently refers
only to the breeding of animals of diverse-kinds, and so presupposes the prohibition of Lv. 19:19 (Maim. *Code, Diverse-Kinds*
9:4).   According to some commentaries (MS, TYT), however, M. also
refers to the law of Dt. 22.10, which prohibits the driving or
leading together of two different kinds of animals (cf. M. 8:2).

In terms of literary structure, M. is identical to M. 1:4D-F
and M. 1:5, for it consists of a list (A), subscription (C) and
gloss (B).   Pairs (5)-(7) alone, however, form a list which differs structurally from the other lists, for the last animal of
each of the first two pairs is the first animal listed in the next
pair.   The list then has the form of A-B, B-C, C-D.   This may be
seen as an elegant way to end the list of M. 1:6, and it is perhaps also intended as an ending to the entire construction of
M. 1:1-6, which now contains thirty-five items in all.

We may note that all of the animals named in A are listed in
the singular, except for those belonging to pairs (3)-(4), which
are given in the plural.   The list of A may thus be divided into
three parts, (1)-(2), (3)-(4), and (5)-(7).   This division is
also on sound taxonomical grounds, since each group represents
a different family of animals.   We shall now consider each of
these families separately.

All of the animals of pairs (1)-(2) belong to the genus *Canis*
of the dog family (Canidae).   Feliks maintains that we cannot
accurately identify the dogs mentioned in M., but suggests that
they may be similar to the dogs of the present day.   One type of
dog has long legs and a rolled-up tail, and is similar in these
respects to the wolf.   Another type is smaller and has pointed
ears along with a hanging, heavy tail.   This type of dog also
walks with its head low, keeps its distance from man, and is
considered almost wild.   On account of these characteristics, this
dog is said to be similar to the jackal.[143]

All of the animals of pairs (3)-(4) belong to the ox family (Bovidae). The animals are not grouped together according to any similarities in overall appearance, for, although the goat and the Nubian ibex belong to the same genus (*Capra*) and resemble each other, they are placed in different pairs. Rather, the animals are apparently paired according to similarities between their horns. All four of the animals have permanent, hollow horns. However, the horns of both the goat and gazelle are short and slender, while those of the Nubian ibex and the sheep are broad and have grooves.[144] Feliks[145] notes that no mating between any two animals of pairs (3)-(4) actually produces offspring, except for the mating of the goat and Nubian ibex (since they belong to the same genus). All of the animals, though, can mate with each other, "particularly in captivity with the aid of man."[146] The mating of these animals is thus prohibited, even though they cannot actually produce an animal of diverse-kinds.[147] This rule is consistent with the general principle that one cannot allow even the appearance of diverse-kinds to take place.

All of the animals of pairs (5)-(7) belong to the horse family (Equidae) and are similar to each other. Matings between any two of these animals may produce offspring, except where one of the animals is a mule, which is sterile.[148] MR explains that the mule is considered to be diverse-kinds with both the horse and the ass because it is the offspring of their mating.

Maimonides (*Code*, *Diverse-Kinds* 9:4) interprets M. to concern wild and domesticated animals which are similar to one another:

> [Concerning] two kinds (*myny*) of domesticated or
> wild animals which are similar to one another--even
> though they conceive from one another and are similar
> to one another, lo, they are [considered] diverse-
> kinds and it is forbidden to cross-breed them (*lhrkybn*).

Maimonides then lists the animals of M. 1:6 as examples (cf. also MR). It is not clear, however, that pairs (2) and (5)-(6) each include one wild and one domesticated animal. We therefore prefer the interpretation given above.

A. (1) A cock[149] [and a] peacock,[150]

(2) a cock [and a] pheasant[151] (*psy'ny*) [first printed ed.: *ps'ny*] [Erfurt, B. B.Q.: The cock and the peacock and the pheasant (*psywny*); Y. Kil. and Y. B.Q.:

The cock with the pheasant (*pysywyn*),
the cock with the peacock (*ṭwws*; Y. B.Q.:
twwst)],

B. even though they are similar to one another,

C. they are [considered] diverse-kinds with one another.

> T. Kil. 1:7 (p. 204, ll. 17-18)
>
> (Y. Kil. 1:6 (27a), B. B.Q. 55a,
>
> Y. B.Q. 5:8 (5a))

T. adds a group of birds to M. 1:6's list of animals which may not be mated with one another (cf. M. B.Q. 5:7). We shall first deal with the different readings of T. As it stands, A consists of two pairs made up of three birds (Y. Kil and Y. B.Q. reverse the order of the pairs). We have inserted the conjunction "and" between the members of each pair, for otherwise the list would make no sense.[152] The law thus reads that the cock is considered diverse-kinds with both the peacock and the pheasant. The readings of Erfurt and B. list a group of three instead of two pairs. They differ in law with the previous reading only in that now the peacock and the pheasant are presumably considered diverse-kinds with each other.[153] This fact is not clear from the other reading of T.

The three birds belong to different genera of the pheasant family (Phasianidae). Feliks[154] explains (following Erfurt and B.) that the female pheasant resembles the hen (of the domestic fowl, or chicken) while the male pheasant, with its long and colorful tail, is similar to the peacock. The reading of two pairs at A may be explained by noting that the female pheasant is similar to the hen of a chicken (A(2)), and that the peahen presumably resembles the hen as well (A(1)). Feliks[155] comments that no mating of these birds produces offspring, for the birds belong to different genera.

A. R. Judah said [B.: says], "A female mule which craved ($\check{s}tb^c h$) a male [mule] [= omitted in B.]--

B. "they do not mate with it ('yn mrby^{c}yn) either [one] of [= omitted in B.] the horses or [one] of the asses, but only [one] of the male mules   [B.: of its own kind]." [Entire pericope omitted in Vienna.]

> T. Kil. 1:8a (p. 204, ll. 18-19)
>
> (B. Hul. 79a = B. Ket. 111b)

T. Kil. 1:8a presents an opinion of Judah which agrees with M. 1:6 as to which animals may not be mated with the mule. Judah assumes that it is permissible to satisfy the mule's sexual desires by mating another animal with it, even though no offspring can result from such a mating. He rules, however, that, although the female mule cannot produce offspring, it still may not be mated with a horse or an ass, but only with another mule.[156] Judah thus again illustrates the principle that animals of different kinds may not be mated with each other, even when no offspring of diverse-kinds can be produced. We note that Judah agrees with the law of M. Kil. 1:6 A(5)-(6), which states that both the horse and the ass are considered diverse-kinds with the mule. He thus attests the substance of M. to Usha.

C. (1) An ox[157] and a wild ox [= omitted in Vienna],[158]
   (2) an ass and a wild ass,[159]
   (3) a hog[160] and a wild boar [= omitted in Y.],[161]
D. even though they are similar to one another [= omitted in Y.],
E. they are [considered] diverse-kinds with one another.

T. Kil. 1:8b (p. 204, ll. 19-20)

(Y. B.Q. 5:8 (28b))

T. Kil. 1:8b adds three pairs of animals to the list of M. 1:6.[162] T.'s three pairs of animals respectively belong to the ox (Bovidae), horse (Equidae), and hog (Suidae) families. Each pair consists of one wild and one domesticated species of the same animal.[163] The point of T. is that, although the members of each pair resemble each other and differ only as to how and where they were raised, they are still considered diverse-kinds with each other. We may point out that Maimonides (*Code, Diverse-Kinds* 9:5) disagrees with the law of T., maintaining that the wild and domesticated species of the same animal are not considered diverse-kinds with each other.

A. Five things were said concerning the wild ox:
   (1) It is prohibited because of [the law prohibiting the slaughter of both] it and its offspring [on the same day],
   (2) and its fat is prohibited,
   (3) and it is offered on the altar,
   (4) and it is liable for the gifts [which must be given to the priests],
   (5) and it is bought with [second] tithe-money for peace-offerings, but not for meat [to satisfy] the appetite [i.e., for use as food[164]].
B. And lo, it is [considered] like a domesticated animal (*bhmh*) in all respects.

C. R. Yosé says, "This is the *t'w* which is written [Erfurt, first printed ed.: said (*h'mwr*)] in the Torah,[165]

D. "(1) and it is permitted because of [i.e., in respect to] [the law prohibiting the slaughter of both] it and its off-spring [on the same day],

"(2) and its fat is permitted,

"(3) and it is disqualified (*pswl*) from [= omitted by First printed ed.: Erfurt: for] the altar,

"(4) and it is exempt from the gifts [which must be given to the priests],

"(5) and it is bought with [second] tithe-money for meat [to satisfy] the appetite [i.e., for use as food], but not for peace-offerings.

E. "And lo, it is [considered] like a wild animal (*ḥyh*) in all respects."

F. And the sages say, "The *t'w* is a creature unto itself, and the wild ox is a creature unto itself."

T. Kil. 1:9 (pp. 204-205, ll. 20-26)

T. presents a dispute between an anonymous opinion and Yosé concerning certain rulings which pertain to the wild ox. The central issue of the dispute concerns whether the wild ox is considered a domesticated or wild animal. T. 1:9 thus supplements T. 1:8b. While the latter states that the ox and the wild ox are considered diverse-kinds, T. 1:9 deals with the related question of whether or not the wild ox is treated like a domesticated animal (i.e., like an ox) in differing legal contexts. As the redactor sees them, then, both pericopae are concerned with the difference between a wild ox and an ox.[166]

A lists five rulings which concern the wild ox, and B glosses A with the general principle behind the list. In C, Yosé intro-duces a new issue, the identification of the *t'w* with the wild ox. D-E then opposes and balances A-B. F opposes C, as the sages say that the *t'w* and the wild ox are two separate animals.[167] We now see that T. is actually composed of two disputes. A-B and D-E differ as to whether the wild ox is a domesticated or wild animal (*bhmh* vs. *ḥyh*), and F disagrees with C concerning the identification of the *t'w* as the wild ox.

Now the issues of these two disputes are somewhat related (we shall see below to what extent this is the case). By identi-fying the *t'w* as the wild ox in C, Yosé implies that the latter is a wild animal, for the *t'w* is listed among the clean wild animals in Dt. 14:5. In fact, Yosé explicitly states in M. Kil. 8:6

that the wild ox is a wild animal. D-E is then consistent with
C. Moreover, since D-E is autonomous of C, and since it perfectly
balances A-B, it is possible that D-E was attached to C in order
to relate the issue of C+F to that of A-B. That is, D-E spells
out C's implication that the wild ox is a wild animal, and at
the same time brings Yosé, who originally disputes only with the
sages in F, into dispute with the anonymous opinion of A-B as
well. T. thereby combines two related issues into a single
pericope.

Let us now turn to the law of T. We shall begin with the
dispute over the five laws in A-B and D-E. As B and E indicate,
the dispute concerns whether the wild ox is a domesticated or
wild animal.[168] All five laws apply only to domesticated
animals, so that A maintains that they do apply in the case of
the wild ox, while D says that they do not. We shall briefly discuss these five laws, and, by referring to their sources, indicate
why they apply only to domesticated animals.

The first four laws are all based on biblical verses. Each
of these verses refers only to domesticated animals, and therefore may be understood as applying to that class of animals alone.
A(1) and D(1) discuss whether or not it is prohibited to slaughter
a wild ox and its offspring on the same day. The relevant law is
based on Lv. 22:28, which reads: *And whether it is an ox or a
sheep, you shall not slaughter both it and its young on the same
day*. The phrase *an ox or a sheep* may be taken to exclude wild
animals, so that the law would not apply to them.[169]

A(2) and D(2) disagree as to whether or not it is permissible
to eat the fat of a wild ox. The prohibition of eating the fat
of an animal is stated in Lv. 7:23: *You shall not eat any of the
fat of an ox, sheep or goat*. Again, since the verse mentions only
domesticated animals, the law is understood to apply only to
them.[170]

Similarly, A(3) and D(3) concern whether or not the wild ox
is an acceptable sacrifice. The law referred to is based on
Lv. 1:2, which states: *Speak unto the Israelite people and say
to them: When any of you presents an offering to the Lord, you
shall bring your offering of cattle from the herd (bqr) or
from the flock (ṣ'n)*. The terms "herd" and "flock" clearly
exclude wild animals, and the law does not apply to them.[171]

A(4) and D(4) dispute whether or not the wild ox is liable
for gifts. The gifts are the portions of the sacrifice which
one is obligated to give the priest (cf. Maimonides, *Code,
First-Fruits* 9:1). The law is stated in Dt. 18:3 as follows:
And this shall be the priests' due from the people: Everyone

who offers a sacrifice, whether an ox or a sheep, must give the
shoulders, the cheeks and the stomach to the priest. Once more,
the verse mentions only domesticated animals, so that only when
one sacrifices such animals is he liable for the gifts. Of
course, the fact that this law applies only to domesticated animals may be inferred from our understanding of Lv. 1:2. If a
wild animal is not an acceptable sacrifice, it clearly is not
going to be liable for the gifts.

A(5) and D(5) deal with what one is allowed to purchase with
second tithe-money which he has brought to Jerusalem. M. M.S.
1:3-4 and T. M.S. 1:9 all assume that domesticated animals may
be purchased only for peace-offerings, while wild animals may be
bought only for use as food. A(5) therefore says that the wild
ox may be purchased only for peace-offerings, while D(5) states
the opposite view.

We now turn to the second dispute of the pericope in C and
F, which concerns the identification of the *t'w* with the wild ox.
The *t'w* is listed among the clean wild animals in Dt. 14:5:
The deer and the gazelle and the antelope and the wild goat and
the adax and the t'w and the wild sheep.[172] In C, Yosé identifies the *t'w* as the wild ox,[173] while in F the sages distinguish
between the two animals. The legal significance of the dispute
is not clear. It is possible that the two sides simply disagree
as to the identification of the *t'w*. It is more likely, however,
that the dispute concerns the wild ox, and is related to the
dispute as to whether the wild ox is a domesticated or wild
animal.[174] Yosé identifies the *t'w* with the wild ox, and would
maintain that the latter is a wild animal. The sages, on the
other hand, maintain that the *t'w* and the wild ox are two separate
animals, and presumably would say that the latter is a domesticated animal. If the dispute of C+F does concern the wild ox,
then it parallels the dispute of M. Kil. 8:6, where an anonymous
opinion says that the wild ox is a *bhmh*, while Yosé maintains
that it is a *hyh*. This means that the dispute of C+F is also
parallel to that of A-B+D-E, even though the two disputes are
phrased in different terms.

1:7

A. They do not graft (*mby'yn*; lit.: bring) [B: *mrkybyn*] [175]
B. [either] a tree onto a tree [of a different kind],
C. [or] a vegetable onto a vegetable [of a different kind],
D. and neither [do they graft] a tree onto a vegetable,

E.   nor a vegetable onto a tree.

F.   R. Judah permits [the grafting of] a vegetable onto a tree.

M. Kil. 1:7

M. Kil. 1:7-8 forms an autonomous subunit within Chapter
One and introduces a new issue, the prohibition of grafting.
M. 1:7 presents a general statement of the law, which M. 1:8
then illustrates with specific examples. We first turn to a
discussion of M. 1:7.

M. 1:7 has a tight literary structure. A serves as the protasis for each of the clauses of B-E. B-E is formed from the four
possible pairings of the words "tree" (*'yln*) and "vegetable"
(*yrq*). Each clause, then, has the same number of syllables (five,
omitting *wl'* in D-E), and it is clear that B-E has been constructed with mnemonic considerations in mind. Furthermore,
the four pairings may be divided into two groups, B-C and D-E.
The members of each pair of B-C are identical with each other
(i.e., tree-tree, vegetable-vegetable). D-E, though, differs from
B-C in that *wl'* is added to each clause, and in that the members
of its pairs are not identical with each other (i.e., tree-
vegetable, vegetable-tree). This grouping of the pairs is
probably also intended as a mnemonic aid. F then glosses and
opposes E, and attests it to Usha.

A indicates that M. concerns the practice of grafting, which
is prohibited when it results in diverse-kinds growing together.
We note that M. nowhere relates the prohibitions of grafting to
the prohibition of diverse-kinds (*kl'ym*). Feliks[176] suggests
that A uses the general term *mby'yn*, "they bring," and not
mrkybyn, "they graft," in order to include different methods of
uniting two plants which may not be technically termed "grafting."[177]
We shall discuss these methods in M. 1:8 and T., where various
examples of them are given.

B-C prohibits the grafting of trees onto trees[178] and vegetables onto vegetables. We assume that the prohibitions apply
only when one of the trees or vegetables is considered diverse-
kinds with the other.[179] D-E prohibits the grafting of trees
and vegetables onto one another. In F, Judah disagrees with E,
saying that it is permitted to graft a vegetable onto a tree.
The reasons for Judah's ruling are not clear, and we offer two
possible explanations. Y. 1:7 (27a) implies that Judah permits
this type of graft because the vegetable and the tree do not
actually unite to form one plant. Rather, the vegetable only
derives its nourishment from the tree, and it is possible that,

according to Judah, this is not prohibited by the laws of diverse-kinds.[180] Alternatively, Feliks explains Judah's position with reference to botanical considerations. A vegetable may be success-fully grafted onto a tree only when the two plants have com-patible structures of cambium tissue (a single cell layer between the bark and the core). The only vegetables which have a cambial structure compatible to that of a tree are certain "grass-like" (i.e., having a soft stem) perennials. However, even the graft of such a vegetable onto a tree is only temporary, for it is success-ful only until the branches of the tree harden into wood. It is possible, then, that Judah permits the graft of a vegetable onto a tree because it does not often succeed, and even when it does succeed, the graft is only temporary.[181]

A. Whence [do I know] that they do not graft
   (1) a barren tree upon a fruit tree,
   (2) nor a fruit tree upon a barren tree,
   (3) nor a fruit tree upon a fruit tree [Y. adds: one kind upon one not of its kind]?
B. Scripture says, *You shall keep my statutes* (Lv. 19:19).

> Sifra Qedoshim 4:17 (ed. Weiss, 89a)
> (Y. Kil. 1:7 (27a))

A-B takes the clause *You shall keep my statutes*, which immediately precedes the prohibition concerning diverse-kinds of crops, to include the prohibition of grafting one kind of tree on another (which is not stated in Scripture). We note that unlike M. 1:7B, which states simply that one may not graft one kind of tree on another, Sifra prohibits only the three possible grafts which involve at least one fruit tree.[182]

1:8

A. They do not plant vegetables in the stump (*šdn*: Geniza fragments: *šdn*;[183] P: *šndn*) of a sycamore tree,[184]
B. [S: and] they do not graft rue[185] onto a trifoliate orange (*qydh lbnh*)[186] [alt. translation: peganum[187]] tree
C. because these are [lit.: it is] [grafts of] a vegetable onto a tree.
D. They do not plant a shoot of a fig [tree][188] in squill,[189]
E. so that [the latter] might cool [the former];
F. [B, S: and] they do not insert a vine shoot[190] into a watermelon,
G. so that [the latter] might pour [lit.: throw] its water into [the former],

H. because these are [lit.: it is] [grafts of] a tree onto a
    vegetable.
I. They do not place [lit.: give] a seed of a gourd in
    mallow,[191]
J. so that it might protect it,
K. because it is [a graft of] a vegetable onto a vegetable
    [of a different kind].

M. Kil. 1:8

M. Kil. 1:8 presents five examples of the categories of
grafts which are prohibited by M. 1:7. M. 1:8 discusses the last
three of the four categories of M. 1:7 in reverse order, and
provides no illustration of the first.[192] M. may then be divided,
according to these categories, into three parts, A-C, D-H, and
I-K. Each of the first two parts contains two examples, while
the third has only one. All three parts have a similar structure,
consisting of a description of the example(s) (A-B, D-F, I) and
an apodosis linking the example(s) to M. 1:7. Both the descriptions and the apodoses follow set patterns (the former begin with
'yn + plural participle, the latter with mpny š). In addition,
each of the examples of D-H and I-K is glossed by a clause
explaining the purpose of the graft (E, G, J).

A states that one may not plant a vegetable on the stump
of a sycamore tree, and C explains that this act falls under the
prohibition of grafting a vegetable onto a tree. Feliks[193] says
that when a sycamore tree was cut down, it was a common practice
to leave a stump (up to ten handbreadths high) and cover it
with dirt. It would therefore be possible to plant a vegetable
on the stump or in the surrounding area.[194] This planting was
prohibited because the vegetable planted on the stump would
receive nourishment from it.[195] The vegetable would then, in
effect, be grafted onto the tree.

B states that one is not allowed to graft rue onto a
qydh lbnh, again because of the prohibition of grafting a vegetable onto a tree. Rue is a perennial shrub of the rue family
(Rutaceae), which has split, pinnate[196] leaves and yellow
flowers. It is probably considered a vegetable, rather than a
tree, on account of its soft stem.[197] Feliks is uncertain as
to the identification of qydh lbnh, and presents two alternative
interpretations.[198] One possibility is that the qydh lbnh is
the trifoliate orange. This plant also belongs to the rue family
and has flowers similar to those of rue. The trifoliate orange
commonly serves as understock (i.e., a plant onto which a graft
is made) for several citrus fruits, and could conceivably perform

the same function for rue as well. However, the identification
of *qydh lbnh* with the trifoliate orange is uncertain, for the
latter originated in China, and it is not known whether it had
already reached Palestine by the time of M.[199]

Alternatively, *qydh lbnh* may correspond to peganum, a plant
which has white flowers but resembles rue in its split leaves.
Since its family (Simaribeae) is systemically close to the rue
family, a graft is botanically feasible. This identification,
though, also poses a problem, for the peganum is a low plant,
and it is not clear whether M. would describe it as a tree (which
qydh lbnh certainly is). The problem of the identification of
qydh lbnh therefore remains unresolved.

D states that one may not plant a fig-shoot in squill, because
of the prohibition of grafting a tree onto a vegetable (H). E
explains that the purpose of such a planting is to keep the
fig-shoot cool.[200] According to Feliks[201] a common means of
spreading the growth of trees involves planting their shoots in
the ground, so that they may strike new roots. In order for
this procedure to be effective, the shoots must obtain a certain
amount of moisture (but also no more). D then describes one
method of assuring that the shoots gain this moisture, namely
the planting of the shoots in squill. Squill is a wild plant
of the lily family (Liliaceae). It has large bulbs with roots
which dig deep into the earth and absorb moisture.[202] Therefore,
by planting a fig-shoot in squill, one could be sure it would
receive the necessary moisture[203] and strike root faster.[204]
The planting is prohibited, though, as the fig-shoot is nourished
from the squill, and it is as if the two are grafted together.

F describes another example of a tree grafted onto a vegetable. One may not insert a vine-shoot into a watermelon, so
that the latter might provide water for the former. Feliks
(following Y. 1:8 (27b))[205] maintains that the vine-shoot is not
cut off from the vine, but rather is bent and inserted into the
watermelon. It is not clear, though, whether the vine-shoot is
inserted into the watermelon plant (i.e., at the stem or the
roots), or into the watermelon itself. There are, then, two
possible interpretations. Sens and Sirillo (both cited by
Feliks[206]) both maintain that the vine-shoot is inserted into
the watermelon plant at a depth of three handbreadths[207] below
the ground (following Y.). Feliks rejects this possibility,
arguing that it describes an actual graft of a vine-shoot onto
a watermelon plant, and such a graft would be unlikely to succeed.
Since M. Kil. consistently deals only with cases which are
practically feasible, it is doubtful that F refers to an actual

graft. Furthermore, the language of F-G ("insert," "throw")
is not that which is usually employed in describing a graft.[208]
We therefore turn to Feliks, who offers an alternative explanation.
Feliks[209] maintains that the vine-shoot is inserted into the
watermelon itself.[210] This may have been done for one of two
purposes. It is possible that the procedure was performed so
that the vine might draw moisture from the watermelon and also
become sweeter from it. Feliks, however, thinks that the act
was done in order to better the taste of the watermelon, by having
the vine pour its liquids into it.[211] We tend to favor the
first alternative, if only because it seems more likely that the
procedure was developed to improve the vine, which is presumably
a more important plant than the watermelon. As to whether the
vine is inserted into the watermelon plant or the watermelon
itself, we lean towards the latter alternative, but only because
the graft described by the former is not likely to succeed. If,
however, M. is not speaking in practical terms (and there is no
reason to think that it must) either interpretation is possible.

I-K states that one may not plant a gourd-seed in mallow
in order to protect it, because this is considered a graft of
a vegetable onto a vegetable. Feliks[212] explains that the
gourd is usually a summer plant, for it needs a certain amount
of warmth. It was also grown in winter, though, because it could
then obtain a higher price. In order to keep the gourd-seed warm,
it was necessary to place it in a winter plant, such as mallow.
This, then, is the procedure which is prohibited by M.

A. They do not plant [either] the shoot (*šrbyt*) of a
    pomegranate [tree][213] or the stalk of pomegranates beside
    the stump of a sycamore tree;
B. and they do not place [lit.: give] [Erfurt: nor (do
    they plant)] a shoot between two beams [of a trunk],
C. so that it might absorb (*štbl^c*; Erfurt: *štybl^c*) [lit.:
    swallow] [nourishment] between them [alt. translation: so
    that it might be absorbed between them];
D. and they do not place two kinds [of tree-seeds][214] in a
    single tube (*špwprt*)
E. so that they might absorb [nourishment] from one another;
F. and they do not graft the branch (*rkb*) of a palm tree[215] onto
    olive [trees][216] [lit.: they do not graft olive [trees] with
    the *rkb* of a palm tree];
G. because [these are grafts] of a tree onto a tree [of a
    different kind].
                        T. Kil. 1:10 (pp. 204-205, ll. 27-30)
                        (F-G: Y. Kil. 1:7 (27b))

T. Kil. 1:10-12 comments on M. 1:7 in the manner of M. 1:8,
i.e., by providing examples which illustrate the categories of
prohibited grafts listed in M. T. presents seven examples for
the first, second, and fourth categories of M., and comments on
the third as well. We shall present and discuss each pericope
of T. individually, and then summarize in a chart the relationship
of T. to M.

T. 1:10 describes four examples of a tree grafted onto another
tree. The pericope has basically the same literary structure as
that of M. 1:8, with descriptions of the examples (A, B, D, F),
and an apodosis (G) relating them to M. 1:7B. Two of the examples,
B and D, are glossed by clauses (C, E) which explain, in similar
language (both use the verb bl^c), the purpose of the graft. B
and D also differ from A and F in that the former deal with
general methods, while the latter are concerned with specific
cases. B-E may then form an autonomous unit within the pericope.
The pericope may be composed of three separate units, A, B-E,
and F, together with the apodosis, G.

A states that one may not plant a pomegranate-shoot or the
stalks of pomegranates beside a sycamore stump. Following GRA
and HD Feliks[217] prefers to read $btwk$ ("in") in A rather than
$b\dot{s}d$ ("beside"), since it makes more sense to have the shoot
planted within the stump itself. Feliks suggests that A refers
to the area surrounding the stump, which, along with the stump,
is covered with dirt when the sycamore tree is cut down (cf.
M. 1:8). It is possible for a pomegranate-shoot to take root
there, and since the area contains some of the trunk's sap, the
shoot will be nourished by the trunk. This planting is therefore
prohibited. Alternatively, Feliks[218] suggests that T. may refer
to the stalk of the pomegranate, which may have been planted in
the dirt which is on top of the stump itself, for there it
could take root and be nourished by the trunk.

B states that one may not place a shoot[219] between two
beams, which presumably are two halves of a trunk. C, which
states the purpose of B, may be explained in one of two ways,
depending on whether tbl^c is understood as an active or passive
verb.[220] If it is taken to be active, then C states that the
shoot absorbs nourishment from the trunk because it was placed
between two beams. Alternatively, C says that the shoot will be
absorbed between the two beams, meaning that it will be united
with the trunk. Either way, it is clear that the shoot will
absorb nourishment from the trunk, and therefore placing it
between the beams is prohibited as a graft of a tree onto a
tree.

D-E states that one may not place two kinds in a single tube[221] so that they may nourish each other. Lieberman[222] states that D refers to two kinds of tree-seeds. He further notes that while different kinds of tree-seeds may be planted next to each other (cf. T. Kil. 1:15), they may not be planted in such a way that they derive nourishment from each other, as is the case here.

The meaning of F is unclear, for the term *rkb* may be understood in various ways. We shall present three interpretations of F, each of which explains this word differently. Lieberman[223] (whom our translation follows), explains that *rkb* refers to a branch of the palm tree. F then says that one may not graft a palm branch onto an olive tree. Lieberman maintains (following Y. 1:7 (27a)) that the purpose of such a graft is to sweeten the taste of the olives. Löw,[224] on the other hand, takes *rkb* to refer to the trunk of a palm tree which lies on the ground. Accordingly, F says that one may not graft an olive-shoot onto the trunk of a palm tree. Löw explains the palm tree was laid on the ground so that the shoots coming out of its trunk would strike roots in the soil. Therefore, one may not graft an olive-shoot onto the trunk, for fear that the palm-shoots would take root and the olive-shoot would be nourished from them.

Finally, Feliks[225] rejects both of these interpretations, for both entail an actual graft involving olive and palm trees. He maintains that such a graft could not succeed, for the two trees differ considerably in structure. Rather, says Feliks, the *rkb* does not refer to a part of the palm tree at all. It refers to a structure of earth which surrounds the tree in such a way that shoots coming out of the trunk of the tree will take root in it. F then prohibits the bending of olive-shoots into this earth so that they may strike roots, for the olive-shoots would then be nourished by the roots of the palm tree (i.e., the roots of its shoots).[226] Feliks's interpretation depends on accepting a new meaning for *rkb*, and it is not clear whether one can legitimately understand the word in this way. If, however, an actual graft between olive and palm trees cannot take place, then it is equally difficult to see how Lieberman or Löw could be correct (unless, again, M. need not refer to grafts which are actually practicable). The problem of understanding *rkb* and interpreting F must therefore remain unresolved.

A. They do not graft dodder[227] onto alhagi,[228]

B. nor [do they graft] a spinach beet onto an amaranth,[229]

C. because [these are grafts] of a vegetable onto a vegetable [of a different kind].

T. Kil. 1:11 (p. 205, ll. 30-31)

T. Kil. 1:11 continues T.'s illustration of M. 1:7 with two examples of a vegetable grafted onto a vegetable. T. has the same literary structure as that of M. 1:8 and T. 1:10, with descriptions of the examples (A-B) followed by an apodosis (C) linking them to M. 1:7C.

A states that one may not graft dodder onto an alhagi plant. Dodder is a wild, parasitic plant of the convolvulus family (Convolvulaceae). It has a unique seed which lacks both a rootlet and cotyledons (the earliest leaves of a plant). Dodder grows in the shape of a thread, and waves in the air until it finds a host plant, around which it then wraps itself. It then sends "suckers" into the stalk of the plant in order to obtain nourishment. At the same time, the dodder is cut off from the ground and becomes entirely dependent on its host.[230] Feliks[231] points out that dodder was actually grafted onto host plants and thereby cultivated (even though the graft destroyed the host), for it had medicinal uses. One of these host plants was alhagi, a low perennial plant of the pulse family (Leguminosae). Alhagi could serve as a host for several types of dodder.[232] It is clear why A prohibits the graft of dodder onto alhagi, for one plant nourishes another of a different kind.

B states that one may not graft a spinach beet onto an amaranth. Feliks[233] points out that the two plants belong to related families (goosefoot [Chenopodiaceae] and amaranth [Amarantaceae], respectively), and therefore B prohibits a feasible graft.

A. They do not graft dodder onto a calycotome ('g'),[234]

B. because [it is a graft] of a vegetable onto a tree.

C. *R. Judah permits [the grafting of] a vegetable onto a tree* [= M. 1:7F].

D. [Concerning the graft of] a tree onto a vegetable --

E. R. Simeon b. Gamaliel permits in the name of R. Judah b. 'Agra [B.: Gamdah] from Kefar ᶜAkko.

T. Kil. 1:12 (p. 205, ll. 31-33)
(D-E [with slight changes]: B.
Sot. 43b)

T. Kil. 1:12 concludes T.'s illustration of M. 1:7 with
an example of a vegetable grafted onto a tree. A describes the
example and B relates it to M. 1:7E. Citing Judah's opinion of
M. 1:7F, C glosses and opposes B. D-E presumably complements C,
for it discusses the case of the tree grafted onto the vegetable,
while C concerns the issue of the vegetable grafted onto a
tree. D-E opposes M. 1:7D.[235]

A states that one may not graft dodder onto the 'g'. We
have already discussed the characteristics of the parasitic dodder
(cf. T. 1:11). From B we learn that the 'g' is considered a
tree.[236] Feliks says that it is probably the calycotome, a
wild, thorny bush of the pulse family (Leguminosae). The calycotome can serve as a host plant for several types of dodder.[237]

C cites Judah's opinion, which we have already discussed
(cf. M. 1:7). In D-E, Simeon b. Gamaliel, in the name of
Judah b. 'Agra, opposes the prohibition of M. 1:7D and permits the
grafting of a tree onto a vegetable. His view may be explained
in the same way that we explained Judah's position. That is, it
is possible that Simeon b. Gamaliel permits the grafting of a
tree onto a vegetable because he does not consider the result
a true graft (since the plants do not actually unite). Alternatively, he permits such a graft because it is often unsuccessful,
and even when it does succeed, the graft is only temporary in
nature.[238]

We shall now summarize T.'s relationship to M. 1:7 with
the following chart:

M. 1:7		*T. 1:10-12*	
A.	They do not graft:		
B.	a tree onto a tree,	T. 1:10A	Planting of pomegran-ate shoots or stalks in a sycamore tree.
		B-C	Placing a shoot between two beams.
		D-E	Placing two kinds of tree-seeds in a single tube.
		F-G	Grafting a palm tree onto an olive tree.

C. a vegetable onto a vegetable,	T. 1:11A(+C)	Grafting dodder onto alhagi.
	T. 1:11B(+C)	Grafting a spinach beet onto an amaranth.
D. a tree onto a vegetable,	T. 1:12D-E	Simeon b. Gamaliel, in the name of Judah b. 'Agra, permits the grafting of a tree onto a vegetable.
E. a vegetable onto a tree,	T. 1:12A-B	Grafting dodder onto calycotome.
F. Judah permits the grafting of a vegetable onto a tree.	T. 1:12C	= M. 1:7F.

Except for T. 1:12D-E, then, T. 1:10-12 follows exactly the order of M. in systematically illustrating each of its clauses.

A. He who places a seed $(m^c h)$[239] of lupine beside a seed of a gourd,

B. so that the earth might be broken open $(\check{s}tybq^c)$ before it,

C. is liable.

T. Kil. 1:13 (p. 205, 11. 33-34)

T. supplements M. 1:8I-K, for it describes another procedure designed to stimulate the growth of gourds. T. follows the basic structure of M. 1:8 and T. 1:10A-C+D-E, for it consists of a description of the act (A), a gloss explaining its purpose (B), and an apodosis (C). T. 1:13 differs from these pericopae,[240] however, in that its apodosis states only that one who performs the act is liable, and does not relate the act to one of the categories of prohibited grafts listed in M. 1:7. We shall see below that this allows for two possible interpretations of T.

According to A-C one may not plant a lupine-seed next to a gourd-seed so that the former might break up the soil for the latter. Feliks[241] explains that a gourd must grow in loose soil. The lupine-seed was well known in ancient times for the way in which it would vigorously bore through the soil.[242] Therefore, if a lupine-seed were to be planted next to a gourd-seed, the latter would be able to grow in the soil loosened by the former. Now the act prohibited by T. does not actually involve grafting, for the two kinds of seeds are simply planted next to one another. Taken by itself, therefore, T. may refer to the prohibition not of

grafting one kind on another, but of sowing seeds of different
kinds together. The redactor of T. has placed it as a comment
on M. 1:8I-K because, like the latter, it involves the seeds of
a gourd. Alternatively, Lieberman[243] maintains that, although
the act described in T. does not involve grafting, it still
falls in the same category as that of a graft of one vegetable
onto another (M. 1:7C). There is little reason, however, to
regard the case of T. as having any similarity with an act of
grafting, and we therefore prefer the first interpretation given
above.

1:9

A. He who buries turnips or (w) radishes [B. Erub. 77a-b: a
turnip or a radish] under the vine --

B. if [B. Erub.: when ($bzmn$)] some of its leaves ($^c lyw$; Geniza
fragments,[244] Geonim and early commentaries:[245] $h^c lywn$
["the upper part"]) were exposed,

C. he does not fear [that he has transgressed (Danby)],

(1) either because of ($m\v{s}wm$; Geniza fragments, K, Ox.: $m\v{s}m$)
[the laws of] diverse-kinds,

(2) or because of [the laws of] the Seventh Year [= omitted
in a Geniza fragment],

(3) or because of [the laws of] tithes [= omitted in S]
[Geniza fragments, K, B. Erub., reverse (2) and (3)];

D. and they are removed ($wny\d{t}lyn$; C, K (before correction),
Mn of B. Shab. 50b-51a: $wnw\d{t}lyn$, ["and they remove them"])
on the Sabbath.

E. He who sows wheat and barley together [lit.: as one],

F. lo, this is [considered a sowing of] diverse-kinds.

G. R. Judah says, "It is not [considered a sowing of] diverse-
kinds,

H. "(1) until there are [either] two [grains of] wheat and
[one of] barley,

"(2) or [one of] wheat and two [of] barley,

"(3) or [one each of] wheat, barley, and rice-wheat."

M. Kil. 1:9 (A-D: B. Erub. 77a-b,
B. Shab. 50b-51a, 13a)

M. is composed of two autonomous subunits, A-D and E-H.
The former concerns the case of one who buries turnips or
radishes under a vine. This pericope thus supplements M. 1:7-8's
discussion of prohibited grafts. E-H then deals with the separate
issue of sowing together different kinds of seeds. Since the

two subunits deal with such entirely different questions,
we shall deal with each of them separately.

The basic unit of A-D consists of the declarative sentence
formed by A+C, with the apodosis C consisting of three parts.
B was then inserted into this completed sentence. This is clear
from the fact that B interrupts the smooth construction of the
sentence, for the subject of B is not that of A and C (i.e., "he
who buries"), but the "turnips or radishes" of A. D, which also
refers to the subject of B,[246] then augments the list of C.
We shall see below that D could not have been added to the
pericope without B, so that it was included in M. 1:9 either
together with B or after the latter had already been inserted
into A+C.

A describes the case of one who buries turnips or[247]
radishes[248] under a vine, presumably in order to protect them
from heat and dryness (Feliks[249]). According to C one who thus
buries these vegetables is exempt from three prohibitions, all of
which apply only to crops which are actually planted, and not
simply buried. We note that the fact that the vegetables are
buried specifically under a vine is relevant only to C(1),
which concerns the prohibition of diverse-kinds, and not to
C(2) or C(3) (Seventh Year and tithes), which need presuppose
only that the vegetables are buried. The pericope has thus
been formulated with special regard to the law of diverse-kinds,
and so concerns the other two prohibitions only secondarily.

Let us now take each of C's rules in turn. C(1) states
that the action described in A is not prohibited by the laws
of diverse-kinds. As we have already indicated, the relevant
law is probably the prohibition against grafting a vegetable
onto a tree (M. 1:7E; cf. Hai Gaon,[250] Maim., *Code, Diverse-
Kinds* 2:11, Rabad [*ad. loc.*], MR, and Feliks[251]).[252] According
to this law it is prohibited to plant a vegetable near a tree
in such a way that it would gain nourishment from the latter.
Since in this instance the turnips or radishes are only buried
and are not actually planted, they will not be nourished by
the roots of the vine, and the action described in A is therefore
permitted. Alternatively, C(1) may refer to the law of diverse-
kinds of the vineyard (Dt. 22:9), which prohibits the planting
of another kind near a vine (Sens, Maim., *Comm.*, Rashi,[253]
Me'iri[254]). Again, since the vegetables are not actually planted,
the law does not apply. While both of these explanations are
plausible, the redactor, by placing M. 1:9A-D immediately after
M. 1:7-8, appears to understand the pericope according to the
first interpretation.

C(2) concerns the prohibition of planting during the
Seventh Year (Ex. 23:10-11, Lv. 25:4). One is permitted to bury
the turnips or radishes because he is not considered thereby to
plant them (Maim., *Code, Seventh Year and Jubilee* 1:15, according
to the interpretation of Ridbaz). Alternatively, C(2) may concern the prohibition of eating that which grows of itself (*spyḥ*)
in the Seventh Year (Sens, Bert., TYY, GRA; cf. M. Shev. 9:1).
Since the vegetables were buried rather than planted, one is
permitted to eat any aftergrowth which may be produced by the
vegetables during this period.

C(3) refers to the obligation of tithing one's crops (Lv.
27:30, Nu. 18:21-24). One who buries turnips or radishes need
not tithe them after removing them from the ground,[255] since
he is obligated to tithe only that which he has planted (Maim.,
Comm.;[256] cf. also Bert.). Alternatively, the relevant law may
again concern the aftergrowth which the turnips or radishes
may produce. Since no planting has taken place, one is not obligated to tithe the aftergrowth.[257]

According to B the rule of A+C holds only if the leaves of
the turnips or radishes are visible aboveground. It is not
clear, however, why one should be exempt from the laws of C only
if the leaves of the vegetables are exposed. Three different
interpretations have been advanced to explain this difficulty.
Some commentaries (Maim., *Code, Diverse-Kinds* 2:11, Rabad
[*ad. loc.*], Maim., *Code, Seventh Year and Jubilee* 1:15) maintain
that one must expose the leaves[258] in order to show that he
intends only to bury the vegetables, but not to plant them.[259]
Feliks,[260] however, disagrees, maintaining that if the leaves
are visible aboveground the vegetables actually appear to be
growing. The point of B, rather, is that the owner is exempt
from the laws of C even if the turnips or radishes appear to have
been planted. This interpretation, though, does not follow from
the language of the text, which reads "if some of its leaves
were exposed," and not, as Feliks wishes to take it, "even if some
of its leaves are exposed." B therefore clearly implies that
the rule of A+C holds only when the leaves are visible. Finally,
a third interpretation maintains that B applies only to D, and
that the rule of A+C holds whether or not the leaves are exposed
(Rashi,[261] Sens, Maim., *Comm.*). This interpretation, however,
is also difficult. It is true that this explanation is supported
by the fact that B and D may have been added together to the
pericope. Even if this is the case, though, one must still explain why B was inserted into the pericope in such a way that it
must be read with C as well as with D. If the glossator had

wished to read B with D alone, he could have placed the former
after C, and not before it. According to its position in the
pericope, then, the point of B can only be that one is exempt from
the laws of C and D solely when the leaves of the vegetables are
exposed. We therefore prefer the first interpretation given
above.

D states that, if their leaves are visible, the buried turnips
or radishes may be removed on the Sabbath. Several commentaries
(Sens, Maim., *Comm.*, *Code*, *Sabbath* 25:14-15, Bert., TYY) state that
the point of D is that one may remove the vegetables by their
leaves even though he may also move some soil (which one is not
permitted to move on the Sabbath) in the process. Since he
moves the soil only indirectly, the one who picks up the vegetables is not considered to violate the Sabbath.[262] We note that,
according to this interpretation, B is clearly necessary to D,
for one cannot remove the vegetables without violating the Sabbath
unless he can pull them out by their leaves.

We now turn to E-H. Like A+C, E-F opens with a singular
present participle ($hzwr^c$). In contrast to the former, however,
E-F does not form a smooth declarative sentence, for the subject
of F is not the sower of E, but the act of sowing itself. Judah
glosses and opposes F at G, which balances the former ($kl'ym$ $vs.$
$'ynw$ $kl'ym$). G in turn is glossed and expanded at H.

According to E-F one who sows a grain of barley and a grain
of wheat together is liable for sowing diverse-kinds.[263] At
G Judah disagrees with this rule, maintaining that one is not
liable for sowing only two grains of different kinds. H explains
that one is liable only if he sows together three grains, with
at least two of the grains being considered diverse-kinds with
the third. Judah and the anonymous rule of E-F thus dispute
concerning the number of grains which one must sow before becoming
liable for sowing diverse-kinds. The issue of the dispute may
concern the definition of the "field" mentioned in the prohibition
against sowing diverse-kinds, which reads: *You shall not sow
your field with diverse-kinds* (Lv. 19:19). E-F takes "field" to
mean simply an area of land, so that the verse prohibits one
from sowing $kl'ym$, i.e., two grains (as indicated by the dual
form) in an empty space. Judah, on the other hand, apparently
understands field to refer to land which has already been sown.[264]
Judah therefore maintains that the verse prohibits one from sowing $kl'ym$, i.e., two grains, in land which has already been sown,
i.e., containing at least one grain. Accordingly, one is not
liable until he has sown three kinds together (Sens, Maim., *Comm.*,
Bert.).

A. He who sows something [i.e., a kind of seed] which sprouts
    [by nature],[265]
B. over (*ʿl gby*) swamps or over rushes (*hylt*),[266]
C. is liable.
D. [If he sows it] over a rock or over a water-channel (*'mt mym*),
E. he is free of liability.
F. and [he who sows] something [i.e., a kind of seed] which
    does not sprout [by nature],
G. whether over swamps, over rushes [Erfurt, first printed
    ed. add: over a rock], or over a water-channel [= omitted
    by Lieberman],[267]
H. he is free from liability.

                            T. Kil. 1:14 (p. 205, ll. 35-37)

        T. Kil. 1:14 supplements M. 1:9E-G, for both pericopae
discuss the conditions under which one becomes liable for sowing
diverse-kinds. While M. discusses the number of seeds one must
sow before becoming liable, T. concerns how such factors as
the condition of the seed and the land determine liability. We
note that T. nowhere explicitly mentions diverse-kinds, and could
just as easily relate to another area of law (e.g., laws of the
Seventh-Year). Our understanding of the pericope here follows
that of the redactor, who has placed the pericope in the context
of T. Kil., and has thus indicated that he interprets it as a
rule of diverse-kinds.
        T. consists of three statements, A-C, D-E, and F-H. D-E,
which depends on A, balances and opposes B-C (swamps and rushes
vs. rock and water channel [B *vs.* D]; *ḥyyb vs. pṭwr* [C *vs.* E]).
F+H balances A+C (*ḥmṣmyḥ vs. š'ynw mṣmyḥ* [A *vs.* F]; *ḥyyb vs. pṭwr*
[C *vs.* H]), but G does not correspond to B, for the former contains an additional item, the water-channel. According to
Lieberman, however, this item has been mistakenly inserted into
G from D, so that G does correspond to B, and F-H balances and
opposes A-C. Alternatively, Erfurt and the first printed edition
add a fourth item, the rock, to G, so that the latter includes
the kinds of land listed in both B and D. It is not likely,
though, that C would list all of these types of land, when, as
we shall see, it need list only those of B. We therefore prefer
the reading suggested by Lieberman.
        A describes a case in which one sows diverse-kinds which sprout
by nature, i.e., seeds which readily germinate. In B-C seeds are
sown over swamps and rushes. Although these areas contain too
much moisture and do not have adequate drainage,[268] it is

sometimes possible for a seed to germinate in the soil found
in them. The actual growth of diverse-kinds thus may result from
the sowing of the seeds, and the sower is therefore liable
(following HD[269]). According to A, then, one is liable for sowing diverse-kinds even if there is only a slight possibility
that the seeds will actually grow. In D-E, on the other hand,
the seeds are sown over a rock or a water-channel. Both such
areas are totally unsuitable for sowing, for the rock offers no
moisture at all, while the water-channel presumably contains too
much water. The seeds will not germinate when sown in such areas,
and therefore the sower is not liable.[270] F-H similarly presents
a case which contrasts with A-D, only this time the case differs
in that the sower uses a different type of seed. In this instance
the seeds of diverse-kinds will not germinate at all, so that the
sower is not liable even if he sows them over swamps or rushes
(or, it logically follows, over a rock or a water-channel as
well). The point of T., then, is that although one is liable for
sowing diverse-kinds, when there is even the slightest possibility
that the growth of diverse-kinds will result, he is not liable
if such growth is not at all likely to occur. It is therefore
not the act of sowing itself, but its probable outcome, which
determines liability.[271]

A. He who sows, weeds, or covers of (*hmnph*; Lieberman,[272]
    following Erfurt, corrects to *hmhph*; first printed ed.:
    hhwph) [Erfurt: He who sows, covers over, or weeds] [seeds
    of diverse-kinds], transgresses a negative commandment
    (*^{c}wbr bl' t^{c}šh*).
B. R. ^{c}Aqiva says, "Even (*'p*) he who allows [plants of diverse-
    kinds] to grow transgresses a negative commandment."
C. And they sow seeds [i.e., either seeds of vegetables, or
    grains] and tree-seeds together [lit.: as one] [Erfurt:
    And they sow tree seeds together].
D. He who sows grape-seeds (*hrsnym*) with wheat [= omitted
    in Y.], lo, he receives forty stripes (*lwqh 't h'rb^{c}ym*).

                    T. Kil. 1:15 (pp. 205-206, ll. 37-40)
                    (A-B: B. M.Q. 2b, B. Mak. 21b,
                    B. A.Z. 64a; C-D: Y. Peah 1:4
                    (16c)[273])

     T. is composed of two separate subunits, A-B, which con-
cerns activities related to the care of sown seeds, and C-D,
dealing with the sowing together of certain kinds of seeds.

Although these two parts are autonomous of M. 1:9E-G they seem to
supplement the latter. A-B expands M.'s prohibition of sowing
diverse-kinds to include related activities as well, and C-D
discusses a situation which is analogous to M.'s care of sowing
wheat and barley together.

A-B consists of a declarative sentence at A, which is glossed
by ^CAqiva's statement at B. The two sayings clearly have been
formulated together, for they each consist of one or more singular present participles and the apodosis "transgresses a negative commandment." Since A and B share the same apodosis, it is
likely that the latter was added to ^CAqiva's saying from A, and
that B originally read simply, "Even he who allows [them] to grow"
(cf. the formulation of B, cited below). In fact, it is possible
that "even" (*'p*) is standard joining-language which may have
been used here to connect an independent saying of ^CAqiva (e.g.,
He who allows [them] to grow + apodosis) with A. B may thus
have not been originally formulated as a gloss of A at all. We
note that the phrase "transgresses a negative commandment"
appears nowhere else in M.-T. Kil., and in fact gives no indica-
tion that the prohibition concerns diverse-kinds (and not, for
example, laws of the Seventh-Year) at all. We understand A-B
to pertain to diverse-kinds only on account of the work of the
redactor, who has placed A-B in T. Kil.

According to A one is prohibited not only from sowing diverse-
kinds, as Scripture itself indicates (Lv. 19:19), but also from
performing any other action, such as weeding or covering with
soil, which may aid the growth of diverse-kinds. A thus extends
the prohibition against sowing diverse-kinds to include the
care of the seeds which have already been sown. In B ^CAqiva
states that one may not allow diverse-kinds to grow. When taken
by itself ^CAqiva's saying simply restates the point of A, *viz.*,
that one may not further the growth of diverse-kinds which have
already been sown. When read together with A, however, B may be
taken to add that one may not allow diverse-kinds to grow, even
if he does not do anything himself to aid their growth. In this
context, then, B may be understood to say that one is liable for
acts of omission (e.g., failing to uproot the diverse-kinds) as
well as acts of commission (e.g., actually aiding the growth
of diverse-kinds).[274]

Let us now compare T.'s version of A-B with that of B.:

T. Kil. 1:15	*B. M.Q. (et al.)*
1. He who sows, weeds or covers over	1. He who weeds or covers over diverse-kinds,
2. transgresses a negative commandment.	2. receives stripes [Mn. of B. Mak.: transgresses a negative commandment].
3. R. ^CAqiva says "Even he who allows [plants of diverse-kinds] to grow	3. R. ^CAqiva says, "Even he who allows [plants of diverse-kinds] to grow."
4. "transgresses a negative commandment."	4. ---

B. differs from T. in several ways. First, B. mentions "diverse-kinds" in (1), and so presents the context of the rule. B. does not mention sowing in (1), presumably because this action is expressly prohibited by Scripture (Lv. 19:19). B. also reads "receives stripes," for T.'s "transgresses a negative commandment" at (2), and so perhaps specifies the punishment connected with the prohibition.[275] Finally, B. omits the apodosis at (4), because it is redundant. B. thus both clarifies the laws of T. (at (1) and (2)) and simplifies its formulation (at (4)).[276]

C and D are formally autonomous of one another, for the subject of C is given in the singular (and is prefaced by the definite article), while that of D appears in the plural. D, however, seems to supplement C, as we shall immediately see. C states that one may sow tree-seeds together with other kinds of seeds. The point of C is that the prohibition of sowing diverse-kinds does not apply to trees, perhaps because the latter are not mentioned in the scriptural formulation of the laws of diverse-kinds (Lv. 19:19, Dt. 22:9). According to Erfurt's reading C permits the sowing of different kinds of tree-seeds together, again because the laws of sowing diverse-kinds do not apply to trees.[277] We note that Sirillo[278] derives both of the above rules from our initial reading of C. Maimonides (*Code, Diverse-Kinds* 1:6) also presents both laws:

> And it is permitted to sow [other kinds of] seeds and tree-seeds together; and similarly it is permitted to mix tree-seeds [of different kinds] and sow them together, for [the laws of] diverse-kinds concern trees only in respect to grafting alone (š'yn lk kl'ym b'ylnwt 'l' hrkbh blbd).

D states that one may not sow wheat together with grape-
seeds, since the sowing of diverse-kinds in a vineyard is expressly prohibited by Scripture (Dt. 22:9). In this context the
point of D is that although vines are regarded as trees (cf.
M. 1:8F-H), one is not permitted to sow other kinds with them.
D thus presents an exception to the rule of C. We note that,
while D supplements M. 1:5 E-G's case of sowing wheat and barley
together, C bears no connection to M., and so has been placed
here only on account of D. If, on the other hand, Erfurt's reading
of C is followed, D is not related to C at all, so that the latter
is autonomous of D as well as of M.

CHAPTER TWO

KILAYIM CHAPTER TWO

Chapter Two concerns the various means by which different
kinds of plants may be sown together without being sown as
diverse-kinds. The chapter actually begins at M. 1:9E-G, which
states that the sowing of two seeds of different kinds (or,
according to Judah, three seeds of two different kinds) at the
same time constitutes a sowing of diverse-kinds. M. 2:1-2 then
discusses how one may sow two or more different kinds of seeds
which have been mixed together. M. 2:1 opens with a rule stating
that if a *se'ah* of one kind of seeds contains a *rova^c* of seeds
of another kind, then the *se'ah* may not be sown until the quantity
of seeds in the *rova^c* is lessened. That is, a field may contain
two different kinds if one kind is present only in very small
quantities, and so does not produce the appearance of diverse-
kinds. Yosé, on the other hand, rules that all of the seeds of
the *rova^c* must be removed from the *se'ah*, for one may not cause
the actual growth of diverse-kinds, regardless of whether or not
the appearance of diverse-kinds would result. As we shall see,
the rest of the chapter presupposes M. 2:1A's view that it is
the appearance of diverse-kinds which must be avoided.

M. 2:3-2:5C forms a subunit dealing with the problem of
sowing one kind in a field already sown with another kind. In
M. 2:3 a man wishes to sow one kind of grain in a field already
sown with grain of another kind, while M. 2:4 has the owner
wishing to plant trees in a field already sown with grain or
vegetables (and vice-versa). M. 2:5A-C concerns one who wishes
to sow grain or vegetables in a field already sown with carum
or arum (which produce fruit for several years after they are
sown). In each case M. rules that the plants already in the field
must be removed before, rather than after, the new plants are
sown. The new plants may not be allowed to grow alongside of
the old ones, for, although the owner intends to remove the latter,
he appears to be sowing diverse-kinds. The subunit thus agrees
with M. 2:1A that it is the appearance of diverse-kinds which
determines liability, and not their actual growth.

M. 2:5D-F deals with wild plants which come up together with
plants that have been sown, and so forms an appropriate appendix
to the foregoing. The issue now is not that of sowing diverse-
kinds, but of allowing them to remain. M. again follows the theory

of M. 2:1A, ruling that since one did not appear to wish the growth of the diverse-kinds, he is not required to weed out the wild plants. Once he begins to weed, however, he must uproot all of the wild plants, for if he were to stop weeding, he would appear to allow diverse-kinds to grow.

M. Kil. 2:6-9 forms a new subunit which concerns sowing different kinds together (i.e., in the same field or in adjacent fields) without producing the appearance of diverse-kinds. The subunit as a whole follows the theory of M. 2:1A. M. 2:6 has a Houses-dispute concerning the minimum width which the rows of different kinds must have in order to be considered autonomous from one another. M. 2:7-8 then interrupts the discussion of sowing different kinds in the same field with a subunit concerning the sowing of different kinds in adjacent fields. According to M. 2:7 the corner of a field of one kind may enter a field of a different kind, and the edge of a field of one kind may be sown with the kind of an adjacent field, for in each instance, the kind which enters the field of another kind appears to mark the end of its own field, so that no appearance of diverse-kinds results. M. 2:8 concerns the related problem of flanking a field of one kind with another kind (in this instance, mustard or safflower) in such a way that the appearance of diverse-kinds is not produced. M. 2:9 reverts to M. 2:6, for it opens with the same sentence-structure ("He who wishes to lay out his field. . ."). Now the field is to be laid out in patches of different kinds. M. again deals with the minimum size a patch must be in order to be considered an autonomous field. A dispute between Meir and the sages, concerning the sowing of mustard patches, is then interpolated into M. The insertion of this dispute may represent an attempt by the redactor to link M. 2:9 and M. 2:8 (which also concerns mustard) together, and so to consolidate the two parts of the subunit (M. 2:6+2:9, M. 2:7-8). M. 2:10A-B, which concerns measuring the area within a patch, is then appended to the subunit.

M. 2:10C-2:11 closes the chapter with rules about sowing different kinds among one another. Both pericopae are tightly constructed, for both describe the ways in which the different kinds may be sown with each other by listing the four possible combinations of the words $tbw'h$ and yrq. M. 2:10C-F defines, for each combination, the minimum area which a secondary kind must cover when it is sown in a field of a primary kind. A space the size of this minimum area constitutes an autonomous field, so that the presence of the secondary kind in the field does not produce the appearance of diverse-kinds. M. 2:11 rules that all plants may be allowed to lean over other kinds of plants, except

for the Greek gourd. The Greek gourd tends to become entangled
in adjacent plants, and so could cause the appearance of diverse-
kinds if it were allowed to lean over other kinds. M. 2:10C-2:11
then also follows M. 2:1A's emphasis on the appearance of
diverse-kinds.

2:1-2

A. [Concerning] every *se'ah* [of one kind of seeds] which
contains a quarter [-*qab*] [most mss.[1]add: of seeds] of
another kind (*mmyn 'ḥr*; B, C, Geniza fragments,[2] K, Pr, V:
of one kind [*mmyn 'ḥd*][3]) -- he shall lessen [the quantity
of seeds of the other kind, so that those seeds form less
than a quarter-*qab*].

B. R. Yosé says, "He shall sift [out the other kind completely]."

C. [And it makes no difference] whether [the quarter-*qab* con-
sists] of one kind or two.

D. R. Simeon says, "They only said [that he must lessen the
quantity of seeds in the quarter-*qab* when the latter consists solely] of one kind."

E. And the sages say, "Everything which is [considered] diverse-
kinds with [the seeds of] the *se'ah* combines (*mṣtrp*) to
[form] the quarter [-*qab*]."

M. Kil. 2:1 (A: B. M.Q. 6a;
A-B: M. B.B. 94a)

F. Under what circumstances?

G. (1) When grain [is mixed] with grain,
   (2) and pulse with pulse,
   (3) grain with pulse,
   (4) and pulse with grain.

H. But they said (*b'mt 'mrw*) [C, K, L, O, P, Pr omit: said],
"Garden-seeds which are not eaten combine (*mṣtrpyn*) [to
form an amount sufficient to prohibit the sowing of the
when they total] one twenty-fourth of [the volume] which is
sown[4] in a *bet se'ah*."

I. R. Simeon says, "Just as they said [this ruling in order] to
make [the law] more stringent [in one case], so did they
say [the same ruling in order] to make [the law] more lenient
[in another]:

J. "Flax[5] [which has been mixed] with [a *se'ah* of] grain combines
[to form an amount sufficient to prohibit the sowing of the
se'ah when it totals] one twenty-fourth of [the volume] which

is sown in a *bet se'ah*."

M. Kil. 2:2

M. Kil.2:1-2 deals with the problem of sowing seeds of
diverse-kinds which have been mixed together, thus continuing the
discussion of sowing diverse-kinds which began at M. 1:9E-G.
M. consists of four parts, A-B, concerning the sowing of different
kinds of seeds with one another, C-E, dealing with the combining
of seeds to form a minimum quantity, F-G, glossing A-B, and H-J,
dealing with mixtures containing garden-seeds or flax. We shall
consider each of these sections in turn. A describes a situation
where a *se'ah* of one kind of seeds (henceforth: principal seeds)
contains a quarter-*qab* (= one twenty-fourth of a *se'ah*[6]) of
another kind of seeds (henceforth: secondary seeds). According
to A one must lessen the quantity of secondary seeds before
sowing the *se'ah*. Y. understands A to mean that one must reduce
the proportion of secondary seeds to principal seeds. Therefore
one may either lessen the quantity of secondary seeds or add to
the amount of principal seeds (Y. Kil. 2:1 (27c), Maim., *Comm.*,
Code, Diverse-Kinds 2:1, GRA). The purpose of this action is to
avoid presenting the appearance of sowing diverse-kinds (TYY,
GRA, MR). It is apparently assumed that the diverse-kinds would
be noticed (later, when the plants actually grew) only if the
secondary seed comprised at least one twenty-four of the *se'ah*.

In B, Yosé disagrees with A and says that one must remove
all of the secondary seeds from the *se'ah*. Yosé apparently
reasons that one may not sow any amount of diverse-kinds, and
therefore one may not leave any secondary seeds in the *se'ah*.
The issue of the dispute thus concerns whether the appearance or
actual sowing of diverse-kinds determines liability. While A
apparently maintains that one need only be concerned about the
appearance of diverse-kinds, Yosé says that the actual sowing of
diverse-kinds is prohibited, even when the appearance of diverse-
kinds will not result.

C-E glosses A-B with a dispute concerning whether or not
several different kinds of secondary seeds may join together
to form the quarter-*qab* mentioned in A. The dispute consists
of three opinions. C states that different kinds of seeds may
combine to form the quarter-*qab*. Simeon, on the other hand, says
in D that the quarter-*qab* may consist of only one kind. In E
the sages basically restate the position of C in the language of
A ("*se'ah*" and "*rova*[c]"), for they maintain that every kind of
seed which is considered diverse-kinds with the principal seeds
combines to form the quarter-*qab*. The dispute then poses a

problem, for it contains two different versions of the same
position. We may resolve this difficulty by noting that C is
only necessary to A because of D. In other words, it is only
necessary to specify that the quarter-*qab* of A may consist of
either one or two kinds because Simeon says that it must be
composed of one kind. Therefore C was added to the pericope
together with D. E, which, without the attributive formula,
restates C as an autonomous rule, was then added to the dispute
of C-D.

The issue of the dispute concerns whether or not the quarter-
qab of seeds must be lessened even when it consists of more than
one kind. According to C and E such a quarter-*qab* must be
lessened, presumably because such a quantity of seeds will produce
the appearance of diverse-kinds even if the seeds themselves are
of different kinds. Simeon, however, disagrees in D, maintaining
the seeds will produce the appearance of diverse-kinds only when
the quarter-*qab* consists entirely of one kind.

F-G glosses A-B, stating that the law of that unit (i.e.,
that one may not sow a *se'ah* which contains a quarter-*qab* of
another kind of seeds) applies only to mixtures involving grain
and/or pulse. G then simply consists of the four possible
combinations of the words *tbw'h* and *qṭnyt*. Feliks explains that
the grains involved are probably wheat, barley, two-rowed barley,
rice-wheat and spelt (all belonging to the grass family
[Graminae]).[7] Pulse refers to certain plants of the pea family
(Papilionaceae). The particular grain and pulse of which M.
speaks have large seeds which are usually sown close together,
so that a relatively high volume of seeds is sown in a given
area (or, they are sown at a high rate [= volume/area]).[8]
According to G, therefore, the law of A-B applies only when all
of the seeds in the mixture are sown at this rate. MR points
out that M. assumes this rate to be a *se'ah* per *bet se'ah*.[9]

H-J concerns the measure in which garden-seeds (H) and flax
(I-J) prohibit the sowing of a *se'ah*. H is connected to G by
the phrase *b'mt 'mrw*, which, according to Lieberman,[10] should
simply read *b'mt*. This phrase usually introduces a particular
case which does not follow a foregoing general rule.[11] In this
instance, then, H is contrasted with G, for the law of A-B, which
applies to grain and pulse, does not apply to garden-seeds, as
we shall now see.

H states that garden-seeds which are not eaten combine at
one twenty-fourth of the volume sown in a *bet se'ah*. The garden-
seeds referred to here are those seeds which are not produced as
the fruits of their plants (e.g., seeds of onions, turnips, etc.;

cf. M. Ma^cas. 5:8). These seeds are said to combine to form a
certain measure. Now the meaning of "combine" in this context
is not clear. It is likely that "combine" has the sense of
"combine to prohibit," or simply "prohibit" (GRA, cited by Feliks,
Mixed Sowing, p. 197).[12] H then says that garden-seeds prohibit
the sowing of a *se'ah* at one twenty-fourth of the volume sown
in a *bet se'ah*. Garden-seeds are then distinguished from grain
and pulse, which prohibit the sowing of a *se'ah* at a quarter-*qab*
(A+G).

Alternatively, the statement may mean that different kinds
of garden-seeds combine to prohibit the sowing of a *se'ah* at
the given measure (Maim., *Comm.*, Sirillo, TAS, MR [latter three
cited by Feliks, *Mixed Sowing*, p. 196]). H then refers back
to E, its point being that while different kinds of grain and
pulse[13] combine to form a quarter-*qab*, different kinds of
garden-seeds combine to form one twenty-fourth of the volume
sown in a *bet se'ah*. According to this interpretation H assumes
that the garden-seeds prohibit the sowing of a *se'ah* when they
amount to the latter measure.

In any event, both of the above interpretations of H agree
that garden-seeds prohibit the sowing of a *se'ah* when they amount
to one twenty-fourth of the volume (of garden-seeds) sown in a
bet se'ah. We must now determine why the law of A-B does not
apply to garden-seeds. The reason for this, in my view, is
as follows. A apparently assumes that every kind of seed in the
se'ah is sown at the same rate. It is only under this condition
that each kind's proportion of the total volume equals the proportion of area which it will cover. A can then say that a
quarter-*qab* of seeds prohibits the sowing of a *se'ah*. For a
quarter-*qab* (= one twenty-fourth of a *se'ah*) of seeds will cover
one twenty-fourth of the area sown, and A apparently determines
that this sowing will result in the appearance of diverse-kinds
(cf. Maim., *Code*, *Diverse-Kinds* 2:7). Now garden-seeds are
smaller than grain or pulse (all commentaries) and so are sown
at a lower rate (i.e., less volume per area). If garden-seeds
are mixed with grain or pulse, their proportion of the total
volume will not correspond to the proportion of area which they
will cover. For example, a quarter-*qab* of garden-seeds will cover
more than one twenty-fourth of the area sown. The law of A
then cannot be applied in this case, for that law does not consider
seeds with different rates of sowing.

The law of H, however, does take the garden-seeds' rate of
sowing into account. As we have already seen, H says that the
measure in which garden-seeds prohibit the sowing of a *se'ah*

is one twenty-fourth of the volume sown in a *bet se'ah*. In
other words, a *se'ah* of grain or pulse may not be sown when
there are enough garden-seeds in it to cover one twenty-fourth
of the area sown by the *se'ah*, for then the garden-seeds will
produce the appearance of diverse-kinds (as in A). Since the
rate of sowing for garden-seeds is less than that for grain or
pulse, the amount described in H is less than a quarter-*qab*.[14]
H then states that the principle of A (that the secondary seeds
may not cover one twenty-fourth of the area sown) also applies
to garden-seeds, only with a different measure.

In I, Simeon glosses H with the comment that, while the
method of calculation used in H results in a stringent ruling in
one case, the same method produces a lenient ruling in another.
That is, it takes *less* than a quarter-*qab* of garden-seeds to
prohibit the sowing of a *se'ah* of grain or pulse, and this
ruling is more stringent than the law of A, which says that it
takes a full quarter-*qab* of seeds to do the same. Simeon then
states in J that flax, like garden-seeds, combines (i.e., prohibits) at one twenty-fourth of the volume sown in a *bet se'ah*.
Now although the law for flax is the same as that for garden-seeds,
the two kinds of seeds prohibit the sowing of a *se'ah* in different amounts. Flax-seeds, although they are the same size as
garden-seeds, are sown closer together because their plants do
not spread out.[15] Therefore flax-seeds are sown at a rate which
is not only higher than that of garden-seeds, but higher than
that of grain and pulse as well.[16] Consequently, it takes more
than a quarter-*qab* of flax-seeds to prohibit the sowing of a
se'ah. The principle of A, when applied to flax, thus produces
a lenient ruling.

A. *[Concerning]every se'ah [of one kind of seeds] which contains
a quarter[-qab]* [Erfurt, first printed ed. add: of seeds]
of another kind(mmyn 'ḥr; first printed ed.: of one kind
[mmyn 'ḥd]) *-- he shall lessen [the quantity of seeds of
the other kinds, so that those seeds form less than a
quarter-qab]* [= M. 2:1A].

B. Under what circumstances?

C. With seeds [lit.: things] which [are sown at the rate of]
three or (*w*) four *qabs* per *bet se'ah* [first printed ed.:
per *se'ah*].

D. *But (b'mt)* [Erfurt adds: they said] *garden-seeds combine
[to form an amount sufficient to prohibit the sowing of the
se'ah when they total] one twenty-fourth of [the volume] which
[is sown] according to its own kind (bnwpl lmynw)* [= M. 2:2H].

E. [And this amount prohibits the sowing of the *se'ah*] whether
it [i.e., the garden-seeds] fell into other [kinds of
seeds] or other [kinds of seeds] fell into it.

T. Kil. 1:16a (p. 206, 11. 40-43)

T. cites and glosses M. 2:1-2. A cites M. 2:1A, and B-C
states that the law of M. applies to seeds which are sown at the
rate of three or four *qabs* per *bet se'ah*. T. then qualifies
M. 1:1a in a way different from the way in which M. explains
itself. While M. 2:2F-G states that M. 2:1A concerns particular kinds of seeds (grain or pulse), T. says that the law applies
to seeds sown at particular rates.[17]

D cites M. 2:2H, but the two statements differ in that the
latter ends with the phrase *bnwpl lbyt s'h* ("of [the volume] which
falls [i.e., is sown] in a *bet se'ah*"), while the former concludes
with *bnwpl lmynw*. According to Feliks *bnwpl lmynw* means
"according to the measure in which they are accustomed to sow
the given kind,"[18] so that both phrases refer to the rate at
which garden-seeds are sown.[19]

E then comments that the same measure (one twenty-fourth
of the volume sown in a *bet se'ah*) prohibits the sowing of a
se'ah both where the garden-seeds are mixed with a larger volume
of seeds of other kinds, and where other kinds of seeds are mixed
with a larger volume of garden-seeds. E clarifies M. 2:2H,
which says only that the law applies to garden-seeds, but does
not describe the composition of the relevant mixtures.

2:3

A. [If] his field was sown [with] wheat, and he decided to sow
it [with] barley,
B. he shall wait until [the wheat] sprouts radicles (*^{c}d šttly^c*;
L: *šytly^c*),[20]
C. and overturn [the soil], and afterwards sow [the barley].
D. If [the wheat] has [already] sprouted [aboveground[21]],
E. he should not say, "I shall sow [the barley] and afterwards
overturn [the soil];"
F. rather, he overturns [the soil], and afterwards sows
[the barley].
G. How much [of the field] should he plow [up] (*ḥwrš*; K, L, P;
ḥryš; Geniza fragment,[22] Ox: *ḥḥryš* ["How much should the
plowing be?"])
H. [He should make furrows] like the furrows [= omitted by N]
[plowed after[23]] a rainfall (*ktlmy hrby^{c}h*; C, Cn, Mn, V: *btlmy*).

I. Abba Saul says, "[He should plow enough] so that he shall
    not leave [alt. trans.: so that there will not be left]
    [unplowed the area which is sown by] a quarter[-*qab* of
    grain] in a *bet se'ah*."

                                                    M. Kil. 2:3

        M. Kil. 2:3-4 continues the discussion of sowing diverse-
kinds. While M. 1:9E-2:2, however, concerns sowing seeds of
diverse-kinds together, M. 2:3-4 deals with sowing one kind of
seeds in a field which has already been sown with another kind.
In M. 2:3, the owner wishes to sow one kind of grain in a field
already sown with a different kind. M. 2:4 then has the owner
wishing either to plant vines in a field of vegetables or grain,
or to sow grain or vegetables in a field already planted with
vines. M. 2:3-4 is probably a unitary composition, for the main
protases of both M. 2:3 and M. 2:4 (M. 2:3A, M. 2:4A+D) are constructed in a similar way (if his field + passive participle +
and he decided + infinitive) and several of the apodoses differ
only in their choice of verbs (M. 2:3E-F, M. 2:4B-C + E-F: "He
shall not say, 'I shall do X and afterwards do Y;' rather, he
does Y and afterwards does X"). We shall discuss M. 2:3 and
M. 2:4 in turn.
        M. 2:3 presents two cases, A-C and D-F, which, when supplied
with "if," are in declarative sentences. D-F depends on A.
G-I then has a dispute between an anonymous opinion and Abba Saul
on a secondary issue.
        A presents the case of one who wishes to sow barley in a
field already sown with wheat. B-C states that, before one may
sow the barley, he must first wait for the wheat to sprout
radicles (i.e., small roots), and then he must overturn the soil.
Following Feliks, we may explain the law of B-C as follows. The
point of M. is that in order to avoid sowing diverse-kinds, one
must destroy the wheat before sowing the barley.[24] Now one can
only destroy the wheat if he overturns the soil after the wheat
sprouts radicles. For if he were to overturn the soil before
the wheat sprouted radicles, the seed would simply begin to grow
wherever it came to rest. Once the radicles sprout, however, the
seeds are attached to the soil and are nourished by it. Therefore when the soil is overturned, the seeds are cut off from
their source of nourishment and consequently die.[25] By overturning the soil after the radicles sprout, one destroys the
previously-sown wheat, and one may sow the barley without being
liable for sowing diverse-kinds.[26]

D-F differs from A-C only in that now the wheat has already
sprouted aboveground. E-F states that one may not say that he
will sow the barley before overturning the soil, but he must still
overturn the soil first, as in A-C. According to TYT one may
reason that since the wheat is now visible, he will be able to
destroy all of it at any time. He may then wish to sow the
barley first, and overturn the soil later when he covers the
grains of barley. Therefore the point of M. is that even when one
may be certain that he can destroy all of the wheat, he must still
overturn the soil before sowing. For otherwise he would actually
be sowing barley in a wheatfield, and so would be liable for
sowing diverse-kinds.

G asks how much of the field must be plowed up, and so introduces a secondary issue into the pericope. H presents a dispute
in response to G. H states that when one plows up his field,
he must make furrows like those which are made after a rainfall.
These particular furrows are wide and deep, for they are made
to hold rain water. More importantly, these furrows do not lie
right next to each other. Between every two furrows there is an
area of unplowed land, upon which dirt is piled to prevent
erosion.[27] The point of H is that when one plows his field,
he need not make the furrows right next to one another, even
though the wheat will remain in the unplowed areas and may still
grow (cf. Maim., *Code*, *Diverse-Kinds* 2:13). Y. explains that
by sowing in this manner one indicates that he does not want
the wheat which he had previously sown in the field, and so he
need not plow up the entire field.[28]

In I Abba Saul says that one must plow up enough of the
field so that less than one twenty-fourth of the area sown by a
quarter-*qab* remains unplowed in a *bet se'ah*. If we assume that
grain is sown at the rate of a *se'ah* per *bet se'ah* (cf. M. 2:1-2),
then Abba Saul says that one may not leave one twenty-fourth
or more of a *bet se'ah* unplowed.[29] Abba Saul apparently reasons
that if the previously-sown wheat were to grow in a one twenty-
fourth of a *bet se'ah*, the field would appear to be sown with
diverse-kinds (as in M. 2:1-2). Abba Saul differs with H in that
he requires a fixed proportion of the land to be plowed, while H
presumably requires only that the furrows cover most of the land.
It appears, though, that H and I are not really in dispute at
all, for their answers to G are phrased in entirely different
terms. H speaks of a type of furrow, while Abba Saul discusses
a proportion of land. It is likely, therefore, that H and I are
two autonomous statements which have been redacted together to
form a dispute (see T. below).

F. [*If*] *his field was sown* [*with*] *wheat, and he decided to*
   sow it [*with*] *barley* [= M. 2:3A],

G. he shall not sow [the barley] until he overturns [the soil;
   HD: the wheat-grains].

H. [If] he did not overturn [the soil; HD: the wheat-grains],

I. *he shall wait until* [*the wheat*] *sprouts radicles* [= M. 2:3B].

J. How long [does it take] until (^{c}d *kmh*) it [i.e., the wheat]
   sprouts radicles (*mtl^{c}t*; Y.: *mzr^{c}t*[30])?

K. [The wheat does not sprout radicles] until it has stayed (*šht*;
   first printed ed.: *yšhh*) in the place [Y.: in the earth]
   for three days [Erfurt: [Not] until three days];

L. [that is, when the wheat is sown] in a moist place (*mqwm
   ḥṭynh*), but not in a dry place (*mqwm hgryd*);

M. for (*š*) part of the day [is considered] like a whole [day]
   [i.e., one may assume that the wheat has already sprouted
   radicles by the third day itself].

> T. Kil. 1:16b (p. 206, ll. 43-46)
> (J-M: Y.Kil. 2:3 (27d);
> L-M: T.Men. 10:31)

N. They do not require him to plow a fine plowing (*ḥryš dq*)
   [i.e., to make narrow furrows], but rather (*'l'*) he plows
   [= omitted by first printed ed.] a coarse plowing[31] (*ḥryš gs*)
   [i.e., he makes wide furrows] [Erfurt: but rather a coarse
   (plowing)] like [the plowing of] the furrows [after] a rainfall [Y.: They do not require (him) to plow finely (*lhywt
   ḥwrš dq*), only (to make furrows) like the furrows (plowed
   after) a rainfall].

O. Rabban Simeon b. Gamaliel says, "[The appearance of the furrows
   which are plowed after a rainfall] was called 'the horse's
   tail[-end],' [for] the end [of the mound] of dirt this
   [furrow] touches the [mound of] dirt of that [i.e., the next]
   [furrow] [First printed ed.: the end (of the mound) of
   dirt touches the (mound of) dirt of that (furrow); Y.: so
   that the end (of the mound) of dirt of this (furrow) touches
   that (furrow), and the end (of the mound) of dirt of that
   (furrow) touches this (furrow)].

P. *If* [*the wheat*] *has* [*already*] *sprouted* [*aboveground*] [=M. 2:3D],
   and he brought an animal down into [= omitted by Erfurt]
   [the field], and [the animal] plucked out (*wlyqṭtw*; Erfurt:
   wlyqtth; Y.: *wqyrṭmth*) [the wheat], lo, this is permitted

[i.e., one is then allowed to sow without overturning the soil].

T. Kil. 1:17 (pp. 206-207, ll. 46-49)

(Y. Kil. 2:3 (27d))

T. Kil. 1:16b-17 concerns issues similar to those raised by M. 2:3. We shall postpone a consideration of T.'s relationship to M. until after we have discussed each section of T. T. consists of four subunits, F-G, presenting the case of one who wishes to sow barley in a field already sown with wheat, J-M and N-O, which discuss secondary issues, and P, which, reverting to A-D, deals with a case in which the wheat has already grown aboveground.

F-I consists of two cases, F-G and H-I, with the former citing and glossing M. 2:3A and the latter citing and glossing M. 2:3B. According to T., therefore, M. 2:3B supplies the apodosis not to M. 2:3A, but to a different case. F-G states that if one wishes to sow barley in a field already sown with wheat, he first overturns the soil and then sows. It is only if he did not overturn the soil, and the wheat has (presumably) started to grow, that he must wait for the seeds to sprout radicles, overturn them, and then sow the barley (H-I). This interpretation of T. is difficult, however, for it is not evident how overturning the wheat before the radicles sprout would in any way destroy it. Furthermore, if the overturning of the soil is supposed to be effective even before the radicles sprout, why should one wait for them to sprout at all? It is not at all clear how T. understands the procedure discussed in M.

Since the above interpretation, which follows the plain sense of the text, presents certain difficulties, we must turn to a different explanation of the pericope. We shall here offer the views of HD. According to the latter B does not refer to the overturning of soil, for such an action is effective only when the wheat has already sprouted radicles. Rather, T. means that one overturns (i.e., shakes) the seeds themselves until they are destroyed and can no longer grow.[32] It is only once the wheat is destroyed that one is allowed to sow the barley. H-I then presents the law of M. 2:3B. If one did not overturn the seeds he waits for the wheat to sprout radicles, overturns the soil, and sows. According to this interpretation T. supplements M. by presenting a case in which one may sow the barley without waiting for the radicles to grow.

J-M refers to D, and concerns how long it takes for wheat to sprout radicles. J states the question, K responds, and

L-M glosses K. We note that H begins with "for" (ש), which makes
no sense in this context. Lieberman[33] points out that L-M also
appears in T. Men. 10:31, where ש is appropriate. Therefore L-M
may be primary to T. Men.

J-K states that it takes three days for wheat to sprout
radicles. This statement is botanically sound, for wheat begins
to germinate within a three-day period, and the radicles are the
first parts to emerge from the seed.[34] L adds that this is true
only where the seed is sown in a moist place, for in a dry place
it presumably takes longer. L's point stands to reason, for the
seed must imbibe water before it begins to germinate.[35] Therefore a seed sprouts radicles faster if it is sown in wet
ground.[36] M introduces a separate issue, stating that part of
the day is considered like a whole day. In this context, the
point of M is that one may assume that the wheat sprouts radicles
by the third day itself, and therefore, one may sow the barley on
that very day.

N-O discusses the method of plowing which is used in overturning the soil. I states that one does not have to plow finely
when overturning the soil, for one may make a coarse plowing
like that which is plowed after a rainfall. This means that
one need not carefully make smooth narrow furrows throughout
the field. Rather, one may plow quickly and make wide furrows
even though he will not overturn all of the soil in the field.
In O, Simeon b. Gamaliel glosses this rule, saying that the
appearance of the furrows described in N was called "the horse's
tail[-end]," for one furrow's mound of dirt touched that of
the next furrow. That is, the two mounds of dirt, when viewed
in cross-section, resemble the backside of a horse.

We shall now compare T. N with M. 2:3G-I:

M. 2:3G-I	*T. 1:17N*
1. How much [of the field] should he plow [up]?	1. ---
2. [He should make furrows] like the furrows [plowed after] a rainfall (*ktlmy hrby^ch*).	2. They do not require him to plow a fine plowing, but rather he plows a coarse plowing like [the plowing of] the furrows [after] a rain-fall (*ktlmy hrby^ch*).

3̂. Abba Saul says, "[He shall   3.   ---
    plow enough] so that he does
    not leave [unplowed the area
    which is sown by] a quarter
    [-*qab*] of grain] in a
    bet se'ah.

M. and T. both say in (2) that one plows furrows like those which
are plowed after a rainfall, but each places this law in a different context. M. presents the law as concerning how much of a
field one must plow up, while T. mentions it in reference to
methods of plowing. It is clear that T. has the law in the more
appropriate context, for the phrase *ktlmy hrby*^{c}*h* describes a type
of furrow, and does not deal with an amount of land (as, for
example, (3) does). T. therefore clarifies M., for it explains
the type of plowing to which *ktlmy hrby*^{c}*h* refers.

P cites M. 2:3D, and concerns a case in which the wheat has
already sprouted aboveground. P states that if one brings an
animal into his field to pluck out the wheat, he may afterwards
sow the barley. The point of P is that by bringing an animal
into the field, one shows that he does not want the wheat which
grows there.[37] Therefore one may afterwards sow the barley
without being liable for sowing diverse-kinds.[38]

Let us now review the relationship of T. to M. F cites
M. 2:3A (the protasis of the case), which G-H then supplements.
I cites M. 2:3B and depends on M. 2:3C, for the citation of B
alone is meaningless. N clarifies M. 2:3H (*ktlmy hrby*^{c}*h*), and
P cites and supplements M. 2:3D. T. thus provides a running
commentary to M. while at the same time slightly rearranging
the order of its topics, placing the discussion of the furrows
(N, M. 2:3H) before that of the wheat growing aboveground
(P, M. 2:3D-F).

2:4

A. [If his field] was sown [with vegetables or grain] and he
    decided to plant it [with vines[39]],
B. he shall not say, "I shall plant and afterwards overturn
    [the soil];"
C. rather, he overturns [the soil] and afterwards plants.
D. [If his field] was planted [with vines] and he decided to
    sow it [with vegetables or grain],
E. he shall not say, "I shall sow and afterwards uproot [the
    vines];

F. rather, he uproots [the vines] and afterwards sows.

G. If he wanted ($r\underset{\cdot}{s}h$; K: $rw\underset{\cdot}{s}h$) [however, to sow first (PM)],
    he cuts ($gwmm$; K: $gwms$; Mn: $gyms$) [the vines] until they
    are less than a handbreadth [high], and sows, and afterwards
    uproots [the vines].

M. Kil. 2:4

M. Kil. 2:4 concerns the planting of a field which is already
sown and the sowing of a field which is already planted. M.
may be divided into three parts, A-C, D-F, and G. A-C and D-F
present two cases in perfectly balanced declarative sentences.
The two protases (A and D) are identical except for the reversal
of nt^{c} and zr^{c}. The apodoses both follow the same pattern (as
given above), so that B-C balances E-F. Furthermore, each apodosis
consists of two clauses which balance each other. The second
clause of each apodosis (C and F) simply reverses the verb-order
of the first (B and E). G glosses D-F and presents an additional case in a simple declarative sentence.

A-C states that if one wishes to plant a field which is
already sown, he first overturns the soil and then plants. The
point of A-C is that one first overturns the soil and thereby
destroys the seeds which are already in the ground,[40] and then
plants without being liable for planting diverse-kinds (as in
M. 2:3). M. then implies that one may not both plant and sow
in the same field. Now M. is not clear as to what is being
planted in this case. While "sowing" ($zry^{c}h$) may be understood
to refer to vegetables or grain, "planting" ($nty^{c}h$) may refer
to either trees or grapevines. If M. refers to the planting of
trees, then M. opposes T. 1:15C, which says that one is permitted
to sow tree-seeds together with other kinds of seeds. It is perhaps more probable, therefore, that M. refers to the planting
of grapevines (most commentaries), as Scripture prohibits the
sowing of other kinds of seeds in a vineyard (Dt. 22:9). We
have interpolated into our translation accordingly.

In D-F, the circumstances of A-C are reversed, so that now
one wishes to sow a field which is already planted. E-F states
that one first uproots the vines and then sows. The law of D-F
is then the same as that of A-C, for in both cases one must remove
whatever is already in the soil before adding the new seeds.

G presents an alternative to E-F. If one wishes to sow
before uprooting the vines,[41] he must first cut the vines down
to a height of less than a handbreadth. He may then sow, for the
vines are no longer easily visible, and there is no appearance of

sowing diverse-kinds (MR).[42] Later, of course, the vines must be uprooted.[43]

A. [*If his field*] *was planted* [*with vines*[44]] *and he decided to sow it* [*with vegetables or grain*],
    he diminishes (*mgry*^{c}; *Erfurt:* *mgr*^{c}; *First printed ed.:* *mgbyh*[45]) [*the vines*] *until* [*they are*] *less than a handbreadth* [*high*], *sows, and afterwards uproots* [*the vines*] [= M. 2:4D+G].
C. [If] he diminishes (*gwr*^{c}; Sirillo: *gr*^{c}[46]) [the vines] until [they are] less than a handbreadth [high],
D. and [later] he came and found its leaves (*^{c}lyw*; First printed ed.: *^{c}lyn*) [growing] on top of grain,
E. [the benefit of the vines and the grain] is permitted for [vines which have already grown on top of grain in] the past (*lš^{c}br*; omitted by Vienna[47]), but [such benefit] is prohibited for [vines which will grow on top of grain in] the future (*l^{c}tyd lb'*; Erfurt: *l^{c}tyd*) [i.e., one may benefit from diverse-kinds which have already grown together, but once one sees the diverse-kinds growing together he may not allow them to continue to grow in this manner];
F. [rather], he uproots whichever of them (*mhn*; Erfurt: *myn* ["which-ever kind"]) he wishes [to uproot], and sustains whichever of them he wishes [to sustain].

                    T. Kil. 1:18 (p. 207, ll. 49-52)
                    (E: Y. Kil. 2:4 (27d))

    T. Kil. 1:18 comments on M. 2:4. T. A-B cites M. D+G (differing only in having the verb *mgry*^{c} for *gwmm*), which T. C-F then supplements with a related case. We note that C-D+F form a simple declarative sentence which is interrupted by E, for the subject of E (understood as "the benefit of the vines and the grain") is not that of the sentence (the "one who diminishes the vines" in C). It appears, then, that E glosses C-D+F.

    C-F describes an instance in which diverse-kinds grow between the time that one sows and the time that one uproots the vines in the case of M. 2:4G. In C-D one diminishes the height of the vines to less than a handbreadth and then sows. Later he finds that the leaves of the vines have begun to grow over the plants which were just sown. F states that one uproots which-ever kind he wishes to uproot, and sustains what is left. The point of F, then, is that one need not uproot the vines, even though his original intention was to do so. Rather, he may

change his mind and uproot those plants which he has just sown.
E then adds that one may benefit from those vines and plants which
are growing together as diverse-kinds at the time that he finds
them,[48] but not from any diverse-kinds which may grow afterwards.
PM explains that since one does nothing wrong by sowing while the
vines are still in the ground, he may benefit from the vines and
plants which are growing together when he finds them. Once, however, he notices the diverse-kinds he may not allow them to continue to grow, for then he would be sustaining diverse-kinds
(prohibited by T. 1:15, M. 8:1).

2:5

A. [If] his field was sown with carum (*qnbws*; Geniza fragment
   [margin], K [after correction], L, Mn, N, P, V: *qnbs*;
   B, C, Cn, Geniza fragment,[49] K [before correction], O, Pr,
   Maim., *Comm.*: *qrbs*),[50] or arum,[51]
B. He should not (*l' yh'*) sow (*zwr^c wb'*) on top of them,
C. for [B, Cn, Geniza fragments, O, Maim., *Comm.*: even
   though] they produce [fruit] only [after] three years
   (*š'yn ^{c}wšyn 'l' lšlš šnym*; B. Men., S, GRA: *šhn ^{c}wšyn*
   [B.: ^{c}wšwt] lšlš šnym* ["for they produce [fruit] for
   three years"]).
D. (1) Grain among which [Geniza fragment: with which] after-
   growths of woad[52] came up,
   (2) and so the threshing-floors [lit.: the place of the
   threshing-floors] in which many kinds came up,
   (3) and so fenugreek[53] which brought up (*šh^{c}lt*; Geniza
   fragment: *š^{c}lt ^{c}m*; B. B. Q.: *š^{c}lth ^{c}m* ["which came up
   with"]; Mn and all mss. of B. B. Q.: *š^{c}lt*) [different]
   kinds of plants (*smhym*; most mss.: ^{c}*šbym* ["grasses"]) --
E. they do not require him to weed (*lnkš*; B. B.Q. *l^{c}qwr*["to
   uproot"]).
F. [But] if he weeded or cut down [some of them (Maim.)], they
   say to him, "Uproot everything, except for one kind."

> M. Kil. 2:5 (A-C: B. Men. 15b
> [in printed ed. only]; D(3)-E:
> Y. Kil. 2:5 (27d), B. B.Q. 81a,
> Y. B.B. 5:1 (15a))

M. Kil. 2:5 continues the discussion of M. 2:3-4, presenting
another case in which one wishes to sow one kind of seeds in a
field which is already sown with another kind. M. 2:5 is divided
into two autonomous parts, A-C and D-F. A-C discusses the case

of one who wishes to sow something in a field already sown with carum or arum. D-F concerns the problem of uncultivated plants which come up and, with or without cultivated plants, produce the appearance of diverse-kinds.

A-C forms a simple declarative sentence. The law of A-C states that one may not sow a field which is already sown with carum or arum, for these plants produce fruit only after three years. In other words, carum and arum do not produce fruit for three years, so that if one were to sow on top of them, no appearance of diverse-kinds would result. Even so, the seeds are still in the ground during the three-year period, and therefore one who sows on top of them is liable for sowing diverse-kinds. Now this reading of C ("for they produce [fruit] only [after] three years") is difficult, for while it may be the case that arum produces fruit only after three years,[54] carum produces fruit no later than two years after it is sown.[55] We therefore prefer the alternate version of C, which reads "for they produce [fruit] for three years." Accordingly, the point of M. is that both carum and arum produce fruit for several years after they are sown. Therefore, if the plants are not visible at any time within this period, one may not simply assume that they have died. On the contrary, one must assume that they will sprout again, and therefore one may not sow on top of them.

D-E, with the order of D and E reversed, forms a declarative sentence. D-F concerns plants which grow wild and produce an appearance of diverse-kinds. D lists three instances in which such plants may come up. In D(1) aftergrowths of woad, growing from seeds or roots which are left behind in the ground,[56] spring up alongside of grain. In D(2) seeds which are dropped on the threshing-floor sprout by themselves, and D(3) has wild grass coming up together with fenugreek. According to E one does not have to weed out the wild plants. Maimonides (*Code, Diverse-Kinds* 2:8-9) explains that since these plants are not cultivated, and since it is known that the owner does not want them (and will eventually have to pull them out anyway [Sens]),[57] the owner may allow them to grow and he will not appear to allow diverse-kinds to grow. F states that if one does begin to weed out or cut down the wild plants, he must remove all but one kind. According to Maimonides (*Code, Diverse-Kinds* 2:10) one who pulls out only some of the surrounding plants implicitly indicates that he wishes the remaining plants to continue to grow. In effect, then, by leaving the plants in the ground, one allows diverse-kinds to grow. If one uproots any plants at all, therefore, he must continue to uproot until there is no longer any appearance of diverse-kinds.

A. [Concerning] a field in which grasses came up --
B. they do not require him to overturn [the soil before
    sowing];
C. rather, he plows when he covers over ($b\check{s}^{c}h$ $\check{s}mhph$; Erfurt:
    $k\check{s}^{c}t$ $hpkh$) [the seeds], and [thus] overturns [the soil].

                    T. Kil. 1:19a (p. 207, ll. 52-53)

     T. Kil. 1:19a supplements M. 2:5D-E, for both pericopae
concern wild plants which come up in a field of crops. A-C, with
the order of A-B reversed, forms a declarative sentence.
     A-C states that if wild grasses grow in a field, one need
not overturn the soil (and so destroy the grasses) before sowing.
Rather, one first sows, and then plows the grasses in while
covering the seeds. The point of T. is then the same as that
of M.[58] Since it is known that one who sows does not want the
wild grasses and will eventually have to pull them out, one may
sow while the grasses still grow without appearing to sow diverse-
kinds. We note that T. is a good supplement to M., for the
latter speaks of wild plants which come up after sowing, while T.
concerns grasses which grow before sowing takes place.

D. He removes thorns ($mkbkb$; Erfurt: $mkrkyb$) and removes the
    large [plant[59]] from before the workers, and this [action]
    is not considered "cutting" ($w'yn$ bzh $m\check{s}wm$ $mk\check{s}h$; Lieberman[60]
    prefers the reading of the First printed ed.: $mk\check{s}h$) [i.e.,
    even though he removes thorns and large plants, this does
    not mean that he must remove all of the wild plants].

                    T. Kil. 1:19b (p. 207, ll. 53-54)

     T. Kil. 1:19b comments on M. 2:5F. M. states that one who
begins to remove wild plants from among cultivated ones must pull
out every kind of plant but one. For if one were to pull out
only some of the plants, it would appear as if he wanted the remaining plants to continue to grow, and so he would appear to be
allowing diverse-kinds to grow. T. then comments that one may
remove thorns or large plants from before the workers (in order
to clear a path for the plow[61]), and such an action is not considered "cutting." That is, one who removes only some of the
thorns or wild plants need not uproot every kind of plant but one.
The point of T., then, is that one who clears away some of the
plants for a specific purpose, does not appear to be allowing

diverse-kinds to grow, and so does not have to uproot all but
one kind of plant.

2:6

A. He who wishes to lay out [so Danby for $l^c\check{s}wt$] his field
    [in] narrow beds ($m\check{s}r$ $m\check{s}r$) [Mn omits:] of every kind [i.e.,
    with each bed containing a different kind] --
B. The House of Shammai say, "[He makes the beds as wide as the
    width of] three furrows of 'opening' ($\check{s}l$ $ptyh$) [i.e.,
    furrows plowed for the purpose of "opening" the field in
    order to collect rainwater[62]]."
C. And the House of Hillel say, "[He makes the beds as wide as]
    the width [so Danby for ml'] of the Sharon yoke."
D. and the words of these [i.e., one House] are near the words
    of those [i.e., the other House] [i.e., there is little
    difference between the two measurements].

M. Kil. 2:6

M. Kil. 2:6 concerns the planting of different kinds of
plants in the same field. A-C presents a Houses-dispute, the
opinions of which are neither balanced nor mnemonically formu-
lated ($\check{s}l\check{s}h$ $tlmym$ $\check{s}l$ $ptyh$ vs. ml' h^cwl $h\check{s}rwny$). D glosses A-C.

A presents the case of one who wishes to lay out his
field in narrow beds,[63] with each bed containing a different
kind of seed. In B-C the Houses dispute a measurement which is
involved in the case of A. We are not told, however, what is
being measured. The commentaries offer two explanations.
According to several commentaries (Sens [who presents both inter-
pretations], R. Yehosaf Ashkenazi [cited by MS], Sirillo [cited
by Feliks[64]], GRA, Lieberman[65]) M. presupposes that one may lay
out his field in beds containing different kinds only if the
beds are of a certain minimum size. In this way, each bed is
considered a field unto itself, and the different kinds are
easily distinguished from one another. Different kinds may then
grow in the same field without producing the appearance of
diverse-kinds. The dispute of M. then concerns the minimum width
which a bed must have in order to be considered an autonomous
field.[66] Alternatively, most commentaries (e.g., Maim., *Comm.*,
TYY, MR) understand M. to assume that the beds of A must be
separated from one another in order to prevent the appearance of
diverse-kinds. The Houses then dispute concerning the distance
by which the beds must be separated. We note, however, that M.
nowhere states that beds (or similar areas of land) of different

kinds must be separated from one another.[67] We therefore
regard this latter interpretation to be less plausible than
the former.

The actual measurements of B-C may be explained as follows
(following Feliks[68]). The House of Shammai say that the beds
must be as wide as the width of three furrows of "opening."
The furrows of "opening" are plowed after the spring harvest
in order to loosen the soil and "open" the ground to collect
rainwater. These furrows do not lie immediately next to one
another, but are separated by a short distance. The House of
Hillel say that the width of the beds must equal that of the
Sharon yoke. This yoke is made for a single animal (and so is
narrower than the average yoke), for it is necessary to use only
one animal to plow the soft soil of the Sharon plain. We see,
then, that the Houses describe the measure of the width of the
beds in completely different terms.

D states that the words of the two Houses are nearly the
same. That is, the breadth of the three furrows of "opening"
is approximately equal to the width of the Sharon yoke.[69]
According to D, then, the Houses do not dispute at all, but only
present the same ruling in different language.[70]

A. *He who wants to lay out his field* [= M. 2:6A] [in] rows of
   grain and rows of many [different] kinds [of plants] --
B. He makes three open furrows[71] (*tlmym mpwlšyn*) [extending]
   from the beginning of the field to its ends.
C. R. Leazar b. R. Simeon and Abba Yosé b. Ḥanan of Vani
   (*w'ny*; Erfurt: *y'ny*; First printed ed.: *ywny*) say, "It
   is sufficient for them (*dyn*; Erfurt: *dyw*) [to measure] fifty
   amot in length."
D. How much is its width (*rḥbw*; Lieberman[72] corrects to *rḥbn*,
   ["their width," i.e., the width of the furrows considered
   collectively]) [GRA: *wrwḥb* ("and of a width [of]")]?
E. *The width (mlw') of the Sharon yoke* [= M. 2:6C], which
   resembles the yoke of the vineyards.
F. Its beginning [i.e., the width at the beginning of the
   furrows] is of this measure, even though its end [i.e., the
   width at the end of the furrows] is not of this measure.

T. Kil. 2:1a (pp. 207-208, ll. 1-5)

(C: T. Kil. 2:4, Y. Kil. 2:6

(28a))[73]

T. Kil. 2:1a comments on M. 2:6. We shall consider T.'s
relationship to M. after our discussion of the substance of T.
A serves as a topic-sentence for the pericope. B states a law
in a declarative sentence, which Leazar b. Simeon and Abba Yosé
b. Ḥanan then gloss in C. D-E depends on A-B and introduces a
secondary issue. F glosses E.

Citing the language of M. 2:6A, A presents the case of one
who wishes to plant rows of both grain and different kinds of
plants in his field. According to B he must plow, presumably for
each kind, three furrows across the entire length of the field.[74]
The point of T. is that these rows must extend across the entire
length of the field, in order to appear as an autonomous field.[75]
In C Leazar b. Simeon and Abba Yosé b. Ḥanan say that the furrows
need extend for only fifty *amot*.[76] These authorities apparently
reason (in this context) that furrows of this length form
autonomous fields, so that the furrows need not extend over the
entire length of the field.[77]

D-E concerns the width of the furrows described in B. E,
apparently referring to the collective width of the three furrows,[78]
states that this width must be equal to the width of the Sharon
yoke [= opinion of House of Hillel, M. 2:6C], which is similar
to the yoke of the vineyards. Feliks[79] points out that both
yokes are narrow and made for one animal. The point of E is
that the furrows must be of a specific width. F, however, states
that the three furrows must be as wide as the width of the
Sharon yoke only at their starting-points. As the furrows
traverse the field, though, this breadth may narrow. According
to F, then, it is necessary for the rows to be of a certain
width only at their beginnings in order to prevent the appearance
of diverse-kinds.

Let us now compare T. to M. 2:6:

M. Kil. 2:6	*T. Kil. 2:1a*
1. He who wants to lay out his field [in] narrow beds of every kind --	1. He who wants to lay out his field [in] rows of grain and rows of many [different] kinds [of plants]--
2. The House of Shammai say, "[He makes the beds as wide as the width of] three furrows of 'opening' (*šl ptyḥ*)."	2. He makes three open furrows (*mpwlšym*) from the beginning of the field to its end.

3.   ---

4.   ---

5. And the House of Hillel
    say, "[He makes the beds
    as wide as] the width
    of the Sharon yoke."

6.   ---

7. And the words of these
    [i.e., one House] are near
    the words of those [i.e.,
    the other House].

3. R. Leazar b. R. Simeon and
    Abba Yosé b. Ḥanan of Vani
    say, "It is sufficient for
    them [to measure] fifty *amot*
    in length."

4. How much is its width?

5. The width of the Sharon yoke,
    which resembles the yoke of
    the vineyards.

6. Its beginnings [i.e., at their
    beginnings, the furrows are]
    of this measure, even though
    its end [i.e., at their ends,
    the furrows are] not of this
    measure.

7.   ---

We note that T. explains M.'s protasis in (1), for T.'s phrase
"rows of grain and rows of many [different] kinds [of plants]"
spells out M.'s "narrow beds of every kind." The more interesting
difference between M. and T. occurs at (2)-(5). M. contains
a Houses-dispute which apparently concerns the width of the rows
of different kinds. T. has neither the attributions to the
Houses nor a dispute, but it does know the measurements of M.
While House of Shammai, for example, state that the width of the
beds must be that of three furrows, T. rules that each kind must
actually be sown in three open furrows (2). Referring to the
view of the House of Hillel, T. then states that the combined
width of these furrows must be equal to that of a Sharon yoke,
or the yoke of the vineyards. According to T., then, each kind
must be planted in three furrows, the total width of which
must be a Sharon yoke. By setting the width of three furrows
equal to that of the Sharon yoke, T. describes an arrangement
which illustrates M.'s statement (7) that "the words of these
are near to the words of those."

2:7

A. [If] the point of the angle of the field [so Danby for
    rwš twr;] of wheat entered (*nkns*; most mss.:[80] [*wnkns*
    "(If) there was a point of an angle of the field of wheat,
    and it entered"]) into [a field[81]] of barley.
B. it is permitted [to grow the wheat in the field of barley];
C. for it [i.e., the point of the angle of the wheat-field]
    looks like the end of his field (*kšwp šdhw*; B, Geniza
    fragment,[82] K (before correction), L, Mn, N: *bšwp šdhw*
    ["for it appears at the end of his field"]) [of wheat].
D. [If] his [field] was [sown with] wheat, and his neighbor's
    [field] was [sown with] another kind,
E. it is permitted to flank[83] (*lsmwk*) it [i.e., his neighbor's
    field (Maim., *Comm.*)] [with some] of the same kind [as that
    of his neighbor's field].
F. [If] his [field] was [sown with] wheat, and his neighbor's
    [field] was [also sown with] wheat,
G. it is permitted to flank it [i.e., his field] [with] a furrow
    of flax, but not (*wl'*; C: *'w* ["or"]; cf. MS) [with] a
    furrow of another kind.
H. R. Simeon says, "It is all the same whether [a furrow of]
    flax-seeds or [a furrow of] any kind [flanks the field]."
I. R. Yosé says, "Even (*'p*; omitted in K[84]) in the middle of
    his field it is permitted to test [the suitability of the
    soil for growing flax] with a furrow (*lbdwk btlm*; C: *lsmwk
    tlm* ["to flank (the field with) a furrow"] of flax.

M. Kil. 2:7

    M. 2:7 concerns the appearances of diverse-kinds which occur
when two fields adjoin one another. M. is divided into two
large units. A-C discusses a case in which the crops of one
field are sown in the other. In D-H the two fields are owned by
different men, and the issue concerns what may be sown at the
common border of the fields. Yosé's saying in I is then attached
to F-H because it deals with a related issue.
    A-B is phrased in a declarative sentence (with "if" supplied).
C glosses A-B. A describes a case in which a *rwš twr* of wheat
enters an adjacent field of barley. *rwš twr* is a technical
term for a triangular or wedge-shaped area, for this is how the
expression is commonly understood[85] in the context of M. Kel.
18:2.[86] A then concerns a triangular area of wheat which
enters a field of barley (Maim., *Comm.*, Rosh,[87] MS; fig. 1[88]).[89]

Alternatively, *rwš twr* may refer to a row of wheat which enters
the barley-field diagonally (following the usage of *rwš twr* in
B. Suk. 7a[90] [as explained by Rashi, *ad. loc.*]; Ribmaṣ [fig. 2[91]],
Sirkes).[92] B then rules that one may allow the *rwš twr* to grow
in the neighboring field, even though wheat and barley are considered diverse-kinds with one another. C explains that the wheat
does not appear to grow in the field of barley at all. Rather,
the *rwš twr* appears to mark the end of the field of wheat,[93] and
so may be seen as belonging to that field, even though it
actually lies in the space of the barley-field (cf. TYT). According to C, then, one may permit the wheat to grow in the field
of barley because there is no appearance of diverse-kinds.

D-I consists of two cases, D-E and F-I, both of which are
presented in declarative sentences (with "if" supplied). The
two protases balance one another (wheat + another kind *vs*. wheat +
wheat). In D-E one man's wheat-field adjoins his neighbor's
field, which is sown with another kind. According to E the
owner of the wheat-field may sow his neighbor's kind at the edge
of his own field (fig. 3). The point of D-E is then the same as
that of A-C. Even though the plants of the neighbor's kind
actually grow among the wheat, these plants appear to mark
the end of the neighbor's field, so that there is no appearance
of diverse-kinds (Maim., *Comm*., Sens, Bert., TYY). Maimonides
(*Code, Diverse-Kinds* 3:16) explains the law as follows:

> Under what circumstances does one require distancing
> (*hrḥqh*) [between plants of diverse-kinds] or something
> which separates [the diverse-kinds from one another]?
> When one has sown diverse-kinds in his [own] field.
> But if his [own] field was sown with wheat, his
> neighbor is permitted to sow barley next to [the wheat];
> for [Scripture] says, *You shall not sow your field [with]
> diverse-kinds* (Lv. 19:19); the prohibition is only that
> he [not] sow his [own] field with diverse-kinds, for
> [Scripture] does not say, "You shall not sow the land
> [with] diverse-kinds." And not only this, but even
> if he sowed barley in his field next to the wheat, and
> the barley-grains extended [further] (*mšk*) until they
> flanked his neighbor's field, which was sown with barley,
> lo, this is permitted, for the barley-seeds in his
> field appeared [to mark] the end of the neighbor's
> field.

F describes a case in which two men own adjacent fields of
wheat. The question now becomes what may be sown at the common
border of the fields without producing the appearance of diverse-

kinds. G states that one may sow a furrow of flax at the common
edge, and that no other kind may be sown there. A furrow of flax
may be placed as a border to the fields because it is known that
the owner would not sow a single furrow for the flax itself
(for the yield would be too small). Rather, it is assumed that
the owner wishes only to test the suitability of the soil for
growing flax, and so there is no appearance of diverse-kinds.
The same may not be said of other kinds, however, for the owner
could sow a furrow of another kind with the intention of growing
that kind. In that case, the owner would be liable for sowing
diverse-kinds (cf. T. 2:4a below).

In H Simeon disputes with G, and so attests it to Usha.
Simeon rejects G's distinction between flax and other kinds,
maintaining that the law is the same in both cases. This statement probably means that one may sow a furrow of any kind at the
common border of the wheat-fields (Sens [following Y.], Rosh,
TYY, GRA). Simeon apparently reasons that a single furrow will
not produce the appearance of diverse-kinds, regardless of what
is sown in it, because a single furrow of any kind looks like
a border.[94]

Yosé states in I that one may test the soil by sowing a
furrow of flax in the middle of a field. The point of Yosé's
saying is that a single furrow of flax may be sown anywhere
without producing an appearance of diverse-kinds, since it is
clear that the owner intends only to test the soil. Yosé's
statement is connected to F-G by 'p, which is standard joining-
language. The statement is autonomous of F-G. Yosé speaks of
testing the soil for growing flax in the middle of a field, but
does not specifically address himself to the case where flax
is sown at the common border of the two fields (although he would
certainly agree with the ruling of F-G). It is probably that
Yosé's saying has been attached to F-G because both statements
concern sowing flax in a field of another kind.

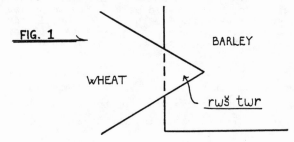

FIG. 1

BARLEY

WHEAT

ruš tur

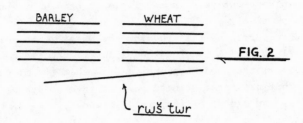

FIG. 2

rwš twr

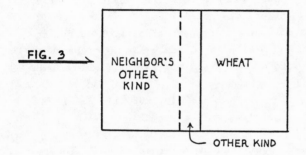

FIG. 3

NEIGHBOR'S OTHER KIND

WHEAT

OTHER KIND

G. [If] one had two fields (*śdwt*; Erfurt: *świwt* ["rows"]), (1) one sown [with] wheat and (2) one sown [with] barley,

H. [and] he would plow and [thereby] bring (1) wheat into a field of barley, or (2) barley into a field of wheat,

I. it is permitted [(1) to grow the wheat in the field of barley, or (2) to grow the barley in the field of wheat];

J. for (1) the wheat appears to be within (*btwk*; Erfurt: first printed ed.: *kswp* ["looks like the end of"]) the field of wheat, and (2) the barley appears to be within (*btwk*; Erfurt: *kswp* ["looks like the end of"]) the field of barley [first printed ed.: for the wheat looks like the end of the field of barley].

                              T. Kil. 2:1b (p. 208, ll. 5-8)

K. R. Liezer b. Jacob says, "Also (*'pylw*) if (1) one grain of wheat after another (*ḥṭh 'ḥr ḥṭh*) enters the field of barley, or (2) [one grain of] barley after another enters the

field of wheat [i.e., the grains of wheat or barley are
sown consecutively in the field of barley or wheat,
respectively],

L. it is permitted [(1) to grow the wheat in the field of
barley, or (2) to grow the barley in the field of wheat];

M. for (1) the wheat appears to be within [= omitted by
Erfurt and first printed ed.] at the end (*bswp*; Erfurt: *kswp*
["as the end"]) of the field of wheat, and (2) the barley
appears to be within (*btwk*; Erfurt: *kswp* ["as the end of"];
first printed ed.: *bswp* ["at the end of"]) the field
of barley [Y.: for (1) the (one grain of) wheat after
another (*ḥṭh 'ḥr ḥṭh*) which enters (the field of) barley
(is considered the end of the field of[95]) wheat, and (2)
the (one grain of) barley after another which enters the
field of wheat (so GRA; printed text: field of barley) (is
considered the end of the field of) barley (following HD,
GRA)].

T. Kil. 2:2 (p. 208, ll. 8-11)

(Y. Kil. 2:7 (28a))

N. [If] one had two [= omitted by Y.] rows (*šwrwt*; Lieberman,
following Y., corrects to *šdwt* ["fields"]), (1) one sown [with]
wheat, and (2) one sown [with] barley,

O. it is permitted to make a furrow (*tlm*; L: *tbn* ["straw"])
between them (*bynyhn*; Erfurt: *mhn* ["of them"]), and to
sow [in it] either wheat or barley [H. adds: (1) for the
wheat looks like the end of the field of wheat, and (2) the
barley (looks like) the end of the field of barley].

P. (1) [If] [Erfurt, first printed ed. add: one (grain of)]
wheat is absorbed (*mwblᶜt*) in the field of barley [i.e.,
the grains of wheat do not fall consecutively in the field
of barley (Lieberman)], or (2) [if] one [grain of] barley
is absorbed in the field of wheat,

Q. it is prohibited [(1) to grow the wheat in the field of barley,
or (2) to grow the barley in the field of wheat].

T. Kil. 2:3 (p. 208, ll. 11-14)

(Y. Kil. 2:7 (28a))

R. [If] one had two fields (*šdwt*; Erfurt: *šwrwt*), (1) one
sown [with] wheat and (2) one sown [with] barley,

S. it is not permitted (*'yn mwtr*; Erfurt: *'swr*) to make a furrow of another kind between them.

T. [first printed ed. adds: And] with [a furrow sown with] flax, it is permitted [to make a furrow between the two fields],

U. because he wishes [only] to test his field [for growing flax];

V. and provided that the furrows be open (mplyš; Erfurt, first printed ed.: mpryš ["separate"] from one end of the field to the other [lit.: from the head of the field to the other head].

W. R. Leazar b. R. Simeon and Abba Yosah b. Ḥanan of Vani say, "It is sufficient [for the furrow] to be fifty amot in length."

T. Kil. 2:4a (p. 208, ll. 14-17)

(W: T. Kil. 2:1a)

T. Kil. 2:1b-2:4a presents a series of cases which supplement M. 2:7. T. may be divided into five units. G-J describes a case where seeds of one kind enter a field of another kind (= M. 2:7A-C). In K-M Eliezer b. Jacob rules on a similar case in which seeds of one kind fall consecutively in a field of another kind. N-O deals with sowing a furrow of one of two different kinds between two fields containing these kinds (M. 2:7D-E). P-Q reverts to K-M and concerns seeds of one kind which fall haphazardly in a field of a different kind. Finally R-W, continuing the theme of N-O, discusses what may and may not be sown in a furrow located between two fields of different kinds (= M. 2:7F-G).

G-J presents its case in a well-developed declarative sentence. The protasis consists of two parts, G and H, each of which is internally balanced (wheat vs. barley in G; wheat + barley vs. barley + wheat in H). J glosses G-I and is also well-balanced (wheat + wheat vs. barley + barley).

In G-H the owner of adjacent fields of wheat and barley plows one of the fields in order to cover the seeds already sown in it.[96] He accidentally propels some of these seeds into an adjacent field of another kind, with the result that either wheat is sown in a barley-field, or barley grows in a field of wheat. According to I the owner may allow the stray seeds to grow in the field of the other kind. J explains that these errant seeds appear to mark the end of the field of their own kind, so that their growth in the field of the other kind does not

produce the appearance of diverse-kinds. T.'s point is then
the same as that of M. G-I (even though the latter concerns only
the case of the *rwš twr*). Although seeds of one kind may actually
grow in a field of a different kind, these seeds appear to
belong to the adjacent field of their own kind, so that there is
no appearance of diverse-kinds.

Eliezer b. Jacob's saying in K-M depends on G, and appears
to gloss G-J. However, K-M is attached to G-J only by *'pylw*,
which is standard joining-language. In fact, the two sayings
are very similar to one another, for they both have the same
apodoses (I and L) and glosses (J and M). They differ only in
their protases. H has "[and] he would plow and [thereby] bring
(1) wheat into the field of barley, or (2) barley into the field
of wheat," while K states "[if] (1) [one grain of] wheat after
another enters the field of barley or (2) [one grain of] barley
after another enters the field of wheat." While H and K do differ
in respect to language, they basically state the same law concerning one kind of seed which enters the field of another kind.
It appears, then, that Eliezer's saying (originally G+K-L) is
autonomous of G-I and that the two sayings were redacted
together because of their interest in the same issue. At a
redactional stage, therefore, A was dropped from Eliezer's saying,
and G-I and K-L were probably glossed by the same hand at J
and M, giving the pericope its present form.

N repeats F. I states that one may sow either wheat or
barley in a furrow located between the fields of these two kinds
(fig. 5).[97] No matter which kind is sown between the two
fields, the furrow of that kind appears to mark the end of the
adjacent field of the same kind (following Y.), so that there
is no appearance of diverse-kinds. The point of T. is similar
to that of M. 2:7D-E. The latter allows one to sow the edge of
a field of one kind with seeds of the kind sown in an adjacent
field (fig. 6 = fig. 3, p. 97), while T. states that one may sow
a furrow of either kind at the common border of the two fields.
In both cases one may sow seeds of one kind in an area which
lies beyond the border of the field of that kind, for that area
appears to mark the end of the field. T. then states the law of
M. 2:7D-E in different language.[98]

P-Q presents another balanced declarative sentence (wheat
+ barley *vs.* barley + wheat). P-Q completes the thought of

K-M,[99] for we are now told that it is prohibited to grow seeds of
one kind in a field of another kind, if the stray seeds do not
fall consecutively.[100] The reason is that stray seeds which fall
haphazardly in the field do not appear to extend from the adjacent
field which contains their own kind, and so produce an appearance
of diverse-kinds.

R-S forms a simple declarative sentence. T-U (with U
glossing T) depends on R-S, while V-W (with W glossing and
opposing V) glosses T-U. We note that W appears verbatim in
T. 2:1a, and so may not originally belong in this context.[101]
R repeats G. S states that one may not sow a furrow of another
kind (i.e., a furrow of something other than wheat or barley)
between the fields of wheat and barley. Such a furrow would
clearly produce an appearance of diverse-kinds. T, however,
adds that one may sow a furrow of flax between the two fields
(= M. 2:7F-G(1)). U explains that one who sows a single furrow
of flax wishes only to test the soil. Therefore, one who sows
a furrow of flax does not appear to be sowing diverse-kinds. U
thus agrees with Yosé (M. 2:7I) that one may test for flax even
in the middle of a field.

Maimonides (*Code, Diverse-Kinds* 3:17) explains the law
as follows:

> [If] his field was sown [with] wheat, and his
> neighbor's field, which was adjacent to it, was
> sown with wheat, it is permitted for him to sow
> one furrow of flax beside his wheat, next to his
> neighbor's field [i.e., between his wheat and his
> neighbor's field]. For one who sees [the furrow
> of flax] knows that it is not the common practice
> (*drk h*^{c}*m*) to sow one furrow of flax, and that he
> intended only to test whether or not his field is
> suitable for sowing flax; and he is [thus] dis-
> covered to be like one who sows [only] for [the
> sake of] destruction. Therefore it is prohibited
> to sow another kind between these two rows, which
> are of one kind, until he distances [the other
> kind from the row which is] in his [field].

According to V the furrow of flax must extend for the length
of the field (i.e., it must be as long as the furrows of wheat
or barley). That is, the flax must be sown in a furrow of
sufficient length to be considered an area unto itself (cf. M.
2:6, T. 2:1a), and so distinct from the fields of wheat and
barley. The flax then does not appear to be sown among the wheat
and barley, and there is no appearance of diverse-kinds. In W,
Eleazar b. Simeon and Abba Yosah b. Ḥanan of Vani say that the
furrow need only be fifty *amot* in length, for a furrow of this

length is already considered an area unto itself (cf. T. 2:1C).[102]
We note, then, that T. R-W both restates (R-T) and supplements
(U-W) M. 2:7F-G.

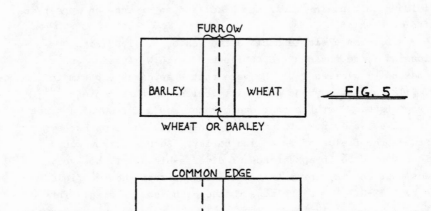

FURROW

BARLEY | WHEAT   FIG. 5

WHEAT OR BARLEY

COMMON EDGE

FIG. 6

OTHER | WHEAT
KIND

OTHER KIND

2:8

A. They do not flank a field of grain [with] mustard or
   safflower,[103]

B. but they flank [Geniza fragments,[104] O: he flanks] a field
   of vegetables [with] mustard or safflower.

C. And he flanks [with diverse-kinds (Maim., *Code, Diverse-Kinds*
   3:15)]

   (1) uncultivated land (*bwr*),
   (2) or newly-broken land [so Danby for *nyr*,[105]]
   (3) or a loose [most comm.[106]] stone wall (*gpph*),
   (4) or a road,
   (5) or a fence (*gdr*) [most mss. add: which is] ten hand-
       breadths high,
   (6) or a ditch which is ten [handbreadths] deep and [Geniza
       fragment omits:] four [handbreadths] wide,
   (7) or a tree which shades the ground,
   (8) or a rock [most mss. add: which is] ten [handbreadths]
       high and four [handbreadths] wide.

                    M. Kil. 2:8 (C(1)-(5): Y. Kil. 2:8 (28a))

M. Kil. 2:8 concerns flanking one kind of seeds with seeds
of another kind, and so continues the discussion of flanking
begun in M. 2:7D-G. M. consists of two units, A-B and C, which
differ from one another both formally and thematically. A-B is
phrased in a declarative sentence using plural present participles,
and concerns flanking fields of grain and vegetables with mustard
or safflower. C, on the other hand, uses the singular present
participle, and presents a list of objects which may be flanked.

A-B states that one may not flank a field of grain, but
only a field of vegetables, with mustard or safflower. Feliks[107]
explains that mustard and safflower were usually sown in small
plots (e.g., patches; cf. M. 2:9) so that it was apparently
customary to sow them at the edges of fields.[108] A prohibits the
sowing of mustard or safflower next to grain, says Feliks,[109]
because the former resembles the latter.[110] Mustard and safflower
both have tall plants with yellow flowers, and so look like
ripened stalks of grain. If the two kinds of plants were to be
sown next to one another, it would become difficult to distinguish
between them, and the field would appear to be sown with diverse-
kinds. In addition, mustard and safflower tend to grow wild once
they are sown,[111] and so could actually enter the field of grain,
making it even more difficult to distinguish between the two
kinds of plants. B, on the other hand, says that one may sow
mustard or safflower next to a field of vegetables. In this
instance the two kinds of plants do not resemble one another, so
that an appearance of diverse-kinds does not result from one kind
being sown next to the other.[112]

C is autonomous of A-B, and the two units have been redacted
together only because both concern the problem of flanking. C
lists eight objects which may be flanked with diverse-kinds (Maim.,
Code, Diverse-Kinds 3:15), that is, eight objects which serve
to separate diverse-kinds from one another. In each instance
the diverse-kinds are to be sown on opposite sides of the object
itself, except in the case of the tree, where one kind is to be
sown under the tree's foliage, and the other is to be sown outside of its shade (following T. 2:5b). We note that seven of
the eight objects[113] are mentioned as dividers in some other
context in M.-T. Some serve to divide a field for the setting
aside of *pe'ah*[114] or for the giving of *bikkurim*,[115] while others
divide a vineyard (in respect to the laws of diverse-kinds of a
vineyard)[116] or divide an area into autonomous domains (in respect
to the laws of carrying on the Sabbath).[117] Finally, the tree
which shades the ground is also said to form a Tent.[118] Our

list, then, consists of objects which are commonly considered
dividers for various purposes.

X. Rabbi [Erfurt adds: Yosé] says, "A man [= omitted by Erfurt]
   is permitted to make a row [Erfurt: rows] of mustard [or]
   [first printed ed. omits:] safflower in his field."
Y. How much is the length of the row [Erfurt: the field]?
Z. Ten and one-half *amot*.

T. Kil. 2:4b (p. 209, ll. 17-19)

(Y. Kil. 2:8 (28a)[119])

    T. Kil. 2:4b presents a saying of Rabbi which opposes the
law of M. 2:8A. Rabbi states in X that one may sow a row of
mustard or safflower in a field of another kind. He apparently
reasons that because mustard and safflower are usually sown in
small plots, a single row of either is considered a field unto
itself (HD). Therefore a row of mustard or safflower which grows
in a field sown with another kind does not produce the appearance
of diverse-kinds. We note that Rabbi agrees with Simeon in T.
2:5a (see below), who says that one may flank any kind with
mustard or safflower. Rabbi will then clearly disagree with the
law of M. 2:8A, which says that mustard or safflower may not
flank a field of grain.
    Y-Z glosses X, and concerns the minimum length which a row
must have in order to be considered an autonomous field. Z
states that the row must be ten-and-a-half *amot* long. This means
that the row must be as long as one side of a *bet rova*[c] (T. Kil.
2:6), which is the minimum size of an area within a field which
may be sown with a kind other than that sown in the field
itself (cf. M. 2:9-10). According to Z, then, the row of
mustard or safflower must be as long (though not as wide) as an
area within a field which is usually considered autonomous.

A. "They edge (*mqypyn*)[120] only [a field of] geophytes[121] (*ḥysyt*)
   alone [with] mustard [or] safflower," the words of R. Meir.
B. R. Judah says, "They edge [a field of] any [kind with] mustard
   [or] safflower, except for [a field of] grain."
C. [Lieberman, following Erfurt, Y., and Sens[122] adds: R.
   Simeon says, "They edge [a field of] any [kind with] mustard
   [or] safflower."]
D. Rabbi Simeon b. Gamaliel says, "They surround small beds
   (*[c]rwgywt*; Erfurt: *[c]rwgwt* ["beds"]; *[c]rwgwt qṭnwt* ["small

beds"]) of vegetables [= omitted by Erfurt] with mustard
[or] safflower."

T. Kil. 2:5a (p. 209, ll. 19-22)

(Y. Kil. 2:8 (28a))

T. Kil. 2:5a comments on M. 2:8A-B, for it presents an
Ushan dispute concerning the flanking of a field with mustard
or safflower (and so assigns M. to Judah). The dispute consists
of four sayings, with those of Judah and Simeon balancing one
another in B-C (both sayings being identical except for the
phrase *ḥwṣ mn htbw'h* in B). It is possible, then, that Judah and
Simeon were originally in dispute, and the sayings of Meir and
Simeon b. Gamaliel later added to form the present dispute.

Meir says in A that one may flank only a field of geophytes
with mustard or safflower. According to Feliks[123] Meir
apparently reasons that since geophytes are not visible aboveground, mustard or safflower may flank them without causing an
appearance of diverse-kinds. Meir maintains, however, that mustard
or safflower may not be sown next to any crops which grow aboveground, for then an appearance of diverse-kinds would result.
Meir thus opposes the law of M. 2:8B, which states that one may
flank a field of vegetables with mustard or safflower.

In B-C, Judah and Simeon dispute as to whether or not one may
flank grain with mustard or safflower. Both men agree (against
Meir) that one may sow these kinds next to anything else, so
that Meir clearly stands outside of their dispute. Judah maintains that one may not flank grain with mustard or safflower (=
M. 2:8A), apparently because an appearance of diverse-kinds
would result. Simeon, on the other hand, permits one to sow
mustard or safflower next to grain. According to his view
mustard or safflower does not produce the appearance of diverse-
kinds even when it flanks grain (Feliks[124]).

Simeon b. Gamaliel's saying in D is autonomous of the
foregoing. Simeon b. Gamaliel says that one may surround small
vegetable-beds with mustard or safflower. The beds do not appear
to be sown with diverse-kinds, for at a distance only the tall
mustard or safflower plants are visible, while upon a closer look,
the vegetables may be easily distinguished from the other plants
(Feliks[125]). Simeon b. Gamaliel then agrees with M. 2:8B that
one may flank vegetables with mustard or safflower.

E. He flanks [with diverse-kinds] tree-roots which have dried
up, [and] [Y. omits:] which are ten handbreadths high.

F. [Concerning] a tree whose foliage is not [i.e., is less than]
    three [handbreadths off the ground]--
G. he sows seed under [the tree], and flanks it [with] another
    kind outside [of the foliage].

                              T. Kil. 2:5b (p. 209, 11. 22-24)
                              (E: Y. Kil. 2:8 (28a))

     T. Kil. 2:5b comments on M. 2:8C(7), which says that one
may flank with diverse-kinds a tree which shades the ground.
T. is divided into two parts, E and F-G. E concerns flanking
the roots of a tree with diverse-kinds, while F-G deals with the
foliage of a tree as a divider of diverse-kinds.
     E states its law in a simple declarative sentence (using,
as M. does, the singular present participle). According to E
one may flank with diverse-kinds dry tree-roots which are ten
handbreadths high. Feliks[126] explains that only dry roots adequately separate diverse-kinds, for moist roots are green and
may be easily confused with the plants growing near them.
Feliks[127] also points out that trees which live long (such as
olive or fig trees) commonly have roots which are ten handbreadths off the ground, for eventually the soil surrounding
the trees erodes and the roots are exposed. E then supplements
M. 2:8C(7), for it adds another way in which a tree may be
flanked with diverse-kinds.
     F describes the case of a tree whose foliage is less than
three handbreadths above the ground.[128] G then explains how
the tree separates diverse-kinds. One kind is sown under the
tree, while the other is sown outside of the tree's foliage, so
that the foliage itself divides the two kinds (following
Lieberman[129]). We note that in this case the two kinds are not
actually sown on two sides of a divider. Rather, one kind is
sown in the autonomous domain created by the tree's shade,
while the other is sown outside of the tree's foliage. F-G then
explains how M.'s "tree which shades the ground" may be flanked
with diverse-kinds, both by stating how low the foliage must be
and by explaining how the foliage itself separates the diverse-
kinds.

A. [If diverse-kinds, separated by a fence (= M. 2:8C(5))]
    extended (mšwkwt; Erfurt: mšwkyn; first printed ed.:
    mwškwt) three handbreadths beyond the fence,
B. he shall not make [the area of each kind] less than [the area
    of] three open furrows [= T. 2:1a],

C. so that [the diverse-kinds] appear [to be sown] in rows
    (*kšwrh*; lit.: "in a row").

                              T. Kil. 2:6a (p. 209, ll. 24-25)

    T. Kil. 2:6a supplements M. 2:8C(5), which says that one
may flank a fence with diverse-kinds. A describes a case in
which diverse-kinds extend three handbreadths beyond the fence
which separates them (following Lieberman[130]). According to B
each kind must cover an area no less than that of three open
furrows. That is, the plot of each kind must have a width equal
to that of three furrows, and each kind must be sown over the
entire length of the field (Feliks[131]). C glosses B, explaining
that each kind then appears to be sown in a row, for the area of
a row is defined as that of three open furrows (T. 2:1a). Now
according to M. 2:6 rows of diverse-kinds may be sown next to
one another, for each row is considered a field unto itself.
The diverse-kinds which extend beyond the fence may therefore
grow in adjacent rows without producing an appearance of diverse-
kinds.

                              2:9

A. He who wishes to lay out his field [in] patches [so Danby
    for *qrḥt*; lit.: bald-spots (cf. M. 4:1)] of every kind
    [i.e., with each patch containing a different kind] --
B. (1) he lays out twenty-four patches to a *bet se'ah*,
    (2) a patch to a *bet rova^c*,
C. and sows in [each patch (Albeck)] any kind that he wishes.
D. "If there were one or two patches [in a field of grain (Sens)],
    he sows them with mustard;
E. "[but if there were] three [patches], he shall not sow
    [most mss.[132] add: them] [with] mustard,
F. "for [then the field as a whole] looks like a field of
    mustard,"
G. the words of R. Meir.
H. And the sages say, "Nine patches are permitted, [but] ten
    are prohibited [i.e., it is permitted to lay out no more
    than nine patches of mustard in a field of grain.]"
I. R. Eliezer b. Jacob says, "Even (*'pylw*) [if] his entire field
    is [the size of] a *bet kor*, he shall lay out only one
    patch in it."

                              M. Kil. 2:9

M. Kil. 2:9 concerns dividing a field into patches of
different kinds, and so continues the discussion of M. 2:6, which
deals with a field laid out in rows of different kinds. M.
consists of three units, A-C, D-H, and I. A-C discusses the
number of patches which may be laid out in a *bet se'ah*. In D-H
Meir and the sages dispute concerning the number of patches of
mustard which may be sown in a single field (an alternative
interpretation of the sages' views will be presented below).
Finally Eliezer b. Jacob glosses A-C in I, and discusses how
many patches may be laid out in a *bet kor*.

A describes the case of one who wishes to divide his field
into patches and sow a different kind in every patch. According
to B(1) one may make twenty-four patches in a *bet se'ah*, while
B(2) adds that each patch must have the area of a *bet rova*^{c}
(= one twenty-fourth of a *bet se'ah*). B(2)'s gloss is important,
for it establishes that each patch must have a minimum area.[133]
These patches are considered fields unto themselves, so that
each may contain a different kind (C). The point of A-C, then,
is that each patch must be of a minimum area, for otherwise the
different kinds would appear to be growing haphazardly and in
confusion, and the field would appear to be sown with diverse-kinds.

Eliezer b. Jacob's saying in I refers to A-C, for the
language of I, *bet kor*, corresponds to the language of A-C,
bet se'ah. Eliezer b. Jacob opposes the law of A-C, for he states
that even if the field is the size of a *bet kor* (= thirty times
the size of a *bet se'ah*), only one patch may be laid out in it.
That is, one may sow in a field only one kind other than that
which is sown in the greater part of the field, no matter how
large the field may be. Eliezer b. Jacob's point is that no more
than two kinds may grow in a single field, for the presence of
even three kinds in a field produces the appearance of diverse-kinds.

D-H presents a dispute between Meir and the sages. The
dispute is not balanced, for the operative language of D-E
(zwr^c/l' yzr^c) differs from that of H ($mwtr/'swr$). Both opinions,
however, contain similar number-sequences, as D-E has two/three
and H has nine/ten (X/X+1). The dispute concerns the number of
mustard patches which may be laid out in a field of grain (Sens).
Meir says in D-E that two, but not three, patches of mustard
may be sown in a single field. Glossing D-E, F explains that
three patches of mustard are enough to determine a mustard-field.
That is, since mustard is usually sown in small quantities (cf.
our discussion of M. 2:8), a field containing even as few as
three patches of it is already considered a field of mustard.

Meir therefore permits only two patches to be laid out, for
otherwise the grain growing in the same field would seem to be
growing in a mustard field, and the appearance of diverse-kinds
would result. The sages, on the other hand, maintain in H that
ten patches of mustard determine a mustard-field, so that one
may lay out as many as nine patches without producing the appearance of diverse-kinds.[134]

2:10

A. Everything which is within [an area the size of] a *bet rova*^{c}
counts within the measure of the *bet rova*^{c}.

B. (1) The ground required for a vine [so Danby for *'kylt hgpn*;
most mss.: *'klt hgpn*; B, Geniza fragment,[135] O, Ox, Pr:
'wklt hgpn],

(2) or the grave,

(3) or the rock,

counts within the measure of the *bet rova*^{c} [even though these
areas may not be sown].

C. (1) Grain [of one kind which is to be sown in a field
containing mostly] grain [of another kind] (*tbw'h btbw'h*)
[must itself cover an area of] a *bet rova*^{c}.

D. (2) Vegetables [of one kind which are to be sown in a field
containing mostly] vegetables [of another kind] (*yrq byrq*)
[must themselves cover an area of] six handbreadths
[square].

E. (3) Grain [which is to be sown in a field containing mostly]
vegetables (*tbw'h byrq*), or

(4) vegetables [which are to be sown in a field containing
mostly] grain (*yrq btbw'h*) [must themselves cover an area
of] a *bet rova*^{c}.

F. R. Eliezer [N, Sn, V: Eleazar[136]] says: "Vegetables [which
are to be sown in a field containing mostly] grain (*yrq
btbw'h*) [must themselves cover an area of] six handbreadths
[square]."

M. Ḳil. 2:10

M. Ḳil. 2:10 concerns the dimensions of an area which is
to be considered an autonomous field. M. is divided into two
units, A-B, and C-F. A-B considers whether or not areas which
cannot be sown are included in the measuring of a *bet rova*^{c}.
C-F concerns the minimum area which one kind of seed must cover
when it is sown in a field of another kind (GRA).

A-B presupposes that the *bet rova*^{c} is an autonomous field,

and so is probably redacted as a comment on M. 2:9 (Albeck).
A states that everything within an area the size of a *bet rova*^{c}
is included in measuring the *bet rova*^{c}. B illustrates A with a
list of three areas which may not be sown but which are nevertheless counted as part of a *bet rova*^{c}. The area surrounding a
vine (six handbreadths [in each direction (TYY)]; cf. M. Kil.
3:7, 6:1) may not be sown, for the presence of other plants in
this area produces the appearance of diverse-kinds of the vineyard. It is prohibited to derive benefit from a grave (TYY;
cf. M. Oh. 18:2), and a rock is clearly not suitable for sowing.
According to B, then, the point of A is that even areas which
cannot actually be sown count as part of the *bet rova*^{c}. This
means that the *bet rova*^{c} need not be completely covered with
crops of the secondary kind in order to be considered an autonomous field.

C-F defines the minimum area which a plot with a larger
field must cover in order to be considered an autonomous field,
and so to be sown with a different kind. The two fields may
contain either different kinds of the same type of crops (i.e.,
both have either grain or vegetables) or different types of
crops (i.e., one has grain while the other has vegetables).
C-F then simply consists of the four possible combinations of
the words *tbw'h* and *yrq*, with each combination having as an
apodosis either *byt rwb*^{c} or * šš̌h ṭpḥym*. C states that if the
two fields contain different types of grain, the smaller, autonomous field must measure a *bet rova*^{c} in area. D, on the other
hand, says that if the two fields are sown with different kinds
of vegetables, then the smaller field need measure only six
handbreadths square. According to E if one field is sown with
grain and the other contains vegetables, the smaller field
(regardless of which type of crop it contains) must measure a
bet rova^c. In F, Eliezer (or Eleazar) disagrees with E(4),
saying that if the smaller field contains vegetables and the
larger one is sown with grain, then the former need measure only
six handbreadths square. According to Eliezer, then, a smaller,
autonomous field of grain always requires the area of a *bet rova*^{c}
while a smaller field of vegetables must always be six handbreadths square, regardless of what the larger field contains.

D. (1) A private road,
   (2) or a public road,
   (3) or a fence which is ten handbreadths high,
       does not count within the measure of the [*bet*] *rova*^{c}.

E. [A fence which is] lower than ten handbreadths counts
within the measure of the *bet rova*^c [Erfurt: The private
road, or the public road, or the fence which is nearly
(*smwk*) ten handbreadths high, counts within the measure
of the *bet rova*^c. But the fence which is higher than ten
(handbreadths) does not count in the measure of the *bet
rova*^c; first printed ed.: The private road, or the public
road, or the fence which is lower than ten handbreadths,
counts within the measure of the *bet rova*^c. But (the fence)
which is higher than ten handbreadths does not count within
the measure of the *bet rova*^c].

F. [Erfurt adds: And] what (*kmh*; lit.: how much) is the
measure of a *bet rova*^c?

G. Ten-and-one-half *amot* by ten-and-one-half *amot*, squared
[Erfurt: Ten-and-one-half *amot* squared].

H. R. Yosah [Erfurt, first printed ed.: Yosé] says, "[An
area may be considered a *bet rova*^c] even ('*pylw*) [if] its
length is about twice its width."

> T. Kil. 2:6b (pp. 209-210, ll.
> 25-29)
> (H: M. Erub. 2:5)

T. Kil. 2:6b is divided into two parts, D-E and F-G. D-E
discusses areas which either are or are not counted as part of
a *bet rova*^c, and so comments on M. 2:10A-B. F-H deals with
the dimension of a *bet rova*^c, and so comments on either T. 2:6D-E,
M. 2:9 or M. 2:10, all of which concern an area of that size.

D-E distinguishes between the private road, the public
road,[137] and the fence which is ten handbreadths high, on the
one hand, and the fence which is lower than ten handbreadths,
on the other. A similar distinction is drawn by M. 4:7, which
rules that the two kinds of road and the fence which is lower
than ten handbreadths do not constitute valid dividers of
diverse-kinds, while the fence which is higher than ten handbreadths does form a valid divider. It appears, then, that our
reading of D-E is difficult, for it groups the two kinds of
roads together with the higher fence, and implies that each
of the two roads forms an autonomous domain within the field
in which it lies. According to M. 4:7, however, the roads do not
serve to separate two kinds from one another, and so cannot be
considered as being separate from the rest of the field. It is
likely, therefore, that D(3) and the apodosis of D should be
reversed with E (as in the first printed ed.)[138], so that T. rules

that the two roads,[139] and the lower fence, do not count within
the measure of *bet rova*^{c}. The point of D-E, then, is that those
areas which do not form domains unto themselves are counted in
the *bet rova*^{c}, since they are regarded as part of the same field,
while those which do constitute a separate domain do not form
part of a *bet rova*^{c}. T. thus qualifies M. 2:10A, which states
that everything within a *bet rova*^{c} is counted as part of the
latter.

F-G defines a *bet rova*^{c} as an area which measures ten-and-
one-half by ten-and-one-half *amot*. In H Yosé says that a *bet
rova*^{c} need not be a square, for he maintains that its length
may equal even twice its width. Yosé's saying, however, may not
refer to a *bet rova*^{c} at all. The identical saying appears in
a different and more appropriate context in M. Erub. 2:5, so
that H is probably not original to the context of T. Kil.[140]

A. The area required for the tillage of vegetables (^{c}*bwdt yrq*)
[of one kind sown] among vegetables of another [kind] is
six handbreadths [square] [Erfurt, Sens add: whether (the
secondary kind is sown) in the middle (of the field of the
primary kind), or whether (it is sown) at the sides (of
the field of the primary kind)].

B. [Erfurt adds: And] they consider (*rw'yn*) it [i.e., the
area sown with the secondary kind] as if it were a square
tablet [even if it is not perfectly square].

C. Even (*'pylw*) if there is only one stalk there [i.e., in
the area sown with the secondary kind], they [Erfurt: he]
allow it the area required for its tillage, six handbreadths [square],

D. [Erfurt, Sens omit:] whether [the stalk is sown] in the
middle [of the square], or whether [the stalk is sown] at
the sides [of the square].

·E. If the stalks leaned [over adjacent plants of another kind]
in four directions [from the square], lo, this is
permitted,

F. for it looks like the end of the field.

T.Kil. 2:7 (p. 210, ll. 29-32)

(A-B: B. Shab. 85b-86a)

T. Kil. 2:7 is divided into three parts, A+C-D, B, and E-F.
A+C-D concerns sowing vegetables of one kind among another
kind of vegetables, and so comments on M. 2:10D. B interrupts
A+C-D with a discussion of an area which is not perfectly

square. E-F, commenting on M. 2:11, deals with vegetables which
lean over vegetables of another kind.

A states that if one kind of vegetable is sown in a field
consisting of vegetables of another kind, the former requires
an area measuring six handbreadths square (following the readings
of Vienna Ms. and first printed ed.[141]). A thus simply restates
M. 2:10D. According to C even if only one stalk of the secondary
kind is to be sown in the field, it must still be given the
full area of six handbreadths square. D adds that the single
stalk must be given the full square even if it is sown at the
edge of the primary kind,[142] that is, in a place where the single
stalk would not by itself appear to form a separate and autonomous
field. The point of C-D is that any quantity of a secondary kind
which is sown among a primary kind must be sown in a field unto
itself, for otherwise the larger field would appear to be sown
with diverse-kinds.

B states that one regards a certain area as if it were a
square tablet. B presumably refers to a plot sown with a
secondary kind, and its point is that such a plot need not be
in a regular shape. That is, if the plants of the secondary kind
extend from an irregularly-shaped area into the field of the
primary kind, so that the plants which extend from it are regarded
as part of it, the plot of the secondary kind is considered a
square (Lieberman[143]). Now B does not refer specifically to the
case of A, and so may be out of place in our pericope. B perhaps
belongs in T. 2:6B, which concerns the size and shape of a
bet rova[c].

E states that stalks of a secondary kind, which are sown in
a square, may be allowed to lean over the plants outside of
the square. E then restates M. 2:11 (plants of one kind may lean
over another kind of plant) in the context of M. 2:10 (a secondary
kind is sown in a square among a primary kind) and its purpose
is to link the two rules. According to F the plants of the
secondary kind are allowed to lean over the other plants for,
although they extend beyond the square, they appear to mark the
end of the square (cf. M. 2:7), and there is thus no appearance
of diverse-kinds.

2:11

A.　(1) [If] grain leans [so Danby for *nwṭh*] over grain [of
　　　　another kind],
　　(2) or vegetables [lean] over vegetables [of another kind],
　　(3) [if] grain [leans] over vegetables,
　　(4) [or if] vegetables [lean] over grain --

B. everything is permitted,

C. except for the Greek gourd [i.e., any plant may be allowed
    to lean over any other plant, while the Greek gourd may
    not be allowed to lean over any plant].

D. R. Meir [C, Geniza fragments,[144] K, L, Mn, Ox, P, S read:
    Rabbi] says, "Even ('p) the chate melon and the cowpea [lit.:
    Egyptian bean] [may not be allowed to lean over any plant];

E. "but I prefer (rw'h) their words to my own."

M. Kil. 2:11

M. Kil. 2:11 discusses allowing plants of one kind to lean
over another kind of plants. A lists all of the ways in which
grain and vegetables may lean over plants, presenting all four
possible combinations of the words tbw'h and yrq. According to
B any plant may be allowed to lean over a plant of another kind.
C glosses B and gives one exception to this rule, the Greek
gourd, which is not permitted to hang over plants of other
kinds. The reason behind B is apparently that most plants do
not spread out very far, so that even if they lean over plants of
other kinds they do not become entangled with them and so do not
cause the appearance of diverse-kinds. The Greek gourd, on the
other hand, spreads out 10-15m.,[145] and tends to become entangled
with the adjacent plants. Since the Greek gourd, then, could
easily produce the appearance of diverse-kinds,[146] it may not
be allowed to hang over nearby plants.[147]

In D Meir (or Rabbi) glosses C and says that the chate
melon and the cowpea also may not be allowed to lean over plants
of other kinds.[148] Both the chate melon and the cowpea are
climbing plants,[149] so that if they were to spread over other
plants, they would become entangled with the latter and cause
the appearance of diverse-kinds. In E, however, Meir states
that he prefers the ruling of C to his own. He apparently
reasons that the Greek groud spreads out farther than do the chate
melon and the cowpea. If the Greek gourd were allowed to lean
over other plants, it would become entangled to a greater extent
than would the other two plants under similar circumstances.
Therefore Meir reasons that the chate melon and the cowpea are
not in the same category as the Greek gourd with respect to
causing the appearance of diverse-kinds.

KILAYIM CHAPTER THREE

Chapter Three, which is concerned with planting vegetables and trailing plants, presents a series of rules defining the minimum area which a secondary kind must cover in order to avoid the appearance of diverse-kinds. The chapter consists of two major units, M. 3:1-2, discussing the garden-bed, and M. 3:3D-G + M. 3:6 + M. 3:7C-E, dealing with rows in a field. The intervening pericopae, M. 3:3A-C, M. 3:4-5, M. 3:7A-B, F-H and J-K, are all brief units attached to the larger formal structure. As we shall see, however, the redactor has largely ignored these formal units and has organized the chapter along thematic lines.

M. 3:1-2 determines the number of different kinds of vegetables which may be sown in a garden-bed measuring six hand-breadths square. An area of this size is considered an autonomous field (M. 2:10), and so may be sown with one kind and flanked with different kinds along its sides. Judah maintains that an autonomous field need be much smaller, and therefore allows six kinds to be sown in the bed itself.

The pericopae of the second major unit exhibit a distinctive formulary pattern in their protases: *hyh śdhw zrw^{c}h* X, *whw'* (or *w*) *mbqš* (or *bqš*) *lṭ^c b* (or (1)) *twkh šwrh šl* Y. This unit deals with the minimum dimensions of rows of one kind which are sown in a field containing a different kind. M. 3:3D-G concerns sowing a row of vegetables in a vegetable field of another kind, while M. 3:6 discusses planting a row of gourds in a field of onions, and M. 3:7C-E rules on planting a row of gourds among grain. Both M. 3:3D-G and M. 3:6 present disputes between Ishmael and ^{c}Aqiva, and so were probably formulated together. The redactor of the chapter then separated the two pericopae by means of M. 3:4+5, which concern planting different kinds of trailing plants in rows and individually.[1] We may understand why the redactor chose to place M. 3:4+5 where he did if we consider the alternatives which lay before him. He could not insert the two pericopae before M. 3:1-2, for then he would have a unit on the garden-bed (M. 3:1-2) interrupting a discussion of planting rows in a field (M. 3:4 and M. 3:3). Nor could the redactor place M. 3:4+5 after M. 3:1-2, for then rulings concerning trailing plants would separate pericopae dealing with vegetables (M. 3:1-3). Similarly, M. 3:4+5 could not be appropriately set

115

between M. 3:6 and M. 3:7, for both of these pericopae deal
with planting rows of trailing plants together with vegetables.
Finally, M. 3:4+5 could not conclude the chapter, for then the
chapter's sequence of themes would not be logical, as a discussion
of planting different kinds of trailing plants with one another
would follow the rules for planting trailing plants with vegetables.
That is, the discussion of planting trailing plants together with
vegetables would then not follow units dealing with the planting
of vegetables and trailing plants separately. The redactor thus
had to insert M. 3:4+5 into the unit of M. 3:3D-G + M. 3:6 +
M. 3:7C-E, because he wanted the chapter to have the thematic
sequence of vegetables (M. 3:1-3) -- trailing plants (M. 3:4-5) --
trailing plants + vegetables (M. 3:6-7). The chapter is thus
organized around thematic considerations rather than formal ones.

3:1

A. A garden-bed which is six handbreadths by six handbreadths --
B. (1) they sow in it five [kinds of] seeds,
    (2) four [along] the four sides (*rwhwt*) of the garden-bed
        and one in the middle.
C. If it [i.e., the garden-bed] had a border [measuring] a
    handbreadth [B, Geniza fragment,[2] L, O, T, Tm omit:] high,
D. (1) they sow in it thirteen [kinds],
    (2) three on each and every border and one in the middle.
E. He shall not plant the head of a turnip in the border,
F. because it fills [i.e., spreads throughout] [the border].
G. R. Judah says, "Six [kinds may be sown] in the middle [of a
    garden-bed]."

                            M. Kil. 3:1 (A-B: M. Shab. 9:2b,
                            B. Pes. 39b; B(2): B. Qid. 39b)

    M. Kil. 3:1 concerns the ways in which different kinds may
be sown around a garden-bed. M. is divided into two parts,
A-B+G and C-F. A-B concerns the number of different kinds which
may be sown in and around a single garden-bed. In G, Judah
glosses and opposes A-B. C-F, which has been inserted between
A-B and G, discusses the number of different kinds which may be
sown around a garden-bed surrounded by a border.
    According to A-B five different kinds may be sown in a
garden-bed which measures six handbreadths square. One kind is
to be sown in the garden-bed itself, while each of the other four

kinds is sown along the outer edge of one side of the square
(GRA; cf. fig. 9[3]).[4] Since an area measuring six handbreadths square is considered an autonomous field (cf. M. 2:10[5]),
the garden-bed is comparable to a field of one kind which is
flanked by different kinds on all four sides. In G., Judah
says that six kinds, rather than one, may be sown in the garden-
bed itself (fig. 13[6]). Accordingly, each of these six kinds
covers an area measuring six by one handbreadths. Judah's
saying here is then consistent with his ruling in M. 3:3, which
states that a row of vegetables of one kind which is sown in
a field of another kind of vegetables need measure about six
by one handbreadths (Bert., GRA).[7]

C-D states that thirteen kinds may be sown in and around
a bed which has a border measuring one handbreadth high. One
kind is to be sown in the bed itself, as in A-B, but now three
kinds may be sown on each side. One kind is sown along the
inner edge of the side, a second kind is sown on the border
itself, and a third kind is sown just outside of the border
(GRA; cf. fig. 15[8]). The border serves to separate the three
kinds from one another, so that there is no appearance of
diverse-kinds. The garden-bed is again comparable to a field
which is flanked by different kinds, only now it is flanked by
three kinds, rather than one, on each side.

E-F depends on C. According to E-F one should not plant the
heads (i.e., the hypocotyls[9]) of turnips in the border of the
garden-bed because they would fill up the border. That is, turnips
may not be planted in the border because their leaves would spread
out beyond the border and become entangled with the adjacent
plants, and so cause the appearance of diverse-kinds.

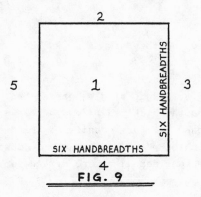

FIG. 9

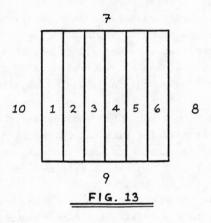

FIG. 13

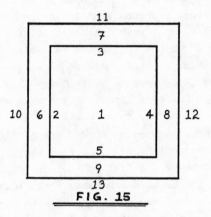

FIG. 15

3:2

A. No kind of seeds do they sow in a [B. adds: single] garden-
    bed,

B. but [= omitted by most mss.[10]] all kinds of vegetables do
    they sow in a [B. adds: single] garden-bed.

C. Mustard and smooth chick-peas (*'pwnym h̆ŭwpyn*; alt. trans.:
    small chick-peas[11])[12] [are considered] kind[s] of seeds,

D. [while] large chick-peas (*'pwnym hgmlnym*; most mss.[13] read
    hgmlwnym) [are considered] a kind of vegetable.

E. A border which was [originally] a handbreadth high and
    became diminished [in height],

F. is fit ($k\check{s}r$),

G. for it was fit from [i.e., at] its inception.

H. The furrow and the [dry] water-channel which are a
    handbreadth deep --

I. (1) they sow in them three [kinds of] seeds,
    (2) one on one [side], one on the other [side], and one
    in the middle.

M. Kil. 3:2 (A-B;   B. Pes. 39b; G-H:

Y. Kil. 3:1 (28c))

M. 3:2 concerns sowing vegetables in a garden-bed and its
borders, and so supplements M. 3:1. M. is divided into three
parts, A-D, E-G, and H-I. A-D lists the kinds of plants which
may and may not be sown in a garden-bed. E-G presents the case
of the border which becomes diminished in height, so that it
no longer separates the different kinds along the sides of
the garden-bed. H-I concerns the number of different kinds which
may be sown in a water-channel or furrow, which, as we shall
see, are analogous in this respect to the border.

A-D consists of two sets of balanced declarative sentences,
A-B and C-D. A and B differ only in that the former reads zr^cym +
$'yn\ zwr^cym$, while the latter has $yrqwt$ + zwr^cym. C and D also
balance one another.

C: $h\d{h}rdl\ w'pwnym\ h\check{s}wpyn\ myn\ zr^cym$

D: $'pwnym\ hgmlnym\ myn\ yrqwt.$

Except for the presence of $hhrdl$ in C, the two sentences
would be in almost perfect balance ($\check{s}wpyn$ + zr^cym vs. $gmlnym$ +
$yrqwt$). $hrdl$ breaks the tightly disciplined structure of C-D
and so appears to be a gloss.

A-B refers to the garden-bed of M. 3:1A-B (all commentaries),
which contains one kind in its center and a different kind along
each of its four sides. According to A-B this garden-bed may
be sown with vegetables (i.e., plants which are sown for the
sake of their leaves or green [i.e., fresh] seeds [cf. T. Kil.
2:8]), but not with seeds (i.e., plants which are sown for the
sake of their dried seeds[14]). The reasoning behind A-B is that
a garden-bed is considered an autonomous field only when it is
sown with vegetables (M. 2:10D). Therefore only a garden-bed

containing vegetables may be flanked with a different kind on
each edge (GRA[15]). Different kinds of seeds, however, may not
be sown in a garden-bed, for then the latter would not be considered a field unto itself. The different kinds of seeds would
simply appear to be sown in confusion, and the appearance of
diverse-kinds would result.

C-D states that mustard and smooth chick-peas are considered
kinds of seeds, while large chick-peas are a kind of vegetable.
C-D clearly intends to contrast the two varieties of chick-peas,
and therefore mustard does not belong in C (even though it is
grown for the sake of its seeds). Feliks[16] explains that the
smooth chick-pea is considered a kind of seed because it is
eaten either cooked or roasted, while large chick-peas are eaten
while still green and so are considered vegetables.[17]

E-F forms a declarative sentence, with G glossing F. The
language of the apodosis (F-G), $k\check{s}r$ ("fit"), appears nowhere
else in M.-T. Kil. E refers to the garden-bed which is surrounded
by a border measuring one handbreadth in height (M. 3:1C-D;
all commentaries). One kind is sown in the center of the bed,
and a different kind is sown on each of the bed's four sides,
on the inner edge of the border, on the border itself, and on
the outer edge of the border. E describes a case in which the
height of the border is diminished, so that the border no longer
separates the three different kinds on each side of the bed.
According to F the border is still fit, and the plants already
sown in and around it are allowed to continue to grow (most
commentaries). G explains that since the border was fit (i.e.,
of sufficient height to separate the different kinds) at its
inception, the plants in the garden-bed need not be uprooted,
even though they may produce the appearance of diverse-kinds.

According to H-I a furrow[18] or water-channel which is one
handbreadth deep may be sown with three different kinds.[19] One
kind is sown in the center of the furrow or channel, while a
different kind is sown at each of the sides. The furrow or
channel is then analogous to the border of M. 3:1C-D, which
may be sown in a similar manner. The analogy, in fact, is
appropriate, for the furrow or water-channel, being one handbreadth deep, is the mirror-image of the border, which is
one handbreadth high.

A. *The mustard and the smooth* [Lieberman,[20] following Y.,
   reads *šwpyn* for *šypwn*; alt. trans.: small[21]] *beans* (*pwlyn;*

Y.:   *'pwnyn* ["chick-peas"]) [Y. adds: are a kind of
      seeds] [= M. 3:2C] --
B. even though [omitted by Y.] he [first printed ed. reads:
    they] sowed them for [the sake of their] greens (*lyrq*),
C. they sow [Lieberman,[22] following Y. and first printed ed.,
    corrects to: they do not sow] them in a garden-bed [Y.
    throughout reads: they do not place them on a garden-bed].
D. [Erfurt omits D-K] [Concerning] *the large beans* (*pwlyn*; Y.:
    'wpnyn ["chick-peas"])   [= M. 3:2D] and the cowpea [lit.:
    Egyptian bean] --
E. when [Y.: which] they sowed them for [the sake of their]
    seeds (*lzr*^{c}),
F. they sow [Lieberman corrects to: they do not sow] them in
    a garden-bed;
G. [when they sowed them for the sake of their] greens (*lyrq*),
H. they do not sow [Lieberman corrects to: they sow] them in
    a single [= omitted by first printed ed.] garden-bed.
I. And [concerning] the rest of the field-vegetables and
    garden-vegetables [Y.: And (concerning) the rest of the
    garden-seeds which are not eaten] --
J. even though he sowed them for [the sake of their] seeds (*lzr*^{c}),
K. they do not sow [Lieberman corrects to: they sow] them in
    a single [= omitted by first printed ed.] garden-bed.

T. Kil. 2:8 (p. 210, ll. 32-35)

(Y. Kil. 3:2 (28c))

T. Kil. 2:8 comments on M. 3:2A-D, which concerns what may
and may not be sown in a garden-bed. T. is divided into three
units, A-C, D-H, and I-K. A-C concerns sowing mustard and the
smooth bean in a garden-bed (M. 3:2C), while D-H deals with the
large bean (M. 3:2D) and the cowpea.   I-K then presents the
rule for sowing a garden-bed with all other kinds of vegetables.
The pericope is well-balanced, for each unit consists of a protasis naming the plants under discussion (A, D, I), a subordinate
clause ("even though/when they sown them [for the sake of their]
seeds/greens;" B,E,G,J), and an apodosis (they sow/do not sow;
C,F,H,K). D-H is internally well-balanced as well, for it
consists of a protasis (D) which is followed by balanced sets
of subordinate clauses and apodoses (E-F [seeds + they do
not sow] vs. G-H [greens + they sow]).
    According to M. 3:2 plants sown for the sake of their seeds

may not be placed in a garden-bed, while those sown for their
greens may be placed there. T. now considers cases in which a
plant usually sown for the sake of one item is actually sown for
the sake of another. T. A-C rules that mustard and the smooth
bean (= smooth chick-pea), both of which are classified by M.
as kinds of seeds, may not be sown in a garden-bed even if they
are sown for their greens (i.e., the plant itself or green seeds).
The point of T., then, is that a plant is considered a kind of
seed or vegetable according to the purpose for which it is
usually sown, regardless of the owner's actual intention in
sowing it.

D-H concerns the large bean (= large chick-pea), which M.
considers a kind of vegetable, and the cowpea.[23] T. states that
these plants may be sown in a garden-bed if they are sown for
the sake of their greens, but not if they are sown for their
seeds. In this case we do take account of the owner's intention
in sowing the plants, for they are apparently not generally
sown for the sake of one item rather than the other. Therefore
they may not be classified as either seeds or vegetables without
determining the owner's purpose in sowing them. The large bean
apparently may be eaten dried as well as green, and both the
dried cowpea and its green pod are edible.[24]

I-K states that all other kinds of vegetables may be sown
in a garden-bed even if they are sown for the sake of their
seeds. The point of I-K is then the same as that of A-C. In
determining whether a plant is a kind of seed or vegetable, we
consider only the usual purpose for which the plant is sown, and
not the owner's intention in sowing them.

3:3

A. [If] the point of the angle of a field (*rwš twr*) of vegetables
    entered a field of another [kind of] vegetables,
B. it is permitted [to grow one kind of vegetables in the field
    of the other kind];
C. for it [i.e., the point of the angle of the vegetable-field]
    looks like the end of his field (*kswp šdhw*; Geniza fragment,[25]
    N: *bswp šdhw* "for it appears at the end of his field").
D. [If] his field was sown with [one kind of] vegetables, and
    he wishes (*mbqš*; Geniza fragment, Mn, Ox: *bqš* ["wished"]) to
    plant in it a row of another [kind of] vegetables --
E. R. Ishmael says, "[He may not do so] unless the furrow is
    open [i.e., extends] from one end of the field to the other."

F. R. ^CAqiva says, "[The row must measure] six handbreadths [in]
    length and fully as wide [so Danby for *rwḥb mlw'w*]."

G. R. Judah says, "The width [of the row] must be as wide as
    the width of the sole of a foot [so Danby for *rwḥb hprsh*]."

M. Kil. 3:3 (A-C: B. Shab. 85b;

G: B. Shab. 85a)

M. Kil. 3:3 concerns sowing different kinds of vegetables
among one another. M. consists of two parts, A-C and D-G.
A-C deals with a triangular area of one kind of vegetables
which grows in a field of vegetables of another kind. D-G concerns
sowing a row of one kind of vegetables in a vegetable-field of
a different kind.

A-C is identical to M. 2:7A-C, except that here M. concerns
two kinds of vegetables instead of wheat and barley. According
to A-C, the point of the angle of a field containing one kind of
vegetables may be allowed to grow in a field of another kind,
since that point appears to mark the end of its own field. There
is therefore no appearance of diverse-kinds, even though vegetables of one kind actually grow in a field of another kind.

D describes the case of one who wishes to sow a row of one
kind of vegetables in a field already sown with vegetables of
another kind. In E-F Ishmael and ^CAqiva dispute concerning the
minimum area which such a row must cover in order to be considered
an autonomous field. Judah glosses ^CAqiva's opinion in G and
so provides it with an Ushan attestation. Now this dispute
poses linguistic, formal, and substantive difficulties. First,
the language of the superscription (D) does not correspond to
that of Ishmael's ruling (E), for the former concerns a row (*šwrh*),
while the latter discusses a furrow (*tlm*). Second, the two
opinions of the dispute (E-F) are not balanced, and they are
phrased in entirely different terms. Ishmael presents his ruling
in terms relative to the field, while ^CAqiva provides a linear
measure. It is clear, then, that the dispute of D-F has been
artificially constructed from two autonomous sayings.

In E Ishmael states that, in a field of one kind of vegetables,
only an open furrow may be sown with a secondary kind. Since
such a furrow extends across the entire length of the field, it
is considered to be marked off from the rest of the field and so
autonomous of it.[26] ^CAqiva says in F that the area covered by
the secondary kind must measure six handbreadths long and fully

as wide, or six handbreadths square. ^CAqiva's rule is identical
to the anonymous law of M. 2:10D, which states that a secondary
kind of vegetables sown in a vegetable-field of another kind
must cover an area measuring six handbreadths square. Such an
area, however, is not a row but a garden-bed (cf. M. 3:1). ^CAqiva
then does not rule concerning a row of one kind in a field containing a different kind, but only concerning a garden-bed which
is autonomous of the surrounding field.

In G Judah glosses ^CAqiva's ruling, for the language of
his saying (*rḥb kml'*) corresponds to that of ^CAqiva's (*rḥb mlw'w*).[27]
According to Judah the width of the area containing the secondary
kind need measure only the width of the sole of a foot. B.
(B. Shab. 85b) and Y. (Y. Kil. 3:3 (28b)) explain that this
width equals a handbreadth. Judah maintains that a row measuring
six by one handbreadths is considered a field unto itself (cf.
M. 3:1G). An autonomous row need be only as long, but not as
wide, as a garden-bed. Judah thus reads the concerns of the
dispute (i.e., the row of another kind) into ^CAqiva's opinion,
and revises that opinion accordingly. Now ^CAqiva and Ishmael
both speak of rows, differing only with respect to the minimum
length of the latter (open furrow *vs.* six handbreadths). Judah
thus attests the entire dispute of D-F to Usha.

3:4

A. He who plants two rows of chate melons, two rows of gourds,
    [and] two rows of cowpeas -- it is permitted.
B. [He who plants] a row of chate melons, a row of gourds,
    [and] a row of cowpeas -- it is prohibited.
C. [He who plants] a row of chate melons, a row of gourds, a
    row of cowpeas and a row of chate melons --
D. R. Eliezer[28] permits,
E. and sages prohibit.

M. Kil. 3:4 (A-B: B. Shab. 85b)

M. Kil. 3:4 concerns planting rows of different kinds of
vegetables next to one another, and so continues the discussion
of M. 3:3D-6, which dealt with sowing a row of one kind of
vegetable in a field of another kind. M. consists of two mildly
apocopated sentences at A and B (in the "he-who. . . it-is"
formulary pattern), and a dispute between Eliezer and sages at
C-E. The pericope is tightly constructed, for the protases are
identical to one another except for the shift of a single variable
from A to B and again from B to C. A has two rows of each kind

(*šty šwrwt*) while B has one row (*šwrh*), and B has a total of
three rows while C has four. In addition, the apodoses use the
same language throughout the pericope (*mwtr/'swr*).

M. discusses different ways in which rows of chate melons,
gourds, and cowpeas may and may not be planted together. All of
these plants are climbing plants, so that the point of M. is to
define when such plants, which may easily become entangled with
each other, may be planted next to one another without producing
the appearance of diverse-kinds. According to A one may plant
two rows of each kind next to one another. Each set of two
rows is considered a field unto itself (Maim., *Comm.* and other
commentaries), and there is therefore no appearance of diverse-
kinds. B states that individual rows of each kind may not be
planted next to each other. A single row of climbing plants is
not considered an autonomous field, and, since the plants in
each row would become entangled with the plants of the next row,
a planting of individual rows next to one another would cause
the appearance of diverse-kinds.

C describes a case in which individual rows of chate melons,
gourds, cowpeas and chate melons adjoin one another. In D
Eliezer permits such an arrangement, for he maintains that the
two rows of chate melons combine to form an autonomous field,
which then contains single rows of gourds and cowpeas (as in
M. 3:3D; Y., Maim., *Comm.*, and other commentaries).[29] Sages
disagree with Eliezer in E, for they say that the two separated
rows of chate melons do not combine to form a field unto itself.
Accordingly, the case of C (four individual rows) is no different
from that of B (three individual rows), and the planting described
in C is prohibited.

A. *One who plants two rows of chate melons, two rows of gourds,*
   two rows of watermelons, and two rows of musk melons, *and*
   two rows of cowpeas -- even his entire field is permitted
   [Erfurt, Sirillo read: *One who plants two rows of chate*
   melons, two rows of gourds, and two rows of cowpeas [= M. 3:4A]
   -- even his entire field is permitted].

                              T. Kil. 2:11 (p. 211, ll. 44-46)

T. Kil. 2:11 comments on M. 3:4A, and follows the apocopated
sentence-structure of M. T. cites M. 3:4A, adding watermelons
and musk melons[30] to M.'s list of climbing plants (the variant
readings cite M. verbatim). T. states that an entire field may
be laid out in sets of two rows of climbing plants. T. then

carries forward the rule of M. 3:4A that one may plant such sets
next to one another. The point of T. is that each set is considered an autonomous field, so that even if many such sets are
planted in a single field there is no appearance of diverse-kinds.

3:5

A.   A man plants a chate melon and a gourd in a single hollow,
B.   provided that one leans to one side, and the other leans
     to the other side;
C.   [most mss.[31] omit C-D] and the foliage [so Danby for $š^cr$;
     lit.: hair] of one leans to this side, and the foliage of
     the other leans to the other side;
D.   for whatever the sages prohibited, they [so] decreed only
     on account of appearances ($mr'yt$ ^cyn).

M. Kil. 3:5

     M. Kil. 3:5 concerns planting chate melons together with
gourds, and so continues the discussion of M. 3:4, which deals
with planting rows of such plants next to one another. M.
consists of a simple declarative sentence (A) followed by a
subordinate clause (B). C then repeats B, and D glosses A-C.
C-D does not appear in most manuscripts, however, and it probably
forms a commentary to A-B which has been mistakenly inserted
into the text (Zachs[32]).
     A-B states that one may plant a chate melon and a gourd
in the same hollow as long as the two plants lean in different
directions. In this way the two climbing plants do not become
entangled with one another, and so do not produce the appearance
of diverse-kinds (Maim., *Comm.*). According to D the point of
A-B is that two plants may be planted even in the same location,
provided that they do not produce the appearance of diverse-kinds.
That is, only the appearance of diverse-kinds, but not their
actual planting, is prohibited.

A.   (1) A man is permitted to make in his field small furrows,
         [each measuring] a handbreadth [by a] handbreadth, and
         to place in them three [Erfurt omits:] *three* kinds,
     (2) *one on one side, one on the other side and one in the
         middle* [= M. 3:2H-I];[33]
B.   [Erfurt omits:]
     (1) A man is permitted to make in his field small garden-beds
         [each measuring] six [by] six handbreadths, and to place
         in them *five* kinds,

(2) *four along the four sides of the garden-bed, and one
in the middle* [= M. 3:1A-B];

C. And a man is permitted to make in his field a small hollow
which is a handbreadth deep, and to place in it four kinds
[Y.: seeds];

D. and he turns them [Y.: and to turn them] to its four sides
[i.e., he turns each plant so that it faces a different
direction].

> T. Kil. 2:9 (pp. 210-211, ll. 36-41)
>
> (C-D: Y. Kil. 3:4 (28d))

E. And a man is permitted to make in his field a furrow in
order to plant [in it] chate melons and gourds, watermelons
and musk melons [Lieberman[34] deletes:] and cowpeas;

F. and he turns some to one side, and others to the other side;

G. provided that there be [following Lieberman[35]] six
handbreadths between one [plant] and its neighbor.

> T. Kil. 2:10 (p. 211, ll. 41-43)

T. 2:9-10 forms a commentary to M. 3:1, 3:2 and 3:5, as
it presents a series of rules concerning the number of different
kinds which may be sown in given areas. The pericope is formally
a unitary composition, for each rule opens with the phrase "A
man is permitted to make in his field. . ." T. is divided into
five parts, four rules (A [sowing in small furrows], B [small
garden-beds], C-D [small hollows], and E-F [furrows]) and G,
which glosses all of the foregoing rules.

A restates M. 3:2H-I (citing I(2) verbatim), which says that
one may sow three different kinds in a furrow or water-channel.
T. differs from M. only in reading "small furrows" in place of
"furrow or water-channel." T. then either clarifies M.'s "furrows" or supplements the list of M. with a third type of area
which may be sown with three different kinds.

B similarly rephrases M. 3:1A-B (citing B(2) verbatim),
which states that one may sow five different kinds in a garden-bed
measuring six handbreadths square. T. reads "small garden-beds"
in place of M.'s "garden-bed," but since both types of beds are
equal in area, this difference in language is of little consequence.

C-D supplements the rule of M. 3:5A-B. The latter states
that one may plant a chate melon and a gourd in a single hollow,
povided that the plants lean in different directions. C-D has
the same rule (in different language), but speaks of planting
four different kinds instead of a chate melon and a gourd. T. then
presents a different version of the rule of M., one which deals

with four kinds instead of two.

E-F supplements C-D. According to E one may plant chate
melons, gourds, watermelons, and musk melons in a single furrow.
E concerns four kinds, as C does, only now these kinds are
planted in a furrow instead of a hollow. F then repeats D.

T. A-F thus links three rules of M.[36] and supplements them,
so that the point of T. is to join together the laws of M. 3:2H-I,
M. 3:1A-B, and M. 3:5A-B. G, however, glosses A-F, adding that
in each case the plants sown together must be separated from one
another by a distance of six handbreadths. Now this condition is
immediately satisfied in the case of B (where the plants are sown
along an area measuring six handbreadths square), but it cannot
be met in the other three cases, the areas of which (small
furrows, small hollows, and a furrow) are too small to allow
for the plants to be separated by such a distance. In fact, the
point of all four rules is that the different kinds may be sown
next to one another without producing the appearance of diverse-
kinds. By introducing a condition which requires the plants to
be separated from one another, G effectively contradicts the
point of the entire pericope.

3:6

A. [If] his field was sown [with] onions, and he wishes
   (*mbqš*; most mss.[37] *bqš* ["wished"]) to plant in it rows
   (*šwrwt*; B, C, Geniza fragment,[38] O, Ox: *šwrh* ["a row"])
   of gourds --

B. R. Ishmael says, "He uproots two rows [of onions] and plants
   one row [of gourds],

C. "and leaves the standing crop of onions over a space of
   two rows [so Danby for *wmnyḥ qmt bṣlym bmqwm šty šwrwt*],

D. "and [again] uproots two rows [of onions] and plants one
   row [of gourds]."

E. R. ᶜAqiva says, "He uproots two rows [of onions] and plants
   two rows [of gourds],

F. "and leaves the standing crop of onions over a space of
   two rows,

G. "and [again] uproots two rows [of onions] and plants two
   rows [of gourds]."

H. And sages say, "If there are not twelve *amot* between one row
   [of gourds] and the next, he shall not allow the seed [sown]
   between [the rows] to grow."[39]

M. Kil. 3:6

M. Kil. 3:6 continues the discussion, begun in M. 3:4-5,
of planting gourds with other kinds. M. is divided into three
parts, a superscription (A), a dispute between Ishmael and
^{C}Aqiva (B-G), and a saying of sages (H). The dispute of B-G is
well-balanced, with each opinion consisting of three clauses
(B-D *vs*. E-G). The first and third clauses balance each other
(two+one/two+one *vs*. two+two/two+two), and the two middle clauses
(C and F) are identical. The two rulings are internally
balanced as well, for the first and third clauses of each opinion
are identical. B-D then has the number-sequence two+one/two/
two+one, while E-G has two+two/two/two+two.

A describes a case in which one wishes to plant gourds in
a field already sown with onions.[40] The planting of gourds
among onions creates a problem in that the former may spread
out and cover most of the latter, and so produce the appearance
of diverse-kinds. Ishmael and ^{C}Aqiva then dispute whether the
planting of gourds need be restricted in order to avoid the
appearance of diverse-kinds, or whether only the actual planting
of diverse-kinds is prohibited. While both authorities agree
that the gourds are to be planted in the space of two rows,[41] or
the area of an autonomous field (cf. M. 3:4), they differ as
to whether or not the two rows are to be fully planted.[42]
Ishmael maintains that only one row of gourds may replace the
two rows of onions (Maim., *Comm*., and others; cf. fig. 17[43]).[44]
He apparently reasons that if two rows of gourds were to be
planted they would spread out to such an extent that they would
cover the majority of the onions. There would then not appear
to be a full two rows of onions between the rows of gourds,
and the appearance of diverse-kinds would result. According to
^{C}Aqiva, however, one may plant the two rows of gourds in place
of the two uprooted rows of onions (fig. 18). Even if these
two rows of gourds were to spread out and obscure the remaining
onions, the latter would still cover the area of two rows and so
continue to form an autonomous domain. The planting of two rows
of gourds is then permitted because it does not cause the actual
growth of diverse-kinds, regardless of the subsequent appearance
of the field.[45]

The opinion of sages in H depends on A. H is connected
to B-G only by the conjunction *w*, which is standard joining-
language, and sages' saying is, in fact, autonomous of the foregoing dispute. According to sages one may allow the onions to

remain between the rows of gourds only if the latter are separated
by twelve *amot*. Sages are then concerned not with the number
of rows of gourds which may be planted together, but with the
distance which must be maintained between the rows. They apparently
reason that the row of gourds must be separated by a fixed distance, so that the gourds do not cover most of the onions between
them and so produce the appearance of diverse-kinds. The point
of sages' saying is then similar to that of Ishmael's (i.e., the
avoidance of the appearance of diverse-kinds), even though the
two opinions are phrased in entirely different terms.[46]

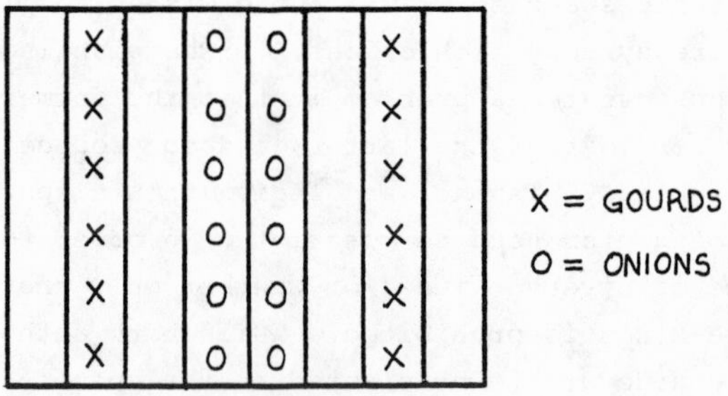

X = GOURDS
O = ONIONS

FIG. 17

FIG. 18

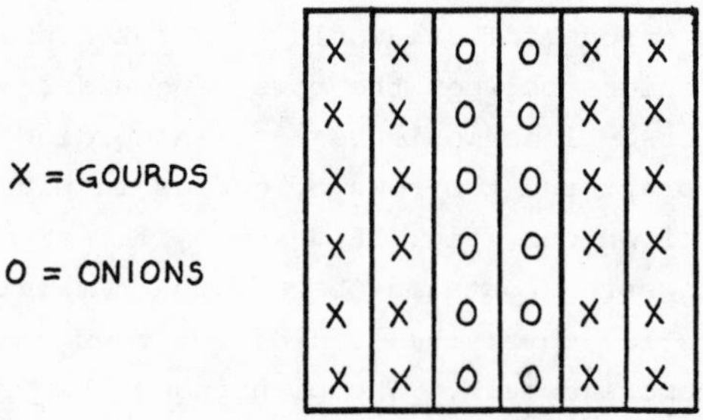

X = GOURDS

O = ONIONS

A. A summary [alt. trans: the essential point[47]] of the
    opinions of both [authorities] (*qṣr dbry šnyhm*; Erfurt:
    hqwṣr šnyhm; first printed ed.: *hqwṣr dbry šnyhm*; Y.:
    hqwṣb dbry šnyhm; Sirillo[48]: *qṣb ldbry šnyhm*):
B. [L omits B-C[49]] R. Ishmael says, "Ten [Y.: Twelve] *amot* [need
    separate the rows of gourds from one another]."

C.　R. ^CAqiva says, "Eight *amot* [need separate the rows of gourds from one another]."

D.　*m^cśh hyh* in Kefar Pegai and R. Neḥemiah ruled [Lieberman,[50] following Erfurt, reads *hwrh* for *hwdh*] according to the opinion of R. Ishmael.

T. Kil. 2:12 (p. 211, ll. 46-48)
(A-C:　Y. Kil. 3:6 (28d))

　　T. Kil. 2:12 comments on M. 3:6.　T. is divided into two parts, A-C and D.　A-C restates the dispute between Ishmael and ^CAqiva in perfect balance (ten *vs.* eight).　According to A B-C summarizes the dispute of M. 3:6.[51]　The dispute, which in M. 3:6B-G concerns the number of rows of gourds which may be planted together among the onions, is now phrased in terms of the sages' opinions in M. 3:6H.　All three opinions (M. H, T. B-C) may be summarized in the number-sequence twelve/ten/eight.

　　Let us now consider how T.'s version of the two opinions is related to that of M.　According to M. Ishmael maintains that one plants a single row of gourds for every two uprooted rows of onions, allows the next two rows of onions to stand, and repeats the process.　T. has Ishmael state that ten *amot* must separate the rows of gourds from one another.　If we assume (following the supposition of Y.) that a row measures four *amot* in width, then T.'s restatement of M. may be explained as follows. One uproots two rows of onions (total width = eight *amot*) and replaces them with a single row of gourds (width = four *amot*), which is planted down the center of the two uprooted rows.　Two *amot*, which are left uncultivated, then flank the row of gourds on each side.　The next two rows of onions (total width = eight *amot*) are left standing, and a row of gourds is then planted adjacent to them.　The two rows of gourds are then separated by ten *amot* (cf. fig. 21).　We note, however, that this distance will not exclusively separate rows of gourds which are planted serially in a field of onions (as the succeeding rows will be alternately separated by fourteen and ten *amot*; cf. fig. 22).　It is therefore possible that Y. and Samuel (cited by Y.)., who read "twelve *amot*," have the better reading, for intervals measuring twelve *amot* do repeatedly separate rows of gourds which are planted throughout a field (cf. fig. 23).[52]　Alternatively, however, Y. may simply correct the reading of T. to agree with the ruling of sages in M. 3:6H (Porton[53]).

In M. 3:6 [C]Aqiva states that two rows of gourds may replace
the two uprooted rows of onions. According to T. 2:12C [C]Aqiva
maintains that eight *amot* must separate the rows of gourds from
one another. If we again assume that a row measures four *amot* in
width, then T.'s version of [C]Aqiva's opinion clearly follows
from that of M. Since the areas which are no longer covered
by onions are now fully planted with gourds, only the two rows
of onions remaining between the gourds, the total width of which
is eight *amot*, separate the paired rows of gourds from one another
(cf. fig. 25).

D is phrased in the form of a $m^c \check{s}h$. D states that in
Kefar Pegai[54] Nehemiah once ruled according to Ishmael's opinion.
In its present context D supports Ishmael's ruling in M. 3:6.
D itself, however, describes neither the details of the case in
Kefar Pegai nor the particular ruling of Nehemiah, and so need
not refer to the case of M. 3:6 at all. Rather, D could support

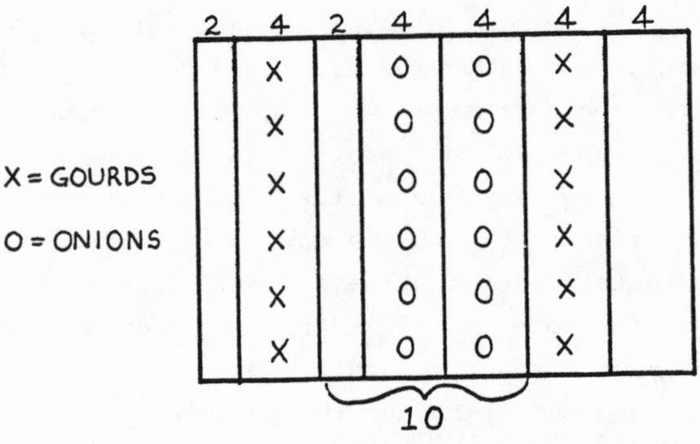

FIG. 21

FIG. 22

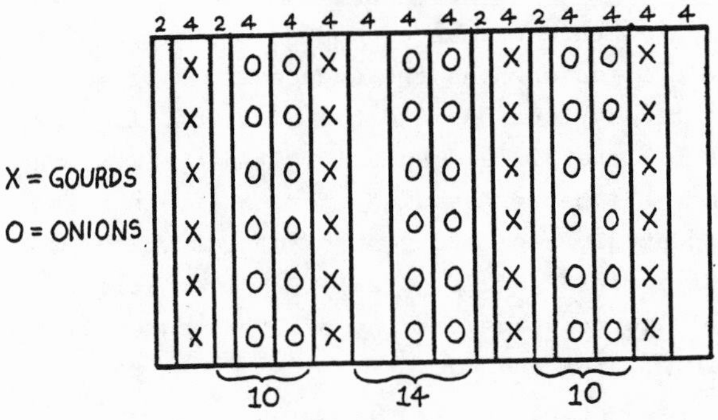

any ruling of Ishmael equally well. D. then does not provide a good attestation for Ishmael's views in M. 3:6.

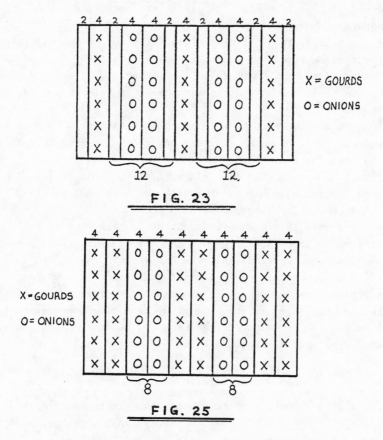

FIG. 23

FIG. 25

3:7

A. Gourds [which are to be planted in a field containing mostly] vegetables [are considered] as vegetables [of one kind which are to be sown among another kind of vegetables] [i.e., the gourds require a space measuring six handbreadths square (= M. 2:10D)].

B. And [concerning gourds which are to be planted in a field containing mostly] grain -- they allow it [i.e., them] a *bet rova*.

C. [If] his field was sown with grain, and he wished to plant in it a row of gourds,

D. they allow it [i.e., the row of gourds], as (*l*; omitted by B, C, Geniza fragments,[55] K, Mn, O, Ox, Pr) the area required for its tillage ([*l*]*bdth*) six handbreadths;

E. and if [the gourd(s)] grew larger [i.e., the gourds
extended beyond the area allotted for its tillage], he shall
uproot ($y^c qr$; most mss.[56]: $y^c qwr$) [the grain (Maim.)[57]] from
before it.

F. R. Yosé says, "They allow it [i.e., the row of gourds] as
the area required for its tillage, four *amot*."

G. They said to him, "Will this [i.e., the rule in the case
of the gourd] be more stringent than [the rule in the case
of] the vine?"

H. He said to them, "We have found that this [i.e., the rule in
the case of the gourd] is more stringent than [the rule in
the case of] the vine,

I. "for to a single vine they allow [L, S, Sn add: as] its
area for tillage, six handbreadths, but (w) to a single
gourd they allow a *bet rova*^{c}."

J. R. Meir says in the name of R. Ishmael, "Wherever (kl)[58]
[there are three gourds *per bet se'ah*, he shall not bring
seed [of another kind] into the *bet se'ah*.

K. R. Yosé b. HaHotef ($hhwtp$; K (before correction), MS, S:
$h^c wtp$; Geniza fragments: $h^c twp$ or $h^c ytwp$) the Ephrathi said
[B, Mn, S: says] in the name of R. Ishmael, "Wherever (kl)
[there are] three gourds *per bet kor*, he shall not bring
seed [of another kind] into the *bet kor*."

M. Kil. 3:7

M. Kil. 3:7 concludes the subunit concerning the planting
of gourds with other kinds. M. is divided into three parts, A-B,
C-I, and J-K. A-B concerns planting an autonomous field of
gourds in a field sown mostly with vegetables or grain and so
continues the interest of M. 3:6 in planting gourds in a field
of another kind. C-I deals with planting a row of gourds in a
field already sown with grain. J-K then discusses sowing another
kind in a field already planted with gourds.

A states its law in a declarative sentence. B depends on
A for its subject ("gourds"), and a reversal of its word-order
would yield a declarative sentence ("They allow gourds [which
are to be planted in a field containing mostly] vegetables a
bet rova^c"). The protases of A-B (gourds + vegetables, gourds +
grain) are similar to those of M. 2:10C-F (e.g., grain + grain,
vegetables + vegetables, etc.) and the apodosis of B, without
the phrase *nwtnyn lh* ("they allow it") is identical to the apodoses
of M. 2:10C+E (*bet rova*^{c}).[59] According to A gourds which are
to be planted among vegetables are considered as vegetables of

one kind which are to be sown in a field of another kind of
vegetables. A then apparently presupposes the law of M. 2:10D,
which says that in the latter case the secondary kind of vegetable
must be sown in an area measuring six handbreadths square. B
states that gourds which are to be planted in a field of grain
must be allowed a *bet rova^c*. Gourds are then treated as vegetables in this instance as well, for M. 2:10D-E gives the same
rule in the case of vegetables which are to be sown among grain.
A-B thus follow ^{C}Aqiva's reasoning in M. 3:6 that gourds are
treated as vegetables.

C-I consists of two parts, a dispute at C-F and a debate
at G-I. C-D presents a law in a declarative sentence which is
then glossed by E. In F Yosé glosses and opposes C-D (and so
attests it to Usha). The dispute is well-balanced, for D and F
differ only in that one has *ššh ṭphym* while the other reads
'rb^c 'mwt. In G-I Yosé debates anonymous authorities (presumably
those behind the ruling of C-D) concerning his opinion in F.
Yosé has the last say in H-I and so wins the debate.

C describes a case in which one wishes to plant a row of
gourds in a field already sown with grain. According to D the
gourds must be planted in an area measuring six handbreadths
square (= ^{C}Aqiva's ruling in M. 3:3F concerning a row of vegetables sown in a vegetable-field of another kind). C-D then
also follows ^{C}Aqiva's view in M. 3:6 that gourds are no different
from other vegetables. E adds that if the leaves of the gourds
extend beyond this space, the adjacent grain is to be uprooted.
The two kinds will then not become entangled with one another
and produce the appearance of diverse-kinds (Maim., *Code, Diverse-
Kinds* 3:13).[60] In F Yosé disagrees with D, saying that the area
of tillage for a row of gourds is four *amot* (presumably) square.
Now the distinction between these two measures of an area of
tillage is made with reference to grapevine or the vineyard
(defined either as five grapevines or two rows [M. 4:5]) (cf.
the debate at G-I). The area of tillage of the former is six
handbreadths square, while that of the latter is four *amot*
square (M. 6:1, following Maim., *Comm.*; cf. also Maim., *Comm.*
to M. 4:1, and Maim., *Code, Diverse-Kinds* 7:1). The dispute of
D+F then concerns whether a row of gourds is analogous to a
grapevine (or a single row of vines) or a vineyard. The reasoning
behind D is that there is no difference between a row of gourds
and a row of vines, so that the former requires an area of only
six handbreadths square. Yosé, on the other hand, apparently
reasons that gourds tend to spread out to such an extent that a
single row of them must be allowed the area usually allotted to

a vineyard. The dispute of D+F thus concerns the area of tillage of a row of gourds, but it has little to do with C's particular problem of planting a row of gourds in a field of grain. The opinions of the dispute do not relate closely to the issue of the superscription.

In G anonymous authorities oppose Yosé's ruling, asking why the law in the case of a row of gourds should be more stringent than that in the case of a row of vines. That is, they ask why, according to Yosé, a row of gourds should require an area measuring four *amot* square, while a row of vines requires an area of only six handbreadths square. In asking about the difference between gourds and vines, the authorities of G focus upon the point of Yosé's ruling, i.e., that a row of gourds is considered as a vineyard rather than as a row of vines. In H-I Yosé answers, in language identical to that of the question, that it is indeed true that the law is more stringent in regard to gourds than it is in respect to vines. The area of tillage of a single gourd need measure a *bet rova*^{c} (B)[61] while that of a single vine need measure only six handbreadths square. Similarly, therefore, the area of tillage of a row of gourds should be larger than that of a row of vines. Now while the argument of H-I supports Yosé's point that the law for gourds is more stringent than that for vines, at the same time it seems to undermine his position at F. For if the area of tillage of a single gourd is a *bet rova*^{c}, it follows that the area of tillage of a row of gourds should measure at least a *bet rova*^{c}, and not merely four *amot* square.[62] Yosé's opinion in F is therefore not supported by the argument of H-I.

J-K is autonomous of the rest of the pericope, but it is related to the foregoing in that it concerns sowing seeds of another kind in a field already planted with gourds. This unit then reverses the circumstances of A-B and C-D, in which gourds are planted in a field already sown with another kind. In J-K Meir and Yosé b. HaHotef present two versions of an Ishmael-tradition which differ from one another in only one word (*se'ah vs. kor*). According to both authorities Ishmael states that one may not introduce a different kind of seed in a field of a specified size which already contains three gourds. Meir maintains that the saying gives the area of the field as a *bet se'ah*, while Yosé b. HaHotef says that the saying concerns a *bet kor*, which is thirty times larger. In either case the point of Ishmael's saying is that once three gourds have been planted in a given area they tend to spread over that area, so that if one were to sow another kind anywhere in the field he would

appear to be sowing diverse-kinds. As in M. 3:6, Ishmael again
takes account of the special properties of gourds and distinguishes
them from vegetables, just as (in M. 3:6) he restricts the
planting of gourds for the same reason.

A. A row of gourds [which is to be planted in a field
    containing mostly] *vegetables* [is considered] [Erfurt,
    first printed ed., Sens omit:] *as* [a row of] *vegetables*
    [of one kind which is to be sown among another kind of
    vegetables] [= M. 3:7A] --

B. [i.e., the row must measure] *six handbreadths* [in] *length
    and fully as wide* [= M. 3:3F].

C. It is all the same whether a row of chate melons [Erfurt,
    Sens, Sirillo, (cited by Lieberman: gourds)] or a row
    of vegetables of another [kind] [Lieberman,[63] following
    Sens, Sirillo, and PM, reads *'ḥr* for *'ḥd*] [is to be sown in
    a field containing mostly] grain --

D. [the row must measure] ten-and-one-half *amot* [in] length
    by a width [of] six handbreadths [Y.: One who wishes to
    make a row of vegetables in a field of grain, lo, this
    one makes (a row) ten-and-one-half *amot* (in length) by
    width (of) six (handbreadths)].

E. And a row of vegetables [which is to be sown in a field
    containing mostly] vegetables [of another kind] --

F. [the row must measure] *six handbreadths* [in] *length and
    fully as wide* [Lieberman,[64] following Erfurt, Sens, and
    Sirillo, reads *rwḥb* for *rhbw*] [= M. 3:3F].

G. [Erfurt and Sens reverse G-I and J-O] [Erfurt and Sens
    add: A row (*šwrh*); Sirillo:[65] A field (*šdh*)] of gourds
    [which is to be planted in a field containing mostly]
    vegetables --

H. *between one row* (*šwrh*; Erfurt, Sens: *šdh* ["field"]) *and the
    next* [there must be] *twelve amot* [= M. 3:6H];

I. and so [the same rule applies] in [the case of a row of
    gourds which is to be planted in a field containing mostly]
    grain [following Lieberman[66]].

J. [A row] of grain [which is to be sown in a field containing
    mostly] vegetables [Lieberman[67] deletes:] of another kind --

K. [the row must measure] from one end of the field to the other
    [Erfurt, first printed ed. omit:] [in] length, by a width
    [of] three open furrows [= T. 2:1B].

L. [first printed ed. omits L-O] [A row] of vegetables [which is
    to be sown in a field containing mostly] vegetables of
    another [kind] --

M.   between one row and the next [there must be] six hand-
     breadths;

N.   [Sens omits:] and a row of grain [which is to be sown in
     a field containing mostly grain of another kind (Lieber-
     man[68])] --

O.   [the row must measure] *three open furrows* in width [= M. 2:6B].

                              T. Kil. 2:13 (pp. 211-212, ll. 48-54)
                              (B: Y. Kil. 2:10 (28b))

      T. Kil. 2:13 comments upon and supplements M. 3:7, which
concerns planting gourds among vegetables and grain. T. is
divided into three parts, A-F, G-I+L-M, and J-K+N-O, which
differ from one another both in their subjects and in the concerns of their apodoses. A-F deals with sowing a single row
of gourds or vegetables in a field of another kind, and its
apodoses concern the linear dimensions of the minimum area which
must be covered by that row. G-I+L-M concern sowing rows of
gourds or vegetables in a field containing a different kind, and
its apodoses are interested in the distance which must separate
the rows from one another. J-K+N-O discuss sowing a single row
of grain in a field of a different kind, and its apodoses deal
with the minimum dimensions of such a row in terms of the measure
ofthe field and its furrows.

      A-F consists of three well-balanced declarative sentences.
The protases (A,C,E) all follow the pattern of *śwrh śl* X *bY* (with
A adding *kyrq* from M. 3:7A and C presenting the pattern twice).
The apodoses (B,D,F) also follow a single pattern, reading
'rk X *w/ᶜl rwḥb* Y. B and D are identical, for both are vebatim
citations of M. 3:3F.

      A-F comments on M. 3:7A-C. A states that a row of gourds
which is to be planted among vegetables is considered as a row
of vegetables which is to be sown among vegetables of a different
kind. B explains that the row of gourds requires an area of
six handbreadths square, as does a row of vegetables according
to the ruling of ᶜAqiva in M. 3:3F. T. then supplements M. 3:7A,
which concerns planting an area of gourds among vegetables, with
a discussion of planting a row of gourds in a vegetable-field.
T. thus links M. 3:7A to M. 3:6 (planting a row of gourds among
vegetables) and M. 3:3 (sowing of a row of vegetables among
vegetables of another kind). According to C-D a row of either
gourds (this reading better fits the context than that of "chate
melons") or vegetables which is to be sown in a field of grain
must measure ten-and-one-half *amot* by six handbreadths. Now

ten-and-one-half *amot* is the measure of one side of a *bet rova*^{c}
(T. 2:6B), so that the length of the row must equal that of a
side of a *bet rova*^{c}, while its width must measure six handbreadths. It appears, then, that in combining these two
measures, T. attempts to harmonize M. 3:7B, which says that an
area of gourds planted among grain must measure a *bet rova*^{c}
(taking B to refer to a row), and M. 3:7C-D,which rules that a
row of gourds planted in a field of grain must cover an area
measuring six handbreadths square. In speaking of rows of vegetables as well, T. may at the same time attempt to harmonize
M. 2:10E(4), which says that vegetables sown among grain must
be given a *bet rova*^{c}, and M. 2:10F, where Eliezer/Eleazar says
that in such an instance the vegetables require an area measuring
only six handbreadths square (again interpreting both rules as
referring to rows). In presenting the same rule (i.e., that a
row must measure ten-and-one-half *amot*) for both gourds and
vegetables, T. follows ^{c}Aqiva's view (M. 3:6) that gourds are to
be treated as vegetables. Finally, E-F clarifies A by presenting
the rule for vegetables sown among vegetables of another kind,
which, of course, is identical to that of A-B (= M. 3:3F).

G-I+L-M are also composed of declarative sentences. G and
L balance one another (*šl dl^{c}wyn byrq vs. šl yrq byrq 'ḥr*) as
do H and M (*štym ^{c}šrh 'mh vs. ššh tpḥym*). I glosses G-H and
depends on it for both its subject ("A row of gourds") and its
apodosis. According to G-H a row or field (i.e., several rows[69])
of gourds planted in a field of vegetables must be separated by
a distance of twelve *amot*. G-H then simply restates the ruling
of sages in M. 3:6H in terms of A-B (a row of gourds planted
among vegetables). I adds that the same rule holds in the case
of rows of gourds which are planted in a field of grain (following Lieberman; we have interpolated accordingly). I then applies
the rule of M. 3:6H to the case of C-D (a row of gourds planted
in a field of grain). L-M states that rows of vegetables of one
kind sown in a vegetable field of another kind must be separated
from one another by six handbreadths. This rule follows from
E-F, for if the vegetables between the rows must be allowed an
area measuring six handbreadths square, then the rows will be
separated by six handbreadths. L-M restates E-F in terms of the
consideration of the distance between rows. G-I+L-M then goes
over the cases of A-F and reads into them the question of the
distance required to separate the rows, which is introduced by
sages in M. 3:6H. Since A-F comments on M. 3:7A-C, T. 2:13 G-I+
L-M effectively link M. 3:6H to M. 3:7A-C.

J-K+N-O deal with sowing a row of grain in a field of
a different kind, and so supplement the foregoing two units,
which concern sowing rows of gourds and vegetables. According
to J-K a row of grain sown among vegetables must extend for the
entire length of the field, and its width must equal that of
three open furrows. J-K then applies the rule of T. 2:1B, which
concerns the minimum size of rows of different kinds sown adjacent to one another, to the case of a row of grain sown in a field
of vegetables. N-O states that a row of grain sown among a
different kind of grain (so Lieberman; we have interpolated
accordingly) must be as wide as the width of three open furrows.
N-O thus assigns the rule of House of Shammai in M. 2:6B, which
concerns the minimum size of adjacent rows of different kinds,
to the case of a row of grain sown among grain of a different
kind. N-O, however, basically repeats J-K, and it is therefore
probable that, following Sens, we should omit it.

A. All the same are [Lieberman,[70] following Erfurt, corrects
   '*ht* to '*hd*] a row of chate melons, and a row of gourds, and
   a row of watermelons, and a row of musk melons, and a row
   of cowpeas --
B. [Erfurt adds: and he who; GRA[71] adds: and one who (*w'hd*)]
   allows a single stalk [= omitted by Erfurt] [of any of
   these kinds] to grow [for the sake of its] seed [besides
   a row of the same kind (HD)],
C. [GRA adds: he must allow the stalk a space measuring a
   bet rova[c]] and [= omitted by Erfurt; GRA: or] he must
   make [between the row and the stalk] a partition ten
   handbreadths high and [with] its width [measuring] four
   handbreadths.

T. Kil. 2:14 (p. 212, ll. 55-57)

(B-C: Y. Kil. 3:6 (29a)[72])

T. Kil. 2:14 supplements M. 3:7J-K, for both pericopae
concern the sowing of seed near trailing plants. A-C, with the
order of A-B reversed, forms a declarative sentence. According
to A-C one who, for the sake of its seed, allows a single stalk
of any kind of trailing plant to grow beside a row of the same
kind (HD) must erect a partition between them.[73] The point of
T. is that even if the plants adjoining one another are of the
same kind, and even if only a single stalk adjoins the row, that
single stalk is considered diverse-kinds with the plants in the
row, if the former is planted for its seed while the latter are

planted for their greens. T. thus supplements in two ways
Ishmael's saying in M. 3:7J-K, which states that one may not
bring seed into an area already containing three gourds. First,
T. rules concerning all kinds of trailing plants and not only
gourds, and T. concerns rows rather than individual plants. T.
may then intend to link M. 3:7J-K with M. 3:4, for the latter
deals with rows of the same kinds of trailing plants as those
mentioned in T.[74] Second, T. interprets "seed" (zr^c) to mean
not merely anything which is sown (as we have interpreted zr^c to
mean in the context of M. 3:7J-K)[75] but specifically that which
is sown for the sake of its seed (as in M. 3:2).[76] With this
interpretation of "seed," T. effectively contradicts the point
of Ishmael's saying. Ishmael presumably reasons that no seed
may be introduced into a field planted with three gourds because
the latter could spread out over the newly-sown plants and so
produce the appearance of diverse-kinds. The point of T., on
the other hand, is that the purpose for which the plants are
sown determines whether or not they are considered diverse-kinds
with one another, regardless of whether or not there is an
appearance of diverse-kinds.[77]

A. A gentile who grafted a peach [bud] onto a quince [tree]
    ($^cwb\check{s}$; Erfurt: ^cwgs ["pear"]) [Y.: (Concerning) a gentile
    who grafted (the bud of) a nut (tree) onto a peach (tree)] --
B. even though he [first printed ed., Y. add: an Israelite;
    Lieberman[78] comments: the gentile] is not [himself] per-
    mitted to do so [i.e., to perform such a graft],
C. he [i.e., the Israelite] takes a shoot [= omitted by Erfurt
    and first printed ed.] from it and [Y. adds: goes and]
    plants it [Erfurt, first printed ed. add: again] in another
    place.
D. [If a gentile] grafted a spinach-beet onto an amaranth
    ($yrbwz$; first printed ed.: $yrbh$; Y. $drkwn$ or $drbwn$ (PM)
    [= T. 1:11B] --
E. even though the Israelite [= omitted by Erfurt] is not
    [himself] permitted to do so [i.e., to perform such a graft],
F. he [i.e., the Israelite] takes a seed from it and sows it
    in another place.

T. Kil. 2:15 (p. 212, 11. 56-60)

(Y. Kil. 1:4 (27a))

T. Kil. 2:15, together with T. 2:16 (which follows), form
an autonomous subunit dealing with the secondary problem of

benefitting from diverse-kinds grown by others.   These
pericopae thus provide a fitting conclusion to T.'s discussion
of diverse-kinds of seeds in Chapters One and Two.   T. 2:15
is a unitary pericope composed of two parts, A-C and D-F.   A-C
concerns the grafting of a tree bud onto a different tree,
while D-F deals with grafting a vegetable onto a plant of a
different kind (following the sequence of M. 1:7).   The two sections are well-balanced, for each of the three clauses of A-C
is almost identical with each of the corresponding clauses of
D-F.

A describes the case of a gentile who performed a graft of
a peach-bud onto a quince tree, a graft which is presumably
prohibited on account of diverse-kinds.   According to B-D an
Israelite may plant a shoot from the hybrid tree, even though
he may not perform the graft itself.[79]   Similarly, D-F states
that an Israelite may sown the seeds of an amaranth which a
gentile has hybridized with a spinach-beet, even though again
the Israelite is prohibited from performing such a graft (T.
1:11B).   The point of T., then, is that one may reproduce a
hybrid which results from a graft performed by a gentile (who
is presumably not prohibited from grafting diverse-kinds), even
though one may not initially produce the hybrid on account of
diverse-kinds.

A.   An Israelite who allowed diverse-kinds to grow in his field --
B.   his brothers [= omitted by Erfurt] the priests do not
     enter it,
C.   but rather consider it [i.e., the diverse-kinds] as a sign
     [Lieberman[80] following Erfurt and OZ, reads *kṣywn* for *bṣywn*]
     [indicating] a graveyard.
D.   They do not produce diverse-kinds with an Israelite [i.e.,
     in the field of an Israelite (Lieberman[81])] [first printed
     ed.: with a gentile[82]] [B. A.Z. 63b: They do not hoe
     (*'yn ᶜwdryn*) diverse-kinds with a gentile],
E.   but they uproot diverse-kinds with him [i.e., they uproot
     diverse-kinds in his field without his permission (Lieber-
     man[83])],
F.   because he diminishes the impropriety (*tplh*; Erfurt, Y.:
     ᶜ*brh* ["transgression"]).
G.   They do not produce diverse-kinds with a gentile [i.e., in
     the fields of a gentile (Lieberman[84])] [Y. adds: either
     diverse-kinds of the vineyard or diverse-kinds of seeds].

H. And in the towns surrounded [Y. adds: by the land
   of Israel], such as Bet ^CAnah [Erfurt: Bat ^CAnah], 'Emah
   [Erfurt, first printed ed.: 'Umah], and its neighbors,
I. they produce diverse-kinds with a gentile.
J. Just as diverse-kinds [are prohibited] in the Land [of
   Israel], so are diverse-kinds [prohibited] outside of the
   Land [of Israel].

> T. Kil. 2:16 (p. 212, ll. 60-65)
> (D-F: B. A.Z. 63b; D-I: Y. Orl.
> 3:7 (63b))

   T. Kil. 2:16 continues the discussion of T. 2:15 concerning
secondary issues of diverse-kinds. T. is divided into two
autonomous parts, A-C and D-J. A-C discusses the significance
of the growth of diverse-kinds in an Israelite's field. D-J,
perhaps continuing T. 2:15's interest in the issue of deriving
benefit from diverse-kinds, concerns the question of sowing
diverse-kinds for an Israelite or a gentile.

   A-C states its law in an apocopated sentence, for the subject
shifts from "the Israelite" in A to "his brothers the priests"
in B. According to A-C priests may not enter a field containing diverse-kinds. The assumption behind this rule is that an
Israelite will always uproot diverse-kinds, unless the circumstances are such that he cannot use them. Since he has in fact
allowed the diverse-kinds to grow, it follows that he did so
only because he could not otherwise derive benefit from them,
and it is therefore presumed that the area is a graveyard (cf.
M. Oh. 18:2-3). The growth of diverse-kinds in an Israelite
field is thus taken to be a sign of a graveyard, and priests
may not enter the field.

   D-J is divided into two parts, D-F and G-J. D and G balance
one another, for they differ only in that D has "Israelite"
while G has "gentile." E-F glosses D (with the subject changing
from plural to singular in F), while H-I qualifies G, with I
balancing and opposing the latter. J then supplements H-I.
According to D one may not grow diverse-kinds (presumably for pay)
with an Israelite, i.e., in the field of an Israelite (Lieberman).
The point of T., then, is that one may not profit from growing
diverse-kinds, even if they are grown in the field of another.[85]
E-F adds that one may uproot diverse-kinds in the field of an
Israelite without his permission (Lieberman),[86] for in this way
one lessens the wrong done by the owner of the field.[87]

   G expands the ruling of D, stating that one may not grow
diverse-kinds in the field of a gentile. Qualifying G, H-I

maintains that one may grow diverse-kinds in a gentile's field
which is located in a gentile city surrounded by the land of
Israel, such as Bet^{C}Anah and 'Emah.[88] These cities are not
considered part of the land of Israel (Lieberman;[89] cf. T. Ah.
18:4), so that one may help a gentile grow diverse-kinds in
them. If we now interpret G in the light of H-I, then the point
of G is that one may not grow diverse-kinds with a gentile in
the land of Israel, for diverse-kinds may not be grown by an
Israelite in the Land, regardless of who owns the field in
question.[90] J, which is autonomous of the foregoing, reverses
the rule of H-I by stating that the law of diverse-kinds apply
both inside and outside of the land of Israel. J then agrees
with M. Qid. 1:9, which states that all commandments which depend
on the land of Israel are not observed outside of it, except
for the laws ^{C}orlah and diverse-kinds.[91]

KILAYIM CHAPTER FOUR

Chapter Four opens M.'s discussion of diverse-kinds of the
vineyard. The chapter consists of two large formal units,
M. 4:1-3 (with M. 4:4 appended to it) and M. 4:5-9. At the head
of each unit stands a pair of Houses-disputes which generates the
law of the chapter. The chapter accordingly concerns two major
themes. M. 4:1-3Q deals with sowing seed in a cleared space within or at the edge of a vineyard, while M. 4:5-7 defines a vineyard in terms of the number of vines and rows it must contain.
M. 4:8-9 both supplements M. 4:5-6 and returns to the concerns
of M. 4:1-3Q with a discussion of sowing seed between rows of
vines. In addition, M. 4:3R-U + M. 4:4 form a small subunit
dealing with rules pertaining to partitions. Now we might have
expected the chapter to begin with its most fundamental rule, the
definition of a vineyard (M. 4:5-7), and then to proceed with a
discussion of sowing seed between rows of vines (M. 4:8-9,
following M. 4:5-7 both formally [opening with $hnwt^c$] and
thematically [dealing with rows]) and cleared areas (M. 4:1-3Q).
The redactor, however, chose to open the chapter with M. 4:1-3Q,
presumably in order to consider, in a logical sequence, the
planting of seeds and vines in separate areas (M. 4:1-3Q) and the
planting of seeds among vines (M. 4:8-9). The definition of a
vineyard in terms of vines and rows thus serves to introduce the
latter section.

M. 4:1-3 consists of a pair of Houses-disputes followed by a
tightly constructed series of glosses in a question-and-answer
pattern. In M. 4:1 the Houses-dispute concerning the minimum
area which a bald spot or an outer space of a vineyard must have
in order to be sown with another kind. The rest of the unit
(M. 4:1G-4:3Q) defines these areas and clarifies the law for each
according to the viewpoint of the House of Hillel. M. 4:3R-U +
M. 4:4 then present several rules concerning partitions.
M. 4:3R-U, following the question-and-answer pattern of
M. 4:1-3Q, offers the minimum measurements which a fence or a
ditch must have in order to be considered a valid partition,
while M. 4:4 discusses partitions which contain gaps. The redactor
has apparently appended this subunit to M. 4:1-3Q only because
the fence is mentioned in connection with the definition of an
outer space (as the area between the fence and the vineyard).

The substance of the subunit, however, is not related to that
of M. 4:1-3Q, and, in fact, does not specifically discuss issues
of diverse-kinds, for it deals simply with rules concerning
partitions.

M. 4:5-9 constitutes a distinct formal unit in that each of
its pericopae begins with the present participle *hnwṭ^c*. M. 4:5
opens with a Houses-dispute concerning the definition of a vineyard. House of Shammai say that a row of five vines is considered
a vineyard, while House of Hillel disagree, maintaining (according to a gloss) that a vineyard consists of two rows. A second
Houses-dispute, which discusses the same issue in another context (the sanctification of a vineyard by the sowing of another
kind), follows. M. 4:6 and M. 4:7 then carry forward the view
of House of Hillel. M. 4:6 discusses how the five vines of
M. 4:5 are arranged in the two rows, and M. 4:7 deals with the
secondary question of combining two separated rows of vines to
form a vineyard.

Continuing the discussion of rows of vines and returning
to the concerns of M. 4:1-3Q, M. 4:8-9 deals with sowing seeds
between rows of vines. M. 4:8 discusses sowing seed between
individual rows arranged in sets of two or three. According
to M. three rows must be set apart by more space than is necessary
to separate two rows, presumably because there is a greater
tendency for the appearance of diverse-kinds to develop in the
former case. M. 4:9 then concerns sowing seeds between rows of
a vineyard. An anonymous opinion maintains that the rule of
M. 4:8, which applies to the spacing of three rows, also obtains
in the case of a vineyard, while Meir and Simeon disagree, saying
that the rows of a vineyard are to be separated according to the
rule which applies to two rows.

4:1-3

A. [The] bald spot (*qrḥt*) of the vineyard --
B. House of Shammai say, "[It need measure] twenty-four *amot*
   [square (following Sens, Bert.)]."
C. House of Hillel say, "[It need measure only] sixteen *amah*
   [P: *amot* (throughout)] [square]."
D. [The] outer space [so Danby for *mḥwl*] of the vineyard --
E. House of Shammai say, "[It need measure] sixteen *amah*."
F. House of Hillel say, "[It need measure only] twelve *amah*."
G. And what is [the] bald spot of the vineyard?
H. [Danby: The part of] a vineyard which is bare [so Danby for
   ḥrb] in its middle (*m'mṣ^c w*; Sn: *b'mṣ^c w*).

I. If there are not there [i.e., in the bald spot] sixteen
   amah [square of space], [then] he shall not put seed
   into it.

J. [If] there were there [i.e., in the bald spot] sixteen *amah*
   [square of space], [then] they allow it [i.e., the vineyard]
   its area of tillage and he sows the rest.

M. Kil. 4:1 (B. Erub. 3b, 93a)

K. What is [the] outer space of the vineyard?

L. [The area] between the vineyard and the fence.

M. If there are not there [i.e., in the outer space] twelve
   amah [of space], [then] he shall not put seed into it.

N. [If] there were there [i.e., in the outer space] twelve *amah*
   [of space], [then] they allow it [i.e., the vineyard]
   its area of tillage and he sows the rest.

M. Kil. 4:2 (B. Erub. 3b, 93a)

O. R. Judah says, "This [i.e., the space between the vineyard
   and the fence] is only [the area of] the fence of the
   vineyard.

P. "And what is the outer space of the vineyard?

Q. "[The area] between two vineyards."

R. What is [considered] a fence?

S. [A fence] which is ten handbreadths high.

T. And [what is considered] a ditch?

U. [A ditch] which is ten [handbreadths] deep and four wide.

M. Kil. 4:3

   M. Kil. 4:1-3 concerns the minimum size which an area in a
vineyard must have in order to be sown with another kind (e.g.,
grain or vegetables). The forms of the unit are highly disciplined.
A-C and D-F present two parallel, balanced Houses-disputes, the
numbers of which, taken together, occur in descending order
according to the sequence a-b-b-c (twenty-four *vs.* sixteen,
sixteen *vs.* twelve). G-J and K-N then balance one another in
respectively glossing A-C and D-F. G-H and K-L both appear in
a question-and-answer pattern, while I-J and M-N form nearly
identical sets of conditional sentences (differing only in that
the former has sixteen while the latter has twelve), with the
protases within each set balancing one another (*'yn šm vs. hyw
šm*). The apodoses of the sentences in each set, however, do not
all correspond to one another, and differ in that the verbs of I

and M appear in the imperfect tense, while those of J and N are
phrased in present participles (l' yby' zr^c $l\v{s}m$ $vs.$ $nwtnyn$ lw
^cbwdtw $wzwr^c$ $'t$ $hmwtr^1$).   In O-Q Judah glosses and opposes K-L,
following in P-Q the question-and-answer pattern of G-H and K-L.
R-S, repeating the same pattern, glosses O, and T-U similarly
supplements R-S.

In A-C and D-F the Houses dispute concerning the minimum size
which areas in and around a vineyard must have in order to be
sown with a different kind.   These areas must cover a certain
amount of space so that the crops sown within them appear to grow
in fields unto themselves and therefore do not produce the appearance of diverse-kinds with the vines.   A-C concerns the bald spot
($qr\d{h}t^2$) of the vineyard, or (according to the gloss at G-H) its
bare inner area, while D-F deals with the vineyard's outer space
($m\d{h}wl^3$), or (according to the gloss at K-L) the area between
the vineyard and the fence.   I and M then restate the views óf
House of Hillel (C and F) in a negative way ("If there are not
there X $amah$"), while J and N rephrase the same rule in an
affirmative manner ("[If] there are there X $amah$").   J and N,
however, do not simply repeat I and M, for, instead of balancing
the latter with the apodosis "he shall put seed into it," J and
N have a more complex apodosis, "they allow it its area of tillage
and he sows the rest."   J and N thus introduce a new consideration
into the pericope, the area of tillage, saying that this area
must separate the vines and the crops sown in the bald spot or
outer space.[4] The reasoning behind the rule appears to be that the
vines must have sufficient space to spread out without becoming
entangled with the crops.   Alternatively, the point of the rule
may be that the vines and crops must be separated from one
another in order to avoid the appearance of diverse-kinds.   We
note that I and M do not relate anything new, and so appear to
be necessary only to introduce, respectively, J and N.

In O-Q Judah disagrees with the gloss at L, saying that the
area between the vineyard and the fence is not the outer space
of the vineyard, but merely the area adjacent to the fence.   The
outer space, rather, is the area between two vineyards.[5]   Judah
thus apparently agrees with L that the $m\d{h}wl$ discussed by the
Houses signifies a border of the vineyard, but he maintains that
this border lies outside of the vineyard and not within its
fences.   R-U then glosses O, describing the minimum dimensions
which a fence or ditch must have in order (according to context,
since R-U itself makes no mention of diverse-kinds) to separate
a vineyard from another kind.   R-U is thus only indirectly
relevant to O, for, although both discuss the fence of the

vineyard, the latter concerns the area between the fence and
the vines while the former deals with the dimensions of the
fence (or the ditch) itself.

A. *What is [the] bald spot of the vineyard?*
B. *A vineyard the middle of which is bare* [= M. 4:1G-H],
C. and there remained in it [i.e., the vineyard] five
    [following Lieberman[6]], five vines [i.e., sets of five
    vines] [Y.: and there remained in it enough (vines to
    constitute) a vineyard],
D. whether [they are found] on [each of] four [Erfurt omits:]
    sides, or [each of] three sides, or [each of] two sides,
E. one [set of vines] opposite the other.
F. *What is the outer space (mḥwl) of the vineyard?*
G. "[*The area] between two vineyards* [= M. 4:3P-Q]," the words
    of R. Judah.
H. And sages say, "*If there are not there [i.e., in the
    outer space] twelve amot, he shall not put seed into it.*
I. "[*If] there were there [i.e., in the outer space] twelve
    amot, they allow it [i.e., the vineyard] its area of tillage
    and he sows the rest* [= M. 4:2M-N]."

T. Kil. 3:1 (p. 213, ll. 1-5)

(A-d: Y. Kil. 4:1 (29c))

    T. Kil. 3:1 comments on M. 4:1-3, with A-E discussing the
bald spot of the vineyard and F-I dealing with the vineyard's
outer space. A-E complements M.'s concern with the minimum
size of a bald spot with a discussion of the minimum amount of
vines which a vineyard with a bald spot must have in order to
continue to be considered a vineyard. A-B cites M. 4:1G-H,
which C+E then augment, with D apparently interpolated between
C and E. According to C a vineyard containing a bald spot must
have sets of five vines on opposite sides (G) in order to continue to be regarded as a vineyard. D clarifies C+E by stating
that the sets of five vines need remain on only two sides of
the vineyard, and need not be found on all four sides.

    F-I presents an apparent dispute concerning the outer space
of the vineyard between Judah, cited at M. 4:3P-Q, and sages,
who are assigned the anonymous opinion of M. 4:2M-N. Judah and
sages, however, do not actually dispute, for Judah discusses
the location of the outer space while sages define its minimum
size. Rather, in juxtaposing the two views T. applies the rule
of M. 4:2M-N (which in M. is attached to M. 4:2K-L's view of

the location of the outer space) to Judah's definition of an
outer space at M. 4:3P-Q. The same law now applies to both of
M.'s descriptions of an outer space.[7]

A. There is in respect to (b) [the law of] the partition of the
    vineyard [a side which enables one] to rule more leniently,
    and [a side which enables one] to rule more stringently [than
    he would in the absence of a partition].
B. How so?
C. [If the] partition is near the vines, he sows outside of it
    [i.e., the partition] until he reaches the base ($^c yqr$) of
    the partition.
D. [In this case one thus rules more leniently,] for were
    there no partition, they [Erfurt: he] would allow the vine-
    yard four *amot* [Lieberman,[8] following Erfurt and first
    printed ed., omits *mǝwkh* here] [Erfurt omits:] and he would
    sow the rest [B. Erub. adds: And this is the partition of
    the vineyard (which enables one) to rule more leniently].
E. [If the partition] extended [around the vineyard] at a
    distance of eleven *amot* [from it], he shall not put seed
    into it [i.e., the area between the partition and the
    vineyard].
F. [In this case one thus rules more stringently,] for were
    there no partition, he would allow the vineyard four *amot*
    and sow the rest [B. Erub. adds: And this is the partition
    of the vineyard (which enables one) to rule more stringently].

                    T. Kil. 3:2 (p. 213, 11. 5-10)
                    (B. Erub. 93a)

T. Kil. 3:2 supplements M. 4:3R-U, which discusses the partition separating grain or vegetables from a vineyard. A serves
as the superscription of the pericope. B introduces C-F, which
consists of two declarative sentences (C and E), each followed
by the identical conditional sentence (D and F). C-D and E-F
illustrate A. In C-D the partition allows one to rule leniently,
for one may sow another kind even up to the base of a partition
standing within the vineyard's area of tillage, which normally
may not be sown. In E-F the partition stands eleven *amot* away
from the vines and creates an outer space (M. 4:2K-L). Following
the rule of M. 4:2M-N, E says that one may not put seed into the
outer space, for it measures less than twelve *amot* wide. The
presence of the partition now causes one to rule more stringently,
for were the partition absent one could sow another kind up to a

point just four *amot* away from the vineyard. The point of
T., then, is that the location of the partition determines whether
the distance between the vineyard and the other kind must be
greater or less than four *amot*, the vineyard's area of tillage.

4:4

A. The partition of reeds --
B. if there are not between [one] reed and the next three
    handbreadths,
C. [i.e.,] sufficient (*kdy*) [space] so that a kid may enter
    (*ykns*; S, MS read *yzdqr* ["leap through"]),
D. lo, this is [considered] as a [valid (Danby)] partition.
E. And a fence which was breached --
F. [if the breach measures] up to ten *amot* [wide],
G. lo, this is [considered] as an opening [and the fence is
    still considered a valid divider];
H. [if the breach measures] more than this [i.e., ten *amot*],
I. opposite the breach it is prohibited [to sow a kind
    different from that on the other side of the fence].
J. [If] many breaches were breached in it [i.e., the fence] --
K. if the [combined measure (Maim., *Comm.*, TYY) of the parts
    of the fence which remain] standing exceeds the [combined
    measure of those parts which were] breached,
L. it is permitted [to sow diverse-kinds on opposite sides
    of the fence];
M. and if the [combined measure of those parts which were]
    breached exceeds the [combined measure of the parts which
    remain] standing,
N. opposite the breach it is prohibited [to sow a kind different
    from that sown on the other side of the fence].

M. Kil. 4:4
(E-N: T. Erub 6(9):13-14[9])

M. Kil. 4:4 continues the interest of M. 4:3R-U in the
divider which separates diverse-kinds. Like M. 4:3R-U, M. 4:4
deals in a general way with rules concerning partitions and has
no particular reference to issues of diverse-kinds (cf. the
parallels to E-N at T. Erub.). M. is composed of two autonomous
parts, A-D and E-N, both of which concern dividers containing
gaps. A-D deals with a partition of reeds, while E-N discusses
a fence which has been breached.

    A-D forms a declarative sentence, with A serving as a protasis,
B+D constituting a conditional clause, and C glossing B. According

to A-B+D a partition made of reeds may not have gaps which measure
three or more handbreadths wide, for then the reeds would not be
regarded as forming a continuous divider. A space smaller than
three handbreadths, though, is not seen as affecting the compact-
ness of the partition (Maim., *Comm.*, Sens, following B. and Y.[10]),
so that a partition containing such gaps is considered valid.
C adds that a gap in the partition must be small enough so as not
to allow a kid to break through it.[11] C thus defines the
validity of the partition in terms of its function, stating that
a partition is considered valid only if it serves to set apart
the enclosed area, e.g., by keeping out animals.

E-N is a unitary composition consisting of two large constructions of declarative sentences, E-I (concerning the fence with
one breach) and J-N (discussing the fence with many breaches).
The two units balance one another, for each is composed of a
protasis (E and J [with J dependent on E]) and a pair of conditional clauses (F-G+H-I, K-L+M-N). In addition both units end
with the same apodosis (I and N). E-I and J-N are also internally
balanced, for within each pair of conditional clauses the protases
(though not the apodoses) correspond to one another (F *vs.* H
[(^{c}d/^{c}śr 'mwt *vs.* ytr mkn] and K *vs.* M (^{c}wmd + prwṣ *vs.* prwṣ +
^{c}wmd]).

F-G describes a case in which a fence contains a gap measuring
up to ten *amot* wide. Such a breach is regarded as an opening in
the fence rather than as an interruption of it, so that the
fence is still considered a valid partition.[12] In H-I, on the
other hand, the breach is wider than ten *amot*, and so is seen as
breaking the continuity of the fence. Now we might expect that
a large breach would invalidate the entire fence as a partition
(with the apodosis reading simply *'swr*), since the fence no longer
sets apart the entire area. I, however, states that it is
prohibited to sow diverse-kinds only on opposite sides of the
breach itself. I thus implies that it is permitted to sow diverse-
kinds on opposite sides of a breached fence where the fence
remains standing, for in these places the fence still functions
as a divider (Sens, GRA).[13] I therefore takes an intermediate
position (with the apodosis, kngd hprṣ *'swr*, a development of the
simple apodosis *'swr*), for it neither completely prohibits nor
completely permits the sowing of different kinds on opposite
sides of the fence.

In J-N the fence has been breached in many places.[14] According
to K-N one must determine whether or not the greater part of the
fence remains standing (Maim., *Comm.*, TYY). If most of the
fence still stands, the fence is considered a valid divider (K-L)

and diverse-kinds may be sown even opposite the breaches (Sens, GRA). If, on the other hand, most of the fence has been breached, one may not sow diverse-kinds opposite the breaches (M-N). Like I, N implies that one may still sow different kinds where the fence remains standing (Sens, GRA), and so again takes an inter-mediate position (with the same apodosis[15]).

We now turn to consider the relationship between the rules of A-D and E-N. A-D concerns the partition of reeds, which is, in effect, an example of the partition with many breaches described in J-N. A-D and J-N, however, do not present the same criteria for determining the validity of such a partition. A-D states that the gaps between the reeds may not be greater than three handbreadths, while J-N rules that the combined measure of the breaches may not exceed that of the standing parts of the parti-tion. A-D and J-N thus differ in that A-D is concerned with the width of the individual breaches, while J-N is interested in the combined measure of the breaches relative to that of the standing parts of the partition.[16]

A. The partition of a vineyard which was breached --
B. they say to him [i.e., the owner of the vineyard], "Repair (*gdwr*) [it]."
C. [If] he repaired it [= omitted by B. B.Q.] and it was breached [B. B.B. adds: again (*ḥzrh wnprṣh*)],
D. they say to him, "Repair [it]."
E. If [= omitted by Erfurt] he became lax [so Lieberman[17] for *nty'š*] as to [repairing] it [i.e., the breached partition] [B. B.Q. adds: and did not repair it (again)],
G. lo, this one has sanctified (*qdš*) [i.e., prohibited the use (so Bokser[18] for *qdš*) of the grain or vegetables which adjoin the vineyard] and is answerable for it [so Danby[19] for *ḥyyb b'hrywth*] [i.e., he is liable for the loss of the other kinds which adjoin the vineyard (MB)].

T. Kil. 3:3a (p. 213, ll. 9-11)
(B. B.Q. 100a-100b, B. B.B. 2a-2b)

T. Kil. 3:3a supplements M. 4:4 with a discussion of the liability for damages resulting from the breaching of a partition, an issue which M. does not raise in its consideration of the breached partition. T. consists of three declarative sentences, A-B (with subject and object in inverted order), C-D, and E-F, with two apodoses, B and D, identical to one another. T. describes a case in which one person's vineyard is surrounded by a partition

and is adjoined by another person's field of grain or vegetables
(cf. B. B.Q. 100a-100b, B. B.B. 2a-2b, and Lieberman, *TZ*, p. 210,
on 1. 10). According to A-D the owner of the vineyard is responsible for repairing the partition regardless of how many times
it may be breached. E-F then states that if at some time the
owner of the vineyard fails to repair the breach he is liable
for the grains or vegetables which become sanctified by the vineyard[20] and which therefore may not be used by their owner (MB;
cf. Maim., *Comm.* to M. 4:5). The point of T. thus is that the
owner of the vineyard is responsible for maintaining the partition
which separates the vines from other kinds, for if the partition
is breached his vineyard causes a loss to the owner of the adjacent field.

4:5

A. He who plants a row of five vines --

B. House of Shammai say, "[It is considered] a vineyard."

C. House of Hillel, say, "[It is] not [considered] a vineyard,

D. "unless there are two rows."

E. Therefore,

F. he who sows [within the] four *amot* which are [allotted as
    the area of tillage] in the vineyard--

G. House of Shammai say, "He has sanctified [i.e., prohibited
    the use of (Bokser;[21] cf. also Maim., *Comm.*)] one row
    [of vines]."

H. House of Hillel say, "He has sanctified [i.e., prohibited
    the use of] two rows [of vines]."

> M. Kil. 4:5 (E-H: Y. Kil. 4:1 (29b);
> F-H: M. Ed. 5:2[22])

M. Kil. 4:5 concerns the definition of a vineyard. M. consists
of two Houses-disputes, A-D and F-H, joined by E. The super-
scriptions of the two disputes are somewhat balanced, for both
open with a present participle (*hnwṭ* vs. *hzwr*) and both contain
four words. Each dispute is internally well-balanced, for A-D
has *krm* vs. *'ynw krm*, while F-H reads *šwrh 'ht* vs. *šty šwrwt*. In
A-D the Houses-dispute concerning the way in which vines must be
arranged in order to constitute a vineyard, and so to require four
amot, (= twenty-four handbreadths) rather than six handbreadths,
as an area of tillage (Maim., *Comm.*, Ribmas, and others; cf.
M. 3:7, 6:1). House of Shammai say that a vineyard consists of
only a single row of five vines, while House of Hillel maintain
in C that such an arrangement of vines is not considered a vineyard.

It is not clear from C, however, whether House of Hillel hold
that a vineyard must consist of more rows, more vines, or more
of each. D, glossing C, explains that House of Hillel require
a vineyard to contain two rows, apparently with a total of five
vines between them (cf. M. 4:6).

F-H is joined to A-D by *lpykk* ("therefore") which functions
as a conjunction, and so may be either autonomous of A-D and
appended to it, or, as we shall see, actually generated by that
dispute. F-H concerns the interpretation of the word "vineyard"
in Dt. 22:9: *You shall not sow your vineyard with two kinds of
seed, lest the whole yield be sanctified, the crop which you
have sown and the yield of the vineyard*. The Houses apparently
dispute concerning the number of rows of vines which constitute
a "vineyard," i.e., the area to be sanctified when another
kind is sown near an (actual) vineyard. House of Shammai say
that one row forms a "vineyard" and therefore is sanctified,
while House of Hillel maintain that the "vineyard" which is
sanctified consists of two rows (Maim., *Comm.*, Bert., GRA, MR).
The opinions of the Houses thus appear to presuppose a prior
definition of a "vineyard," so that F-H may depend on A-C. Alternatively, the two disputes are separate from one another and
simply phrase the same issue in different terms. In any event,
we note that D may have been added to A-C together with F-H,
for D allows House of Hillel in C to agree with the corresponding
view in H.

4:6

A. He who plants two [vines] opposite two [others] and one
    extending out [like a] tail [so Bokser[23] for *w'ḥt ywṣ'h znb*] --
B. lo, this is considered a vineyard,
C. [If there are] two [vines planted] opposite two [others] and
    one is between [two of the opposing vines],
D. or [if there are] two [vines planted] opposite two [others]
    and one is in the middle [i.e., equidistant from all
    four vines] --
E. this [i.e., the vines in these patterns] is not [considered]
    a vineyard,
F. unless there are two [vines planted] opposite two [others]
    and one extending out [like a] tail.

M. Kil. 4:6
(A: B. Sot. 43b, B. B.B. 14a)

M. Kil. 4:6 presupposes the opinion of House of Hillel in
M. 4:5 (MR), for it concerns the manner in which five vines are
to be arranged in two rows in order to form a vineyard. M. 4:6
is a unitary pericope composed of two parts, A-B and C-F, with
the latter glossing the former. A-B is slightly apocopated,
following the *he-who* formulary pattern, while C-F forms a conditional sentence[24] consisting of a double protasis (C+D), an
apodosis (E), and a gloss (F). A-B and C-E balance one another,
for A, C and D all contain the same number sequence (2-2-1),
differing only in their final clauses (*ywṣ'h znb vs. bntym vs.
b'mṣ[c]*). The apodoses, B and E, are fixed and so also balance
one another. F then repeats A.

According to A-B the five vines mentioned in M. 4:5C-D must
be arranged in such a way that two pairs of vines are set
opposite each other and the fifth vine extends outward from them.
A-B may be taken to mean either that the fifth vine is attached
to one of the rows (Sens, Ribmaṣ, Bert., TYY, TYT, GRA, PM;
cf. T. 3:3a; fig. 32[25]), or that it is located opposite the space
between the rows (Rashi to B. Sot. 43a, Maim., *Comm.*, KM to
Maim., *Code, Diverse-Kinds* 7:7, TYY [gives both interpretations],
TYT [gives both interpretations], MR; fig. 33).[26] The point of
A-B apparently is that five vines must be planted exclusively in
two rows. According to the first interpretation, then, the
fifth vine belongs to one of the two rows, while according to
the second explanation this vine, located outside of the set of
four vines but between the two rows, may be regarded as belonging
to either of the rows. C-F then rephrases the law of A-B in a
negative manner. C states that the fifth vine may not be planted
between two opposing vines, meaning either that this vine may not
be located between the vines themselves (Ribmaṣ, Maim., *Comm.*,
KM to Maim., *Code*, Kil. 7:8, TYY, TYT; fig. 34[27]), or that it
may not be planted opposite the space between the two vines (Bert.
[according to TYT], TYY [gives both interpretations]; fig. 35[28]).
According to D the fifth vine may also not be planted in the
middle of the four vines, or equidistant from all of them (figs.
36,[29] 37[30]).[31] In all of these instances the fifth vine is
located in the midst of the other four vines, and so does not
belong to either of the two rows.[32] Since the five vines are not
arranged in two rows alone, they are not regarded as constituting
a vineyard.

```
* * *              * * *
* *              * * *
```
FIGURE 32   FIGURE 33

```
*   *              * * *
* * *              * * *
```
FIGURE 34   FIGURE 35

```
*   *                *
 *               * * *
*   *                *
```
FIGURE 36   FIGURE 37

4:7

A. He who plants one row [of vines] in his own [field],

B. and one row [of vines also grows] in his neighbor's [field]--

C. and [even though (Maim., *Code, Diverse-Kinds* 7:5, TYY)] a private road or a public road are in the middle [i.e., between the two rows of vines] --

D. or a fence lower than ten handbreadths [separates the two rows of vines] --

E. lo, these [two rows] combine [to form a vineyard].

F. [If the fence] is higher than ten handbreadths,

G. they do not combine [to form a vineyard].

H. R. Judah says, "If [= omitted by B] he trained [so Danby for ^crsn] [the vines] over [the fence],

I. "lo, [the two rows of vines] combine [to form a vineyard]."

M. Kil. 4:7

M. Kil. 4:7, again presupposing House of Hillel's view (M. 4:5C-D) that two rows constitute a vineyard, discusses the question of combining two separated rows to form a vineyard. A-E is an apocopated sentence (with A in the *he-who* formulary pattern) consisting of a double protasis, A-B (with A and B balanced) and C+D, with A-B serving the two separate protases,

C and D. E functions as an apodosis for both sets of protases
(A-B+C, A-B+D). E-G then glosses and balances D-E (*nmwk vs.*
gbwh; *mṣtrpyn vs.* *'yn mṣtrpyn*), and is itself glossed by Judah
in H-I (with I balancing G).

In A-D two adjacent rows of vines which are owned by different
people are separated by either a public or private road on the
one hand, or a low fence on the other. These two rows combine
to form a vineyard, for separate ownership does not prevent the
vines from combining (A-B), while (taking C and D separately)
apparently neither a road nor a low fence is considered a valid
divider with regard to a vineyard.[33] F-G then states that if the
fence is higher than ten handbreadths, the two rows do not combine
to form a vineyard, for such a fence is considered a valid
divider.[34] In H-I Judah glosses F-G, saying that if the vines
are trained over the high fence the rows do combine to form a
vineyard, for the fence no longer serves to separate them.[35] We
note that F-G does not relate anything new, and so apparently
serves only to introduce H-I.

4:8

A. He who plants two rows [of vines] --
B. if [Geniza fragment,[36] K, Ox: and] there are not between
    them eight *amot*, he shall not put seed into it.
C. [If] there were three rows [of vines] --
D. if [C: and] there are not between one row and the next
    sixteen *amot*, he shall not put seed into it.
E. R. Eliezer b. Jacob says in the name of Ḥananiah b. Ḥakinai,
    "Even if the middle [row] was laid waste, and [Geniza
    fragments: if] there are not between one row and the next
    sixteen *amot*, he shall not put seed into it,
F. "though if [so Danby for *š'ylw*] from the outset he had
    planted [two rows], lo, this [i.e., sowing seed between the
    rows] is permitted with eight *amot* [between the rows]."

M. Kil. 4:8

M. Kil. 4:8 discusses sowing seeds between rows of vines, and
so returns to the interest of M. 4:1-3Q in sowing seeds in a vineyard. M. consists of two balanced (two *vs.* three; eight *vs.*
sixteen) sentences, A-B, a slightly apocopated sentence following
the *he-who* formulary pattern, and C-D, which forms a conditional
sentence.[37] Eliezer b. Jacob in the name of Ḥananiah b. Ḥakinai
then glosses A-D and E-F. According to A-B seed may be sown
between two rows of vines only if the rows are separated by eight

amot. The seed then grows in an area unto itself and does not produce the appearance of diverse-kinds with the nearby vines. C-D states that three rows must be set apart by sixteen *amot*, or twice as much space as must separate two rows, for since there are more vines, the seeds must be allowed twice as much area in order to avoid the appearance of diverse-kinds.

Alternatively, the commentaries interpret M. 4:8 in the light of M. 4:5-7, and regard M. as concerning the problem of the combining of rows to form a vineyard. Two rows which are separated by eight *amot* do not combine to form a vineyard, so that seed may be sown between them (with the allowance of six handbreadths per row as the area of tillage). Three rows, however, at first sight resemble a vineyard, and therefore must be separated by sixteen *amot* if they are not to combine and actually form a vineyard (Sens, Ribmas, Bert., MS, GRA; cf. also T. 3:3b, 3:5c).[38] This interpretation, however, does not follow the plain sense of M. 4:8, for M. deals with sowing seed between rows of vines, and does not discuss the issue of the combining of rows to form a vineyard. We therefore favor the first interpretation given above.

In E-F Eliezer b. Jacob, in the name of Ḥananiah b. Ḥakinai, describes a case which lies in a gray area between the cases of A-B and C-D. Three rows of vines are planted, but the middle one is laid waste, so that two rows remain. The problem deals with the distance which must separate these rows if seed is to be sown between them. Are these rows still to be separated by sixteen *amot*, since they originally formed part of a set of three rows, or need they be set apart by only eight *amot*, since they are now only two in number? Eliezer b. Jacob rules that the two remaining rows must be separated by sixteen *amot*, for only if they were planted as two rows at the outset could one separate them by eight *amot* alone (F). The point of Eliezer b. Jacob is that the actual planting of diverse-kinds determines the spacing of the rows, regardless of the appearance of diverse-kinds. While the remaining rows may be separated by only eight *amot* without producing the appearance of diverse-kinds, the same amount of the different kind as was originally sown between the three rows remains between the two rows, so that they must still be separated by sixteen *amot*.

4:9

A. He who plants his vineyard by [intervals of] sixteen *amah* [most mss.[39] omit *amah*], sixteen *amah* [i.e., in rows sixteen

amot apart (so Danby and all commentaries)] -- it is
permitted to put seed into it [i.e., the area between
the rows].

B.   Said R. Judah, "$m^c \delta h$ b: In Salmon one planted his vineyard
by [intervals of] sixteen [B, S, Sn add: amah], sixteen amah,

C.   "and he would turn the foliage [so Danby for $\delta^c r$] of two
rows to one side and sow the cleared land [so Danby for
nyr[40]].

D.   "And in the next year he would turn the foliage to another
place [i.e., to the area which he had sown in the previous
year] and sow the uncultivated land [so Danby for bwr[41]].

E.   "And the case came before sages and they permitted [his
actions]."

F.   R. Meir and R. Simeon say, "Even ('p) he who plants his
vineyard by [intervals of] eight [B, S, and B. B.B. add:
amot], eight amot [Cn, Geniza fragment,[42] L, O, Sn, and V
read only: eight amot] -- it is permitted [to put seed
into the area between the rows]."

M. Kil. 4:9
(A-B: B. B.B. 82b; C: B. B.B.
83a)

Continuing the discussion of M. 4:8, M. 4:9 turns to the
question of sowing seed between rows of a vineyard. A is a slightly
apocopated sentence in the he-who formulary pattern. Judah
glosses A in B-E (with C and D roughly balanced) with a precedent
introduced by the formula $m^c \delta h$ b, while in F (joined to the foregoing by 'p) Meir and Simeon gloss A with a saying which almost
perfectly balances and opposes it. It appears, then, that B-E
has been inserted into the balanced dispute A+F.

The dispute of A-B apparently concerns the application of
the rules of M. 4:8, which deal with sowing between individual
rows to the case of sowing between rows of a vineyard. According
to A the rows of a vineyard must be separated by sixteen amot
(all commentaries), or the distance which must separate three
individual rows (M. 4:8C-D). The point of A is that a vineyard,
like a set of three rows, contains many vines which spread over
a large area, so that the seed must be sown in a large field unto
itself if it is not to produce the appearance of diverse-kinds.
In F Meir and Simeon disagree, maintaining that the rows of a
vineyard need to be set apart by only eight amot, or the distance
required to set apart two rows (M. 4:8A-B). Meir and Simeon
perhaps reason that the rows of a vineyard are separated by

regular intervals, so that seeds sown even in smaller spaces
clearly grow in areas unto themselves and do not produce the
appearance of diverse-kinds.[43]

In B-E Judah cites a precedent in support of A. A man in
Salmon[44] would separate the rows of his vineyard by sixteen *amot*
in order to sow seed between them (B). He would also turn the
foliage of every two rows of vines to the space between the
rows (alternating this space with the next one every other year),
so that alternate intervals would be completely free of vines
and could be sown (C-D). In this manner he would both allow the
seed more space to grow (Maim., *Comm.*) and prevent the seed and
the vines from becoming entangled and producing the appearance
of diverse-kinds. The point of B-E, then, is that one must turn
the foliage of the vines away from the seeds in order to avoid
the appearance of diverse-kinds. B-E thus only indirectly supports
A, for it presupposes the rule of A but does not primarily
concern it.

CHAPTER FIVE

KILAYIM CHAPTER FIVE

Chapter Five consists of two subunits, M. 5:1-3A-F+5:4N-P
(with M. 5:4G-M+5:4Q-R appended) and M. 5:5-6+5:7C-8 (with M.
5:7A-B attached). The first unit discusses two themes, the
arrangement of vines in a vineyard (a continuation of the interests
of Chapter Four; M. 5:1-2) and the sowing of different areas within a vineyard (M. 5:3-4). The second subunit discusses the prohibited acts of sowing and allowing another kind to grow in a
vineyard.

All of the protases of the first subunit (M. 5:1A, 5:1E,
5:2A, 5:3A, 5:4N, five in all) follow the formulary pattern
X *šhw'* + participle (while M. 5:1A omits *hw'*), with those of
M. 5:1-2 opening with *krm*. M. 5:1A-D discusses the number (and,
according to a gloss, the arrangement) of vines that a vineyard
which lay waste must have in order to remain in the status of
a vineyard. M. 5:1E-K+M. 5:2 then deals with the irregularly-
planted vineyard and with the vineyard containing rows separated
by less than four *amot*. M. discusses in each instance whether
the internal arrangement of the group of vines or its overall
appearance determines its status as a vineyard. Meir (M. 5:1K)
favors the latter view (along with sages, M. 5:2C), while Simeon
(M. 5:2B) appears to stand behind the former (along with the
anonymous law of M. 5:1E-J).

M. 5:3-4 consists of Eliezer b. Jacob's saying at M. 5:3A-F,
followed by a brief unit at M. 5:3G-M+5:4Q-R, and an interpolated
unit at M. 5:4N-P. The protases of M. 5:3G-M+5:4Q-R (M. 5:3G,
5:3J, and 5:4Q, three in all) all follow the pattern X *šbkrm*,
while the apodoses all read *zwr^cm btwkh*. In M. 5:3A-F Eliezer
b. Jacob rules that one may sow a ditch of a specified size
only if it extends across the entire length of the vineyard,
for then it appears to divide the vineyard and so forms an
autonomous domain. If the ditch is not open, however, it is considered like a winepress, i.e., a depression in the ground, which
may not be sown. The redactor here attaches Eliezer's rule
(M. 5:3G-H) that one may sow a winepress in a vineyard, assigning
to sages (M. 5:3I) Eliezer b. Jacob's opposing view concerning
the winepress (which has been dropped from his saying in order
to introduce Eliezer's opinion). The rest of the appended unit
(M. 5:3J-M+5:4Q-R) concerns sowing other areas of the vineyard

(e.g., the watchman's hut or mound, or the house). M. 5:4N-P
then complements M. 5:3G-I by discussing the sowing of another
kind with a vine in a winepress or hollow.

The protases of the second subunit (M. 5:5-6+5:7C-8) all
open with the third-person singular present participle (M. 5:5A
[*hnwṭ'*], M. 5:6A [*hrw'h*], M. 5:7C [*hzwr^c*], and M. 5:8A [*hmqym*],
four in all). M. 5:5A-B presents a basic rule concerning the
number of vines which are sanctified by vegetables planted or
allowed to grow in a vineyard. M. 5:5C-G then qualifies this
rule, maintaining that it applies only when the vines are planted
close together. When, however, the vines are spaced farther
apart, the vegetables sanctify an area of the vineyard rather
than a quantity of the vines. As we shall see, the commentaries
offer various explanations to account for M.'s distinction between
the different arrangements of vines.

M. 5:6-8 complements the discussion of M. 5:5 concerning
sowing and allowing another kind to grow in a vineyard by defining
those actions. According to M. 5:6 one may allow diverse-kinds
to grow until he reaches them in the course of his work. Once
he comes upon the diverse-kinds, however, he may not leave without
uprooting them, for by leaving he would appear to indicate that
he wished them to grow. M. 5:7 distinguishes between one who
accidentally and unknowingly sows another kind in a vineyard (e.g.,
the wind scatters the seeds behind him into the vineyard), who
does not sanctify the vines, and one who accidentally and know-
ingly sows in a vineyard (e.g., the wind scatters the seeds
before him into the vineyard), who is liable. In M. 5:8A-D
Eliezer and sages dispute concerning whether or not one who allows
thorns to grow in a vineyard sanctifies the vines. Eliezer maintains that thorns, like other plants, sanctify the vines, while
sages disagree, maintaining that one who allows the useless
thorns to grow does not thereby appear to desire that they grow.
M. 5:8E-K, which in part illustrates the view of sages, then
discusses whether or not certain plants are considered diverse-
kinds in a vineyard.

5:1

A. A vineyard which lay waste--
B. if there are in it (*'m yš bw*; Mn adds: *kdy*) [enough vines
    to enable one] to gather ten vines *per bet se'ah*,
C. and [= omitted by a Geniza fragment[1]] they are planted
    according to the rule [pertaining to] them (*khlktn*),

D. lo, this is called a "lean"[2] vineyard (*krm dl* [Danby: "poor vineyard"]; Cn, N, Sn: *krm* ["a vineyard"]).

E. A vineyard which is planted in an irregular manner [so Blackman for ^{c}*rbwby*'[3]] --

F. if there are in it [vines which are so arranged that is able] to align (*lkwyn*) two [vines] opposite three [others],

G. lo, this is [considered] a vineyard.

H. And if not [i.e., if two vines may not be aligned opposite three others],

I. it is not [considered] a vineyard.

J. R. Meir says, "Since it [i.e., the irregularly-planted vineyard] looks [in form] like the pattern (*ktbnyt*) of the vineyards [in general],

K. "lo, this is [considered] a vineyard."

M. Kil. 5:1

M. Kil. 5:1 continues the discussion of M. 4:5-7 concerning the manner in which vines must be arranged in order to form a vineyard. M. 5:1 is a unitary pericope composed of two parts, A-D, discussing the vineyard which lay waste, and E-K, dealing with the irregularly-planted vineyard. The two sections are similar to one another in that both contain conditional sentences (A-D and E-G) following the same formulary pattern (*'m yš bw*). A-D and E-G somewhat balance one another, for their protases differ only to a small degree (*krm šhrb* vs. *krm šhw' ntwᶜ*; cf. M. 5:2), while the apodosis of A-D is slightly more complex than that of E-G (*hry zh nqr' krm dl* vs. *hry zh krm*).

A-D consists of a declarative sentence, A-B+D (with subject and object in inverted order), which is glossed by C. According to A-B+D a vineyard which lay waste and which still contains ten vines *per bet se'ah* is called a "lean" vineyard, and so apparently remains in the status of a vineyard (cf. other mss. readings at D). C adds that the ten must be planted according to the rule applying to them, i.e., the law of M. 4:6 (all commentaries; cf. T. 3:3b).[4] The latter states that five vines constitute a vineyard if they are so arranged that two pair of vines face one another, and the fifth vine extends outward from them. C thus rules that the ten vines discussed in B must form two sets[5] of five vines, ordered in the pattern described in M. 4:6. The point of C is that the arrangement of the remaining vines, as well as their number, determines whether or not a vineyard which lay waste continues to be considered a vineyard.

E-K is composed of a declarative sentence, E-G (with
subject and object again in inverted order), a gloss at H-I, and
Meir's gloss of H-I at J-K (with the fixed apodoses of G, I,
and K balancing one another). E-G describes a case in which the
vines of a vineyard are planted irregularly, that is, without
being arranged in rows (Maim., *Comm.*, *Code*, *Diverse-Kinds* 7:9,
Sens, and others). According to F-G such an area may be considered
a vineyard only if a row within it containing two vines may be
aligned opposite a row of three vines. In other words, five
vines in the vineyard must be so arranged that two pair of vines
stand opposite one another, and the fifth extends outwards. The
five vines are thus laid out in the pattern described in M. 4:6,
and so form a vineyard, which is extended to include the entire
irregularly-planted area. H-I then restates the rule of E-G
in a negative manner. In J-K Meir opposes H-I (and E-G as well),
maintaining that an irregularly-planted area is considered a
vineyard even if it does not contain two vines aligned opposite
three others, for the area has the overall appearance of a vineyard. According to Meir, then, the appearance of an area planted
with vines determines its status as a vineyard, regardless of
the actual arrangement of the vines. We note that H-I relates
nothing new, and so apparently serves only to introduce Meir's
statement at J-K.

T. Kil. 3:3b-3:9 forms a sustained commentary to M. 5:1.
The following chart shows the relationship of M. to T.:

T.	M.	Issue
T. 3:3b	M. 5:1A-D	Distance allowed between vines of a vineyard which lay waste
T. 3:4	M. 5:1E-I	The parts of the vine which must be aligned in order for the vines to be considered to be lined up
T. 3:5a	M. 5:1A-D	The circular espalier which is not considered an espalier
T. 3:5b	M. 5:1E-I	The alignment of vines in an irregularly-planted vineyard
(T. 3:5c	M. 5:2)	
T. 3:6	M. 5:1E-I	The odd row in the regularly-planted vineyard
T. 3:7-8+9	autonomous	The status of the slope of the terrace in respect to adjacent fields

T. thus groups together and presents first those pericopae which
comment on M., closing with a set of autonomous materials.
T. 3:3b-3:6 is well-organized. Except for T. 3:5c, which

comments on M. 5:2, and T. 3:4, which appears to be out of place,
T. comments on M. 5:1A-D and M. 5:1E-I in sequence. T. 3:3b
and T. 3:5a both interpret M. 5:1C, which states that the ten
vines of a vineyard which lay waste must be "planted according
to the law [pertaining to] them." T. 3:3b explains that this
rule deals with the distance which may separate the remaining
vines. T. 3:5a presents a counter-example to M. 5:1C, describing
the case of a circular espalier, which is not regarded as an
espalier even though it is properly planted. T. 3:4, 3:5b, and
3:6 then comment on M. 5:1E-I, which states that five vines of
an irregularly-planted vineyard may combine (if correctly
aligned) to form a vineyard. T. 3:4 discusses the part of the
vines which must be aligned in order for the vines to form a
vineyard. T. 3:5b cites the rule of M. and presents it in the
context of a $ma^{c}a\acute{s}eh$, while T. 3:6 presents the contrasting
case of a properly-planted vineyard containing a row which is out
of place.

 T. 3:7-8+9 concerns the relationship of the slope of a
terrace to adjacent fields. T. 3:7-8 rules than an individual
vine or plant of another kind which is planted on a slope is not
considered to be attached to the vineyard or field below. T. 3:9
similarly rules that a slope separates a vineyard on one terrace
from a field of another kind on the other. The point of T. 3:7-
8+9 thus is that the slope is considered to be autonomous of
the terraces which it joins.

A. How much [i.e., how many vines] shall its [i.e., a vineyard's] planting be?
B. Three [vines] opposite three [others].
C. [If] one of the outer [vines] is removed, how much [space]
   may there be between them [i.e., the remaining five vines]?
D. Two [vines which are] opposite two [others may be separated
   from the latter by a distance measuring] from four *amot* to
   eight [*amot*],
E. and the [one extending out like a] tail [may be separated
   from each pair of vines by a distance measuring] from four
   amot to eight [*amot*].
F. [If the] two [vines which are] opposite [the] two [others]
   were [separated from the latter by a distance measuring]
   [Erfurt, first printed ed. omit: less than] from four
   amot to eight [*amot*],
G. and the [one extending out like a] tail [Erfurt adds through
   H [to "tail"] (Vienna omitting[6]):] [is separated from each

pair of vines by a distance measuring] less than four *amot*
or more than eight [*amot*];

H. or [if the] two [vines which are] opposite [the] two
[others] were [separated from the latter by a distance
measuring] less than [= omitted by first printed ed.] four
amot or more than eight [*amot*],

I. and [the one extending out like a] tail [was separated from
each pair of vines by a distance measuring] from four [*amot*]
to eight [*amot*],

J. [Erfurt omits:] lo, this is not [considered] a vineyard,

K. unless [the] two vines [which are] opposite [the] two
[others are separated from the latter by a distance measuring]
from four *amot* to eight [*amot*] [= Efurt omits],

L. and the [one extending out like a] tail [is separated from
each pair of vines by a distance measuring] from four *amot*
to eight [*amot*].

T. Kil. 3:3b (pp. 213-214, 11. 11-17)

T. Kil. 3:3b comments on M. 5:1A-D, explaining M.'s phrase
"planted according to the rule [pertaining to] them" as referring
to the distance which may separate the vines of a "lean" vineyard from one another. T. is a unitary pericope composed of two
parts, A-E and F-L, with the latter glossing the former. A-B
and C-E follow a question-and-answer pattern, with D and E somewhat balancing one another (both ending with the phrase "from
four [*amot*] to eight [*amot*]"). F-L consists of two balanced
conditional clauses, F-G and H-I (which balance D-E as well),
an apodosis at J, and K-L, which glosses F-J by repeating D-E.
We note that F-L forms an apocopated sentence, for the subject
of F-I, the individual sets of vines, is not that of J, which
concerns the vineyard as a whole.

A-B describes a vineyard which contains two opposing rows
of three vines each.[7] In C an outer vine is removed, so that
the vineyard now lies waste, with its five remaining vines
arranged in the pattern described in M. 4:6. C then asks how
much space may separate the vines if they are to form a "lean"
vineyard. Following the language of M. 4:6 ("Two [vines]
opposite two [others], and one extending out [like a] tail"),
D-E states that the rows may be separated from one another and
from the fifth vine by a distance covering from four to eight
amot. F-L then simply restates D-E in a negative manner (i.e.,
the distance may not be less than four or more than eight *amot*),
perhaps following the pattern of M. 4:6 (rule + two rejected

alternatives + repetition of rule). In addition to reading
M. 4:6 into M. 5:1A-D (as we have already noted), T. reads two
other rules into M. The law of T. also includes Meir and
Simeon's view (M. 4:9) that one may not sow another kind between
two rows of vines separated by less than eight *amot*,[8] and Simeon's
rule (M. 5:2) that the rows of a vineyard must be separated by
more than four *amot* (cf. also T. 3:5c). T. effectively links
these four pericopae of M. (M. 4:6, 4:9, 5:1, and 5:2) together.

A. [If] the stem[s](so Lieberman[9] for *kwwrt*)[of the vines are]
   aligned and the foliage [of the vines] is not aligned --
B. lo, this is [considered] a vineyard.
C. [If] the foliage [of the vines] is aligned, and the stem[s
   of the vines are] not aligned --
D. lo, this is not [considered] a vineyard.
E. [Erfurt reverses E-G and H-M[10]] [If the stems (MB)] were
   thin and were not aligned,
F. [and then] became thick and became aligned --
G. lo, this is [considered] a vineyard.
H. How does he know if [the stems] were aligned or not?
I. He stretches a thread to the base of the vines [*l^cyqr hgpnym*;
   Erfurt: *^cl gby hgpnym* ("over the vines")] --
J. if they [i.e., the vines] all touch the thread [*bḥwṭ*;
   Erfurt: *k'ḥt* ("if they all touch as one")] [on the same
   side] --
K. lo, this is [considered] a vineyard;
L. if one [vine] stands inside (*nknst*) and the other stands
   outside (*ywṣ't*) [of the thread] --
M. lo, this is not [considered] a vineyard.

                    T. Kil. 3:4 (p. 214, ll. 17-22)
                    (A-I: Y. Kil. 5:1 (29d))

     T. Kil. 3:4 comments on M. 5:1E-G,[11] which states that vines
which are irregularly planted form a vineyard only if two of
the vines are aligned opposite three others. T. consists of
two subunits, A-G, concerning the parts of the vines which must
be aligned with one another, and H-M, glossing the foregoing
with a discussion of the method of determining whether or not
the vines are aligned. A-G is composed of three declarative
sentences, A-B, C-D, and E-G. A and C balance one another
(*kwwrt + nwp vs. nwp + kwwrt*), while E-F is internally balanced
(*dq + l' mkwwn vs. h^cbw + mkwwn*). All three apodoses (B, D,
and G) are fixed (*krm vs. 'ynw krm*), and so balance one another

as well. H-M consists of a question, H, and an answer, I-M,
with the latter forming an apocopated sentence composed of a
protasis, I, and a pair of conditional clauses, J-K and L-M
(with fixed apodoses at K and M).

According to A-D the vines are considered to be aligned
with one another if their stems, presumably their principal parts,
oppose each other, regardless of whether or not their foliage,
a secondary feature, is also lined up. E-G adds that if stems
which are not aligned at the outset grow thicker and become
aligned, then at that point the vines form a vineyard. Explaining
the rule of A-D, H-M describes the manner in which one determines
whether or not the vines are aligned. One stretches a thread
between the two rows at the base of the vines. If the vines all
touch one side of the thread they are considered to be aligned,
but if they make contact with the thread on different sides
("inside" and "outside") they clearly are not lined up with one
another.

A. R. Simeon says, "An espalier [so Lieberman[12] for *ḥryṣ*;
    Erfurt: *ᶜrys*] which [was] planted according to the rule
    [pertaining to] it,
B. "or [Lieberman[13] suggests instead: but (*'l'*)] which was
    circular (*mwqp*; Erfurt: *mkwwn* ["aligned"]) like that dove-
    cote [which is] round (*kšwbk hzh ᶜgwl*),
C. "lo, this is [= omitted by Erfurt] not [considered] an
    espalier."

T. Kil. 3:5a (p. 214, ll. 22-23)

T. Kil. 3:5a comments on M. 5:1A-D. While M. states that
ten vines which are planted according to the rule pertaining
to them constitute a "lean" vineyard, T. presents a contrasting
case in which vines planted according to the law applying to them
do not combine to form a single group. Simeon maintains that
trained vines which are properly planted, or properly spaced
(Lieberman[14]), do not constitute an espalier if they are arranged
in a circle. Simeon apparently reasons that the vines of an
espalier must be planted in a straight line (cf. M. 6:1).

A. *A vineyard which is planted in an irregular manner--*
B. *if there are in it [vines which are so arranged that one
    is able] to align (lkwyn) two [vines] opposite* [Lieberman,[15]
    following first printed ed., omits: *two*] *three* [= omitted
    by Erfurt] *[others]*,

C. *lo, this is [considered] a vineyard.*

D. *And if not [i.e., if two vines may not be aligned opposite
    three others],*

E. *it is not [considered] a vineyard* [= M. 5:1E-I].

F. [Erfurt omits F-L] *zh hyh m^{c}šh w*: They came and asked
    Rabban Gamaliel [concerning the irregularly-planted
    vineyard].

G. And he said to them, "(1) Go and ask Yosah b. Geali [first
    printed ed.: Gulai], (2) who is excellent[16] and expert
    (*br wbqy*) in the rules [pertaining to] the vineyard."

H. They went and asked him [concerning the irregularly-planted
    vineyard].

I. He said to them, "*If there are in it [vines which are so
    arranged that one is able] to align (lkwyn) two [vines]
    opposite three [others],*

J. "*lo, this is [considered] a vineyard.*

K. "*And if not [i.e., if two vines may not be aligned opposite
    three others],*

L. "*it is not [considered] a vineyard* [= M. 5:1F-I]."

T. Kil. 3:5b (p. 214, ll. 23-27)

T. Kil. 3:5b comments on M. 5:1E-I. A-E cites M., which
F-K then supplements with a precedent introduced by the formula
m^{c}šh w. F-L is attached to A-E by the phrase *zh hyh*,[17] and
depends on A-E for its context. The point of F-L is to support
the rule of M. 5:1E-I, perhaps in response to the opposing
view of Meir at M. 5:1J-K (HD). In F-G Gamaliel, who was asked
concerning the irregularly-planted vineyard, refers the question
to Yosé b. Geali, whom he considers (according to G(2), perhaps
a gloss) to be an expert in the laws of the vineyard. Yosé
then presents what we have in M. 5:1F-I. T. thus attributes
M. to this Yavnean Yosé.

A. A vineyard which is planted according to the rule [pertaining
    to] it --

B. and one row extends from it [i.e., one row is longer than
    the others] --

C. when he measures [the area of tillage] of the vines,

D. he allows the vineyard four *amot* and the [extended] row
    four [GRA and Lieberman[18] (following Erfurt) correct to:
    six] handbreadths.

E. [Erfurt omits E-H[19]] [If the vineyard] was planted according
    to the rule [pertaining to] it --

F.   and the outer vines [i.e., the vines of the outer row] are
     visible through [the spaces] between [the vines of the
     other rows] --

G.   when he measures [the area of tillage] from within [i.e.,
     between the outer row and the rest of the vineyard],

H.   he allows the vineyard four *amot* and the [outer] row six
     handbreadths.

                              T. Kil. 3:6 (p. 214-215, ll. 28-33)

        T. Kil. 3:6 supplements M. 5:1E-G. While M. discusses the
irregularly-planted vineyard which contains five vines aligned
to form a vineyard, T. presents the reverse case of the regularly-
planted vineyard which has one row out of place. T. is not
directly relevant to M., however, for T. is concerned not with
the status of the vines as a vineyard but with the areas of
tillage of the vineyard and the odd row (although, as we shall
see, the latter issue presupposes the former). T. is a unitary
pericope composed of two parts, A-D, concerning the row which
extends beyond the vineyard, and E-H, discussing a row the vines
of which are out of phase with the other vines of the vineyard.
A-D appears in apocopation, while E-H forms a conditional
sentence.[20] The two units somewhat balance one another, for A
differs only slightly from E (which depends on it for its meaning), while C-D is virtually identical to G-H (differing only
in that G adds the phrase "from within").
        A-B describes the case of a properly-planted vineyard con-
taining one row which extends further than the others. According
to C-D this row is granted its own area of tillage of six handbreadths (= the area of tillage of a single vine [M. 6:1]), while
the vineyard is allowed its four *amot*. In other words, the
extended row is not considered part of the vineyard. In E-H
a vineyard which is properly planted contains an outer row which
is so arranged that its vines stand opposite the spaces of the
vines in the other rows. G-H again rules that the vineyard
and the outer row are allowed separate areas of tillage. The
gloss "from within" in G, interpreting H to apply to a single
area, explains that both areas of tillage are granted in the
area between the vineyard and the outer row.[21] The point of T.
once more is that the odd row of vines does not belong to the
vineyard. T. thus would probably not agree with the rule of
M. 5:1E-H. While M. rules that the irregularly-planted vines
belong to the vineyard formed by the five regularly-planted vines,
T. maintains that vines which are planted irregularly in respect
to a vineyard are not considered part of the vineyard.

A. A vine which is planted on [the slope of (HD)] a terrace
   [above a vineyard (Lieberman[22])] --
B. he [Erfurt, first printed ed.: they] allows it its [own]
   area of tillage [apart from that of the vineyard].

T. Kil. 3:7 (p. 215, ll. 31-32)

C. Seeds or vegetables which are planted on [the slope of]
   a terrace [above a field of the same kind (Lieberman)] --
D. he [Erfurt, first printed ed.: they] allows them their
   [own] area of tillage [apart from that of the field].

T. Kil. 3:8 (p. 215, ll. 32-33)

   T. Kil. 3:7-8, together with T. 3:9 (which immediately
follows), form an autonomous subunit concerning the relationship
of the slope of a terrace to adjacent fields. T. 3:7-8 consists
of two balanced, apocopated sentences, A-B and C-D, which differ
only in that A-B has *gpn* while C-D reads *zr^{c}ym wyrqwt*. A-B
describes the case of a vine which is planted on a slope above
a vineyard (Lieberman). A-B rules that this vine is considered
to be planted in an autonomous area, and so is allowed its own
area of tillage. C-D similarly states that seeds or vegetables
planted on a slope above a field of the same kind are not
regarded as belonging to the field, and therefore are allowed
their own area of tillage. The point of T., then, is that the
slope of a terrace is not considered to be connected to the
fields adjoining it, but rather forms an autonomous domain.

A. [If] he had two fields, one above another --
B. [if] the lower one is planted [with] a vineyard, and the
   upper one is not planted [with] a vineyard,
C. he sows [first printed ed. adds through "he sows" in E
   (Vienna omitting):] the upper [field] until he reaches the
   base of the lower [field];
D. [if] the upper one is planted [with] a vineyard, and the lower
   one is not planted [with] a vineyard,
E. he sows the lower [field] and the [slope of the (HD)]
   terrace until he reaches the base of the vines [in the
   upper field].

T. Kil. 3:9 (p. 215, ll. 33-36)
(D-E: Y. Kil. 6:2 (30a))

T. Kil. 3:9 continues the discussion of T. 3:7-8 concerning
the status of the slope of the terrace. T. consists of a protasis, A, and a pair of conditional clauses, B-C and D-E. These
clauses almost perfectly balance one another, differing only in
that E adds "the [slope of the] terrace," which may be a gloss.
T. concerns the case of two neighboring terraces which are planted
with different kinds. In B-C a vineyard is planted in the upper
field and another kind is sown in the lower terrace, while in
D-E the circumstances are reversed. In both instances T. rules
that one may sow the other kind on the slope right up to the
beginning of the vineyard, presumably even within the latter's
area of tillage. The point of T. is that the slope of the terrace
is considered to be autonomous of the fields which it joins, so
that the crops sown in it are not regarded as being connected to
either of the adjoining terraces. We note that T.'s rule, in
allowing the other kind to be sown right up to the vineyard itself, is concerned only that there be no actual planting of
diverse-kinds, regardless of whether or not the appearance of
diverse-kinds may result.

5:2

A. A vineyard which is planted by [intervals of] less than
    four *amot*--

B. R. Simeon says, "[It] is not [considered] a vineyard [B. B.B.
    83a reads: the words of R. Simeon]."

C. And sages say, "[P, B. B.B. 37b add: Lo, this is (considered)]
    a vineyard."

D. And they [i.e., sages] regard the middle [rows] as if they
    are not [there].

M. Kil. 5:2 (B. Erub. 37b, 83a, 102b,
Y. Shev. 1:3 (32b), Y. Naz. 9:3 (57d))

M. Kil. 5:2 discusses the minimum distance which must separate rows of a vineyard, and so continues the interest of M.
5:1E-K in the arrangement of a vineyard. M. presents a dispute
consisting of a protasis at A (following the formulary pattern
of M. 5:1E [*krm šhw' nṭwᶜ*]), two fixed, balanced opinions of
Simeon and sages at B-C, and a gloss of C at D. The dispute
concerns whether or not the rows of a vineyard must be set apart
by a fixed distance, so that they may be differentiated from
one another and the vineyard may appear to be planted in an
orderly manner.[23] Simeon maintains that the rows must be
separated by four *amot*, the area of tillage of a vineyard, for
then the rows will surely appear to be distinct from each other.

Sages, on the other hand, maintain that rows may form a vineyard
even if they are separated by less than four *amot*. Sages therefore will agree with Meir (M. 5:1J-K) that the vines of a vineyard need only produce the overall appearance of a vineyard, but
need not actually be planted in a regular arrangement. D explains
that sages, ignoring the actual planting of the vineyard, maintain that the middle rows, or the rows which (individually) lie
between any two rows separated by four *amot*, are regarded as if
they do not exist, so that all vineyards are considered to be
arranged by intervals of four *amot*. D thus brings the opinion
of sages in line with that of Simeon, for now all agree that the
rows of a vineyard must be separated by four *amot*.

A.   R. Simeon says, "*A vineyard which is planted by* [*intervals
     of*] *less than four amot* [= M. 5:2A] or more than eight *amot*,
B.   "lo, this is [= omitted by Erfurt] *not* [*considered*] *a
     vineyard* [= M. 5:2B]."

                    T. Kil. 3:5c (p. 214, 11. 27-28)

     T. Kil. 3:5c restates M. 5:2A-B, incorporating M.'s pro-
tasis (M. 5:2A) into Simeon's saying and adding the rule that a
vineyard's rows must be separated by less than eight *amot*.
T. derives this rule from M. 4:9F, where Meir and Simeon state
that one may sow another kind between rows of a vineyard which
are set apart by eight *amot*. T. interprets this saying to mean
that rows which are separated by eight *amot* do not combine to
form a vineyard, and therefore another kind may be sown between
them without producing a planting of diverse-kinds of the vineyard. T. thus combines the rules of M. 4:9F and M. 5:2B, and
so has Simeon presenting both the minimum and maximum distances
which may separate the rows of a vineyard.

                              5:3-4

A.   A ditch which passes through a vineyard [and measures] ten
     [handbreadths] deep and four wide --
B.   R. Eliezer b. Jacob says, "If [= omitted in Sn] [the ditch]
     was open [= omitted in M] [i.e., extending] from the
     beginning of the vineyard to its end (*swpw*; most mss.,
     MS: *r'šw* ["from one end of the vineyard to the other"]),
C.   "lo, this appears as [if it extends] between two vineyards,
D.   "and they sow [another kind] in it.
E.   "And if not [i.e., if the ditch is not open],

F.   "lo, this is [considered] like the winepress."

G.   And [= omitted by most mss.] the winepress which is in
     the vineyard [and measures] ten [handbreadths] deep and
     four wide --

H.   R. Eliezer says, "They sow [another kind] in it."

I.   And sages prohibit [sowing another kind in it].

J.   The watchman's booth [so Danby for *šwmrh*; alternatively,
     a mound or hill upon which a watchman stands (most commen-
     taries)] which is in the vineyard [and measures] ten
     [handbreadths] high and four wide --

K.   they sow [another kind] in it [i.e., on top of it (Maim.,
     Code, Diverse-Kinds 7:22)].

L.   And if it is overhung by interlaced foliage [so Danby for
     š^cr kwtš],

M.   it is prohibited [to sow another kind in it].

                                             M. Kil. 5:3

N.   A vine which is planted in the winepress or in the hollow
     (*nq^c*)^{24} --

O.   they allow it its area of tillage and he sows the rest.

P.   R. Yosé says, "If there are not there four *amot* [of space],
     he shall not put seed into it."

Q.   And the house which is in the vineyard --

R.   they sow [another kind] in it.

                                             M. Kil. 5:4

     M. Kil. 5:3-4 discusses sowing another kind in different
areas of the vineyard. A-F concerns sowing a ditch, while G-M+Q-R
deals with seeding a winepress (G-I), a watchman's booth or
mound (J-M), and a house (Q-R). As we shall show, N-P is an
interpolated unit which concerns sowing another kind together with
a vine in a winepress or hollow, and so complements G-I.

     A-F consists of a protasis, A, following the formulary
pattern of M. 5:1E and M. 5:2A (X *šhw'* + participle), and Eliezer
b. Jacob's saying at B-F. The latter is composed of a pair of
conditional sentences, B-D (forming, with A, a mildly apocopated
sentence) and E-F. These two sentences are not well-balanced,
as we see from the following chart:

B. R. Eliezer b. Jacob says,
"If the ditch was open [i.e.,
extending] from the beginning
of the vineyard to its end,

C. "lo, this appears as [if it
extends] between two vineyards,

D. "and they sow [another kind]
in it."

E. "And if not,

F. "lo, this is [considered]
like the winepress."

While E-F corresponds to B-C, we would expect the phrase "they
do not sow [another kind] in it" to follow F and balance D.
This phrase has been dropped so that F, which by itself simply
compares the "closed" ditch to the winepress, may introduce
Eliezer's opposing view (G-H) that one may not sow in a winepress. The ruling of Eliezer b. Jacob is not obscured, however,
for the redactors both preserves it and increases its prominence
by assigning it to sages (I), thus giving it the status of a
majority opinion.

    The three parts of G-M+Q-R (G-I, J-M, and Q-R) all open with
protases in the formulary pattern X *šbkrm*. Two of the protases
(G and S) also give the dimensions of the area discussed with
nearly identical phrases ("ten [handbreadths] deep (or high)
and four wide"), while Q lacks such a specification of size
because of the substance of its rule.[25] The apodoses of the unit
(H, K, and R) all read *zwr*c*ym btwkh* (with L-M glossing K). The
protasis of N-P follows the formulary pattern of M. 5:1E, 5:2A,
and 5:3A. Since N follows a distinctive formulary pattern, but
not that of the protases of G-M+Q-R, it appears that N-P is
separate from the foregoing. Furthermore, the apodosis of the
unit, O (= the apodoses of M. 4:1J, 4:2N), differs from the
apodoses of G-M+Q-R in introducing the consideration of the area
of tillage. N-P is therefore an autonomous unit which has been
inserted into G-M+Q-R to complement the discussion of the winepress in G-I.

    Eliezer b. Jacob rules in A-F that a ditch measuring ten
handbreadths deep and four wide may be sown only if it extends
across the length of the vineyard. The ditch then forms an
autonomous domain, both because of its size and because it appears
to divide two separate vineyards. If the ditch is not open,
however, it is regarded as a winepress, which may not be sown
(regardless of its size) because it lies entirely within the
vineyard and is not adequately set apart from it (as it would be,

for example, by partitions). In G-H Eliezer[26] disagrees with
Eliezer b. Jacob, maintaining that, because of its size, the
winepress measuring ten handbreadths deep by four wide does
constitute an area unto itself in the vineyard.

According to J-K one may sow on top of a *šwmrh*, i.e., a
watchman's booth or mound, which measures ten handbreadths high
and four wide, for a mound of such dimensions forms an autonomous
domain within the vineyard.[27] L-M then qualifies J-K by saying
that a *šwmrh* covered by an overhang of interwoven vines may not
be sown,[28] for now the booth or mound clearly belongs in the
domain of the vineyard.[29] Q-R states that one may sow in the
house of a vineyard (presumably under a partially-open roof),
for the house is separated from the vineyard by its walls and
roof, and so constitutes an area unto itself.

The point of N-O is that a vine and another kind may be
sown even in a small, bounded area, as long as they are separated
by the vine's area of tillage (Maim., *Comm.*). Yosé then qualifies N-O by saying that the winepress may be sown only if it contains four *amot* of space, or (presumably) enough space to allow
both the vine and a substantial amount of the other kind to grow.
Albeck apparently understands "four *amot*" to mean "four square
amot (rather than four *amot* in one direction or four *amot*
square)," so that Yosé refers to the vine's area of tillage
(= one *amah* in each direction). Yosé then makes the obvious
point that the winepress or hollow may not be sown unless it is
large enough to contain the vine and its area of tillage.

A. *A vine which is planted in a hollow* [measuring] ten [hand-
    breadths] deep and four wide --
B. *they allow it its area of tillage* [i.e., the area between
    the vine and another kind] below [i.e., within the hollow
    itself (HD)].
C. [If the hollow measures] less than this,
D. *they allow it its area of tillage* [i.e., the area between
    the vine and another kind] above [i.e., outside of the
    hollow (HD)].

                    T. Kil. 3:10a (p. 215, ll. 36-38)

     T. Kil. 3:10a cites and glosses M. 5:4N-O. T. consists of
a declarative sentence, A-B, followed by a conditional sentence,
C-D, which depends on A-B for its context. The two apodoses
are glossed citations of M. 5:4O, and so perfectly balance one
another (*mṭh vs. m^c lh*). M. 5:4N-O states that one may sow
another kind near a vine planted in a winepress or hollow,

provided that he allows the vine its area of tillage, which here refers simply to the distance which must separate a vine from another kind. T. now assumes that a vine planted in a hollow will eventually climb out of it, and therefore asks whether in this case the area of tillage is to be allowed within the hollow or outside of it. According to T. the answer depends on the size of the hollow. If the hollow measures ten handbreadths deep and four wide, then the vine is considered to grow in a distinct, autonomous area (cf. M. 5:3A-F+G-I), so that the area of tillage is to be allowed within the hollow itself (A-B). If, however, the hollow is smaller than the specified size, the vine is not considered to grow in a separate area unto itself, and the area of tillage is to be allowed aboveground (C-D). In the latter case T. takes the middle position between permitting the area of tillage to be allowed within the hollow (as in A-B), and not permitting the area of tillage to be allowed at all (i.e., prohibiting another kind from being sown near the vine). T. thus introduces the consideration of the hollow's size within the framework of M.'s rule that a vine in a hollow is allowed its area of tillage. T. therefore concerns not whether or not the area of tillage is to be allowed, but where it is to be granted.

A. *A ditch which passes through a vineyard and measures ten handbreadths deep and four wide* [= M. 5:3A] --

B. R. Liezer [Erfurt, first printed ed.: Eliezer] says, "They sow in it three seeds (*zr^{c}wnyn*; Erfurt: *mynyn* ["kinds"]),

C. "one on one [side], one on the other [side], and one in the middle."

D. Said R. Liezer [Erfurt, first printed ed.: Eliezer] b. Jacob [first printed ed.: R. Eliezer b. Jacob says], "The words of R. Eliezer [Lieberman,[30] following Erfurt, first printed ed., omits: b. Jacob] appear [correct (Neusner[31])] with [regard to] a breached ditch [so Neusner for *ḥryṣ mbwrṣ*]."

T. Kil. 3:10b (p. 215, ll. 38-40)

(C: M. Kil. 3:2)

T. Kil. 3:10b cites and glosses M. 5:3A. A's citation
of M. is glossed by Eliezer in B-C, whose opinion is then glossed
in turn by Eliezer b. Jacob in D. In B-C Eliezer applies the
rule of M. 3:2H-I to M. 5:3A (Lieberman[32]), saying that one may
sow the ditch described in A with three kinds of seeds, one on
either side and a third in the middle. Eliezer thus presupposes
that one may sow a ditch of the specified size which passes
through a vineyard, and so is consistent with his rule (M. 5:3H)
that one may sow a winepress of the same size in a vineyard (for
both areas are simply depressions in the ground). Eliezer b.
Jacob in D qualifies Eliezer's ruling, saying that it applies
only in the case of a breached, or open (Lieberman[33]), ditch.
Eliezer b. Jacob then brings Eliezer into accord with the view
attributed to Eliezer b. Jacob at M. 5:3A-D. T. thus links the
rules of Eliezer and Eliezer b. Jacob, which appear in different
contexts in M. (concerning the winepress and the ditch, respectively), so that both authorities now discuss a single issue,
the sowing of a ditch in a vineyard.

5:5

A. He who plants vegetables in the vineyard or allows them
   to grow,
B. lo, this one sanctifies [i.e., prohibits the use of] forty-
   five vines.
C. When [is this the case]?
D. When [the vines] were planted by [intervals of] four, four [amot,
   i.e., the vines were separated from one another by four amot
   in four directions (most commentaries)], or by [intervals
   of] five, five [amot, i.e., the vines were separated from one
   another by five amot in four directions].
E. [If the vines] were planted by [intervals of] six, six [amot,
   i.e., the vines were separated by six amot in four directions],
   or by [intervals of] seven, seven [amot, i.e., the vines were
   separated from one another by seven amot in four directions],
F. lo, this one sanctifies [i.e., prohibits the use of the
   vines planted within] sixteen amah in each direction,
G. [measured] in circles and not in squares [following Danby for
   ^{c}gwlwt wl' mrwb^{c}wt; Danby adds (p. 34, n. 1): The vines are
   forfeit that lie within a circle of sixteen cubit radius,
   not within the square that contains the circle].

M. Kil. 5:5

M. Kil. 5:5 continues the discussion of M. 5:3-4 concerning
the sowing of another kind in a vineyard, turning from the
instances of permitted sowing to the case of prohibited sowing.
M. consists of A-B, a declarative sentence which is glossed by
C-G. The latter is a unitary construction composed of C-D, which
appears in a question-and-answer pattern, followed by a conditional sentence at E-F (with E balancing D [four + five *vs.* six +
seven]), and an internal gloss at G.

A-B describes the case of one who plants vegetables or allows
them to grow among vines (i.e., within a vineyard), ruling that
the sower thereby sanctifies forty-five vines. Now we have
already seen that one who sows another kind within the vineyard's
area of tillage, i.e., at the edge of the vineyard, sanctifies
either one (House of Shammai) or two (House of Hillel) rows of
vines (M. 4:5F-H). This rule follows from the Houses' respective
definitions of a vineyard as consisting of either one or two
rows (M. 4:5A-D), and Dt. 22:9, which states that, by sowing
another kind, one sanctifies a vineyard: *You shall not sow your
vineyard with two kinds of seeds, lest the whole yield be sanctified, the crop which you have sown and the yield of the vineyard.*
A-B then complements M. 4:5F-H. While the latter defines the
"vineyard" which is sanctified when one sows another kind at
the edge of the vineyard, A-B determines this "vineyard" when one
sows the other kind among the vines. It is not clear, however,
why A-B should define the "vineyard" to consist of exactly
forty-five vines. In order to understand A-B, therefore, we must
first turn to the explanation presented in C-G.

C-D states that the rule of A-B applies only when the
vines of the vineyard are set apart by four or five *amot* in each
direction. When the vines are separated by six or seven *amot*,
however, all of the vines which lie within a radius of sixteen
amot from the vegetables are sanctified (E-G). Maimonides (*Comm.*)
explains the significance of the spacing of the vines as follows.
The rule of A-B, as interpreted by C-D, is a particular instance
of E-G, for the latter, although referring to vines separated
by six or seven *amot*, actually presents a general rule applying
to all arrangements of vines. A-B thus gives the number of vines
which happen to lie within the specified radius when the vines

are separated by four or five *amot*. Now while forty-five vines do lie in a circle of radius sixteen *amot* when four *amot* separate the vines (fig. 38),[34] only thirty-seven vines are actually contained in such a circle when the vines are set apart by five *amot* (fig. 39). Maimonides here explains that the circle is considered to be wholly planted with vegetables, so that the row immediately outside of the circle but within four *amot* of it is also sanctified, since this row lies within the sanctified vineyard's area of tillage. In this case as well, then, the number of sanctified vines totals forty-five (fig. 40).

A-B is thus shown to be an example of the rule of E-G. Maimonides summarizes his view as follows (*Code, Diverse-Kinds* 6:1-2):

> [6:1] He who sows vegetables or grain in the vineyard, or he who allows them to grow until they have increased by one two-hundredth [cf. M. 5:6], lo, this one sanctifies [i.e., prohibits the use of] vines which [lie] around it [i.e., the vegetables or grain] sixteen *amot* in each direction, [measured] in circles and not in squares [= M. 5:5F-G]. And they regard the entire circle, the width [i.e., the diameter] of which is thirty-two *amah*, as if it is full of vegetables throughout. And every vine which is within this circle is sanctified with the vegetables, and all vines which are outside of the circle are not sanctified.

> [6:2] Under what circumstances? When there were between the circumference of this circle and the row of vines which [lies] outside of it more than four *amot*. But if there were between them exactly (*mswmṣmwt*) four *amot* or less, they regard the circle as if it reaches the [outside] row nearest to it, and as if the circle's width [i.e., diameter] is forty *amah*. And as to [lit.: they regard (*rw'yn*)] every vine which falls within this circle of [diameter] forty *amot*, lo, this one is sanctified.

Maimonides' reading of A-B as an instance of E-G is somewhat difficult, though, for he must maintain that, when the vines are separated by five *amot*, vines outside of the circle of sixteen *amot* are also sanctified. M., however, nowhere states that vines lying outside of a radius of sixteen *amot* are sanctified (Rabad to *Code, Diverse-Kinds* 6:2).[35] We therefore turn to the alternative interpretation based on TAS.

According to TAS both A-B (as explained by C-D) and E-G describe cases in which vegetables are sown or allowed to grow around the vine which is located at the very center of the vineyard (Samuel in Y. Kil. 5:5 (30a)).[36] A-B+C-D states that when the vines are separated by four or five *amot*, forty-five vines

are sanctified, while E-G rules that when the vines are six or
seven *amot* away from each other, all vines within a radius of sixteen *amot* from the vine in the center are sanctified. Now TAS
agrees with Maimonides that E-G states a general rule applying to
all arrangements of vines. We maintain, however, that such a
position raises the same problems mentioned above with reference
to Maimonides' opinion (i.e., only thirty-seven vines are contained in a radius of sixteen *amot* when the vines are set apart
by five *amot*).[37] We shall therefore modify the view of TAS and
not read A-B as an instance of E-G. The two rules then disagree
because of the difference in the spacing of the vines. In the
case of A-B the vines are separated by four or five *amot* (C-D),
so that the vegetables lie within the area of tillage (= four
amot) of both the vine at the center and the eight surrounding
vines (cf. fig. 41), and are regarded as being sown near each of
these nine vines. We have already seen that, according to House
of Hillel (M. 4:5H), vegetables which lie within the area of
tillage of a vineyard sanctify a "vineyard" consisting of two
rows of vines.[38] This rule is here applied to each of the nine
vines, so that every vine which may combine with one or more of
these vines to form a vineyard (consisting of two rows of vines,
with two vines aligned opposite three others [M. 4:6]) is sanctified. The number of vines which are sanctified when the vines
are separated by four or five *amot* thus turns out to be forty-
five (fig. 42).

At E-G, on the other hand, the vines are set apart by six
or seven *amot*, and the vegetables sown around the vine in the
center lie within the area of tillage of that vine alone. In
this instance, then, only those vines are sanctified which may
combine with the central vine to form a vineyard. Now we may
support the interpretation of TAS by showing that all of these
sanctified vines, and these vines alone, lie within a radius of
sixteen *amot* from the vine in the center. We may demonstrate
that all of the sanctified vines are contained in the circle of
radius sixteen *amot* by showing that the sanctified vine which
lies furthest from the center is less than sixteen *amot* away
from it. We may similarly show that only the sanctified vines
are contained in the circle by determining that the vine which
is closest to the center and yet not sanctified lies more than
sixteen *amot* away from the center. In each case the distance
between the vine in the center and the outer vine may be measured

by constructing a right triangle with the hypotenuse drawn
between the two vines. The measure of the hypotenuse is then
equal to the square root of the sum of the squares of the measures
of the triangle's other two sides (Pythagorean Theorem).

The proof proceeds as follows. First, the perpendicular
sides of a right triangle with a hypotenuse drawn from the center
to the furthest sanctified vine respectively measure either
6 and 12 *amot* (with the vines spaced at intervals of six *amot*)
or 7 and 14 *amot* (with the vines spaced at intervals of seven
amot) (fig. 43). The distance between the furthest sanctified
vine and the center is then either

$$13.41 = \sqrt{6^2 + 12^{12}} \qquad \text{or} \qquad 15.65 = \sqrt{7^2 + 14^2} \qquad amot,$$

so that this vine lies within the circle of radius sixteen *amot*.
Since the sanctified vine furthest from the center lies within
the circle, all other sanctified vines are contained in the circle
as well. Second, the perpendicular sides of a right triangle with
a hypotenuse drawn from the vine in the center to the nearest
vine which is not sanctified respectively measure either 12 and
12 *amot* (with the vines spaced at intervals of six *amot*) or 14
and 14 *amot* (with the vines spaced at intervals of seven *amot*)
(fig. 43). The vine which is closest to the center and yet not
sanctified is either

$$16.97 = \sqrt{12^2 + 12^2} \qquad \text{or} \qquad 19.79 = \sqrt{14^2 + 14^2} \quad amot$$

away from the center, and thus lies outside of the circle of
radius sixteen *amot*. Since the nearest vine to the center which
is not sanctified is not contained in the circle, no vine which
is not sanctified lies within the circle. We have thus accounted
for the rule of E-G by first determining which vines are sanctified, and then showing that the circle of radius sixteen *amot*
exclusively contains all of these vines.

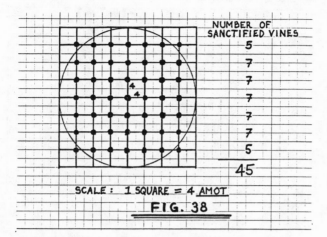

NUMBER OF
SANCTIFIED VINES

5
7
7
7
7
7
5
___
45

SCALE : 1 SQUARE = 4 AMOT

FIG. 38

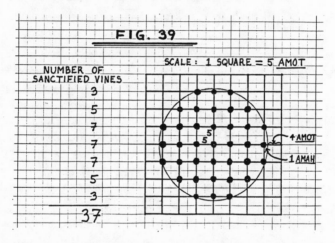

FIG. 39

SCALE : 1 SQUARE = 5 AMOT

NUMBER OF
SANCTIFIED VINES

3
5
7
7
7
5
3
___
37

4 AMOT
1 AMAH

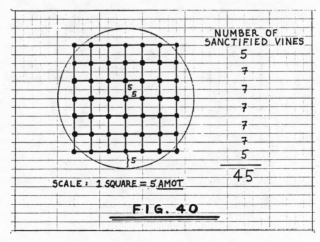

NUMBER OF
SANCTIFIED VINES

5
7
7
7
7
7
5
___
45

SCALE : 1 SQUARE = 5 AMOT

FIG. 40

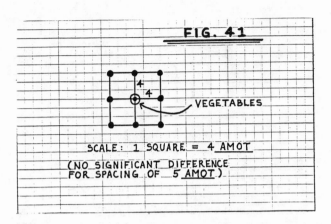

FIG. 41

SCALE: 1 SQUARE = 4 AMOT

(NO SIGNIFICANT DIFFERENCE
FOR SPACING OF 5 AMOT)

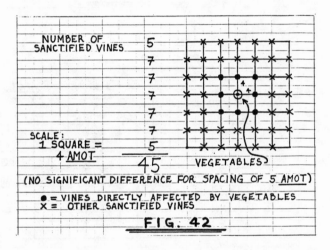

NUMBER OF
SANCTIFIED VINES

5
7
7
7
7
7
‾‾
45

SCALE:
1 SQUARE =
4 AMOT

VEGETABLES

(NO SIGNIFICANT DIFFERENCE FOR SPACING OF 5 AMOT)

● = VINES DIRECTLY AFFECTED BY VEGETABLES
X = OTHER SANCTIFIED VINES

FIG. 42

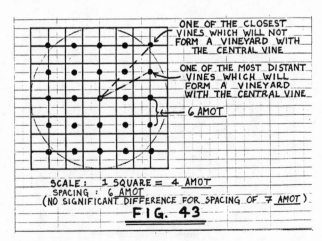

ONE OF THE CLOSEST
VINES WHICH WILL NOT
FORM A VINEYARD WITH
THE CENTRAL VINE

ONE OF THE MOST DISTANT
VINES WHICH WILL
FORM A VINEYARD
WITH THE CENTRAL VINE

6 AMOT

SCALE: 1 SQUARE = 4 AMOT
SPACING : 6 AMOT
(NO SIGNIFICANT DIFFERENCE FOR SPACING OF 7 AMOT)

FIG. 43

A. *He who plants vegetables in the vineyard or allows them to grow,*

B. *lo, this one sanctifies [i.e., prohibits the use of] forty-five vines.*

C. *When [is this the case]?*

D. *When [the vines] were planted by [intervals of] four, four [amot, i.e., the vines were separated from one another by four amot in each direction], or by [intervals of] five, five [amot, i.e., the vines were separated from one another by five amot in each direction].*

E. *[If the vines] were planted by [intervals of] six, six [amot, i.e., the vines were separated from one another by six amot in each direction], or by [intervals of] seven, seven [amot, i.e., the vines were separated by seven amot in each direction],*

F. *lo, this one sanctifies [i.e., prohibits the use of the vines planted within] sixteen amah in* [Erfurt omits the following through I] *each direction,*

G. *[measured] in circles and not in squares* [= M. 5:5A-G].

H. R. Simeon b. Eleazar says, "He drives [GRA[39] adds: a stake (*ytd*)] into the ground [at the spot at which the vegetables grow], and measures from it *sixteen amah in each direction,*

I. "*[measuring] in circles and not in squares* [HD: (measuring) in squares and not in circles],

J. "because they [i.e., the vines in the corners of the square] appear [as if they are] in [Erfurt, first printed ed.: like] the corner[s] of a tablet [i.e., they are considered to be part of the whole] [Erfurt: it (i.e., the vineyard) is regarded (to be) like a curved horn (*kqrn ᶜgwlh*)[40]]."

T. Kil. 3:11 (pp. 215-216, ll. 41-45)

T. Kil. 3:11 cites M. 5:5 at A-G, with Simeon glossing and opposing G at H-J. The reading of H-J is somewhat difficult. According to our present text Simeon b. Eleazar agrees with G and H-I, saying that F refers to a circle and not to the square in which it is inscribed. At J, however, he states that the vines in the corners of the square are regarded as being in corners of a tablet, or as part of a whole (cf. T. Ah. 15:2 [Neusner, *HMLP*, IV, pp. 292-293] for a similar use of the phrase *qrn ṭbl'*).

These vines would not be contained in a circle, so that Simeon
b. Eleazar here appears to oppose H-I. We therefore follow HD
and emend I to read "[measuring] in squares and not in circles."
Simeon b. Eleazar then opposes G, maintaining that F describes
the square rather than the circle inscribed within it, for the
corner-vines are to be sanctified along with the other vines.

5:6

A. He who sees vegetables [growing] in the vineyard and said
    [Mn, N: says], "When I shall reach it [i.e., the vege-
    tables] I shall pluck it [so Danby for '$lqtnw$]" --
B. it is permitted [i.e., the vegetables and surrounding
    vines are not sanctified].
C. [If he said,] "When I shall return I shall pluck it"--
D. if [in the meantime] it [i.e., the vegetables] increased
    [in size] by [one] two-hundred[th] [all commentaries],
E. it is prohibited [i.e., the vegetables and the surrounding
    vines are sanctified].

M. Kil. 5:6

M. Kil. 5:6 defines the act of allowing diverse-kinds to
grow in a vineyard, and so complements the discussion of M. 5:5
concerning, "He who plants vegetables in the vineyard or allows
them to grow." M. is a unitary pericope consisting of A-B, a
declarative sentence and C+E, a conditional sentence dependent
on A for its context. D glosses C+E. C balances the latter
part of A ($k\check{s}'gy^c$ lw $vs.$ $k\check{s}'h\text{z}r$), while the apodoses at B and
E are fixed. We note that A opens with a participle and then
uses the perfect tense, a shift which may indicate that A has
been revised to follow the formulary pattern of M. 5:5.

According to A-B one who spots vegetables growing in his
vineyard need not immediately remove them, but may allow them to
grow until he reaches them in the course of his work. Since he
has not overtly indicated that he wishes the vegetables to grow
in the vineyard, it does not appear as if he allows diverse-kinds
to grow, and he therefore need not make a special effort to
uproot them. C+E, on the other hand, states that, having
reached the vegetables, one may not leave the area with the intent of returning to remove them. By leaving one makes it appear
as if he wishes the vegetables to continue to grow, and he is
thus regarded as one who allows diverse-kinds to grow in the vine-

yard. D adds that one may not leave and allow the vegetables to
remain if, in the meantime, they grow by one two-hundredth.

A. The owner (*b^cl hbyt*) [of a vineyard] who allowed wild
    vegetables (*yrqwt śdh*) to grow in the vineyard--
B. it [i.e., the use of the vegetables or vines] is prohibited
    for him and prohibited for everyone [else] [Y.: whether
    for him or for anyone else].
C. Another [person] from any place [Y.: a worker] who allowed
    wild vegetables to grow in [someone else's] vineyard--
D. it [i.e., the use of the vegetables or vines] is prohibited
    for him and permitted for everyone [else].

T. Kil. 3:12b (p. 216, ll. 47-49)

(Y. Kil. 5:5 (30a))

T. Kil. 3:12b comments on M. 5:6, introducing a distinction
between the owner and the passerby who allow diverse-kinds to
grow in the vineyard. T. is composed of two well-balanced
declarative sentences, A-B and C-D. T. concerns the case of wild
vegetables which grow in a vineyard, and thus underlines the fact
that the vegetables involved are not sown.[41] According to A-B
the owner who allows the vegetables to grow in his vineyard
renders them prohibited, or sanctifies them (along with the
surrounding vines), for everyone. C-D then states that one who
sees vegetables growing in another's vineyard but fails to remove
them, as he is allowed to do (cf. T. 2:16 [cited by *TZ*, p. 216,
on l. 48]), renders them prohibited for himself but not for others.
In this instance one may not himself use diverse-kinds which he
has allowed to grow, but he does not render them prohibited for
others, presumably because one cannot sanctify that which is not
his (cf. M. 7:4-5). T. thus effectively understands sanctification
in a relative sense, for in the latter case the vegetables and
vines do not become absolutely prohibited, but are forbidden
only to certain individuals.

5:7

A. [If]he was passing through the vineyard, and seeds fell from
    him [i.e., from those which he was carrying]--
B. or [if seeds] went out [into the vineyard] with the dung
    [used in manuring the vineyard] or with the water [which
    irrigated the vineyard]--

C. he who sows [in a field of grain (Y.)] and the wind blew
    ($s^c rtw$) [the seeds] behind him [into the nearby vineyard]--

D. it is permitted.

E. [If] the wind blew ($s^c rtw$; most mss.: $syy^c tw$ ["aided him
    (in spreading)"]) [the seeds] before him [Bert. (according
    to MS), KP[42] add: --it is prohibited]--

F. R. ^{c}Aqiva says, "If [he allowed the seeds to grow until they
    yielded] blades [so Danby for $^c \check{s} bym$], he shall overturn
    [them].

G. "If [he allowed the seeds to grow until they reached] an
    early stage of ripening [so Primus[43] for 'byb], he shall
    break [the ears] off [following Danby for $ynps$].

H. "And if [he allowed the seeds to grow until they] yielded
    [Primus adds: ripened] grain--it shall be burnt."

M. Kil. 5:7

M. Kil. 5:7 discusses the act of sowing diverse-kinds in a
vineyard, and so further complements M. 5:5. M. is composed of
A-D, consisting of three protases (A-C) with a single, fixed
apodosis (D), and E-H, containing a protasis (E) which balances
C and a saying of ^{c}Aqiva (F-H). Since E responds only to C,
and since C (rather than A-B) follows the formulary pattern of
M. 5:5A and M. 5:6A, it appears that C originally opened the
pericope, and that A-B was later attached to it. The balance of
C and E leads us to expect D to be balanced by the fixed apodosis
'swr, which has apparently been dropped in favor of ^{c}Aqiva's
saying at F-H. The latter is then not primary to the pericope,
and we shall see, in fact, that it does not deal with the issue
of M. 5:5E at all. T. 3:12a, furthermore, assigns to Simeon,
an Ushan, a different version of M. (lacking ^{c}Aqiva's saying), so
that it is unlikely that the pericope is of Yavnean origin. M.
then appears to have originally consisted of C-E + the apodosis
'swr.

A-B describes cases in which seeds accidentally enter a
vineyard without being sown. C and E then contrast two cases of
accidental sowing in a vineyard, distinguishing between the
appearances of intentional and unintentional sowing. In both
instances the wind blows into an adjacent vineyard seeds which
are sown in a field of grain (Eleazar in Y. Kil. 5:7). If the
wind blows the seeds behind the sower into the vineyard (C) the
sowing is considered to be unintentional. Since the sower
clearly does not want the wind to blow the seeds away from the

spot of sowing, it does not appear as if he wishes the seeds to
go into the vineyard. This sowing is therefore permitted (D),[44]
i.e., it does not sanctify the vines.[45] It is now clear that
A and B have been added in order to illustrate the case of C.
If, on the other hand, the wind blows the seeds before the
sower (E), the sowing is considered to be intentional. Since
the sower desires the wind to blow from behind him and scatter
the seeds, he thus appears to wish that the seeds be blown into
the vineyard. In this instance, then, the sowing is presumably
prohibited.

In F-H [C]Aqiva describes that method of destroying seeds which
is appropriate to each stage of the seeds' development. [C]Aqiva's
saying is then not relevant to the case of E. While the latter
concerns only the sowing of seeds in a vineyard, [C]Aqiva's saying
presupposes that the seeds have been allowed to grow as well.
F-H perhaps better fits the context of M. 5:6, which specifically
discusses the question of allowing diverse-kinds to grow in a
vineyard. M. 5:6 would then read as follows:

A. He who sees vegetables [growing] in the vineyard and said,
    "When I shall reach it [i.e., the vegetables] I shall
    pluck it"--
B. it is permitted [i.e., the vegetables and surrounding vines
    are not sanctified].
C. [If he said,] "When I shall return I shall pluck it"--
D. if [in the meantime] it [i.e., the vegetables] increased
    [in size] by [one] two-hundred[th]--
E. R. [C]Aqiva says, "If [the seeds yielded] blades, he shall
    overturn [them].
F. "If [they reached] an early stage of ripening, he shall
    break [the ears] off.
G. "And if [they] yielded [ripened] grain--it shall be burnt."

[C]Aqiva's methods of destroying the seeds may be described
as follows. If one allows the seeds to sprout only blades, he
may destroy them by simply overturning them (F). If, however,
the plants have reached an early stage of ripening ('byb), in
which they already have ears containing partially-ripened grains,[46]
then they are not to be overturned. Although the ears, by being
overturned, would be detached from the ground, they would still
continue to provide nourishment to the grains within them. One
must therefore break off the ears (G), and thereby dislodge the

grains, which will then dry up.[47] Finally, grains which are
fully ripened are able to survive even outside of the ears, so
that these grains can only be destroyed by being burnt (H).

A.   R. Simeon b. Judah says in the name of R. Simeon, *"He who
      sows [in a field of grain] and the wind blew (sy^crtw) [the
      seeds] behind him [into the nearby vineyard]*--

B.   *"it is permitted* [= M. 5:7C-D],

C.   "for it is [a case of] an unavoidable accident [so Danby[48]
      for *'wns*].

D.   *"[If] the wind aided him [in spreading]* (syy^ctw; first
      printed ed.: sy^crtw ["blew"]) [*the seeds*] *before him*
      [= M. 5:7E],

E.   [Erfurt, first printed ed., add:]   "it is prohibited."

                    T. Kil. 3:12a (p. 216, ll. 45-47)
                    (A-C: Y. Kil. 5:7 (30a))

        T. Kil. 3:12a attributes M. 5:7C-E, with slight differences,
to Simeon b. Judah in the name of Simeon. T.'s version of
the pericope differs from that of M. in two places. C glosses
A-B, explaining that the sowing described in the latter is considered to be an unavoidable accident, since the wind scatters
the seeds in the direction opposite to that in which the sower
intends them to fall. At E T. presents the apodosis *'swr*,
which the presence of *mwtr* in M. 5:7D (= T. 3:12a/B) had led
us to expect.

R.   [*You shall not sow your vineyard with diverse-kinds lest
      the whole yield be sanctified,*] *the seed* [*which you have
      sown and the yield of the vineyard* (Dt. 22:9)]--

S.   excluding [the cases of] seed which went out [into the
      vineyard] with the dung [used in manuring the vineyard] or
      with the water [which irrigated the vineyard],

T.   [or the case of] he who sows in a white field and the wind
      blew (the seeds) behind him (into the nearby vineyard)
      [= M. 5:7B-C].

U.   Might one say that I should exclude [as well the case of]
      he who sows and the wind aided him [in spreading] ($msyy^ctw$;
      London, Hillel, GRA: $ms^ărtw$ ["blew"]) [(the seed) before
      him] [= M. 5:7E]?

V.   Scripture says, *Which you have sown.*

                Sifré Dt. 230e (ed. Finkelstein, p. 263, ll. 5-6)

Sifré Dt. 230e supplies proof-texts from Dt. 22:9 to M. 5:7B-C+E. R-T takes the phrase *the seed* to exclude all but the seed which the owner desires to be sown, and so to exclude the cases of S-T. At U-V the relative clause *which you have sown* is understood to include all cases of intentional sowing, and thus to include the case of E.

5:8

A. He who allows thorns to grow in the vineyard--

B. R. Eliezer [B. B.B. 156b: Eleazar] says, "He has sanctified [the surrounding vines of the vineyard]."

C. And sages say, "He does not sanctify [the surrounding vines of the vineyard],

D. "except [when he allows to grow] something the like of which they [Danby: ordinarily] allow to grow."

E. (1) Iris,[49] and (2) ivy,[50] and (3) a white lily,[51]

F. and all kinds of [plants grown for the sake of their] seeds [Geniza fragments,[52] P, Pr (cf. also T. 3:12c, MS, and Lieberman[53]): are kinds of seeds and],

G. are not [GRA: are] [considered] diverse-kinds in the vineyard.

H. (4) Hemp[54]--

I. R. Tarfon says, "It is not [considered] diverse-kinds [in the vineyard]."

J. And sages say, "[It is considered] diverse-kinds [in the vineyard]."

K. (5) And the globe artichoke[55] is [considered] diverse-kinds [in the vineyard].

M. Kil. 5:8 (A-D: B. Shab. 144b, B. B.B.
156b, Y. Kil. 1:1 (26d))

M. Kil. 5:8 consists of two parts, A-D and E-K, which may be distinguished from one another by the language of their apodoses. A-D concerns the sanctification of vines by the growing of another kind in the vineyard, and its operative language is *qdš/l' qdš*. E-K determines whether or not certain kinds of plants are considered diverse-kinds in a vineyard, and its apodoses read *kl'ym/ 'ynn kl'ym (± bkrm)*.

A-D is composed of a well-balanced dispute at A-C (with A in the formulary pattern of M. 5:5A, 5:6A, 5:7C), with D glossing C. According to D the dispute concerns whether or not one who allows useless plants, such as thorns, to grow in a vineyard thereby sanctifies the vines. Eliezer says that he does sanctify

the vines, for any kind which he allows to grow is considered
to be diverse-kinds in the vineyard. Sages, on the other hand,
maintain that the vines are sanctified only by a kind which is
usually allowed to grow, i.e., a kind which is beneficial to the
owner (D), for only then does it appear as if the owner wishes
the other kind to grow in the vineyard. According to Eliezer,
then, the actual growth of diverse-kinds determines the status
of the vines, while sages say that one sanctifies the vines only
when one desires the diverse-kinds to grow, and thus one may
allow certain kinds to grow without sanctifying the vines.

E-K consists of a list of three plants at E+G (glossed by
F), a balanced dispute concerning another plant at H-J, and a
declarative sentence dealing with a fifth plant at K. According
to E+G iris, ivy, and the white lily are not considered diverse-
kinds in a vineyard, apparently because they serve no useful
purpose for the owner (following Rabad, Maim., *Code, Diverse-kinds*
5:19). E+G then illustrates the position of sages in C-D (and E-K
is related to A-D). F states that plants grown for the sake of
their seeds are also not considered diverse-kinds in the vineyard.
The reasoning behind this rule is difficult, for presumably any
kind of plant is considered diverse-kinds in a vineyard (cf. the
emendation of GRA). The point of F is perhaps analogous to that
of D, maintaining that since the owner desires the seeds but not
the plants themselves, the latter are not considered diverse-kinds
in a vineyard. Alternatively, some manuscripts (perhaps following
T.) read F as referring to E. F then states that even though the
three plants of E are grown for the sake of their seeds, they are
not considered diverse-kinds in the vineyard because they are not
usually allowed to grow (Rabad).[56]

The dispute of H-J apparently concerns whether or not hemp
is grown primarily for the sake of its seeds or for its plant.
Tarfon maintains that hemp is grown mainly for its seeds, which
produce an oil, and therefore is not considered diverse-kinds in
a vineyard (F). Sages, however, say that hemp is grown primarily
for its fibers, which are used in the manufacture of rope and
clothing,[57] and thus is considered diverse-kinds in the vineyard.[58] K concerns the globe artichoke, of which both the leaves
and flowers may be eaten.[59] The point of K apparently is that
the plant is grown primarily for the sake of its leaves, and
therefore is considered diverse-kinds in a vineyard.

A. (1) Chrozophorae,[60] and (2) spurges,[61] and (3) cudweed
(*brkwyyr*),[62] and (4) muscari,[63] and (5) dyer's reseda,[64]
and (6) saffron,[65]

B.   and (7) *a globe artichoke* [= M. 5:8K] and (8) ammi,[66]
     and (9) mallow,[67]

C.   and (10) savory,[68] and (11) hyssop,[69] and (12) thyme,[70]

D.   and (13) chate melons, and (14) gourds, and (15) watermelons,
     and (16) musk melons, and (17) a cowpea,

E.   [even though they are] kinds of [plants grown for the
     sake of their] seeds,

F.   lo, they are [considered] diverse-kinds in the vineyard.

T. Kil. 3:12c (p. 216, ll. 49-53)

G.   (18) *Iris, and* (19) *ivy, and* (20) *a white lily*

H.   are kinds of [plants grown for the sake of their] seeds,

I.   and *are not [considered] diverse-kinds in the vineyard*
     [= M. Kil. 5:8E-G].

J.   R. Dosethai b. Judah says, "Kinds of grasses [are considered]
     diverse-kinds in a vineyard."

T. Kil. 3:13 (p. 216, ll. 52-53)

K.   (21) A cat-tail flag,[71] and (22) a juncus,[72] and (23) a
     papyrus plant,[73]

L.   and everything which grows in the dirt [i.e., in meadow-grass
     (Lieberman)],

M.   are kinds of grasses,

N.   [and] lo, they are [Erfurt: are not] [considered] diverse-
     kinds in the vineyard.

T. Kil. 3:14 (pp. 216-217, ll. 53-54)
(Y. Kil. 5:8 (30a))

O.   (24) Reeds,[74] and (25) alhagi,[75] and (26) the hawthorns,[76]
     and (27) buckthorns,[77]

P.   are kinds of trees,

Q.   and are not [considered] diverse-kinds in the vineyard.

R.   This is the general rule: Every [plant] which sends out its
     leaves from its base, lo, this is [considered] an herb (*yrq*).

S.   And every [plant] which does not send out its leaves from
     its base, lo, this is considered a tree.

T. Kil. 3:15 (p. 217, ll. 55-57)
(O-Q: B. Erub. 34b, Y. Kil. 5:8 (30a))

T.   (28) Squill[78]-

U. R. Ishmael [Erfurt: Simeon] says, "It is [considered] diverse-kinds in the vineyard."

V. And sages say, "It is not [considered] diverse-kinds in the vineyard."

W. (29) Dodder[79]--

X. R. Tarfon says, "It is not [considered] diverse-kinds [in the vineyard]."

Y. And sages say, "It is [considered] diverse-kinds [in the vineyard]."

Z. Said R. Tarfon, "If [it is considered] diverse-kinds in the vineyard, let [it be considered] diverse-kinds [when planted] with seeds.

AA. "And if it is not [considered] diverse-kinds [when planted] with seeds, let it not be [considered] diverse-kinds in the vineyard."

T. Kil. 3:16 (p. 217, ll. 57-60) (W-Y: B. Shab. 139a)

BB. (3) Caper[80]--

CC. House of Shammai say, "It is [considered] diverse-kinds [Erfurt, first printed ed. omit:] in the vineyard."

DD. House of Hillel says, "It is not [considered] diverse-kinds."

EE. And both agree that [the caper] is liable in [respect to the laws of] *ᶜorlah*.

T. Kil. 3:17 (p. 217, ll. 60-61) (B. Ber. 36a, Y. Kil. 5:8 (30a))

T. Kil. 3:12c-17 complements M. 5:8E-K with a large construction concerning whether or not certain plants are considered to be diverse-kinds in a vineyard. T. consists of three major subunits, A-I, J-N, and O-EE. A-I lists twenty kinds of seeds which either are or are not considered diverse-kinds in a vineyard. J-N then discusses the status of three kinds of grasses which grow in a vineyard, and O-EE concerns whether or not seven kinds of plants are treated as trees and are thus not considered diverse-kinds in a vineyard. T. therefore discusses thirty plants in all.

A-I complements M. 5:8F by contrasting those kinds of seeds which are considered diverse-kinds in a vineyard (A-F) with those that are not so considered (G-I) (Lieberman[81]). A-F lists seventeen plants, which may be arranged in sublists of six (A), three (B), three (C), and five (D). The five trailing-plants of D,[82] however, are clearly not grown for the sake of their seeds, and so apparently do not belong on the list. The remaining

twelve plants are all presumably grown for their seeds. Four
of the six plants of A (1-2,5-6) are grown for their dyes.[83]
The identification of *brkwyyr* (3) as cudweed, an herb, is tenta-
tive. Muscari (4) is grown for its edible bulbs. It is possible,
then, that plants 3 and 4 do not belong on the list of A, so
that A should contain four plants and A-D should list ten in all.

The three plants of B are all grown for use as food. The
globe artichoke, the leaves and flowers of which are edible, is
mentioned in M. 5:8K as being considered diverse-kinds in a
vineyard. T. then perhaps contrasts the globe artichoke with
the plants of G, so relating M. 5:8K to M. 5:8E-G. Ammi (8) is
used as flavoring,[84] while mallow is similar to the globe artichoke in that both its leaves and its flowers may be eaten.[85]
All of the plants of C belong to the mint family (Labiateae),
and so are grown for use as spices. G-I then cites M. 5:8E-G
(reading M. 5:8F as referring to M. 5:8E), saying that iris, ivy,
and white lily are kinds of seeds, and are not considered diverse-
kinds in the vineyard. A-I may read M. 5:8A-D into M. 5:8F[86]
in order to qualify the latter. T's point then is that although
the plants of both A-D and G are kinds of seeds, the former are
beneficial to the owner and are considered diverse-kinds in the
vineyard, while the latter are not usually allowed to grow and
thus are not so considered.

J-N consists of Dosethai b. Judah's ruling at J, followed
by a list at K+M-N, which is perhaps glossed by L. Dosethai b.
Judah rules that kinds of grasses are considered diverse-kinds
in a vineyard. K+M-N then either illustrates his rule, or,
according to the reading of Erfurt Ms., presents exceptions to
it, following the pattern of A-I (Lieberman[87]). All of the
plants of K grow in or near water, so that L simply generalizes
the rule of K.

O-EE is composed of O-Q, a list of trees, R-S, a well-
balanced general rule for distinguishing between trees and herbs,
and T-EE, a series of three disputes (T-V, W-AA, and BB-EE) concerning whether certain plants are considered trees or herbs.
O lists four plants which are regarded as trees and so are not
considered diverse-kinds in a vineyard.[88] These plants are
treated as trees either because their leaves do not come out
of their roots (R-S), or because they have hard stems (Lieberman[89]). R-S then differentiates between herbs and trees, ruling
that plants with leaves coming directly out of their bases or roots
are considered herbs, while those with leaves coming out of other
parts (e.g., branches) are regarded as trees.[90]

In T-V Ishmael and sages dispute concerning whether squill
is considered an herb or a tree. Squill is a bulbous plant with
a two-part growth-cycle. In late summer it sprouts a stem containing many flowers. When the fruits of the plant ripen and
its seeds scatter, the stem withers and dies, and all that
remains of the plant is the underground bulb. In the fall leaves
then sprout up directly from the bulb.[91] Ishmael apparently
maintains that squill is an herb because its leaves grow out
of its base in the fall, while sages say that because of its
summer stem squill is considered a tree.[92]

W-AA consists of a dispute between Tarfon and sages at W-Y,
followed by an argument of Tarfon at Z-AA which appears to be the
beginning of a debate. Sages, however, are not assigned a
response to the argument, so that the redactor of W-AA appears
to favor Tarfon's position.[93] The dispute of W-Y deals with
dodder, a parasitic plant which abandons its own roots upon
latching onto a host plant.[94] Tarfon perhaps reasons that dodder
is considered a tree because once it becomes attached to the
host its leaves do not appear to come out of its base. Sages,
though, maintain that dodder is considered an herb,[95] presumably
because its leaves originally grow out of its roots. Tarfon then
determines the status of the plant on the basis of its appearance,
while sages take account of its actual process of growth. In Z-AA
Tarfon argues that sages' views are inconsistent, for while they
do not regard dodder as being diverse-kinds among seeds (thus
considering dodder to be a tree), they do regard it as being
diverse-kinds in a vineyard (thus treating it as an herb). The
view attributed by Tarfon to sages, which states that dodder is
considered to be diverse-kinds among seeds, is not found anywhere
else in M.-T.[96]

The Houses-disputes at BB-DD (which is glossed by EE) concerns caper, which, like squill, has a two-part growth cycle.
During the summer its leaves and flowers grow on branches. The
latter then dry up and disappear,[97] and a new stem sprouts from
the roots in spring.[98] House of Shammai apparently consider
caper to be an herb because its leaves and flowers grow directly
from the base of the plant in spring. House of Hillel, on the
other hand, maintain that because the plant grows branches in the
summer it is regarded as a tree.[99] According to EE both sides
agree that caper is considered a tree in respect to the laws of
corlah, so that EE effectively brings House of Shammai over
to the position of House of Hillel.

W. He who allows thorns to grow in the vineyard--

X. R. Eliezer says, "He has sanctified [the surrounding vines of the vineyard] [= M. 5:8A-B],

Y. [GRA, Nesiv[100] reverse C and E] "as it is written, [*The seed*] *which you have sown* (Dt. 22:9)."

Z. And sages say, "*The seed* (Dt. 22:9),

AA. excluding He who allows thorns to grow in the vineyard."

Sifré Dt. 230f (ed. Finkelstein, p. 263, ll. 6-8)

Sifré Dt. 230f, citing M. 5:8A-B, provides proof-texts from Dt. 22:9 for both sides of M.'s dispute. In X-Y Eliezer's view that thorns which are allowed to grow in a vineyard sanctify the vines is supported by the phrase *Which you have sown*. Since this phrase on the surface adds nothing to the preceding phrase, *The seed*, it is taken to include every plant which is allowed to grow among the plants which sanctify the vines (Hillel). Sages' view that the thorns do not sanctify the vines is supported in Z-AA by the phrase *The seed*, which is understood to include as plants which sanctify the vines only those plants which one usually allows to grow. According to the alternate reading of GRA and Nesiv, Eliezer's view is supported by the phrase *The seed*, which is taken to include all plants, while sages' opinion is supported by the phrase *Which you have sown*, which is understood to exclude everything which one would not normally allow to grow.

CHAPTER SIX

KILAYIM CHAPTER SIX

Chapter Six presents an essay dealing with the relationship
between a trained vine and its supporting structure. M. discusses this question in a logical sequence, considering first
the structure which actually supports the vine (M. 6:1+2A-C
[with M. 6:2D-F appended]), then that part of the structure which
is not covered by the vine (M. 6:3-5+6+7), and finally those
parts of either the vine or structure which project beyond the
whole (M. 6:8-9). The chapter opens (M. 6:1-2A-C) and closes
(M. 6:6+7+8+9) with a discussion of the espalier, or row of
trained vines, and treats at its center the single trained vine
(M. 6:3-5).

The chapter logically begins with the definition of an
espalier as a row of five vines trained on a fence (M. 6:1).
Like a vineyard, an espalier is allowed four *amot* as its area of
tillage. The Houses then dispute whether these four *amot* are
measured from the vines or from the fence, i.e., whether the
former or the latter constitutes the principal part of the espalier.
This dispute is based on the Houses-dispute of M. 4:5, which concerns whether one (House of Shammai) or two (House of Hillel)
rows of vines form a vineyard. House of Shammai reason here that
the vines are regarded as being primary to the espalier, for they
maintain that the row of vines itself forms a vineyard and would
thus be allowed four *amot* even without a fence. House of Hillel,
on the other hand, maintain that the espalier's chief component
is the fence, without which, in their view, the row of vines would
be allowed the area of tillage of a single vine, six handbreadths.
M. 6:2A-C then augments M. 6:1 with a discussion concerning the
area of tillage which is allowed to an espalier planted on a
terrace, and is itself complemented by M. 6:2D-F, which discusses
another problem related to planting vines on a terrace.

The attention of M. now turns to that part of the structure
which does not support the vine. The discussion of this part of
the structure is opened by M. 6:3-5, a subunit characterized by
its distinctive formulary pattern (*hmdlh*, at M. 6:3A, D, 6:4A),
and by its subject, the single trained vine. The issue of M. 6:3-5
concerns whether the entire supporting structure is considered
to be merely an extension of the vine (as in the case of the

espalier), so that one may not sow even under that part which is
not covered by the vine, or whether the structure retains its
own aspect, and one may sow under the part which does not serve
the vine. M. at first distinguishes between an inanimate
structure (e.g., a latticework of laths), which is considered
to be entirely "taken over" by the vine trained upon it, and an
animate structure (e.g., a fruit tree), which keeps its own aspect.
A glossator, however, redraws this distinction, contrasting
instead a non-fruit-bearing structure (e.g., a barren tree), which
is regarded as an extension of the vine, and a fruit-bearing
structure (e.g., a fruit tree), which is not so regarded.

M. 6:6+7 then raises the question of M. 6:3-5, i.e., whether
one may sow under that part of the structure which does not support
the vine, with respect to uncovered areas in the middle (M. 6:6)
or at the end (M. 6:7) of an espalier's wall. M. rules that
one may sow at such spots along the wall after allowing the vines
their area of tillage, and so disagrees with the rule of M. 6:3-5,
according to which one would not be able to sow at all along any
part of the wall (since the latter is neither animate nor fruit-
bearing). M. 6:6+7 therefore appears to be interested not in
the issue of the status of the supporting structure, but in the
entirely different question of separating the vines from the
other kind in order to prevent the appearance of diverse-kinds.
We note that M. 6:7 follows the formulary pattern of M. 6:2A
($^c rys\ hyw\d{s}'\ mn$ X), so that the two pericopae were originally
redacted together. A redactor then separated the two pericopae,
which are not related to each other in substance, by inserting
between them M. 6:2D-F, which augments M. 6:2A-C, and M. 6:3-5+6,
which (as we have just seen) discusses the same issue as does
M. 6:7.

Reversing the formulary pattern of M. 6:7 ($^c rys\ hyw\d{s}'\ mn$ X
[M. 6:7] $vs.$ X $hyw\d{s}'\ mn\ h^c rys$ [M. 6:8A,6:9E]), M. 6:8-9 concludes
the chapter with a sub-unit dealing with the projections of an
espalier. The issue of the sub-unit concerns whether part of
the espalier which projects beyond it may nevertheless be regarded
as belonging to an espalier, so that one may not sow under such
a projection. Reeds projecting from the supporting structure,
on the one hand, do not at all serve the vines and so are considered to be separate from the espalier. A projecting vine-blossom,
on the other hand, will eventually produce grapes, and therefore
is regarded as part of the espalier.

6:1

A.   What is an espalier (^{c}rys)?

B.   He who plants a row of five vines beside a fence which is
     ten handbreadths high, or beside a ditch which is ten hand-
     breadths deep and four wide--

C.   they allow it its area of tillage of four *amot*.

D.   House of Shammai say, "They measure four *amot* from the base
     of the vines to the field."

E.   House of Hillel say, "From the fence to the field."

F.   Said R. Yohanan b. Nuri, "All err who say so [tr. Danby].

G.   "Rather, [the four *amot* are measured as follows:] If
     there are four *amot* from the base of the vines to the fence,
     they allow it its area of tillage and he sows the rest."

H.   And how much is the area of tillage of a [single] vine?

I.   Six handbreadths in all directions.

J.   R. ^{c}Aqiva says, "Three [handbreadths]."

                              M. Kil. 6:1 (A-B [until "vines"]:
                              Y. Kil. 4:1 (29b); J: Y. Kil. 7:1 (30d))

       M. Kil. 6:1 opens the chapter's discussion of the espalier
by dealing with the distance which must separate the vines from
another kind. M. begins with a question at A, followed by a
mildly apocopated sentence (in the *he-who*-formulary pattern)
at B-C. The latter, however, does not respond to A, for it concerns not the definition of an espalier but the extent of its
area of tillage. Furthermore, B-C contains both a protasis and
an apodosis, and so can stand without A. It is possible that
A was originally answered by a phrase such as "A row of five vines
beside a fence, etc.," which was then absorbed by B-C when the
latter was attached to A. We note that B follows the formulary
pattern of M. 4:5A ("He who plants a row of five vines"). Since
M. 6:1B-C and M. 4:5A are both followed by Houses-disputes, it
is possible that the two pericopae were redacted together. At
D-E a Houses-dispute glosses B-C, with the superscription of
the dispute included in the opinion of House of Shammai. In its
primary, balanced formulation, the dispute probably read
^{c}*yqr vs. gdr*.[1] Yohanan b. Nuri glosses B-E at F-G, and so attests
it to Usha (or late Yavneh). H-J then glosses F-G with a balanced
(six *vs.* three) Yavnean dispute concerning a secondary issue.

     B-C states that a row consisting of five vines trained cn
a fence or in a ditch of a specified size (i.e., according tc A,
an espalier) must be separated from another kind by an area of
tillage of four *amot*, or the area of tillage of a vineyard. Now

we have already seen that, while House of Shammai consider a
row of five vines to be a vineyard, House of Hillel require a
vineyard to contain two rows of vines (M. 4:5A-D). House of
Hillel would presumably agree here that a row of trained vines is
to be treated as a vineyard, reasoning that the structure upon
which the vines are trained, which forms an autonomous domain,
joins the individual vines together to constitute a single group
of vines (HD to T. 4:1). At D-E the Houses dispute concerning
the secondary problem of where to allow the four *amot* of the
espalier. According to Maimonides (*Comm.*) and GRA the dispute
concerns which part of the espalier is considered to be primary
to it. House of Shammai rule that one measures the four *amot* from
the base of the vines to the field (both of which lie on the same
side of the fence or ditch[2]). Since the vines themselves are
considered to be a vineyard, they, rather than the fence (or
ditch), are considered to be primary to the espalier. House of
Hillel, on the other hand, maintain that, since the vines are
considered to be a vineyard only when they are trained on a
fence, the latter is considered to be the primary part of the
espalier, and the four *amot* are measured from the fence to the
field.

In F-G Yoḥanan b. Nuri revises B-E so that the position of
House of Hillel in E does not conflict with House of Hillel's
view (M. 4:5C-D) that a single row of vines does not form a vineyard. According to Yoḥanan b. Nuri the four *amot* mentioned in
connection with the row of vines refer not to its area of tillage
(C), but to the area between the vines and the fence. If this
area measures four *amot*, then the row is allowed its area of
tillage (= six handbreadths [J]), and the rest of the space may
be sown. An area measuring less than four *amot* may not be sown,
presumably because the other kind would then not cover enough
area and so would produce the appearance of diverse-kinds.
Yoḥanan b. Nuri thus does not discuss an espalier at all (since
it is not likely that he would permit sowing under trained
vines), but rather refers to the outer space of a row of vines,[3]
which has been defined as the space between the vineyard and
the fence (M. 4:2L). He thus supplements House of Hillel's view
(M. 4:1F) that the outer space of a vineyard must contain twelve
amot in order to be sown, ruling that the outer space of a row may
be sown if it contains four *amot*. Although Yoḥanan b. Nuri does
not present House of Shammai's opinion, it is clear that, since
they regard a row of five vines as a vineyard, they would require
an outer space of a row to contain sixteen *amot* in order to be
sown (M. 4:1E). Yoḥanan b. Nuri thus resolves the conflict

between the two views of House of Hillel by revising B-F so
that it deals with the outer space, rather than the area of
tillage, of such a row.

H-J glosses F-G with a dispute concerning the secondary
issue of the area of tillage of a single vine. While the anonymous opinion in I holds that this area of tillage measures six
handbreadths in each direction (= two *amot* square), ^CAqiva maintains that it measures only half as much, or three handbreadths
(= one *amah* square). ^CAqiva's rule is consistent with his view
that trailing plants are allowed no more space than are vegetables (M. 3:6E-G), for according to his opinion, the vine's
area of tillage is equal in size to a vegetable's autonomous domain
(when sown with vegetables of another kind) (= one *amah* square;
M. 3:3F). ^CAqiva apparently maintains that a vine is allowed
no more space for its area of tillage than is required to constitute an autonomous domain for vegetables.

T. Kil. 4:1-7a consists of two parts, T. 4:1-2, which comments on M. 6:1, and T. 4:3-7a, an autonomous subunit dealing
with rules concerning the construction of partitions. T. 4:1a
comments on M.'s discussion of the area of tillage of an espalier.
T. 4:1b-2 (repeated by T. 4:9b) then continues this interest
in the area of tillage, asking whether vines need be allowed their
area of tillage if they are already separated from another kind
by a partition. T. 4:3-7a supplements the foregoing by presenting
a separate set of rules which, although formally diverse, all pertain to the construction of partitions. The point of T. is that
a partition must be so constructed that it clearly appears to
separate different parts of a field. T. 4:3 lists the types of
materials from which a partition must be built. T. 4:4-5 then
supplements T. 4:3 with sayings of Eleazar and Yosé, who discuss
whether, because of the nature of their materials, certain kinds
of supporting structures of an espalier may serve as partitions,
and so separate the vines of the espalier from another kind on
the other side. We note that although both T. 4:4 and M. 6:1
deal with an espalier, the former does not appear to serve as a
comment on the latter, for T. 4:4 is interested in the materials
of the espalier's supporting structure, and not in the vines of
the espalier. T. 4:6, discussing a partition composed of sections,
concerns how large a breach may separate the sections without
invalidating the partition. Finally, T. 4:7a, returning to the
concerns of T. 4:3, presents a dispute between an anonymous
opinion and Yosé b. Judah as to whether a partition is considered
to be adequate if its materials extend in only one direction (i.e.,

either perpendicular or horizontal to the ground; e.g., a partition of reeds [anonymous opinion]), or whether a valid partition
must be constructed out of materials extending in both directions
(e.g., a partition of mats [Yosé b. Judah]).

A. Rabban Gamaliel and his court ordained (*htqynw*) that they
    shall allow a distance [of] four *amot* from the base of the
    vines to the fence.

                    T. Kil. 4:1a (p. 217, ll. 1-2)

     According to T. Gamaliel and his court ordained that one
must separate vines from a nearby fence by four *amot*, presumably
in order to sow another kind between them.[4] T. thus attributes
to Gamaliel and his court the rule of Yohanan b. Nuri in
M. 6:1F-G (Lieberman[5]).

B. He who makes a partition for the vineyard [measuring] ten
    [handbreadths] high and four wide, has annulled (*btl*) the
    [requirement of allowing] four *amot* [as the area of
    tillage] of the vineyard.

                    T. Kil. 4:1b (p. 217, ll. 2-3)

C. He who makes a partition for the vine [measuring] ten
    [handbreadths] deep [Erfurt, GRA, and Lieberman[6] read: high]
    and four wide, has annulled (*btl*) the [requirement of allow-
    ing six] handbreadths [as the area of tillage] of the vine.

                    T. Kil. 4:2 (p. 217, ll. 3-4) (B-C:
                    T. Kil. 4:9b)

     T. 4:1b consists of a pair of well-balanced declarative
sentences. According to T. the area of tillage, or the area which
separates a vine from another kind, need not be allowed to a
vine (B) or a vineyard (C) which is already set apart from the
other kind by a partition, since the partition is regarded as
adequately separating the two kinds. T. complements M. 6:1's
rule concerning the separation of two kinds growing on the same
side of the fence with a discussion of separating the two kinds
which grew on opposite sides of a partition.

A. He who makes a partition for the vineyard [measuring] ten
    handbreadths high and [with] its width not [measuring] four
    [handbreadths], has not annulled [Vienna omits the following

until "six handbreadths"; first printed ed:] the
[requirement of allowing] four *amot* [as the area of tillage]
of the vineyard.

B. He who makes a partition for the vine [measuring] ten
handbreadths high and [with] its width not [measuring] four
[handbreadths], has not annulled the [requirement of
allowing] six handbreadths [as the area of tillage] of the
vine.

T. Kil. 4:9b (p. 219, ll. 33-34)

T. 4:9b simply restates the rules of T. 4:1b-2 in a negative manner. I cannot account for the location of T. 4:9b in
T. Chapter Four, for this pericope is not at all related to the
pericopae surrounding it (e.g., T. 4:8-9a, which discusses
sowing in the gaps of an espalier[7]).

A. With all [kinds of materials] they make a partition [T. Sheb.:
enclosures (*śhryn*)]:
B. with (1) stones, and (2) mats, (3) straw, and (4) reeds,
and (5) stalks,
C. even [with] three ropes [strung] one above another,
D. provided that there not be between one reed [T. Sheb.:
rope] and the next three handbreadths,
E. [i.e.,] sufficient [space] so that a kid may enter.

T. Kil. 4:3 (pp. 217-218, ll. 4-6)
(T. Shev. 2:19; A-B(1)-(3):
Y. Shev. 3:3; B(3)-(5)+C-D:
T. Erub. 2:1;[8] C: Y. Kil. 4:4
(29b); C-D: M. Erub. 1:9a;[9]
D: M. Erub. 1:10a;[10] D-E:
M. Kil. 4:4B-C, T. Kil. 4:6C-D)

T. Kil. 4:3 consists of a superscription at A, a list of
five items at B which is augmented by a sixth at C (joined to
the foregoing by *'pylw*), and D-E, which qualifies B(4) (or,
according to T. Shev., C). The point of T. apparently is that
the items listed in B are suitable for use in the construction
of partitions (in this context) between diverse-kinds, for such
materials clearly appear to divide a field. Three ropes strung
above one another similarly form a valid partition (C). D-E,
which also appears (in the same context) in M. 4:4B-C and
T. 4:6C-D, then comments on B(4), ruling that a partition of
reeds must be sufficiently compact, so that it does not contain

breaches measuring three or more handbreadths wide, or spaces
large enough to allow a kid to enter.

A. [Erfurt reverses the order of A-C and D-G] R. Leazar [Erfurt:
    Eliezer; first printed ed.: Eleazar] says, "An espalier
    [so Lieberman[11] for *ḥryṣ*; Erfurt: *ᶜryṣ*][i.e., trained
    vines] which he passed over lattice-work (*rypyn*),[12]

B. "and [= omitted by Erfurt] lo, the lattice-work is [considered]
    as a [valid] partition,

C. "provided that there not be between it [i.e., one slat of
    the lattice-work] and the next [an area] fully as wide [as
    the slat itself (HD)]."

                    T. Kil. 4:4 (p. 218, ll. 6-8)

D. R. Judah says, "An espalier (*ḥryṣ*; Erfurt: *ᶜryṣ*) [i.e.,
    trained vines] which he passed over reeds,

E. "and [= omitted by Erfurt] lo, [Erfurt adds: the] reeds
    are [considered] as a [valid] partition,

F. "[but] it is necessary that there not be between one reed
    and the next three handbreadths,

G. "[i.e.,] sufficient [space] so that a kid may enter."

H. R. Yosah [Erfurt, first printed ed.: Yosé] says, "If the
    reeds were pronged (*mdwqrnyn*) [i.e., split at the top] and
    he made for them (*lhm*; Erfurt: *'wtn* ["(of) them"]) a plait
    (*py'h*) at the top [by running a string through them (Lieber-
    man[13])], it is permitted [i.e., the plaited reeds form a
    valid partition]."

                    T. Kil. 4:5 (p. 218, ll. 8-11)
                    (F: M. Erub. 1:9a; F-G: M. Kil.
                    4:4B-C, T. Kil. 4:3D-E; H: T. Kil.
                    4:6S+U)

    T. concerns an espalier, which, because it is constructed
out of certain kinds of materials, may also serve as a partition.
T. is composed of two sayings, A-C (attributed to Eleazar) and
D-G (attributed to Judah), with the latter glossed by Yosé at H.
A-C and D-G balance one another, for both consist of nearly
identical sentences in mild apocopation (A-B and D-E; *rypyn vs.*
qnym) followed by similar qualifying clauses (C and F-G [= M. 4:4
B-C, T. 4:3D-E]: *kmlw'w vs. šlšh ṭphym*). It appears, then,
that both sayings were formulated together. We note that H also
appears anonymously at T. 4:6S+U. H is apparently primary to
T. 4:4-5, however, since T. 4:6 does not deal specifically with

the partition of reeds. We also note, though, that H is not
particularly concerned with the espalier of reeds of T. 4:4-5,
and could fit equally well in the context of M. 4:4A-C (with
M. 4:4B-C = T. 4:5F-G), which deals simply with the partition
of reeds.

According to Eleazar and Judah an espalier constructed out
of lattices or reeds may serve as a partition and separate the
vines on the espalier from another kind on the other side of
the structure (Lieberman[14]). The point of T. is that the materials of the espalier appear to separate the vines from another
kind, so that the structure may serve as a partition as well.
C and F-G then qualify their respective preceding rules, stating
that the espalier must have a certain degree of solidity in order
to serve as a partition. An espalier constructed from lattices
must not contain gaps wider than the width of the lattice itself
(C), while an espalier of reeds may not contain breaches measuring
three or more handbreadths wide, or enough space to allow a kid
to enter, again so that the partition may appear to separate
the different kinds. In H Yosé qualifies D-G, saying that if the
reeds are tied together at the top they form a satisfactory
partition, even if the reeds are separated by gaps measuring
three or more handbreadths wide. The reeds which are tied
together in this fashion are not easily breached, so that the
partition is valid regardless of the size of the gaps within it.[15]

A. The result is (nmṣ't 'wm[r]) [that there are] three measures
    of the partition:

B. (1) All [sections of a partition] which [measure] less than
    three [handbreadths wide]--

C. it is necessary that there not be between it [i.e., one
    section of the partition] and the next three handbreadths,

D. [i.e.,] sufficient [space] so that a kid may enter [B. Erub.:
    may leap headlong (yzdqr hgdy bbt r'š)].

E. (2) And all [sections of a partition] which [measure] three
    [Erfurt adds: or (w)] three to four [handbreadths wide]--

F. it is necessary that there not be between it [i.e., one
    section of the partition] and the next [a space] fully as
    wide [as one section of the partition],

G. so that (kdy) [the measure] of the breaches may not equal
    [that of] the structure itself (bnyn; E. Erub.: 'wmd ["that
    which stands"] [throughout]).

H. [Erfurt, B. Erub. add: If (the measure) of the breaches]
    exceeded [that of] the structure,

I. even opposite the structure it is prohibited [to sow diverse-kinds].

J. (3) All [sections of a partition] which [measure] four [Erfurt adds: or (w)] from four [handbreadths] upwards [other versions:[16] from four (handbreadths) to four *amot*, and from four *amot* to ten (*amot*)]--

K. it is necessary that there not be between it [i.e., one section of the partition] and the next [a space] fully as wide [as one section of the partition],

L. so that [the measure of] the breach[es] may not equal [that of] that which stands.

M. If [the measure of] that which stands is [equal to that of] the breach[es],

N. opposite that which stands it is permitted [to sow diverse-kinds],

O. but opposite the breach[es] it is prohibited [to sow diverse-kinds].

P. If [the measure of] that which stands exceeded [that of] the breach[es],

Q. even opposite the breach[es] it is permitted [to sow diverse-kinds],

R. provided that the breach[es] do not exceed ten *amot* [in width] [B. Erub. reads instead of R: (If the partition) was breached by (a breach) greater than ten *amot*, it is prohibited].

S. If the reeds were pronged (*mdwqrnyn*) [i.e., split at the top], and he made for them a plait (*py'h*) at the top [by running a string through them (Lieberman[17])],

T. even [if the breaches] exceed ten *amot*,

U. it is permitted [to sow diverse-kinds opposite the breaches].

> T. Kil. 4:6 (pp. 218-219, ll. 11-19)
> (B. Erub. 16a; A-R: Y. Kil. 4:4
> (29b), Y. Erub. 1:8 (9b), Y. Suk.
> 1:1 (52b);[18] E-K: T. Erub. 2(3):
> 2a;[19] S+U: T. Kil. 4:5H; S-U:
> B. Erub. 11a)

    T. Kil. 4:6 A-R is a unitary pericope consisting of a superscription, A, and three parts, B-D, E-I, and J-R, with the latter glossed by S-U. Each part is composed of a protasis in the pattern *kl šhn* X (B,E, and J), and an apodosis following the pattern *sryk. . .kdy* (C-D, F-G, and K-L). In addition, the rules of E-G and J-L are supplemented by one or more conditional

sentences (H-I, M-O, and P-R, with N balancing O, and P-Q
corresponding to M+O), the apodoses of which all follow the same
formulary pattern, $kngd\ h^cwmd/hprws\ +\ 'swr/mwtr$.

B-D, E-I, and J-R concern a partition which is composed of
sections. Each rule discusses how large a gap may separate
sections of a particular size if the partition is to be considered
valid. B-D states that sections measuring three handbreadths
or less in width may not be separated by gaps measuring the same
width (i.e., three handbreadths), or by a space large enough to
allow a kid to enter (cf. M. 4:4A-C, T. 4:3D-E, for the same
rule applied to a partition of reeds). A partition containing
gaps of such size would not appear to separate the diverse kinds.
E-F then similarly rules that sections measuring from three to
four handbreadths wide may not be set apart by breaches equal in
width to the sections themselves. G, glossing E-F, explains that
the rule of E-F does not allow the measures of the breaches to
equal those of the sections of the standing structure of the
partition. If, on the other hand, the breaches measure more than
do the sections of the standing structure, it is prohibited to
sow diverse-kinds on different sides of the entire partition (H-I),
for now the partition as a whole does not seem to divide the
diverse-kinds, and so is not considered valid. We note that I,
in stating that "even opposite the structure it is prohibited,"
perhaps follows the language of L-R, which distinguishes between
sowing opposite the structure and opposite the breaches. The
language, however, while appropriate to the context of L-R, has
little significance at E-I, which does not make such a distinction. I then could have read simply "it is prohibited."

J-L applies the rule of E-G (with a slight variation in
language from $prwswt$ to $prws$ and from $bnyn$ to ^cwmd) to the
partition made up of sections measuring four or more handbreadths
wide. M-O then discusses the case in which the width of the
breaches equals that of the sections, with N-O taking an intermediate position between prohibiting and permitting the sowing
of different kinds on opposite sides of the partition. One may
sow diverse-kinds on opposite sides of the standing structure,
which itself serves as a partition, but not opposite the breaches,
which do not set the diverse-kinds apart. If the width of the
sections exceeds that of the breaches, then one may sow diverse-
kinds even opposite the breaches (P-Q), for the partition as a
whole is considered as serving to separate the different kinds.
R glosses the foregoing, stating that the rule of P-Q applies
only when the breaches measure less than ten $amot$ in width, presumably because a partition containing a gap of that size no

longer appears to serve as a partition (although it is not clear
whether one may still sow opposite the standing structure[20]).
The following chart summarizes the rules of B-R:

T.	Measure of Sections	Measure of Breaches	Rule
B-D	less than three handbreadths	three or more hand-breadths	prohibited
E-I	three to four handbreadths	less than that of sections	permitted
		greater than that of sections	prohibited, even opposite sections
J-R	four or more handbreadths	less than that of sections	permitted
		equal to that of sections	permitted opposite sections prohibited opposite breaches
		less than that of sections	permitted, even opposite breaches (measuring less than ten *amot*)

S-U, supplementing R, consists of S+U, an anonymous
version of Yosé's saying concerning the partition of reeds (T.
4:5H), and T, which has apparently been interpolated into the
pericope in order to relate S+U to R. In its present context
the point of S-U is that a breach measuring more than ten *amot*
does not invalidate a partition of reeds, provided that the reeds
are tied together at the top and so serve to close the breach and
to separate the different kinds from one another.

A. Every partition which is made [of materials extending]
   perpendicularly [so Danby[21] for *šty*; lit.: "warp"] and is
   not made [of materials extending] horizontally [so Danby
   for *ᶜrb*; lit.: "woof"],
B. [or which is made of material extending] horizontally and
   is not made [of materials extending] perpendicularly,
C. lo, this is [considered a valid] partition.
D. R. Yosah [Erfurt, first printed ed.: Yosé] b. R. Judah
   says, "It is not [considered a valid] partition unless it is
   made [of materials extending both] perpendicularly and
   horizontally."

                      T. Kil. 4:7a (p. 219, ll. 19-21)

A. "Every partition which is not [made of materials extending both] perpendicularly and horizontally is not [considered a valid] partition," the words of R. Yosé b. Judah.

B. And sages say, "[A partition need have only] one of the two things [i.e., characteristics; the partition need only be made of materials extending either perpendicularly or horizontally]."

M. Erub. 1:10b (Y. Erub. 1:8 (19b))

T. consists of A-C, a declarative sentence with a duplicated subject (with A and B balanced: $st\breve{y}$ + $'yn\ ^{c}rb$ vs. ^{c}rb + $'yn\ \breve{s}ty$), and Yosé b. Judah's saying at D, which glosses and opposes the foregoing (balancing A+B with $\breve{s}ty$ + ^{c}rb). M. Erub. 1:10b presents the same dispute in a different variation of the dispute form, as we see from the following chart:

T. Kil. 4:7a	*M. Erub. 1:10b*
1. Every partition which is made [of material extending] perpendicularly and is not made [of materials extending] horizontally,	1. (see 5)
2. [or which is made of materials extending] horizontally and is not made [of materials extending] perpendicularly,	2. (see 5)
3. lo, this is [considered a valid] partition.	3. (see 5)
4. R. Yosah b. Judah says, "It is not considered a valid partition unless it is made [of materials extending both] perpendicularly and horizontally."	4. "Every partition which is not [made of materials extending both] perpendicularly and horizontally is not [considered a valid] partition," the words of R. Yosé b. Judah.
5. (see 1-3)	5. And sages say, "[A partition need have only] one of the two things [i.e., characteristics]."

M. Erub. 1:10b differs from T. Kil. 4:7a in presenting the opinions of the dispute in reverse order, for sages gloss Yosé b. Judah's view with the anonymous opinion of T. 4:7a/A-C. M. Erub. 1:10b

also makes no attempt to balance the opposing views. The two
versions of the dispute, however, do not differ in substance.
The dispute apparently concerns whether a partition appears to
separate diverse-kinds if it is composed of materials extending
in only one direction. According to A-C the materials of a partition may extend either horizontally (e.g., a partition of three
ropes [T. 4:3]; cf. TYY to M. Erub. 1:10; MB) or vertically
(e.g., a partition of reeds [M. 4:4, T. 4:3]). Yosé b. Judah,
on the other hand, maintains that a partition is valid only if
it is constructed out of materials extending in both directions
(e.g., a partition of mats [T. 4:3]), for only then does it have
enough surface area to divide the diverse-kinds. Yosé b. Judah
would then disagree with T. 4:3, which allows a partition to be
made out of materials extending in only one direction. We note
that A-C has apparently been generated by D, for it is necessary
to state that the materials of a partition may extend either
horizontally or vertically only in response to the view that they
must extend in both directions.

6:2

A. An espalier which projects from [so Danby for *ywṣ' mn*]
    a terrace--

B. R. Eliezer b. Jacob says, "If he [can] stand on the ground
    and harvest all of it [i.e., harvest all of the grapes of
    the espalier's vines], lo, this [espalier] prohibits four
    amot in the field [below].

C. "And if not [i.e., if he cannot harvest all of the grapes
    of the espalier's vines while standing on the ground], [the
    espalier] prohibits only that [part of the field which lies]
    opposite [i.e., under] it."

D. R. Eliezer [Ox, P, Rosh,[22] MS: Eleazar; L: Leazar] says,
    "Even (*'p*) [= omitted by Pr] he who plants one [row of vines
    (Maim., *Comm.*, *Code*, *Diverse-Kinds* 7:6, others)] on the
    ground and one on the terrace--

E. "if [the row on the terrace] is ten handbreadths higher
    [C, Geniza fragment,[23] K, L, Mn, Ox, P, and S omit:] than
    the ground, it does not combine with it [i.e., with the row
    on the ground] [to form a vineyard].

F. [Mn omits:] "And if not [i.e., if the row on the terrace is
    not ten handbreadths higher than the ground], lo, this [row on
    the terrace] combines with it [i.e., the row on the ground]
    [to form a vineyard]."

                                        M. Kil. 6:2

M. consists of two rules, Eliezer b. Jacob's saying concerning the espalier planted on a terrace (A-C), and Eliezer/
Eleazar's statement dealing with planting one row of vines on
a terrace and another on the ground (D-F, joined to the foregoing
by 'p). Both sayings consist of a protasis (A,D) followed by a
pair of conditional sentences (B-C, E-F). The two rules appear
to be autonomous, however, for they open with different formulary
patterns (^{c}rys šhw'[A] vs. hnwṭ^c[D]) and concern different
arrangements of vines (espalier [i.e., one row] [A-C] vs. two
rows [D-F]). We note that, since the question of terraces is
discussed by Eliezer b. Jacob, an Ushan, at A-C, the Eliezer/
Eleazar of D-F is probably an Ushan as well.

A-C continues the interest of M. 6:1 in the area of tillage
of an espalier, asking whether the same area of tillage, four
amot, is required for an espalier which is planted on a terrace
but hangs over the field below. The issue of A-C concerns
whether the espalier, because it is planted on a terrace, is
considered separate from the field and so does not require four
amot in the field below, or whether, because it hangs over the
field, the espalier is regarded as belonging to the latter and so
requires its full area of tillage. Eliezer b. Jacob rules in
B-C that the criterion for deciding this question is the proximity
of the overhanging vines to the field, which is measured in
terms of one's ability to harvest the grapes of the espalier.
If the vines hang so low that one may harvest all of their grapes
while standing in the field, then for all practical purposes these
vines may be regarded as if they were planted in the field itself (Maim., Comm., Code, Diverse-Kinds, 8:8). That is, the
vines of the espalier may produce the appearance of diverse-kinds
with the other kind in the field equally as well as if the vines
were actually planted in the field itself, and they therefore
must be allowed four amot in the field (presumably measured
either from the terrace [Maim., Code, Diverse-Kinds 8:8, MS[24]]
or from the spot where the vines meet the field[25]). If, on the
other hand, the vines of the espalier hang so far above the field
that one cannot pick all of their grapes while standing in the
field, then the espalier is not regarded as if it were planted
in the field. One then need allow as its area of tillage only
that part of the field which lies directly below the espalier, for
only in that area could the vines of the espalier produce the
appearance of diverse-kinds with the kind sown in the field.

In D-F Eliezer/Eleazar discusses whether or not two rows of
vines, one planted on a terrace and the other planted in the
field below, combine to form a vineyard (following the definition

of a vineyard as two rows, given by House of Hillel, M. 4:5C-D).
The issue of D-F concerns whether or not the terrace is considered
part of the field. Eliezer-Eleazar rules that if the terrace
measures ten handbreadths higher than the field, it forms a
domain unto itself (R. Mena in Y. Kil. 6:2; cf. M. 2:8, 5:3;
cf. also T. 3:7-8[26]) and the two rows do not combine. If, on
the other hand, the terrace measures less than the specified
height above the ground, then it is considered part of the field
and the two rows do combine to form a vineyard. Eliezer/Eleazar
thus simply goes over the anonymous law of M. 4:7C-G, concerning
two rows of vines which are separated by a fence, and presents
it in terms of the question of the terrace.

Let us now turn to consider the redactor's view of the relationship between the sayings of Eliezer b. Jacob and Eliezer/
Eleazar. If, as we have already shown, the two rulings are autonomous of one another, why did the redactor decide to join them
together? We may explain this decision by showing that the
pericope may have actually undergone two stages in its history.
At first a redactor may have simply juxtaposed the rulings, viewing
them as two separate answers to the same question, i.e., whether
or not a terrace is considered to be part of the field below it.
Eliezer b. Jacob presents one criterion, concerning one's ability
to work from the field on the terrace's vines, and Eliezer/
Eleazar offers another rule, dealing with the height of the
terrace. At some later point a (presumably different) glossator
then added 'p ("even") to Eliezer/Eleazar's saying in D, making
the latter appear to be a restatement of Eliezer b. Jacob's
rule of B-C. When read together with 'p, Eliezer/Eleazar's saying
may be taken to mean that a terrace ten handbreadths higher than
the field is considered to be separate from the latter because one
standing in the field cannot reach vines which are planted on
a terrace of that height. The two sayings may thus have been
viewed differently at separate stages in their history, being
regarded first as autonomous opinions and then as statements
of the same rule.

6:3-5

A. He who trains [so Danby for *hmdlh*] a vine over some of the
laths [of a latticework] shall not put seed under the
remaining [laths].

B. If he did put [seed there], he has not sanctified [the
seeds underneath].

C. And if the new growth (*ḥḥdš*; Danby: tendrils) [of the vine] spread [over the rest of the laths], it is prohibited [i.e., the seeds underneath are sanctified].

D. And so [is the rule for] he who trains [a vine] over part of a barren tree (*'yln srq*).

M. Kil. 6:3

E. He who trains a vine over part of a fruit tree (*'yln m'kl*)-- it is permitted to put seed under the remainder [of the tree].

F. And if the new growth [Danby: tendrils] [of the vine] spread [over the rest of the tree], he shall turn it [i.e., the new growth] back (*yḥzyrnw*).

G. *mᶜśh š*: R. Joshua went to R. Ishmael at Kefar Aziz,[27] and he showed him a vine which was trained over part of a fig tree.

H. He [i.e., R. Joshua] said to him, "May I put seed under the remainder [of the tree]?"

I. He [i.e., R. Ishmael] said to him, "It is permitted."

J. And he brought him up from there to Bet Hamaganyah,[28] and he showed him a vine which was trained over part of a branch [so Porton[29] for *qwrh*] and [K (after correction), Mn, Sirillo:[30] in (*btwk*)] a trunk of a sycamore tree, in which there were many branches.

K. He [i.e., R. Ishmael] said to him, "Under this branch it is prohibited [to put seed], and under the rest [of the branches] it is permitted."

M. Kil. 6:4

L. What is [considered] a barren tree (*'yln srq*)?

M. Every [tree] which does not produce fruit.

N. R. Meir says, "Every tree is [considered] a barren tree, except for the olive tree and the fig tree."

O. R. Yosé says, "Every [tree] the like of which they do not plant as whole groves, lo, this is [considered] a barren tree."

M. Kil. 6:5 (N: Y. Orl. 1:1 (60c))

M. 6:3-5 forms a new subunit dealing with single trained vines. M. opens with three rules, A-C (vine trained on a lattice-work of laths), D (vine trained on a barren tree), and E-F (vine trained on a fruit tree), all of which begin with the formulary pattern *hmdlh*. A and E somewhat balance one another (*'ppywrwt vs. 'yln m'kl*, *l' yby' vs. mwtr lhby'*), although C and

F do not closely correspond to each other (*mwtr vs. yḥzyrnw*, as
we shall see below). B's language differs from that of C (*qydš*
vs. 'swr),[31] and B has no corresponding clause in E-F, so that B
appears to be secondary to the construction. D (joined to A-C
by *wkn*) and the protasis of E are almost perfectly paired (*'yln*
srq vs. 'yln m'kl). D, however, lacks an apodosis, and states no
new rule of its own. It appears, therefore, that D has been added
to the pericope in order to present a contrast for E (barren
tree *vs.* fruit tree). D thus serves the redactional function of
linking A+C to E+F. G-K then augments E-F with a *m^{c}šh*. L-O
glosses D, and thus is also secondary to the original construction, which may now be seen to have consisted of A+C+E-F. L-O
was probably placed after G-K and not immediately after D so
that it would not interfere with the contrast between D and E.

A and E describe cases in which a vine is trained over part
of some structure. The question discussed in both instances is
whether one may sow another kind under that part of the structure
which remains uncovered by the vine. The issue of A and E concerns whether or not the uncovered part of the structure is considered to be "taken over" by the trained vine, so that the vine
and the entire structure are deemed to form a single entity
(as in the case of the espalier [M. 6:1]), under which one may
not sow. M. here distinguishes between a latticework of laths
(A), which is regarded as an extension of the vine (cf. MR,
Albeck), and a fruit tree (E), which is not so considered. The
reasoning behind M. appears to be that the laths are inanimate,
and therefore lose their aspect to the animate vines, while the
animate fruit tree retains its own aspect in supporting the vine.
The glossator responsible for D, though, apparently sees the
issue differently, for he compares the barren tree, which is
animate, to the latticework of laths, which is not. According
to D, therefore, M. distinguishes between the non-fruit-bearing
structure (latticwork of laths, barren tree), which is "taken
over" by the fruit-bearing vine, and the fruit tree, which,
because it bears fruit itself, keeps its own aspect while
supporting the vine.

B then weakens the force of A, saying that one who actually
does sow under the uncovered part of a latticework of laths
does not thereby sanctify the seeds. We may understand the function of B in the pericope only after turning to C. The latter
states that if one sows under the remaining part of the structure,
and the vine subsequently spreads out over that part, the seeds
are prohibited, or sanctified, for the vine now hangs directly
over seeds which should not have been sown at that spot in the

first place. A has already told us, however, that one may
not sow under the remaining part, and it should follow from A that
any seeds which are sown there are sanctified. The rule of C
thus appears to be unnecessary. C, however, is already part of
the original construction, for it balances F (*kngdw mwtr vs.*
kngdw yḥzyrnw). B therefore has apparently been added to the
pericope in order to clarify A+C. B explains that, although A
does not allow sowing under the remaining part of the latticework
of laths, such an action does not sanctify the seeds, presumably
because they do not lie directly under the vine. The rule of C
then logically follows that of B.

Like C, F rules concerning the vine which spreads over seeds
previously sown under the uncovered part of the fruit tree.
Now we might expect F to read *mwtr* in order to balance C's *'swr*.
F, however, reads *yḥzyrnw* ("he shall turn it back") and so takes
an intermediate position, in which the seeds are neither entirely
permitted or prohibited. The seeds are not prohibited, or sanctified, for it was originally permitted to sow them under the fruit
tree. At the same time, though, the seeds and the vine may not
continue to grow in their respective positions, for they would
then produce the appearance of diverse-kinds. The vines must
therefore be turned back, so that they do not cover the seeds.

G-K presents a $m^{e}\check{s}h$ in which Joshua asks Ishmael (or *vice*
versa[32]) concerning two cases of sowing under a tree which supports a vine. In G-I Ishmael permits Joshua to sow under that
part of a fig tree which is not covered by the vine. In J-K
Ishmael prohibits sowing under a sycamore branch upon which a
vine is trained, but he permits sowing under the other branches
which grow out of the same trunk. G-I and J-K thus both illustrate
E, for in both instances Ishmael permits one to sow under the
uncovered part of the fruit tree (for the sycamore bears a fig-
like fruit[33])[34]. Alternatively, Maimonides (*Comm.*)[35] notes that,
although J states that the vine is trained over only part of the
sycamore branch, Ishmael in K prohibits sowing under the entire
branch. Maimonides therefore reasons that the sycamore, which
yields fruit but is grown primarily for its lumber,[36] is considered partly like a barren tree, so that one may not sow under
any part of the branch supporting the vine (a rule analogous to
that of A), and partly like a fruit tree, so that one may sow
under the uncovered part of the tree (as in E). According to
this interpretation the point of G-K may be to contrast the status
of the fig tree with that of the sycamore, for both trees are
members of the same botanical genus (*Ficus*, of the nettle family
[Urticaceae][37]) and both yield similar fruits. It is not clear,

however, that one may read J-K to imply that a sycamore is considered a barren tree. J-K may not intend to place any emphasis
at all on the fact that, although the vine is trained on only
part of the branch, Ishmael prohibits sowing under the whole
branch. We therefore prefer the first interpretation given above.

L-O glosses D with a dispute concerning the definition of
a barren tree. The dispute consists of three opinions, an anonymous saying (M), and the views of Meir and Yosé (N-O), all of
which respond to the question at L. M and N-O, however, deal
with entirely separate issues. While M presents the obvious[38]
definition of an 'yln srq as a tree which does not produce fruit,
Meir and Yosé define the 'yln srq not in terms of a tree's ability
to bear fruit but in terms of the economic importance of its
fruit. Meir maintains that all but fig and olive trees are considered "barren," or economically insignificant, for these two
trees, together with the vine, alone produce the most important
fruits of the Mediterranean area.[39] Yosé, on the other hand,
states that any tree with which one would not plant an entire
grove is considered a "barren" tree, for only those trees for
which one would invest a whole grove are regarded as important.
Yose thus encompasses and relativizes Meir's definition of a
"barren" tree, making it dependent on the value of the tree's
fruit. In defining a "barren" tree in terms of a tree's economic
importance, Meir and Yosé effectively revise the criterion for
determining whether a tree supporting a vine is "taken over" by
the vine or whether it retains its own aspect. The barren tree
of D, which is considered an extension of the vine trained upon
it, now refers to all economically unimportant trees, and the
fruit tree of E, which keeps its own aspect, now describes either
the fig or olive tree (Meir), or any fruit-bearing tree of significance (Yosé). We note that it is possible that L-M, which
merely states the obvious and is not interested in the concerns
of N-O, serves only to introduce N-O and to underline the
latter's divergence from the standard definition of an 'yln srq.

A. *m*ᶜ*šh š: R. Joshua went to R. Ishmael at Kefar Azin [Erfurt:
   Aziz], and he showed him a vine which was trained on part
   of a fig tree.*
B. *He [i.e., R. Joshua] said to him, "May I put seed under the
   remainder [of the tree]?"*
C. *He [i.e., R. Ishmael] said to him, "It is permitted [= M. 6:
   4G-I],*
D. *"for a man does not set his fig tree at nought (mbṭl) before
   his vine."*

E. *He brought him up from there to Bet Hameganin,*40 *and*
    he showed him there a vine which was trained on part of
    a branch, and with it was a trunk of a sycamore tree, and
    in it [i.e., the trunk] were many branches.

F. *He [i.e., R. Ishmael] said to him, "Under this branch it is*
    prohibited to [to put seed], and [under] the rest [of the
    branches] it is permitted [= M. 6:4J-K],

G. "for I regard each and every branch [Erfurt omits: "in
    the tree"] in the tree as a tree unto itself."

H. R. Simeon b. Leazar [first printed ed.: Ishmael] says, "If
    [the vine] was climbing (*mpsy^c*; Erfurt: *mpsy^c*) from one
    branch to another, [the branches are all considered] as
    [belonging to] a single tree."

                        T. Kil. 4:7b (p. 219, ll. 21-25)
                        (H: Y. Kil. 4:3 (30c)^{41})

        T. cites and glosses M. 6:4G-K, presenting reasons at D
and G for the two rulings of the *m^{c}śh* (A-C, F-H). D has Ishmael
explain that one may sow under the uncovered part of a fig tree
which supports a vine because he is not assumed to set his fig
tree at nought for the vine, i.e., to regard the fig tree as
losing its own aspect and taking on that of the vine (= M. 6:4E).
G has Ishmael state that one may sow under the uncovered branches
of a sycamore tree if a vine is trained on one branch, because
each branch is considered a tree unto itself. In making the
point that each branch is considered a separate tree, T. apparently
presupposes that the sycamore is considered as a barren tree.
T. thus explains that one may not sow under the entire tree upon
which the vine is trained, but that the tree in question refers
only to the supporting branch and not to the whole sycamore.
At H Simeon b. Eleazar glosses E-G, saying that if the vine begins
to climb from one branch to another, all of the branches are considered part of one tree, for now the branches are all regarded
as serving the vine and thus are no longer considered as separate
trees. In this instance, therefore, one may not sow under any
part of the sycamore.^{42}

                            6:6

A. Gaps [so Danby for *psqy*] of an espalier [must measure] eight
    amot and a little more [so Danby for *w^{c}wd*] [in order to be
    sown with another kind].

B. And all of the dimensions of which sages spoke in [reference
    to] the vineyard--there is no [mention of] "and a little
    more" in them, except for [the dimensions of] the gaps of
    an espalier.

C. What are [considered] the gaps of an espalier?
D. An espalier which lies waste at its center [following
    Danby for ḥrb m'mṣ'ᶜw], and there remained in it five vines
    on one side [of the center] and five vines on the other--
E. if there are there [i.e., between the two groups of vines]
    eight *amot*, he shall not put seed there.
F. [If there are there (i.e., between the two groups of vines)]
    eight *amot* and a little more, they allow it [i.e., each
    group of vines] enough [space] for its area of tillage, and
    he sows the rest.

                                                    M. Kil. 6:6

    Returning to the subject of the espalier, M. consists of
a statement at A, which is then glossed separately by B and C-F.
Apparently referring to the issue of sowing, A states that the
gaps of an espalier must measure "eight *amot* and a little more."
B points out that similar rules concerning the minimum area which
may be sown among vines (e.g., M. 4:1-2, 8-9 [Albeck], M. 5:4) do
not include the phrase "and a little more," giving instead an
exact measurement of the area. C-F explains that A concerns an
espalier which contains more than ten vines. The middle of
the espalier is destroyed, and two groups of five vines each,
or two espaliers (cf. M. 6:1B), remain on either side of the
gap. E-F (following the formulary pattern of M. 4:1I-J,
4:2M-N) then spells out the rule of A. One may not sow in the
gap if it measures only eight *amot* (E), for then there would be
enough space only for the areas of tillage of the two espaliers
(four *amot* each [M. 6:1A-C]), but not for the other kind. If,
on the other hand, there is more than eight *amot* of space in the
gap, one allows each espalier its area of tillage and sows the
rest (F), for then there is enough space for both the areas of
tillage and the other kind (the latter being sown in the space
referred to by the phrase "and a little more" in A). By interpreting A to refer to two espaliers which are separated by a
gap, C-F thus explains why the gap must contain "eight *amot* and
little more" in order to be sown.[43]

A. *What are [considered] the gaps of an espalier (hrys)?*[44]
B. *An espalier which lies waste at its center and there remained
    in it five vines on one side [of the center] and five vines
    on the other--*
C. *if there are not there [i.e., between the two groups of vines]
    [Lieberman:[45] if there are there only] eight amot, he shall
    not put seed there.*

D.   [*If there are there (i.e., between the two groups of vines)*]
     eight amot and a little more, they allow it its area of
     tillage and he sows the rest   [= M. 6:6C-F].

T. Kil. 4:8 (p. 219, ll. 28-30)

E.   How much is "and a little more?"
F.   One of six handbreadths of an *amah* [Sens, Ribmaṣ: one-sixth
     of an *amah*; Maim., *Comm., Code, Diverse-Kinds* 5:5, others:[46]
     one-sixtieth of an *amah*].

T. Kil. 4:9a (p. 219, ll. 30-31)

     T. cites and glosses M. 6:6C-F, specifying at E-F the
measure meant by the phrase "and a little more (D)." T. states
that this phrase refers to one of the six handbreadths of an *amah*,
or simply one handbreadth. In phrasing its answer in this manner,
T. disagrees with Meir's view that the *amah* mentioned in
reference to the gaps of an espalier measures five handbreadths
(T. Kel. B.M. 6:13). We note that the reading of Sens and Ribmaṣ
avoids the question of the number of handbreadths in an *amah*
by stating simply "one-sixth of an *amah*."[47]

6:7

A.   An espalier which projects [so Danby for *ywṣ'*] along [so
     Danby for *mn*; B, Cn, Geniza fragment,[48] O, Ox, P: *^cm*]
     a wall from (*mtwk*) the corner [formed by two walls] and
     stops (*wklh*) [in the middle of the wall]--they allow it its
     area of tillage and he sows the rest.
B.   R. Yosé says, "If there are not there four *amot*, he shall
     not put seed there."

M. Kil. 6:7 (B: Y. Kil. 6:1 (30b))

     M. consists of A, a declarative sentence in the formulary
pattern of M. 6:2A (*^crys hywṣ' mn* X), followed by Yosé's gloss
at B. The language of A, "An espalier which projects along a
wall from the corner and stops," describes a case in which an
espalier, located in a walled area, begins in one corner, goes
along a wall, and stops before reaching the next corner (cf.
fig. 44). The issue which A discusses concerns whether one may
sow another kind between the end of the espalier and the next
corner without producing the appearance of diverse-kinds.[49] A
rules that one may sow in this space after allowing the espalier
its area of tillage, for then the two kinds are adequately

separated (or, alternatively, they grow in separate domains) and
do not appear to grow as diverse-kinds.[50] Yosé states in B
that the area between the end of the espalier and the far corner
must cover four *amot* in order to be sown, for only then will
there be enough space to allow the espalier its area of tillage
of four *amot* (M. 6:1C).

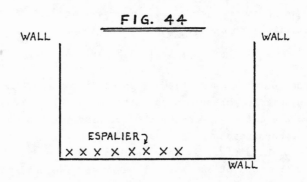

FIG. 44

WALL   WALL

ESPALIER⌐
X X X X X X X X
                          WALL

6:8-9

A. The reeds which project beyond the espalier--
B. and [= omitted by most mss.[51]] he refrains from cutting
   them short [so Danby for *hs* ^{c}*lyhm lpsqn*]--
C. opposite [i.e., under] them, it is permitted [to sow another
   kind].
D. [If] he prepared them [following Danby for ^{c}*š'n*] so that the
   new growth [of the vines] would spread over them, it is
   prohibited [to sow another kind under them].

M. Kil. 6:8

E. The blossom [of the vine] which projects beyond the espalier--
F. they regard it as if a plummet [so Danby for *mṭwṭlt*; B, C,
   Mn: *mṭwlṭlt*] were suspended from it--
G. opposite [i.e., under] it, it is prohibited [to sow another
   kind].
H. And so (*wkn*) [is the rule] for [a blossom which projects
   beyond] a trained vine (*dlyt*).
I. He who extends (*hmwṭh*) a vine-shoot from tree to tree--
J. under it, it is prohibited [to sow another kind].
K. [If] he attached to it [so Jastrow[52] for *spkh*] rope or
   reed-grass (*gmy*),

L. [the space] under that which is attached (*spwk*), it is permitted [to sow another kind].

M. [If] he prepared it so that the new growth [of the vines] would spread over it, it is prohibited [to sow another kind under it].

M. Kil. 6:9

M. opens with two apparently apocopated sentences, A-C and E-G, both of which follow the same formulary pattern (X *hywṣ'/hywṣ'm mn hᶜrys*). The two sentences partially balance each other in that A corresponds to E (with a shift from singular to plural; *qnym hywṣ'm vs. prḥ hywṣ'*) and C balances G (*mwtr vs. 'swr*). B and F, however, the clauses which actually produce the apocopation, are not at all balanced, and so appear to be secondary to the original construction of the declarative sentences A+C+E+G. H then glosses E-G. I-L augments A-G with a separate rule following its own formulary pattern (*he-who. . . it-is* apocopation [*hmwth*]). D and M are identical glosses of A-C and I-L, respectively, and thus were added to the pericope after the insertion of I-L. The addition of identical glosses to A-C and I-L supports our claim that I-L is to be regarded as related to that which precedes it.

A-C and E-G both describe cases in which some part of the espalier projects outwards. Both ask whether one may sow under the projection. The issue of A-C and E-G concerns whether the projection is considered part of the espalier.[53] A-C concerns sowing under projecting reeds, which, B explains, one did not wish to cut for fear of destroying the espalier (Maim., *Comm.*; cf. also Maim., *Code, Diverse-Kinds* 6:14). These reeds do not serve the vine and thus are not regarded as belonging to the espalier, so that one may sow under them (C). D adds, however, that if one arranges the extended reeds in such a way that the vines will eventually spread over them, he may not sow under them, for, since the reeds will ultimately support the vines, they are considered part of the espalier. In contrast to A-C, E-G rules that one may not sow under a vine-blossom which projects from an espalier, for, since the blossom will eventually yield grapes, it is considered an integral part of the espalier. F notes that one determines the extent of the prohibited area underneath the vine-blossom by imagining that a plummet is dropped from the blossom to the ground. All of the space between the imaginary plummet and the espalier is then considered the area under the vine-blossom. H adds that the rule of E-G applies also

in the case of a blossom which extends not from an espalier,
but from an individual trained vine.

I-L complements A-G with another case concerning sowing under
something which is connected to a vine. I-L consists of two
declarative sentences, I-J and K-L, with the latter dependent on
the former for its context. I-J describes the case of a vine-
shoot which is extended from one tree to another, ruling that
one may not sow under the shoot, for one would then produce the
appearance of diverse-kinds. In K-L the shoot is attached to
one of the trees by rope or reed-grass. Now we might expect L
to read *thtyh mwtr* in order to balance J's *thtyh 'swr*. L,
however, reads *tht hspwk mwtr*, emphasizing that it is permitted
to sow only under the attached rope or grass, and implying that
one may not sow under the vine. The reasoning behind I-L appears
to be that, since the vine does not actually grow on the attached
connector, the latter is not considered merely as an extension
of the vine, and one is permitted to sow under the rope or reed-
grass. The point of the glossator who inserted I-L into the
pericope is apparently that the rope or reed-grass "projects"
from the vine rather than supports it, so that the case of I-L
is analogous to that of A-C. M then repeats D. We note that
the rule of I-J makes a rather obvious point, and so may serve
only to introduce the case of K-L (Ridbaz to Maim., *Code, Diverse-
Kinds* 6:15).

A. A vine-shoot which was trained over grain,
B. even if it is a hundred *amah* [in length]--
C. the entire vine is prohibited [i.e., sanctified],
D. [i.e.], it [i.e., the vine] and its fruit.

T. Kil. 4:10a (p. 220, ll. 34-35)

T. complements M. 6:9I-J, turning from the latter's discussion of sowing under a vine-shoot to deal with a vine-shoot
which is trained over grain. T. consists of an apocopated
sentence, A+C, with B and D respectively glossing A and C.
According to A+C a vine-shoot which is trained over grain prohibits, or sanctifies, the entire vine, including the main stem
and the fruit (D). T. takes M.'s case and extends it, maintaining
that if any part of a vine, even a shoot, overshadows grain, the
entire vine is sanctified. B presents an extreme case, maintaining
that the whole vine is sanctified even if the shoot is a hundred
amot long and the grain which it overshadows is distant from
the main stem of the vine (Lieberman[54]).

OO. [Some mss.[55] omit OO-PP+QQ-SS] [Hillel[56] reads OO-PP here:]
Another matter [= omitted by R. Hillel]: *Lest the whole
yield be sanctified* (Dt. 22:9)--

PP. "Lest the whole yield be prohibited," according to the words
of R. Josiah [other mss.:[57] Judah].

> Sifré Dt. 230m (ed. Finkelstein,
> p. 264, ll. 2-3)

QQ. He who extends (*hmwth*) a vine-shoot over seeds--
RR. even [if it is] a hundred *amah* [in length]--
SS. the vine is prohibited [GRA omits:] and its fruit [as well]
[= T. 4:10a].

> Sifré Dt. 230j (ed. Finkelstein,
> p. 263, ll. 11-12)

In OO-PP Josiah defines the term *sanctified* to mean "prohibited," or forbidden for use. QQ-SS then cites T. 4:10a with
mostly minor variations. The one major difference occurs at
QQ, which opens with the language of M. (*hmwth*) rather than
that of T. (*hmwdlh*), and so links M. and T. by reading the
former into the latter. Hillel's reading[58] juxtaposes OO-PP
and QQ-SS, and thus implicitly connects QQ-SS to Dt. 22:9.
The rule that a shoot extending over grain sanctifies the entire
vine is then deduced from the phrase *the whole yield*, which is
taken to refer to the entire vine.

and an interest in the question of sowing above a sunken vine-
shoot (M. 7:1), and thus serves to relate its own subunit
(M. 7:2D-F+3) to M. 7:1-2C. Eleazar b. Ṣadoq (M. 7:2F), however,
differs with M. 7:1's view of the problem of sowing above a sunken
shoot. He takes the issue of such a case to concern not whether
the seeds which are sown actually grow together with the vine as
diverse-kinds (as in M. 7:1), but whether the seeds and the vine
produce the appearance of diverse-kinds. M. 7:3 complements
M. 7:2D-F with two contrasting lists. One describes cases in which
seeds sown near a vine produce only the appearance of diverse-
kinds and so do not sanctify the vine, while the other presents
instances in which such seeds do grow as diverse-kinds with the
vine and thus sanctify the latter.

M. 7:4-5+6-7 discusses cases in which the growth of diverse-
kinds actually takes place, but against the desire of the owner.
M. 7:4 presents a dispute between an anonymous opinion, on the
one hand, and Yosé and Simeon (augmented by a $m^c\check{s}h$ involving
^{c}Aqiva [M. 7:5]), on the other, concerning one who trains a
vine over his neighbor's grain. The issue of the dispute concerns
whether sanctification occurs automatically with the growth of
diverse-kinds, so that the neighbor's grain is sanctified (anonymous opinion), or whether the process of sanctification is relative to the intention of the owner, in which instance the grain
is not sanctified, for one cannot sanctify that which does not
belong to him (Yosé and Simeon). M. 7:6-7, a subunit characterized
by its apocopated sentences (M. 7:6A, 7:7A,D), then complements
the view of Yosé and Simeon. M. 7:6 illustrates the position of
these authorities, ruling that one who usurps and sows a vineyard
does not sanctify the latter. The rightful owner need only cut
down the other kind, lest he appear to allow diverse-kinds to grow.
A gloss adds that he must do so immediately upon regaining his
property. M. 7:7 turns from the above cases, which concern a
person who sows diverse-kinds against the owner's wishes, to one
in which the owner himself separately sows the two kinds, which
accidentally (e.g., by being blown together by the wind) grow
together as diverse-kinds. M. 7:7 follows Yosé and Simeon's
principle that sanctification is relative to the intent of the
owner, ruling that, since the owner clearly does not wish the
different kinds to grow together, no sanctification takes place,
and the owner need only remove the appearance of diverse-kinds.

Returning to the interests of M. 7:2D-F+3, M. 7:8 presents
a dispute between an anonymous opinion and Simeon concerning
whether, when placed in a vineyard, a perforated pot containing
another kind produces the actual growth, or only the appearance,

of diverse-kinds. According to the anonymous opinion the roots of the seeds in the pot can penetrate to the vineyard's soil and be nourished from it, so that the seeds actually grow as diverse-kinds with the vines and therefore sanctify the latter. Simeon, on the other hand, maintains that the seeds in a perforated pot are not regarded as being attached to the vineyard's soil, so that, like seeds in an unperforated pot, they produce only the appearance of diverse-kinds when placed in a vineyard. According to Simeon, then, it is prohibited to place either a perforated or unperforated pot containing another kind in a vineyard, and the seeds in the former, like those in the latter, do not sanctify the vines.

7:1

A. He who sinks (*hmbryk*) a vine-shoot into the ground--

B. if the soil on top of it does not [measure] three hand-breadths [high],

C. he shall not put seed on top of it [i.e., the underground vine],

D. even if he sank it in a [Maimonides, *Comm.*: dried] gourd or pipe (*sylwn*).

E. [If] he sank it in stony ground [so Danby for sl^c; Maim., *Comm.*: hard ground]--

F. even though the soil on top of it [measures] only three fingerbreadths [high]--

G. it is permitted to put seed on top of it [i.e., the underground vine].

H. The "knee" (*h'rkwbh*; B. B.B.: *hrkbh*) of the vine-shoot [i.e., the part of the vine that is bent under the ground]-- they measure for it [most mss.:[1] they measure] [its area of tillage] only from the second root (*^{c}yqr*) [i.e., from the spot at which the vine grows new roots].

> M. Kil. 7:1 (A-C: B. B.B. 19b; H:
> B. B.B. 83a)

M. is composed of two declarative sentences, A-C (glossed by D) and E-G, with the latter dependent on the former for its content. The two sentences somewhat balance one another (*h'rs* vs. *hsl^c* [A vs. E], *šlšh tphym* vs. *šlšh 'sb^{c}wt* [B vs. F], and *l' yby'* vs. *mwtr lhby'* [C vs. G]). H complements A-G with a separate rule.

M. concerns the method of plant propagation known as lay-ering,[2] which consists (in the case of vines) of sinking a

vine-shoot into the ground so that it may develop new roots.
The shoot (also called the layer) is then separated from the
parent vine and grows from its own roots. M. asks whether one
may sow another kind above the sunken shoot without sowing diverse-
kinds. M. here distinguishes between the types of soil in which
the vine-shoot may be sunk. A-C rules that one may sow over a
vine-shoot which has been sunk into the ground only if three handbreadths of soil cover the vine. This amount of soil prevents
the roots of the seeds from penetrating into the vine and gaining
nourishment from it, for then the seeds would be considered to
be grafted onto the vine (Sens, Ribmaṣ; cf. M. 1:7-8; cf. also
Lieberman, *TK*, II, p. 644, on 1. 40). D adds that when the shoot
is sunk into a dried gourd or a pipe, presumably in order to hold
it in place,[3] three handbreadths of soil must nonetheless cover
the vine, for the roots of the seeds may perforate the casing
and penetrate into the vine. In E-G the vine-shoot is sunk into
rocky or hard ground, in which the roots of the seeds cannot
penetrate as deeply as they can in ordinary soil. In contrast
to the rule of A-C, therefore, one may sow on top of the vine even
if it is covered by only three fingerbreadths (= three-quarters
of a handbreadth). This contrast is underlined by the language
of F-G, which balances that of B-C:

B. if the soil on top of it does   F. even though the soil on
    not [measure] three hand-   top of it [measured] only
    breadths [high],   three fingerbreadths
                                          [high],

C. he shall not put seed on it.   G. it is permitted to put
                                          seed on it.

F's "three fingerbreadths" is clearly meant to contrast with
B's "three handbreadths," and so to emphasize the difference
between the two rulings.

H augments the interest of A-C, sowing above a sunken shoot,
with a discussion of measuring the area of tillage of the new
vine which rises aboveground. The new vine is here referred to as
the "knee" of the vine-shoot, or that part of the shoot which is
bent and which produces roots as the shoot turns upwards.[4] The
"knee" may then be said to represent the point at which the new
vine begins. H deals with the question concerning whether one
measures the area of tillage of the new vine from the parent vine,
to which the former is still attached, or from the roots of the
new vine itself. H rules that, although the new vine is still
connected to the parent vine, once it has its own roots it is

KILAYIM CHAPTER SEVEN / 233

considered a separate plant and its area of tillage is measured
from the new roots.

A. *He who sinks a vine-shoot into the ground* [= M. 7:1A]--
B. if there is on top of it soil [in] only the least amount
    (*kl šhw'*), it is permitted to sow on either side (*mykn wmykn*),
    but it is prohibited to sow [Vienna omits following to "it is
    permitted to sow"; first printed ed.:] on top of it.
C. *"If he sunk it into stony ground (slᶜ)* [= M. 7:1E]--
D. "even though the soil on top of it measures only two
    fingerbreadths [high]--
E. "it is permitted to sow on top of it," the words of R. Meir.
F. R. Yosah says, "[The soil must measure] three fingerbreadths
    [high]."
G. R. Simeon b. Gamaliel says, "(1) House of Shammai say, 'Ten
    [Erfurt omits:] *amot* [GRA: Ten handbreadths],' and (2) House
    of Hillel say, 'Six [Erfurt: ten] handbreadths.'"

T. Kil. 4:11 (p. 220, 11. 39-43)

T. comments on M. 7:1, with A-B citing and glossing M. 7:1A,
C-F relating to M. 7:1E-G, and H complementing M. 7:1A-C. A-B
turns from M.'s interest in the problem of sowing on top of a
sunken shoot to the related question of sowing beside such a
shoot. B somewhat follows the formulary pattern of M. 7:1B
('*m 'yn ᶜpr ᶜl gbh* [M. 7:1B] vs. *ᶜm 'yn ᶜl gbh ᶜpr 'l'* [T. 4:11B]).
B rules that one may not sow upon a sunken vine-shoot which is
covered by only a little soil (thus agreeing with M. 7:1A-C), but
one is permitted to sow on either side of the vine-shoot, for one
does not assume that the roots of the seed will penetrate the vine
from the side (Lieberman[5]).

At C-F Meir and Yosé dispute concerning how much soil must
cover a vine-shoot which is sunk into rocky soil. T. attributes
the language, though not the rule, of M. 7:1E-G to Meir at C-E,
who maintains that two fingerbreadths must cover the shoot, while
assigning to Yosé at E M.'s view that three fingerbreadths of
soil are required.

At G Simeon b. Gamaliel presents a balanced Houses-dispute
concerning the amount of soil which must cover a sunken shoot.
Both Houses disagree with the rule of M. 7:1A-C that only three
handbreadths of soil need cover the vine (Lieberman[6]). They both
maintain that the issue of sowing above a sunken vine-shoot concerns not the prevention of the roots of the seeds from penetrating
into the vine, but the separation of the other kind from the vine

by some fixed distance. House of Shammai maintain that ten
handbreadths (according to the readings of Erfurt, GRA, and
Lieberman[7]) must cover the vine. House of Shammai apparently
reason that, because the other kind is to be sown above the
sunken shoot (and not, for example, beside it), it must be sown
in a domain unto itself, or in a space ten handbreadths[8] above
the vine-shoot. House of Hillel, on the other hand, do not distinguish between the space above the vine and the space beside
it, ruling that in all cases one separates the other kind from
the vine by the latter's area of tillage, six handbreadths.[9]

7:2

A. (1) He who sinks three vine-shoots (2) and their roots
    [i.e., the roots of the layers (new vines)] are visible--
B. R. Eleazar b. Sadoq says, "If there are between them [i.e.,
    between the layers and the parent vines] from four to eight
    amot, lo, these [i.e., the layers and the parent vines]
    combine [to form a vineyard].
C. "And if not, they do not combine [to form a vineyard]."
D. A vine which withered [so Danby for *ybšh*] is prohibited [i.e.,
    it is prohibited to sow near it], but does not sanctify
    [the seeds sown near it].
E. R. Meir says, "Also (*'p*) [the] cotton (*smr gpn*) [tree[10]] is
    prohibited, [i.e., it is prohibited to sow near it], but
    it does not sanctify [the seeds sown near it]."
F. R. Eleazar b. Sadoq says in his name, "Also (*'p*) on top of
    the vine-shoot it is prohibited [to sow], but it [i.e., the
    vine-shoot] does not sanctify [the seeds sown above it]."

M. Kil. 7:2 (A-C: B. B.B. 83a;

D: Y. Kil. 2:3 (27d),

Y. Bes. 5:2 (63a)[11])

M. consists of Eleazar b. Sadoq's saying at A-C (in the
formulary pattern of M. 7:1A [*hmbryk*]), followed by a rule at D,
which is augmented by both Meir and Eleazar b. Sadoq in Meir's
name at E-F (both joined to D by *'p*). A-C and D-F are autonomous
of one another, for the former deals with an issue concerning
sunken vine-shoots, while the latter discusses the entirely
separate question of whether the act of sowing near certain vines
sanctifies the seeds. A-C and D-F were probably joined together
because of F, which, like A-C, is attributed to Eleazar b. Sadoq,
and which concerns whether sowing over a sunken shoot sanctifies
the seeds, thus serving to link together the interests of both
parts of the pericope.

A(1) describes a case in which one sinks three vine-shoots (from three different vines) into the ground in order to produce a set of new vines, or layers, alongside the standing vines. A(2), which perhaps glosses A(1), states that the roots of the layers are exposed, so that the layers appear to be vines unto themselves, even though they may still be attached to the parent vines. In B-C Eleazar b. Ṣadoq discusses whether the layers may combine with the parent vines to form a vineyard consisting of two rows (following House of Hillel, M. 4:5C-D). The issue of B-C concerns whether or not the layers and the parent vines appear to be aligned in two separate rows. Following Simeon's view concerning the spacing of rows in a vineyard (M. 4:9F [with Meir] + 5:2B; T. 3:5), Eleazar b. Ṣadoq rules that the layers and the parent vines combine to form a vineyard only if they are separated by a distance measuring between four and eight *amot*. The reasoning behind the rule is that rows which are separated by less than four *amot* do not appear to be distinct from one another, and rows which are set apart by more than eight *amot* do not appear to constitute a single entity.

D-F presents three instances of an act of sowing which is prohibited but does not sanctify the seeds of the other kind. In each case the point of M. is that the sowing is prohibited because it creates the appearance of diverse-kinds, but, since no actual sowing of diverse-kinds takes place, the seeds are not sanctified. In the case of D sowing near a withered vine produces only the appearance of diverse-kinds, for, since the vine no longer bears fruit, two kinds do not actually grow at the spot which is sown. Similarly, Meir maintains in E that one may not sow near a cotton tree without producing the appearance of diverse-kinds, for the cotton tree resembles a vine (Rosh[12]). The seeds are not sanctified, of course, for they and the cotton tree do not grow as diverse-kinds of the vineyard.[13] According to Eleazar b. Ṣadoq (in the name of Meir) at F sowing above a sunken vine-shoot produces the appearance of diverse-kinds, presumably because such a sowing takes place between the parent vine and the layer. Eleazar b. Ṣadoq apparently holds that sowing above a vine-shoot is not considered an actual sowing of diverse-kinds, perhaps because he believes sowing above a vine to differ from sowing beside it (an act which does sanctify the seeds [C]). In prohibiting the sowing of another kind above a sunken shoot, Eleazar b. Ṣadoq disagrees with the rule of M. 7:1A-C, which permits one to sow above a sunken shoot as long as the latter is covered by soil measuring three handbreadths deep. Eleazar b. Ṣadoq sees the issue to concern not whether the roots of the seeds will penetrate into the vine (as in M. 7:1A-C), but whether the seeds produce the appearance of diverse-kinds.[14]

GG. [(*Lest the whole yield be sanctified, the crop which you have sown and) the yield of the vineyard* (Dt. 22:9)--]

HH. I know only [concerning] a vineyard which bears fruit [i.e., that one may not sow in it].

II. Whence [do I know concerning] a vineyard which does not produce fruit [i.e., that one may sow in it]?

JJ. Scripture says, [*You shall not sow your*] *vineyard* [*with diverse-kinds* (Dt. 22:9)]--in every instance (*mkl mqwm*).

Sifré Dt. 230h
(ed. Finkelstein, p. 263,
ll. 9-10)

GG-JJ discusses whether the prohibition of sowing another kind in a vineyard (Dt. 22:9) applies in the case of a vineyard which does not bear fruit. GG-HH deduces that this prohibition applies to the fruit-bearing vineyard from the phrase *yield of the vineyard* (Dt. 22:9), which implies that the vineyard discussed in the verse does bear fruit. II-JJ then states that the phrase [*your*] *vineyard* in the opening of the same verse may be taken to include all vineyards. In maintaining that the rule (i.e., that sowing sanctifies the seeds) is the same for both fruit-bearing and barren vineyards, Sifré disagrees with M. 7:2D, which distinguishes between sowing near a fruit-bearing vine, which does sanctify the seeds, and sowing next to a withered vine, which is prohibited but does not sanctify the seeds.

7:3

A. These prohibit but (*w*) do not sanctify [the seeds sown in them]:

B. (1) The remainder of the waste-state [so Neusner[15] for *ḥrbn*; Danby: patch] of the vineyard, (2) the remainder of the outer space (*mḥwl*) of the vineyard, (3) the remainder of the gaps of an espalier, (4) the remainder of the [latticework of] laths.

C. But (1) [the area] under the vine, and (2) the area of tillage of the vine, and (3) the four *amot* of the vineyard, lo, these sanctify [the seeds sown in them].

M. Kil. 7:3 (B: T. Kel.
B.M. 6:13[16])

M. augments M. 7:2D-F's discussion of acts of sowing
near a vine which do not sanctify the seeds, presenting both
further instances and contrasting cases of the same rule. M.
consists of a superscription at A, a list of four items (all
beginning with the word *mwtr*) at B, and a list of three at C
(joined to B by *'bl*), thus enumerating seven items in all.

B discusses four instances in which one who sows near a vine
does not sanctify the seeds. B(1)-(3) refers to cases in which
one is permitted to sow the "remainder" of an area of a specified
size, or that space which remains after the nearby vines are
allowed their respective areas of tillage. M. rules that if the
area is of insufficient size, and one nevertheless sows in its
"remainder," the seeds are not sanctified. In the cases of the
vineyard's waste-state or bald spot (B(1)),[17] and the outer space
of the vineyard (B(2)),[18] the reasoning behind M. is that one who
sows in the "remainder" of an area which is too small appears to
sow diverse-kinds, for the other kind does not appear to be sown
in an area unto itself. Like M. 7:2D-F, therefore, M.'s point
is that one who produces only the appearance of diverse-kinds
does not sanctify the seeds.

The rule of B(3), which concerns sowing the "remainder" of
an espalier's gap, is difficult. According to M. 6:6A the gap
must measure eight *amot* and "a little more" in order to be sown,
and M. 6:6D-F explains that an area of this size is required
because the gap lies between two espaliers, each of which is
allowed an area of tillage of four *amot*. If, therefore, the gap
measures less than the specified size, the area to be sown actually
lies within one of the areas of tillage of the vines. C(2)-(3),
however, explicitly states that one who sows within a vine's (or
vineyard's) area of tillage does sanctify the seeds. B(3) may
therefore follow Yoḥanan b. Nuri's view (M. 6:1F-G) that the area
of tillage of an espalier is only six handbreadths. Alternatively,
B(3) may reject M. 6:6D-F's explanation that the gap mentioned
in M. 6:6A lies between two espaliers, maintaining that it lies
simply between two parts of the destroyed espalier. In any event
B(3) apparently holds that the vines on either side of the gap
are allowed only six handbreadths as their respective areas of
tillage, and that the "remainder" refers to the rest of the eight
amot and "a little more." If the gap then initially measures
less than the specified measure, one who sows in the "remainder"
produces the appearance of diverse-kinds, for again the other kind
does not lie in an autonomous area. As in the case of B(1)-(2),
therefore, the seeds sown in the "remainder" are not sanctified.

B(4) rules that sowing under the "remainder" of a latticework of laths does not sanctify the seeds. In this instance the term "remainder" refers not to the area remaining after the vines are allowed their areas of tillage (as in B(1)-(3)), but to that part of the latticework which remains uncovered by the vine trained on the laths. According to M. 6:3A one may not sow under the "remainder" of the latticework, for the entire latticework is regarded as an extension of the vine. M. 6:3B then rules that one who does sow under the "remainder" does not sanctify the vines, presumably because the seeds are not sown directly under the vine.[19] Like B(1)-(3), therefore, the point of B(4) is that the seeds are not sanctified because no actual sowing of diverse-kinds takes place.[20]

C augments B with three instances in which sowing near a vine does sanctify the seeds. One who sows either under a vine (C(1); e.g., by trellising his vines over grain [M. 7:4], or by sowing under a vine-shoot extended between trees [M. 6:9I-J (Ribmaṣ, Bert., MS, TYY)]) or within the area of tillage of a vine (C(2)) or a vineyard (C(3)) sanctifies the seeds, for in these cases he sows within the domain of the vine and thus actually sows diverse-kinds. By ruling that the seeds are sanctified by the actual sowing of diverse-kinds, C thus complements B's principle that the appearance of diverse-kinds does not sanctify the seeds.

F. [*You shall now sow your vineyard with diverse-kinds* (Dt. 22:9)--]
G. I know only [that the prohibition against sowing a vineyard with diverse-kinds applies to] a full vineyard.
H. Whence [do I know that the prohibition applies] even [to] a single vine which bears fruit?
I. Scripture says, [*Lest the whole yield be sanctified, the crop which you have sown and the yield of*] *the vineyard* (Dt. 22:9) [So Nesiv]--under all circumstances.

> Sifré Dt. 230b (ed. Finkelstein, p. 262, l. 12, to p. 263, l. 1)

G understands the word *vineyard* (Dt. 22:9) to mean that it is prohibited to sow diverse-kinds only in a full vineyard. H-I then takes the second mention of *vineyard* in the verse to include in the prohibition the act of sowing near an individual vine which bears fruit (Nesiv; cf. also Ish-Shalom[21]). Sifré thus agrees

both with M. 7:3C's rule that a single vine sanctifies another
kind sown near it, and with M. 7:2D's statement that a withered
vine does not sanctify diverse-kinds which are sown nearby.

7:4-5

A. He who trellises [so Bokser[22] for *mškk*] his vine over the
grain of his neighbor, lo, this one has sanctified [the grain
underneath the vines] and is liable [B. B.Q. omits:] to
replace it [so Bokser for *ḥyyb b'ḥrywth*].

B. R. Yosé and R. Simeon say, "A man does not sanctify (*mqdš*;
Y. Kil. 2:5, 4:5, 5:5: *mqdyš*) something which is not his own."

M. Kil. 7:4 (B. Yev. 83a,
B. B.Q. 100a; B: Y. Kil. 2:5
(28a), 4:5(28c), 5:5 (30a))

C. Said R. Yosé, "*m^{c}šh b*: One sowed his own vineyard in the
Seventh Year, and the case came before R. ^{c}Aqiva, and he
said, 'A man does not sanctify something which is not
his own.'"

M. Kil. 7:5

M. consists of a declarative sentence at A, which Yosé and
Simeon gloss and oppose at B. Yosé then augments B with a *m^{c}šh*
at C. A discusses whether one who trellises a vine over his
neighbor's grain sanctifies the latter, even though it does
not belong to him. The issue of A is whether sanctification
always takes place whenever another kind grows near a vine, or
whether other considerations, such as the ownership of the different kinds, must be taken into account as well. A rules that the
owner of the vine does sanctify his neighbor's crop and must
compensate his neighbor for them (for the crops must now be burnt
along with the vine). A thus maintains that sanctification occurs
automatically with the sowing of diverse-kinds of the vineyard,
regardless of the circumstances of the sowing. Yosé and Simeon
disagree at B, saying that one may not sanctify that which is not
his. These authorities thus regard sanctification to be relative
to other factors, such as (in this instance) the ownership of
the two kinds which grow together. We note that B does not respond
directly to the case of A, and need not even refer to a problem
concerning diverse-kinds.[23] A and B are therefore autonomous sayings which have been juxtaposed in order to create the semblance
of a dispute.

Unlike B, the $m^c\check{s}h$ cited by Yose relates specifically to
the question of A (i.e., diverse-kinds of the vineyard), and thus
was probably added to B when the latter was joined to A. The
$m^c\check{s}h$ has ^{C}Aqiva present verbatim the saying of B in ruling that
one who sows his vineyard in the Seventh Year does not sanctify
it. C presupposes that one's fields are considered ownerless
in the Seventh Year (Maim., *Comm.*; cf. Ex. 23:10-11, Lv. 25:7), so
that, since one may not sanctify that which is not his own, he
who sows his vineyard cannot sanctify it. The $m^c\check{s}h$ thus illustrates
B. C is curious, however, for it assigns to ^{C}Aqiva, a Yavnean,
a saying which is attributed at B to the Ushans Yosé and Simeon.
Now it is unlikely that Ushans would be assigned a saying which
had originally been attributed to a Yavnean. It is therefore
more probable that the $m^c\check{s}h$, which perhaps originally read "and
he permitted it," was revised to include B and thus to serve
more clearly as a precedent for the rule of B.

[KK.   *(You shall not sow) your vineyard (with diverse-kinds)*
       (Dt. 22:9)--]
LL.   I know only [concerning] your [own] vineyard [i.e., that
       you may not sow in it].
MM.   Whence do I know [concerning] a vineyard belonging to
       others [i.e., that you may not sow in it]?
NN.   Scripture says, *You shall not sow your vineyard with
       diverse-kinds* --in every instance (*mkl mqwm*).

Sifré Dt. 230i (ed. Finkelstein,
p. 263, ll. 10-11) (Y. Kil. 7:3
(30d)[24])

Sifré discusses whether one may sow a vineyard which belongs
to someone else. KK deduces from the phrase *your vineyard* that
the prohibition of sowing a vineyard refers to one's own vineyard.
NN then extends the prohibition to apply to all vineyards by
taking the phrase *You shall not sow* to refer to all cases of
sowing in a vineyard. Sifré would thus agree with M. 7:4A's rule
that one does sanctify that which does not belong to him.

7:6

A.   The usurper [following Danby for *h'ns*] who sowed a vineyard--
B.   and it left his possession (*wys' mlpnyw*) [Danby: and it
     was recovered from him]--
C.   he [i.e., the rightful owner] cuts down [the other kind],

D. even (*'pylw*) on [the intermediate days (Maim., *Comm.*,
    Code, *Diverse-Kinds* 5:12) of] a festival.

E. How much more does he pay the workers [for cutting down the
    other kind on the intermediate days of a festival]?

F. Up to a third [more than their usual wages].

G. [If they demand] more than this,

H. he continues to cut [it] down in his [usual] manner,

I. even [if he does not finish cutting it down until] after
    the festival.

J. At what point is [the vineyard] called [that of the] usurper?

K. At the point that [the vineyard] settles (*mšyšq^c*) [firmly
    into the usurper's possession and the rightful owner may no
    longer recover it from him (Albeck)].

M. Kil. 7:6

   M. opens with an apocopated sentence, A-D, dealing with a
vineyard which has been sown by a usurper. E-I and J-K then
separately gloss A-D. Now E-I responds only to D (with I somewhat
balancing D [*'pylw bmw^{c}d vs. 'pylw l'ḥr mw^{c}d*]), for D alone
shares E-I's interest in the issue of cutting down the other kind
during a festival. Along with E-I, then, D actually glosses
A-C, which presents a perfectly intelligible rule by itself.
It therefore appears that the gloss D-I, introducing the issue
of work which may be done during a festival, has been inserted
into the unit A-C+J-K, which concerns simply the problem of the
usurper who has sown a vineyard.

   A-C complements M. 7:4B with another instance of Yosé's
and Simeon's rule that one cannot sanctify that which is not his
own. A-C describes a case in which one recovers his vineyard
from one who had illegally seized it and had sown it with another
kind. The issue of A-C concerns whether the usurper sanctified
the vineyard by sowing it, so that the rightful owner must burn
the other kind together with the vines. According to A-C the
owner must cut down the other kind, lest he appear to allow
diverse-kinds to grow. A-C does not rule, however, that the two
kinds must be burnt, and thus implies that the vineyard was not
sanctified by the usurper, presumably because he could not sanctify
that which did not belong to him. J then asks concerning the point
at which the usurper is regarded as the owner of the vineyard,
so that he does sanctify it by sowing it (Bert., TYY).[25] K
answers that the usurper is considered the vineyard's owner once
the property rests firmly in his possession, for he then has control
over the vineyard and so effectively functions as its owner.

D introduces the consideration of the haste with which the owner must clear the vineyard of the other kind. According to D the owner must immediately cut down the other kind, even if he must do so during the intermediate days of a festival, when such work is usually prohibited. The point of D is that one must act as soon as possible to destroy the appearance of diverse-kinds. E-I then augments D with a discussion of the maximum amount which the owner is required to pay the workers in order to induce them to work during the festival. E-F states that the owner must pay the laborers up to a third more than their regular wages. He need not offer more than this amount, however, even if these wages will not attract workers and the vineyard thus will not be entirely cleared of the other kind until after the festival (G-I). According to G-I, then, one need not suffer a great economic loss in order to remove the other kind, which after all produces only the appearance of diverse-kinds. G-I thus qualifies D, for it rules that, under certain circumstances, one may allow the other kind to remain in the vineyard until after the festival.

7:7

A. Wind which hurled [so Danby for $^{c}l^{c}lh$] vines on top of grain--

B. he should cut them [i.e., the vines] down at once ($ygdwr$; V, Sens: $ygrwr$;[26] B, Cn, O,P, Maim., *Comm.*, *Code*, *Diverse-Kinds* 5:11 [some mss.[27]]: $ygrwd$ ["he shall remove them (Maim., *Comm.*)"]; Geniza fragment,[28] S, other commentaries:[29] $ygdwd$).

C. If an unavoidable accident (*'wns*) befell him [and he could not immediately cut down the vines], it is permitted [i.e., the grain is not sanctified].

D. Grain which sways [so Danby for $nwth$] under the vine,

E. and so [is the rule] in [the case of] vegetables [which sway under the vine]--

F. he returns [the grain or the vegetables to their original positions] and does not sanctify [i.e., forfeit the vines].

G. At what point does grain become sanctified?

H. At the point that it strikes root ($m\breve{s}t\breve{s}ry\breve{s}$; many mss. and commentaries:[30] $m\breve{s}t\breve{s}ly\breve{s}$ ["at the point that it reaches one-third of its growth"]).

I. And [at what point do] grapes [become sanctified]?

J. At the point that they become like [i.e., the size of] a hyacinth bean.

K. Grain which has become fully dried or (*w*) grapes which have fully ripened do not become sanctified.

M. Kil. 7:7

M. continues its discussion of diverse-kinds of the vineyard
which grow against the wishes of the owner, turning from the
case of the usurper who sows a vineyard (M. 7:6) to instances in
which vines accidentally hang over another kind. M. 7:7 opens
with an apocopated sentence, A-B (glossed by C), concerning
vines which are blown on top of grain by the wind. D+F (glossed
by E), which is also in apocopation, then presents a separate
rule characterized by a differed apodosis, dealing with grain
which sways under a vine. D+F has been joined to A-B because it
reverses the circumstances of the latter, discussing grain which
extends under the vine, rather than the vine which hangs over
grain. G-J then augments A-F, and is itself complemented by K.

A describes a case in which the wind blows vines on top of
some nearby grain. The issue of A concerns whether sanctification
occurs automatically with the growth of diverse-kinds, even though
the owner could not have prevented such a growth. B rules that
the owner must cut down the overhanging vines at once so that he
not appear to allow diverse-kinds to grow. B does not state,
however, that the two kinds must be destroyed, and so implicitly
rules that the grain is not sanctified by the vine. A-B thus
agrees with M. 7:6A-C's principle that sanctification takes place
only when diverse-kinds are sown intentionally. C then makes
this point clear, stating that the grain is not sanctified even
if one is unable immediately to cut down the vines, for in any
case the owner did not wish the diverse-kinds to grow.

D presents a similar case, in which grain (or, according to
E, vegetables) sways under a vine. Like A, D concerns whether
sanctification takes place regardless of the intentions of the
owner. According to F the vines are not sanctified if the owner
returns the grain to its original position, for he then does not
appear to allow diverse-kinds to grow. D+F then agrees with the
principle of A-B, i.e., that sanctification occurs only when
diverse-kinds are sown intentionally, but differs from the actual
rule of A-B, maintaining that the kind which has moved from its
original position need only be returned to its proper place, but
need not be cut down.

G-J augments A-F with a discussion of the points in their
respective growth processes at which grain and grapes can become
sanctified. According to one reading of H (mǎtǎryǎ) grain can
become sanctified once it has struck root, presumably because
at that point it visibly begins its process of growth.
Alternatively, H (when mǎtǎlyǎ is read) maintains that grain
cannot become sanctified until it reaches a third of its projected
size,[31] presumably because only then does it begin to acquire

distinctive characteristics of grain. I-J then rules that
grapes can become sanctified as soon as they reach the size of
hyacinth beans, for only at that point may they be properly called
grapes. K then augments G-J by defining the points at which grain
and grapes can no longer be sanctified. According to K one cannot
sanctify grain which has fully dried or grapes which are fully
ripe, for in either case the crop has ceased to grow. The point
of K thus is that diverse-kinds are sanctified only if they
actually grow together, so that a kind which has stopped growing
can no longer be sanctified.

A. *Grain which sways under the vine*--

B. *he returns it [to its original position] and does not sanctify*
    [= M. 7:7D+F] the vines.

C. *And vegetables* [= M. 7:7E] which sway into (*ltwk*; Erfurt:
    tḥt ["under"]) the vine [Erfurt, first printed ed. omit:
    grain]--

D. Abba Saul says [= omitted by Y. Kil. 7:5], "(1) R. ^CAqiva
    says, 'He shall return [them to their original positions],'
    and (2) Ben ^CAzzai says, 'He shall cut [them] down (*yspr*).'"

E. If their [i.e., the vegetables'] roots extended [from outside
    of the vineyard's area of tillage] into the four *amot* [Erfurt,
    first printed ed. add:] of the vineyard, all agree [Erfurt,
    first printed ed. add:] that he shall uproot them [first
    printed ed.: *y^cqwr*; Erfurt: *^cwqr*].

F. Roots of madder [so Lieberman,[32] reading *pw'h* for *py'h*]
    which extended [from outside of the vineyard's area of
    tillage] into the four *amot* of the vineyard [even (= omitted
    by Y. Kil. 1:8, 5:3, 6:2; GRA[33])] more than three handbreadths
    below [the surface]--it is permitted [i.e., the madder does
    not sanctify the vine].

                                    T. Kil. 4:10b (p. 220, ll. 35-39)
                                    (D: Y. Kil. 7:5 (31a); F: Y. Kil.
                                    1:8 (27b), 5:3 (29d), 6:2 (30c))

     T. cites M. 7:7D+F at A-B, adding "the vines," an obvious
gloss, at B. C-D cites and glosses M. 7:7E, filling out its
protasis and augmenting it with a dispute between ^CAqiva and
Ben ^CAzzai (cited by Abba Saul). The dispute concerns how one
removes the appearance of diverse-kinds which is produced when
vegetables sway under vines. The issue of the dispute is whether
one need deal only with the current appearance of diverse-kinds,
or whether one must also ensure that the appearance of diverse-kind
will not reoccur in the future. According to ^CAqiva one has only

to return the vegetables to their original positions, for one need be concerned only with the present appearance of diverse-kinds and not with the possibility that the vegetables might again sway under the vines. ^{C}Aqiva is thus assigned the view of M. 7:7E (= M. 7:7D+F). Ben ^{C}Azzai, on the other hand, maintains that one must cut down the vegetables in order to prevent them from again producing the appearance of diverse-kinds. Ben ^{C}Azzai's view is similar to M. 7:7A-B's rule that one must cut down vines which the wind has blown on top of grain. T. thus perhaps links M. 7:7A-B to M. 7:7D-F by placing the two rules in dispute with one another in the context of M. 7:7E.

E then augments C-D with a case in which vegetables are sown outside of a vineyard's area of tillage, but their roots then extend into the four *amot* of space surrounding the vines.[34] The vegetables thus actually grow with the vines as diverse-kinds, although, of course, they do not sanctify the vines, since they were originally sown outside of the vineyard's area of tillage. In this instance all of the parties to the dispute of D agree that the vegetables must be uprooted, for only in this way can the growth of diverse-kinds be stopped. F[35] complements E with an exception to its rule. If the roots of madder[36] extend from outside of the vineyard's area of tillage into the four *amot* at a depth of three handbreadths below the surface, they do not sanctify the vines, since the two sets of roots do not touch one another.

A. Grain which has struck root, lo, (1) this is prohibited [i.e., it is prohibited to plant vines near it], and (2) it sanctifies [vines growing near it], and (3) it is sanctified [by vines growing near it].

B. Vines which have struck root, lo, (1) these are prohibited [i.e., it is prohibited to sow grain near them] (*'swryn*; GRA:[37] *'wsryn* ["prohibit"]), and (2) they sanctify [grain growing near them], but (3) they are not sanctified [by grain growing near them].

C. until *they* [i.e., their grapes] *shall become like* [*i.e., the size of*] *a hyacinth bean* [= M. 7:7J].

D. (1) If some of the vines produced [grapes] like [i.e., the size of] a hyacinth bean, and (2) others did not produce [grapes like (i.e., the size of) a hyacinth bean].

E. (1) those [vines] which produced [grapes] like [i.e., the size of] a hyacinth bean are prohibited [i.e., sanctified], and (2) those [vines] which did not produce [grapes] like [i.e., the size of] a hyacinth bean are permitted [i.e., not sanctified].

T. Kil. 4:12 (p. 221, ll. 44-47)

T. complements M. 7:7G-J's interest in the points at which
grain and vines can become sanctified, presenting additional rules
concerning the instants at which each of these two kinds may not be
sown with each other and can sanctify one another. A-B forms a
well balanced pair of declarative sentences, with A and B differing only at their respective openings (*tbw'h vs. gpn*) and at A(3)
and B(3) (*mtqdš vs. 'ynw mtqdš*). B(3) is then glossed by C, which
cites M. 7:7J. D-E augments the latter with a conditional sentence,
the protasis and apodosis of which are each internally balanced
(D(1) *vs.* D(2), E(1) *vs.* E(2)).

A restates and expands the rule of M. 7:7G-H, saying that
once grain has struck root it not only can become sanctified
(A(3)), but it can also sanctify vines growing around it (A(2)),
and one may not plant vines near it (A(1)). This last rule
appears to be unnecessary, for it appears to follow clearly
from A(2) and A(3) that one is not permitted to plant vines near
grain. T. perhaps follows the language of M. 7:3A (*'lw 'wsryn
wl' mqdšyn*) and thus simply joins together the two phrases *'swrh*
and *mqdšt*, even though the latter (+A(3)) makes the former
redundant. B extends the rule of A to the case of vines, maintaining that, like grain, vines which have struck root can sanctify,
and it is prohibited to sow near them. The rule for vines differs
from that for grain, however, for vines cannot become sanctified
until their grapes grow to the size of hyacinth beans (= M. 7:7J[C])
D-E then augments C with an intermediate case in which only some
of the vines of a sanctified vineyard have produced grapes as
large as hyacinth beans. The issue of D-E concerns whether
sanctification[38] takes place with respect to the vineyard as
a whole, even though some of the vines do not contain grapes of
the specified size, or whether sanctification affects each vine
separately. According to E only those vines which have produced
grapes of the size of hyacinth beans are sanctified, so that
sanctification may be said to take effect only in respect to
single vines, and not in regard to the entire vineyard.

M. *Lest be sanctified the fullness of seed (hml'h hzrᶜ) [which
    you have sown and the yield of the vineyard (Dt. 22:9)]*
    [Alternatively: *Lest the whole yield be sanctified (hml'h)
    (, the seed which you have sown and the yield of the
    vineyard)*].

N. At what point does *the fullness of seed (hml'h hzrᶜ)*
    [some mss.:[39] the whole yield *(hml'h)*] become sanctified?

O. *At the point that it strikes root (mštšryš; Hillel:
    mštšlyš* ["At the point that it reaches one-third of its
    growth"]).

P. And [at what point do] grapes [become sanctified]?

Q. At the point that they become like i.e., the size of a
    hyacinth bean [= M. 7:7G-J].

> Sifré Dt. 230d (ed. Finkelstein,
> p. 263, ll. 4-5)

Sifré cites M. 7:7G-J at N-Q and links it to Dt. 22:9 (M).
According to one reading of B Sifré connects M. to the words
hml'h hzr^c (substituting them for *tbw'h* in its citation of
M. 7:7G), which are read as a single phrase meaning *the fullness
of seed*. Sifré takes this phrase to indicate that grain cannot
be sanctified until it reaches a certain "fullness," and thus
cites M. at O to define when this instant occurs. Alternatively,
Sifré links M. at N to the word *hml'h* (substituting it for
tbw'h in citing M. 7:7G), which, read by itself, is taken to
mean *the whole yield* and to refer to grain (Nesiv). According
to this reading of B Sifré understands Scripture to say that
grain cannot be sanctified until it is regarded as producing a
"yield," and so cites M. at O to describe the point in the growth-
process of the grain at which this development takes place. We
note that although Sifré cites M. 7:7G-J, it is relevant only
to M. 7:7G-H.

BB. [*The seed which you have sown and*] *the yield of the
     vineyard* (Dt. 22:9).

CC. At what point does grain become sanctified?

DD. At the point that it strikes root.

EE. And [at what point do] grapes [become sanctified]?

FF. At the point that they become like [i.e., the size of]
     a hyacinth bean [= M. 7:7G-J].

> Sifré Dt. 230g (ed. Finkelstein, p. 263, ll.
> 8-9) (EE-FF: cf. Y. Kil. 7:5[40])

Sifré cites M. 7:7G-J (CC-FF), linking M. 7:7I-J to Dt. 22:9.
Sifré thus complements Sifré Dt. 230d, which connects M. 7:7G-H
to the same verse. Sifré here specifically links M. to the
phrase *the yield of the vineyard* (*tbw't hkrm*), taking this phrase
to indicate that the vines cannot be sanctified until they
produce a "yield." Sifré then cites M. 7:7I-J at EE-FF to specify
the point at which such a "yield" is produced.

7:8

A. A perforated pot [containing another kind] sanctifies [the
    vines when located] in the vineyard.

B. And that [pot containing another kind] which is unperforated
    does not sanctify [the vines when located in the vineyard].

C. And [= omitted by most mss.[41]] R. Simeon says, "Both
    [perforated and unperforated pots containing another kind]
    prohibit ('wsryn; some mss.:[42] 'swryn ["are prohibited"])
    [i.e., it is prohibited to place them in a vineyard] but
    (w) do not sanctify [the vines when located in the vineyard]."

D. He who carries a perforated pot [containing another kind]
    through the vineyard--

E. if [while he carried the pot through the vineyard] it [i.e.,
    the seeds of the other kind] increased in size by [one]
    two-hundredth--

F. it is prohibited [i.e., it sanctifies the vines].

                    M. Kil. 7:8 (A-B: Y. Dem. 5:8 (25a), Y. Shab.
                    10:6 (12d); D-F; B. Pes. 25a, B. Hul. 116a)

        M. opens with a pair of well-balanced declarative sentences,
A-B (nqwb + mqdš vs. 'ynw nqwb + 'ynw mqdš), concerning a
perforated pot containing seeds which is located in a vineyard.
Simeon glosses and opposes A-B at C. Following its own formulary
pattern (he-who . . . it-is apocopation [hmᶜbyr]), D+F (glossed
by E) then complements A-C with a separate rule dealing with the
perforated pot which is carried through a vineyard.

        A-B discusses whether seeds which grow in a pot located in
a vineyard are regarded as growing in the vineyard itself, and
so sanctify the surrounding vines. The issue of A-B concerns
whether or not the seeds contained in the pot derive nourishment
from the soil of the vineyard. M. here distinguishes between
those seeds which are planted in a perforated pot and those which
grow in a pot without any holes. In the first instance the roots
of the seeds can penetrate through the holes in the pot to the
vineyard's soil, from which they may be nourished. The seeds
are thus regarded as growing in the vineyard itself and so
sanctify the vines.[43] If the pot has no holes, on the other hand,
the seeds within it do not sanctify the vines. Since in this
case their roots cannot come into contact with the soil of the vineyard, the seeds are not considered to grow in the vineyard itself.

        At C Simeon disagrees with the view of A-B, maintaining that
the rule is the same whether or not the pot containing the seeds
is perforated.[44] In either case it is prohibited to place the
pot in the vineyard, but the seeds within the pot do not sanctify
the vines. One may not place the pot in the vineyard lest the
seeds within it appear to grow as diverse-kinds with the vines
(e.g., if the pot should be hidden from view). According to this
interpretation, then, Simeon follows the principle of M. 7:2D-F+3,

i.e., that the appearance of diverse-kinds does not sanctify the
seeds or the vine. In ruling that seeds in either type of pot do
not sanctify the vines, Simeon implies that the seeds contained in
a perforated pot, like those which grow in a pot without holes, are
not regarded as growing in the vineyard itself. Simeon may reason
here that the seeds in the perforated pot may be sustained from the
soil of the pot alone. One therefore need not assume that the seeds
are actually nourished by the vineyard's soil, even if their roots
can penetrate into that soil. The seeds contained in the perforated
pot are thus considered to grow in the pot,[45] and not in the vineyard, so that they do not sanctify the vines.

    According to D+F it is prohibited for one to carry a perfora-
ted pot containing another kind through a vineyard, for it would
then seem as if he intended to place the pot in the vineyard, and
he would thus appear to sow diverse-kinds. This rule is separate
from that of A-C, for in this instance the perforated pot is only
carried through the vineyard, while in the case of A-C the pot
is actually set down there. Both Simeon and the anonymous authority
behind A-B, who disagree concerning whether or not the pot sanctifies the vines of the vineyard, would presumably be in accord
with the rule of D+F. Both authorities would agree that carrying
a perforated pot through a vineyard produces only the appearance
of diverse-kinds, and thus does not sanctify the vines. Glossing
D+F, E states that the rule of the latter applies only when the
seeds in the pot grow by one two-hundredth while being carried
through the vineyard. The significance of the figure "one two-
hundredth" may be explained as follows (cf. also M. 5:7). Only
that part of a plant which actually grows while the pot is in
the vineyard is considered to be prohibited. This additional,
prohibited part of the plant is regarded as if it were in a mixture
with other, permitted parts of the plant. Now one prohibited
part may be neutralized in a mixture containing two hundred permitted parts (M. Orl. 2:1). If, therefore, the prohibited part
of the plant measures less than one two-hundredth of the whole,
that prohibited part is neutralized by the rest of the plant. If
the plant grows one two-hundredth or more, however, the prohibited
part is not neutralized by the remainder of the plant (for the
ratio of permitted to prohibited parts is less than 200:1), and
the entire plant is prohibited. The point of E is that the issue
of D+F concerns not the appearance of diverse-kinds, but their
actual growth in the vineyard. Accordingly, E may take 'swr
(F) to mean "it [i.e., the plant in the pot] is sanctified"
rather than simply "it is prohibited," and thus follows the view
of A-B (i.e., that a perforated pot can sanctify [and be sanctified
by] the vines of a vineyard).

A. *He who carries a perforated pot [containing another kind] through the vineyard* --

B. *if [while he carried the pot through the vineyard] it [i.e., the seeds of the other kind] increased in size by [one] two-hundredth--*

C. *it is prohibited* [= M. 7:8D-F],

D. but (1) it does not become sanctified (2) until he places it under the vine.

E. R. Simeon says [= omitted by Y. Kil.], "The perforated pot differs from that which is not perforated only in [respect to] rendering seeds susceptible."

> T. Kil. 4:13 (p. 22, 11. 47-49)
>
> (E: Y. Kil. 7:6 (31a), B. Shab. 95a)

T. cites and glosses M. 7:8D-F at A-D, complementing M.'s case of one who carries a perforated pot through a vineyard with the instance of one who actually sets down such a pot in a vineyard. T. understands '*swr* in M. 7:8F to mean simply that it is prohibited to carry a perforated pot through a vineyard, and thus adds in D(1) that such an act does not sanctify the seeds in the pot. D(2), which may gloss D(1), then states that the pot does become sanctified when it is actually set down in the vineyard, as in the case of M. 7:8A ("A perforated pot [containing another kind] sanctifies [the vines when located] in the vineyard"). T. thus links M. 7:8A-C to M. 7:8D-F by reading the former into the latter.

At E T. augments Simeon's saying of M. 7:8C, having Simeon extend to every case but one his principle that one does not distinguish between perforated and unperforated pots. The one instance in which Simeon does make such a distinction concerns rendering seeds susceptible to uncleanness. Simeon here refers to M. Uqs. 2:10, which states that seeds planted in a perforated pot may not be rendered susceptible to uncleanness (by being wet down), for the seeds are considered to be attached to the ground. Seeds contained in an unperforated pot, on the other hand, are regarded as being detached from the ground, and thus may be rendered susceptible to uncleanness, when wet down. Simeon thus reasons that the tenuous connection (through the seeds' roots) between the seeds in a perforated pot and the ground is considered to be significant only in regard to the issue of rendering seeds susceptible to uncleanness, perhaps because in this instance even the slightest connection is considered to attach the plant to the ground (M. Uqs. 3:8H [Lieberman][46]).[47]

KILAYIM CHAPTER EIGHT

Chapter Eight is divided into two parts, M. 8:1, which
introduces the chapter with a series of rules concerning various
types of diverse-kinds, and M. 8:2-6, which discusses prohibitions
dealing specifically with diverse-kinds of animals. M. 8:1
serves to link M. 8:2-6 to Chapter Seven, for it opens with a
rule concerning diverse-kinds of the vineyard, the subject of
the previous chapter, and closes with the prohibition against
breeding animals of diverse-kinds, a concern of M. 8:2-6.
M. 8:1 thus serves a clear redactional purpose. This last rule
is glossed by the statement, "Diverse-kinds of animals are prohibited with the another (M. 8:1J)." This statement apparently
means that diverse-kinds of animals, i.e., animals born of the
union of different kinds, may not be mated with one another, for
such a union would surely be a pairing of different kinds. We
shall immediately see, however, that at least one redactor
apparently understood M. 8:1J differently, and that his understanding of this rule had a direct bearing on the redaction of
the chapter.

M. 8:2-6 consists of three parts, M. 8:2-4B, concerning
the prohibition of yoking animals of different kinds to do work,
M. 8:4C-E+5A-B, discussing the mating of mules with one another,
and M. 8:5C-G, dealing with animals of doubtful status (e.g.,
animals which may be regarded as either wild or domesticated).
Now it is not clear why M. 8:2-4B, which concerns the yoking
of animals to do work, separates M. 8:1J and M. 8:4C-E+5A-B,
both of which discuss the mating of animals of diverse-kinds.
If M. 8:1J were immediately to be followed by M. 8:4C-E+5A-B,
then the former's prohibition against the mating of animals of
diverse-kinds would be augmented with the latter's discussion of
the mating of mules, i.e., particular animals of diverse-kinds.
M. 8:1J and M. 8:4C-E+5A-B would thus together form a coherent
subunit. It is therefore likely that M. 8:1J and M. 8:4C-E+5A-B
were at one point juxtaposed with one another, and that M. 8:2-4B
was later inserted between them. The redactor responsible for
this insertion apparently understood M. 8:1J to have a meaning
different from that presented above. It is likely that he took
the phrase "diverse-kinds of animals" in M. 8:1J to refer not
to animals born of the union of different kinds, but simply to

251

different kinds of animals. He could not, however, understand
M. 8:1J to refer to the mating of such animals with one another,
for that act is already prohibited by the rule which M. 8:1J
glosses. The redactor therefore took M. 8:1J to concern the
yoking together of different kinds of animals to do work, and so
attached to it M. 8:2-4B.

M. 8:2-4B opens with the prohibition against joining together
animals of different kinds to do work (M. 8:2), and then turns
to two secondary problems. M. 8:3A-C presents a dispute between
an anonymous opinion and Meir concerning whether or not one is
liable for being passively pulled by animals of different kinds.
M. 8:3D+4A-B then rules that an animal of one kind may not be
attached to any part of a wagon drawn by another kind of animal,
for, although the two animals are not actually yoked together,
they are still considered to be joined to one another.

M. 8:4C-E+5A-B presents Judah's view that mules born of
dams of the same kind may be mated with another. Judah maintains
that animals of diverse-kinds themselves form different "kinds"
and so may be mated with other members of their own kind. Judah
thus opposes M. 8:1J's rule that animals of diverse-kinds may
not be mated with each other.

M. 8:5C-G and M. 8:6 present two lists (respectively containing two and five items, or seven in all) of animals of doubtful status. Although neither list explicitly raises concerns
of diverse-kinds, and each is relevant to such other considerations as uncleanness (as indicated by glosses), the context of
the lists allows us to interpret them as referring to matters
of diverse-kinds. M. 8:5C-G thus concerns whether certain
creatures are regarded as wild animals and not as either men (in
one case) or creeping things (in the other), and so subject to
the rules of diverse-kinds. M. 8:6A-G then considers whether
certain animals are regarded as wild or domesticated, i.e.,
whether certain animals are considered to be diverse-kinds with
similar kinds living in a different environment (e.g., the ox and
the wild ox). M. 8:6H glosses the list with the rule that man
may join together with animals to do work, for the rules of
diverse-kinds do not apply to man. Following the language of
M. 8:2, M. 8:6H serves to relate M. 8:6A-G, which implicitly concerns the mating of animals of different kinds, to M. 8:2, which
discusses the joining together of different kinds to do work, and
so ties together the subunit of M. 8:2-6, a good piece of
secondary redaction.

8:1

A. Diverse-kinds of the vineyard [i.e., another kind growing in a vineyard] are prohibited from being sown and being allowed to grow,

B. and are prohibited in respect to benefit [i.e., one may not profit from them in any way].

C. Diverse-kinds of seeds [i.e., two kinds of seeds growing together] are prohibited from being sown and being allowed to grow,

D. but (w) are permitted in respect to eating [i.e., one may eat the produce of the seeds],

E. [most mss.[1] omit:] and all the more so in respect to benefit [i.e., one may profit from them].

F. Diverse-kinds of garments [i.e., garments composed of a mixture of wool and linen] are permitted in every respect [e.g., one may manufacture them],

G. and are prohibited only from being worn.

H. Diverse-kinds of animals [i.e., the offspring of the mating of two kinds of animals] are permitted to be reared and maintained,

I. and are prohibited only from being bred [following Danby for $mlhrby^c$] [i.e., one may not breed one kind of animal with another].

J. Diverse-kinds of animals [i.e., the offspring of the mating of two kinds of animals] are prohibited [i.e., may not be mated] with one another [zh bzh; many mss.:[2] zh ^cm zh].

M. Kil. 8:1

M. is a unitary pericope consisting of four rules, A-B, C-D (glossed by E), F-G, and H-I (glossed by J). All of the rules open with the formulary pattern $kl'y$ X, and all contain a double apodosis composed of one or both of the contrastive predicates $'swr$ and $mwtr$. The four rules may be divided into two pairs, for the apodoses of A-B and C-D open with $'swryn$, while those of F-G and H-I begin with $mwtryn$. The rules of each pair also balance one another. A and C are almost identical to each other ($hkrm$ $vs.$ zr^cym), and B balances D ($'swryn$ $bhn'h$ $vs.$ $mwtryn$ $b'kylh$). Now F and H only roughly correspond to one another ($kl'y$ X + $mwtryn$ in each), but G closely balances I ($mllbwš$ $vs.$ $mlhrby^c$), so that these two rules may be considered a pair as well.

M. presents fundamental rules concerning the creation and use of the four different types of diverse-kinds. A-B and C-D

compare and contrast the case of diverse-kinds of the vineyard
with that of diverse-kinds of seeds. According to A and C the
two cases are similar in that one may neither sow nor maintain
either type of diverse-kinds. B and D, on the other hand, distinguish between these two instances, maintaining that one may
not derive any benefit from diverse-kinds of the vineyard, which
are sanctified and must be burnt, while one is permitted to eat
the produce of diverse-kinds of seeds, to which the law of
sanctification does not apply. We should expect D to balance B
and so read *mwtryn bhn'h*. D, however, reads *mwtryn b'kylh*,
thus making the further point that one may not only derive benefit
from diverse-kinds of seeds, e.g., sell them, but one may even
eat their produce, and thus use them for the purpose for which
they were sown. E, which is omitted in most manuscripts, then
supplies the expected phrase *bhn'h*.

F-G states that one is prohibited only from wearing garments
of diverse-kinds, and thus follows Scripture, which prohibits
only the wearing of such garments: *Nor shall there come upon
you a garment of cloth made up of two kinds of stuff* (Lv. 19:19);
You shall not wear a mingled stuff, wool and linen together
(Dt. 22:11). H-I similarly follows Scripture in prohibiting only
the breeding of animals of diverse-kinds, for Scripture refers
only to breeding such animals: *You shall not let your cattle
breed with a different kind* (Lv. 19:19). H-I thus rules that one
may rear and maintain animals of diverse-kinds. Glossing H-I,
J adds that one may not breed animals of diverse-kinds with one
another, for such breeding would certainly represent a mating
of different kinds.

A. Diverse-kinds of the vineyard are permitted with regard to
    [the law of]robbery [i.e., one may steal diverse-kinds from
    another's vineyard] and are exempt from tithes.

                    T. Kil. 5:1 (p. 221, l. 1)

                    (T. Sheq. 1:3)

B. Diverse-kinds of seeds are prohibited with regard to [the
    law of] robbery [i.e., one may not steal diverse-kinds
    from another's field] and are liable for tithes.

                    T. Kil. 5:2 (p. 221, ll. 1-2)

                    (T. Sheq. 1:3[3])

    T. augments M. 8:1A-F, extending the latter's comparison of
diverse-kinds of the vineyard with diverse-kinds of seeds to

include the considerations of liability for robbery and for
tithes. Like M., T consists of well-balanced declarative
sentences. The issue of T. concerns whether or not diverse-kinds
are regarded as ownerless, so that a robber is not liable for
stealing them, and the owner is not obligated to tithe them (as
to the latter, cf. M. Hal. 1:3). Diverse-kinds of the vineyard,
on the other hand, are sanctified and cannot be used by their
owner (M. 8:1B), who is therefore assumed to renounce his rights
of ownership over them.[4] Diverse-kinds of seeds, on the other
hand, may be eaten by their owner (M. 8:1D). The latter is
therefore assumed to want the diverse-kinds for himself, so that
they may not be stolen without penalty and are liable for
tithes.[5]

A. [Erfurt, Ribmaṣ, Sens, and OZ[6] reverse A-B and C-D] A
   horse which brought forth [a foal of] a kind [resembling]
   [following Ribmaṣ, Sens, and MB;[7] who read *myn* for *mn*;
   OZ:[8] *kmyn* ("[a foal] like") (throughout)] an ass--[the
   foal] is permitted [to be mated] with its dam [i.e., with
   a horse].
B. And if its sire was an ass, [the foal] is prohibited [from
   being mated] with its dam.
C. An ass which brought forth [a foal of] a kind [resembling] a
   horse--[the foal] is permitted [to be mated] with its dam
   [i.e., with an ass].
D. And if its sire was a horse, [the foal] is prohibited [from
   being mated] with its dam.
E. [Erfurt, Ribmaṣ, Sens, and OZ[9] reverse E-F and G-H] A fat-
   tailed sheep which brought forth [a foal of] [Vienna omits,
   Erfurt and first printed ed. read:] a kind [resembling] a
   member-goat--[the foal] is permitted [to be mated] with its
   dam [i.e., with a fat-tailed sheep].
F. If its sire was a member-goat, [the foal] is prohibited
   from being mated with its dam.
G. A member-goat which brought forth [a foal of] a kind
   [resembling] a fat-tailed sheep--[the foal] is permitted [to
   be mated] with its dam [i.e., with a member-goat].
H. If its sire was a fat-tailed sheep, [the foal] is prohibited
   [from being mated] with its dam.
I. And [whether a fat-tailed sheep or member-goat only appears
   to be of a kind different from that of its dam or whether
   it actually is the offspring of diverse-kinds (Sens,[10] HD)],
   it is not sacrificed upon the altar.

                    T. Kil. 5:3 (pp. 221-222, ll. 2-7)

T. complements M. 8:1J, which concerns the mating of one animal of diverse-kinds with another, with a discussion of the mating of such an animal with an animal similar in kind to the former's dam. T. consists of four perfectly balanced sets of rules, A-B, C-D, E-F, and G-H, each composed of one rule presented in *that-which* . . . *it-is* apocopation, and a second stated in a conditional sentence. The four groups form two internally-balanced pairs (A-B+C-D, E-F+G-H), with the second set of each pair reversing the order of animals of the first (horse + ass [A] *vs.* ass + horse [C], fat-tailed sheep + member-goat [E] *vs.* member-goat + fat-tailed sheep [G]). I clearly stands outside of the well-balanced construction of A-H and thus apparently glosses the entire unit. Since, however, I discusses only those animals which are fit for sacrifices, it relates only to E-F+G-H, which alone refers to such animals. Alternatively, I may be read as glossing H alone.

Each set of rules discusses the case of an animal which, although produced from the union of two animals of the same kind, actually resembles an animal of a kind different from that of its dam. In each instance the issue of T. concerns whether such an animal is regarded as being of its dam's kind or as an animal of diverse-kinds. A, for example, states that if a horse gives birth to a foal resembling an ass, the foal may be mated with its dam, i.e., with any horse, for it is considered to be a horse in spite of its appearance. If, however, the foal was sired by an ass, it may not be mated with a horse (B), for now the foal is the offspring of a mating of different kinds. The point of T., then, is that an animal is regarded as being of diverse-kinds only if it is actually produced by the union of different kinds, regardless of its appearance. C-D repeats the rule of A-B but reverses the order of the animals, so that now an ass brings forth a foal resembling a horse. E-F and G-H then repeat the sequence of A-B and C-D, with the fat-tailed sheep and the member-goat, respectively, replacing the horse and the ass.

As we have already mentioned, I apparently glosses the completed unit E-F+G-H, and so refers to the member-goat or fat-tailed sheep which either only appears to be of diverse-kinds or actually is the product of a mating of different kinds (Sens, HD). I thus applies to both apparent and actual instances of diverse-kinds the rule that animals of diverse-kinds are not fit to be sacrificed (cf. M. Zeb. 9:3, 14:2, M. Tem. 6:1). In not differentiating between those animals which only appear to be of diverse-kinds and those which actually are of diverse-kinds, I

opposes the principle behind A-H, which does draw such a
distinction. Alternatively, if I is taken to gloss H alone, then
it applies the rule concerning the sacrifice of animals of
diverse-kinds to a fat-tailed sheep which actually is of diverse-
kinds, and thus does not oppose the principle of A-H. If I is
to be read in this way, though, it is not clear why I was not also
attached to F, for the member-goat does not differ from the fat-
tailed sheep in its fitness for sacrifice. It is more probably
that I is to be understood as glossing E-H, and we therefore
prefer the first interpretation given above.

A. *When a bull or ('w) sheep* [Vatican Codices 31,66 add: *or
     goat*] [*is born, it shall remain seven days with its mother;
     and from the eighth day on it shall be acceptable as an
     offering by fire to the Lord*] (Lv. 22:26)--
B. excluding [an animal of] diverse-kinds.
C. [Vatican Codices 31,66 omit C-D] *Or ('w) goat*--
D. excluding [the animal] which appears [to be of diverse-kinds].

> Sifra Emor VIII:3a
> (ed. Weiss, 99a)
> (B. B.Q. 77b,
> B. Hul. 38a, B. Nid. 41a,
> B. Bek. 12a, 57a)

Sifra comments on Lv. 22:26, which mentions several
different kinds of animals in its discussion of the age at which
animals are fit to be sacrificed. A-B considers the word "or"
('w) in the opening of Lv. 22:26 to add nothing to the meaning of
the verse, and so takes it to exclude animals of diverse-kinds
from among the animals mentioned in the verse, i.e., those animals
which are fit to be sacrificed. C-D similarly understands the
second "or" in the verse to exclude from the same category those
animals which only appear to be of diverse-kinds. Sifra thus
agrees with T. 5:3I's rule that neither animals which only appear
to be of diverse-kinds nor animals which actually are of diverse-
kinds are fit to be sacrificed. Alternatively, the Vatican
codices read the phrase *or goat* as part of A, and thus take both
instances of "or" to exclude the animal of diverse-kinds.
According to this reading, then, Sifra discusses only the animal
which actually is of diverse-kinds.

A. *Koy*--they place upon it two stringencies.

> T. Kil. 5:4a (p. 222, l. 7)

T. complements M. 8:1I, turning from the latter's general prohibition against breeding animals of diverse-kinds to the special case of the *koy*. The *koy* is an animal which is not clearly defined to be either wild (i.e., a *hyh*) or domesticated (i.e., a *bhmh*; cf. M. Bik. 2:8). T. relates to M. Bik. 2:11, which states that a *koy* is considered to be diverse-kinds with both wild and domesticated animals. The two stringencies mentioned in T. therefore refer to the dual prohibition against mating a *koy* with either wild or domesticated animals.

A. *You shall now sow your vineyard with diverse-kinds* (Dt. 22:9)--
B. Why do I need [this rule]?
C. Is it not already stated, *You shall not sow your field with diverse-kinds* (Lv. 19:19)?
D. This [additional rule] teaches that everyone who allows diverse-kinds to grow in a vineyard transgresses two prohibitions.
[GRA:[11]
A. Another matter: [*You shall not sow your vineyard with*] *diverse-kinds* (Dt. 22:9).
B. Why is this [rule] stated?
C. Is it not already stated, *You shall not sow your field with diverse-kinds* (Lv. 19:19)?
D. This [additional rule] is to render [the sower of diverse-kinds of the vineyard]˙liable both an account of [the prohibition of sowing diverse-kinds in] a field and on account of [the prohibition of sowing diverse-kinds in] a vineyard.
E. This teaches that everyone who sows diverse-kinds in a vineyard transgresses two prohibitions.]

Sifré Dt. 230a (ed.
Finkelstein, p. 262, ll. 11. 11-12)

A-C regards as unnecessary Dt. 22:9's prohibition against sowing diverse-kinds in a vineyard, for this rule is considered to be implicit in Lv. 19:19, which prohibits sowing diverse-kinds in a field (which is taken to include a vineyard). D therefore understands Dt. 22:9 to state that one who allows diverse-kinds to grow in a vineyard transgresses two prohibitions, that of having diverse-kinds in a field (Lv. 19:19), and that of maintaining them in a vineyard (Dt. 22:9). D is difficult, for it apparently combines two separate answers to the question of A-C, viz., that the verse refers to one who allows diverse-kinds to grow, and that the sower of diverse-kinds in a vineyard transgresses two prohibitions. Alternatively, GRA presents a less problematic reading of Sifré,[12] in which the verse is taken to state that the sower of diverse-kinds transgresses two prohibitions.

YY. Another matter: [*You shall not sow your vineyard with*] *diverse-kinds* (Dt. 22:9)--

ZZ. This [phrase] is to render [the sower of diverse-kinds in the vineyard] liable both on account of [the prohibition of sowing diverse-kinds in] a vineyard and on account of [the prohibition of sowing diverse-kinds in] a field.

> Sifré Dt. 2301
> (ed. Finkelstein, p. 264,
> 1. 2)

Sifré considers the phrase *diverse-kinds* in Dt. 22:9 to be unnecessary, for one who sows a vineyard clearly sows diverse kinds. *Diverse-kinds* is therefore understood to refer to the prohibition of sowing diverse-kinds in a field (which is taken to include a vineyard; Lv. 19:19), so that one who sows a vineyard is liable on account of this rule as well as the prohibition of sowing diverse-kinds in a vineyard. The pericope is similar in substance to Sifré Dt. 230a, differing only in basing its exegesis on the phrase *diverse-kinds*, rather than on the entire verse, and in reading the verse to refer to the sower of diverse-kinds, rather than to one who allows them to grow.[13]

AAA. [*You shall not sow your vineyard with diverse-kinds, lest the whole yield be sanctified, the crop*] *which you have sown* [*and the yield of the vineyard*] (Dt. 22:9)--

BBB. I know [that he is liable] only [in the case] that he [himself] sowed.

CCC. Whence [do I know that one is liable if] his neighbor sowed [another kind in the former's vineyard] and he [i.e., the owner] wanted to allow it to grow?

DDD. Scripture says, *You have sown (tzr^c; GRA: hzr^c* ["*the crop*"])--under all circumstances.

> Sifré Dt. 230n (ed. Finkelstein,[14]
> p. 264, 11. 3-4)

AAA-BBB understands the phrase *which you have sown* (Dt. 22:9) to mean that one is prohibited only from actually sowing diverse-kinds in a vineyard. CCC-DDD then takes the phrase *you have sown* to prohibit one from maintaining diverse-kinds sown in his

vineyard by someone else. It is not clear, however, how Sifré
can read the same phrase, *you have sown*, to yield two opposing
rulings at AAA-BBB and CCC-DDD. GRA therefore reads *the crop*
(*hzr^c*) for *you have sown* (*tzr^c*) at DDD.[15] According to this
reading CCC-DDD understands the phrase *the crop* to include all
crops which are sown in the vineyard, whether or not they are
sown by the owner of the vineyard himself. Sifré thus agrees
with M. 8:1A that one may not allow diverse-kinds to grow in a
vineyard.

J. Whence [do we know that] diverse-kinds of the vineyard
    are prohibited in respect to benefit?

K. Here "sanctified" (*qdš*) is mentioned [*Lest the whole yield
    be sanctified* (Dt. 22:9)] and there "sanctified" (*qdš*) is
    mentioned [*If any one commits a breach of faith and sins
    unwittingly in any of the holy things* (*qdšy*) *of the Lord*
    (Lv. 5:15) (Hillel)].

L. Just as [the phrase] "sanctified" mentioned there [refers
    to that which] is prohibited in respect to benefit, so [the
    phrase] "sanctified" mentioned here [refers to that which]
    is prohibited in respect to benefit.

> Sifré Dt. 230c (ed. Finkelstein,
> p. 263, ll. 1-3) (Y. Kil.
> 8:1 (31b)[16])

Sifré bases the rule that one may not benefit from diverse-
kinds of the vineyard on an analogy (*gezerah shavah*) between
the use of the root *qdš* in Lv. 5:15 (Hillel) and the use of the
same root in Dt. 22:9. Just as one may not use those items
which are dedicated to God and thus regarded as sanctified, so
one may not derive benefit from diverse-kinds of the vineyard,
which are also said to be sanctified. Sifré thus agrees with
M. 8:1A's rule that one is prohibited from deriving benefit from
diverse-kinds of the vineyard.

A. *Your field you shall not sow* [*with diverse-kinds*] (Lv.
    19:19)--

B. I know only that he should not sow [diverse-kinds].

C. Whence [do I know that] he should not allow [diverse-kinds]
    to grow?

D. Scripture says, *Not . . . diverse-kinds.*

E. [B. M.Q., B. Mak., B. A.Z., GRA omit:] I have said [this]
   only on account of [the law of] diverse-kinds.

                              Sifra Qedoshim 4:16
                              (ed. Weiss, 89a)
                              (B. M.Q. 2b, B. Mak. 21b,[17]
                              B. A.Z. 74a; cf. Y. Kil 8:1
                              (31b))

   Sifra deduces the prohibition of allowing diverse-kinds to
grow in a field from the word-order of Lv. 19:19. Since *not*
precedes *diverse-kinds* as well as *sow*, it is taken to be read with
the former as well as with the latter (D). The verse is thus
understood to state not only that one may not sow diverse-kinds
(as it explicitly rules [A-B]), but also that one may not have
diverse-kinds in his field, i.e., allow diverse-kinds to grow
(QA[18]). E explains that the point of the verse is to prohibit
the growing of diverse-kinds rather than the particular act of
sowing them (QA). Sifra thus agrees with M. 8:1C's rule that one
may not allow diverse-kinds of seeds to grow.

A. Were it stated [only], *You shall not let your cattle breed*
   [Vatican Codices 31,66, B. B.M., Hillel, GRA omit: *with
   a different kind*] (*l' trby[c] bhmtk*) (Lv. 19:19), one might
   think that he should not take hold of the [female] domesticated
   animal and make it stand before the male [domesticated
   animal so that they may mate] [B. B.M.: I might say that a
   man should not hold [down] the [female] domesticated animal
   when the male [domesticated animal] mounts her].
B. Scripture says, *With a different kind*--
C. I have said [this] to you only on account of [the law of]
   diverse-kinds.

                              Sifra Qedoshim 4:13
                              (ed. Weiss, 89a)
                              (B. B.M. 91a; cf. Y. Kil. 8:2)

   According to A[19] the phrase *You shall not let your cattle
breed* could be understood to mean that one may make a female
animal stand before a male animal so that they may mate. B-C
thus explains that the phrase *with a different kind* was included
to prohibit not the holding of the female animal during mating,
but the mating of animals of diverse-kinds.

[A. *You shall not let your cattle breed with a different kind* (Lv. 19:19).]

B. I know only [that you may not make] your [own] domesticated animal [mount] on your [own] domesticated animal.

C. Whence [do I know that you may not make] your [own] domesticated animal [mount] on a domesticated animal of others, [nor make] a domesticated animal of others [mount] on your [own] domesticated animal?
[GRA omits "whence," and so reads: [nor] your [own] domesticated animal on a domesticated animal of others, nor a domesticated animal of others on your [own] domesticated animal.]

D. Whence [do I know that you may not make] a domesticated animal of others [mount] on a domesticated animal of others?

E. Scripture says, *You shall keep my statutes* (Lv. 19:19).

> Sifra Qedoshim 4:14
> (ed. Weiss, 89a)

B understands the phrase *your cattle* in Lv. 19:19 to mean that one is prohibited from mating animals of different kinds with one another only when both animals are one's own. C-E then takes the clause *You shall keep all my statutes* to imply that the prohibition covers all matings of animals of different kinds, including those instances in which either only one of the animals is one's own or both animals belong to someone else.[20] Alternatively, according to GRA's reading *your cattle* is taken to include all cases in which at least one of the animals is one's own. The clause *You shall keep my statutes* is then understood to include the mating of another's animals of different kinds.

8:2

A. (1) A domesticated animal with a domesticated animal,
(2) and a wild animal with a wild animal,
(3) a domesticated animal with a wild animal,
(4) and a wild animal with a domesticated animal,

B. (1) an unclean [animal] with an unclean [animal],
(2) and a clean [animal] with a clean [animal],
(3) an unclean [animal] with a clean [animal],
(4) and a clean [animal] with an unclean [animal],

C. are [each] prohibited [from being joined together] to plow, draw (*lmšwk*) [e.g., a wagon], or be led (*lhnhyg*).[21]

> M. Kil. 8:2 (C: Gn. R. 7:4)

M. 8:2 continues M. 8:1H-J's discussion of the pairing of
animals of different kinds, turning from the issue of the mating
of such animals to the question of joining them together to do
work. M. consists of a two-part protasis, A-B, served by the
apodosis at C. A and B balance one another and are internally
balanced as well, for each lists four pairs of animals in the
sequence a+a/b+b/a+b/b+a.

M. presupposes the rule of Dt. 22:10, *You shall not plow
with an ox and an ass together*. According to A-B this prohibition
includes all possible pairings of wild and domesticated or clean
and unclean animals.[22] C rules that one is prohibited not only
from plowing with such pairs of animals, but also from having
them draw objects and from leading them together, that is, from
having them do any work at all.

[A. *You shall not let your cattle (bhmh) breed with a
different kind* (Lv. 19:19).]

B. I know only that [one may not let] a domesticated animal
(*bhmh*) [mount] on a domesticated animal [= M. 8:2A(1)].

C. Whence [do I know that one may not let] a domesticated
animal [mount] on a wild animal, nor a wild animal [mount]
on a domesticated animal? [GRA omits "whence" and so reads:
(nor) a domesticated animal on a wild animal, nor a wild
animal on a domesticated animal.] [= M. 8:2A(3)-(4)]

D. Whence [do I know that one may not let] an unclean [animal
mount] on a clean [animal], nor a clean [animal] on an
unclean [one] [= M. 8:2B(3)-(4)]?

E. Scripture says, *You shall keep my statutes* (Lv. 19:19).

Sifra Qedoshim 4:15
(ed. Weiss, 89a)

Sifra cites M. 8:2A(1) at B, M. 8:2A(3)-(4) at C, and
M. 8:2B(3)-(4) at D. Unlike M., however, Sifra concerns not the
joining of animals of different kinds to do work, but the mating
of such animals with one another. A-B takes Lv. 19:19, which
refers to the *bhmh*, to prohibit the mating of different kinds of
domesticated animals alone. C-E then understands the clause
You shall keep my statutes to include in the prohibition the mating
of all animals of different kinds, and thus to prohibit the
mating of both domesticated with wild animals and clean with
unclean animals. Alternatively, according to GRA's reading
A-C understands Lv. 19:19 to refer to all matings which involve
at least one domesticated animal. The clause *You shall keep my*

statutes is then understood to include in the prohibition the matings of clean with unclean animals alone.

[TT. *You shall not plow with an ox and an ass* (Dt. 22:10).]

UU. One might think that [the prohibition] "he shall not plow" refers to [plowing with] this [animal] by itself and that [animal] by itself.

VV. Scriptures says, *Together*--

WW. But [plowing with] this [animal] by itself and that [animal] by itself is permitted.

> Sifré Dt. 230k (ed. Finkelstein, p. 263, 1. 12 to p. 264, 11. 1-2[23])

TT-UU states that if Scripture were to read simply *You shall not plow with an ox and an ass*, one could understand it to mean that it is prohibited to plow at all with either animal. Scripture therefore adds *together*, and thus prohibits plowing only with both animals together, but not with each animal separately (VV-WW).

A. *You shall not plow with an ox and an ass* [Hillel omits:] *together* (Dt. 22:10)--

B. One might think [that the prohibition of plowing with an ox and (i.e., or) an ass applies] under all circumstances ($l^c wlm$).

C. Since (k) it [i.e., Scripture] states, [*Six days you shall do your work, but on the seventh day you shall rest;*] *that your ox and your ass may have rest* (Ex. 23:12), [we] already [know that] an ox and [i.e., or] an ass do work [during the rest of the week (Hillel)].

D. If so, why is it stated, *You shall not plow with an ox and an ass?*

E. [To prohibit working the animals] with one another.

> Sifré Dt. 231a (ed. Finkelstein, p. 264, 11. 5-7)

A-B states that the clause *You shall not plow with an ox and an ass* could be understood to mean that it is prohibited to plow with either animal under any circumstances (cf. Sifré Dt. 230k above). According to C, however, Ex. 23:12, which rules that one must rest his ox and ass on the Sabbath, implies that one is

permitted to do work with these animals during the rest of the
week (Hillel). D-E therefore states that the clause cited in A
can mean only that it is prohibited to plow with both animals
together, as the last word in the verse, *together*, in fact
indicates (Hillel).

8:3

A. He who leads [a pair of animals of different kinds] incurs
   [so Danby for *swpg*; lit.: absorbs] the forty lashes.
B. And he who sits in a wagon [drawn by a pair of animals of
   different kinds] incurs the forty [lashes].
C. R. Meir exempts [one sitting in the wagon from the forty
   lashes].
D. And a third [animal] which is tied to the harness [so Danby
   for *rsw^cwt*] of a wagon drawn by a pair of animals of
   another kind] is prohibited.

M. Kil. 8:3

(A-C: B. B.M. 8b)

M. 8:3 continues M. 8:2's interest in the question of pairing
animals of different kinds to do work. The opening word of
M. 8:3, in fact (*hmnhyg*), has the same root (*nhg*) as the closing
word of M. 8:2. M. opens with A-B, a pair of nearly identical
declarative sentences (differing only in their respective subjects) *hmnhyg vs. hywšb bqrwn*. Meir then glosses and opposes
B at C. D, which depends on B for its context (the drawing of
a wagon by animals), augments the latter with a separate rule
following a different formulary pattern (*that-which* + *'swrh*).
According to A-B one who leads a pair of animals of different
kinds and one who merely sits in a wagon drawn by such a team
are both liable for forty lashes. The point of A-B is that one
may not make any use of a pair of animals of different kinds,
whether one actually leads the animals and thus forces them to
work together, or whether one merely sits as a passenger in a
wagon drawn by such animals. Meir disagrees at C, maintaining
that, since the passenger in the wagon does not overtly act to
lead or direct the animals together, he is not liable for the
forty lashes.
D supplements B, which concerns a wagon drawn by animals of
different kinds, with a case in which a wagon is drawn by animals
of a single kind, but a different kind of animal is attached to
the harness, presumably so that it will not stray. D rules that
one may not tie the third animal to the other two in this manner.

Although the third animal does not actually pull the wagon together with the team (since it is not harnessed to the wagon
itself), it nevertheless moves along with the animals of the
other kind and so is considered to be joined with the latter.
The point of D, then, is that animals which are attached to one
another are considered to be joined together, whether or not the
animals actually function as a team and work together.

L.   *You shall not plow [with an ox and an ass together]*
     (Dt. 22:10)--

M.   I know only [that this rule applies to] one who plows.

N.   Whence [do I know] to include one who (1) threshes, (2) sits
     [in a wagon], or (3) leads [a pair of animals]?

O.   Scripture says, *Together*--under all circumstances.

P.   R. Meir exempts [from liability] one who sits [in a wagon
     drawn by a pair of animals of different kinds] [= M. 8:3C].

> Sifré Dt. 231c (ed.
> Finkelstein, p. 264, ll. 11-12)

According to L-M Dt. 22:10 prohibits the pairing of animals
of different kinds only for the purpose of plowing, for this is
the sole activity explicitly mentioned in the verse. N-O then
deduces from the word "together" that one may not join animals
of different kinds for any purpose, so that one may neither
thresh with them, sit in a wagon drawn by them, nor lead them.
N(2)-(3) thus agrees with M. 8:3A-B, which states that one who
leads a pair of animals of different kinds or sits in a wagon
drawn by such a pair is liable for forty lashes. P cites Meir's
opposing view (M. 8:3C), which maintains that a passenger in a
wagon drawn by such a pair of animals is not liable, since the
passenger himself does not lead or direct the animals.

8:4

A.   They do not tie a horse either to the sides of a wagon or to
     the rear of a wagon [drawn by a pair of animals of another
     kind],

B.   nor [do they tie] a Libyan ass [so Jastrow, Danby, for
     lwbdqs[24]] to camels.

C.   R. Judah says, "All offspring of a [female] horse, even though
     their sires are ass[es], are permitted with one another.

D.   "And so (*wkn*; most mss.:[25] *wkl* ["All"]) offspring of a
     [female] ass, even though their sires are horse[s], are
     permitted with one another.

E.   "But the offspring of a [female] horse with [i.e., and]
     the offspring of a [female] ass are prohibited with
     one another."

                              M. Kil. 8:4 (C+E: B. Hul. 79a)

     M. consists of two autonomous parts, A (glossed by B) and
C-E. The two sayings discuss entirely separate issues, for A-B
continues M. 8:3D's discussion of an animal tied to a wagon drawn
by another kind, while C-E presents a saying of Judah concerning
the pairing of different kinds of mules. A-B and C-E, in fact,
need not relate to the same prohibitions at all. Unlike A-B,
C-E does not explicitly refer to the joining of animals to do
work, and thus probably concerns the mating of animals with one
another. There are two possible views concerning the relationship
of C-E to A-B. As we shall see, Judah's saying apparently belongs
after M. 8:1J (cf. MR), which prohibits the mating of animals
of diverse-kinds (i.e., animals born of a union of different
kinds) with each other. On the other hand, by juxtaposing A-B
and C-E the redactor perhaps indicates that he understands C-E
to refer to the joining of mules (i.e., the product of the union
of horses and another kind) to do work, and thus to complement
A-B, which concerns the joining of a horse to animals of another
kind.

     A concerns a case in which one wishes to tie a horse to the
side or rear of a wagon, presumably so that the horse will not
stray. According to A one may not attach the horse to the wagon
in this manner if the wagon is drawn by an animal (or animals)
of another kind. The point of A, like that of M. 8:3D, is that,
although the horse does not actually help draw the wagon, it is
still attached to the latter and moves with it, and so is considered to be joined with the animal of the other kind. B adds
that one may not tie a Libyan ass to camels in order to lead
them or have them pull a load (Lieberman[26]), even though these
animals do not work together well. B thus complements A with
another case in which animals are considered to be joined with
one another even though they do not actually work together as
a team.

     At C-E Judah discusses the pairing of mules with one
another. According to Judah two mules which were born of dams
of a single kind (and, of course, of sires of a single kind as
well) may be paired with one another (C-D), for these animals
themselves form a single "kind." If, on the other hand, the
mules were born of dams of different kinds, they do not share a
similar parentage and are not regarded as belonging to a single

"kind." In this instance, therefore, the pairing of mules would
be a pairing of different kinds, and thus would be prohibited
(E). If Judah here refers to the mating of mules, he may be
regarded as qualifying M. 8:1J, which states that animals of
diverse-kinds may not be mated with another. Judah maintains
that animals of diverse-kinds themselves form "kinds" according
to parentage, so that animals of diverse-kinds belonging to the
same "kind" may be mated with one another.

A. *They do not tie a horse either to the sides of a wagon or
to the rear of a wagon [drawn by a pair of animals of
another kind],*

B. *nor [do they tie] a Libyan ass to camels* [= M. 8:4A-B].

C. R. Meir permits [Y.: exempts (from liability)].

D. If they [i.e., the horse or the Libyan ass] aided (*msy^{c}yn;*
Erfurt, first printed ed.: *msyy^{c}yn*) [the other animals]
in descending and ascending, all agree that it [i.e., tying
the horse to the wagon or the Libyan ass to camels] is
prohibited.

T. Kil. 5:4b (p. 222, ll. 7-9)

(Y. Kil. 8:3 (31c))

A-B cites M. 8:4A-B, which Meir then glosses and opposes at
C. The issue of the dispute concerns whether one is prohibited
from joining together animals of different kinds even if they do
not work together as a team. As we have already seen, A-B rules
that one may not tie either a horse to a wagon or a Libyan ass
to camels, even though in each case the two kinds do not work
together. Meir, on the other hand, permits one to join together
the different kinds mentioned in A-B, maintaining that one is
prohibited only from having animals of different kinds actually
work together. D then glosses A-C, saying that, if the animals
aid each other in ascending or descending (e.g., the horse pushes
the wagon uphill or slows its descent [PM], or the Libyan ass
and the camels pull each other along [following Lieberman[27]]),
then Meir agrees that they may not be joined, for now they do
function as a team. D thus serves to underline the fact that the
issue of the dispute deals with animals of different kinds which
are attached to one another but do not actually work together.

A. One should not tie (1) *a horse to a mule, nor (2) a mule to
an ass, nor (3) an ass to an Arabian onager* [= M. 1:6A(5)-(7)],

B. because they lead one another along.

C. If he did so--

D.   R. Meir declares [him] liable,

E.   and sages exempt.

F.   R. Judah says, "The [mule-]offspring of a female horse and
     the [mule-]offspring of a female ass, [GRA[28] omits:] [when
     used] as one [i.e., together (Lieberman[29])], prohibit
     [Erfurt: are prohibited with] one another."

G.   And sages say, "All mules are [regarded as belonging to]
     a single kind."

                              T. Kil. 5:5 (p. 222, ll. 9-12)
                              (G: Y. Kil. 8:4 (31c), Y. Shab.
                              5:1 (7b))

     T. complements M. 8:4, with A-E referring to M. 8:4A-B and
F-G augmenting M. 8:4C-E. A-B cites and glosses M. 1:6A(5)-(7),
a sublist consisting of three pairs of animals. According to
M. 1:6 the members of each pair are considered to be diverse-kinds
with one another even though they resemble each other. A rules
that one may not tie one member of a pair to another, and thus
has the sublist, which in the context of M. 1:6 refers to the
mating of animals of different kinds, deal with M. 8:3's issue
of joining together different kinds of animals. B, which perhaps
glosses A, then explains that in each case the two members of the
pair tend to lead each other along, so that the animals of
different kinds actually work together. B therefore follows
Meir's view (T. 5:4b/C) that one is prohibited from joining
together animals of different kinds only if they actually function
as a team. A-B thus complements M. 8:4A-B, which prohibits one
from joining together animals of different kinds under all circumstances, by illustrating Meir's opposing position.

     C-E supplements A-B with a balanced (ḥyyb vs. pṭwr) dispute
between Meir and sages. The dispute deals with the liability of
one who actually joins together two members of one of A's pairs.
The issue of the dispute is not clear, but it may concern whether
the actual joining of animals of different kinds or only the
appearance of such a joining ultimately determines liability. Meir
maintains that, since the members of each pair are actually considered to be diverse-kinds with one another, one is liable for
joining them together. Sages, on the other hand, say that since
the animals belong to the same family (Equus) and resemble one
another (M. 1:6), one who ties one to the other does not appear
to join together animals of different kinds. Sages therefore rule
that, although one may not join together such a pair of animals at
the outset, one is not liable for actually doing so.

F-G complements Judah's saying of M. 8:4C-E with a dispute
between Judah and sages concerning whether or not mules may be
divided into different kinds according to parentage. In F Judah
restates his view of M. 8:4C-E, this time with reference to the
question of joining animals together. T. thus links M. 8:4C-E
to M. 8:4A-B, which also discusses the issue of joining animals
together to do work. Alternatively, according to GRA's reading
(omitting "as one") F, like M. 8:4C-E, refers to no particular
prohibition of diverse-kinds. In any event, Judah states that
mules may be classified into two categories, those mules born of
a female horse and those born of a female ass, with each kind of
mule considered to be diverse-kinds with the other. At G sages
disagree, maintaining that one does not take account of differences in the parentage of mules, so that all mules are considered
to belong to a single kind, defined as consisting of all animals
born of the union of a horse and an ass.

A. Isi the Babylonian says, "It is prohibited to ride on the
    back of a mule,
B. "[as we learn] from an argument *a fortiori*: If, in a case
    in which it is permitted to wear two garments [i.e., one of
    wool and one of linen] as one [i.e., together], lo, he
    [Erfurt: it] is prohibited in respect to [wearing a garment
    composed of] their mixture [i.e., a mixture of the two
    materials], in a case in which it is prohibited to lead two
    animals [of different kinds] as one [i.e., together], is
    it not logical that it should be prohibited in respect to
    [using an animal composed of] their mixture [i.e., a mixture
    of the two kinds of animals]?"
C. They said to him, "Lo, it [i.e., Scripture] says, [*Take with
    you the servants of your lord,*] *and cause Solomon my son to
    ride on my own mule, and bring him down to Gihon* (I Kings
    1:33)."
D. He said to them, "They do not respond from Tekoa [i.e., they
    do not rule on the basis of the practices of townspeople
    (e.g., David, who was not a legal authority)]."
E. They said to him, "Lo, it [i.e., Scripture] says, *And David
    did what was right in the eyes of the Lord, and did not turn
    aside from anything that he commanded him all the days of his
    life, except in the matter of Uriah the Hittite* (I Kings 15:5)."

T. Kil. 5:6 (pp. 222-223, ll.
12-19) (Y. Kil. 8:2 (31c)[30])

T. augments T. 5:5's interest in the joining of mules to
other kinds with a discussion of the permissibility of riding on
a mule. T. consists of a saying of Isi the Babylonian at A,
followed by a debate between Isi and anonymous authorities at
B-E. The anonymous authorities are given the last word at E and
thus are allowed to win the debate.

At A Isi states that one may not ride on the back of a mule.
He thus opposes M. 8:1H-I, which rules that one is prohibited
only from breeding animals of diverse-kinds. Isi then supports
his position at B with an argument *a fortiori* in which he compares
the prohibition of diverse-kinds of animals to that of diverse-
kinds of garments. Isi reasons that if, in the case of diverse-
kinds of garments, where one is permitted to wear garments of
different kinds together (i.e., one on top of the other), one is
prohibited from wearing a garment composed of a mixture of two
kinds, in the case of diverse-kinds of animals, where one may not
join together animals of different kinds, one should surely be
prohibited from using an animal born of the union of two kinds.
The anonymous authorities reply at C, not by responding to the
argument at B, but by citing a scriptural verse (I Kings 1:33)
which tells that David ordered Solomon to be taken to Gihon on
his (i.e., David's) mule. Isi answers at D with the curious
expression, "They do not respond from Tekoa." Referring to the
small town southeast of Jerusalem, this saying apparently means
that the actions of people of a small town are not considered
to be authoritative. In this case, then, the point of Isi is
that the actions of David, who was not a legal authority, cannot
be cited as precedent.[31] At E Isi's opponents cite I Kings 15:5,
which states that David's only transgression occurred in the case
of Uriah the Hittite. The verse thus implies that all of David's
other actions, including his order to have Solomon ride on a
mule, were correct. David's actions thus do establish an authoritative precedent, and the anonymous authorities win the debate.

S. [*You shall not plow with an ox and an ass*] *together* (Dt.
    22:10)--

T. Excluding one who ties a horse to the sides of the wagon or
    to the rear of the wagon,

U. and [one who ties] a Libyan ass to camels [= M. 8:4A-B].

Sifré Dt. 231e (ed. Finkelstein,
p. 264, ll. 12-13)

Sifré cites M. 8:4A-B at T-U, linking it to Dt. 22:10 (=S). The phrase *together* in Dt. 22:10 is taken to indicate that the verse's prohibition of joining together animals of different kinds applies only if the animals actually work together as a team. This phrase thus excludes from the prohibition the cases of M., for neither the horse and the animal pulling the wagon nor the Libyan ass and the camels work together and function as a team. Sifré thus disagrees with M., which rules that animals of different kinds may not be joined together even if they do not work well as a team.

8:5

A. Mules of unknown parentage [following Sens for *prwṭywt*; alternatively: mules (Maim., *Comm.*)] are prohibited [from being mated with one another].

B. But (*w*) a mule foaled by a ĥorse [so Danby (following Bert.) for *rmk*; alternatively: a wild horse (Maim., *Comm.*; cf. also *Code, Diverse-Kinds* 9:5)] is permitted [to be mated with a like animal].

C. (1) And "wild men" [so Danby for *'dny hŝdh*] are [considered a kind of] wild animal.

D. R. Yosé says, "[When dead] they convey uncleanness in a tent like a man."

E. (2) A hedgehog (*qpd*) and (3) a weasel[32] (*ḥwldt ḥsnyym*) are [each considered a kind of] wild animal.

F. The weasel--

G. R. Yosé says, "House of Shammai say, '[When dead] it conveys uncleanness in an olive's bulk by being carried, and in a lentil's bulk by contact [to the person touching it].'"

M. Kil. 8:5

M. consists of two autonomous parts, A-B and C-G. The former continues M. 8:4C-E's discussion of the mating of mules with one another while the latter opens a new subunit, continued at M. 8:6, concerning whether or not certain creatures are regarded as wild animals.

A-B is composed of two declarative sentences with contrasting apodoses (*'swr vs. mwtr* [cf. M. 8:4C-E]). The two sentences differ, however, in that the subject of A appears in the plural while that of B is presented in the singular. A and B do not appear originally to have been formulated together as a unit. A states that one may not pair *prwṭywt* together, with B adding that one may mate a *rmk* with an animal of the same kind. Now the identification of these two animals is not clear. According to one interpretation the term *prwṭywt* refers to mules of unknown parentage, and a *rmk* is a mule born of a female horse (Bert. [following Sens[33] in first instance; cf. also TYY]). The point of A, therefore, is that mules of unknown parentage may not be mated with one another, lest a mule born of a female horse

be paired with one born of a female ass. B then complements A with
the rule that mules born of dams of the same kind may be mated with
each other. A-B thus illustrates Judah's view (M. 8:4C-E) that only
mules of similar parentage may be mated with one another. Alternatively, Maimonides (*Comm.*) explains that *prwtywt* refers to mules of
any parentage, and that a *rmk* is a kind of wild horse. According to
this interpretation A maintains that mules may not be mated with
each other at all, with B adding that pairings of wild horses
are permitted.[34] A thus follows M. 8:1J's rule that diverse-kinds
of animals may not be mated with one another, and B then adds the
obvious rule that animals of the same kind may be mated with each
other (PM). A-B then augments Judah's view of M. 8:4C-E by
presenting the opposing view of M. 8:1J.

C-G concerns certain animals of doubtful status. The pericope
consists of a three-item list composed of C, discussing a creature
which may be regarded as either a man or a wild animal, and E,
concerning whether two different animals are considered either
creeping things or wild animals. Yosé then respectively glosses
each part of the list at D and F-G, introducing in each instance
the consideration of uncleanness. We note that C+E itself need
not concern issues of diverse-kinds, for the determination of an
animal's status is relevant to other issues as well, as Yosé's
glosses indicate. In placing C-G in the context of a discussion
of diverse-kinds, however, the redactor implies that he understands the pericope to concern whether or not the specified
animals are considered to be wild animals, and thus, unlike men
or creeping things, to be subject to the laws of diverse-kinds.

C discusses the "wild man," which is apparently an ape-like
creature resembling a human being.[35] According to C the "wild
man" is regarded as a wild animal, so that (in this context) the
laws of diverse-kinds apply to it. At D Yosé qualifies C, maintaining that, like a man, the "wild man" conveys uncleanness in a
tent (cf. M. Kel. 1:4). According to Yosé, then, the "wild man"
is not treated simply as a wild animal, for, at least in regard
to matters of uncleanness it is regarded as a man.

E states that the hedgehog and the weasel are regarded as
wild animals. The point of E apparently is that even though
these animals crawl on the ground and thus could be considered
creeping things, they are actually considered to be wild animals,
perhaps because both are animals of prey.[36] Yosé then glosses
E with F-G, which consists of a superscription and a saying of
House of Shammai, and so appears to be a defective Houses-dispute.
House of Shammai maintain that, like a wild animal, a dead weasel
conveys uncleanness in an olive's bulk by being carried (cf. M.
Kel. 1:2, M. Oh. 1:7). In this regard a weasel is not considered

a creeping thing, which, when dead, does not convey uncleanness in
this manner at all (M. Kel. 1:1). The weasel is regarded as a creeping thing, however, in that its carrion conveys uncleanness in a
lentil's bulk by contact (i.e., when a person touches it; cf. M.
Kel. 1:1, M. Oh. 1:7). The weasel differs in this respect from the
wild animals, the carrion of which does not convey uncleanness by
contact (M. Kel. 1:2). House of Shammai thus hold that, since the
weasel is of doubtful status and may be regarded either as a creeping thing or a wild animal, it is subject to the stringencies of
both categories. By citing House of Shammai's opinion Yosé qualifies E, maintaining that, as in the case of C, the specified animals are not regarded simply as wild animals, but are actually
considered to belong to two separate classes.

Q. [*You shall not plow with an ox and an ass*] *together*
   (Dt. 22:10)--

R. Excluding the mule foaled by a horse (*rmk*; alternatively:
   the wild horse; GRA: *prd* ["the mule"]).

Sifré Dt. 231d (ed. Finkelstein, p. 264, l. 12)

Sifré takes the word *together* in Dt. 22:10 to exclude from
the verse's prohibition the *rmk*, or the mule born of a female
horse, presumably because this animal will not work together with
animals of other kinds. Sifré thus agrees with Meir (T. 5:4b)
that it is prohibited to join together animals of different kind
only when the animals actually function as a team. It is not
clear, however, why Sifré should exclude from the prohibition
only a specific kind of mule, and GRA therefore reads *prd*, which
refers to any kind of mule, in place of *rmk* at R. Alternatively,
if *rmk* refers to a kind of wild horse, then Sifré's point again
is that such an animal will not work well with other animals and
so may be joined with them. Sifré thus agrees with M. 8:5B
that the *rmk* may be paired with a second animal. Sifré, however,
relates M., which concerns the mating of animals, to the prohibition of joining together animals of different kinds to do work.
Sifré thus refers to pairing the *rmk* not with another animal of
the same kind (as in M.), but with a different kind of animal.

8:6

A. (1) A wild ox is [considered] a kind of domesticated animal.
B. And R. Yosé says, "[It is considered] a kind of wild animal."
C. (2) A dog is [considered] a kind of wild animal.
D. R. Meir says, "[It is considered] a kind of domesticated
   animal."
E. (3) A swine is [considered] a kind of domesticated animal.
F. (4) An Arabian onager is [considered] a kind of wild animal.

G. (5) An elephant and a monkey are [considered] kind[s] of
    wild animal[s].

H. And a man is permitted [to be joined] with all of them [i.e.,
    with either a wild or domesticated animal] to pull [e.g.,
    a wagon], plow, [some mss.,[37] B. Shab., B. B.Q., TYT, and
    MS reverse the order of the preceding verbs and omit:] or
    be led.

                              M. Kil. 8:6 (A-B: B. Sanh.
                              25b, B. Hul. 80a; H: B. Shab.
                              54a, B. B.Q. 54b)

    M. continues M. 8:5C-G's discussion of animals of doubtful
status. While M. 8:5C-G concerns whether certain animals are
regarded as either men or creeping things, on the one hand, or
wild animals, on the other, M. 8:6 turns to discuss those
creatures which may be considered either wild or domesticated
animals. M. consists of a list of five items at A+C+E-G, with
A and C respectively glossed and opposed by Yosé and Meir at B
and D. H glosses the entire list with a rule concerning man.
The list of six animals (presented as five items) may be divided
into two sublists, A+C+E-F, a catalogue of four items which
repeats the formulary pattern x + *bhmh*/y + *hyh*, and G, a
sentence consisting of a compound subject. In addition, the
apodoses of the first sublist, together with those of the glosses
of Yosé and Meir, follow the pattern ab/ba/ab. Like M. 8:5,
M. 8:6A-G need not specifically concern questions of diverse-
kinds.[38] In this context, however, M. concerns whether certain
animals, which are found in both domesticated and wild states,
may be distinguished either from wild animals of the same kind
(in the first instance) or from their domesticated counterparts
(in the second). Repeating the language of M. 8:2C (as we shall
see), H then serves to relate the list to the issue of joining
together animals of different kinds to do work.

    At A-B an anonymous opinion and Yosé dispute concerning
the status of the wild ox. According to the anonymous opinion
of A the wild ox may be successfully domesticated, so that it is
considered a domesticated animal, and thus (in this context) is
not considered to be diverse-kinds with the domesticated ox.
Yosé, on the other hand, maintains that, regardless of the possibility of domesticating the animal, the wild ox retains its
status of a wild animal, and so may not be mated with the ox.
C-D then presents a dispute between an anonymous opinion and Meir
concerning the dog. C maintains that even domesticated breeds of
dogs are regarded as wild animals, while Meir argues that such

dogs are considered domesticated animals and thus may not be
paired with wild dogs (Y. Kil. 1:6 (27a)). According to E the
swine is regarded as a domesticated animal, and so is considered
to be diverse-kinds with the wild boar (cf. T. 1:8b). F then
states that although it may be domesticated,[39] the Arabian onager
is still regarded as a wild animal and may not be mated with the
domesticated ass (cf. M. 1:6[40] [MR]). Finally, G rules that even
though elephants and monkeys may survive in captivity and so be
domesticated, they are still regarded as wild animals (GRA), and
may be mated with wild members of their respective kinds.

    H states that one may join a man together with any animal,
whether the latter is wild or domesticated, to pull a load, to
plow, or to be led. The point of H is that the prohibition
against joining together different kinds refers only to animals,
and thus does not bar man, who is not considered an animal, from
being joined to an animal to do work. This point is underlined
by the fact that the language of H is identical to that of
M. 8:2C (with a slight change in word-order), which states the
prohibition against joining together different kinds of animals.
The phrase "to be led," however, is not appropriate to H, for it
is not likely that one would lead a man carrying a load together
with a burdened animal. It appears, then, that the phrase was
mistakenly inserted into H because of M.8:2C, and it is
therefore omitted by some manuscripts and commentaries.

A. *A dog is [considered] a kind of wild animal.*

B. *R. Meir says, "[It is considered] a kind of domesticated
animal [M. 8:6C-D]."*

C. What is the difference between [the views of] R. Meir and
sages?

D. [The difference is] only that (*'l' š*) [in the case of] he
who assigns[41] [ownership of] his wild animal to his son--

E. R. Meir says, "He has not assigned him [ownership of his]
dog."

F. And sages say, "He has assigned him [ownership of his] dog."

G. [Erfurt, Sens, KP[42] omit G-I] He who assigns [ownership of]
his domesticated animal to his son--

H. R. Meir says, "He has assigned him [ownership of his] dog."

I. And sages say, "He has not assigned him [ownership of his]
[Vienna omits, first printed ed. reads:] dog."

                                T. Kil. 5:7 (p. 223, ll. 19-22)

T. cites M. 8:6C-D at A-B and augments it with C-I, which
consists of a question at C and a pair of disputes at D-F and G-I
(joined to C by *'l' š*). The two disputes balance one another
(*ḥyh* vs. *bhmh*) and are balanced as well (*l' ktb* vs. *ktb*).

A-B cites the dispute between the anonymous opinion of
M. 8:6C and Meir concerning the status of the dog. C then asks
concerning the practical significance of this dispute and thus
introduces D-F, which spells out the dispute between Meir and
sages (= anonymous opinion of M. 8:6C). This dispute concerns
whether one who, in a document, assigns the ownership of his wild
animal to his son intends to give the latter the rights to his
dog. Maintaining that the dog is regarded as a domesticated
animal, Meir rules that the father does not intend to give his
son ownership of the dog. Sages, on the other hand, consider
the dog to be a wild animal, and therefore argue that the document
written by the father does give the son the rights to the dog.
G-I, which is omitted in some versions, then reverses the circumstances of D-F. The dispute now concerns one who assigns his
domesticated animal to his son, and the positions of Meir and
sages are therefore reversed as well. T. thus complements M. by
illustrating the dispute of M. 8:6C-D with a concrete case.

A. A wild dog is [considered] a kind of wild animal.
B. A *yerodin* (*yrwdyn*; Lieberman[43] [following Erfurt]: *yrwryn*)
    and an ostrich[44] (*n^{c}myt*; Erfurt: *n^{c}mywt*; first printed ed.:
    n^{c}mwt), lo, they are [considered] as birds [Erfurt omits:]
    in every respect.

                    T. Kil. 5:8a (p. 223, 11. 22-23)
                        (B: Y. Kil. 8:5 (31c))

T. consists of two autonomous declarative sentences, A and B,
each of which complements M. 8:6's list of animals of doubtful
status. A augments M. 8:6C-D's dispute concerning the status of
the dog with the rule that the wild dog is regarded as a wild
animal. It follows that the anonymous opinion of M. 8:6C, which
views the dog as a wild animal, would not consider the dog to be
diverse-kinds with the wild dog, while Meir, regarding the dog as
a domesticated animal, would prohibit the pairing of the two
dogs. Like T. 5:7, then, T. 5:8a apparently serves to illustrate
the significance of the dispute of M. 8:6C-D.

B adds two animals to M.'s list of animals of doubtful status.
Unlike M., however, B concerns not whether the specified animals
are considered to be wild or domesticated, but whether they are

regarded as birds or as (presumably) wild animals. According
to B the *yerodin* and the ostrich are considered to be birds in
every respect. The identity of the first creature is not clear,
as it is apparently either some legendary bird or a member of
the ostrich family (Lieberman[45]). If the *yerodin* is similar to
the ostrich, then the point of B is that these two creatures
are regarded as birds, even though they cannot fly. The phrase
"in every respect" perhaps refers to matters of uncleanness, in
regards to which birds are distinguished from other animals.[46]

A. For [= omitted by Lieberman[47]] an unclean animal does not
    bear [offspring] [B. Bek.: become pregnant] from (*myn*;[48]
    Erfurt, first printed ed.: *mn*) [mating with] a clean
    [animal],

B. nor does a clean [animal bear offspring] from [mating with]
    an unclean [animal].

C. And a large [animal] does not [bear offspring] from
    [mating with] a small [animal],

D. nor does a small [animal bear offspring] from [mating with]
    a large [animal].

E. And a man does not [bear offspring] from [mating with] any
    of them [i.e., any animal],

F. nor do any of them [bear offspring] from [mating with] a man.

T. Kil. 5:8b (p. 223, ll. 23-25)
(T. Bek. 1:9;[49] A-D: B. Bek.
7a[50])

T. is composed of three pairs of balanced declarative
sentences, A-B, C-D, and E-F. According to T. the matings of clean
and unclean animals, large and small animals, and men with all
animals do not produce offspring, presumably because each union
involves two entirely different types of creatures. In noting
that the union of a man and an animal cannot produce offspring,
E-F serves to complement M. 8:6H. While the latter rules that a
man may be joined together with any animal to do work, E-F discusses another type of pairing of man and animal. Because of E-F,
therefore, the entire pericope was redacted as a comment on
M. 8:6.

A. Every [animal] which is [found] in inhabited places (*byyšwb*)
    is [found] in the desert;

B. many [animals] are [found] in the desert which are not [found]
    in inhabited places. T. Kil. 5:9 (p. 223, ll. 25-26)

C. Every [animal] which is [found] on dry land is [found]
    in the sea;
D. many [animals] are [found] in the sea which are not [found]
    on dry land.
E. There is no kind of weasel in the sea.

> T. Kil. 5:10 (p. 223, ll. 26-27)
> (C-E: Y. Shab. 14:1 (14c);
> C+E: B. Hul. 127a)

    T. consists of two declarative sentences, A-B and C-D, which
both balance one another (inhabited places + desert *vs*. dry land +
sea) and are internally balanced as well (inhabited places +
desert *vs*. desert + inhabited places [A *vs*. B], dry land + sea
vs. sea + dry land [C *vs*. D]). E glosses C. A-B and C-E discuss
the correspondence between kinds of animals belonging to one
setting and similar kinds living in a different environement.
According to A-B every kind of animal found in inhabited places,
i.e., every kind of domesticated animal, has a counterpart in
the desert, or among the wild animals.[51] The converse of this
statement, however, is not true, for not every kind of wild
animal corresponds to a kind of domesticated animal. Similarly,
C-D states that all land-animals have counterparts in the sea,
but not all sea-animals correspond to similar land-animals.
E then presents an exception to C, stating that no animal of
the sea is similar to the weasel. In discussing the correspondence
between kinds of wild and domesticated animals, A-B serves to
complement M. 8:6, which discusses whether certain animals are
considered to be wild or domesticated, i.e., whether certain
animals are considered to be diverse-kinds with similar animals
of a different environment. We note that C-E is not relevant to
M. 8:6, so that the pericope as a whole was redacted as a comment
on M. 8:6 on account of A-B alone.

A. (1) He who muzzles a cow, and (2) he who pairs [i.e., joins
    together] diverse-kinds [of animals] is [i.e., are] exempt
    [from liability].
B. You find that one is liable only [in the case of] the one
    who leads or drives [diverse-kinds of animals].

> T. Kil. 5:11 (p. 223, ll. 27-28)
> (T. B.M. 8:12, T. Mak. 5(4):1,
> B. B.M. 90b[52])

T. consists of A, a declarative sentence with a double
protasis, and B, which glosses A(2) (but cf. B. B.M., which has
B gloss A(1) as well). According to A(1) one who merely muzzles
a cow but does not himself thresh with it is exempt from
liability, for Scripture prohibits one not from muzzling an ox
but only from actually threshing with a muzzled ox: *You shall
not muzzle an ox when it treads out the grain* (Dt. 25:4) (Rashi,
B. B.M. 90b, s.v. *hḥwsm 't hprh*[53]). A(2) similarly states that
one is not liable for merely joining together a pair of animals
of different kinds, for Scripture prohibits one only from working
such a pair: *You shall not plow with an ox and an ass together*
(Dt. 22:10) (Rashi, B. B.M. 90b, s.v. *wkn hmzwg šwr whmwr*). B
then illustrates this last point, saying that one is liable only
for leading or driving the animals, i.e., for using them to do
work. B thus serves to complement M. 8:6H, which rules that man
may be joined with animals to do work, with the prohibition against
joining different kinds of animals. B perhaps also serves to
link M. 8:6H to M. 8:2, which presents the same prohibition. We
note that A is not relevant to M. 8:6H, so that the entire
pericope was redacted as a comment on the latter because of B
alone.

F. [*You shall not plow with*] *an ox and an ass* [*together*] (Dt.
22:10)--

G. I know only [that one is prohibited from plowing with] an
ox and an ass.

H. Whence [do I know] to make (*lˁšwt*; some mss.:[54] *lrbwt*
["to include"]) other pairs of domesticated animals, wild
animals, or fowl [of different kinds] like an ox and an ass
[in respect to the rule against joining together animals
of different kinds]?

I. Scripture says, *You shall not plow*--under all circumstances.

J. If so, why is it stated, *With an ox and an ass*?

K. With an ox and an ass [together] you may now plow, but you
may plow with a man and an ass [together] [Y.: With an ox
and an ass (together) you may not plow, but you may plow
with an ox and a man together or with an ass and a man
(together)].

> Sifré Dt. 231b (ed. Finkelstein,
> p. 264, ll. 7-10) (J-K: Y. Kil.
> 8:6 (31d))

F-G understands the phrase *an ox and an ass* (Dt. 22:10) to
include in the verse's prohibition only the two specified animals.

H-I therefore takes the phrase *You shall not plow* to include in the prohibition all other animals which one may join together, or all domesticated animals, wild animals, and birds. J then asks why, if the prohibition includes all animals, the verse explicitly names two in particular. K answers that the phrase *an ox and an ass* serves to exclude man, for man is not subject to the laws of diverse-kinds and so may be paired with an animal. J-K thus agrees with M. 8:6H's rule that a man may be joined together with animals to do work.

CHAPTER NINE

KILAYIM CHAPTER NINE

The closing chapter of our tractate discusses diverse-kinds
of garments. The chapter is divided into three parts, M. 9:1-2B,
which concerns the mixing of wool and flax, M. 9:2C-7, which
deals with the definition of a garment, and M. 9:8-10, which returns to the concerns of the opening of the chapter and discusses
ways of combining and connecting wool and flax together.
M. 9:1A-C opens the chapter by presenting a unitary set of three
general rules concerning wool and flax, with the first stating
that wool and flax alone combine to produce diverse-kinds. M.
then turns to two secondary cases, one discussing the status of
wool or flax which is mixed with another kind (M. 9:1D-H), and
the other dealing with fibers which resemble wool and flax and
thus produce the appearance of diverse-kinds in a mixture
(M. 9:2A-B). M. 9:2A establishes the formulary pattern which is
followed by M. 9:2C-7, and so has been formulated to provide a
smooth transition to the succeeding subunit.

M. 9:2C-7 presents an essay exploring some of the criteria
of the definition of a garment. The subunit is constructed
around four rules, all of which follow the same formulary pattern
('yn bhm/bw mṧwm kl'ym [M. 9:2C, 9:3A, 9:4A, 9:7E]). Each rule
discusses items which are not regarded as garments and thus not
subject to the laws of diverse-kinds. These four rules are
arranged in a series in such a way that each successive group of
items satisfies an additional criterion of the definition of the
garment. M. 9:2C opens the series with the rule that items
which are neither designed to serve as garments nor actually worn
(e.g., mattresses and cushions) are not regarded as garments.
According to M. 9:3A the same rule applies to items which, although
not made to be worn, may actually function as garments (e.g.,
towels). (Eliezer glosses and opposes this rule, maintaining
that items which secondarily serve as clothing are regarded as
garments.) M. 9:4A then turns to items which are made to be worn,
but not by man (e.g., pack-saddles). Such items are not subject
to the laws of diverse-kinds, for they are not used as garments
by those who are prohibited from wearing diverse-kinds. Finally,
M. 9:7E discusses an item which is designed to be worn by man,
but which, because it does not stay securely on the body, is not
regarded as a garment (e.g., a heelless cloth slipper). In

addition, an interpolated unit (M. 9:5-6) introduces the consideration of intention, discussing whether one's purpose in using an
article of clothing affects its status as a garment (cf. also
M. 9:2G, 9:4C).

Opening with a rule (M. 9:8A) in the formulary pattern of
M. 9:1A, M. 9:8-10 returns to the interests of M. 9:1-2B with a
discussion of the ways in which wool and flax may combine to
form diverse-kinds. The subunit is divided into two parts,
M. 9:8-9D and M. 9:9E-10. The former discusses methods of combining wool and flax during the process of manufacturing garments
(e.g., hackling, spinning, and weaving), while the latter concerns
different ways of attaching finished items (e.g., garments) of
wool and linen to one another. The two parts are joined smoothly
at Yosé's saying of M. 9:9E-F, which follows the formulary pattern
of M. 9:9A-D but concerns the problem of attaching a woolen cord
to a linen garment.

9:1

A. Nothing is prohibited on account of [the laws of] diverse-
   kinds except [a garment composed of a mixture of] wool and
   linen.
B. Nor is anything susceptible to uncleanness through plagues
   except [a garment composed of either] wool or linen.
C. Nor do priests wear anything to serve in the Temple except
   [garments composed of either] wool or linen.
D. Camel's hair and sheep's wool which one hackled [so Danby
   for *trpn*] [i.e., combed] together--
E. if the greater part is from the camels, it is permitted [to
   mix the fibers with flax (Maim., *Comm.*)].
F. But if the greater part is from the sheep, it is prohibited
   [to mix the fibers with flax].
G. [If the quantity of camel's hair and sheep's wool is divided]
   half and half--it is prohibited [to mix the fibers with flax].
H. And so [is the rule for] flax and hemp which one hackled
   together [i.e., if at least half of the hackled fibers are
   of flax, it is prohibited to mix them with wool].

M. Kil. 9:1 (D-H: M. Neg. 11:2[1])

M. consists of A-C, a series of three rules concerning
wool and linen, and an autonomous pericope concerning the status
of wool or linen which is mixed with another kind. A-C is composed
of three declarative sentences, all of which follow the same
formulary pattern (*'yn* + present participle + *'l'* + *ṣmr wpštym*).

We note that the phrase *ṣmr wpštym* in A concerns a mixture of wool and linen, while the same phrase in B and C refers to garments composed of either wool or linen (although, as we shall see, C concerns the mixture of the two kinds as well). According to A the prohibition of diverse-kinds of garments applies to mixtures of wool and linen alone, for only such mixtures are specifically mentioned by Scripture: *You shall not wear a mingled stuff, wool and linen together* (Dt. 22:11).[2] B then states that only garments composed of either wool or linen are susceptible to uncleanness through plagues, for again Scripture explicitly mentions these two fibers alone: *When there is a leprous plague in a garment, whether a woolen or a linen garment* (Lv. 13:47). Finally, C states that, when serving in the Temple, priests wore only garments composed of either wool or linen or a mixture of both (Maim., *Comm.*), for Scripture states (with reference to the materials used in fashioning Aaron's garment[3]): *They shall receive gold, blue and purple and scarlet stuff, and fine twined linen* (Ex. 28:5). All of the priest's garments were thus made of either *blue and purple and scarlet stuff*, or dyed wool (Maim., *Comm.*) (e.g., the robe of the *ephod* [Ex. 28:31-35]), linen (e.g., the coat and turban [Ex. 28:39]), or a mixture of dyed wool and linen (e.g., the *ephod* [Ex. 28:6ff.]). We note that, when serving in the Temple, the priest is permitted to wear garments of diverse-kinds. It follows, then, that the laws of diverse-kinds paradoxically do not apply to priests engaged in the performance of cultic duties.

D-H discusses the status of wool or flax which is mixed with another kind of fiber. D-H consists of a protasis at D and a pair of balanced conditional sentences at E-F (*gmlyn + mwtr* vs. *rhlym + 'swr*), followed by G. H then glosses D-G. D describes a case in which camel's hair and sheep's wool are hackled,[4] or combed, together, so that the two kinds are indistinguishable from one another (MR; cf. T. 5:12). E-G discusses whether or not the wool is considered to be annulled by the camel's hair, so that the hackled fibers may be accorded the status of the latter and may be mixed with flax (Maim., *Comm.*). According to E-F the status of the hackled fibers follows that of the majority of fibers in the mixture. G adds that if equal amounts of both kinds have been hackled together, we rule stringently and regard the hackled fibers as wool, so that they may not be mixed with flax. H then states that the same rule applies to flax and hemp which have been hackled together, so that the combined fibers may be mixed with wool only if the greater part of them derives from hemp.

A. (1) A poultice (*'stplnyt*; Lieberman,[5] following Erfurt
and commentaries, reads *'ysplnyt*),
(2) a plaster (*mlwgm'*),
(3) and a compress (*rtyyh*)
are not subject to [the laws of] diverse-kinds.

T. Kil. 5:25 (p. 225, l. 52)

B. (1) A corpse,
(2) and an animal,
(3) and tents,
(4) and a comb (*'ksylwn*),
(5) and [first printed ed. omits:] a *grgs*,
(6) and a wreath (*'stm'*),
(7) and a hanging of a curtain [i.e., a cloth upon which
a curtain is hung (Lieberman,[6] reading *wqlc wwylwn* for *wqlc
w'ylwn*; alternatively: a sail and a curtain (HD))],
(8) and the garments of priests,
(9) and the garments of the high priest
are not subject to [the laws of] diverse-kinds.

T. Kil. 5:26 (pp. 225-226, ll. 53-54)

T. is composed of two lists (consisting respectively of
three [A] and nine [B] members) of items which are not subject
to the laws of diverse-kinds.   According to A three kinds of
dressings which may be made with cloth, a poultice (containing
grease and wax[7]), a plaster,[8] and a compress (containing medi-
cation[9]), do not come under the laws of diverse-kinds.[10]   The
reasoning behind A is that all of these dressings are simply
placed on the wound but apparently are not tied securely to the
body, and thus are not worn as garments (cf. T. 5:23).[11]
    The list of nine items at B is divided into three parts,
(1)-(2), concerning items which are permitted to bear diverse-
kinds, (3)-(7), dealing with items which are not designed to serve
as garments, and (8)-(9), discussing items which function as
garments but which nevertheless are not subject to the laws of
diverse-kinds.   According to B(1)-(2) one is permitted to place
diverse-kinds upon a corpse or animal, for the prohibition against
wearing diverse-kinds applies only to living people (cf. M. 9:4A).
We note that in this instance the language "are not subject to
[the laws of] diverse-kinds" refers to something which bears
diverse-kinds, and not to something which may be worn.
    B(3) rules that a tent does not come under the laws of
diverse-kinds, for, although it serves to protect man, it is not

designed to be worn as a garment. B(4) concerns the *'ksylwn*, which Lieberman[12] identifies as the ϲάνιν or ϲάνιον, a type of comb used as a head-ornament. According to Lieberman such a comb was attached to a piece of cloth (which protected the head) and then set in the hair. The point of B(4), then, is that the comb and the cloth are regarded as forming an ornament, and not a garment, and thus are not subject to the laws of diverse-kinds. The meaning of *grgs* (B(5)) is not known (Lieberman[13]). B(6) rules that, like a comb, a wreath is regarded as an ornament,[14] and thus does not come under the laws of diverse-kinds. We note that, since B(4) and B(6) refer to types of ornaments, it is possible that B(5) concerns a kind of ornament as well. B(7) refers to the term *ql^c wwylwn*, which may be interpreted in one of two ways. According to Lieberman[15] *ql^c wwylwn* refers to a single item, the hangings of curtains, i.e., cloths upon which curtains were suspended. These hangings are not subject to the laws of diverse-kinds, for they cannot be worn as garments. Alternatively, the first *w* of *wwylwn* may be taken as a conjunction, so that *ql^c wwylwn* may refer to two separate items, a sail (*ql^c*) and a curtain (*wylwn*) (HD), neither of which is designed to serve as a garment.

B(8)-(9) rules that the garments of priests and of the high priest are not subject to the laws of diverse-kinds, for priests were required to wear diverse-kinds while serving in the Temple. T. thus augments M. 9:1C's rule that priests wear only garments of wool and linen in the Temple (cf. also T. 5:27).

A. Garments of the high priest--
B. he who goes out [while dressed] in them to the provinces [i.e., outside the Temple] is liable.
C. But [following Lieberman,[16] who reads *w* for *š* ("for")] [he who wears them] in the Temple,
D. whether [he does so] to serve [i.e., to participate in the Temple service] or not to serve [i.e., while he does not participate in the Temple service],
E. is exempt [from liability],
F. because they [i.e., the garments] are fit (*r'wyyn*) for the Temple service.

T. Kil. 5:27 (p. 226, ll. 54-56)
(B. Yoma 69a, Tamid 27b[17])

T. augments the rule of T. 5:26B(8)-(9) concerning the status of priestly garments. T. consists of declarative sentences at A-B and C+E, with the latter glossed by D and F. According

to A-C+E the high priest may not wear priestly garments, which
include garments of diverse-kinds (cf. our discussion of M. 9:1C,
above), outside of the Temple, for, as F explains, he is required
to wear such garments while participating in the Temple service.
D then appears to gloss C+E-F, explaining that, although the
high priest wears the garments only because he must perform certain cultic actions,he may keep the clothes on even when he does
not actually take part in the service. We note that the separate
glosses of D and F create a difficulty in the final version of
the pericope, for these two statements, when read together, imply
that the high priest may wear his garments even when he does not
serve because the garments are fit for the Temple service.

A. *Camel's hair and sheep's wool* [GRA adds: *which one hackled
    together*] [= M. 9:1D]
[B. (GRA adds:) *if the greater part is from the camel, it is
    permitted (to mix the fibers with flax)*[18] (= M. 9:1E).]
C. Under what circumstances?
D. When he [first] hackled them [i.e., the camel's hair
    and the sheep's wool] together, and [then] introduced flax
    into the mixture and hackled [it together with them] [Erfurt,
    Sens:[19] When he (first) brought flax and hackled (it)
    together with them (i.e., with the camel's hair[20]) and (then)
    hackled them (i.e., the camel's hair combined with the
    flax, and the sheep's wool) together].
E. But he who makes a shirt (ḥlwq) wholly of camel's hair or
    (w) wholly of hare's hair [so Lieberman, following Erfurt[21]],
    and wove into it one thread of [sheep's] wool on one side,
    and another ('ḥr; Erfurt, first printed ed.: 'ḥd ["one"])
    thread of flax [first printed ed. and commentaries[22] add:
    on the other side[23]]--it is prohibited [i.e., the shirt
    is considered a garment of diverse-kinds].

T. Kil. 5:12 (pp. 223-224, ll. 28-31)

T. cites M. 9:1D at A (with GRA completing the citation at
A and adding M. 9:1E at B), which is then augmented by C-E.
According to C-D M. 9:1D-E's rule that wool mixed with a greater
quantity of camel's hair may be combined with flax applies only
when the wool is hackled together with the camel's hair.[24] In
this case the wool becomes indistinguishable from the camel's
hair, so that the latter annuls the former (Lieberman[25]), and
the combined fibers may be mixed with flax. One may not, however,
weave separate threads of flax and wool into a garment composed

wholly of camel's or hare's hair (E). In this instance the flax
and wool remain recognizable when mixed with the third kind, and
so are not annulled even when woven into a garment composed
entirely of that third kind. The shirt is therefore regarded as
containing a mixture of flax and wool, and thus is prohibited
as a garment of diverse-kinds.

9:2

A. Silk and bast-silk [so Danby for *šyryym wklk*] are not
   subject to [the laws of] diverse-kinds,

B. but are prohibited for appearance's sake.

C. Mattresses [so Danby for *krym*; alternatively: pillows (Maim.,
   Comm.[26])] and cushions [so Danby, following Maim., *Comm.*,[27]
   for *kstwt*] [composed of a mixture of wool and linen] are not
   subject to [the laws of] diverse-kinds,

D. provided that one's flesh not be touching them [while one
   sits or lies on them].

E. There is no [rule permitting] temporary use (*^cr'y*) in respect
   to diverse-kinds [of garments].

F. And one shall not wear [a garment of] diverse-kinds even
   [= omitted by B. B.Q. 113a and most mss.[28]] on top of ten
   [garments],

G. even (*'pylw*) to avoid (*lgnwb*; B. B.Q. 113a: *lhbryḥ*) [paying]
   customs-dues [so Danby for *lgnwb 't hmks*].

M. Kil. 9:2 (E: B. Men. 41a;
F-G: B. B.Q. 113a)

M. opens a large subunit (extending through M. 9:7) dealing
with a series of issues related to the problem of defining a
garment. M. begins with two autonomous rules, A-B and C-D.
Although A and C contain identical apodoses (*'yn bhm mšwm kl'ym*
[continued at M. 9:3-4,7]), the two rules are clearly not related
to one another in substance. While A-B concerns whether certain
kinds of fibers produce mixtures of diverse-kinds, C-D discusses
the entirely separate question of whether the laws of diverse-
kinds apply to certain types of objects. C-D is then augmented
by the autonomous rules of E and F-G.

A-B concerns *šyryym*, a kind of silk resembling flax,[29] and
klk, i.e., bast-silk, which apparently is similar to wool (Maim.,
Comm.). A may be understood in one of two ways. According to
one interpretation (Maim., *Code, Diverse-Kinds* 10:1, Bert., TYY)
A rules that it is permitted to mix *šyryym* with wool or *klk*
with flax, for, although appearing to consist of diverse-kinds,

such mixtures are not actually composed of wool and flax.
Alternatively, A may be taken to mean that one is permitted to
mix *šyryym* and *klk* with one another, for again such a mixture would
only appear to contain wool and flax (Maim., *Code, Diverse-Kinds*
10:1, MS, TYY[30]). According to either interpretation, then, the
point of A is that a mixture of fibers is prohibited only if it
actually contains diverse-kinds, regardless of its appearance.
Glossing A, B then reverses the latter's rule. B maintains that
the mixtures (or mixture) described in A are prohibited because
they appear to consist of wool and flax. B thus holds that a
mixture is prohibited even if it produces only the appearance
of diverse-kinds, regardless of the actual presence or absence
of diverse-kinds within it.

According to C one is permitted to use mattresses (or
pillows [Maim., *Comm.*]) or cushions composed of diverse-kinds,
for Scripture prohibits one from using only garments (i.e.,
items which are usually worn) of diverse-kinds: *Nor shall there
come upon you a garment of cloth composed of two kinds of stuff*
(Lv. 19:19), and *You shall not wear a mingled stuff, wool and
linen together* (Dt. 22:11). D then qualifies C, ruling that one
may not allow his flesh to touch the articles of diverse-kinds
while he sits or lies upon them. The reasoning behind D apparently
is that diverse-kinds which come into direct contact with the
flesh serve to warm the latter, and thus function as articles of
clothing. One who allows his flesh to touch the mattresses or
cushions of diverse-kinds is therefore considered to be wearing
a garment of diverse-kinds.[31]

E states that one is not permitted to wear diverse-kinds even
temporarily. In this context E serves to contrast items which
are not designed to function as garments (e.g., mattresses and
cushions) (C-D) with items which are so designed. While the
former may be used as long as they do not function as clothing (D),
the latter may not be used even momentarily, i.e., under any
circumstances. F-G then makes a similar point with a separate
rule. According to F-G one may not wear a garment of diverse-
kinds on top of ten other garments, even if he thereby wishes
only to avoid paying customs-dues (which were not levied on one's
personal apparel), and thus does not intend to use the garments
as clothing at all (Sens). By itself, F-G states simply that one
may not wear diverse-kinds even when they lie upon many layers
of clothing and thus do not serve the functions of garments. In
this context, however, the point of F-G, like that of E, is to
contrast items which are not designed to function as clothing
(C-D) with articles which are so designed. The former may be

used as long as they are not directly touched (D), while the
latter may not be worn even if they lie upon ten layers of
clothing and thus cannot touch the flesh of their bearer.

A. Linen which one dyed with blacking [so Jastrow for *ḥrt*]--
B. he shall not sell it to a gentile,
C. and he shall not make it into a recognizable border [Y. Kil.
   9:2 omits:] of linen.
D. [If he made it into a border] for mattresses and cushions,
   lo, this is permitted.

T. Kil. 5:24 (p. 225, ll. 50-52)

(A+C-D: Y. Kil. 9:2 (32a))

T. is composed of a mildly-apocopated sentence (A-C) with
a compound apodosis (B-C; cf. T. 5:19). D then glosses C. A
concerns linen which is dyed with blacking, a substance usually
applied only to wool (Sens to M. 9:2). According to B one may
not sell such a dyed piece of linen to a gentile, lest the
latter in turn sell it to an Israelite. Thinking the fabric to
be wool, the Israelite might then attach it to a garment of wool,
and so unknowingly produce a garment of diverse-kinds (as in
T. 5:19; Lieberman[32]). C then rules that one may not make the
dyed piece of linen into a recognizable border of a garment
composed of undyed linen. The point of C is that, although the
two pieces of linen do not actually form a garment of diverse-kinds,
they appear to constitute a garment of linen which is bordered
with wool, and they therefore may not be joined together.
According to C, then, one is liable for producing the appearance
of diverse-kinds whether or not the wool and linen are actually
mixed together (cf. M. 9:2B). D adds that one may make the dyed
pieces of linen into a border of a mattress of cushion (Lieberman[33])
which is presumably also composed of linen.[34] The point of D is
that a mattress or a cushion is not subject to the laws of diverse-
kinds (M. 9:2C), and we are therefore not concerned if it appears
to contain diverse-kinds. T. thus augments M. 9:2C-D's rule concerning the status of mattresses and cushions.

A. A garment which contains diverse-kinds at one end--
B. he shall not cover himself with the other side [i.e., with
   the other end of the garment],
C. even though the [end containing the] diverse-kinds [thus]
   rests on the ground.

T. Kil. 5:13 (p. 224, ll. 32-34) (Y. Kil. 9:1 (31d)[35])

T. consists of an apocopated sentence, A-B, which is glossed
by C. T. presupposes the scriptural rule, *Nor shall there come
upon you a garment of cloth made up of two kinds of stuff*
(Lv. 19:19), taking it to prohibit one from covering himself
with diverse-kinds. A describes a garment which contains diverse-
kinds at only one end. B states that one may not cover himself
with the other end of the garment, even if the end containing
the diverse-kinds would then rest on the ground and thus not
cover the person at all (C). T. thus augments M. 9:2F-G, which
prohibits one from wearing diverse-kinds on top of ten layers
of clothing, even though he receives no benefit from the diverse-
kinds, with the rule that one is prohibited from covering himself
with garments of diverse-kinds, even if the mixed fibers themselves do not serve to cover him.

A.   A shirt of wool which was torn (*šnyprs*), and which one
     fastened [Rosh[36] omits "and," reading: he wraps (*kwrkw*[37])]
     [together] with a thread of flax--
B.   or (*w*) a shirt of linen which was torn, and which one
     fastened it [together] with a thread of wool--
C.   if he sewed them [i.e., the torn ends of the shirt] together,
     they [i.e., the shirt and the thread] are prohibited on
     account of [the laws of] diverse-kinds.
D.   And they go out [from one domain to another] with them [i.e.,
     the shirt and the thread] on the Sabbath.

                    T. Kil. 5:14 (p. 224, ll. 33-35)

     T. 5:14 and 5:15 (which immediately follows) form an
autonomous subunit concerning whether certain ways of joining
together wool and flax produce a garment of diverse-kinds. T.
consists of a balanced double-protasis at A-B (wool + flax *vs.*
flax + wool), followed by a conditional sentence at C, which
is augmented by D. A-B describes a case in which a shirt of wool
or linen is torn, and the torn ends are tied together, or fastened,
with a thread of either flax (in the first case) or wool (in
the second). C then rules that if one sews up the tear with the
thread, the latter is considered to be connected to the shirt,
which thus becomes prohibited as a garment of diverse-kinds. D
adds that one may wear the shirt[38] from one domain to another on
the Sabbath, for he is not regarded as carrying the thread, which
is considered to be part of the shirt.[39] Now the rule of C-D,
concerning a thread which is sewn onto a shirt, implies that if
the thread is only fastened onto the shirt, as in the case of A-B,

it is not considered to be connected to the shirt. In this
instance, then, the shirt is not considered a garment of diverse-
kinds, and one is not permitted to wear it from one domain to
the other on the Sabbath. The version of Rosh renders explicit
this understanding of T., for Rosh omits "and" and replaces the
perfect verb in A with a present participle, thus reading A and C
as two separate rules. Maimonides[40] similarly explains A+C[41]
as follows (*Code, Diverse-Kinds* 10:10):

> A garment of wool which was torn--it is permitted to
> fasten it together with threads of flax. And he ties
> [the garment together], but he shall not sew [it
> together].[42]

A. A man wears two shirts, [one of wool and one of linen (Maim.,
    Code, Diverse-Kinds 10:11)] one on top of the other,

B. even though his belt (*pwndtw*) is tied on [i.e., around] him
    on the outside,

C. provided that he does [not (following Lieberman[43])] take
    (*ytn*; Rosh and Maim., *Code, Diverse-Kinds* 10:11:[44] *ytrwp*
    ["wind"[45]]) the cord (*ḥmṣyḥḥ*) [i.e., the cords of the two
    shirts (Lieberman[46])] and tie [the two shirts together]
    between the shoulders.

T. Kil. 5:15 (p. 224, ll. 35-36)

T. continues T. 5:14's discussion concerning whether various
ways of joining together wool and linen yield a mixture of
diverse-kinds. T. opens with a declarative sentence at A, which
is then separately glossed by B and C. According to A one is
permitted to wear two shirts, one of wool and one of linen (Maim.,
Code, Diverse-Kinds 10:11), on top of one another, for the two
garments are not connected to each other (e.g., they may be
removed separately [Rosh; cf. also Lieberman[47]]) and thus are not
considered to constitute a single garment of diverse-kinds. B
adds that one may even tie a belt around the two shirts, for once
the belt is unfastened the shirts are no longer connected (e.g.,
they may be removed separately). The belt thus represents only
an extrinsic connection, and does not alter the status of the
shirts as distinct garments. C, however, rules that one may not
tie the cords belonging to each shirt (Lieberman) together at the
shoulders, for then the shirts are intrinsically connected to
one another (e.g., they cannot be removed individually), and so
are considered to form a single garment of diverse-kinds. The
point of T., then, is that one is permitted to wear separate garments of wool and linen on top of one another, provided that he
does not so connect them that they are considered a single garment.

I. Since it [i.e., Scripture] says, *Nor shall there come upon you* [*a garment of cloth made up of two kinds of stuff*] (Lv. 19:19), might I think that he shall not tie [a garment of diverse-kinds] in a bundle [and throw it] behind him [i.e., over his shoulder]?

J. Scripture says, *You shall not wear* [*a mingled stuff, wool and linen together*] (Dt. 22:11).

K. *You shall not wear*--

L. I know only that he shall not wear [a garment of diverse-kinds].

M. Whence [do I know] that he shall not cover himself [with such a garment]?

N. Scripture says, *Nor shall there come upon you.*

O. [It follows that] you are permitted to spread it (*lhṣy^{c}w*) [i.e., a garment of diverse-kinds] under you.

P. But sages said, "You shall not do so, lest a single fringe (*nym'*) [of the garment of diverse-kinds] come upon (*thyh ^{c}wlh*; B. Yoma, Bes., and Tamid: *tkrk* ["wind itself around"]) his [i.e., your] flesh."

> Sifra Qedoshim 4:18b (ed. Weiss, 89b) (N-P: B. Yoma 69a, B. Bes. 14b, B. Tamid 27b)

I-N discusses why Scripture presents two prohibitions concerning diverse-kinds of garments (Lv. 19:19 and Dt. 22:11). According to I the phrase *Nor shall there come upon you* (Lv. 19:19) by itself implies that one may not bear diverse-kinds on his body in any way, so that one may not even tie his garments of diverse-kinds in a bundle and throw them over his shoulder. J therefore cites the phrase *You shall not wear* (Dt. 22:11), which serves to limit the prohibition of garments of diverse-kinds to concern only the act of wearing such garments. I-J thus agrees with M. 9:5C, which states that the more scrupulous clothes-sellers would carry diverse-kinds in a bundle over their shoulders in order to avoid carrying them on their backs. K then states that the phrase *You shall not wear* by itself indicates that one is prohibited only from wearing garments of diverse-kinds. L-M therefore maintains that the rule of *Nor shall there come upon you* is necessary in order to include in the prohibition the act of covering oneself with diverse-kinds as well. The point of Sifra, then, is that the prohibitions of Lv. 19:19 and Dt. 22:11 serve to qualify one another.

O then takes the phrase *Nor shall there come upon you* to imply that, while one is not permitted to cover himself with diverse-kinds, he is permitted to sit or lie on them. Sages, however, reverse this ruling in P, maintaining that one may not sit or lie on garments of diverse-kinds, for a fringe of one of the garments might come to rest upon him, and he would then be liable for covering himself with diverse-kinds. P thus presents a more stringent view than M. 9:2C-D, which permits one to sit or lie on mattresses or cushions of diverse-kinds, provided that he does not allow his flesh to come into contact with them.

E. *You shall not wear [a mingled stuff, wool and linen together]* (Dt. 22:11)--

F. I know only that he shall not wear [a garment of diverse-kinds].

G. Whence [do I know] that he shall not cover himself [with such a garment]?

H. Scripture says, *Nor shall there come upon you [a garment of cloth made up of two kinds of stuff]* (Lv. 19:19).

I. I might think that [according to this verse (Hillel)] he shall not tie it [i.e., a garment of diverse-kinds] in a bundle [and throw it] behind him [i.e., over his shoulder].

J. Scripture says, *You shall not wear.*

K. [The act of] wearing was [included] in the general principle [i.e., *Nor shall there come upon you a garment of cloth made up of two kinds of stuff*].

L. And why was it [i.e., the act of wearing] specified (*yṣ't*)?

M. To compare [the general principle] to it [i.e., the prohibition against wearing garments of diverse-kinds], and to tell you that just as [the act of] wearing is distinctive (*mywhdt*) because it [involves] the comfort of the body (*hnyt hgwp*), so too every [act of placing diverse-kinds upon oneself] which [involves] the comfort of the body [is prohibited].

> Sifré Dt. 232b (ed. Finkelstein, p. 265,
> ll. 4-7) (A-B+D-F+I: Y. Kil. 9:1 (31d))

E-H = Sifra Qedoshim 4:18K-M, and (H+)I-J = Sifra Qedoshim 4:18I-J, so that Sifré simply restates Sifra Qedoshim 4:18I-M in reverse order. K-L then asks why the act of wearing diverse-kinds, which is presumably included in Lv. 19:19's prohibition against having diverse-kinds upon oneself, is specifically prohibited at Dt. 22:11. M answers that this particular prohibition

is mentioned so that it may qualify the general prohibition
against having diverse-kinds upon one's body. Just as the
act of wearing concerns the pleasure or comfort of the body, so
the act of placing diverse-kinds upon oneself in any way is
prohibited only when it benefits the body. We note that Sifré
disagrees with M. 9:2F as interpreted by Maimonides (*Code*,
Diverse-Kinds 10:18), for according to Maimonides the point of M.
is to prohibit the wearing of diverse-kinds even when such an act
does not add to the body's pleasure at all.

N. [*You shall not wear a mingled stuff, wool and linen*] *together*
   (Dt. 22:11)--
O. I might think that he shall not wear a shirt of wool on top
   of a shirt of linen, nor (*w*) a shirt of linen on top of
   a shirt of wool.
P. Scripture says, *Together*.

> Sifré Dt. 232c (ed. Finkelstein,
> p. 265, ll. 7-8)

According to N-O, were Dt. 22:11 to omit the word *together*
and to read simply *You shall not wear a mingled stuff, wool and
linen*, one might conclude that it is prohibited to wear separate
garments of wool or linen on top of one another (i.e., at the
same time). P therefore cites the word *together*, which implies
that one is prohibited from wearing only garments composed of a
mixture of wool and linen. Sifré thus agrees with T. 5:15,
which rules that one may wear separated garments of wool and linen
on top of one another, provided that he does not connect them to
form a single garment.

U. [*You shall not wear a mingled stuff,*] *wool and linen
   together* (Dt. 22:11)--
V. but [wearing] this one [i.e., a garment composed of one
   fiber] by itself and that one [i.e., a garment composed of
   the other fiber] by itself is permitted.

> Sifré Dt. 232e (ed. Finkelstein,[48]
> p. 265, l. 11)

U-V takes the word *together* in Dt. 22:11 to prohibit one
from wearing only garments composed of a mixture of wool and
linen, and so implicitly to permit one to wear garments consisting of either wool or linen alone.[49]

9:3

A. (1) Hand-towels (*mṭpḥwt hydym*), (2) scroll-wrappers
   (*mṭpḥwt sprym*), and (3) bath-towels [so Danby for *mṭpḥwt
   hspg*] are not subject to [the laws of] diverse-kinds.
B. R. Eliezer prohibits [i.e., they are subject to the laws
   of diverse-kinds].
C. And barbers' towels (*mṭpḥwt hsprym*) are prohibited on
   account of [the laws of] diverse-kinds.

M. Kil. 9:3

A consists of a list of three items which are not subject
to the laws of diverse-kinds, with each member of the list
presented in the formulary pattern *mṭpḥwt* X. Eliezer then
glosses and opposes A at B. C augments A with a contrary case,
presenting an article which, although similar to those listed
in A (and presented in the same formulary pattern), does come
under the laws of diverse-kinds.

A-B turns from M. 9:2C-D's discussion of items which are
not designed to serve as garments and deals with items which,
although not designed to be worn, may still serve as clothing.
The issue of A-B concerns whether one takes account of the
secondary functions of such items in determining whether or not
they are regarded as garments. According to A hand-towels,
scroll-wrappers, and bath-towels do not come under the laws of
diverse-kinds, for, like the mattresses and cushions of M. 9:2C-D,
these articles are not designed to be worn as garments. A thus
holds that an item's status is determined by its primary function
alone. Eliezer disagrees at B, maintaining that, although the
items of A are not made to be worn, they may still function as
garments, for one may use a hand-towel or scroll-wrapper to warm
one's hands,[50] and one may cover his body with a bath-towel
(cf. Y. Kil. 9:3). According to Eliezer, then, the items of
A do come under the laws of diverse-kinds. Eliezer thus argues
that one does take account of the secondary function of an item
in determining whether or not it is regarded as a garment.

C states that one may not put on a barber's towel which is
composed of diverse-kinds, for such a towel is designed to
protect a person and his clothing from cut hair, and so is intended
to function as a garment. C thus serves to contrast the barber's
towel, which is designed to serve as a garment, and does come
under the laws of diverse-kinds, with the three cloths of A,
which are not made for such a purpose and so are not subject to
the laws of diverse-kinds. C therefore serves to underline A's

view that an article's primary function alone determines whether
or not it is subject to the laws of diverse-kinds.

A. Women's bath-towels [following Lieberman[51] for *bl'ry nšym*]
    are not subject to [the laws of] diverse-kinds.
B. And if he sewed them [i.e., if he sewed two ends of the
    towel together],
C. they receive uncleanness, and
D. they are prohibited on account of [the laws of] diverse-kinds.

T. Kil. 5:16 (p. 224, ll. 36-38)

(Y. Kil. 9:3 (32a)[52])

T. augments M. 9:3A(3), which states that a bath-towel is
not subject to the laws of diverse-kinds, with a discussion of
a similar item, the women's bath-towel. According to A a women's
bath-towel does not come under the laws of diverse-kinds, for,
like the bath-towel of M.9:3A(3), it is intended to be used only
to dry off the body, and it is not designed to be worn as a
garment (Lieberman[53]). If, however, one sews together two ends
of a women's bath-towel, it is regarded as a garment, for it
is now made to stay securely on the body and to be worn like an
article of clothing. In this case, therefore, the women's bath-
towel, which formerly was not used for lying or sitting and thus
was not susceptible to *midras*-uncleanness, is now treated as a
garment and thus is susceptible to this type of uncleanness
(Lieberman[54]) (C). Similarly, like any garment, the women's
bath-towel is now subject to the laws of diverse-kinds (D).[55]
By distinguishing between the different ways in which the women's
bath-towel may be designed, T. illustrates M. 9:3A's view that
an item's primary purpose alone determines whether or not it comes
under the laws of diverse-kinds.

A. Wrappers of cases (*mtphwt tybh*) [of scrolls (Lieberman[56])]
    are not subject to [the laws of] diverse-kinds.
B. *"Hand-towels, and scroll-wrappers, and bath-towels are not
    subject to [the laws of] diverse-kinds [= M. 9:3A].*
C. *"And R. Liezer prohibits [= M. 9:3B]," the words of R. Meir.*
D. R. Judah says, "R. Liezer permits,
E. "and sages prohibit."

T. Kil. 5:17 (p. 224, ll. 38-40)

A augments M. 9:3A(2)'s discussion of scroll-wrappers with
a rule concerning another type of cloth which is used to protect

scrolls, the wrapper of a case of scrolls. Such a cloth was
used either to cover the case itself (Lieberman[57]) or to line
the case and thus protect the scrolls placed within it (OZ[58]).
According to A the wrappers of cases do not come under the laws
of diverse-kinds, for like wrappers of scrolls, they are not
designed to be worn as garments.

   B-E presents a dispute between Meir and Judah concerning the
correct version of M. 9:3A-B's dispute between an anonymous
opinion and Eliezer. B-C attributes M.'s version of the dispute
to Meir. Judah then glosses B-C, reversing the opinions assigned
by M. to the two parties of the dispute.[59]

9:4

A.   (1) Shrouds and (2) a pack-saddle ($mrd^c t$) of an ass are
     not subject to [the laws of] diverse-kinds.
B.   One shall not place a pack-saddle [of diverse-kinds] on
     his shoulder,
C.   even to carry out dung upon it.

M. Kil. 9:4

   M. turns from the discussion of items which are not designed
to serve as garments (M. 9:2C-D, 9:3A) to a consideration of
articles which are made to be worn, but not by man. M. opens
with A, a sentence containing a compound subject, and glosses
A with the autonomous rule of B-C. According to A shrouds and
asses' pack-saddles do not come under the laws of diverse-kinds,
for, although these items are designed to be worn, they are made
to be used respectively on corpses and animals, to which the
prohibition against wearing diverse-kinds does not apply. The
point of A, then, is that the only items which are subject to the
laws of diverse-kinds are those designed to serve as garments for
man, the only one who is prohibited from wearing diverse-kinds.
B-C then serves to qualify A, ruling that one may not place a
pack-saddle of diverse-kinds on his shoulder, for the pack-saddle
would then cover and protect the shoulder and so function as
a garment (MR).[60] Like M. 9:2C-D, B thus rules that one may use
an item which is not subject to the laws of diverse-kinds only
as long as it does not serve as a garment. We shall see that
T. takes A and B to be in dispute with one another, for T. understands A to imply that the shroud and the pack-saddle may be used
in any way at all, even as a garment. Glossing B, C adds that
one may not place a pack-saddle of diverse-kinds on his shoulder
even if he wishes only to carry out dung upon it, and thus does
not intend to use it as a garment at all (as in M. 9:2G).

A.   *He shall not place a pack-saddle [of diverse-kinds]*
     [Erfurt, first printed ed. add:] *on his shoulder,*
B.   *even to carry out dung upon it* [= M. 9:4B-C].
C.   And R. Liezer b. Simeon permits.

                    T. Kil. 5:18 (p. 224, ll. 40-42)

        A-B cites M. 9:4B-C, which Eliezer b. Simeon glosses and
opposes at C.   Eliezer b. Simeon maintains that one is permitted
to place a pack-saddle of diverse-kinds on one's shoulder, even
though the pack-saddle then serves as a garment.   Eliezer b.
Simeon thus takes up the position of M. 9:4A, which states that
a pack-saddle is not subject to the laws of diverse-kinds, and
therefore implies that such an item may be used in any manner,
even to serve as a garment.   T. thus presents the views of
M. 9:4A and 9:4B-C in the form of a dispute, and so renders
explicit the disagreement between the two rules which is only
implicit in M.

A.   A garment in which diverse-kinds were lost [some commen-
     taries:[61]   A garment in which one wove (*š'rg*) diverse-
     kinds]--
B.   he shall not sell it to a gentile,
C.   and he shall not make it into a pack-saddle of an ass.
D.   R. Simeon b. Leazar says, "He shall not make it into a recog-
     nizable border (*'ymr' hmpwrsmt*) [of another garment],
E.   "but he may make [Erfurt: makes] it into a shroud."

                    T. Kil. 5:19 (pp. 224-225, ll. 42-44)
                    (A-C+E: B. Pes. 40b, A.Z. 65b,
                    Nid. 61b)

        T. consists of a mildly-apocopated sentence at A-C, which is
glossed and continued by Simeon b. Eleazar at D-E.   A describes
a case in which threads of flax are woven into a garment of
wool (or *vice versa*) in such a way that the flax becomes "lost"
in the garment and cannot be distinguished from the wool
(Lieberman [citing commentaries][62]).   According to B one may not
sell such a garment to a gentile, lest the latter in turn sell
it to an Israelite.   Being unable to spot the flax among the
wool, the Israelite would then put on the garment, and so unknowingly wear an item of diverse-kinds.   C then states that one may
not make the garment of A into an ass' pack-saddle, for one might
pick up such a pack-saddle and place it on one's shoulder, and
so unknowingly have an item of diverse-kinds serve as a garment

(as in M. 9:4B-C). Simeon b. Eleazar adds at D that one may not
make the garment of A into a recognizable border, i.e., a border
of a garment which is composed of a different kind. The point of
Simeon b. Eleazar here is that one may not make a woolen garment
containing threads of flax into a border of a garment of flax,
even though the two garments together now clearly combine to form
a garment of diverse-kinds, which one should be permitted to sell
to a gentile. Simeon b. Eleazar apparently reasons that if one
were to make such a garment of diverse-kinds and sell it to a
gentile, the latter might remove the border and sell it separately
to an Israelite, who again would unknowingly wear diverse-kinds
(Lieberman[63]). Simeon b. Eleazar also rules that one may make
the garment of A into a shroud (E), for the latter does not come
under the laws of diverse-kinds, and we thus need not be concerned lest someone using it transgress the prohibition against
wearing diverse-kinds. By ruling that one may make the garment
of A into a shroud, but not into a pack-saddle, T. serves to make
explicit a distinction between these two items which is implicit
in M. In juxtaposing the rule of M. 9:4A (i.e., pack-saddles
and shrouds are not subject to the laws of diverse-kinds) with
that of M. 9:4B-C (i.e., one may not place a pack-saddle of
diverse-kinds on one's shoulder), M. has been understood by T.
to imply that the latter rule applies specifically to the pack-
saddle, and not to the shroud, so that one is not liable for
wearing a shroud of diverse-kinds.

9:5-6

A. Clothes-dealers sell [garments of diverse-kinds] in their
    usual manner [i.e., while carrying them on their backs
    (Maim., *Comm.*)],

B. provided that they do not intend, in a hot sun, [for the
    garments to protect them] from the hot sun, or (w), in the
    rain, [for the garments to protect them] from the rain.

C. And the more scrupulous ones [so Danby for snw^cym] tie
    [the garments of diverse-kinds] on a stick [B. Shab. 29b,
    46b, B. Pes. 26b, explain: (and throw the garments) behind
    them (i.e., over their shoulders)].

M. Kil. 9:5 (B. Shab. 29b, 46b,
B. Pes. 26b; B: Y. Kil. 9:2 (32a))

D. Tailors sew [garments of diverse-kinds] in their usual
    manner [i.e., with the garments resting on their laps (Bert.)],

E. provided that they do not intend, in a hot sun, [for the

garments to protect them] from the hot sun, or (w), in
the rain, [for the garments to protect them] from the rain.

F. And the more scrupulous ones sew [while sitting] on the
ground [i.e., with the garments resting on the ground
as well].

M. Kil. 9:6

M. consists of two perfectly-matched subunits, A-C and D-F.
The two subunits balance one another at A and D (mwkry vs. twpry)
and at C and F (mpšylyn bmql vs. twpryn b'rṣ [plural present
participle + b- in each]), and are glossed by the same clause
at B and E.   Since B and E are identical to one another, it is
probable that they were respectively added together to the
completed subunits A+C and D+F.

Reverting to the concerns of M. 9:2G (and M. 9:4C), M.
discusses whether one is liable for wearing diverse-kinds even
if he does not intend for them to serve as garments.   According
to A and D clothes-dealers, who usually carry their merchandise
around on their backs, and tailors, who tend to rest clothes on
their laps while they work on them, may bear diverse-kinds upon
themselves just as they would bear any garment, for they do not
intend for the diverse-kinds to function as their own clothing.
B and E then underline this point, ruling that clothes-dealers
and tailors may not intend to use the diverse-kinds to protect
themselves from heat or rain, for then the diverse-kinds would
surely serve as their personal garments.   According to M., then,
one's intention determines whether or not he is liable for wearing
diverse-kinds.   M. thus disagrees with M. 9:2G (Sens and others),
which states that one may not wear a garment of diverse-kinds
even if he wishes only to avoid paying customs-dues for it,
and thus does not intend for it to function as clothing (cf. also
M. 9:4C).   C and F then augment respectively A and D, adding that
the more scrupulous clothes-dealers and tailors do not bear
diverse-kinds upon themselves at all.   Such clothes-dealers tie
the diverse-kinds onto a stick and thus carry them over their
shoulders, and not on their backs, and such tailors sew while
sitting on the ground, and so allow the diverse-kinds to rest on
the latter, and not on their laps.

9:7

A. (1) A birrus (hbrsyn[64]), and (2) a bardaicus [so Windfuhr[65]
for hbrdsyn], and (3) a dalmatic (hdlmṭqywn), and (4) shoes
of coarse wool (mn^{c}ly hpynwn;[66] alternative translation:
shoes of pinna)--

B.   he shall not put them on until he shall examine [them for diverse-kinds].

C.   R. Yosé says, "Those [of the above items] which come from the seacoast or from distant lands (*mmdynt hym*) do not require examination [for diverse-kinds],

D.   "for the presumption concerning them is [that they are composed] of hemp [and not flax]."

E.   A cloth shoe [following Maim., *Code, Diverse-Kinds* 10:15 for *mn^{c}l šlzrd*[67] (some mss.:[68] *mn^{c}l šlzrb*); alternative translation: a cloth-lined shoe (Y. Kil. 9:5)] is not subject to the laws of diverse-kinds.

M. Kil. 9:7

M. consists of two autonomous parts, A-D, which discusses whether certain types of garments are likely to contain diverse-kinds, and E, which returns to the issues of M. 9:2-4 and concerns whether a certain kind of shoe is subject to the laws of diverse-kinds. A-D is composed of a mildly-apocopated sentence, A-B, which is glossed by Yosé at C-D. A-B lists four types of garments, the birrus, the bardaicus, the dalmatic, and shoes of coarse wool,[69] all of which must be examined for diverse-kinds before being worn. The birrus and the bardaicus are types of heavy,[70] hooded cloaks[71] which were apparently made of wool,[72] and the dalmatic is a robe or tunic which could be made of either wool or linen.[73] In the case of the birrus, bardaicus, and the shoes of coarse wool, then, the point of A-B is that the heavy or coarse wool of these garments may contain flax beneath its surface, so that the garments must be thoroughly inspected before they can be worn. The point of A(3) is not clear, for A(3) may be interpreted in one of two ways. If M. refers specifically to a dalmatic made of wool, then such a garment, like the other three items of A, may contain hidden flax and so must be carefully inspected. Alternatively, if M. refers to a dalmatic made of any kind of material, then A(3)'s point is that one must examine the garment to be certain that it consists of wool or linen alone, and not of a mixture of diverse-kinds.

Yosé qualifies A-B and C-D, maintaining that any of the garments of A which come from the seacoast or from distant lands are presumed to be free of diverse-kinds. These garments, which are composed mainly of wool,[74] are assumed to contain hemp rather than flax (e.g., in their stitching [Sens]) (D). Yosé here apparently assumes that on the seacoast and in distant lands hemp, a coarse fiber used mainly for rope or sacking, is cheaper or more readily available than flax, and thus is substituted for the latter in the manufacture of clothing.[75]

E consists of a simple declarative sentence following the formulary pattern *'yn bhm mšwm kl'ym* (M. 9:2-4) and thus serving to close the subunit begun at M. 9:2. E concerns the $mn^c l$ *šlzrd* (or *šlzrb*), which apparently refers to a kind of heelless cloth shoe or slipper (Maim., *Code, Diverse-Kinds* 10:15). According to E such a slipper is not subject to the laws of diverse-kinds, for, although it is clearly designed to be worn, it does not completely enclose the foot.[76] Unlike a garment, then, such a shoe is not made to stay securely on the body.[77] E thus complements M. 9:2-4's discussion of items which are not regarded as garments because they are not designed to be worn (or to be worn by man [M. 9:4]), turning to deal with an item which is made to be worn, but, because of the way it is worn, is not regarded as a garment.[78]

9:8

A. Nothing is prohibited on account of [the laws of] diverse-kinds except [wool and flax which are] spun (*twwy*) or (*w*) woven (*'rwg*) [together],

B. as it is written, *You shall not wear sha^c atnez* (Dt. 22:11)--something which is hackled (*šw^c*), spun (*twwy*), or (*w*) woven (*nwz*).

C. R. Simeon b. Eleazar says, "It [i.e., a fabric of diverse-kinds (Albeck)] is turned away (*nlwz*), and turns (*mlyz*) his Father in Heaven against him."

M. Kil. 9:8 (A: Y. Kil. 9:5
(32d); B: B. Yev. 5b, Nid. 61b)

M. opens with a declarative sentence, A, which is augmented by B-C, an autonomous unit consisting of an exegesis of Scripture at B and Simeon b. Eleazar's gloss of B at C. Reverting to the formulary pattern of M. 9:1A (*'yn 'swr mšwm kl'ym 'l* X), A begins a new subunit dealing with the ways in which wool and flax may be combined or connected with one another. According to A a union of wool and flax is prohibited only if the two fibers have been spun or woven together, for only through being combined in these ways are the fibers regarded as forming a mixture of diverse-kinds. B then augments A with an exegesis of the word *sha^c atnez* (*š^c tnz*) of Dt. 22:11. Using the exegetical method of *notarikon*, B divides *š^c tnz* into three parts, *š^c*, *t*, and *nz*, and takes these parts to represent respectively the words *šw^c* (i.e., hackled), *twwy* (i.e., spun), and *nwz* (i.e., woven). According

to B, then, a union of wool and flax is prohibited if the fabrics
have been either hackled, spun, or woven together.[79] B has thus
been juxtaposed with A because it agrees with the latter's rule
that wool and flax which are spun or woven together are prohibited. B disagrees with A, however, in maintaining that wool
and flax which are hackled together are also prohibited. B is
thus not an entirely appropriate gloss of A.

At C Simeon b. Eleazar glosses B with another interpretation
of the word *nwz* ("woven"). Apparently taking the letters *n*
and *l* to be interchangeable,[80] Simeon b. Eleazar reads *nwz* as
lwz, a verb meaning "to turn or bend." He then interprets
sha^c atnez to refer to the notion of "turning" in two ways. First,
a mixture of diverse-kinds is called *nlwz*,[81] i.e., turned awry,
for it represents a deviation from the natural order, which is
based on a system of distinct kinds (Albeck). Second, such a
mixture is called *mlyz*, i.e., that which turns (something else),
for it serves to turn or estrange God from its bearer.

A. Wool which one put into flax [i.e., to which one attached
   flax] in order to weave upon it [i.e., wool]--lo, this
   [i.e., the act of combining wool and flax] is prohibited,
B. for at the same time that he would comb [following Lieberman,[82] who reads *lwgyz* for *lygwz*] [the wool] it would
   become spun [with the flax].

                              T. Kil. 5:21a (p. 225, l. 45)

     T. serves to illustrate M. 9:8A's rule prohibiting wool
and flax from being spun together. A describes a case in which
one wishes to weave a fabric upon a warp of woolen threads. He
therefore attaches pieces of flax to the ends of groups of
woolen threads, presumably so that the threads would be weighted
down[83] and kept in place.[84] According to A one may not join
wool and flax in this manner, for in combing the wool (to separate
the threads) and attaching the flax to it, one twists the threads
of the fabrics together, and so, in effect, spins them together
(following the commentary attributed to Sens, Sifra Qedoshim
4:18[85]).[86]

A. Said R. Simeon b. Leazar, "Why is it called *sha^c atnez*?
B. *"Because it turns (mylyz) his Father in Heaven against*
   him [= M. 9:8B]."

                              T. Kil. 5:21b (p. 225, ll. 46-47)

T. restates Simeon b. Eleazar's gloss of M. 9:8B as an autonomous saying in a question-and-answer pattern. T. clarifies M. 9:8C by explicitly stating that the subject of the saying is the diverse-kinds, and not the person wearing them. T. also omits *nlwz* ("turned awry") at B, perhaps because the term more appropriately describes a person than the subject of the sentence, a fabric.

A. *You shall not wear sha^c aṭnez* (Dt. 22:11)--

B. Might I think that he shall not wear pieces of shorn wool (*gyzy ṣmr*) and bundles of flax-stalks (*'nyṣy pštn*) together?

C. Scripture says, Sha^C aṭnez--something which is hackled (*šw^c*), spun (*ṭwwy*), or woven (*nwz*).

D. R. Simeon b. Eleazar says, "It [i.e., a fabric of diverse-kinds] is turned awry (*nlwz*), and turns (*mlyz*) his Father in Heaven against him [= M. 9:8B-C]."

> Sifré Dt. 232a (ed. Finkelstein, p. 265, ll. 1-3)

A-B cites the clause *You shall not wear sha^c aṭnez* (Dt. 22:11), taking it to mean that one may not wear anything made of diverse-kinds, even pieces of shorn wool which are joined to bundles of flax-stalks. C-D therefore presents the exegesis of *sha^c aṭnez* (= M. 9:8B-C[87]), which prohibits one from wearing only wool and linen which have been hackled, spun, or woven together, but not pieces of wool and flax which have been simply fastened together.[88]

9:9

A. Felted stuffs [composed of wool and linen] are prohibited,

B. because they are hackled [i.e., their fibers are hackled together].

C. A fringe (*pyw*; most mss:[89] *pyp*) of wool [fastened] onto [a garment of] flax is prohibited,

D. because they [i.e., the threads of the fringe] interlace the web [of the garment] [so Danby for *ḥwzryn b'ryg*; some readings:[90] *l'ryg*; printed ed.: *k'ryg* ("they come up as if woven [together with the flax][91]")].

E. R. Yosé says, "Cords [composed] of purple [wool] are prohibited [to be worn on a garment of flax],

F. "because one bastes (*mwll*) [the cord to the garment] before tying [the ends of the cord together]."

G. One shall not tie a strip (*srṭ*) of wool to one of linen
    in order to gird his loins,
H. even though a [leather (most comm.)] strap is between them.

M. Kil. 9:9 (A-B: Y. Kil. 9:5
(32d); E: Y. Kil. 9:5 (32d)[92])

M. consists of four rules, A-B, C-D, E-F and G-H. The
first three rules all follow the same formulary pattern (X +
'*swrym/'swr* + *mpny š*) and thus were formulated together. These
rules, however, differ with one another in substance, for A-B
and C-D augment M. 9:8's discussion of mixing together wool and
flax, while Yose at E-F deals with the separate question of
attaching discrete items of wool and linen with one another. G-H
then continues the discussion of this issue with an autonomous
rule (following its own formulary pattern [*l'* + imperfect +
'*p* ᶜ*l py š*]). It appears, then, that a redactor has so formulated E-F that it presents the issue of G-H in the formulary
pattern of A-B and C-D, and thus serves to link the pericope (and
the subunit of M. 9:8-10) together.

A-B concerns felt, a fabric consisting of fibers which have
simply been compressed together.[93] According to A felted stuffs
composed of wool and linen are prohibited as fabrics of diverse-
kinds, for, although the fibers of such cloths are not spun or
woven together, they are hackled with one another (B). A-B thus
illustrates the rule of M. 9:8B, which, unlike M. 9:8A, prohibits
one from wearing wool and linen which are hackled together. C
then rules that one may not attach a fringe or border of wool to
a garment of linen, for the woolen threads would then become
entangled with the web of the garment (D) and so appear to be
woven together with the linen. C-D thus augments M. 9:8A-B's
prohibition against wearing wool and linen which are woven
together, maintaining that the wool and linen may not even appear
to be woven with one another, regardless of whether or not they
actually form a mixture of diverse-kinds.

At E Yosé states that one may not wear cords composed of
purple wool on a garment of flax (Ribmas, Sens, Rosh), for such
cords would be temporarily stitched to the garment under them and
thus held in place before being tied (F). In this case, then, the
cords would be attached to the garment of flax, and so would
combine with the latter to form a garment of diverse-kinds.[94]
G then rules that one may not tie a strip of wool and flax to
one another and thus make a belt, for the two strips would then
be connected to one another and so combine to form a single garment

of diverse-kinds. Glossing G, H adds that the strips of wool
and flax are considered to be connected to each other even if they
are attached to opposite ends of a leather strap, and thus do
not touch one another at all.[95]

A. R. Hananiah b. Gamaliel says, "*One shall not tie a strip
    (srq) of wool and [a strip] of linen [together] in order
    to gird his loins,*
B. "*even though a [leather] strap is between them* [= M. 9:9G-H]."

                              T. Kil. 5:22 (p. 225, ll. 47-49)

    A-B cites M. 9:9G-H with only minor differences (e.g.,
reading *srq* for *srt*[96]), attributing the anonymous rule of M. to
Hananiah b. Gamaliel.

W. Felted stuffs [composed of wool and linen] are prohibited
    [= M. 9:9A] on account of [the laws of] diverse-kinds,
X. [for] even though they do not come under [the category of]
    woven [fibers], they do come under [the category of]
    hackled [fibers].
                              Sifré Dt. 231f (ed. Finkelstein,[97]
                              p. 265, ll. 11-12)

    W cites and glosses M. 9:9A. Presupposing the prohibition
against wearing wool and linen which are hackled, spun, or woven
together, X then simply restates and slightly expands M. 9:9B.

A. *Nor [shall] a garment of cloth made up of two kinds [of stuff
    come upon you]*[98] (Lv. 19:19)--
B. Why does Scripture say so?
C. Since Scripture says, *You shall not wear a mingled stuff,
    wool and linen together* (Dt. 22:11), might I [not] think that
    one shall not wear pieces of shorn wool (*gyzy smr*) and
    bundles of flax-stalks ('*nysy pštn*) together?
D. Scripture says, *A garment.*
E. I know [from this phrase] only [that the laws of diverse-kinds
    apply to] a garment.
F. Whence [do I know] to include felted stuffs [in the prohibi-
    tion]?
G. Scripture says, [*A garment of cloth made up of two kinds*] *of
    stuff (sha^c atnez)--something which is hackled (šw^c), spun
    (twwy), or woven (nwz).*

H. R. Simeon b. Eleazar says, "It [i.e., a fabric of diverse-
    kinds] is turned awry (*nlwz*), and turns (*mlyz*) his Father
    in Heaven against him [= M. 9:8B-C].

                    Sifra Qedoshim 4:18a (ed. Weiss, 89a)

       A-B cites Lv. 19:19, asking why it is necessary for Scripture
to state this verse, since Dt. 22:11 also prohibits one from
wearing diverse-kinds (Hillel). C-D answers that Dt. 22:11,
which states simply *You shall not wear a mingled stuff*, may
be taken to mean that one may not wear anything which is composed
of diverse-kinds, even pieces of shorn wool and stalks of flax
which have been joined together. Lv. 19:19 therefore specifically
mentions the word *garment*, and so includes in the prohibition
only garments, and not other items composed of vegetable or
animal fibers.[99]
       E-F then takes the word *garment* to refer only to items which
are woven, and thus asks whether the prohibition of Lv. 19:19
applies also to felted stuffs which are composed of wool and
linen. G-H answers by citing[100] the exegesis of *sha*^{c}*aṭnez*
(= M. 9:8B-C), which rules that hackled fibers of wool and linen
are also prohibited as fabrics of diverse-kinds. E-H thus agrees
with the rule of M. 9:9A-B, and directly links this rule to the
exegesis of *sha*^{c}*aṭnez* at 9:8B-C.

                            9:10

A. Marks of weavers [so Danby for *hgrdyn*] and marks of
    washermen [which are composed of wool or linen and sewn
    respectively onto garments of linen or wool] are prohibited
    on account of [the laws of] diverse-kinds.
B. He who fastens [wool and linen together] with a single
    fastening [of thread] [following I. Epstein[101] for *htwkp*
    tkyph 'ḥt] [i.e., with an incomplete stitch]--
C. it [i.e., the fastening] is not considered a connector
    [for uncleanness],
D. and it [i.e., the fabrics joined by the fastening] is not
    subject to [the laws of] diverse-kinds,
E. and he who undoes it [i.e., the fastening] on the Sabbath
    is exempt [from liability for tearing a stitch in order
    to sew another].
F. [If] he brought both ends [of the thread] to one side
    [i.e., if he completed the stitch]--
G. it [i.e., the stitch] is considered a connector [for
    uncleanness],

H. and it [i.e., the fabrics joined by the stitch] is subject
    to [the laws of] diverse-kinds,

I. and he who undoes it [i.e., the stitch] on the Sabbath
    is liable.

J. R. Judah says, "[The above rules do not apply] unless he
    makes three [fastenings] [i.e., one complete and one
    incomplete stitch]."

K. A sack and a basket [that are patched, one with wool and the
    other with linen, and then bound together,] combine to
    produce diverse-kinds.

> M. Kil. 9:10 (B-C: B. Shab. 54a,
> Men. 39a; F: Y. Kil. 9:6 (32d),
> Y. Shab. 7:2 (10c); J: Y. Kil. 9:6
> (32d); K: Y. Shab. 13:1 (14a))

M. consists of three autonomous rules, A, B-I (glossed by
J), and K, all of which deal with the problem of attaching wool
and linen to one another. A concerns threads which weavers and
washermen would sew into garments in order to mark them for
identification. According to A one may not for this purpose
sew a woolen thread into a linen garment (or *vice versa*), for
the garment would then contain diverse-kinds. The point of A
is that, although the thread is actually extrinsic to the garment
(i.e., it is added after the garment is completed) and serves
no function for the owner (cf. Maim., *Code*, *Diverse-Kinds* 10:23),
it is nevertheless connected to the garment, which thus is
regarded as containing diverse-kinds.

B-I presents a series of rules related to the question of
the connection of fabrics. The pericope has been redacted here
because it is relevant to the issue of diverse-kinds at D and H.
B-I is a unitary construction consisting of a mildly-apocopated
sentence, B-E, and a conditional sentence, F-I, the apodoses
of which balance one another (C-E *vs.* G-I). Judah then glosses
F-I at J. According to B-E a thread which is inserted through
two fabrics (taken, in this context, to be wool and linen) only
once does not serve to connect them together. The thread thus
is not considered a connector (C), presumably for uncleanness
(most commentaries), the fabrics of wool and linen do not combine
to form a garment of diverse-kinds (D), and one is permitted
to undo the fastening on the Sabbath (E). In this instance
one is not liable for tearing a stitch in order to sew it again,
since the stitch has not been completed (Sens, Bert.).[102] If,
on the other hand, one brings the thread through the fabrics

again (F), and thus completes a full stitch, the thread is
regarded as connecting the two fabrics together and the rules
of C-E are reversed.[103] Judah then opposes F-I at J, maintaining
that the fabrics are not considered to be connected unless the
thread is inserted through them an additional time, or three
times in all.

K describes a case in which a sack and a basket are patched,
one with wool and one with linen, and then joined together.
According to K these two items combine to produce diverse-kinds
and so, for example, may not be carried on one's back (Maim.,
Comm.; cf. M. 9:4B-C). The point of K is that, although the wool
and linen patches are not directly attached to each other, they
are fastened to items which are joined together, and which thus
serve to connect them with one another. K thus carries forward
the rule of M. 9:9G-H, turning from a case in which wool and
linen are fastened to the same item (the leather strap) to an
instance in which the two fabrics are attached to separate items
which are joined together.

A. A woolen fringe [so Jastrow for $^c y \underline{t}$; alternatively: a
    wrapper (Lieberman[104])] which one put into flax [i.e.,
    which one attached to flax] is permitted.
B. [*If*] *he brought both ends* [*of the fringe*] *to one side*
    [= M. 9:10F], it is prohibited.

                              T. Kil. 5:20 (p. 225, ll. 44-45)

T. describes a case in which an $^c y \underline{t}$ of wool is attached
to a linen garment. The meaning of $^c y \underline{t}$ is not clear, and the
term has been taken to refer either to a fringe or a kind of
wrapper. According to A one is permitted to attach a woolen $^c y \underline{t}$
to a linen garment by inserting it into the latter, for a simple
fastening is not considered to connect the two fabrics together.
If, on the other hand, one inserts the wool into the linen and
brings it out again, so that both ends of the $^c y \underline{t}$ lie on the
same side of the garment, the two fabrics are considered to be
connected with one another, and they thus combine to form a garment
of diverse-kinds (B). T. thus complements M. 9:10B-I (citing
M. 9:10F at B). While the latter discusses whether a thread
inserted into two garments serves to connect one to the other,
T. concerns whether an item which is itself inserted into a
garment is considered to be connected to the latter. We note that
if the *cy* $\underline{t}$ does refer to a fringe, then T. apparently reads
the rule of M. 9:10B-I into the case of M. 9:9C-D, which concerns

one who attaches a woolen fringe to a linen garment. According
to this interpretation, then, T. serves to link M. 9:10B-I to
M. 9:9C-D.[105] If T. does concern a woolen fringe, though, it
does not deal with the issue of M. 9:9C-D, for the latter prohibits one from attaching a woolen fringe to a linen garment,
lest the two fabrics appear to be woven together.

Q. R. Ḥananiah b. Gamaliel says, "Whence [do I know that] one
shall not tie a strip (srṭ) of wool to one of linen in order
to gird his loins,

R. "even though a [leather] strap is between them [= T. 5:22]?

S. "Scripture says, [*You shall not wear a mingled stuff, wool
and linen*] *together* (Dt. 22:11)--under all circumstances."

T. It follows that (kštmṣ' lwmr) a sack and a basket [that
are patched, one with wool and the other with linen, and then
bound together,] combine to produce diverse-kinds
[= M. 9:10K].

Sifré Dt. 232d (ed. Finkelstein,
p. 265, ll. 8-10)

Q-R cites T. 5:22 (= the anonymous rule of M. 9:9G-H),
adding the word "whence" to the saying and so rephrasing it as
a question. S then presents an exegetical basis for the rule
of Q-R, taking the word *together* of Dt. 22:11 to indicate that
wool and linen may not be joined together under any circumstances,
even if the two fabrics are separated by a leather strap and thus
not directly attached to one another. T then cites M. 9:10K
and links it to S. According to T, then, the reasoning behind
M. 9:10K is that wool and linen may not be joined together in
any manner, even if they are attached to separate items (i.e.,
the sack and the basket) which have been joined together. Sifré
thus links M. 9:10K to M. 9:9G-H by showing that both cases
illustrate the same principle.

A. A tuft [of wool] (hpwqryt) and a strip [of wool] (ṣyph) are
not subject to [the laws of] diverse-kinds.

B. And if he sewed them [i.e., if he sewed the ends together
in each case],

C. they receive uncleanness,

D. and are prohibited on account of [the laws of] diverse-kinds.

T. Kil. 5:23 (p. 225, ll. 49-50)

T. is an autonomous pericope concerning whether or not
pieces of wool used as dressings for wounds are subject to the
laws of diverse-kinds. T. exactly follows the language of
T. 5:16's rule concerning the status of women's bath-towels.
According to A tufts or strips of wool,[106] which were usually
placed on wounds (Lieberman[107]), do not come under the laws of
diverse-kinds. The point of A is that these pieces of wool are
simply put on the wound, but are not bound securely to it, so
that, unlike a garment, they are not made to stay on the body.
If, however, one ties the ends of the tufts or strips together
(B), then the pieces of wool are designed to stay on the body,
and therefore are regarded as garments.[108] Like garments, therefore, they receive *midras*-uncleanness (C),[109] and are subject
to the laws of diverse-kinds.[110]

NOTES

INTRODUCTION

[1]The tractates which discuss man's role in ordering the
sacred deal with his ability to bring objects into (or, in some
cases, remove them from) a process of sanctification and uncleanness. In the Division of Agriculture the tractates Terumot and
Ma^{c}aśerot in particular state that man is able to designate
heave-offering and tithes. For an analysis of Mishnah's conception of agricultural offerings, see R.S. Sarason, "Mishnah and
Scripture: Preliminary Observations in the Law of Tithes,"
now published in W.S. Green, ed., *Approaches to the Study of
Ancient Judaism*, II (Missoula: Scholars Press, 1980). The
tractates Zebaḥim and Menaḥot in the Division of Holy Things deal
with the effect of man's intention upon the designation of sacrifices and meal-offerings; see the analysis of J. Neusner, *A
History of the Mishnaic Law of Holy Things* (Leiden: E.J. Brill,
1978-80), VI, Chapters 2-3. Finally, in the Division of Purities
the tractates Kelim and Makhshirin in particular claim that man
is able to render objects susceptible to uncleanness, while the
tractates Parah and Miqvaot deal with man's role in the process
of purification; see the analysis of J. Neusner, *A History of
the Mishnaic Law of Purities* (Leiden: E.J. Brill, 1974-77),
XXII, pp. 269-303.

[2]BDB (p. 476) explains *kl'ym* as meaning "two", and as having
cognates in Arabic and Ethiopic. M. Noth (*Leviticus: A
Commentary*, trans. J.S. Anderson, The Old Testament Library
[Philadelphia: Westminster Press, 1965], p. 142) notes that the
term perhaps originally meant "double," but here has the sense
of "of two different kinds."

[3]BDB (p. 1043) notes that A. Knobel derived the word *š^{c}ṭnz*
from the Coptic *saht* (woven) and *nudj* (false). Lv. 19:19
appends to *š^{c}ṭnz* the term *kl'ym*, "of two kinds," and so takes
š^{c}ṭnz to refer to a garment composed of any mingled stuff. Dt.
22:11, on the other hand, explains *š^{c}ṭnz* with the phrase
ṣmr wpštym yḥdyw, "wool and linen together," and so defines the
term as referring to the mingling of these two kinds alone.

[4]Cf. J. Soler, "The Dietary Prohibitions of the Hebrews,"
New York Review of Books, June 14, 1979 (26:10), p. 29.

[5]For a detailed study of this phenomenon in the Division of
Purities, cf. J. Neusner, *A History of the Mishnaic Law of
Purities*, XXI, Chapter Two.

[6]*Tosefta Ki-fshutah. A Comprehensive Commentary on the
Tosefta. I. Order Zera^{c}im* (New York: Jewish Theological
Seminary, 1951).

[7]*The Six Orders of Mishnah. I. The Order of Zera^{c}im*
[Heb.] (Jerusalem and Tel Aviv: Bialik Institute and D^{e}vir,
1957), pp. 95-129.

[8]*M. Zera^{c}im* (Jerusalem: Makhon HaTalmud HaYisraeli
HaShalem, 1972-75), I, pp. 219-305.

[9]*The Mishnah* (London: Oxford University Press, 1933),
pp. 28-39.

[10]*Mishnayot. I. Order Zeraim* (2nd ed.; New York: Judaica Press, 1964), pp. 273-299.

[11]*The Babylonian Talmud: Seder Zera^{c}im. II. Kilayim* (London: Soncino Press, 1948), pp. 130-144.

[12]*The Tosefta. I. Order Zera^{c}im* (New York: Jewish Theological Seminary, 1955), pp. 203-226.

[13]*Sifra debe Rab* (1862; rpt. New York: Om, 1946).

[14]*Sifrê on Deuteronomy* (Berlin, 1939; rpt. New York: Jewish Theological Seminary, 1969).

CHAPTER ONE

[1]Either *Triticum durum* ("hard" wheat) or *Triticum aestivum* (*vulgare, turgidum*) ("soft" wheat). For all Latin names, see Yehuda Feliks, *Mixed Sowing, Breeding and Grafting* [Heb.] (Tel Aviv: D^{e}vir, 1967), p. 17.

[2]Tare is also called bearded darnel (both names are given by Danby). Its Latin name is *Lolium temulentum.*

[3]*Hordeum vulgare, genuinum; hexastichum.*

[4]*Hordeum distichum.*

[5]*Triticum diococcum.*

[6]*Triticum spelta.*

[7]*Vicia faba.*

[8]*Vicia narbonensis.* This is apparently the only place this bean appears in rabbinic literature (Feliks, *Mixed Sowing,* p. 35). The identification was first made by Immanual Löw, *Die Flora der Juden* (Vienna: R. Löwit, 1926), II, p. 503.

[9]*Lathyrus cicera.*

[10]*Lathyrus sativus.*

[11]*Dolichos lablab.*

[12]*Vigna nilotica.*

[13]Although Maimonides presents this interpretation only with reference to C(3), we assume that it applies to the entire pericope.

[14]This is true, of course, only if we assume that our identifications (which follow those of Feliks, *Mixed Sowing*) are correct. We admit that the method of identification may sometimes be circular in nature, for one member of a pair may be identified on the basis of its resemblance to the second. It is possible, however, to identify members of pairs by other methods (e.g., the endives and wild endives of M. 1:2) and to infer from these cases that the members of each pair resemble one another, thus avoiding the circularity.

[15]Feliks, *Mixed Sowing*, p. 22.

[16]Cf. the parable of the wheat and tares, Mt. 13:24-30.

[17]Jonah in Y. 1:1 (26d) presents the view that tares constitute an inferior variety of wheat, comparing the name *zwnyn* to the root *ZNH*, "to go astray."

[18]S. G. Harrison, G. B. Masefield, and Michael Wallis, *The Oxford Book of Food Plants* (London: Oxford University Press, 1969), pp. 4-5.

[19]Feliks, *Mixed Sowing*, p. 29.

[20]*Ibid.*, p. 35.

[21]*Cucumis melo var. Chate.* For all Latin names, see Feliks, *Mixed Sowing*, p. 44.

[22]*Cucumis melo L.*

[23]*Lactuca sativa, longifolis.*

[24]*Lactuca scariola.*

[25]This reading is given by several Geniza fragments and the commentary of R. Nathan, the Head of the Academy. See Zachs, pp. 220, on 1.4. Cf. also Erfurt's reading of T. 1:1C.

[26]*Cicorium intybus.*

[27]*Cicorium pumilum.*

[28]*Allium porrum.*

[29]*Allium ampeloprasum.*

[30]*Coriandrum sativum.*

[31]*Bifora testiculata.*

[32]*Brassica nigra.*

[33]*Sinapsis alba.*

[34]*Lagenaria vulgaris forma Asiatica.*

[35]This gourd probably has the same name as that given in the previous note.

[36]*Vigna sinensis Savi.*

[37]*Vigna sesquipedalis.* This is also called the yard-long bean (Feliks, *Mixed Sowing*, p. 73, n. 77).

[38]Cf. also Maimonides, *Code, Diverse-Kinds* 3:3.

[39]Y. Kil. 1:2 (27a) reads as follows:

    A. (1) Chate melons, and (2) watermelons, and (3) musk melons
    B. are not [considered] diverse-kinds with one another.
    C. R. Judah says, "[They are considered] diverse-kinds."

Y. thus differs from M. in adding watermelons at A (perhaps

from T. 1:1H; see above p. 30) and thus has A contain three melons rather than two.

[40]Pair (8) presents a problem, for its seems to make the same distinction that (9)-(11) make. Its language, however, is slightly different, and it thus does not appear originally to have belonged with the group of three pairs. (8), therefore, either stands alone or is part of a group of five ((8)-(12)), depending on how we read (12).

[41]Feliks, *Mixed Sowing*, p. 52.

[42]*Ibid.*, p. 63.

[43]Cf. George E. Post, *Flora of Syria, Palestine and Sinai*. Second edition. Ed. by J. E. Dinsmore (1896; Beirut: American Press, 1932-3), I, p. 123.

[44]Feliks, *Mixed Sowing*, p. 65.

[45]*Ibid.*, p. 70. For Amoraic interpretations of the name *rmwṣh*, see B. Bokser, *Samuel's Commentary on the Mishnah* (Leiden: E.J. Brill, 1975), I, pp. 34-38.

[46]*Lageneria vulgaris*.

[47]*Citrullus vulgaris*. This identification follows Feliks in *Mar'ot HaMishnah* (Jerusalem: *Midrash Bnei Siyon*, 1967), p. 2. In *Mixed Sowing*, p. 52, Feliks identifies *'bṭyḥ* as *Citrullus colocynthis*, the colocynth.

[48]Concerning the different attributions, see Lieberman, *TK*, II, p. 597 on 1.5.

[49]But cf. Tos., B. Shab. 85b, s.v. *'yṭybyh*, which rules the opposite, and MR to M. Kil. 3:4.

[50]Lieberman, *TK*, II, p. 597, on 11. 3-4.

[51]*Ibid.*, p. 597, n. 10.

[52]Cf. T. 1:1a and Lieberman, *TZ*, p. 203, n. to 1. 1.

[53]*TK*, II, pp. 596f., on 11. 3-4.

[54]This reading of T. returns us to the same problem of the chate melons and the gourds which we discussed above. T. implies that since neither the chate melon nor the gourd is considered diverse-kinds with the musk melon, the chate melon and the gourd are also not considered diverse-kinds with each other. As we have already mentioned, M. Kil. 3:4-5 implies that the chate melon and the gourd are considered diverse-kinds. Again we may offer two explanations. We may simply say that T. disagrees with M. Alternatively, Lieberman argues (*TK*, II, pp. 596-597, on 11. 3-4) that one may not infer from T. that the chate melon and the gourd are not considered diverse kinds. Although the chate melon is not considered diverse-kinds with the musk melon, it still may be considered diverse-kinds with the gourd (or the watermelon). T. then does not oppose M. 3:4-5.

In order to justify this way of reading T.'s list, Lieberman analyzes the treatment of the baraita given in Y. 1:2 (27a), which adds "watermelons" to M. 1:2A-C (cf. above n. 39). Y. begins by asking what Judah would say concerning the chate melon and the watermelon, since he offers no explicit opinion as to whether or not they are considered diverse-kinds. Y. then cites the baraita and asks whether Judah's opinion may be deduced from it. The conclusion is that Judah's opinion refers to two pairs, the first and third melons on the one hand, and the second and third on the other. However, his opinion concerning the first two melons themselves (the chate melon and the watermelon) cannot be deduced (following PM, GRA). Lieberman interprets the conclusion of Y. as referring to the anonymous opinion of the baraita as well, so that no ruling at all concerning the first and second melons is deducible. Lieberman thus reads T. in the same way, and concludes that chate melons and gourds need not be considered diverse-kinds with one another.

[55] *Brassica rapa.* For Latin names see Feliks, *Mixed Sowing*, p. 74.

[56] *Brassica napus.* Feliks gives the English name in *Mar'ot HaMishnah*, p. 89. In *Mixed Sowing*, p. 78 n. 13, he called the plant a turnip. For mss. reading *npws* see Zachs, I, p. 221, on 1.7.

[57] *Brassica oleracea var. acephala.*

[58] Possibly *Brassica oleracea var. Capitata* (Feliks, *Mixed Sowing*, p. 81, n. 28).

[59] *Beta vulgaris var. cicla.*

[60] *Rumex acetosa.* Feliks, p. 85, n. 38, credits Löw, I, p. 358, with the identification. The English name is given by Feliks in *Mar'ot HaMishnah*, p. 82.

[61] For a full list see Zachs, I, p. 222, on 1. 8.

[62] *Allium sativum.*

[63] *Allium schoenoprasum.*

[64] *Allium cepa.*

[65] *Allium ascalonicum.*

[66] *Lupinus termis.*

[67] *Lupinus luteus.*

[68] Although M. 1:4 lists two pairs which also seem to belong on the list, these pairs are actually part of a separate list of fruits of M. 1:4.

[69] Y. N. Epstein, *Introduction to Amoraitic Literature* [Heb.] (Jerusalem: Magnes Press, 1962), p. 401, n. 3.

[70] Feliks, *Mixed Sowing*, p. 79. Cf. also Y. 1:5 and Maimonides, *Code, Diverse-Kinds* 3:6.

[71] Feliks, *Mixed Sowing*, p. 85.

[72] *Ibid.*, pp. 88-89.

[73] This explanation may also account for the lack of a subscription following T. 1:2A (for Simeon's comment would make little sense after M. 1:3D as we have already seen).

[74] Cf. Feliks, *Mixed Sowing*, pp. 77-78.

[75]*Pirus communis.* For Latin names, see Feliks, *Mixed Sowing,* p. 90.

[76]*Pira crustamina.*

[77]*Cydonia oblonga* (= *C. vulgaris*).

[78]*Crataegus azarolus.*

[79]*Malus sylvestris* (=*Pyrus malus* = *Malus communis*).

[80]*Pirus syriaca.*

[81]See Zachs, I, p. 223, on l. 11.

[82]*Persica vulgaris* (= *Prunus persica*).

[83]*Amygdalus communis* (= *Prunus amygdalus*).

[84]*Zizyphus jujuba* (= *Z. vulgaris*).

[85]*Zizyphus spina-Christi.* The English name is given by Feliks, *Mar'ot HaMishnah,* p. 138.

[86]We note that, although we assume that B lists two pairs, Y. presents a dispute concerning this very point. In Y. Kil. 1:4 (27a) Rav and Joshua b. Levi argue as to whether B contains two pairs or a single group of four. Y. apparently concludes that B speaks of two pairs. The four fruits do appear as a single group, however, in other contexts in M.-T. Zera^{c}im (M. Ma^{c}as. 1:3, T. Shev. 7:16), so that it is possible that they should be so considered here as well.

[87]Feliks, *Mixed Sowing,* pp. 93-96.

[88]Löw, III, p. 245.

[89]Feliks, *Mixed Sowing,* pp. 93-96.

[90]*Ibid.,* p. 96. Cf. M. Dem. 1:1, where ^{c}*wzrr* is considered one of the *qlyn šbdm'y.*

[91]Feliks, *Mixed Sowing,* pp. 99-101.

[92]*Ibid.*

[93]As we have noted above (p. 27) it was probably his interpretation of M. 1:4 (and M. 1:5-6 as well) which is based on M. 1:4E, that led Maimonides to his interpretation of M. 1:1-3.

[94]M. Avi-Yonah places Ariah on the shores of the Sea of Galilee, southwest of Tiberias. Cf. *Carta's Atlas of the Period of the Second Temple, the Mishnah and the Talmud* [Heb.] (Jerusalem: Carta, 1966), map 131. Elsewhere, Avi-Yonah mentions the accepted identification of Bet Yerah as Philoteria, but expresses doubts about this identification. Cf. *Historical Geography of Palestine from the End of the Babylonian Exile up to the Arab Conquest* [Heb.] Second edition (Jerusalem: Bialik Institute, 1951), p. 139, n. 2.

[95]*Raphanus sativus.* Feliks, *Mixed Sowing,* p. 79. The English name is given by Feliks in *Mar'ot HaMishnah,* p. 120.

[96]*Brassica napus.*

[97]For a full list see Zachs, I, p. 224, on l. 13.

[98]*Brassica nigra* (M. 1:2 above (p. 317, n. 32)).

[99]*Sinapsis arvensis*. Feliks, *Mixed Sowing*, p. 63. In *Mar'ot HaMishnah* Feliks translates it (more literally than we have) as "field mustard."

[100]An African variety of *Lagenaria vulgaris*. Feliks, *Mixed Sowing*, p. 70.

[101]*Lagenaria vulgaris forma Asiatica* (M. 1:2, above (p. 28 and n. 34)).

[102]For a full list see Zachs, I, p.224, on l. 14.

[103]See n. 101 above.

[104]Maimonides, *Code*, *Diverse-Kinds* 3:5-6, interprets taste as a major criterion for determining diverse-kinds (the other criterion being similarity in appearance) only in the case of two plants which are not of the same kind (*myn*). If they are of the same kind, they are not considered diverse-kinds even if they are not similar in appearance or taste. MR (to M. 1:1), however, takes taste as a significant criterion (along with appearance) for all determinations of diverse-kinds and interprets M. accordingly. The plants listed in M. 1:1 are thus not considered diverse-kinds, for, while they differ slightly in taste (and therefore might be considered diverse-kinds), they are similar in appearance. If, however, two plants differ greatly in taste (or slightly in taste but greatly in appearance) they are considered diverse-kinds. And if the two plants do not differ at all in respect to taste, even if they differ greatly in appearance, they are not considered diverse-kinds.

[105]Feliks, *Mixed Sowing*, p. 66.

[106]*Ibid.*

[107]*Ibid.*, p. 70.

[108]We assume this because they are both varieties of the same species of gourds.

[109]Cf. Feliks, *Mixed Sowing*, p. 70.

[110]It does not appear likely that a third list, relating the plants which are common to both M. 1:1-3 and M. 1:5, (e.g., Egyptian mustard and wild mustard) may be generated from the two lists before us. We cannot determine the status of plants B and C, even knowing that A and B are not considered diverse-kinds, and that A and C are so considered. While we may assume that B and C resemble each other, we cannot know whether or not they might form a pair which would be considered diverse-kinds in spite of a similarity of appearance. Therefore, I do not believe that we can logically derive a third list. Y. 1:2 does not discuss one pair which would be on such a list, the turnip and the radish, but its conclusion is unclear (see Maimonides, *Code*, *Diverse-Kinds* 3:5-6, Rabad's comments there and MR to M. 1:2).

[111]*Anethum graveolens*. For all Latin names see Lieberman, *TK*, II, p. 596, notes 1, 2, 4, 5, and Harrison, Mansfield and Wallis, *The Oxford Book of Food Plants*, p. 148.

[112] *Foeniculum vulgare.*

[113] *Apium graveolens.*

[114] Lieberman, *TK*, II, p. 596, on 1.2, says that the four plants belong to Umbellaceae. Post, pp. 327ff., lists them under Umbelliferae, as does Michael Zohary, *A New Analytical Flora of Israel* (Tel Aviv: Am Oved, 1976), pp. 270, 273.

[115] Harrison, Mansfield and Wallis, *op.cit.*, p. 138.

[116] Feliks, *Mixed Sowing*, p. 63.

[117] *TZ*, p. 204, note to 1.14.

[118] Bokser, pp. 35f.

[119] Y.'s version differs from that of T. in that the order of its items is 1, 4, 2, 3, 5.

[120] Feliks, *Mixed Sowing*, p. 308, n. to 1. 3.

[121] Y. 2:11 (28b) explains that T. refers only to actual contact between the Greek gourd and the other plants, but the Greek gourd may be allowed to overshadow them.

[122] *TK*, II, p. 599, on 1. 15. Cf. also Bert. to M. Uqs. 1:6.

[123] That is, one does not take account of the volume of the stalk in calculating the volume of the gourd. An item of food becomes unclean only when it has the volume of an egg (cf. Bert. to M. Uqs. 1:1).

[124] M. comments at the end of the list that the prohibition involved is either ʿ*orlah* (fruit of the first three years after planting) or diverse-kinds of the vineyard. Since ʿ*orlah* applies only to the fruit of the tree (Maim., *Comm.*, *ad. loc.*), the Greek gourd can become prohibited only because of the diverse-kinds of the vineyard.

[125] Cf. Dt. 22:9, M. Kil. 5:5, 8:1, and Maim., *Code, Diverse-Kinds*, 5:7.

[126] *A History of the Mishnaic Laws of Purities* (Leiden: E. J. Brill, 1974-1977), IV, p. 190.

[127] Presumably because an item possessing one property need not possess the other. Cf. M. Oh. 8:3-4.

[128] According to Lieberman (*TK*, II, p. 599, on 1. 16) there is some question as to whether this law belongs on the list of five rulings. Erfurt and Sens omit "and" before the law, which may imply that it is not connected to the list, and Erfurt even has a space between (4) and (5). HD points out that (5) states the only law of the list which is not found in M. In addition, Bar Qappara does not include this law on his list. If (5) does not belong on the list, then it is possible that (4) may be considered as two laws (conveying the uncleanness and interposing before it), so that the list would still contain five items.

[129] Cf. Feliks, *Mixed Sowing*, p. 65, n. to 1. 84.

[130] *Canis lupus.* For Latin and English names, see Feliks, *Mixed Sowing*, pp. 117ff., and Feliks, *The Animal World of the Bible*,

trans. Pinhas Irsai (Tel Aviv: Sinai, 1962), and *HaḤai BaMishnah* (Jerusalem: Institute for Mishnah Research, 1972).

[131] *Canis familiaris putiatini.*

[132] Same as in note 131. The translation of "wild dog" is given by Danby and Israelstam.

[133] For the list of Geniza fragments see Zachs, I, p. 224, on l. 15.

[134] *Canis aureus.*

[135] *Capra hircus mambrica.*

[136] *Gazella subguttorosa* (yellow) or *Gazella gazella* (red).

[137] *Capra nubiana.*

[138] *Ovis vignei platyura.*

[139] *Equus caballus orientalis.*

[140] *Equus asinus mulus.*

[141] *Equus asinus.*

[142] *Equus hemionus.*

[143] Feliks, *Mixed Sowing*, p. 122.

[144] *Ibid.*, pp. 126-127.

[145] *Ibid.*, pp. 127-128.

[146] *Ibid.*, p. 128.

[147] The fact that it is the mating of animals of diverse-kinds which is important, and not the possible product of such a union, is further illustrated by M. 8:1, which states that it is permitted to raise the offspring of animals of diverse-kinds.

[148] Cf. Feliks, *Mixed Sowing*, p. 128.

[149] *Gallus gallus domesticus.* For Latin names, see Feliks, *Mixed Sowing*, p. 132.

[150] *Pavo cristatus.*

[151] *Phasianus colchicus.*

[152] The cock, or the hen, always stands as a separate bird throughout M.-T. Neither word (*trngwl* or *trngwlt*) is used to simply denote the gender of any bird, as cock and hen are used in English.

[153] We assume that, according to Erfurt and B., the cock and the peacock are still considered diverse-kinds. But see our discussion of T. 1:1c for Lieberman's way of reading a list of three items. Lieberman claims that one cannot deduce anything concerning the first two items from such a list.

[154] *Mixed Sowing*, p. 132.

[155] *Ibid.*, p. 134.

[156]Cf. M. 8:4, where Judah distinguishes between the mule (the dam of which is a mare) and a hinny (the dam of which is a she-ass), and does not allow one to be mated with the other. T. (which makes no such distinction) and M. thus represent two different traditions of Judah concerning the same issue.

[157]*Bos taurus.* For all English and Latin names see Feliks, *The Animal World of the Bible.*

[158]*Bos primogenius* (so Feliks, *ibid.*, says s.v. *šwr hbr*; but in *HaHai BaMishnah*, p. 156, Feliks identifies the "wild ox" as the European bison, *Bison bonasus.*

[159]*Equus asinus hemionus.*

[160]*Sus domestica.*

[161]*Sus scropha.*

[162]Y. Kil. 8:6 (31c) attributes T. C(1) to Yosé, based on the dispute in M. Kil. 8:6 between Yosé and an anonymous opinion. The latter states that the wild ox is a domesticated animal (*bhmh*), while Yosé claims that it is considered to be a wild animal (*ḥyh*). Y. reasons that the ox and the wild ox could be considered diverse-kinds only according to Yosé's opinion (since one would be a *bhmh*, and one a *ḥyh*), and assigns T.'s ruling to him. While one may not actually wish to attribute (1) to Yosé, it is certainly true that Yosé would agree with the ruling of T.

We may note further, that M. 8:6 also mentions members of two other pairs of T., the hog and the Arabian onager (see note 163 below). M. calls the hog a *bhmh* and the onager a *ḥyh*. If we follow Y. and assume that a *bhmh* and a *ḥyh* are considered diverse-kinds with each other, then T. agrees with M.'s classification. The hog (a *bhmh*) is paired with the wild boar (presumably a *ḥyh*), while the ass (presumably a *bhmh*) is grouped with the wild ass (= Arabian onager, a *ḥyh*). It is possible, therefore, that the list of T. is related to that of M. 8:6.

[163]The wild ass of A(2) may be identical to the Arabian onager of M. 1:6A(7) (Lieberman, *TK*, II, p. 600, on 1. 19). If so, then T. simply has the same law as M. in a different tradition.

[164]Following Blackman's translation of M. M.S. 1:3-4.

[165]Cf. Sifré Dt. 100 (ed. Finkelstein, p. 160): "*And the t'w* (Dt. 14:5), R. Yose says, '*The t'w* -- this is the wild ox.'"

[166]Although we have stated that T. 1:9 was meant to supplement T. 1:8b, we also note that T. 1:9A-B actually opposes the law of T. 1:8b. It is possible that the redactor also meant for T. 1:9 to comment upon and oppose T. 1:8b. This is probably not the case, though, since T. 1:9D-E does agree with T. 1:8b. Rather, it is more likely that T. 1:9 was placed after T. 1:8b because both pericopae deal with similar issues.

[167]We understand the sages in F as saying that the *t'w* is one creature and the wild ox is another. The phrase "a creature unto itself" simply means that each animal is to be distinguished from the other. A less likely interpretation of the sages' statement is that the *t'w* and the wild ox are each a species unto itself, being neither a *ḥyh* or a *bhmh*. While it is true that the

phrase *bryh bpny ᶜ ṣmh* (not *lᶜ ṣmh*) may indicate that the
subject belongs to its own, unique species (cf. B. Shab. 28b
[concerning the *thš*], B. Yoma 74b, and B. Ḥul. 80a [concerning
the *kwy*]), the phrase is used in different ways as well. It
may, for example, mean simply that the animal is an independent
creature, and not considered merely a part of its mother (B.
Nid. 22b). Therefore *bry'lᶜ ṣmh*, as used here, need not
mean that the *t'w* and the wild ox are each a unique kind of
animal. In addition, as we shall see, M. Kil. 8:6 records a
dispute in which an anonymous opinion says that the wild ox is
a *bhmh*, and Yosé maintains that it is a *ḥyh*. Although it is
possible that the sages in F would take the middle position that
the wild ox is neither a *bhmh* nor a *ḥyh*, it does not seem likely
that they would dispute with both of the positions given in M.
We therefore maintain that our interpretation is the more plausible
of the two.

[168]This dispute parallels the dispute of M. Kil. 8:6, which
we have described in note 167 above. See also our discussion
below of the second dispute of the pericope.

[169]Cf. Sifra Emor VIII:8 (ed. Weiss, p. 99a), where the word
"ox" is taken to exclude the wild animal.

[170]Cf. Sifra Ṣav X:2 (ed. Weiss, p. 38b), where the animals
listed in the verse are taken to exclude the unclean animal
(*bhmh ṭm'h*), the wild animal, and birds.

[171]Cf. Sifra Wayiqra II:6, (ed. Weiss, p. 4b), where the
animals listed in Lv. 1:2 are taken to exclude wild animals.

[172]For English names (and alternates) see Feliks, *The Animal
World of the Bible*.

[173]Feliks, *ibid.*, p. 21, states that the *t'w* is to be
identified with either the bison (*Bison bonasus*) or the bubalis
antelope (*Bubalis boselaphus*).

[174]Cf. also B. Ḥul. 80a, where the dispute of Yosé and the
anonymous opinion in M. Kil. 8:6 is related to the issue of the
meaning of *t'w* in Dt. 14:5.

[175]B has this as a corrected reading. See Zachs, I, p. 225,
on l. 17.

[176]Feliks, *Mixed Sowing*, p. 139.

[177]As a matter of convenience, however, we shall continue
to use "graft" to designate any method of uniting two plants.

[178]Lieberman (*TK*, II, p. 601, on l. 27) points out that B
only prohibits any union by which two trees are nourished by
the same roots. One is, however, permitted to plant tree-seeds
of diverse-kinds near each other (separated by a space of three
handbreadths), for this is not considered a planting of diverse-
kinds (whereas it would be so considered in the case of vegetables
or grains in a field). See also T. Kil. 1:10D.

[179]According to Rosh and Sens (Bert. and MR also give this
interpretation) the prohibition of B concerns only cases in which
at least one of the trees involved produces edible fruit. Two
barren trees, however, are considered to be of a single kind
and may be grafted onto one another. This interpretation is
apparently inferred from Y. 1:7 (27b), which specifically prohibits
grafts involving one tree which bears edible fruit, but says

nothing concerning two barren trees. See Feliks, *Mixed Sowing*, pp. 139-140.

[180]Feliks, *Mixed Sowing*, p. 147, n. to l. 84.

[181]*Ibid.*, pp. 149-150.

[182]Cf., however, Sirillo's version of Y. and Sens' alternate version (both cited by Feliks, *Mixed Sowing*, p. 139), which prohibits grafts involving two barren trees as well.

[183]See Zachs, I, p. 225, n. to l. 19.

[184]*Ficus sycomorus*, or the mulberry family (Moraceae; so Post, p. 514. But cf. also Zohary, p. 78, who places the genus *Ficus* in Ulmaceae, the elm family). For Latin names, see Feliks, *Mixed Sowing*, p. 151.

[185]*Ruta bracteosa*, of the rue family (Rutaceae).

[186]*Poncirus trifoliata*, of the rue family (Rutaceae). See Feliks, *Mar'ot HaMishnah*, p. 122. Feliks, *Mixed Sowing*, p. 159, n. 26, gives *Citrus trifoliata* as a synonym.

[187]*Peganum harmala*, of the caltrope family (Zygophyllaceae).

[188]*Ficus carica* of the mulberry family (Moraceae).

[189]*Urginea maritima*, of the lily family (Liliaceae). The English name is given by Feliks, *Mar'ot HaMishnah*, p. 55.

[190]*Vitis vinifera*, of the vine family (Malvaceae).

[191]*Malva silvestris*, of the mallow family (Malvaceae).

[192]See M. 1:4D-F for examples of forbidden grafts of a tree onto a tree. The presence of the examples in M. 1:4 does not account for their absence in M. 1:8, for the context of the former is entirely different. See also T. Kil. 1:10.

[193]Feliks, *Mixed Sowing*, p. 153.

[194]Cf. T. Kil. 1:10.

[195]Feliks, *Mixed Sowing*, p. 153.

[196]That is, in a feather-like arrangement.

[197]Feliks, *Mixed Sowing*, p. 157. Feliks also notes (p. 158) that Josephus (*BJ* 7. 178f) mentions the rue as being larger than a fig-tree. Feliks suggests that Josephus may be describing a rue grafted onto a tree.

[198]Feliks (*ibid.*, p. 158) rejects Löw's identification (*Die Flora der Juden*, II, p. 114) of *qydh lbnh* as calycotome (*Calycotome villosa*). Feliks claims that the calycotome is not related systematically to rue, and therefore the grafting described in M. could not take place. Feliks rejects the identification under the assumption that M. deals only with cases which are practically feasible.

[199]Feliks, *Mixed Sowing*, p. 159. Cf. also p. 160, n. 27, where Feliks discusses other plants of M. which originated in China.

[200]Feliks, *ibid.*, p. 162, disagrees with this interpretation of E. He maintains that *mqrr* should be understood in the sense of "flow" (*nwb^c*), and that E means that the plant will "flow forth," or spread rapidly.

[201]*Ibid.*, pp. 161-162.

[202]*Ibid.*, p. 162.

[203]Apparently, this is what E means in saying that squill will keep the fig-shoot cool.

[204]Cf. also Theophrastus, *Historia Plantarum* 2.5.5., (cited by Feliks, *Mixed Sowing*, p. 162, n. 35), where he says that the fig grows faster if placed in a squill bulb, and 7.13.4, where he describes how cuttings strike root faster if placed in squill.

[205]Feliks, *Mixed Sowing*, p. 162, bases this assumption on Y., although he does not explain his inference. Y. 1:8 (27b) discusses why it is necessary to state F-G, which appears to describe a simple case of diverse-kinds of the vineyard, rather than a type of graft. Yosé answers that F-G speaks of a case where the two plants unite at a depth of three handbreadths (for the earth below this depth is not considered part of the vineyard; cf. Feliks, *ibid.*, p. 152, n. to l. 26), and where the plants are six handbreadths apart. Feliks apparently assumes that since the plants are united at that depth, one is not speaking of a vine-shoot which is cut off (which could not be grafted under ground), but one which is still attached to the vine.

[206]Feliks, *Mixed Sowing*, pp. 163-164. See especially the illustrations on p. 163.

[207]See n. 205 above. Sens differs from Sirillo in requiring that the vine and the watermelon plant also be separated by three handbreadths above ground (reading three for six in Y. 1:8). Sirillo's edition of Y. apparently lacked this additional requirement (Feliks, *Mixed Sowing*, p. 166).

[208]Feliks, *Mixed Sowing*, pp. 163-164.

[209]*Ibid.*, p. 164.

[210]This interpretation forces Feliks to re-interpret Yosé's saying in Y. that one deepens the roots below three handbreadths. According to Feliks, Yosé refers to digging around the vine or the watermelon and cutting all roots which are above three hand-breadths deep. This is done so that the other roots will grow deeper. According to this view, then, Yosé says that if its shorter roots are cut, the watermelon is not actually planted in a vineyard (as the vineyard does not extend below three hand-breadths) and does not fall under the prohibition of diverse-kinds of the vineyard.

[211]Feliks, *Mixed Sowing*, p. 165, claims that the preposition *ltwkw* in G must refer to the watermelon, since it has a masculine antecedent, and a vine (*gpn* or *zmwrh*) is always referred to in the feminine. Several mss. however, do read *ltwkh*, which has a feminine antecedent (cf. Mss. B, Cn, O).

[212]*Mixed Sowing*, p. 167.

[213]*Punica granatum*, of the loosestrife family (Lytharieae).

[214]Following Lieberman, *TK*, II, p. 601, on ll. 28-29.

[215]*Phoenix dactyfera*, of the palm family (Palmae).

[216]*Olea europea*, of the olive family (Oleaceae).

[217]Feliks, *Mixed Sowing*, p. 154.

[218]*Ibid.*

[219]Feliks, *ibid.*, p. 151, n. to l. 10, notes that B refers to a vine-shoot which is either attached to the vine or cut off from it. He does not, however, give any reasons for his comment.

[220]That is, the difference between *tibla* (*qal* imperfect) and *tibāla* (*niph^cal* imperfect).

[221]Feliks, *Mixed Sowing*, p. 151, n. to l. 12, notes that the tube is made from either a reed or clay.

[222]*TK*, II, p. 601, on ll. 28-29.

[223]*Ibid.*, p. 601, on l. 29.

[224]Immanuel Löw, *Die Flora der Juden*, II, p. 324 (not 234 as cited in Feliks, p. 155, n. 11). We follow the interpretation of Feliks, p. 155. Löw maintains that T. cannot refer to a *Block* of the palm tree which has taken root, for the graft of an olive-shoot onto it would not be successful. Rather, he says that *rkb* refers to a trunk of a palm tree which lies on the ground. Löw cites Pliny (*Historia Naturalis*, 13.8.36), who records that in Assyria they used to lay a palm tree on the ground so that its shoots would strike root in the ground (although shrubs, rather than trees, would result, so that the cutting of the new plants would have to be transplanted). Löw's interpretation presents difficulties, however, for it is not clear why the olive graft should succeed in this case and not in the previous one, where the palm tree is rooted in the ground.

[225]*Mixed Sowing*, p. 156.

[226]*Ibid.*, pp. 156-157.

[227]*Cuscuta sp.*, of the convolvulus family (Convolvulaceae). For Latin names, see Feliks, *Mixed Sowing*, pp. 144-145.

[228]*Alhagi maurorum*, of the pea family (Papilionaceae).

[229]*Amaranthus retroflexus*, of the amaranth family (Amarantaceae

[230]Feliks, *Mixed Sowing*, pp. 145-146.

[231]*Ibid.*, p. 146. Feliks also refers to Pliny (*Historia Naturalis*, 13.46.129) who says that a species of dodder is used in making spiced wine.

[232]*Ibid.*

[233]*Ibid.*, pp. 108-109.

[234]*Calycotome villosa*, of the pulse family (Leguminosae).

[235]D-E may attest M. 1:7D to Yavneh, if we assume that Judah b. 'Agra is a Yavnean. In *Mekilta de Rabbi Ishmael*, ^cAmalek 4 (ed. Lauterbach, II, p. 180, ll. 14-19), Judah of Kefar ^cAkko asks a question of Gamaliel. If the attribution to Gamaliel is

reliable, then Judah b. 'Agra is a Yavnean. However, it is possible that Gamaliel should be Simeon b. Gamaliel, and in that case Judah b. 'Agra would be an Ushan. The evidence, therefore, that Judah b. 'Agra is a Yavnean is not conclusive, and it is only possible that he attests M. 1:7D to Yavneh.

[236]Lieberman, *TK*, II, p. 602, on l. 32, identifies the *'g'* with the *hgyn* of T. 3:15, which is explicitly called a tree.

[237]Feliks, *Mixed Sowing*, pp. 147-148.

[238]*Ibid.*, p. 150.

[239]Cf. Feliks, *Mixed Sowing*, p. 152, n. to l. 28.

[240]Actually, T. 1:19 differs from the other pericopae in both its opening and its apodosis. T. 1:13 opens with a singular participle while the others begin with *'yn* + plural participle. T. 1:13 then closes with *hyyb*, which the other pericopae do not need, since they already have *'yn* in the opening clause. Rather, the other pericopae close with *mpny š* + the appropriate category of M. 1:7. T. 1:13 is then similar to the other pericopae only in its structural outlines, but otherwise it differs significantly.

[241]*Mixed Sowing*, p. 167.

[242]Cf. Theophrastus, *Historia Plantarum*, 1.7.3 and 8.11.8 (cited by Lieberman, *TK*, II, p. 602, on l. 34, and Feliks, *Mixed Sowing*, p. 167, n. 58). Cf. also Pliny, *Historia Naturalis*, 18.36.133-136 (cited by Lieberman, *TK*, II, p. 602, on l. 33).

[243]*TK*, II, p. 602, on l. 34.

[244]For a list of Geniza fragments of the pericope, cf. Zachs, I, p. 227f.

[245]*Ibid.*, p. 227, n. 61. Cf. also MS.

[246]Even according to the alternate reading of D (*nwṭlyn* for *nyṭlyn*) the subject of D is still not that of A, for the verb of D is in the plural rather than in the singular.

[247]Most of the commentaries take the *w* in A to mean "or." The one exception is Bert., who takes *w* to mean "and," maintaining that A concerns turnips and radishes which are buried together. It is not clear, however, what the point of M. would be in such a case (it is not even clear whether turnips and radishes are considered diverse-kinds with one another, although one might argue from M. 1:3A and M. 1:5A that they are). We therefore follow the view of the majority of commentaries and read *w* as "or."

[248]The sense of A implies simply that one may bury even a single turnip or radish under a vine (Rabad to Maim., *Code*, *Diverse-Kinds* 2:11; cf. the reading of B. Erub. 77a-b; "a turnip or a radish"). Several commentaries, however, following Y. Kil. 1:9(27b), maintain that the turnips or radishes must be buried in bunches (Sens, Maim., *Code*, *Diverse-Kinds* 2:11, TYY), for in this way the owner indicates that he intends only to bury the vegetables, and not to plant them. Sens and TYY, in fact, maintain that B applies only to D, so that growing the vegetables in bunches is the only means of avoiding the appearance of diverse-kinds. This interpretation, then, agrees with Rabad that the owner must avoid even the appearance of transgressing the laws of C, but disagrees as to how this goal is to be achieved. Compare the views of GRA and MR, though, who maintain that all vegetables

(or at least turnips and radishes) are planted in bunches, so
that Y. does not wish to make a particular point in mentioning
this fact.

[249]*Mixed Sowing*, p. 169.

[250]Cited by Feliks, *ibid.*, p. 170. Cf. B. M. Lewin, ed.,
Otzar HaGᵉonim (Haifa: 1930), II, part 2, p. 22.

[251]*Mixed Sowing*, p. 170.

[252]Cf. also the explanation of TYY, which relates C(1) to
T. Kil. 1:15's rule that one may plant seeds of vegetables or
grains near tree-seeds, but not near a vine.

[253]On B. Erub. 77b, ş.v. *'ynw ḥwšš*.

[254]*Beth HaBeḥirah on the Talmudical Treatise Shabbath*, ed.
by Isaak S. Lange (Jerusalem: 1971), p. 185 (on B. Shab. 50b).

[255]We note, of course, that the radishes or turnips must
presumably still be tithed after they are first harvested and
before they are buried.

[256]Maimonides derives this ruling from an exegesis of Lv.
27:30, which reads: *All the tithe of the land, whether of the
seed of the land or of the fruit of the trees, is the Lord's;
it is holy to the Lord*. The phrase *of the seed of the land* is
taken to include only those things which are planted, and to
exclude those which are not.

[257]The commentaries actually give three different cases
in which the after-growth could be obligated for tithes. Rashi
(B. Erub. 77b, s.v. *wl' mšwm mᶜśr*), TYY, and Sirillo (cited by
Feliks, *Mixed Sowing*, p. 173), all say that the case concerns
an after-growth which may be liable for first tithe. Sens con-
structs the case differently, stating the vegetables are planted
in the second year of the seven-year cycle, and therefore are
liable for second tithe. They are then buried in the third year,
during which time they produce after-growths. According to Sens
the point of C(3) is that while one is obligated to give second
tithe, one need not give poorman's tithe (which would be given
in the third year) for the after-growths. Similarly, R. Tam
(cited by Feliks, *Mixed Sowing*, p. 173) maintains that vegetables
are planted in the third year, and therefore are liable for poorman's tithe. They are then buried in the fourth year and produce
after-growths. The point of C(3), accordingly, is that the
after-growths need not be redeemed in the fourth year as second
tithe.

[258]Cf. also the explanation of Hai Gaon (B. M. Lewin, ed.,
Otzar HaGᵉonim, v. II, part 2, p. 22), who says that what B means
is that the top of the actual plant is exposed, as this is not
the way in which vegetables are usually planted. Cf. also the
explanation of the reading *hᶜlywn* given by MS.

[259]We note that Maimonides requires one to bury the vegetables
in bunches in addition to exposing the leaves, while Rabad believes
that it is sufficient to expose the leaves in order to avoid the
appearance of diverse-kinds.

[260]*Mixed Sowing*, p. 170. See also Sens, who rejects a
similar interpretation.

[261]On B. Erub. 77b, s.v. *mqşt ᶜlyw mgwlyn*.

262
      T. Shab. 16(17):10 (cited in Y. Kil. 1:9 (27b)), which
presents a similar case of one who is permitted to remove a fig
from straw or cake from coals, provided that the fig or the cake
is partially exposed. The point again is that the straw or the
coals may be moved indirectly. Maimonides (*Code, Sabbath* 24:14-15)
explains this law as follows:

      If two articles are situated side by side,
      or one on top of the other, or one inside the other,
      in such a way that whenever one is moved the other
      is moved also, and one of these articles may not be
      moved while the other may, the rule is as follows:
      If one needs the article which may be moved, he may
      move it, even though the forbidden article is moved
      together with it. But if one needs the forbidden
      article, he may not move it by moving the permitted
      article.

      Thus one may insert a spindle or a whorl into
      a fig stored in straw, or into a cake baked over coals,
      and lift it out, even though the straw or the coals
      will be stirred up on the Sabbath at the moment of
      lifting. Similarly, if turnips or radishes are
      stored in soil with some of the leaves showing, they
      may be lifted out by the leaves on the Sabbath, even
      though the soil will be shaken off in the process. . .
                              (Trans. S. Gandz and H. Klein)

263 This interpretation reads E-F in the light of G. E-F
could be taken to mean simply that one who sows wheat and barley
together is liable on account of diverse-kinds. Such a statement,
however, would be trivial. We therefore understand E-F as it
appears in context.

264 The commentaries compare Judah's understanding of *śdh* with
the exegesis of *krm* which lies behind Josiah's statement (Y. Kil.
8:1) that "One is not liable [for sowing diverse-kinds in a
vineyard] until he sows two kinds in the vineyard." The relevant
verse, Dt. 22:9, states *You shall not sow your vineyard with
diverse-kinds.* Just as Josiah understands "vineyard" to refer
to a vineyard which has already been planted (i.e., already in
existence), so does Judah take "field" to mean a field which
has already been sown.

265 Following *TK*, II, p. 603, on l. 36.

266 See Abraham Eben-Shoshan, *HaMilon HaHadash* (Jerusalem:
Kiryat-Sefer, 1969), v. 2, p. 757, s.v. *ḥylt*. Eben-Shoshan
cites B. Sot. 49b as his source for understanding *ḥylt* to mean
"rushes."

267 *TZ*, p. 205, on l. 37.

268 Cf. Hudson T. Hartmann and Dale E. Kester, *Plant Propagation: Principles and Practices*, Second ed. (Englewood Cliffs:
Prentice-Hall, 1968), p. 135.

269 We differ from the view of HD only in understanding *ḥylt*
to refer to rushes, not, as HD says, to sandy soil (as derived
from *ḥwl*).

270 Cf. Y. Kil. 1:9 (27b), where it is said that Resh Laqish,
who holds a stringent position with regard to areas which may be
sown, would agree that there is no liability for sowing diverse-kinds

over water or rocks, among other places.

271In *TK*, II, pp. 602-603, on ll. 35-36, Lieberman offers a completely different interpretation of T. According to Lieberman the point of T. is that one is liable for sowing diverse-kinds only if the act of sowing immediately results in the growth of the seeds. In A-C seeds which readily germinate are sown over swamps or rushes. These areas contain a great deal of water, so that upon being sown, the seeds promptly stick together and begin to grow. The sower is therefore liable. In D-E, on the other hand, the same seeds are sown over a rock or a water-channel. Now the seeds cannot stick together until either rain falls (in the case of the rock) or water starts to flow through the water-channel. Since growth does not occur instantly after sowing, there is no liability. Finally, F-G describes a case where the seeds are dormant. Even though they are sown over swamps or rushes where they immediately become attached to one another, these seeds do not germinate at all. Therefore, in this case as well, the sower is not liable (Lieberman's reference to seeds sticking together is apparently based on a passage in B. Zeb. 94b, which speaks of flax-seeds sticking to each other in water [following Rashi]).

According to Feliks (*Plant World of the Bible* [Heb.] [Tel Aviv: Masada, 1957], p. 281), they used to sow flax above the ground, and then the seeds would become attached to the ground by rain. However, Lieberman speaks of the seeds sticking to each other, and not to the ground. Furthermore, it is not clear whether other grains besides flax grow in the same way (although B. Zeb. 94a does imply that both wheat and barley may also be sown in water). A study has shown that some seeds can actually germinate in water, but only under special conditions (e.g., where additional oxygen is provided). Cf. Toshitaro Morinaga, "Germination of Seeds under Water," *American Journal of Botany*, 13 (1926), pp. 126-140.

272*TZ*, p. 205, on l. 37.

273Lieberman (*TK*, II, p. 604, on ll. 38-39) cites this source as Y. 1:5.

274Cf. C. Primus, *cAqiva's Contribution to the Law, I, Zeracim* (Leiden: E. J. Brill, 1977), p. 35. Primus also notes that this position is consistent with that taken by cAqiva at M. 5:7, where he states that one must actually destroy diverse-kinds growing in his field.

275According to T. Mak. 5(4):10, however, each apodosis has a different legal significance. T. states that one who sustains diverse-kinds of the vineyard (Vienna, first printed ed. omit "vineyard") transgresses a negative commandment, but does not receive stripes. T. then states a general rule that one receives stripes only when he actually performs an act. For attempts to harmonize T. Mak., T. Kil., and B., see Lieberman, *TK*, II, p. 603, on l. 38. Cf. also Sifré Dt. 230a (ed. Finkelstein, p. 263; see below p. 258) where mss. also give the same two different apodoses (cited by Lieberman, *TK*, II, pp. 603, n. 41).

276Primus, p. 36, notes that T. and B. Mak. 21b are interested in different aspects of the rule: "The *baraita*-editor shifts the focus of the pericope away from the issue of intention. Instead he emphasizes the punishment for the violation of biblical law, a separate issue." Primus goes on to say that this shift is made clear by the changing of the apodoses in the pericope.

[277]The reason for this exemption may be that trees generally are clearly recognizable when planted next to grain or vegetables, so that they would not appear to grow as diverse-kinds when sown with the latter. Similarly, trees which are planted together need room in which to grow, so that different kinds of trees appear to be distinct from one another even when planted in the same field. It is necessary to point out, however, that a tree may not always be distinct from other types of plants (as in the case of the vine), so that the validity of the above explanation rests on the question of such a definition. Cf. S. Lieberman, "The Natural Science of the Rabbis," in *Hellenism in Jewish Palestine* (New York: The Jewish Theological Seminary of America, 1950), pp. 180ff.

[278]Cited by Lieberman, *TK*, II, pp. 603ff, on 11. 38-39.

CHAPTER TWO

[1]For the list of mss., see Zachs, I, p. 229, on 1. 1, and Y. N. Epstein, *Introduction to the Text of the Mishnah* [Heb.]. Second edition (1948; Jerusalem: Magnes Press, 1964), p. 78.

[2]For the particular Geniza fragments, see Zachs, *ibid.*

[3]According to Zachs, I, p. 229, n. 4, this reading is due to a copyist's error.

[4]Lieberman (*TK*, II, p. 605, n. 49) notes that the verb "falls" has the sense of "sown in a known area." Cf. also Feliks, *Agriculture in Palestine in the Period of the Mishna and Talmud* [Heb.] (Jerusalem: Magnes Press, 1963), p. 157.

[5]*Linum usitatissimum*, of the flax family (Linae). See Feliks, *Mixed Sowing*, p. 198.

[6]A *se'ah* (= 0.565 l.) consists of six *qabs* (one *qab* = 1.427 l.), so that a quarter-*qab* (= 356.896 cc.) is one twenty-fourth of a *se'ah*.

[7]Feliks, *Mixed Sowing*, pp. 194-195. Feliks adds that rice, sorghum and millet were also considered grains, except that they were sown at a rate lower than that of the others. For this reason, Feliks suggests that M. does not refer to these three grains when it speaks of a mixture of grain and pulse (for then the rate of the former would not correspond to that of the latter).

[8]*Ibid.*

[9]A *bet se'ah* is an area of fifty by fifty *amot*, or 784 square metres (Feliks, p. 186). MR reasons as follows: One twenty-fourth of the volume sown in a *bet se'ah* prohibits the sowing of a *se'ah* (see M. 2:2H+J). According to A a quarter-*qab* prohibits the sowing of a *se'ah*. Therefore one twenty-fourth of the volume sown in a *bet se'ah* equals a quarter-*qab* and the volume sown in a *bet se'ah* then equals one *se'ah*.

[10]*TK*, II, p. 605, on 1. 41.

[11]Cf. M. Ter. 2:1, M. Shab. 1:3, 10:4, M. Naz. 7:3, M. B.M. 4:11, and M. B.B. 2:3.

[12]While this interpretation gives an unusual sense to the word "combine" we shall see below that, in the case of J, it is the only possible interpretation of the word. J says that flax combines at a certain measure, and since flax only refers to one kind of seeds, "combines" must have the sense of "prohibits." The word may then have the same meaning here.

[13]If F-H is read as a unitary text, then, according to this interpretation of H, F-G may be read as glossing E, and not A-B.

[14]Y. cites a *baraita* which says that garden-seeds are sown at the rate of one or 1½ *qabs* per *bet se'ah*. Garden-seeds would then prohibit the sowing of a *se'ah* at one twenty-fourth or one-sixteenth of a *qab*.

[15]Feliks, *Mixed Sowing*, p. 197, on l. 31. Cf. also TYY.

[16]According to Y. flax is sown at three times the rate of wheat, so that its rate is presumably three *se'ahs* per *bet se'ah* (cf. also Bert.). Flax then prohibits the sowing of a *se'ah* at three-quarters of a *qab*. Following T. Kil. 1:16a, though, Feliks (*Mixed Sowing*, p. 201) points out that wheat may have been sown at three or four *qabs* per *bet se'ah*, and that it may have prohibited the sowing of a *se'ah* at three-eighths or one-half of a *qab*. Either way, though, it takes more than a quarter-*qab* of flax-seeds to prohibit the sowing of a *se'ah*.

[17]Alternatively, Lieberman (*TK*, II, p. 605, on l. 41), following Y.,understands T. as extending the law of M. 2:1A to apply to smaller seeds of pulse which are sown at relatively low rates (three or four *qabs* per *bet se'ah* as opposed to a *se'ah* per *bet se'ah*). T. then says that a quarter-*qab* of seeds which are sown at three or four *qabs* per *bet se'ah* also prohibits the sowing of a *se'ah*. This is so even though in this case a quarter-*qab* is one-twelfth of the volume sown in a *bet se'ah*, and not one twenty-fourth (cf. M. 2:2H). That is, the law of M. 2:1A applies to these seeds, even though this means that it takes double the usual volume to prohibit the sowing of a *se'ah*.

[18]*Mixed Sowing*, p. 196, on l. 22.

[19]Alternatively, Lieberman (*TK*, II, p. 605, on l. 42) understands *bnwpl lmynw* in the sense of *bnwpl bmynw* ("that which falls in its own kind"). He therefore says that D describes the case of garden-seeds which are mixed with another kind of seeds "of the same family," i.e., seeds which are sown at the same rate.

[20]Rosh, TYY, and Feliks (*Mixed Sowing*, p. 202, on l. 2) explain that *ttly^c* is related to *twl^c t* ("worm"), for the radicles resemble small worms.

[21]Following Feliks, *ibid.*, p. 202 on l. 3.

[22]See Zachs, I, p. 231, on l. 11.

[23]Following Sens, Bert., TYY, and Feliks, *Mixed Sowing*, p. 202, on l. 5. Alternatively, Maim., *Comm.* and MS maintain that the furrows are dug before the rainfall.

[24]It is clear that one may not sow the barley with the intention of later destroying the wheat. For in that case one would be sowing the barley without having performed any act to indicate this intention. He thus would actually be sowing diverse-kinds (cf. Feliks, *Mixed Sowing*, p. 206).

[25]We may compare M. to Pliny's description of the method of "plowing in" (*Historia Naturalis*, 18.49.182-183):

> We will not omit one additional method of ploughing that has been devised in Italy north of the Po owing to damage caused by war. When the Salussi were devastating the farms lying below the Alps they made an attempt to destroy the crops of panic and millet that were just appearing above the ground: but after Nature proved contemptuous of their efforts, they ploughed in the crops: these however came up in multiplied abundance, and thus taught us the practice of ploughing in -- *artrare* as it is now called, that as I believe being the form at that time in use of the word *aratrare*. This is done either when the stem is beginning to grow or when it has already shot up as far as the second or third set of leaves. Nor will be withheld a recent instance that was ascertained two years ago in Trier country: the crops having been nipped by an extremely cold winter, in March they actually sowed the fields again, and had a very bounteous harvest (trans. H. Rackham, Loeb ed., V, pp. 303-305).

In the first case which he presents, Pliny clear states that the crops which were plowed in came back up again. It appears, then, that Pliny disagrees with M.'s presupposition that a seed (or a plant, as in D-F) is destroyed by plowing in.

[26]Feliks, *Mixed Sowing*, pp. 204-206.

[27]*Ibid.*, pp. 209-210.

[28]*Ibid.*, p. 210, adds that the opinion of H assumes that the field will be plowed up again later, when the barley is covered. Therefore even the wheat in the unplowed areas will eventually be destroyed, and the entire field will be free of diverse-kinds.

[29]Sens points out that Abba Saul may be understood in two different ways. I means either that one may not leave unplowed a continuous area the size of one twenty-fourth of a *bet se'ah*, or that the sum of all the unplowed areas in the field may not total one twenty-fourth of a *bet se'ah*.

[30]According to GRA and Lieberman (*TK*, II, p. 606, on l. 44) Y.'s reading is an error.

[31]So Reuben Alcalay, *The Complete Hebrew-English Dictionary* (Tel Aviv: Massadah, 1965), p. 374, s.v. ḥryš gs.

[32]Alternatively, T. may mean that one plows the seeds deeper into the soil, so that they cannot grow under any circumstances.

[33]*TK*, II, p. 606, on ll. 45-46.

[34]Cf. John Percival, *The Wheat Plant: A Monograph* (London: Duckworth & Co., 1921), p. 24: "A normally ripened wheat grain, sown an inch or an inch and a half deep in good soil, early in September, begins to germinate in two or three days, the coleoptile [i.e., the plumule-sheath] and first leaf appearing above ground in about two days." Percival goes on to say that the first part to emerge from the seed when it bursts is the coleorhiza,

or root-sheath, which contains several of the radicles (see also p. 14).

[35]Hartmann and Kester, *Plant Propagation: Principles and Practices*, p. 118.

[36]Cf. n. 34 above and Feliks, *Agriculture*, pp. 169-170.

[37]Cf. Lieberman, *TK*, II, p. 606, on 11. 48-49, and Feliks, *Mixed Sowing*, p. 203 on 1. 11.

[38]Feliks (p. 207) points out that K allows one to sow barley after bringing the animal into the field, even though the animal will not pull the wheat out by its roots. According to Feliks T. assumes that the wheat will be uprooted anyway when the barley is covered, and the purpose of bringing the animal into the field is only to show that one does not want the wheat.

[39]Following most commentaries. See our discussion below.

[40]Feliks (*Mixed Sowing*, p. 211 on 1. 2) points out that in order to destroy the seeds one must wait for them to sprout radicles before overturning the soil (cf. M. 2:3B). Feliks accordingly maintains that this condition is understood by M. 2:4 even though it is not specifically stated. Cf. also TYT.

[41]HD explains that by sowing first, one is able to test the soil for grain or vegetables without necessarily losing his vines. If the grains or vegetables grow well, he uproots the vines. If the grains or vegetables do not grow well, then he uproots them and allows the vines to grow.

[42]MR also cites M. Shev. 1:8 and states that when the vine is less than a handbreadth it is as if it does not exist (i.e., it is no longer in the category of a tree).

[43]Ridbaz (to Maim., *Code, Diverse-Kinds* 6:6) points out that one who sows before uprooting does not perform extra work (by cutting and then uprooting), for one may uproot when he covers the newly-sown seeds.

[44]Following Lieberman, *TK*, II, p. 607, on 11. 49-50.

[45]According to Lieberman (*TK*, II, p. 607, on 1. 50) this reading is a mistake.

[46]Cited by Lieberman, *TZ*, p. 207, on 1. 50, and *TK*, II, p. 607, on 1. 50.

[47]Lieberman (*TK*, II, p. 607, on 1. 51) states that this omission is a mistake.

[48]The law that one may benefit from diverse-kinds is understandable if one maintains that T. refers to trees (and not vines), for M. 8:1 states that one may benefit from diverse-kinds of seeds (and M. perhaps may be interpreted to include tree-seeds). The same M., however, also states that one may not benefit from diverse-kinds of the vineyard. If T. refers to grapevines, as we have assumed, then T. apparently opposes M. 8:1. Alternatively, we must assume that vines which are less than a handbreadth high do not sanctify seeds which are sown in a vineyard (B. Sot. 43b, Maim., *Code, Diverse-Kinds* 6:4). Both sources are cited by Lieberman, *TK*, II, p. 607, on 11. 49-50.

[49]For Geniza fragments, see Zachs, I, p. 232, on ll. 16ff.

[50]*Carum carvi*, of the parsley family (Umbelliferae). Carum is commonly known as caraway. We follow Feliks (*Mixed Sowing*, pp. 220-221), who says that the correct reading is *qrbs* (cf. also Albeck, p. 105). For the different readings of the commentaries, see Feliks, *ibid.*, and Zachs, I, pp. 232-233, n. 27. For all Latin names, see Feliks, *ibid.*, p. 220, and M. Zohary, *A New Analytical Flora of Israel*, *passim*.

[51]*Arum palaestinum* of the arum family (Arordeae or Araceae).

[52]*Isatis tinctoria*, of the mustard family (Cruciferae).

[53]*Trigonella foenum-graecum*, of the pea family (Papilionaceae).

[54]According to Feliks (*Mixed Sowing*, pp. 221-222), arum may be propagated by means of its tubers (underground stem-like structures). The tubers separate from the main plant and grow on their own. They are able to produce fruit only after three or four years. However, it is possible that they produce fruit earlier (cf. T. Shev. 4:3, cited by Feliks, *ibid.*, p. 220) a fact which will support the alternate reading below.

[55]Carum is either biennial (S. G. Harrison, *et. al.*, *The Oxford Book of Food Plants*, p. 138) or perennial (Albert F. Hill, *Economic Botany: A Textbook of Useful Plants and Plant Products*, 2nd ed. (1937; rpt. New York: McGraw-Hill, 1952), pp. 455-456), so that it produces fruit within at least two years after it is sown.

[56]Feliks, *Mixed Sowing*, p. 226.

[57]In the case of D(2), the owner does not want the wild plants on the threshing-floor because the floor must be kept smooth (Feliks, *Mixed Sowing*, p. 218, on l. 4). In the cases of D(1) and D(3), one does not want the wild plants because they harm the growth of the cultivated ones. If this interpretation of M. is sound, however, then M. opposes the view of Pliny in regard to fenugreek. Pliny (cited by Feliks, *Mixed Sowing*, p. 232) writes (*Historia Naturalis*, 18.39.40 [trans. H. Rackham, Loeb ed., v. 5, p. 279]): ". . .the worse it [i.e., fenugreek] is treated the better it comes on -- a singular proposition that there is something which is benefitted by neglect." According to Pliny, then, wild plants do not appear to harm the growth of fenugreek, and may, in fact, even help it.

[58]Cf. Lieberman, *TK*, II, p. 607, on l. 52.

[59]Following Lieberman, *TK*, II, p. 607, on ll. 53-54.

[60]*TZ*, p. 207, on l. 54.

[61]Lieberman, *TK*, II, p. 607, on ll. 53-54.

[62]Following Feliks, *Mixed Sowing*, p. 233, on l. 2.

[63]For the etymology of *mĕr*, see Feliks, *ibid.*, p. 235.

[64]*Mixed Sowing*, p. 238.

[65]*TK*, II, p. 608, on l. 1.

[66]The reasoning and evidence for this view are presented by GRA (long commentary) as follows:

> The rule in this [matter is] that it is not necessary [to have] any distancing at all with [regard to] seeds [of diverse-kinds]. Only because of [the possibility of the appearance of] confusion is it necessary for every kind [to be sown in an area of] a size like that of a field. For example, with [regard to] grain [sown among grain of a diferent kind, each area must measure] a *bet rova^c*, and with [regard to] vegetables [sown among vegetables of a different kind, each area must measure] six handbreadths [M. 2:10]. And each according to its measure is considered a field unto itself, and then there is no [appearance of] confusion. And [this follows the law] as it is explicitly stated in M. 3:4, that "two rows of chate-melons, etc., it is permitted" [i.e., it is permitted to sow two rows of one kind next to two rows of another kind], but "one row, it is still prohibited" [i.e., it is prohibited to sow one row of one kind next to one row of another kind, for one row is not considered a field unto itself]. But [concerning] one who wishes to make a narrow bed (*myšwr*) -- that is, not [an area the size of] a *bet rova^c*, which is ten-and-a-half [*amot* squared], but he wishes only to make furrows and to sow a different kind in each furrow -- he is permitted to do so.

[67]M. does know the notion that diverse-kinds must be separated from one another (cf. M. 2:8, which says that one may flank certain objects with diverse-kinds, and M. 3:4,6, which state that one may now sow a single row of one kind next to another row of a different kind). M. does not, however, discuss the separation of diverse-kinds when the different kinds are sown in plots of land of significant size (e.g., two rows, beds, or patches [M. 2:6,9, 3:4,6]). It appears that the commentaries derive such a notion from an exegesis of M. 2:9. According to the commentaries M. 2:9 presents a dispute between Meir and the sages concerning how many patches may be laid out in a *bet se'ah*. Meir says that twenty-four patches may be laid out (with each the size of a *bet rova^c*, or one twenty-fourth of a *bet se'ah*), while the sages allow only nine patches to be arranged. The commentaries (following Y.) then maintain that the dispute concerns the separation of diverse-kinds, with Meir requiring no separation and the sages limiting the number of patches in a field in order to separate one from the next with uncultivated land. The issue of the dispute, however, may not concern the separation of diverse-kinds at all. GRA maintains that the sages only say that more than nine patches in a single field produce the appearance of diverse-kinds. It is then not likely that the requirement of separating diverse-kinds originates in M. itself.

[68]Feliks, *Mixed Sowing*, p. 236.

[69]Feliks, *ibid.*, maintains that both measures equal about two *amot*.

[70]Cf. Jacob Neusner, *The Rabbinic Traditions about the Pharisees before 70* (Leiden: E. J. Brill, 1971), II, p. 167.

[71]So Reuben Alcalay, *The Complete Hebrew-English Dictionary*, p. 2051, s.v. *tlm mpwlš*.

[72]TZ, p. 207, on l. 3.

[73]Y.'s version reads as follows:

> R. Leazar b. R. Simeon [and] Abba Yosé b. Yohanan
> of Yavneh said, "In a large [field the furrows
> are] fifty amot [in length], and in a small
> [field the furrows run] according to [i.e., for]
> the greater part (rwbh) of the field [GRA:
> according to the entire (field)]."

[74]Alternatively, three furrows are to be placed between the
rows, so that the latter are then separated from one another and
the field does not appear to be sown with diverse-kinds (HD, MB;
following the alternate interpretation of M. 2:6 [above, p. 90]).

[75]Cf. Lieberman, TK, II, p. 608, on l. 1, and Feliks,
Mixed Sowing, p. 233, on l. 6.

[76]According to Y.'s version above (n. 73), the rule of
fifty amot applies only to large fields. In small fields, however,
the furrows must extend across either most of the field or all
of it (depending on the reading of Y.).

[77]Feliks (Mixed Sowing, p. 233, on l. 8), following the
alternative interpretation, explains that a furrow which is fifty
amot long and two amot wide (see our discussion of M. 2:6)
covers about the area of a bet rova (= one hundred square amot
= one twenty-fourth of a bet se'ah). Feliks then relates T.
to M. Kil. 2:10 which says that a bet rova of one kind of grain
may be sown next to a bet rova of a grain of another kind.

[78]According to our interpretation of the pericope T. should
be interested in the width of all three furrows taken together,
rather than in the width of each individual furrow. We assume
that this is how Lieberman understands T., for he prefers the
reading of rhbn ("their width") to rhbw ("its width"). It is of
course still possible that T. refers to the width of each
individual furrow. According to the alternative interpretation
of T., D-F does refer to individual width (cf. Feliks, Mixed
Sowing, p. 233, on l. 10).

[79]Mixed Sowing, p. 236.

[80]Cf. Epstein, ITM, p. 1093; cited by Zachs, I, p. 235,
n. 49*.

[81]Following Albeck, I, p. 106.

[82]For Geniza fragments, see Zachs, I, p. 235, on l. 25.

[83]So Danby for lsmwk.

[84]Cf. Epstein, ITM, p. 1008; cited by Zachs, I, p. 236, n. 56.

[85]Cf. most commentaries to M. Kel. 18:2 and Neusner, HMLP,
II, p. 125.

[86]The relevant part of M. concerns measuring the volume of
the space covered by an arch (qmrwn) attached to a chest (šydh).
M. says that this volume is measured by a rwš twr, which is
understood to involve the description of a triangle with its apex
at the highest point of the arch (cf. Danby's comment, cited by
Neusner, ibid.).

[87]Rosh differs from the other commentaries who explain
rwš twr as a triangle in that he maintains that such a triangle
is created at the end of each furrow (as the farmer turns his
plow around). Accordingly, more than one *rwš twr* enters the
field of barley (cf. Feliks, *Mixed Sowing*, p. 243, fig. 118,
no. 1).

[88]Figure 1 is given by Joseph Qappah, *Mishnah with the
Commentary of R. Moses b. Maimon* (Jerusalem: Mossad HaRav Kook,
1963), I, p. 108. Cf. Feliks, *Mixed Sowing*, p. 243, for an
alternate interpretation of the view of Maimonides.

[89]The commentaries who maintain that a *rwš twr* is a triangle offer two etymologies for the term. Maimonides (*Comm.*),
citing Cant. 1:11, identifies *twr* as a triangular earring.
A more widely-held explanation says that *rwš twr* is equivalent
to *rwš šwr*, or "ox-head" (Rosh, MS). MS explains that the head
of an ox is broad at its horns and becomes progressively narrower
until it reaches a point. The ox-head is then shaped like a
triangle (cf. G. Dalman, *Arbeit und Sitte in Palästina* [1928-42;
rpt. Hildesheim: George Olms, 1964], II, p. 114 [cited by
Feliks, p. 243]), who identifies *twr* as the turtle-dove, whose
head may similarly come to a point). I am not certain as to
how much weight should be given to any of these etymologies.

[90]Cited by Albeck, p. 360. B. Suk. 7a presents a discussion concerning the third wall of a *sukkah* (of three walls).
Kahane and Assi suggest to Rav that the third wall should be
placed opposite the other two, *krwš twr*, or as a diagonal.

[91]Figure 2 is presented by Ribmaṣ himself in the Romm ed.

[92]It is also possible that the expression *rwš twr* is equivalent to *rwš šwrh*, "the head of a row." The term then refers
to a row of wheat which extends beyond the borders of the wheat-
field, and enters the field of barley (so Sens, following
T. 2:2; cf. figure 4 [given by Feliks, *Mixed Sowing*, p. 243,
fig. 118, no. 2]).

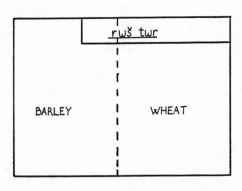

FIG. 4

[93]We note that in the alternative explanations of *rwš twr* (in which the term is considered a single row), M. is taken to refer to the last row of the field.

[94]Alternatively, Simeon may be understood as saying that one may not sow either flax or anything else at the common edge of the two fields (Maim., *Comm.*). Simeon then differs with G as to whether or not a furrow of flax will produce an appearance of diverse-kinds (MR). We do not regard this understanding of Simeon's saying as probable, for Simeon's statement that there is no difference between flax and other kinds follows G's statement that flax is permitted. If Simeon then says that it is all the same whether flax or another kind, it is reasonable to assume that he means that all kinds should be permitted. We therefore believe that the interpretation presented in the text is the more probable one.

[95]Following Feliks, *Mixed Sowing*, p. 245, ll. 34-35.

[96]So Feliks, *ibid.*, p. 241, on l. 10.

[97]Figure 5 appears in Feliks, *ibid.*, p. 250, fig. 128.

[98]Our interpretation follows that of Feliks, *ibid.*, p. 245, on l. 23, and p. 250, fig. 128. Alternatively, Lieberman (*TZ*, p. 208, on l. 11) understands *'ht hyth w'ht šᶜwrh* to mean "both wheat and barley." That is, both wheat and barley may be sown in a single furrow between the fields of the two kinds. The half of the furrow which is adjacent to the wheat-field may contain wheat, while the half next to the field of barley may be sown with barley (fig. 7). Accordingly, the point of law is that, in the case of adjacent fields containing different kinds, the two kinds may be sown together in a single furrow between the fields without producing the appearance of diverse-kinds, for each kind appears to mark the end of the field adjacent to it. This interpretation, however, does not appear to be very plausible, for it is based on a non-idiomatic translation of the phrase *'ht . . . w'ht.* This phrase usually has the sense of "either . . . or" (cf. C. Y. Kosowsky, *Thesaurus Mishnae* [Heb.] (Jerusalem, Massadah, 1956), I, pp. 57-58, s.v. *'ḥd . . . 'ḥd*). We therefore favor the interpretation given above in the text.

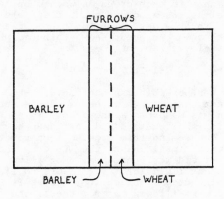

FURROWS

BARLEY   WHEAT

BARLEY ⌐   ⌐ WHEAT

FIG. 7

[99]Y. apparently attributes P-Q as well as K-M to Eliezer b. Jacob (following Feliks, *Mixed Sowing*, pp. 249-250).

[100]Following Lieberman, *TK*, II, p. 611 on ll. 12-13.

[101]In fact, since the law here apparently follows that of T. 2:1a (as explained below), it is probably that T. 2:4a does not provide the original context of the sayings.

[102]We note that if T. 2:4a is related to T. 2:1a, then the former must understand the latter according to our alternate interpretation (but cf. Erfurt's reading of P). That is, T. 2:1a is taken to concern the rows themselves, and not the separation between them. The question in both T. 2:1a and T. 2:4a then becomes how long the rows must be in order to be considered autonomous areas. This appears to be the most plausible way of explaining T. 2:4a (although, of course, both interpretations of T. 2:1a still remain viable).

[103]*Carthamus tinctorius*, of the composite family (Compositae). Cf. Feliks, *Mixed Sowing*, p. 261, n. 5.

[104]For the relevant Geniza fragments for this pericope, see Zachs, I, pp. 236-237, on ll. 29, 31.

[105]*nyr* is land which is plowed for more than one year in order to ready it for sowing in the following year (Feliks, *Mixed Sowing*, p. 269; cf. T. B.M. 9:7, cited by Feliks, *ibid.*, n. 26).

[106]Most commentaries maintain that *gpph* refers to a loose stone wall, and that a *gdr* is a wall whose stones are plastered. Feliks (*Mixed Sowing*, p. 270), however, says that a *gpph* is a plastered wall, and that a *gdr* is a loose stone wall.

[107]*Mixed Sowing*, p. 261.

[108]Cf. P. F. Knowles' statement about the cultivation of safflower in India ("Safflower-Production, Processing and Utilization," in *Economic Botany* 9 (1955), p. 274): "In these regions [i.e., Bombay, Madhya, Pradesh and Hyderabad] it is often found in association with such crops as wheat, barley, and chick peas, being sown either as a border about the field or as a few rows alternating with a larger number of those of the main crop. Its purpose in such an arrangement seems to be to provide protection from stray cattle, sheep, or goats."

[109]*Mixed Sowing*, pp. 261-262.

[110]The only other possible explanation of A-B is given by Maimonides. In fact, Maimonides gives two different and opposing interpretations in his *Commentary* and *Code*. In his *Commentary* Maimonides maintains that mustard and safflower harm the growth of grain, so that one seeing them growing next to grain will assume that the owner himself wants them to grow there (for the owner of the grain-field would certainly not allow his neighbor [who owns the adjacent field (cf. M. 2:7D-G)] to flank the grain-field with a damaging crop). Since it looks as if the owner wishes the mustard or safflower to grow there, the owner appears to be growing diverse-kinds. One may, however, flank a field of vegetables with mustard or safflower, since these plants do not harm vegetables, and those who see them will think that the neighbor has sown them.

In his *Code* (*Diverse-Kinds* 3:18) Maimonides presents a contrary interpretation. Here he says that mustard and safflower are harmful to everything but grain. If mustard or safflower were to be sown next to grain, it would appear as if the owner himself sowed them (since there is no reason why he should not have) and so the owner would appear to be sowing diverse-kinds. One may flank vegetables with mustard or safflower, though, for since the latter are harmful to the former, one may assume that the owner himself did not wish the two crops to be sown next to one another. One seeing them growing together will assume that the neighbor has sown the mustard or safflower, so that the owner of the grain-field does not appear to be sowing diverse-kinds.

In any event, we do not accept either of the interpretations given by Maimonides (and later commentaries). M. nowhere states that mustard or safflower are damaging to crops. Furthermore, there appears to be no botanical evidence which supports the claim that mustard or safflower damages one (grain or vegetables) and not the other. We therefore favor the interpretation of Feliks given above.

[111]Feliks, *Mixed Sowing*, p. 262, n. 14. Cf. also Pliny, *Historia Naturalis*, 19.54.170 (trans. H. Rackman, Loeb Classical Library ed., v. 5, p. 529):

> It [i.e., mustard] grows entirely wild, though it is improved by being transplanted; but on the other hand when it has been sown once it is scarcely possible to get the place free of it, as the seed when it falls germinates at once.

[112]Feliks, *Mixed Sowing*, p. 262.

[113]The one exception is the loose stone wall (3), which is not mentioned elsewhere in M.-T. as a divider.

[114]These are uncultivated land (1), newly broken land (2), and the road (4) (M. Peah 2:10). We note that wherever the road is mentioned as a divider in M.-T. a distinction is usually made between public and private roads, although M. does not make the distinction here.

[115]This is the road (4) (M. Bik. 1:1).

[116]These are the road (4), the fence (5) and the ditch (6) (M. Kil. 4:3, 4:7, 5:3, 6:1).

[117]These are the fence (5) (M. Erub. 1:8, 7:2), the ditch (6) (M. Erub. 7:3), the tree which shades the ground (7) (M. Erub. 10:8), and the rock (8) (M. Shab. 11:2).

[118]M. Oh. 8:2.

[119]Y. reads: "A man is permitted to sow a row of mustard or safflower in his field, provided that he makes the length of the row ten-and-one-half *amot* and *rwḥb mlw'w*." For the various interpretations of Y. (i.e., for an explanation of the phrase *rwḥb mlw'w*) see Lieberman *TK*, II, pp. 611-612, on ll. 18-19, and Feliks, *Mixed Sowing*, pp. 263-266. Cf. also our discussion of M. Kil. 3:3, and Primus, p. 31.

[120]Our translation of *mqypyn* as "edge" follows the interpretation of Epstein (*ITM*, p. 446; cited by Feliks, *Mixed Sowing*, p. 263, and Lieberman, *TK*, II, p. 611 on ll. 17-18), who suggests that the word may have the same sense as *swmkyn*, "they flank."

The term then does not indicate encirclement, but "bringing near" (cf. Jastrow, II, p. 934, s.v. *nqp*, I). Cf. Epstein and Lieberman, however, for the distinction made by Y. between *mqypyn* and *swmkyn* (the former term implies actual contact between the plants, while the latter implies some separation between them). In the case of D, however, Simeon b. Gamaliel does refer to the actual encirclement of the small beds (Lieberman, *TZ*, p. 209 on ll. 21-22, and *TK*, II, p. 612, on ll. 21-22). Feliks (p. 263) points out that the phrase used in D is *mqypyn 'wtn* ("they surround them," the phrase having a direct object), and not *mqypyn lhn* ("they bring [mustard or safflower] near to X," the phrase having an indirect object), as in A-C.

[121]Geophytes are those plants which grow underground. T. Ter. lists arum, garlic, onions and leek as geophytes. Cf. Löw, II, p. 125 (cited by Lieberman, *TK*, I, p. 444, on l. 12), and Feliks, *Mixed Sowing*, p. 262.

[122]Erfurt actually reads as follows:

> B. R. Judah says, "They edge [a field of] any
> [kind with] mustard [or] safflower."
> C. R. Simeon says, "They edge [a field of] any
> [kind with] mustard [or] safflower, except
> for [a field of] grain."

According to Lieberman, (*TK*, II, p. 612, on ll. 20-21) however, the last phrase of Simeon's saying actually belongs to Judah's statement (as the other mss. read it).

[123]*Mixed Sowing*, p. 262.

[124]*Ibid.*

[125]*Ibid.*

[126]*Mixed Sowing*, p. 278. Cf. also Sirillo (cited by Lieberman, *TK*, II, p. 612, on l. 22), who makes a similar comment.

[127]*Ibid.*

[128]Cf. M. Erub. 10:8 (cited by Lieberman, *TK*, II, p. 612, on l. 23) and T. Erub. 10:5, which state that a tree whose foliage is less than three handbreadths above the ground forms an autonomous domain, so that one may carry within it on the Sabbath. Cf. also M. Oh. 8:2, where a tree's foliage clearly forms a Tent.

[129]*TK*, II, pp. 612-613, on l. 23.

[130]*TK*, II, p. 613, on l. 24.

[131]*Mixed Sowing*, p. 272, on l. 35.

[132]Cf. Zachs, I, *ad. loc.*

[133]The commentaries present several different ways in which a *bet se'ah* may be laid out so as to contain twenty-four patches, with each patch the size of a *bet rova`*. We shall briefly summarize the two major interpretations. Maimonides explains in his *Commentary* that each patch is a square measuring 10.2 by 10.2 *amot*. The area of the entire field is then 2,496.96 square *amot* (compared with the area of a *bet se'ah*, 2,500 square *amot*). (Maimonides assumes that the *bet se'ah* is a square

measuring 50 by 50 *amot*.) Feliks (*Mixed Sowing*, p. 282),
however, cites TYT as saying that a square *bet se'ah* cannot
be divided into twenty-four square *batê rova^c*. Feliks then
shows how twenty-four square patches may be laid out (in six rows)
in a rectangular *bet se'ah*.

Alternatively, Ribmas and Sens (following T. 2:6b; for an
explanation as to how theẏ follow T., see Feliks, *Mixed Sowing*,
p. 281) maintain that each patch measures 10 *amot* and 2.5 handbreadths by 10 *amot* or 10.42 by 10 *amot*. According to this
interpretation the total area of the field is 2,500.8 square *amot*.

[134]Alternatively, the dispute between Meir and the sages
concerns not the number of mustard-patches which may be sown in a
field (D-G vs. H), but the number of patches which may be laid out
in a *bet se'ah* (A-C [also attributed to Meir] *vs*. H; this
approach, taken by most commentaries, follows Y.). Meir says
that twenty-four patches, each the size of a *bet rova^c*, may be
laid out in a *bet se'ah*, while the sages allow only nine patches
to be sown in a field of that size. According to most commentaries
(e.g., Maim. [*Comm., Code, Diverse-Kinds* 4:7], Sens, etc.),
the dispute concerns the necessity of separating diverse-kinds
from one another. Meir maintains that the patches need not be
separated from each other, even though each patch may contain
a different kind. Accordingly, the patches may cover the entire
area of the *bet se'ah*. The sages, on the other hand, require
the patches to be separated, and so limit the number of patches
to nine.

The commentaries conceive of how the sages separate the
diverse-kinds in many different ways. We present here only the
explanation of Maimonides (*Comm*.) which is illustrated in figure
8 (found in Qappah, p. 109; the units are *amot*). According
to Maimonides each patch must be separated from its neighbor by
nearly a *bet rova^c*, so that only nine square patches may be sown.
For the other interpretations of the commentaries and for diagrams
illustrating their positions, see Feliks, *Mixed Sowing*, pp. 287-
291.

FIG. 8

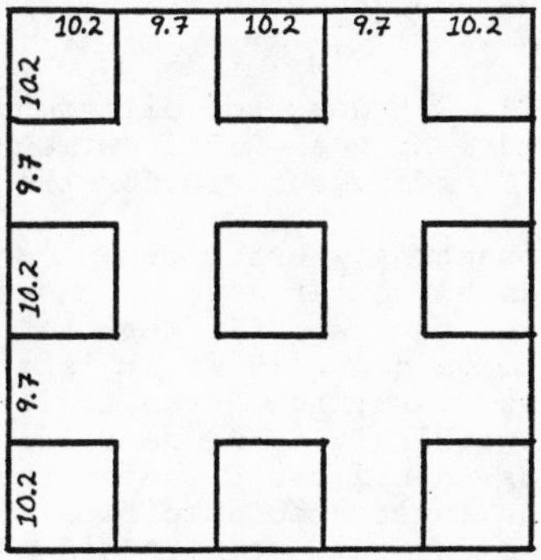

GRA presents yet another alternative interpretation of the dispute, maintaining that the latter concerns simply how many kinds may be sown in one field without producing the appearances of diverse-kinds. Meir says that twenty-four different kinds may be sown, while the sages permit only nine kinds to grow in a single field, for the presence of ten different kinds in one field would already produce the appearance of diverse-kinds.

Albeck (I, p. 361), compares the ruling of sages to M. Shev. 1:4, 6, which says that ten trees determine a field of trees. Albeck argues that the sages similarly maintain that ten patches determine a field, which in turn, because it contains different kinds, appears to be sown with diverse-kinds.

These interpretations of M. do not appear to be plausible, for they require a reconstruction of the text. In order to form a dispute between A-C and H, this approach must maintain that D-F appears in the wrong place (since it interrupts the dispute) and that A-C is to be attributed to Meir. We see no reason to read M. in this way, particularly since M. makes sense as it stands. D-H is presented in a variation of the dispute form (opinion + words of X/Y says + opinion), so that the dispute simply consists of D-G vs. H. We further argue that D-H forms a dispute because both opinions make use of similar number-sequences, as we have shown. We therefore favor the interpretation given earlier.

[135]For Geniza fragment, see Zachs, I, p. 238, on 1. 39.

[136]Neusner (*Eliezer*, I, p. 352) lists F among the traditions which cannot be reliably assigned to Eliezer b. Hyrcanus.

[137]A public road clearly cannot be located in a *bet rova^c*, for the former is sixteen *amot* wide (M. B.B. 6:7), while the latter is only ten-and-one-half *amot* wide (see T. D below). Therefore Lieberman (*TK*, II, p. 613, on l. 25) maintains that the road narrows as it enters the *bet rova^c* and widens as it leaves.

[138]Erfurt's reading agrees with the law of the reading of the first printed ed., but is formulated in order to emphasize the fact that the height of ten handbreadths distinguishes between the two classes of walls.

[139]Although M. Kil. 2:8 does not differentiate between public and private roads, M. Peah 2:1 does mention both types of roads in reference to dividing a field for the giving of *pe'ah*.

[140]M. Erub. 2:5 concerns whether or not one may carry on the Sabbath within a garden and outer area of a specified size. The garden is said to be square. Eliezer states that one is allowed to carry in the garden only if it is a perfect square. Yosé then glosses Eliezer, saying, "Even if its length is twice its width, they carry within it." Since Yosé's saying is more intelligible as a gloss to Eliezer's saying than as a gloss to T. 2:6F-G (which is not interested specifically in the fact that the *bet rova^c* is a square), we maintain that Yosé's saying belongs primarily in the context of M. Erub. 2:5.

[141]We follow Lieberman (*TK*, II, p. 614, on 1. 29) in preferring the readings of Vienna Ms. and first printed ed. to those of Erfurt and Sens.

[142]Following Lieberman, *TK*, II, pp. 614-615, on 1. 30.

[143]*TK*, II, p. 614, on l. 29.

[144]For Geniza fragment, see Zachs, I, p. 239, on l. 43.

[145]Feliks, *Mixed Sowing*, p. 70.

[146]Cf. *ibid.*, p. 308, on l. 3.

[147]Cf. T. Kil. 1:6: "It is prohibited to train [the Greek gourd] over plants."

[148]Although D reads only (without *'p*, which is standard joining-language), "The chate melon and the cowpea," and could conceivably refer to any law at all, we see no alternative but to follow the redactor and interpret it in this context.

[149]Feliks, *Mixed Sowing*, p. 310.

CHAPTER THREE

[1]M. 3:4 and M. 3:5 do not, however, comprise a major unit, for each contains a different formulary pattern in its protasis (*hnwt*^{c} [M. 3:4] *vs.* *nwt*^{c} *'dm* [M. 3:5]).

[2]For the Geniza fragment, see Zachs, I, p. 241, on l. 3.

[3]Alternatively, other commentaries maintain that all five kinds are to be sown within the bed itself. In addition, all of the kinds are said to be separated from one another by (for the most part) one-and-a-half handbreadths, so that they should not nourish one another (Sens, Maim., *Code, Diverse-Kinds* 4:9). Maimonides (*Comm.*), for example, presents two ways in which the five kinds may be sown in the garden-bed (figures 10-11 [the shaded portions are uncultivated]; from Qappah, I, pp. 110-111). The main difference between the two figures concerns whether or not the corners of the bed are sown. Sens, following Y., gives yet another figure (fig. 12; from Romm ed. of M. Zera^{c}im, in Babylonian Talmud).
For yet other interpretations of M., cf. Ribmas and MS. We do not accept these interpretations of M. because they do not follow from the plain sense of the text. M. nowhere says that the different kinds must be separated from one another, and so does not imply that the beds are to be arranged in such complex patterns. We therefore prefer the more straightforward explanation of GRA.

FIG. 10

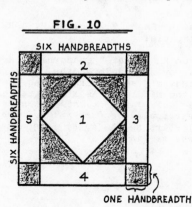

ONE HANDBREADTH

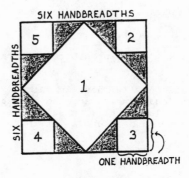

SIX HANDBREADTHS

SIX HANDBREADTHS

ONE HANDBREADTH

FIG. 11

FIG. 12

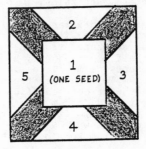

[4]We note that M. Shab. 9:2b cites M. A-B and provides it with a Scriptural basis:

> Whence, do we know that "[Concerning] a garden-bed which is six by six handbreadths, that they sow in it five [kinds of] seeds, from along the four sides and one in the middle?" As it is written, *For as the earth puts forth its blossom and like a garden causes its seeds (zrwᶜyh) to sprout* (Is. 61:11), "Its seed" (zrᶜh) is not stated, but *its seeds (zrᶜyh)*.

That is, the plural noun "its seeds" implies that more than one kind of seeds may be sown in a bed (Albeck). Cf. also B. Shab. 84b-85a for Judah's saying, which has the verse yield exactly five kinds.

[5]While it is true that an area six handbreadths square is only mentioned as an autonomous field with reference to vegetables, M. 3:2 states that only vegetables are sown in a garden-bed.

[6]Maimonides (*Comm.*) gives the following figure to illustrate M. 3:1G (fig. 14; from Qappaḥ, I, p. 111):

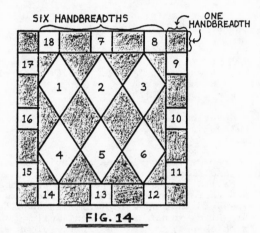

FIG. 14

[7]This interpretation reads M. 3:1 in the light of M. 3:2, which says that only vegetables are sown in garden-beds.

[8]Maimonides (*Comm.*) gives the following figure to illustrate M. C-D (fig. 16; from Qappaḥ, I, p. 111):

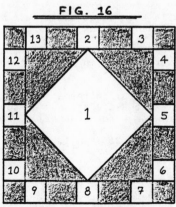

FIG. 16

EIGHT HANDBREADTHS

[9]The hypocotyl of a turnip is the swollen "root" which lies between the plant's first leaves (cotyledons) and its true root (S. G. Harrison, et al., *The Oxford Book of Food Plants*, p. 172).

[10]Cf. Zachs, I, p. 243, on l. 6.

[11]*Cicer arietinum*, of the pea family (Papilionaceae). For this identification see Löw, *Die Flora der Juden*, II, pp. 727ff., and Feliks, *Mar'ot HaMishnah*, p. 15.

[12]Cf. Lieberman, *TZ*, p. 210, on l. 32, and *TK*, II, p. 615, on l. 32.

[13]Cf. Zachs, I, pp. 243f., on l. 7.

[14]Feliks, *Agriculture*, p. 118.

[15]Cf. also Lieberman, *TK*, II, p. 616, on l. 38.

[16]*Plant World of the Bible*, p. 162.

[17]Pliny describes the different types of chick-peas as follows (*Historia Naturalis*, 18.22.124 [Loeb ed., trans. H. Rackham, v. 5, p. 265]):

> There are several varieties differing in size, colour, shape, and flavour. One resembles a ram's head and so is called 'ram's chick-pea;' of this there is a black variety and a white one. There is also the dove-pea, another name for which is Venus's pea, bright white, round, smooth and smaller than the ram's chick-pea; it is used by religious ritual in watchnight services. There is also the chickling vetch, uneven in shape and with corners like a pea. But the chick-pea with the sweetest taste is one that closely resembles the bitter vetch; the black and red varieties of this are firmer than the white.

It is possible that M.'s "smooth chick-pea" is identical with Pliny's dove-pea, while the "large chick-pea" may be the "ram's chick-pea." Cf. also Theophrastus, *Enquiry into Plants*, 8.5.1.

[18]Feliks (*Agriculture*, p. 323) suggests that the furrow of H is an irrigation-furrow (i.e., a furrow which leads water from the water-channel to the fields).

[19]We note that Y. Kil. 3:3 cites a *baraita* in which Bar Qappara opposes the law of H-I, saying, "He sows only one kind in it [i.e., the furrow or water-channel]."

[20]Cf. Lieberman, *TZ*, p. 210, on l. 32, and *TK*, p. 615, on l. 32.

[21]*Ibid.*

[22]For all of Lieberman's corrections, cf. *TZ*, p. 210, on ll. 32ff., and *TK*, II, p. 615, on ll. 33ff. Lieberman suggests (*TK*, II, p. 615, on l. 33) that Erfurt's omission of D-K may account for the transposition of apodoses. C may have originally followed J, but when D-J was dropped, C may have been attached to A-B.

[23] On sowing the cowpea for its seeds, cf. M. Shev. 2:8.

[24] Feliks, *Mixed Sowing*, pp. 71f.

[25] Cf. Zachs, I, *ad.loc.*, for Geniza fragments.

[26] Cf. also T. Kil. 2:1a, 2:4a, where an open furrow is also considered a field unto itself.

[27] G. Porton (*The Traditions of Rabbi Ishmael* [Leiden: E. J. Brill, 1976] I, p. 34) observes that the dispute of D-G is arranged so that the dimensions discussed in the unit appear in this order: length, length-width, width.

[28] Neusner (*Eliezer*, I, p. 352) lists M. Kil. 3:4 among the traditions which may not be reliably attributed to Eliezer b. Hyrcanus.

[29] Alternatively, Eliezer reasons that since the first kind appears again after the third, the different kinds are planted in a regular sequence (1-2-3-1), and there is therefore no appearance of diverse-kinds (Albeck). This interpretation is interesting, but there is no evidence in M. that the sequence of planting has anything to do with the appearance of diverse-kinds.

[30] The four plants mentioned in T. often appear together in T. Kil. (cf. T. 1:1c, 2:10). For other places in M.-T. where these plants appear as a group, see Lieberman, *TK*, II, p. 597, n. 10.

[31] For the list of mss. see Zachs, I, p. 247, on 1. 21.

[32] *Ibid.*, p. 247, n. 34.

[33] Erfurt transposes T. 2:9A with T. 2:9C-D. Cf. Lieberman, *TK*, II, p. 616, on 11. 36-37.

[34] Lieberman (*TZ*, p. 211, on 1. 42, and *TK*, II, p. 616, on 1. 42) maintains that "cowpeas" has been mistakenly inserted here from T. 2:11.

[35] Lieberman (*TZ*, p. 211, on 1. 43) understands *wblbd šl' yh'* as "provided that there be."

[36] The order in which T. joins these three rules is difficult. T. clearly does not follow the order of M., nor does it follow any order which takes account of the substance of the rules. The rules are not listed according to the order of the size of the area involved, for a garden-bed is larger than both a furrow and a hollow, and yet it follows the former and precedes the latter. The order of T. also does not follow the order of the number of different kinds which may be sown in a given area, for the sequence of numbers in A-D is three/five/four. It is perhaps possible that the original sequence was three/four/five (i.e., C-D preceded B), and C-D was then placed immediately before E-G because of their similarity in substance (e.g., both have four kinds, and F=D). Alternatively, if we follow Erfurt's reading and omit B, T. then follows both the order of M. and a three/four number sequence (or the reverse, as Erfurt transposes A and C-D). We see no reason, though, to prefer Erfurt's reading to those readings which do include B.

[37] For the list of mss. see Zachs, I, p. 247, on 1. 23.

[38]For Geniza fragment, see Zachs, *ibid.*

[39]Our translation of H follows that of Primus, p. 30.

[40]We note that A (and M. 3:7C below) describes a plausible situation, in that the two crops involved (gourds and onions/ grain) are sown in late winter, and so begin to grow before the planting-time of gourds, which is in the spring. Cf. Theophrastus, *Enquiry into Plants*, 7.1.2 (Loeb, ed., trans., Arthur Hort, v. 2, p. 61), Columella, *De Re Rustica*, 11.15 (Loeb ed., trans. E. S. Forster and Edward Heffner, v. 3, p. 139), and Pliny, *Historia Naturalis*, 19.24.69 and 19.32. 105-107 (Loeb ed., trans. H. Rackham, v. 5, pp. 467, 487f.). Cf. also Feliks, *Agriculture*, pp. 148, 153f.

[41]We assume (following [C]Aqiva) that a row of onions is equal in width to a row of gourds. Cf. Maimonides (*Comm.*), who says (following the assumption of Y.) that both types of rows measure four *amot* in width.

[42]An autonomous field, of course, need not be fully planted. Cf. T. 2:7.

[43]Fig. 17 follows the interpretation of Maimonides (*Comm.*), who maintains that the row of gourds is planted in the middle of the space formerly occupied by the two rows of onions. Cf. Kahane's statement in Y., though, which gives the various possibilities for planting the row in a space of two rows (discussed below at T. 2:12, n. 52).

[44]Alternatively, Sens, Ribmas, and Rosh maintain that the row of gourds is planted beside the space formerly occupied by the onions, which is then left uncultivated (fig. 19). Sirillo (cited by MS) points out that this interpretation is difficult, for presumably other onions adjoin the uprooted rows, and the gourds cannot be planted there. In any event, this interpretation seems to read into the text a concern for the distance between the rows of gourds (perhaps following H), and so does not follow the plain sense of the text.

FIG. 19

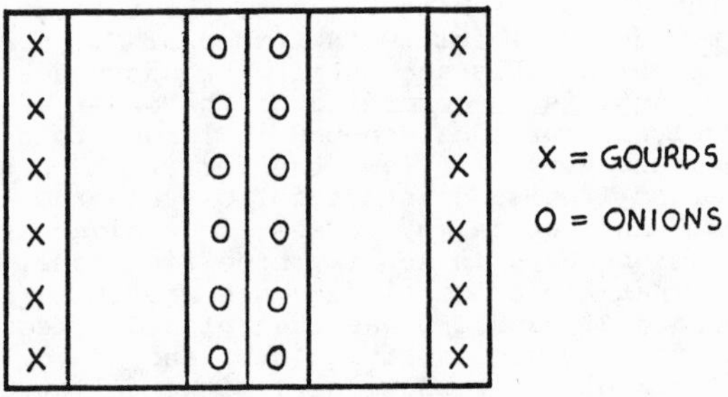

X = GOURDS

O = ONIONS

[45]Alternatively, Maimonides (*Comm.*) and others say that the issue of the dispute concerns the separation of the gourds from the onions. Ishmael maintains that a single row of gourds is planted between the two uprooted rows of onions, so that it is flanked by two *amot* of uncultivated land on each side (since the row of gourds is four *amot* wide, and it is planted in the middle of two uprooted rows of onions [= 8 *amot*]). The gourds must then be separated from the onions by two *amot*. [c]Aqiva, though, requires only a nominal separation (by a single furrow) between the two kinds, and therefore allows two rows of gourds to separate the two rows of onions (cf. figs. 17-18). This interpretation introduces into M. the consideration of separating the different kinds which adjoin one another (a consideration which Maimonides introduces throughout Chapters Two and Three), and perhaps also represents a reading of the dispute in light of sages' opinion on H. This explanation, though, does not follow the plain sense of the text, and we therefore find it less plausible than the one which we have suggested above.

[46]According to Maimonides (*Comm.*) and others the view of sages is identical with that of Ishmael, for in each case the rows of gourds are separated by twelve *amot* (fig. 20; units are *amot*). Maimonides (following Y.), reading A-H as a unitary pericope, maintains that sages differ from Ishmael only in that they do not agree that the gourds must be separated from the onions by more than a nominal distance (and in this respect they agree with [c]Aqiva; cf. especially MR for a good summary of this interpretation). We do not agree, of course, that A-H forms a unitary pericope, and that sages are therefore in dispute with Ishmael and [c]Aqiva. We therefore do not consider this interpretation to be as plausible as the one which we have presented in the text.

FIG. 20

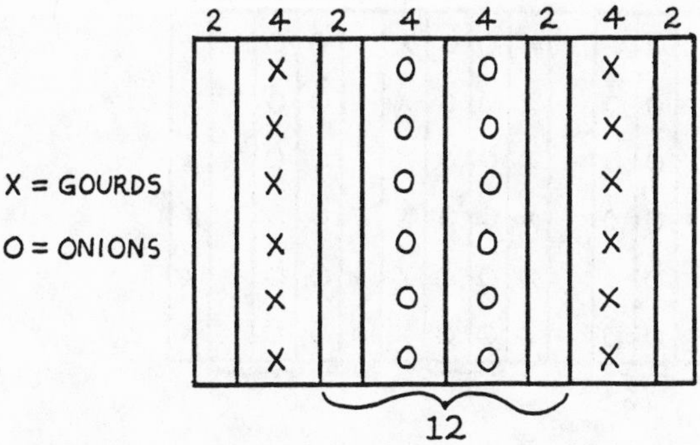

[47]Our translation follows Lieberman's understanding of *qṣr* as *tmsyt* or *šwrš* (*TK*, VIII, p. 763, on ll. 52-54; cited by Bokser, I, p. 46, n. 114).

[48]Cited by Lieberman, *TZ*, p. 211, on l. 46, and *TK*, II, p. 617, on l. 46. Lieberman originally emended the text on the basis of Sirillo's reading, but he later explicitly changes his mind and follows Vienna's reading. Cf. *TK*, VIII, p. 763, n. 32.

[49]L adds B-C in the margin. Bokser, I, p. 45, n. 109 explains that B-C may have been omitted because of a *homoioteleuton*, as "R. Ishmael said, 'Twelve,'" appears again in Y. after the citation of T.

[50]*TZ*, p. 211, on l. 47, and *TK*, II, p. 617, on l. 47.

[51]Alternatively, Y. and Sirillo have *qṣb* (or *hqwṣb*) for *qṣr*, so that A reads "The opinions of both of them are fixed," i.e., given in fixed (linear) measurements. This reading seems to be particularly appropriate to the context in which Y. cites T. Y. presents a "dispute" (cf. Bokser, I, pp. 45f) between Kahane and Samuel concerning the ways in which Ishmael's opinion in M. may be translated into linear measurements. Kahane presents three possibilities, while Samuel gives only one. T. is then cited in support of Samuel's view that the rule of Ishmael is fixed and not variable. The reading of *qṣb* thus allows T. to fit nicely into Y.'s discussion of M., and, since it makes little sense outside of the context of Y., it is possible that this reading arises out of the context of the citation.

[52]In Y. Kil. 3:6 (28d) Kahane presents three distances which could separate the rows of gourds planted according to the opinion of Ishmael. This distance may either be sixteen *amot* (if the row of gourds is planted on the outer side of the area of uprooted rows of onions; cf. fig. 24), twelve *amot* (if the gourds are planted down the middle of the area; cf. fig. 20 above), or eight *amot* (if the gourds are planted on the inner side of the area; cf. fig. 25 below) (following PM). We note that the distance of sixteen *amot*, like that of ten *amot*, does not occur exclusively in a field planted serially with gourds and onions.

FIG. 24

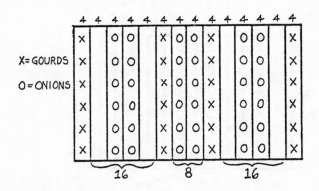

[53]*Ishmael*, I, p. 36.

[54]Kefar Pegai is located about 15 km. north of Lod. It was also known as Antipatris. The location derives its several names (πήγαι, Rosh Ha^cayin, and Arethusa) from the fact that it is situated above several springs. Cf. M. Avi-Yonah, *Historical Geography*, p. 42 (map, 129).

[55]For Geniza fragments, see Zachs, I, p. 249, on l. 31ff.

[56]For a list of mss., see Zachs, I, p. 249, on l. 31.

[57]Maimonides, *Code, Diverse-Kinds* 3:13. Cf. Maim., *Comm.*, *ad. loc.*, where it is stated that the leaves of the gourds are to be cut off (see note 60 below).

[58]Following Danby, who translates *kl* as "where," and Porton (*Ishmael*, I, pp. 36ff.), who translates *kl* as "whenever."

[59]If. M. 3:7A-B depends on M. 2:10 (as seems to be the case), then the reasons that the apodosis of B does not also read *kyrq* (and so refer to M. 2:10E) may be due to the fact that E is opposed by Eliezer/Eleazar in M. 2:10F. If B were to read *kyrq*, it could refer to either of the two rulings of M. 2:10, and the law would be ambiguous. The apodosis of B therefore had to present the ruling of M. 2:10E.

[60]Alternatively, Maimonides says in his *Commentary* that in this instance one should uproot (i.e., cut off) the leaves of the gourds from before the grain. It is more likely, however, that the antecedent of *mlpnyh* is "the gourds" rather than "the grain," so that the explanation given in the *Code* is more plausible.

[61]Although B speaks of an area of gourds (plural), a single gourd requires an area of the same size. Cf. our interpretation of T. 2:7 above.

[62]Sens, Rosh, and Bert. explain in another context (that of harmonizing B and D) that the law concerning a row of gourds is more lenient than the law regarding a single gourd. A row is clearly demarcated as an entity unto itself, and therefore requires less area of tillage than does a single gourd, which, without enough surrounding area, would appear to be planted as diverse-kinds. This line of reasoning, however, has no basis in the text, and there is no reason to assume that it is a consideration in Yosé's argument in H-I.

[63]*TZ*, p. 211, on l. 49, and *TK*, II, p. 617, on l. 49.

[64]*TZ*, p. 211 on l. 51, and *TK*, II, p. 618, on l. 51.

[65]Cited by Lieberman, *TK*, II, p. 618, on l. 51.

[66]*TZ*, p. 211, on l. 52.

[67]*TZ*, p. 211, on l. 52. The word *'hr* is clearly unnecessary in the context of J (where grain is sown among vegetables), and Lieberman maintains that it was mistakenly introduced into J from C and L.

[68]*TZ*, p. 212, on l. 54, and *TK*, II, p. 618, on l. 54.

[69]Since G clearly refers to several rows of gourds, there is no significant difference between the two readings of *śwrh* and *śdh*.

[70]*TZ*, p. 212, on l. 55, and *TK*, II, p. 618, on l. 55.

[71]According to GRA's glosses, which are printed in the back of the Romm ed. of the Babylonian Talmud, GRA reads here simply "one who." "And" (*w*), however, is cited as part of GRA's gloss by MB and Lieberman (*TZ*, p. 212, on l. 56, and *TK*, II, p. 618, on ll. 56-57).

[72]Y. reads as follows:

> B.   One who allows single moist stalks to grow
>   [for the sake of their] seed,
> C.   must clear [a space] for them [measuring]
>   a *bet rova^c*, or make for them a partition
>   ten handbreadths high.

[73]Cf. M. 2:8 for the dimension of the partition.

[74]If it is the case that T. links M. 3:7J-K to M. 3:4,
then the link is only formal (i.e., the two pericopae are similarly
formulated) and not substantive. M. 3:4 concerns planting rows
of different kinds together, while the point of T. is that its
law applies to any of the kinds (individually).

[75]Cf. M. 3:6H, where sages use *zr^c* in a general sense to
refer to that which is sown between the rows of gourds.

[76]Cf. Albeck's comment on M. 3:7J-K, where he interprets
Ishmael's saying to concern sowing grain in a field of gourds.
Albeck may follow T. in interpreting *zr^c* to mean that which is
sown for the sake of its seed, i.e. (in many cases), grain.

[77]Although it appears that GRA interprets T. as we have
explained it (cf. MB), we note that Lieberman may understand
GRA differently. Lieberman (*TZ*, p. 212, on l. 55, and *TK*, II,
pp. 618f., on ll. 56-57) seems to maintain that GRA, in adding
w'ḥd to B, sees B as part of the protasis, so that the pericope
reads as follows:

> A.   All the same are a row of chate melons, and
>   a row of gourds and a row of watermelons, and
>   a row of musk melons and a row of cowpeas,
> B.   [and] one who allows a single stalk [of any of
>   these kinds] to grow for [the sake of their] seed --
> C.   [he must allow the stalk a space measuring] a
>   *bet rova^c*, or he must make a partition [between
>   one kind and the next] ten handbreadths high and
>   [with] its width [measuring] four handbreadths.

According to this reading the point of T. is that whether one
plants single stalks or individual rows of trailing plants next
to one another, he must separate the different kinds, by either
the distance of a *bet rova^c* (following Y.) or a partition. T.
then supplements M. 3:4 by saying that individual stalks of
different kinds of trailing plants, as well as individual rows,
are considered diverse-kinds with one another. This interpretation of T., however, is difficult, for it does not allow any
significance to the fact that the single stalk is planted for the
sake of its seed. We therefore maintain that the explanation
given above in the text is the more plausible one.

[78]*TK*, II, p. 619, on l. 58.

[79]Alternatively, Lieberman (*ibid.*), following the readings
of Erfurt and Vienna Mss., suggests that B refers to the gentile
of A, and not to the Israelite. According to this interpretation
the gentile is presumed to be liable for the grafting of trees
of diverse-kinds (cf. Eliezer's ruling, Y. Kil. 1:7 (27b),
B. Sanh. 56b; cf. Lieberman for sources of later discussions
of this issue). The point of T., then, is that one may reproduce
the product of a gentile's graft, even though the gentile is
prohibited from performing such a graft. If this is the point of
T., though, it is not clear why the pericope chose to speak of a

graft performed by a gentile, and not one made by an Israelite.
We thus prefer our first interpretation of T., which takes
account of the fact that it is the gentile and not the Israelite
who performs the graft.

[80]*TZ*, p. 212, on l. 62, and *TK*, II, p. 620, on l. 62.

[81]*TZ*, p. 212, on l. 63, and *TK*, II, p. 620, on ll. 62-63,
and on l. 63.

[82]Lieberman (*TK*, II, p. 620, on l. 62) suggests that the
first printed ed. has corrected T. on the basis of B. A.Z. 63b.

[83]*TZ*, p. 212, on l. 62, and *TK*, II, p. 620, on l. 62-63.

[84]*TZ*, p. 212, on l. 63, and *TK*, II, p. 620, on l. 63.

[85]This point seems to be somewhat obvious, and Lieberman
(*TK*, II, p. 620, on l. 62) suggests that D appears only because
of what follows (either E or G [Lieberman is not clear on this
point]).

[86]Lieberman (*ibid.*) notes that E-F contradicts A-C, for
the latter implies that diverse-kinds which grow in an Israelite's
field should not be uprooted. The opposition between A-C and
D-F may account for the juxtaposition of the two pericopae, which
present entirely separate rules.

[87]Alternatively, B. A.Z. 63b has D-F refer to a gentile's
field. According to this reading the point of D-F is that one
may not hoe diverse-kinds with a gentile, but one may uproot
them for him (for pay), even though one then wishes the diverse-
kinds to continue growing until he has a chance to uproot them.
This reading, however, is less plausible than that given by T.,
for it is not clear how diverse-kinds become an impropriety
(*tplḥ*) in the field of a gentile.

[88]According to Lieberman (*TK*, II, p. 621, on l. 64) these
two cities are located to the north, on the eastern side of
the Jordan River.

[89]*TZ*, p. 212, on l. 64. T. Ah. states that "surrounded
cities" are exempt from the laws of tithes and the seventh-year,
but are not considered as part of the "land of the peoples" for
purposes of cleanness.

[90]Similarly, Lieberman (*TK*, II, p. 620, on l. 63) explains
that G follows the principle that "a gentile does not acquire
possession of real estate in the land of Israel (attributed
to Meir, Y. Kil. 7:3)." That it, it is prohibited to grow diverse-
kinds with a gentile because the latter does not actually own
his field. One who would grow diverse-kinds for a gentile, would,
in effect grow them for an Israelite (the true owner of the field),
and such an act is prohibited (D).

[91]Lieberman (*TZ*, p. 212, on ll. 64-65, and *TK*, II, p. 621,
on ll. 64-65) following Y. Orl. 1:9 and B. Qid. 39a, says that
both M. Qid. 1:9 and T. Kil. 2:16J apply only to diverse-kinds of
the vineyard but not to diverse-kinds of seeds. Neither M. Qid.
1:9 nor T. Kil. 2:16J, however, offers any support to this interpretation. Cf. also Y. Orl. 1:9, where Samuel says that diverse-
kinds of seeds are permitted outside of the land of Israel,
while Yoḥanan prohibits them.

CHAPTER FOUR

[1]We note that the apodosis of the first sentence in each set is phrased in the singular (*yby'*), while that of the second opens in the plural (*nwtnyn*). The second apodosis, however, shifts to the singular (*zwr*ᶜ), which suggests that *nwtnyn lh* ᶜ*bwdth* may be an idiomatic phrase which always appears in the plural (cf. M. Kil. 3:7, 5:4, 6:1, 6:2, and 6:7).

[2]The term "bald spot of the vineyard" is actually a metaphor, for a bald spot (*qrḥt*) literally refers to a bare, hairless area of a head.

[3]For various etymologies of *mḥwl*, see Maim., *Comm.* (from *mḥl* "to leave, abandon"). Sens (from *mḥwl*, "dance" i.e., the area of the vineyard set aside for dancing) and Meiri to B. Erub. 93a (cited by Lieberman, *TK*, II, p. 622, on l. 3) (from *ḥlwl*, "empty space").

[4]If we follow the commentaries (e.g., Maim., *Comm.*, Sens, etc., all following M. 6:1) and assume the area of tillage of a vineyard to be four *amot*, then in a bald spot either sixteen (House of Shammai; fig. 26) or eight (House of Hillel; fig. 27) *amot* square are sown. Similarly, in an outer space either twelve (House of Shammai; fig. 28) or eight (House of Hillel; fig. 29) *amot* wide may be sown.

FIG. 26

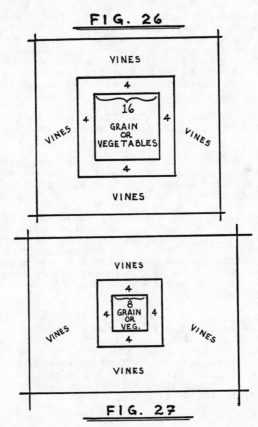

FIG. 27

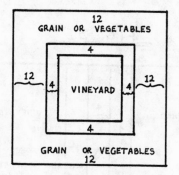

FIG. 28

FIG. 29

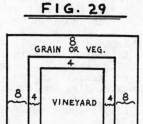

[5]If we apply the measurements of the Houses to Judah's conception of an outer space, we find that an area either eight (House of Shammai; fig. 30) or four (House of Hillel; fig. 31) *amot* wide may be sown.

FIG. 30

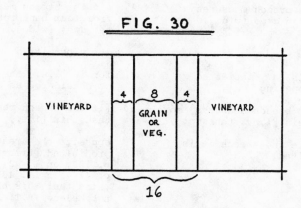

FIG. 31

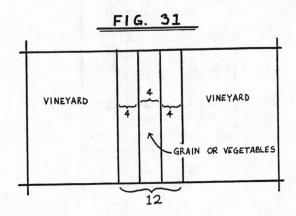

[6]Lieberman, (*TK*, II, p. 621, on ll. 1-2) maintains that through a scribal error "five," represented by the letter *h*, was incorrectly copied as "four and (*dw*)."

[7]Alternatively, Lieberman (*TZ*, p. 213, on ll. 3-4, and *TK*, II, p. 622, on ll. 3-4), following HD, maintains that H-I abbreviates M. and should actually read: "And sages say (The area between the vineyard and the fence. If there are not there twelve *amot*, etc.'" Such a reading would incorporate into the opinion of sages the definition of an outer space of M. 4:2K-L, and so would create an actual dispute between Judah and sages. There is, however, no reason to suppose that the definition of the outer space is implicitly part of sages opinion, and in my view it is more likely that T. reads one rule in light of another, and does not simply repeat the dispute of M.

[8]*TZ*, p. 213, critical apparatus to l. 8.

[9]T. Erub. 6(9):13-14, compared with M. Kil. 4:4E-N, reads as follows:

M. Kil. 4:4	T. Erub. 6(9):13-14
1. And a fence which was breached --	1. The wall of a courtyard which was breached --
2. [if the breach measures] up to ten *amot* [wide],	2. [if the breach measures] from four handbreadths to ten *amot* [wide],
3. ---	3. it is permitted,
4. lo, this is considered as an opening.	4. for it [i.e., the breach] is considered as an opening
5. [if the breach measures] more than this [i.e., ten *amot*],	5. [if the breach measures] more than this [i.e., ten *amot*],
6. opposite the breach it is prohibited.	6. opposite the breach it is prohibited [Lieberman (*TM*, p. 122, on l. 42, *TK*, III, p. 426, on ll. 43-44) maintains that this phrase does not belong in T. Erub. and

M. Kil. 4:4	T. Erub. 6(9):13-14
	has been mistakenly inserted here from M. Kil. 4:4].
7. [If] many breaches were breached in it [i.e., the fence] --	7. [If] many breaches were breached in it [i.e., the wall] --
8. if the [combined measure of the parts of the fence which remain] standing exceeds the [combined measure of those parts which were] breached,	8. if the [combined measure of the parts of the wall which remain] standing exceeds the [combined measure of those parts which were] breached,
9. it is permitted;	9. it is permitted;
10. and if the [combined measure of those parts which were] breached exceeds the [combined measure of the parts which remain] standing,	10. and if the [combined measure of those parts which were] breached exceeds the [combined measure of the parts which remain] standing,
11. opposite the breach it is prohibited.	11. opposite ten houses [Lieberman (TM, p. 122, on 1. 44 and TK, III, p. 426, on 1. 44) suggests that T. may read: at a height of ten amot] the partition is considered invalid.

We see that, except for the protasis (1) and several apodoses ((6) and (11)), the two pericopae are identical. The unit concerning partitions thus does not appear to be primary to either the problem of diverse-kinds or the issue of the cerub. Rather, the pericope is an autonomous unit which the redactors have inserted (with slight modifications) into various appropriate contexts.

[10] B. Ber. 25b, Y. Kil. 4:4, B. Shab. 97a, B. Erub. 16a, 79b, Y. Erub. 1:8, and B. Suk. 7a, 16b all state (with minor variations): "Every [space measuring] less than three [handbreadths] is [considered] as a solid (klbwd) [i.e., as nonexistent]."

[11] Maim., Comm. and Rashi to B. Erub. 16a (s.v., kl šhw' cited by Qappah, I, p. 117, n. 10) note that C concerns a partition which will keep out a kid under normal conditions, that is, when the kid does not apply an unusual amount of force to the partition.

[12] Sens, Bert., and TYY, reading H-I into F-G, maintain that in this instance one may sow different kinds even on opposite sides of the breach itself.

[13] Maimonides (Code, Diverse-Kinds 7:16; cf. also Ribmas, Sens, and MR) points out that in the case of a vineyard one may still sow another kind opposite the breach, but now he must allow the vineyard four amot as its area of tillage (and he may not sow up to the base of the partition itself).

[14] Sens, TYY, and GRA, reading E-I into J-N, point out that each gap in the wall must be ten amot or less wide, for otherwise

it would be prohibited to sow different kinds opposite the breaches (H-I).

[15]It is clear here that the more developed apodosis (*kngd hprws 'swr*) has been chosen over the simpler one (*'swr*), for the latter would have balanced L's *mwtr*.

[16]Cf. also MR, who harmonizes the two rules by stating that, in the case of A-D, the spaces between the reeds which measure less than three handbreadths are considered as if they were actually solid (*lbwd*) (B. Erub. 16a and parallels). The measure of the standing part of a partition of reeds is then greater than that of the breaches, for the latter are not even considered to exist. According to this interpretation the rule of A-D agrees with that of J-N that a partition is valid only if the measure of its standing part exceeds that of its breaches.

[17]Lieberman (*TZ*, p. 213, on 1. 10, and *TK*, II, p. 623, on 11. 10-11) understands *nty'š* to mean *htrph wntršl*.

[18]Cf. his translation of M. Kil. 5:5a (apparently following Maim., *Comm.* to M. Kil. 4:4), I, p. 50.

[19]Cf., for example, his translation of M. Bik. 1:9, 2:4.

[20]The basis for the rule that a vineyard sanctifies adjacent crops (and that crops sanctify a vineyard) is found in Dt. 22:9: *You shall not sow your vineyard with two kinds of seed, lest the whole yield be sanctified (tqdš), the crop which you have sown and the yield of the vineyard.*

[21]Cf. Bokser, I, p. 50.

[22]Yosé cites F-H in M. Ed. 5:2 (and so attests it to Usha).

[23]I, p. 47.

[24]Except for the presumed "if," and with the phrase "He who plants" understood, C-F would also appear in slight apocopation.

[25]Figure 32 is found in Ribmas, TYY, and TYT.

[26]Figure 33 is found in Maim., *Comm.*, KM to Maim., *Code, Diverse-Kinds* 7:7, TYY, and TYT.

[27]Figure 34 is found in Maim., *Comm.*, KM to Maim., *Code, Diverse-Kinds* 7:7, Ribmas, TYY, and TYT.

[28]Figure 35 is given by TYY and TYT.

[29]Figure 36 is given by Maim., *Comm.*, KM to Maim., *Code, Diverse-Kinds* 7:7, Ribmas, TYY and TYT . Sens also presents this interpretation of D. This arrangement of vines was common in Roman viticulture, where it was known as the *quincunx* (= the form of five spots on dice [D.P. Simpson, *Cassell's New Latin Dictionary* (New York: Funk and Wagnall's, 1960), p. 496]). Cf. Columella, *De Re Rustica*, 3.13.3, E.B. White, *Roman Farming* (Ithaca: Cornell University Press, 1970), p. 237, and Lieberman, *TK*, II, p. 624, on 1. 12 (all cited by BOkser, I, p. 48, n. 120).

[30]Figure 37 is given by TYT, TYY (both of whom give both interpretations of D). According to TYT Bert. holds this view as well.

[31]For further sources of the different interpretations of M. 4:6, cf. Lieberman, *TK*, II, p. 624, on 1. 12.

[32]We note that the commentaries clearly disagree concerning the pattern represented in both figures 33 and 35, for some maintain that vines planted in such an arrangement do constitute a vineyard, while others say that they do not. According to our interpretation of M. the difference of opinion concerns whether the fifth vine, being outside of the set of four, belongs to one of the two rows, or whether this vine, being between the two rows, belongs to neither. We see no reason to favor one interpretation over another.

[33]In connection with C-D Sens refers to M. Peah 2:3, which states in part:

> All [of the items mentioned above (M. Peah 2:1-2)]
> divide [a field for the purpose of giving *pe'ah*]
> for [the case of a field sown with] seeds, but
> only a fence divides [a field for the purpose
> of giving *pe'ah*] for [the case of a field planted
> with] trees.

According to Sens the latter rule applies to the vineyard as well as to trees.

[34]Sens and GRA again refer to M. Peah 2:3 in explaining F-G.

[35]Sens and GRA regard the substance of the law of H-I as similar to that of the latter part of M. Peah 2:3, which reads as follows:

> If the branches of the trees were intertwined (so
> Danby for *šᶜr kwtš*) [the fence] does not divide
> [the field of trees], but (*'l'*) one gives [one]
> *pe'ah* for all.

[36]For Geniza fragments referred to in B and E see Zachs, I, p. 256, on 1. 26, and p. 257, on 1. 29, respectively.

[37]C-D would also appear in apocopation if the phrase "there were" [and the presumed "if"] were dropped, and the phrase "he who plants" were understood.

[38]We also note that Maim., *Comm.* (and others), reading M. 4:8 in light of M. 4:1, see C-D as describing a bald spot of the vineyard, which also (according to House of Hillel) requires sixteen *amot*. M. 4:1, however, discussed a cleared space within a vineyard, while M. 4:8 concerns the spaces between rows (cf. also Albeck, p. 364). Cf. also MR, who distinguishes between the two cases by noting that in the instance of the bald-spot four *amot* are allowed the vines as area of tillage, while in the case of the space between the rows only six handbreadths are allowed as the area of tillage.

[39]For the list of mss., see Zachs, I, p. 257, on 1. 31.

[40]Cf. also Danby's translation of *nyr* in M. 2:3 as "newly-broken land."

[41]Danby thus translates *bwr* in M. 2:8. Cf. also his translation of M. 4:9, where he renders *bwr* as "fallow land."

[42]For Geniza fragment, see Zachs, I, p. 258 on l. 36.

[43]We note that M. 4:9, like M. 4:8, is interpreted by many commentaries as concerning the issue of the combining of rows to form a vineyard.

[44]Salmon (or Salamin) may refer to one of two cities. One is located in the south, approximately fifteen km. northeast of Sepphoris (cf. M. Avi-Yonah, *Historical Geography*, p. 177 [map, p. 173] [for first Salmon], and *Carta's Atlas*, pp. 107-108, 131 [for the second Salmon], 145 [for the first]).

CHAPTER FIVE

[1]See Zachs, I, p. 259, on l. 1.

[2]Cf. R. Alcalay, p. 437, s.v. *krm dl*.

[3]Danby similarly translates *crbwby'* as "in irregular fashion."

[4]Most commentaries maintain that C also refers to the rule that the vines must be separated by a distance measuring from four to sixteen *amot* (M. 4:9 and M. 5:2). Since, however, this rule is actually a composite of several (explicit [M. 5:2] or inferred [M. 4:9]) rules of M., we maintain that it is not likely that C makes reference to it. But cf. T. 3:3b, where the issue of the distance between the vines is raised in reference to M. 5:1.

[5]MR, on the other hand, states that a vineyard need not be composed of two sets of five vines arranged in the pattern of M. 4:6, for one such set by itself is considered a vineyard. He therefore maintains that only five of the ten vines need be arranged in the pattern of M. 4:6, and that on account of these five the entire area is considered a vineyard.

[6]Lieberman (*TK*, II, p. 624, on ll. 14, 15, and 16) explains that the omissions by Vienna Ms. in E-F, by the first printed ed. in F, and by Erfurt Ms. in G-H are all the result of copyist's errors.

[7]Alternatively, Lieberman (*TK*, II, p. 623, on ll. 11-12) follows Maimonides' reading of M. in the light of T. (*Code, Diverse-Kinds* 7:8):

> A vineyard which lay waste--if there are in it [enough vines to enable one] to gather ten vines per an entire *bet se'ah*, and they are planted [in rows of] two [vines] opposite two [others], and one extending out [like a] tail; or [if] there are in it [enough vines to enable one] to align three [vines] opposite three [others], lo, this is called a "lean" vineyard, and it is prohibited to sow [another kind] in any [part of] it.

Lieberman accordingly interprets A-B, which has three vines opposing three others, as referring (along with C-D) to the "lean" vineyard. C, however, appears to describe how the vineyard is laid waste, so that it is more likely that A-B discusses the vineyard in its original shape.

[8]T. apparently reasons here that two rows separated by more than eight *amot* do not constitute a vineyard (cf. our discussion of M. 4:8).

[9]*TZ*, p. 214, on l. 17; cf. also *TK*, II, p. 625, n. 22.

[10]Lieberman (*TK*, II, p. 625, on l. 19) maintains that Erfurt reverses the order of E-G and H-M by mistake.

[11]Alternatively, Lieberman (*TK*, II, pp. 624 f., on ll. 17-18) argues that T. 3:4 precedes T.'s citation of M. 5:1E-G at T. 3:5b, and therefore actually comments on M. 5:1A-D, adding another rule pertaining to the "lean" vineyard. M. 5:1A-D, however, does not explicitly require the vines of a "lean" vineyard to be aligned (as does M. 5:1E-G, although this is required by the interpretation of M. 5:1A-D in the light of M. 4:6), so that we consider it more likely that T. 3:4 comments on M. 5:1E-G.

[12]*TZ*, p. 214, on l. 22, and *TK*, II, p. 625, on l. 22.

[13]*Ibid.*

[14]Lieberman (*TK*, II, p. 624, on l. 22) states that the vines of an espalier may be separated by a distance measuring from four to eight *amot*. Cf. M. 6:6 (and T. 3:3b).

[15]*TZ*, p. 214, l. 24.

[16]Following Lieberman (*Greek in Jewish Palestine* [New York: Jewish Theological Seminary, 1942], p. 51 [cited by Lieberman, *TK*, II, p. 626, n. 25]) who translates *br* in various contexts as "select."

[17]It is not clear whether *zh hyh* has been appended to the formula *m^c śh w* or is actually part of the formula itself. We claim only that by its very meaning ("this was") the phrase *zh hyh* serves to join F-K to A-E, regardless of whether or not *zh hyh* is part of the formula.

[18]*TZ*, p. 215, on l. 30, and *TK*, II, p. 626, on l. 30.

[19]Lieberman (*TK*, II, p. 626, n. 27) suggests that Erfurt mistakenly omits E-H because both D and H end with similar phrases.

[20]We note that, except for the presumed "if" in E and with *krm* understood, E-H may be considered to appear in apocopation as well.

[21]Following Y., Lieberman (*TK*, II, p. 626, on ll. 30-31) reasonably assumes that the outer row and the vineyard are separated by more than four *amot* (and less than eight), for otherwise the two areas of tillage would overlap.

[22]*TZ*, p. 215, on l. 32, and *TK*, II, pp. 626-627, on ll. 31-32, 32. Lieberman further maintains that T. 3:7-8 continues the discussion of T. 3:6 concerning the row which is not considered part of the vineyard and therefore is allowed its own area of tillage. T. 3:7-8, however, appears to introduce a new issue dealing specifically with the slope of a terrace, and does not seem to concern the set of problems involved with the "vineyard which is planted according to the rule [pertaining to] it." We therefore maintain that T. 3:7-9 forms an autonomous subunit concerning the problem of the slope of the terrace.

[23]Alternatively, the commentaries maintain that the dispute concerns whether or not the vines of a vineyard need be allowed sufficient room to grow (Maim., *Comm.*), or whether or not the rows of a vineyard need be separated by enough space to allow a plough and its animals to pass through (Rosh, Bert., PM; cf. Columella, *De Re Rustica* 5.5.3 (Loeb ed., II, p. 31), who also cites this reason as a consideration in the spacing of rows of a vineyard). Cf. also B. B.B. 102b for another interpretation based on D. We do not see, however, why any of these considerations should affect the status of the vines as a vineyard.

[24]Our translation follows Maim., *Comm.*, Rosh, and others, who understand nq^{a} to mean gwm' ("hollow").

[25]Since the area within the house is clearly separated from that of the vineyard by the walls and the roof, a house of any size presumably forms an autonomous domain within the vineyard.

[26]Cf. Neusner, *Eliezer*, I, pp. 354f., who maintains that this Eliezer is not Eliezer b. Hyrcanus. Since Eliezer here (indirectly) disputes with Eliezer b. Jacob concerning the winepress, he is probably an Ushan as well.

[27]Y. explains (cf. also Ribmas, Rosh, Albeck) that the case of the watchman's booth or mound differs from that of the winepress in that the seeds on the booth or mound grow outside of the vineyard's airspace, while those sown in the winepress remain within it. The difference may also be explained with regard to the appearance of diverse-kinds. One may sow on top of a booth or mound because the plants are visible above the surrounding vines. Since, however, plants sown in a winepress would not grow higher than the vines (and so could produce the appearance of diverse-kinds), they may not be sown there.

[28]According to Maimonides (*Code, Diverse-Kinds* 7:22) the overhanging vines will touch the vegetables sown on top of the šwmrh, so that sowing on top of the šwmrh is clearly prohibited.

[29]Cf. M. Peah 2:3 and M. Kil. 4:7H-I, which state that a divider covered by interlaced vines is no longer considered a valid divider.

[30]*TZ*, p. 215, critical apparatus to l. 40, and *TK*, II, p. 628, on l. 40.

[31]*Eliezer*, I, p. 354.

[32]*TK*, II, p. 628, on l. 39.

[33]*TZ*, p. 215, on l. 40, and *TK*, II, p. 628, on l. 40.

[34]Figures 38-40 are found in Qappaḥ, I, pp. 121-122.

[35]Cf. also TYT and GRA, who explain the case of vines separated by five *amot* as follows. One cannot distinguish between the appearance of vines set apart by five *amot* and that of vines separated by four *amot*. If, therefore, one were to destroy only thirty-seven vines which are separated by five *amot*, it would appear as if he were allowing eight sanctified vines to grow in a vineyard with the vines separated by four *amot*. Therefore forty-five vines are sanctified in both cases.

[36]Cf. also Yosé b. Ḥaninah's comment in Y. that the vegetables are sown opposite the central vine. For further discussion of Y., see Bokser, I, pp. 50-54.

[37]TAS solves this problem by maintaining that several circles of radius sixteen *amot* are drawn, each with its center at either the vine at the center of the vineyard or one of the eight vines surrounding it. Those vines are sanctified which both lie in one of those circles and form a vineyard with one of the nine vines (see interpretation in text). We maintain, however, that this interpretation does not follow the plain sense of M., which nowhere mentions that several circles are drawn. Furthermore, the reading of A-B as an instance of E-G does not appear to be necessary to the interpretation of A-B itself. We therefore omit this point in following the interpretation of TAS.

[38]According to this interpretation there is no difference between sowing at the edge of a vineyard and sowing within it. A-B then does not complement M. 4:5H, but provides an instance of the view of the House of Hillel.

[39]Cited by Lieberman, *TZ*, p. 216, on 1. 44, and *TK*, II, p. 629, on 1. 44.

[40]Lieberman (*TK*, II, p. 629, on 1. 45) rejects Erfurt's reading (which perhaps follows the present reading of I) in favor of the reading in Vienna Ms. and the first printed ed.

[41]*TK*, II, p. 629, on 11. 47-48.

[42]Cited by Lieberman, *TK*, II, p. 629, on 1. 47.

[43]Primus, p. 33.

[44]We note that Maimonides (*Code*, *Diverse-Kinds* 5:17 [see n. 45 below]; cf. also TYY) maintains that although the sowing itself is permitted, one must still uproot the other kind as it grows, lest one allow diverse-kinds to grow in the vineyard. Maimonides here perhaps reads M. 5:6 into M. 5:7, for the pericope itself does not discuss allowing the other kind to grow.

[45]According to Maimonides, who perhaps reads F-H (which discusses the destruction of seeds) into A-E, the sowings of C and E affect only the seeds, and not the vines (*Code*, *Diverse-Kinds* 5:17):

> [If] he was passing through the vineyard and seeds fell from him, or [if] the seeds went out [into the vineyard] with the dung or with the water, or [if] he was sowing or scattering [seeds] in a white field, and the wind blew [the seeds] behind him, and the seeds fell into the [nearby] vineyard and sprouted--lo, this [i.e., these seeds] have not been sanctified, as it is written [*You shall not sow your vineyard with two kinds of seed lest the whole crop be sanctified, the crop*] *which you have sown* [*and the yield of the vineyard* (Dt. 22:9], and this he did not sow. And he is obligated to uproot it when he sees it [growing]. And if he allowed them to grow, lo, this one has sanctified [them]. If the wind blew [the seeds] before him and he sees the seeds which fell into the vineyard, lo, this one is [considered] as one who sows [diverse-kinds]. And what shall he do if they have sprouted? The blades he shall overturn with a plow, and it is sufficient [i.e., the plants are thereby destroyed]. And if he found that they developed into an early state of ripening (*'byb*),

> he shall break [the ear] off in order to destroy
> it, for all of it is prohibited in [respect to]
> deriving benefit from it. And if he found that
> it developed into grain, lo, this shall be burnt.
> And if he saw them [growing] and allowed them to
> grow, lo, these shall be burnt with the vines
> which are near them.

Maimonides thus rules that the vines are destroyed only when the
seeds are allowed to grow, but not when they are only sown. It
appears, then, that Maimonides does not regard the sowing which
is aided by the wind as an intentional sowing of diverse-kinds
(Ridbaz, *ad.loc.*; Albeck, p. 366). If we read A-E without F-H,
however, D (and the missing apodosis *'swr*) appear to discuss the
status of both the seeds and the vines.

[46]Feliks, *Agriculture*, p. 171.

[47]*Ibid.*

[48]Cf. his translation of M. B.M. 7:9.

[49]*Iris pallida*, of the iris family (Iradaceae). For identification of all plants, cf. Feliks, *Mar'ot HaMishnah*.

[50]*Hedera helix*, of the aralia family (Araliaceae).

[51]*Lilium candidum*, of the lily family (Liliaceae).

[52]For Geniza fragments, cf. Zachs, I, p. 265, on l. 26.

[53]*TK*, II, p. 631, on ll. 52-53.

[54]*Cannabis sativa*, of the nettle family (Urticaceae; so
Post, s.v. *Cannabis*). Cf. also Feliks, *Maro't HaMishnah*, p. 131,
who identifies the plant as belonging to Cannabinaceae.

[55]*Cynara scolymus*, of the composite family (Compositae).

[56]For Rabad's views cf. Lieberman, *TK*, II, p. 632, on ll.
52-53. It is not clear to me, however, whether these plants
would be grown for the sake of their seeds. For further discussion of the various explanations of F presented by the commentaries, cf. MR and *TK*, II, pp. 631-633, on ll. 52-53.

[57]For the uses of hemp, cf. Feldman, *Simḥé HaMishnah*,
pp. 279ff., and Feliks, *Mar'ot HaMishnah*, p. 131.

[58]Alternatively, the dispute concerns whether hemp is considered a tree or an herb. Tarfon maintains that the plant has the
appearance of a tree, and so is not considered diverse-kinds in a
vineyard. Sages, on the other hand, say that since the leaves of
hemp sprout directly from its roots it is considered an herb
(T. 3:15), and thus is considered diverse-kinds in a vineyard.
While this explanation of the dispute is plausible, it requires
a reading of M. in the light of T. 3:15, while we prefer to
attempt to explain M. in terms of its own issues.

[59]Feliks, *Mar'ot HaMishnah*, p. 127.

[60]*Chrozophora tinctoria*, of the spurge family (Euphorbiaceae).
Cf. Löw, I, pp. 595ff., *TK*, II, p. 549, on l. 11, and Feldman,
pp. 324ff.

[61]*Euphorbia tinctoria*, of the spurge family (Euphorbiaceae). Cf. Löw, I, pp. 597ff., cited by Lieberman, *TK*, II, pp. 549ff., on l. 12, who gives a full discussion of this identification. Cf. also Feldman, p. 22.

[62]*Gnaphalium luteo-album*, of the composite family (Compositae). This is the identification tentatively made by Löw, IV, p. 506. Feldman, pp. 319f. rejects this identification and lists various other possibilities, concluding that the plant has not been identified with any certainty.

[63]*Muscari comosum*, of the lily family (Liliaceae). Cf. Löw, II, pp. 184f. (cited by Lieberman, *TK*, II, pp. 548f., on l. 7), and Feldman, pp. 159-160.

[64]*Reseda luteola*, of the mignonette family (Resedaceae). Cf. Löw, III, p. 130 (cited by Lieberman, *TK*, II, p. 630, on l. 50), Feldman, pp. 339f., and Feliks, *Mar'ot HaMishnah*, p. 139.

[65]*Crocus sativus*, of the iris family (Iridaceae). Cf. Löw, II, pp. 7ff., Feldman, pp. 322f., and Feliks, *Mar'ot HaMishnah*, p. 75.

[66]*Ammi*, of the parsley family (Umbelliferae). Cf. Löw, III, p. 421 (cited by Lieberman, *TK*, II, p. 630, on l. 50).

[67]Cf. M. 1:8.

[68]*Satureia thyumbra* of the mint family (Labiatae). Cf. Löw, II, p. 103, Feldman, pp. 291ff., and Feliks, *Mar'ot HaMishnah*, p. 90.

[69]*Origanum maru*, of the mint family (Labiatae). Cf. Löw, II, pp. 84ff., and Feldman, pp. 295ff. For English name see Feliks, *Mar'ot HaMishnah*, p. 8, who gives the Latin name as *Majorana syriaca*.

[70]*Thymus capitatus*, of the mint family (Labiatae). Cf. Löw, II, p. 77, Feldman, pp. 311ff., and Feliks, *Mar'ot HaMishnah*, p. 123.

[71]*Typha angustata*, of the cat-tail family (Typhaceae). Cf. Löw, I, p. 579 (cited by Lieberman, *TK*, II, p. 633, on ll. 53-54), and Feldman, pp. 27ff. For English name, cf. Post, p. 314.

[72]*Juncus*, of the rush family (Juncaceae). Cf. Löw, I, p. 572, and Feldman, pp. 17ff.

[73]*Cyperus papyrus*, of the sedge family (Cyperaceae). Cf. Löw, I, p. 569, Feldman, pp. 320ff., and Feliks, *Mar'ot HaMishnah*, p. 28.

[74]*Arundo donax*, of the grass family (Graminae). Cf. Löw, I, p. 663, Feldman, pp. 281ff., and Feliks, *Mar'ot HaMishnah*, p. 132.

[75]Cf. T. 1:12.

[76]Cf. M. 1:4.

[77]*Lycium europaeum*, of the nightshade family (Solanaceae). Cf. Löw, IV, p. 28, Feldman, pp. 231f., and Feliks, *Mar'ot HaMishnah*, p. 11.

[78]Cf. M. 1:8.

[79]Cf. T. 1:12.

[80]*Capparis spinosa*, of the caper family (Capparidaceae).
Cf. Löw, I, p. 323, Feldman, pp. 255f., and Feliks, *Mar'ot HaMishnah*, p. 118.

[81]*TK*, II, p. 632, on 11. 52-53.

[82]These plants frequently appear together in M.-T. Kil.
Cf. M. 3:4, T. 2:10-11.

[83]For more information concerning these and other plants,
refer to the sources given in the notes.

[84]Cf. Pliny (*Historia Naturalis*, 20.163 [Loeb ed., trans.
Jones, v. 6, p. 97]), who states that *ammi* grains were sprinkled
on bread or used as flavoring.

[85]Feliks, *Mar'ot HaMishnah*, p. 49.

[86]It makes no difference here whether or not F is read as
being separate from E, for either understanding of F yields the
point that all kinds of seeds are considered diverse-kinds in
a vineyard.

[87]*TK*, II, p. 632, on 11. 52-53.

[88]Cf. Maim., *Code*, *Diverse-Kinds* 1:6, who rules that trees
are considered diverse-kinds only in respect to cases involving
grafting.

[89]*TK*, II, pp. 634f., on 1. 55.

[90]Theophrastus (cited by Lieberman, *Hellenism in Jewish
Palestine*, p. 181 [Gereboff, *Tarfon*, p. 48, n. 7], and *TK*, II,
p. 636, n. 81) draws a similar distinction between herbs and
plants (*Historia Plantarum*, 1.3.1 [Loeb ed., trans. Hort, I,
pp. 23-25]):

> A tree is a thing which springs from the root with a
> single stem, having knots and several branches, and
> it cannot easily be uprooted; for instance olive
> fig vine. A shrub is a thing which rises from the
> root with many branches; for instance, bramble
> Christ's thorn. An under-shrub is a thing which
> rises from the root with many stems as well as
> many branches; for instance, savory rue. A herb
> is a thing which comes up from the root with its
> leaves and has no main stem, and the seed is borne
> on the stem; for instance, corn and pot-herbs.

[91]Cf. Feldman, pp. 23f., and Feliks, *Mar'ot HaMishnah*, p. 54.

[92]Cf. M. 1:8, where squill is considered a tree in the
context of grafting.

[93]Cf. Gereboff, *Tarfon*, p. 28. Gereboff also notes that
B. perhaps drops Z-AA in order to improve T.

[94]Cf. T. 1:11.

[95]Cf. T. 1:11, where dodder is assumed to be an herb in the
context of grafting.

[96]Cf. Gereboff, *Tarfon*, p. 29. Gereboff also notes that according to Feldman (p. 353; perhaps following Rashi and R. Gershom) *kswt* may alternatively refer to *Humulus lupulus*, of the nettle family (Urticaceae), or hops. Hops are cones which grow on vines and resemble grape clusters. According to this interpretation the dispute concerns whether hops are considered diverse-kinds in the vineyard because they are similar in appearance to grapes. But cf. Feliks, *Mixed Sowing*, p. 146, who opposes this identification on the grounds that T. 1:11 clearly refers to a parasitic plant, which a hop is not.

[97]The branches, however, may also harden and remain. Cf. Feliks, *Plant World of the Bible*, p. 132.

[98]*Ibid.* Cf. also Löw, I, p. 327 (cited by Lieberman, *TK*, II, p. 636, n. 81).

[99]Alternatively, the disputes dealing with dodder and alhagi may concern whether or not they resemble trees. Cf. Lieberman, *TK*, II, pp. 636ff., on l. 60. We prefer the interpretation given above, however, for M.-T. offers no criterion besides that of T. 3:15 for distinguishing between trees and herbs.

[100]Cf. also Maim., *Comm.* to M. Kil. 5:8.

CHAPTER SIX

[1]Neusner, *Pharisees*, II, p. 70.

[2]Alternatively, Maimonides (*Code, Diverse-Kinds* 8:2; cf. also Sens), following Y., maintains that the fence or ditch lies between the vines and the field. Since, however, the vines are trained on the fence, the latter is not considered a partition, and the area of tillage must still separate the vines from the other kind on the opposite side of the fence. KM supports this interpretation by arguing that, according to our first interpretation, House of Hillel would hold the unlikely opinion that the foliage of the vines would be further removed from the field than would be the base of vines. Cf. also Ridbaz (*ad.loc.*) for a further argument against our first interpretation. B-C does not, however, indicate that the fence lies between the vines and the field, and we therefore see no reason to interpret it in this manner.

[3]Cf. M. 6:3-4, Maim., *Comm.* (M. 6:1), R. Yehosaf Ashkenazi (cited by MS, M. 6:1), and Lieberman, *TK*, II, p. 637, on l. 1.

[4]Alternatively, the four *amot* mentioned in A refer to the area of tillage of the vines (Maim., *Comm.* to M. 4:3 [cited by Lieberman, *TK*, II, p. 637, on l. 1], MB). The case discussed in A then concerns vines which are separated from another kind by a fence, and Gamaliel and his court rule that even in this instance one must allow the vines their area of tillage. The reasoning behind A would be that the partition does not annul the requirement of the area of tillage (cf. T. 4:1b-2), perhaps because a partition is not deemed to separate vines, which are trailing plants, from another kind. T. 4:1a would then complement T. 4:1b-2, which presents the opposing view. We regard our first interpretation to be the more plausible one, however, both because it places T. in an appropriate context (that of M) and because T. nowhere mentions the issue of area of tillage.

[5]*TZ*, p. 217, on ll. 1-2, and *TK*, II, p. 637, on l. 1.

[6]*TZ*, p. 217, on l. 3.

[7]Alternatively, Lieberman (*TK*, II, p. 642, on l. 31) maintains that, because of the proximity of T. 4:9b to T. 4:8-9a, both T. 4:9b and T. 4:1b-2 are to be understood in the context of the issue of sowing the gaps of an espalier. It is not at all clear, however, how the two issues (i.e., the issue of the area of tillage with a partition, and that of sowing the gap of an espalier) may be related to one another, and we therefore think that it is more likely that the two questions are to be considered separately.

[8]T. Erub. 2:1 reads:

A. A caravan which rested (*šrth*) in the valley and they surrounded it with (1) camels, or (2) pack saddles [so Neusner, *HMLP*, II, p. 215, (M. Kel. 23:2) for *ᶜbyṭ*], or (3) saddles (*'kypwt*), or (4) sacks, or (5) reeds, or (6) straw, or (7) stalks,

B. even [with] three ropes [strung] one above another--

C. he carries within it [i.e., the enclosed area],

D. provided that there not be (1) between one camel and the next [an area] fully as wide as a camel, nor (2) between one pack-saddle and the next [an area] fully as wide as a pack-saddle, nor (3) between one saddle and the next [an area] fully as wide as a saddle, nor (4) between one reed and its neighbor three handbreadths, [i.e.,] sufficient [space] so that a kid may enter.

T. Erub. thus differs from T. Kil. in that it includes additional items which are relevant to its subject-matter and not to that of T. Kil.

[9]M. Erub. 1:9a reads: They surround [an area] with three ropes [strung] one above another, provided that there not be between one rope and the next three handbreadths.

[10]M. Erub. 1:10a reads: They surround [an area] with reeds, provided that there not be between one reed and the next three handbreadths.

[11]*TZ*, p. 218, on l. 7, and *TK*, II, p. 638, on ll. 6-7.

[12]Following HD, Lieberman (*TZ*, p. 218, on l. 7, and *TK*, II, p. 638, on l. 7) identifies *rypyn* as *rppyn*, or lattice-work constructed of willow branches. He also identifies the term with the Greek ρίψ, ρίπος [mats]. These branches were used because their flexibility allowed them to be shaped to the growth of the trained plants.

[13]*TZ*, p. 218, on l. 10.

[14]*TK*, II, pp. 638-639, on l. 7.

[15]Alternatively, MB explains that when the reeds are tied together at the top the breaches appear to be openings rather than gaps, so that the partition is considered valid. This interpretation, however, appears to be based on M. 4:4 (which discusses gaps which appear like openings), and does not necessarily follow from the plain sense of T.

[16]For reading of J., cf. Lieberman, *TK*, II, p. 640, on ll. 14-15.

[17]*TK*, II, p. 639, on ll. 10-11.

[18]Y. Kil. 4:4 (29b), Y. Erub. 1:8 (9b), and Y. Suk. 1:1 (52b), with minor variations from T. Kil. at many points, all read as follows:

A. The result is (*nmṣ't 'wmr*) in [regard to] the issue of diverse-kinds:

B. (1) All [breaches] which [measure] less than three [handbreadths wide] are [considered] as solid (*kstwm*).

C. (2) And all [sections of a partition] which [measure] [Y. Suk. adds: (from) less than] three to four [handbreadths wide]--

D. if [the measure of] that which stands exceeds [that of] the breach[es] it is permitted [to sow diverse-kinds on opposite sides of the partition].

E. And if [the measure of] the breaches exceeds [that of] that which stands, it is prohibited [to sow diverse-kinds on opposite sides of the partition].

F. (3) [If the sections of the partition measured] from four [handbreadths] to ten [*amot*]--

G. if [the measure of] that which stands exceeds [that of] the breach[es], it is permitted [to sow diverse kinds on opposite sides of the partition].

H. If [the measure of] the breach[es] exceeds [that of] that which stands,

I. opposite that which stands it is permitted [to sow diverse-kinds],

J. opposite the breach[es] it is prohibited [to sow diverse-kinds].

K. [If the breaches measured] more than ten [*amot*],

L. even though [the measure of] that which stands exceeds [that of] the breach[es],

M. opposite that which stands it is permitted [to sow diverse-kinds],

N. opposite the breach it is prohibited [to sow diverse-kinds].

All three passages then present a similar pericope concerning laws pertaining to carrying on the Sabbath in an area enclosed by partitions.

[19]For the possible readings of T. Erub., cf. Lieberman, *TK*, III, p. 318, on ll. 5-6.

[20]Y. Kil. 4:4 (29b), Y. Erub. 1:8 (9b), and Y. Suk. 1:1 (52b) state that if the breach measures more than ten *amot* in width it is prohibited to sow diverse-kinds opposite the breaches (cf. n. 18 above).

[21]Cf. his translation of M. Miq. 6:9.

[22]Cited by Zachs, I, p. 269, n. 9.

[23]*Ibid.*, p. 269, on l. 12.

[24]MS explains that since the vines lean over the terrace, the latter is considered as if it were a fence supporting the vines, so that the four *amot* are measured from it (following the view of House of Hillel, M. 6:1E). This view, however, presupposes that M. 6:1 concerns sowing on the side opposite that of the vines of the espalier (cf. our discussion of M. 6:1).

[25]If the spot at which the vines meet the ground is considered the spot at which the vines would be regarded as growing out of the ground (cf. Maim., *Comm.*, *Code*, *Diverse-Kinds* 8:8), it follows that the four *amot* should be measured from that spot.

[26]T. Kil. 3:7-8 maintains that a terrace is considered separate from the field below, but does not discuss whether or not the terrace must be a specific distance above the ground.

[27]Kefar Aziz is located about 12 km. south of Hebron. Cf. M. Avi-Yonah, *Historical Geography*, p. 115, and *idem.*, *Carta's Atlas*, pp. 87, 116, and 128.

[28]For variant readings see Zachs, I, p. 270, on 1. 19. Bet Hameganyah was apparently a private estate (Sirillo, cited by Lieberman, *TK*, II, p. 640, on 1. 24).

[29]Cf. Porton, *Ishmael*, I, p. 38.

[30]Cited by Zachs, I, p. 271, n. 28.

[31]Cf. Porton, *Ishmael*, I, p. 38.

[32]We here follow the commentaries in assigning the questions to Joshua and the replies to Ishmael, although there is no reason why these attributions may not be reversed (following William S. Green, *The Traditions of Joshua b. Hananiah*, I, p. 21).

[33]Cf. Theophrastus, *Enquiry into Plants*, 4.2.1 (trans. Arthur Hort, Loeb ed., v. I, p. 293; cited by Feliks, *Plant World of the Bible*, p. 55), who compares the fruit of the sycamore to the fig as follows:

> . . . in size it [i.e., the fruit of the sycamore] is as large as a fig, which it resembles also in appearance, but in flavour and sweetness it is like the 'immature figs,' except that it is much sweeter and contains absolutely no seeds, and it is produced in large numbers.

Cf. also Pliny, *Historia Naturalis*, 14. 56-57 (cited by Hort, p. 291, n. 6).

[34]Porton (p. 38) notes, however, that E and J-K were formulated separately, for the language of K, $\check{s}'r$ ("the rest [of the braches]"), differs from that of E, $mwtr$ ("the remainder [of the tree]").

[35]Cited by Lieberman, *TK*, II, pp. 640f., on 11. 26-27, who discusses Maimonides' interpretation in the light of T. 4:7b. Cf. our discussion of T. below.

[36]Cf. Feliks, *Plant World of the Bible*, p. 54, and *Mixed Sowing*, pp. 153-154, and Feldman, *Şimḫê HaMishnah*, pp. 135-138.

[37] The sycamore's botanical name is *Ficus sycamorus*, while that of the fig tree is *Ficus carica* (Feliks, *Mixed Sowing*, pp. 153, 160, and *Mar'ot HaMishnah*, pp. 152-153). For both trees as members of the nettle family, cf. Post, *Flora of Syria, Palestine, and Sinai*, s.v. *Ficus*. Feliks, however, places both trees in Moraceae (mulberry family) (*Mar'ot HaMishnah*, pp. 152-153).

[38] Cf. M. Oh. 18:3.

[39] K.D. White, *Roman Farming*, p. 224. Olives or olive oil were used as food, as a source of illumination, and for anointing. Figs were used mainly as food (e.g., dried figs, bread).

[40] For variant readings cf. Lieberman, *TZ*, p. 219, critical apparatus on 1. 24, and *TK*, II, p. 640, on 1. 24.

[41] In Y. Kil. 4:3 (30c) the saying of Simeon b. Eleazar appears in the context of a discussion of a vine trained over laths, and the saying there reads as follows:

> R. Simeon b. Leazar says, "If it was its [i.e., the vine's] manner to climb from lath to lath, [all of the laths together are considered] as [belonging to] a single lath."

[42] Alternatively, Lieberman (*TZ*, p. 219, on 1. 27, and *TK*, II, pp. 640-641, on 11. 26-27, 27) explains that in G each branch is considered as separate from the others because the sycamore tree is considered partly as a fruit tree, so that one may sow under the branches which do not support the vine. At H Simeon b. Eleazar then states that if the vine climbs from one branch to the next, all of the branches are considered to belong to a single tree, for now the entire tree is regarded as serving the vine, and is now treated as a barren tree. This interpretation is difficult, however, for it does not account for T.'s specific language at G ("a tree unto itself"), nor does it explain why the status of the sycamore should change so that it should be considered a fruit tree at G but a barren tree at H. We therefore prefer the first explanation offered above.

[43] Alternatively, one may adopt Yohanan b. Nuri's view (M. 6:1F-G) that the area of tillage of an espalier is six handbreadths, or that of a single vine. The area which is to be sown then measures at least six *amot* (cf. Maim., *Comm.*). (Cf. also GRA, who maintains than an espalier is allowed four *amot* as its area of tillage, but only in respect to the area facing it. At the sides of the espalier, on the other hand, it is allowed only six handbreadths.) Although there is no reason to rule out such an interpretation, we prefer the one given above, for it explains the significance of the phrase "eight *amot* and a little more." According to the view which maintains that an espalier is allowed six handbreadths as its area of tillage, the measure of "eight *amot* and a little more" appears to have no particular significance at all.

[44] Cf. our translation of T. 4:4-5, above.

[45] *TZ*, p. 219, on 1. 29, and *TK*, II, p. 641, on 1. 29.

[46] Cited by Lieberman, *TK*, II, p. 642, on 11. 30-31.

[47] Lieberman (*TK*, II, p. 642, on 1. 30) cites the version presented by Nathan, the Head of the Academy, which reads,

"one-fifth of an *amah*." This reading agrees with Meir's view
in T. Kel. B.M. 6:13, and perhaps reads into T. both that view
and that of Yoḥanan (Y. Kil. 6:5 (30c)) that the phrase "and a
little more" refers to a handbreadth. Lieberman proposes to
conflate the readings of Nathan and the text before us to read,
"one-sixth of five handbreadths of an *amah*" meaning five-sixths
of a handbreadth. We see no reason, however, to conflate the
two readings. We therefore prefer the reading in the text
before us, for there does not appear to be sufficient reason
to change it.

[48]Cf. Zachs, I, p. 273, on l. 29.

[49]Cf. MS and Ribmas (second interpretation), who perhaps
give interpretations similar to our own (the language of both
is unclear).

[50]We shall here present three alternative explanations offered by the commentaries. Maimonides (*Comm.*) explains that A
refers to an espalier which extends diagonally from a corner and
stops, thus forming an imaginary triangle with one of the walls
(cf. fig. 45 [adapted from Qappaḥ, I, p. 127]). The question discussed by A concerns whether one may sow between this triangle
(the area of which is regarded as part of the espalier [Qappaḥ])
and the second wall at the point where the espalier stops, even
though sowing another kind between the espalier and the wall may
produce the appearance of diverse-kinds. A rules that one may
sow in the specified space after allowing the espalier its area
of tillage (which Maimonides takes to be six handbreadths [follow-
ing Yohanan b. Nuri, M. 6:1]), for the area of tillage separates
the other kind from the vines and so prevents them from appearing
to be sown as diverse-kinds. Referring to the distance between
the end of the espalier and the second wall, Yosé states in B
that if this distance does not measure four *amot*, the area may not
be sown, presumably (although Maimonides does not explicitly state
this) because sowing in such a small, bounded area would produce
the appearance of diverse-kinds. Maimonides states his views in
the *Code* (*Diverse-Kinds* 8:9) as follows:

> Two walls are near one another, and the vines are
> planted in the angles between them, and the espalier
> projects along (ʿm) the walls from the corner and
> stops--he allows a space from the base of the vines
> according to the [appropriate] measure and sows at
> the place where the espalier stops, [i.e., the place]
> upon which there is no espalier. And even though
> the seed is aligned (mkwwn) between the two walls
> between which the espalier [lies], since he allowed
> a space [from the espalier] according to the appro-
> priate measure, he sows between the two walls.

Maimonides' interpretation is difficult, however, for it is not
clear how vines extending diagonally from a corner may continue
to be trained on a wall and so remain in the status of an
espalier.

Sens and Ribmas both interpret A to concern an espalier
which is divided into two parts, with each beginning at an opposite end of the wall and with a gap separating them (cf. fig. 46).
A discusses an issue similar to that of M. 6:6A, namely whether
one may sow in a gap of an espalier without causing the appearance
of diverse-kinds. A rules that one may do so after allowing the

vines their area of tillage of six handbreadths (for the vines
do not join together to form an espalier). In B Yosé maintains
that the area between the two sections of the espalier must cover
four *amot* in length, just as he rules in M. 5:4P that one may sow
near a vine located in a hollow or winepress only if four *amot*
are present. This explanation is difficult, however, for while
it speaks of two rows of vines coming out of two separate corners,
M. mentions only one row extending from one corner.

TYY explains that A concerns a group of vines which is planted
in a corner, with some vines trained along one wall, and some
along the other wall (cf. fig. 47 [Romm ed., *ad.loc.*]). The
issue of A is whether one may sown between the two groups of vines
without appearing to sow diverse-kinds. A rules that one may sow
in this space after allowing each group of vines its area of
tillage of six handbreadths (since the two groups do not combine
to form an espalier). Yosé, however, disagrees with A, maintaining
that the vines are joined by the corner to form an espalier, so
that four *amot* must be present between them in order to allow
for their area of tillage. We find this interpretation to present
problems as well, though, for M. does not appear to speak of two
rows of vines extending out of a corner in opposite directions. It
is therefore not clear how closely the interpretation of TYY is
based on the plain sense of M.

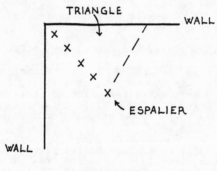

FIG. 45

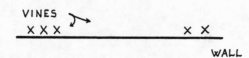

FIG. 46

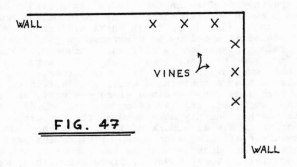

FIG. 47

[51]Cf. Zachs, I, p. 273, on l. 32.

[52]Jastrow, II, p. 1015, s.v. *spk* I.

[53]We note that M. 6:8-9 is not interested in the consideration of the espalier's area of tillage.

[54]*TZ*, p. 220, on l. 34, and *TK*, II, pp. 642ff., on l. 34.

[55]Cf. Finkelstein, p. 263, on l. 11. Finkelstein maintains
that the section containing OO-PP+QQ-SS (p. 263, l. 11, to p. 264,
l. 4) is actually a marginal gloss which has been erroneously
inserted into the text of Sifré. Since this section does appear
in some manuscripts, however, we have decided to include it in
our discussion of Sifré.

[56]*Ibid*., p. 263f., on l. 11. Hillel places OO-PP at the
opening of the discussion of the citation *Lest the whole yield
be sanctified*. We note that Neṣiv places OO-PP after QQ-SS.

[57]*Ibid*., p. 264, on l. 3.

[58]GRA places QQ-SS in the middle of a discussion of the citation *You shall not sow your vineyard* (Dt. 22:9). It is not
clear, however, whether GRA intends to link the rule to the
verse, for there is no obvious connection between them.

CHAPTER SEVEN

[1]Cf. Zachs, I, p. 275, on l. 4.

[2]Layering may be defined as "the development of roots on a
stem while it is still attached to the parent plant" (Hartmann
and Kester, *Plant Propagation: Principles and Practices*,
p. 481).

[3]Cf. Hartmann and Kester, p. 487, who indicate that the layer
should be held in place underground by such an item as a wooden
peg, a bent wire, or a stone placed underground beside the shoot.

[4]Figure 48 is adapted from Hartmann and Kester, p. 486.

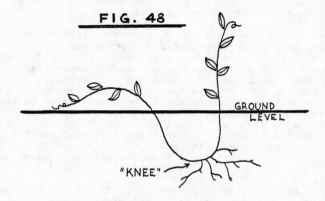

FIG. 48

GROUND LEVEL

"KNEE"

[5]*TK*, II, p. 644, on 1. 40.

[6]*Ibid.*, p. 644, on 11. 42-43.

[7]*TZ*, p. 220, on 1. 41, and *TK*, II, p. 644, on 1. 43.

[8]For the height of ten handbreadths as marking a separate domain, cf. M. 2:8, 4:7, 5:2, and 6:2D-F.

[9]Alternatively, Lieberman (*TK*, II, p. 644, on 1. 43) maintains that House of Shammai reason that a sunken shoot, like a vine which grows aboveground, must be allowed an airspace of ten handbreadths. House of Hillel, though, argue that, since the "airspace" of a sunken shoot is actually composed of soil, the amount of soil allowed above the vine should not differ from the amount of soil allowed beside it, which is six handbreadths. This interpretation is difficult, however, for the notion that a vine must be allowed ten handbreadths of airspace is found in Y. (e.g., Y. Kil. 6:2, 7:2), but not, as far as I am able to determine, in M.-T. itself. We therefore prefer the first explanation given above.

[10]*Gossypium herbaceum* or *Gossypium arboreum*, of the mallow family (Malvaceae). Cf. Feldman, p. 119, and Feliks, *Mar'ot HaMishnah*, p. 285.

[11]Y. Bes. 5:2 attributes D to Meir.

[12]Cf. Theophrastus, *Enquiry into Plants*, 4.7.7 (cited by Feliks, *Plant World of the Bible*, p. 286), and Pliny, *Historia Naturalis*, 12.21.38, who note that the leaves of the cotton tree resemble those of the vine.

[13]Alternatively, Maimonides (*Comm.*, *Code*, *Diverse-Kinds* 5:19) understands Meir to refer not to sowing another kind near a cotton tree, but to sowing a cotton tree near a vine. Feliks (*Plant World of the Bible*, p. 285) explains that, although it is prohibited to plant a cotton tree in a vineyard, such a tree is not actually considered diverse-kinds in a vineyard, for it is regarded as a tree rather than simply as a bush. It is not clear, however, why the cotton tree, if it is a tree, should be prohibited at

all in a vineyard. Furthermore, this interpretation does not
follow the view of the redactor, who, in formulating D and E
in a similar manner, and in juxtaposing them, clearly regards
the two sayings to be related in substance. We therefore prefer
the first interpretation given above, according to which E
presents another instance of the rule of D.

[14]Alternatively, most of the commentaries read M. 7:1A-C
into M. 7:2F. For example, Maimonides (*Comm*.) and Bert. maintain
that Eleazar b. Ṣadoq refers to a case in which three handbreadths
of soil do not cover the sunken shoot. These commentaries,
however, do not explain why the seeds are not sanctified in this
instance. According to TYB, on the other hand, Eleazar b. Ṣadoq
discusses a case in which there are three handbreadths of soil
above the shoot. One may not sow even in this instance, however, for it may appear that less than three handbreadths of
soil cover the sunken shoot. Since three handbreadths of soil
are in fact present, though, the seeds are not sanctified. There
is no reason, however, to believe that the rule of Eleazar b.
Ṣadoq is at all interested in the considerations of M. 7:1A-C.

MR explains that Eleazar b. Ṣadoq and M. 7:1A-C disagree
as to whether the sower is liable if the roots of the seeds
penetrate into the vine. Eleazar b. Ṣadoq maintains that the
sower does not intend for the seeds to be nourished from the
vine, and that the penetration of the roots does not occur immediately after sowing. The sower therefore is not liable and
the act of sowing, although prohibited, does not sanctify the
seeds. M. 7:1A-C, on the other hand, rules that, since the sower
knows that the roots will definitely penetrate into the vine,
he is liable and the seeds are sanctified (unless, of course,
he separated the two kinds by three handbreadths of soil). Again,
however, there is no reason to assume that Eleazar b. Ṣadoq's
saying is related to M. 7:1A-C, and we therefore prefer our first
interpretation to all of the explanations given above.

[15]Cf. Neusner's translation of T. Kel. B.M. 6:13A, *HMLP*,
II, p. 102.

[16]In T. Kel. B.M. 6:13 Meir presents the list of B (omitting
mwtr at B(1)-(3)) in a discussion of the length of an *amah* used
in measuring certain areas.

[17]The bald spot (= patch) of a vineyard must measure either
twenty-four (House of Shammai) or sixteen (House of Hillel) *amot*
square in order to be sown (M. 4:1A-C).

[18]The outer space of a vineyard must be either sixteen (House
of Shammai) or twelve (House of Hillel) *amot* wide in order to
be sown (M. 4:1D-F).

[19]Cf. M. 6:3C, which rules that the seeds are sanctified
if the vine spreads over them, thus implying that the seeds are
not sanctified as long as they do not lie under the vine. We
also note that, unlike M. 7:3, M. 6:3C uses *'swr* in the sense
of "sanctified." Cf. our discussion of M. 6:3-5, above.

[20]Cf. GRA (M. 6:3), who explains that one who sows under
the "remainder" of the latticework does not sanctify the seeds
because he produces only the appearance of diverse-kinds (i.e.,
it appears that the vines will spread over the latticework).
According to this interpretation the rule of B(4) follows the
principle of M. 7:2D-F and M. 7:3B(1)-(3). We have not accepted
this interpretation of M. 6:3-5, however, for it does not account
for the difference between the "remainder" of the latticework of

laths and the "remainder" of the fruit tree. We fail to see why the appearance of diverse-kinds is not produced in the case of the latter as it is in the instance of the former. We therefore prefer the interpretation presented in our discussion of M. 6:3-5, above.

[21]Cited by Finkelstein, p. 263, on l. 1.

[22]Bokser, I, p. 54.

[23]The term *qdš* is used in several contexts besides that of diverse-kinds, e.g., in reference to the mixture of *ᶜorlah*-fruit and permitted fruit (M. Orl. 3:7).

[24]Y. Kil. 7:3 differs from Sifré mainly at NN, where Y. reads as follows:

> NN. Scripture says, [*your*]*vineyard* (Dt. 22:9)-- and not *diverse-kinds* [i.e., the prohibition *You shall not sow* precedes the phrase [*your*] *vineyard* and not the phrase *diverse-kinds* (PM); GRA reads: Scripture says, [*The produce of the*] *vineyard* (Dt. 22:9)--and not *your vineyard*].

PM explains that, unlike the prohibitions of Lv. 19:19, which place the verb after the direct object and before the phrase *kl'ym* (e.g., *bhmtk l' trbyᶜ kl'ym, śdk l' tzrᶜ kl'ym*), Dt. 22:9 places the verb before the direct object (*l' tzrᶜ krmk kl'ym*). Y. takes the proximity of the direct object to the verb in Dt. 22:9 to mean that the prohibition applies to any act of sowing in a vineyard (reading *your vineyard* as simply *vineyard*). According to GRA's reading the point of Y. is that the phrase at the end of Dt. 22:9, *the produce of the vineyard*, refers to all vineyards, rather than only to *your vineyard*, as the verse states at its beginning.

[25]Alternatively, GRA understands J to read, "At what point is he [i.e., the man who seized the vineyard] called a usurper?" According to this reading J-K distinguishes between one who has seized the vineyard but does not yet have full control of it, and the usurper, who does have a firm hold on the land. J-K cannot then gloss only A-C, for it is difficult to distinguish between the two thieves in respect to the question of the sanctification of the vineyard. If, according to A-C, a usurper does not sanctify the vineyard which he sows, it does not follow that the thief who does not have control of the property should be able to sanctify it. This reading of J-K thus requires a unitary interpretation of the pericope, an interpretation which GRA provides as follows. The usurper is effectively the owner of the vineyard at the time that he sows it, and he therefore renders the vineyard prohibited by his act of sowing. For this reason the rightful owner must cut down the other kind as soon as possible. He need not burn the other kind with the vines, however, for the vineyard has not actually been sanctified. If, on the other hand, a thief who did not have complete control over the property sowed the vineyard, he does not sanctify it even at the time of sowing, since he may not be said to have "owned" the vineyard. The rightful owner, therefore, need not hurry to remove the other kind. This explanation, however, presents several difficulties. First, as I have said, it presupposes a unitary reading of the pericope, which we have rejected for the reasons given above. Second, GRA attempts to distinguish between the usurper, who may be said to "own" the land, and the thief, who does not have firm control over the property and thus is not considered its "owner." Ultimately, however, the vineyard is not sanctified

by either thief, so that it is not clear why the owner should
hurry to remove the other kind in one case and not in the other.
We can see no relationship between the fact that the usurper
actually functions as an owner and the rule that the rightful
owner need hurry to remove the other kind which the usurper
sowed. We therefore see no reason to distinguish between the
two thieves, and so prefer the translation and explanation of
J-K presented above.

[26]All cited by Zachs, I, p. 280, n. 25.

[27]*Ibid.*, p. 280, n. 26.

[28]*Ibid.*, p. 280, on l. 20.

[29]*Ibid.*, p. 280, n. 27.

[30]*Ibid.*, p. 281, n. 31. Cf. also Y. Kil. 7:7, which records
both readings of M.

[31]Cf. M. Ma^{c}as. 1:3 (and M. Hal. 1:3), which states that
grain becomes liable for tithes once it has reached one-third
of its projected size.

[32]Following Sirillo and Elijah Fulda, in *TK*, p. 220, on l. 31,
and *TK*, II, p. 643, on l. 38. The Latin name of madder is
Rubia tinctorum (*TK*, II, p. 643, n. 31), of the madder family
(Rubiaceae). Cf. Feliks, *Mar'ot HaMishnah*, p. 102.

[33]Cited by Lieberman, *TK*, II, p. 643, on l. 39.

[34]Alternatively, Lieberman (*TZ*, p. 220, on l. 37, and *TK*,
II, p. 643, on l. 37), following Maimonides (*Code, Diverse-Kinds*
8:11), maintains that E refers to the roots of the vines rather
than to those of the vegetables. According to this interpretation E states that if the roots of the vines extend from the
latter into the four *amot* of the vineyard, the vegetables must
be uprooted, for now the roots of the vegetables (which are
apparently presumed to have entered the four *amot* as well) may
gain nourishment from the roots of the vines, and the two kinds
thus grow together as diverse-kinds. This interpretation is
difficult, however, for the language "[If] their roots extended
into the four *amot* of the vineyard" seems to apply more appropriately to the vegetables, which lie outside of the vineyard's
area of tillage, than to the vines, which are already located in
the four *amot* of the vineyard. Furthermore, Maimonides' interpretation of E may have been influenced by his reading of F.
According to Maimonides (*Code, Diverse-Kinds* 8:11; cf. Lieberman,
TK, II, p. 643, on l. 37) F refers to roots of grain (*py'h*)
which enter the four *amot* of the vineyard. Maimonides perhaps
reasoned that if F refers to roots of grain, E, which gives the
opposite rule, must refer to roots of vines. Since, however,
we do not accept Maimonides' reading of F, we see no reason to
interpret E to refer to the vines. We therefore prefer the
interpretation given above.

[35]We follow Y. and GRA in omitting "even" (*'pylw*) at F,
for otherwise F would make no sense. When read with "even" F
states that the roots of madder do not sanctify the vines even
if they are more than three handbreadths below the surface. F
thus implies that the roots of madder also do not sanctify the
vines if they are less than the specified depth below the surface.
Now the point of F can only be that the vines are not sanctified
because the madder's roots do not come into contact with those
of the vines. The two sets of roots will surely meet, however, if

the roots of the madder are less than three handbreadths under the ground. F thus cannot be read with "even," and we therefore follow those readings which omit it.

[36]Lieberman (*TZ*, p. 220, on l. 38, and *TK*, II, p. 643, on l. 38) notes that F specifically mentions madder because its roots have a tendency to spread out.

[37]Commentary to M. 7:7, cited by Lieberman, *TK*, II, p. 645, on ll. 44-45.

[38]It is clear from B-C, which states that vines can become sanctified once their grapes grow to the size of hyacinth beans, that "prohibited" in E(1) can mean only "sanctified."

[39]Cf. Finkelstein, p. 263, on l. 4.

[40]In Y. Kil. 7:5 Hananiah b. Hillel first cites EE-FF and then quotes BB.

[41]Cf. Zachs, I, p. 282, on l. 25.

[42]*Ibid.*

[43]For other instances in which a plant growing in a perforated pot is considered to be attached to the ground, cf. M. Dem. 5:10 and M. Shab. 10:6.

[44]For other instances in which Simeon does not distinguish between perforated and unperforated pots, cf. T. Shev. 8:10 (one may write a *prozbol* for either type of pot [cited by Lieberman, *TK*, II, p. 646, on ll. 48-49]), and M. Shab. 10:6 (one may uproot a plant on the Sabbath from either type of pot [cited by Y., MS, and TYT]).

[45]Simeon's view may be related to his rule at M. Uqs. 2:9 (cited by TYT), which read as follows (trans. Neusner, *HMLP*, XX, pp. 61-62):

A. A cucumber [which was rendered susceptible to uncleanness] which one planted in a pot and grew, and [the root of which grew and] went outside of the pot is [thereby] insusceptible to uncleanness.

B. Said R. Simeon, "What is its character that it should be insusceptible to uncleanness?"

C. "But that which is susceptible to uncleanness remains on its status of susceptibility to uncleanness, and that which is insusceptible to uncleanness is eaten."

A states that a plant growing in an unperforated pot (Neusner) is rendered insusceptible to uncleanness if a shoot grows into the soil outside of the pot, for the plant is now considered to be attached to the ground. Simeon, however, maintains that the plant in the pot remains susceptible to uncleanness and the shoot alone is rendered insusceptible, for only the latter is actually attached to the ground and clearly derives nourishment from it. In both M. Kil. 7:8 and M. Uqs. 2:9, therefore, Simeon apparently reasons that a plant which begins to grow in a pot can be sustained by the soil in that pot alone. The plant thus is not assumed to derive nourishment from a source outside of the pot if a part of the plant becomes attached to the ground around the pot. In

both cases, then, Simeon rules that the plant inside the pot is
not considered to be attached to the ground outside of the pot.

[46]*TK*, II, p. 646, on l. 49. M. Uqs. 3:8H states (trans.
Neusner, *HMLP*, XX, p. 67), "Grain which was uprooted, and is
attached even by a small root, is insusceptible to uncleanness."

[47]In B. Shab. 95b (cf. also Y. Kil. 7:6) Rav explains that
Simeon's position is based on an interpretation of Lv. 11:37,
which reads, *And if any part of their carcass falls upon any seed
for sowing that is to be sown, it is clean.* According to Rav
the repetition of the root zr^c in the phrase *any seed for sowing
that is to be sown* is taken to mean that anything which is in
any way connected to the earth cannot be rendered susceptible
to uncleanness (Rashi, *ad loc.*).

CHAPTER EIGHT

[1]Cf. Zachs, p. 283, on l. 2.

[2]*Ibid.*, p. 285, on l. 5.

[3]T. Sheq. 1:3 reads as follows:

A.   On the fifteenth of it [i.e., Adar] the
     messengers of the court go out and declare
     the diverse-kinds ownerless,

B.   for that which is declared to be ownerless
     by the court is [considered to be] ownerless,

C.   and is exempt from tithes.

D.   [If] he found diverse-kinds in the vineyard,
     it [i.e., the diverse-kinds] is permitted
     with regard to [the law of] robbery and exempt
     from tithes.

E.   [If he found diverse-kinds] in the field, it
     [i.e., the diverse-kinds] is prohibited with
     regard to [the law of] robbery and liable for
     tithes.

A-C and D-E can each stand by itself, and it appears that they
have been joined because of C. Since D-E does not depend on A-C
for its context, it is probable that D-E is primary to T. Kil.
(where it appears by itself), rather than to T. Sheq.

[4]HD (to T. Sheq. 1:3; cited by Lieberman, *TK*, II, p. 646,
on l. 1) points out that diverse-kinds of the vineyard are
considered to be ownerless even if they grow without being sown
and have not yet sanctified the vineyard (i.e., the owner is not
yet aware of their growth). In this instance it is assumed
that the owner, who would have to destroy the diverse-kinds
anyway, wishes them to be uprooted by someone else, and so
renounces his rights of ownership over them.

[5]Cf., however, T. 2:16, which, without distinguishing between
the types of diverse-kinds, rules that one may uproot another's
diverse-kinds without permission because he thereby "lessens
the impropriety (*mm^{c}t 't htplh*)."

[6]Cited by Lieberman, *TK*, II, p. 647, on ll. 2-3.

[7]Cited by Lieberman, *ibid.*

[8]Cited by Lieberman, *ibid.*

[9]Cited by Lieberman, *ibid.*, on ll. 4-5.

[10]Cited by Lieberman, *ibid.*, on ll. 6-7.

[11]Cited by Finkelstein, pp. 262-263, on l. 11.

[12]On D in GRA's reading of Sifré, see Sifré Dt. 2301.

[13]Cf. GRA, who reads the present pericope (without its exegesis of *diverse-kinds*) in the context of Sifré Dt. 230a, while taking the latter to refer to one who sows a vineyard. We note that Finkelstein (p. 263, on l. 11) considers the present pericope to be a marginal gloss of Sifré.

[14]We note that Finkelstein (p. 263, on l. 11) regards this pericope to be part of a long marginal gloss on Sifré.

[15]Cf. also Neṣiv, who reads *which you have sown* at D and takes the word *which* to include the act of allowing diverse-kinds to grow.

[16]Y. offers two versions of the pericope. The first is garbled and refers to a non-existent verse (cf. GRA, PM, *ad loc.*). The second differs from Sifra (according to Hillel's interpretation) in referring to another verse in the *gezerah shavah*:

A. Here *Lest [the whole yield] be sanctified* (Dt. 22:9) is said, and there *Neither shall there be a cult prostitute (qdš) of the sons of Israel* (Dt. 23:18) is said.

B. Just as [the phrase] "sanctified" mentioned there [refers to that which] is prohibited in respect to benefit, so [the phrase "sanctified" mentioned] here [refers to that which] is prohibited in respect to benefit.

Y. thus reasons that just as one may not derive benefit from a cult prostitute, so may one not benefit from diverse-kinds of the vineyard. This reading of the pericope is somewhat less plausible than that of Hillel, for the prohibition against deriving benefit is related more directly to the law of "holy things" (which is concerned with the proper and improper use of such items) than to the law of the cult prostitute (the issue of which is the proper conduct of the cult, not deriving benefit or pleasure from the prostitute). It is thus more likely that Sifré would choose to draw an analogy between the sanctified diverse-kinds of the vineyard and the "holy things to the Lord" than between the diverse-kinds and the cult prostitute. We therefore prefer the interpretation of Hillel given above.

[17]B. M.Q. 2b and B. Mak. 21b read D as follows:

D. Scripture says, [*Your cattle you shall not let breed with*] *a different kind; your field [you shall] not [sow with diverse-kinds]* (Lv. 19:19).

According to this reading the rule that one may not derive benefit from diverse-kinds is derived from the juxtaposition of *a different kind* (the last word in the previous clause), *your field*, and *not*. These three phrases are read together and taken

to mean that one may not have diverse-kinds in his field, so
that one is prohibited not only from sowing diverse-kinds but
from allowing them to grow as well.

[18]QA also offers an alternative explanation (which he prefers to the one given above), basing upon the phrase *your field*
the rule that one may not allow diverse-kinds to grow. This
phrase is regarded as unnecessary, for the prohibition against
sowing diverse-kinds may be easily understood from the rest of
the verse (*You shall not sow with diverse-kinds*). *Your field*
is therefore taken to indicate that one is prohibited not only
from sowing diverse-kinds, but also from having them in one's
field, i.e., allowing them to grow. This explanation of the
pericope is difficult, however, for D does not include *your field*
in its citation of Lv. 19:19, and there is no reason to assume
that this phrase figures in the exegesis of Sifra. We therefore
prefer the first interpretation given above.

[19]We here follow the reading which omits *with a different
kind*, for this phrase clearly does not belong in A.

[20]Rabad understands "others" in C and D to refer to gentiles.
We see no basis for this interpretation in the text itself, though,
and we therefore prefer to read "others" to refer simply to
other people.

[21]Referring to Gn. R. 7:4, Albeck (p. 368) maintains that
lmšwk refers to leading the animals, and that *lhnhyg* refers to
driving them from behind (cf. also Danby, *ad loc.*). We here
simply follow the view of the majority of the commentators.
In any event, though, the difference in translation does not
affect our exegesis of the pericope.

[22]Alternatively, Maimonides (*Comm.*; cf. also GRA) takes
Dt. 22:10, which specifically mentions an ox and an ass (both
of which are domesticated animals), to prohibit the pairing of
clean and unclean animals alone. He therefore understands A
to continue the discussion of M. 8:1J and thus to refer to the
mating of animals of different kinds, so that C, which refers
to the yoking together of animals, serves B alone. Maimonides'
reconstruction of M.'s exegesis of Scripture is interesting,
but A and B are perfectly matched, and it is difficult to see
any good reason to separate them. We therefore prefer our first
interpretation given above.

[23]We note that Finkelstein (p. 263, on l. 11) regards this
pericope to be a marginal gloss of Sifré.

[24]For variant readings of *lwbdqs*, cf. Epstein, *ITM*, pp.
97ff. (cited by Lieberman, *TK*, II, p. 648, on l. 8). Feliks
(*Mixed Sowing*, p. 130, fig. 74) identifies the Libyan ass as
Equus asinus (cf. our discussion of M. 1:6).

[25]Cf. Zachs, I, p. 288, on l. 13.

[26]*TK*, II, p. 648, on l. 8.

[27]Cf. *TZ*, p. 222, on l. 9.

[28]Cited by Lieberman, *TK*, II, p. 650, on ll. 11-12.

[29]*TZ*, p. 222, on l. 12.

[30]The version of Y. may be compared to that of T. as follows:

T. Kil. 5:6	_Y. Kil. 8:2_
1. Isi the Babylonian says, "It is prohibited to ride on the back of a mule,	1. Isi b. ^cAqavyah says, "It is prohibited to ride on the back of a mule,

1. Isi the Babylonian says, "It is prohibited to ride on the back of a mule,

2. "[as we learn] from an argument *a minori*: If, in a case in which it is permitted to wear two garments as one, lo, he is prohibited in respect to their mixture, in a case in which it is prohibited to lead two animals as one, is it not logical that it should be prohibited in respect to their mixture?"

3. They said to him, "Lo, it [i.e., Scripture] says, [*Take with you the servants of your lord,*] *and cause Solomon my son to ride on my own mule, and bring him down to Gihon* (I Kings 1:33)."

4. He said to them, "They do not respond from Tekoa."

5. They said to him, "Lo, it [i.e., Scripture] says *And David did what was right in the eyes of the Lord, and did not turn aside from anything that he commanded him all the days of his life, except in the matter of Uriah the Hittite* (I Kings 15:5)."

1. Isi b. ^cAqavyah says, "It is prohibited to ride on the back of a mule,

2. "[as we learn] from an argument *a minori*: If, in [the case of] two garments which you are permitted to wear one on top of the other, you are prohibited in respect to their mixture, [in the case of] an animal which you are prohibited to lead [i.e.,] one [kind] with another, all the more so should you be prohibited from riding on it."

3.   And is it not written, [*Then all the king's sons arose,*] *and each mounted his mule and fled* (II Sam. 13:29)?

4.   They do not learn [the law] from royalty.

5.   And is it not written, [*Take with you the servants of your lord,*] *and cause Solomon my son to ride on my own mule, and bring him down to Gihon* (I Kings 1:33)?

6. This mule was a creature from the six days of creation [i.e., it was created as a mule, and was not born of the union of a horse and an ass (PM)].

Y. significantly differs with T. at (3)-(6). While T. cites David's action (I Kings 1:33) as precedent at (3) and supports it with I Kings 15:5 at (5), Y. cites the action of David's sons (II Sam. 13:29) as precedent at (3) and supports it by citing David's own action (I Kings 1:33) at (5). In Y.'s version, then, David's authority is not questioned (as it is in T.), but in fact is used to support the argument of Isi's opponents (and is not challenged by Isi). We note that Y. clarifies T.'s reading of (4) by replacing "Tekoa" with "royalty." Y. also adds (6), and thus has Isi win the debate. Isi now responds that David's action does not set a precedent, for his mule was created at the creation of the world and, unlike other mules, was not born of the union of a horse and an ass (PM). Y. here presupposes Isi's statement at (2), which specifically states that one is prohibited from using an animal born of the union of two kinds, so that Y. perhaps links (2) and(3)-(6).

³¹Alternatively, Sirkes (cited by Lieberman, *TK*, II, p. 651, on l. 17) explains that "Tekoa" refers to Ira the son of Iqqesh of Tekoa, one of David's advisers (II Sam. 23:26). This

reference, however, is obscure, and thus not likely to provide
the basis for the idiomatic saying of D. Following Sens (who
reads $htqw^c$ at D) and Rosh (who reads $htwq^c$ at D), Lieberman
interprets tqw^c as $htqw^c$, meaning one who establishes ($htwq^c$) the
law for himself (cf. B. Yev. 109b). It is not clear, however,
why such a description should be applied to David in particular.
We therefore prefer the explanation given in the translation as
the most probable one.

[32]For the identification of the hedgehog and the weasel,
cf. Danby, who follows the views of most of the commentaries. As
to the identification of the weasel, cf. also Feliks, *Animal
World of the Bible*, p. 42, who argues that the $h\underaccent{.}{l}dh$ is not a weasel
but a rat.

[33]Sens maintains that the parentage of $prwtywt$ cannot be
ascertained because such mules do not exhibit the characteristics
which generally distinguish one kind from another (cf. also TYY,
who explains the $prwtywt$ are mules which are too young to display
such characteristics). Sens here refers to signs which distinguish a mule born of a female horse from a mule born of a
female dam in respect to the sound of the voice and the length
ofthe ears and tail (B. Hul. 79a). Cf. Varro, *On Agriculture*
2.8.6 (trans. W.D. Hooper, rev. Harrison Boyd, Loeb ed., p. 395),
who states:

> The so called hinny is the offspring of a horse
> and a jenny; smaller than the mule, usually rather
> redder, with ears like a horse's, but with mane
> and tail like those of the ass.

[34]Maimonides actually states with respect to A-B only that
"it is prohibited or permitted to allow them to mate ($lhrkyb$)."
Since Maimonides presumably takes A to mean that mules may not
be permitted to mate with each other, we assume that he understands B to mean that wild horses may be mated with each other.
Alternatively, MR takes B to mean that wild horses may be
paired with other horses. Neither M. nor Maimonides mentions
other horses, however, and we therefore prefer the first interpretation of Maimonides given above.

[35]So Louis Ginzberg, "Beiträge zur Lexikographie des
Aramaischen," in *Festschrift Adolf Schwartz*, ed. Samuel Krauss
(Berlin: R. Löwit, 1917), pp. 329ff. (cited by Albeck, p. 379).
Cf. also Danby (p. 37, n. 4), who suggests that the creature may
be identified as a chimpanzee or an ape. TYY identifies the
"wild man" as the orangoutang (which, in fact, means "wild man"
in Malay), but, since the latter is found only in Borneo and
Sumatra, it is probable the TYY actually refers to the ape, to
which the name "orangoutang" was often mistakenly applied (cf.
Oxford English Dictionary [Oxford: Oxford University Press, 1933],
v. 7, p. 172, s.v. orangoutang).

[36]Hedgehogs feed on mice, birds, lizards, and snakes, as
well as insects (J[ames Smith] Fi[ndlay], "Insectivora,"
Encyclopaedia Britannica 15th ed., Macropedia, 9:623) and weasels
prey on rodents, fish, frogs, and birds' eggs ("Weasel,"
Encyclopaedia Britannica, 15th ed., Micropedia, 10:588).

[37]Cf. Zachs, I, p. 281, on 1. 20.

[38]Cf. T. Kil. 1:9, M. Bik. 2:8-11 for other issues related
to the distinction between wild and domesticated animals.

[39]Cf. Feliks, *Animal World of the Bible*, p. 30.

[40]The point of M. 1:6, though, is that the Arabian onager and the ass are considered to be diverse-kinds with one another even though they resemble each other. Cf. also T. 1:8b, which states that the wild ass, which MR identifies as the Arabian onager, is considered to be diverse-kinds with an ass.

[41]Our translation of *hkwtb* follows that of Danby in M. Bik. 2:11.

[42]All cited by Lieberman, *TK*, II, p. 652, on ll. 21-22.

[43]*TZ*, p. 223, on l. 22.

[44]For the identification of the ostrich, cf. Feliks, *Animal World of the Bible*, p. 91.

[45]*TK*, II, p. 652, on ll. 22-23.

[46]Cf. M. Kel. 17:14, T. Kel. B.M. 7:5-6, and M. Toh. 1:3 (cited by Lieberman, *TK*, II, p. 652, on l. 23).

[47]*TZ*, p. 223, on l. 22, and *TK*, II, p. 652, on l. 23. Lieberman maintains that "for" was mistakenly inserted into T. Kil. 5:8b from T. Bek. 1:9 (see below, n. 49).

[48]Alternatively, A could be translated as "an unclean animal does not bear a kind of clean animal." At E-F, however, *mn* clearly means "from" and not "a kind of" (for there is only one kind of man), and we therefore prefer to translate it as "from" throughout the pericope.

[49]T. Bek. 1:9 reads as follows:

    A. R. Simeon says, "Why does Scripture say, *camel* (Lv. 11:24), *camel* (Dt. 14:7) twice?

    B. "To include the camel which is born of a cow as one which is born of a female camel.

    C. "And if its head and greater part resemble its dam, it is permitted in [respect to] eating."

    D. And sages say, "That which comes from an unclean animal is [considered to be] unclean,

    E. "and that which comes from a clean animal is [considered to be] clean;

    F. "for an unclean animal does not bear [offspring] from [mating with] a clean [animal],

    G. "nor does a clean [animal] bear [offspring] from [mating with] an unclean [animal].

    H. "And a large [animal] does not [bear offspring] from [mating with] a small [animal],

    I. "nor does a small [animal bear offspring] from [mating with] a large [animal].

    J. "And a man does not [bear offspring] from [mating with] any of them [i.e., any animal],

    K. "nor does any of them [bear offspring] from [mating with] a man."

T. Bek. 1:9F-K, which corresponds to T. Kil. 5:8b, supports sages' position (T. Bek. 1:9D-E, a citation of M. Bek. 1:2), which states that any offspring of an unclean animal is considered unclean (and *vice versa*). T. Bek. 1:9F-K is thus presented only

because of T. Bek. 1:9F-G, for only this part of the pericope
is relevant to sages' views. In addition, T. Bek. 1:9D-E and
F-K can each stand without the other. It appears, then, that
T. Bek. 1:9F-K is an autonomous unit which has been appended to
T. Bek. 1:9D-E because of T. Bek. 1:9F-G. At the same time,
however, we note that the pericope does not explicitly raise the
issue of diverse-kinds, and thus need not be primary to T. Kil.
The pericope could thus primarily concern either the issues of
M.-T. Bekorot (e.g., the status of a first-born of one kind born
to a dam of another kind) or questions of diverse-kinds (e.g.,
the results of the mating of different kinds of animals with one
another).

[50]B. Bek. 7a attributes C-H to Joshua b. Levi.

[51]Cf. Pliny, *Historia Naturalis* 8.79.213f. (trans. H. Rackham, Loeb ed., v. III, p. 149), who states:

> . . .But not only in pigs but in all animals as
> well whenever there is any tame variety of a genus
> there is also found a wild one of the same genus,
> inasmuch as even in the case of man an equal number
> of savage races have been predicted to exist.

[52]B. B.M. 90b reads B as follows:

> B. One incurs forty lashes only [in the case of]
> he who threshes [with a muzzled cow] and he
> who drives [diverse-kinds of animals].

B. thus replaces T.'s mention of liability with the specific
punishment for the act. B. also replaces the verb "leads"
with "threshes," so that B refers to A(1) as well as to A(2).
Cf. also the version of *Sefer HaEshkol* (cited by Lieberman, *TK*,
II, p. 653, on l. 28), which adds *hmšk* ("he who pulls") to
B.'s version, and so brings B. closer to the language of
M. 8:2C ("plowing, pulling [e.g., a wagon], and being led").

[53]Cited by Lieberman, *TK*, II, p. 653, on l. 28.

[54]Cf. Finkelstein, p. 264, on l. 8.

CHAPTER NINE

[1]M. Neg. 11:2 reads as follows (trans. Neusner, *HMLP*, VI,
p. 199):

> A. Camel's hair [which is not susceptible to plagues]
> and sheep's wool which one hackled together--
>
> B. if the larger part is from the camels, they
> are not susceptible to uncleanness through plagues.
>
> C. If the greater part is from the sheep, they are
> susceptible to uncleanness through plagues.
>
> D. Half and half--they are susceptible to uncleanness
> through plagues.
>
> E. And so the flax and the hemp which one hackled
> together.

M. Neg. 11:2 differs from M. Kil. 9:1D-H only in its apodoses,
reading "are/are not susceptible to uncleanness through plagues"
for the latter's "it is permitted/prohibited [to mix the fibers
with flax]." The two versions thus use the same case to illustrate

different rules, with M. Kil. 9:1D-H augmenting M. Kil. 9:1A, and M. Neg. 11:2 referring to M. Kil. 9:1B. The pericope could have originally appeared in either context, and it is thus impossible to tell whether M. Kil. 9:1D-H or M. Neg. 11:2 represents the primary formulation of the pericope.

[2]All scriptural references for A-C are cited by Maim., *Comm.*

[3]Cf. also Ex. 29:27ff. (cited by Sens), which states that the garments of Aaron's sons were also composed of wool or linen.

[4]Hackling, or combing, involves the separation of fiber from unwanted parts of the stem (in the case of vegetable fibers), or the removal of tangles and impurities from the fibers (in the case of animal fibers). This process represents the last stage of the preparation of the fibers for spinning (cf. J.P. Wild, *Textile Manufacturing in the Northern Provinces* [Cambridge: Cambridge University Press, 1970], pp. 24, 28). For a discussion of Pliny's account of hackling (*Historia Naturalis* 19.16-18) and a description of the type of hackle mentioned by him, cf. J.P. Wild, "The Roman Flax-Hackle (*AENA*)," *Museum Helveticum* 25(1968), pp. 139-142 (cited by Wild, *Textile Manufacture*, p. 29, n. 1). Cf. also R.J. Forbes, *Studies in Ancient Technology*, IV, second ed. (Leiden: E.J. Brill, 1964), p. 32. Forbes, however, relates hackling to the Hebrew root *srk*, and does not mention the root *ṭrp* (or M. Kil. 9:1) at all.

[5]*TZ*, p. 225, on l. 52.

[6]*TZ*, p. 225, on l. 53, and *TK*, II, pp. 663f., on l. 53. Lieberman here follows the reading of Rabad. Cf. also GRA (cited by Lieberman, *ibid.*), who presents the same reading.

[7]Lieberman, *TK*, II, p. 663, on l. 52 (following B. Shab. 133b).

[8]*Ibid.*

[9]*Ibid.*

[10]These three types of dressings also appear together at T. Kel. B.B. 6:3.

[11]Alternatively, cf. Maimonides (*Code, Diverse-Kinds* 10:19; cited by Lieberman, *ibid.*), who explains that the dressings do not serve to warm the body and thus do not function as garments.

[12]*TK*, II, p. 663, on l. 53.

[13]*TZ*, p. 225, on l. 53, and *TK*, II, pp. 663f., on l. 53.

[14]Cf. T. Shab. 4:5(7), which also states that a wreath is not subject to the laws of diverse-kinds.

[15]*TK*, II, p. 663f., on l. 53.

[16]*TK*, II, p. 664, on l. 55. Lieberman here follows the readings of Erfurt, first printed ed., B. Yoma and Tamid, and the commentaries.

[17]B. Yoma 69a and B. Tamid 27b actually read as follows:

A. Garments of the high priest--

B. he who goes out [while dressed] in them to the provinces [i.e., outside of the Temple]--it is prohibited.

    C.   And [he who wears them] in the Temple,

    D.   whether [he does so] at the time of the
[Temple] service or not at the time of the
[Temple] service--

    E.   it is permitted,

    F.   because the priestly garments were intended
to be enjoyed [i.e., to be used privately].

B. differs with T. mainly at F. B. replaces T.'s version of
F, which, as we shall see, cannot be read together with D, with
a version which does take account of the rule of D. B. thus
resolves the difficulty which occurs in T. when D and F are
read together.

[18]Cf. also *Sefer HaEshkol* (cited by Lieberman, *TK*, II,
p. 653f., on ll. 28-29), which reads, "Camel's hair and sheep's
wool are permitted."

[19]For other commentaries which follow this reading, cf.
Lieberman, *TK*, II, p. 654, on ll. 29-30.

[20]Alternatively, Lieberman (*ibid.*) maintains that "them"
refers to the sheep's wool, and so takes Erfurt's reading of T.
to say that wool and flax may be hackled together and then
combined with camel's hair. It is not likely, however, that one
would be permitted to hackle together sheep's wool and flax
under any circumstances, and we therefore prefer the interpretation given above in the translation.

[21]Lieberman (*TK*, II, pp. 654-655, on l. 30) cites Erfurt's
reading as the key to understanding the reading of Vienna.
Erfurt reads *kwlw smr hgmlyn wkwlw smr 'rnbyym* for Vienna's
smr gmlym kwlw wkwlw smr 'rnbyym, and so clarifies the latter's
reading by placing the first *kwlw* at the outset of the phrase.
For various other readings of E, cf. Lieberman, *ibid.*

[22]For the commentaries which add the same phrase, cf.
Lieberman, *TK*, II, p. 655, on l. 31.

[23]For the secondary question (generated by this reading)
of whether E applies only when the threads touch one another
(Sens) or even when the threads are at opposite end of the shirt
(Maim., *Code, Diverse-Kinds* 10:9), cf. Lieberman, *TK*, II,
pp. 655-656, on l. 31.

[24]According to the reading of Erfurt and Sens the flax is
first hackled with the camel's hair, and the combined fibers
and then mixed with wool. This reading, though, does not differ
in substance from that of Vienna.

[25]*TK*, II, p. 655, on ll. 29-30.

[26]Cf. Qappaḥ, p. 133, n. 9.

[27]*Ibid.*, n. 10.

[28]For the list of manuscripts, cf. Zachs, I, p. 294, on
l. 8.

[29]Classical sources describe a silk, known as amorginon, as
being similar to linen. For such sources, cf. Forbes, p. 52.
Forbes cites the description of this silk as given in the lexicon
Suidas:

> Amorginon is like linen and very dear. . .
> Amorgis is like unhackled linen, they strip
> it and work it. It is much finer than cotton
> (byssos) or linen (karpasos).

[30]Maimonides (*Code, Diverse-Kinds* 10:1) and TYY offer both
interpretations, which, of course, do not mutually exclude one
another.

[31]Alternatively, the rule of C-D may be based on an exegesis
of Lv. 19:19 (Sens and others, following Sifra Qedoshim 4:18b
and B. Yoma 69a). C takes the phrase *Nor shall there come upon
you* to imply that it is prohibited to place diverse-kinds only
upon, but not under, one's body, so that one is permitted to sit
or lie on mattresses or cushions of diverse-kinds. D then states
that one may not allow his flesh to touch the mattress or cushions,
lest a fringe of diverse-kinds wrap itself around the flesh. In
that case diverse-kinds would rest upon the body, and one would
transgress the prohibition of *Nor shall there come upon you*.
This interpretation is somewhat difficult, however, for it does
not explain why one is prohibited specifically from touching
diverse-kinds. According to this explanation one should also be
liable if a fringe of diverse-kinds were to wrap itself around
a covered part of the body, for in this instance as well the
fringe would lie upon the body. We therefore prefer the interpretation given above in the text.

[32]*TK*, II, p. 662, on l. 51.

[33]*TK*, II, p. 662, on ll. 51-52.

[34]We assume that the mattresses and cushions are also
composed of linen, for if they were made of wool one could not
attach a linen border to them. In such a case one would be
concerned lest someone think them to be composed entirely of
wool and so unknowingly allow his skin to touch diverse-kinds
(cf. M. 9:2D). If the mattresses and cushions are made of linen,
on the other hand, one may use them even if they appear to be
bordered with wool, as long as he does not allow his flesh to
touch them.

[35]Y's version reads as follows:

A. R. Neha b. Sabbah, R. Yohanan in the name
of R. Ze^{c}ira [say], "For if there was a
large garment--

B. "one end of it contains diverse-kinds and
rests on the ground, and the [other] end of
it does not contain [diverse-kinds]--

C. "he shall not cover himself with the other
side [i.e., with the end which does not contain
the diverse-kinds]."

Y. thus differs from T. mainly in that it describes the garment
as being large, and incorporates the gloss of T. 5:13C into the
description of the case at B.

[36]*Laws of diverse-kinds of garments*, 19 (cited by Lieberman,
TK, II, p. 656, on l. 33).

[37]Lieberman (*ibid.*) presents the alternative reading of
pwrpw ("he fastens").

[38]D, of course, disregards C's prohibition against wearing a
garment of diverse-kinds (HD).

[39]This is apparently the view of HD (for the discussion of this issue in M., cf. M. Shab., Chapter Six). Alternatively, Lieberman (*TK*, II, p. 657, on ll. 34-35) maintains that if the shirt were only fastened together, one would be liable for carrying not the thread, but the torn end, from one domain to the other on the Sabbath. According to his interpretation, then, the point of D concerns not whether or not the thread is considered to be connected to the shirt, but whether or not the torn end of the shirt is considered to be attached to the rest of the shirt. While this explanation is possible, we consider it to be more likely that the issue of D is identical to that of C, so that both rules concern whether or not the thread is regarded as part of the shirt. We therefore prefer the first interpretation given above.

[40]Lieberman (*TK*, II, p. 656, on l. 33) suggests that Maimonides' text of T. was probably similar to that of Rosh (who, in fact, cites Maim., *Code, Diverse-Kinds* 10:10 in support of his reading).

[41]We note that both Maimonides and Rosh omit reference to B and D.

[42]Cf. also the version of Rabbenu Tam (presented by Lieberman [citing Ravyah] *TK*, II, p. 656, on l. 33) which reads A as follows:

> A shirt [of wool] which was torn and he fastened it [i.e., the shirt] [together] with a thread [of flax]--it [i.e., the shirt] is prohibited.

This version omits the phrase "if he sewed it," and so reads A and C as a single rule. According to this reading one is prohibited even from fastening together the torn ends of a woolen shirt with a thread of flax. The rule of this version thus clearly opposes that given by the version of Rosh.

[43]*TZ*, p. 224, on l. 36, and *TK*, II, p. 657, on l. 36.

[44]According to Lieberman (*TK*, II, p. 657, on l. 36) this reading is found in the oldest printed edition and in the manuscripts of the *Code* (in place of the present reading of *ykrwk*). The reading of Rosh is also cited by Lieberman.

[45]Following Lieberman, *TZ*, p. 224, on l. 36, who takes *trp* to be synonymous with *k̤rk̤*.

[46]*TZ*, p. 224, on l. 36, and *TK*, II, p. 657, on l. 36.

[47]*TK*, II, p. 657, on l. 36.

[48]We note that Finkelstein (p. 265, on l. 11) considers this pericope to be part of a marginal gloss of Sifré.

[49]Cf. Sifré Dt. 230k for a similar exegesis of the word *together* in Dt. 22:10 (*You shall not plow with an ox and an ass together*).

[50]According to Sens' version of Y. the scroll-wrapper may also be placed on one's lap (under the scroll) and thus may serve to warm the lap.

[51]*TZ*, p. 224, on l. 36. Cf. also *TK*, II, pp. 657f., on ll. 36-37, where Lieberman describes *bl'ry nšym* as sheets, and identifies them with the Greek βαλναρία or βανιάρια.

52
Y. reads as follows:

> R. Abbahu in the name of R. Yohanan says,
> "Women's bath-towels (*blnry nšym*) àre prohibited
> on account of [the laws of] diverse-kinds."

Y. thus disagrees with A, perhaps following Eliezer's view
(M. 9:3B) that bath-towels are subject to the laws of diverse-kinds.

53 *TZ*, p. 224, on l. 36, and *TK*, II, p. 658, on l. 37.

54 *TK*, II, p. 658, on l. 37.

55 The same apodosis appears at T. 5:23.

56 *TZ*, p. 224, on l. 38.

57 *Ibid.*; cf. also *TK*, II, p. 658, on l. 38.

58 Cited by Lieberman, *TK*, II, p. 658, on l. 38. In his
account OZ specifically refers to the placing of Torah-scrolls
in the ark of a synagogue. T., however, does not appear to
refer to a particular case of scrolls, and we therefore apply
the interpretation of OZ to any such case.

59 We note that the dispute of B-E attests that of M. 9:3A-B
to Usha, so that the Eliezer of M. is clearly a Yavnean (Neusner,
Eliezer, I, p. 39).

60 Alternatively, the rule of B may be based on an exegesis
of Lv. 19:19. According to Albeck B may take the phrase *Nor
shall there come upon you* [*a garment of cloth composed of two
kinds of stuff* (Lv. 19:19)] to mean that one may not bear
diverse-kinds on his body in any manner at all. One may therefore
not place a pack-saddle of diverse-kinds on his shoulder, even
though the pack-saddle is not designed to be worn by man. This
interpretation is somewhat difficult, however, for it does not
allow for the importance of C (and for the force of *'p*). If
the point of B is that one is not permitted to bear diverse-kinds
at all, then C's point, that he may not put a pack-saddle on his
shoulder even to carry out the dung, becomes obvious, and serves
only to illustrate B. We therefore prefer the first interpretation
given above, according to which C refers to the intention of the
bearer of the pack-saddle, and thus introduces a new consideration
into the pericope.

61 Cited by Lieberman, *TK*, II, p. 659, on l. 42.

62 *Ibid.*

63 *TK*, II, p. 659, on l. 43.

64 For other readings, cf. Zachs, I, p. 297, on l. 17.

65 Cf. his note to T. Kel. B.B. 5:11, in *Die Tosefta*
(Stuttgart: Kohlhammer, 1960), VI.1, p. 172, n. 42.

66 For other readings, cf. Zachs, I, p. 298, on l. 17.

67 In the *Code* Maimonides speaks simply of a shoe which is
composed of diverse-kinds, and we therefore take him to refer
to a cloth shoe. Cf. also Ridbaz, who cites Maimonides' reference
to slippers in the latter's *Commentary* and maintains that
Maimonides refers to the same type of slippers in the *Code* (for
the citation of the passage in the *Code*, see below, n. 76).

[68]For the list of manuscripts, cf. Zachs, I, p. 298, on l. 19.

[69]According to this interpretation, *pynwn* is derived from the Greek πίνος, which means dirt or filth. In this instance *pynwn* refers to coarse wool which contains dirt or foreign substances (cf. S. Krauss, *Talmudische Archaeologie* [Leipzig: G. Fock, 1910], I, p. 628, n. 712). Alternatively, *mn^{c}ly hpynwn* may refer to shoes made of pinna (cf. Krauss, *ibid.*), a fiber produced by the mollusk *Pinna nobilis* (cf. J.P. Wild, *Textile Manufacture*, p. 20). According to this explanation the point of A apparently is that one must examine the shoes in order to be certain that they are actually composed of pinna, and not of a mixture of wool and flax. It is not clear, however, why these shoes in particular have to be examined for diverse-kinds. We therefore prefer the first interpretation given above, for according to that explanation (as we shall see), the reasoning behind the rule for the *mn^{c}ly hpynwn* follows that of the rule for the birrus and bardaicus.

[70]Cf. T. Kel. B.B. 5:11, which states that the birrus and the bardaicus were composed of heavy or thick material. Cf. also T. Neg. 5:14, which also implies that these two types of cloaks were composed of heavy material.

[71]The birrus was a cloak which apparently also had a cowl (cf. L.M. Wilson, *The Clothing of the Ancient Romans* [Baltimore: Johns Hopkins Press, 1938], pp. 125ff. henceforth: *Clothing*). We assume that the bardaicus is identical with the bardocucullus, a hooded cloak named after the Bardaei, a people of Illyria (cf. Wilson, *ibid.*, p. 85; cf. also Krauss, *Talmudische Archaeologie*, I, p. 611, n. 586).

[72]For the composition of the birrus, cf. *Edict of Diocletian* 19.25ff., which in fixing prices for different type of garments, lists the birri only among the woolen garments (cf. *The Edict of Diocletian*, trans. S.R. Graser, in Tenney Frank, ed., *An Economic Survey of Ancient Rome* [Baltimore: Johns Hopkins Press, 1940], V, pp. 374ff.). For the composition of the bardaicus, cf. Wilson, *Clothing*, p. 95, who cites an epigram of Martial (I,53) referring to a bardocucullus composed of greasy wool.

[73]Cf. *Edict of Diocletian*, 19.28-31 (trans. Graser, *ibid.*, p. 374), which lists dalmatics of wool, and *Edict*, 26.5ff. (trans. Graser, pp. 390ff.), which lists dalmatics composed of linen.

[74]Yosé's saying clearly assumes that all of the garments of A, including the dalmatic (and the shoes of A(4)) were composed of wool. Alternatively, Yosé may gloss an earlier version of the list which did not contain the dalmatic (or the shoes of A(4), if these are taken to refer to shoes of pinna). Since the identities of the final two items of A's list are not certain, it is not possible to make a definite statement concerning the relationship between A-B and C-D.

[75]The extent to which this assumption accords with our knowledge of the clothing industry in the Roman Empire is not clear. While it is probably true that hemp was cheaper than flax in many places, it is also true that by the first century A.D., flax was grown even in the western provinces (cf. Pliny, *Historia Naturalis* 19.27ff., who refers to flax which was grown in Spain and Gaul). Our evidence thus does not give us reason to believe that hemp was regularly substituted for flax in the manufacture of clothing (for a survey of cloth manufacture in the Roman Empire, cf. A.H.M. Jones, "The Cloth Industry in the Roman Empire,"

reprinted in P.A. Brunt, ed., *The Roman Economy* [Oxford: Basil Blackwell, 1974], pp. 350-364). We note, however, that Egypt and Syria were known for their fine linens, which were exported throughout the empire (cf. Wild, *Textile Manufacture*, p. 15). It is possible, then, that knowledge of such trade led to the supposition that flax was not readily available in distant lands. We repeat, however, that our evidence does not allow us to make an accurate judgment of this assumption.

[76]Cf. Ridbaz, who raises a similar consideration. Maimonides himself presents a different reason for E (*Code, Diverse-Kinds* 10:15):

> A shoe which is [composed of] diverse-kinds
> and lacks a heel--it is permitted to wear it. For
> the skin of the [sole of the] foot is hard and
> does not receive comfort [from the shoe] like the
> rest of the body.

It is not clear, however, that the foot receives no comfort from the sole of the shoe (cf. Sirillo's comment [cited by Zachs, I, p. 298, n. 32]), and it is thus difficult to accept Maimonides' interpretation (cf. also the objections discussed by Ridbaz). We therefore prefer the interpretation given above in the text.

[77]Cf. T. Kil. 5:16, which states that a women's bath-towel is not considered a garment unless it is sewn together at the ends and thus designed to stay on the body.

[78]Alternatively, following Y. Kil. 9:5, Ribmaṣ, Sens and Rosh maintain that E refers to a cloth-lined shoe. According to this interpretation the point of E is simply that one need not be concerned lest the lining of the shoe contain diverse-kinds. It is not clear, though, why one should assume that such a lining is free of diverse-kinds. We therefore prefer the interpretation of Maimonides given above.

[79]B. Yev. 5b and B. Nid. 61a discuss whether B refers to three separate acts of combining diverse-kinds or to three parts of a single process (i.e., the wool and flax must be hackled, spun, and woven together in order to be prohibited as a mixture of diverse-kinds). We maintain that it is more likely that B refers to three separate acts, for otherwise A and B would completely oppose one another. While A would maintain that wool and flax must be spun and woven together in order to be regarded as a mixture of diverse-kinds, B would argue that these fibers must be hackled together as well. Now it is true that, according to our interpretation, A and B also disagree, but at the same time they also agree concerning wool and flax which is spun or woven. It is therefore possible to explain why B was placed after A. According to the alternative interpretation, however, no such explanation is possible, for A and B simply oppose one another. We therefore prefer the interpretation given above in the text (for a summary of the views of the commentaries, cf. Albeck, p. 372).

[80]Cf. Lieberman (*TZ*, p. 225, on l. 47), who explains that Simeon b. Eleazar reads *šᶜtnz* as *šᶜtlz* and so derives *mlyz* from the latter (*nlwz* does not appear in T.). Alternatively, Albeck suggests that Simeon b. Eleazar simply adds a *l* to *nwz* and so reads it as *nlwz*.

[81]Alternatively, most commentaries consider the subject of *nlwz* and *mlyz* to be the wearer of diverse-kinds. We assume, however, that Simeon b. Eleazar simply continues B, and so depends on the latter for its subject, which is "something" composed of

diverse-kinds. We therefore agree with the interpretation of
Albeck (cf. also T. 5:21b).

[82]*TZ*, p. 225, on l. 46.

[83]This interpretation of T. assumes that the weaving described
in A is done on a warp-weighted loom. We note, however, that such
looms were usually operated with weights (e.g., of stone), so
that it is not clear whether our interpretation of T. accords
with our knowledge of weaving techniques. We see no better explanation of T., however, and therefore present this one as the
most plausible explanation.

[84]The point of weighing down the wool is not only to keep
it in place, but also to keep all of its threads under the same
degree of tension, as Forbes explains (p. 198):

> The spacing of the warp threads on the loom
> governs to a large degree the texture of the fabric
> to be woven. Their tension must be uniform or else
> the fabric will be uneven.

[85]Cited by Lieberman, *TK*, II, p. 660, on l. 46. Sens actually takes A to mean that one places both wool and flax on a
warp of another kind so that the weaver (*h'wrg*) will not lose
the threads of the warp (his language is somewhat difficult
at this point). We maintain, however, that A describes a case
in which the wool is used for the warp, so that the flax is
attached to it in order to weigh it down.

[86]Alternatively, Lieberman (*ibid.*) maintains that A concerns
wool which is being combed in order to be spun. The point of B,
then, is that in combing wool one may accidentally mix it with
some of the flax which lies under it, and thus spin wool and
flax together. Lieberman apparently takes A to mean that the
wool is being prepared for weaving, i.e., it is being spun. The
phrase *lhywt 'wrg ᶜlyw*, though, implies that the wool has
already been prepared for weaving, and thus has already been spun.
We therefore prefer the interpretation given above in the text.

[87]It is not clear whether one pericope depends on the
other. We have already shown (cf. our discussion of M. 9:8)
that M. does not provide the original context of the exegesis
of *shaᶜaṭnez*, so that it is possible that M. cites Sifré, to
which an exegesis of a verse in Dt. is surely appropriate. It
is not possible to prove such dependence, however, and it is
therefore difficult to arrive at a definite conclusion concerning
the relationship between M. and Sifré in this instance.

[88]We note that Sifra Qedoshim 4:18a asks the same question
as does A-B, but answers it by citing the word *garment* (Lv. 19:19),
which it takes to exclude pieces of wool and flax from the
prohibition.

[89]For the list of manuscripts, cf. Zachs, I, p. 301, on l. 23.

[90]Cf. Zachs, I, p. 301, on l. 24.

[91]Our translation here follows that of Blackman.

[92]Y. presents E as an anonymous saying.

[93]Cf. Wild, *Textile Manufacture*, p. 60: "Felt consists of a
sheet of compressed woollen or other fabrics, not spun, but held
together by the surface irregularities of the fabric alone."

[94]Alternatively, Maimonides (*Comm.*) takes *mwll* to mean "twisted" (cf. MR, M. Ma^{c}as. 4:5). He thus understands F to say that threads of wool would be gathered together and twisted with threads of flax in order to make the cord. The point of E-F, then, is that the cords of purple wool are prohibited because they would be twisted, or spun, together with the flax. According to this interpretation, E-F serves to illustrate M. 9:8A-B's prohibition against wearing wool and flax which have been spun together. This explanation of F, however, is not as plausible as the one presented above in the text. The term *mwll* appears to refer to an act which is done immediately before the cord is tied. It is thus more likely that *mwll* refers to the basting of the cord, which holds the cord in place until it is tied, than to twisting the threads of the cord, which is not directly related to the act of tying. We therefore prefer the first interpretation given above.

[95]Some commentaries (e.g., Sens, Rosh, TYY) maintain that one may not attach strips of wool and linen to opposite ends of a leather strap because one must still connect the strips together in tying the belt. According to this interpretation, however, the gloss of H is pointless, for if the strips are to be connected when the belt is tied, it makes no difference whether or not they are directly connected when the belt is not tied (MS). We therefore prefer the first interpretation given above, according to which H introduces the issue of (indirect) connection.

[96]The reading of *srq* is also found in Ms. Munich of M.

[97]We note that Finkelstein (p. 265, on l. 11) considers W-X to be a marginal gloss of Sifré.

[98]We here follow the word order of the MT, rather than that of the RSV (*Nor shall there come upon you a garment of cloth made up of two kinds of stuff*).

[99]Cf. Sifré Dt. 232a, which bases the same rule concerning pieces of shorn wool and stalks of flax on the exegesis of *sha^{c}atnez*, maintaining that the pieces of wool and flax are neither hackled, spun, nor woven together.

[100]The relationship between Sifra and M. here is not clear. We note that while Sifra at G-H presumably bases its exegesis of *sha^{c}atnez* on Lv. 19:19, M. 9:8B cites Dt. 22:11 in its version of the same exegesis. It is thus not likely that M. here cites Sifra, for M. would have no reason to change the verse of the exegesis from Lv. 19:19 to Dt. 22:11. It follows, therefore, either that Sifra cites M. or that both Sifra and M. know the exegesis without one being dependent on the other. Now since Sifra knows M. 9:9A-B's rule concerning felted stuffs and links this rule to the exegesis of *sha^{c}atnez*, it is likely that Sifra knows the exegesis as well from M., and that Sifra has simply changed the verse of the exegesis from Dt. 22:11 to Lv. 19:19 (for the relationship between M. and Sifré Dt. 232a, cf. above n. 87).

[101]Cf. his translation of B. Shab. 54a in *The Babylonian Talmud: Seder Mo^{c}ed* (London: Soncino, 1938), I, p. 249.

[102]Cf. M. Shab. 7:2, 13:2.

[103]For the rule of I, cf. M. Shab. 7:2 (cited by Albeck).

[104]TZ, p. 225, on l. 44.   Both in TZ and in TK (II, p. 660, on l. 44), however, Lieberman states that he does not know the meaning of ᶜyṭ, and that his identification of the item as a wrapper is only a suggestion.

[105]We note that, whether T. complements M. 9:10B-I alone, or links the latter to M. 9:9C-D, it is not clear why T. was redacted between T. 5:19, which complements M. 9:4, and T. 5:21, which comments on M. 9:8.

[106]We here follow Lieberman's identification of pwqryt ṣyph (TZ, p. 225, on l. 49, and TK, II, p. 662, on l. 49). Alternatively, HD (following Rashi, B. Shab. 50a, s.v. pwqryn wṣyph) maintains that pwqryt refers to pieces of combed flax, and that a ṣyph is a piece of beaten wool.   According to HD the point of A is that one is permitted to wear a pwqryt and ṣyph together on a wound, for the two items are not considered to be connected and to form a garment of diverse-kinds.   (He also notes that the two strips now receive uncleanness as a utensil, for they were already considered garments before being joined.)   We maintain, though, that B refers to tying together the ends of each item (as in T. 5:16), and not to tying the two items together. We therefore prefer the first interpretation given above in the text.

[107]Cf. his comment to T. Shab. 5(6):2 (TK, III, p. 72, on l. 5).

[108]Cf. T. Shab. 5(6):2 (cited by Lieberman, TK, II, p. 662, on l. 49), which states that one may bear tufts or strips of wool from one domain to the otheron the Sabbath only if the wool is dyed in oil (apparently to make it clear that it serves as a garment [cf. Rashi, B. Shab. 50a, s.v. bzmn šṣbᶜn bšmn]) and tied together with a cord.

[109]We assume that, as in the case of T. 5:16, T. refers to midras-uncleanness, to which the tufts and strips are not susceptible because they are used only to cover wounds.   Cf. Lieberman, TK, II, p. 658, on l. 37.

[110]Alternatively, Lieberman (TK, II, p. 662, on ll. 49, 50), referring to Sifré, maintains that A concerns pieces of wool which have not been hackled, and thus do not come under the laws of diverse-kinds (M. 9:8B), even if they are tied together with cords of flax.   The point of B-D, then, is that pieces of wool which are sewn together are considered to form a garment, and thus are prohibited because of the flax which they contain.   It is not clear, however, how unhackled wool can be subject to the laws of diverse-kinds at all.   In addition, T. makes no mention of cords of flax which may be used to tie the pieces of wool together.   We therefore maintain that the issue of T. concerns not whether or not the wool is hackled, but, as in the case of T. 5:16, whether the specified items are regarded as garments.

GENERAL INDEX